German-Language Children's and Youth Literature
In The Media Network 1900–1945

Petra Josting • Marlene Antonia Illies
Matthias Preis • Annemarie Weber
Editors

German-Language Children's and Youth Literature In The Media Network 1900–1945

Editors
Petra Josting
Faculty of Linguistics and Literary Studies
German Studies
Bielefeld University
Bielefeld, Germany

Matthias Preis
Faculty of Linguistics and Literary Studies
German Studies
Bielefeld University
Bielefeld, Germany

Marlene Antonia Illies
Faculty of Linguistics and Literary Studies
German Studies
Bielefeld University
Bielefeld, Germany

Annemarie Weber
Bielefeld, Germany

ISBN 978-3-476-05891-1   ISBN 978-3-476-05892-8   (eBook)
https://doi.org/10.1007/978-3-476-05892-8

© Springer-Verlag GmbH Germany, part of Springer Nature 2024
This book is a translation of the original German edition "Deutschsprachige Kinder- und Jugendliteratur im Medienverbund 1900–1945" by Josting, Petra, published by Springer-verlag GmbH DE in 2020. The translation was done with the help of artificial intelligence (machine translation by the service DeepL.com). A subsequent human revision was done primarily in terms of content, so that the book will read stylistically differently from a conventional translation. Springer Nature works continuously to further the development of tools for the production of books and on the related technologies to support the authors.
This work is subject to copyright. All rights are reserved by the Publisher, whether the whole or part of the material is concerned, specifically the rights of translation, reprinting, reuse of illustrations, recitation, broadcasting, reproduction on microfilms or in any other physical way, and transmission or information storage and retrieval, electronic adaptation, computer software, or by similar or dissimilar methodology now known or hereafter developed.
The use of general descriptive names, registered names, trademarks, service marks, etc. in this publication does not imply, even in the absence of a specific statement, that such names are exempt from the relevant protective laws and regulations and therefore free for general use.
The publisher, the authors, and the editors are safe to assume that the advice and information in this book are believed to be true and accurate at the date of publication. Neither the publisher nor the authors or the editors give a warranty, expressed or implied, with respect to the material contained herein or for any errors or omissions that may have been made. The publisher remains neutral with regard to jurisdictional claims in published maps and institutional affiliations.

This Palgrave Macmillan imprint is published by the registered company Springer-Verlag GmbH, DE, part of Springer Nature.
The registered company address is: Heidelberger Platz 3, 14197 Berlin, Germany

Preface

Without the generous funding from the Deutsche Forschungsgemeinschaft spanding four years, our project and thus this volume could not have been realised. We would like to express our sincere thanks to their referee, Dr. Thomas Wiemer, for his manifold support. We would also like to thank many others who supported the project work in various ways.

First and foremost, the Bielefeld University Library, namely its director Barbara Knorn and her deputy Dirk Pieper, without whose willingness to cooperate and support a project that has opened up to the Digital Humanities with its online portal would have never been possible. Our cooperation began in the course of the application, continued after the project was approved with the development of the metadata structure (Edith Rimmert) and, in parallel, with the conception and development of the online portal, which offers a variety of innovative research and visualisation possibilities. We appreciate the commitment of Friedrich Summann, who, as head of the LibTec department, was always available for discussions and programmed the portal dispite his many other mandatory tasks! We would also like to thank Artur Nold (Drupal system administration) and Sebastian Wolf (Web design) for the extended technical support on the part of the University Library.

We would like to thank three institutions for providing journals, archival materials, etc.: the Bundesfilmarchiv in Berlin, the Deutsche Kinemathek in Berlin, and especially the Deutsches Rundfunkarchiv in Frankfurt am Main, with which the project was continuously connected. Ms. Susanne Hennings supported us with research in the archives and with digitisation requests, Ms. Marion Gillum and Dorothee Fischer provided audio copies, and Ms. Julia Weber helped clarify usage rights.

The extensive source material could not have been handled by the project staff alone. Therefore, Dilek Çıkrıkcıoglu, Elham Moghadas, Jenny Petermann, Natalie Regier and Kevin Richardt helped us with the digitalisation, the input of data and their linking. Support in the evaluation of sources was provided by staff members Alina Wanzek and Linda Schrader-Grimm. Annika Behler joined the project in its fourth year as a competent research assistant.

After sufficient material was available around the halfway mark of the project, we approached researchers of children's and youth literature in Germany and Switzerland with the request to present selected media networks at a joint conference at the Center for Interdisciplinary Research (ZiF) in Bielefeld and to publish them later in our volume. They agreed, which we are very grateful for, because as a project team alone we would not have been possible to accomplish this task due to time constraints. Our colleagues had to deal with a lot of unknown material, they searched film archives, did research and presented their first results in the form of a lecture. The thorough working atmosphere and the substantial contributions will positively remain in our memories. Many of them travelled to Bielefeld a second time a few months later for an exchange on media theories, in order to write down their results on this basis. Thank you to all of them!

No project and no conference can do without secretarial support. Therefore, we would also like to thank our secretary Dorothea Meerkamp for her organisational talent and for remaining calm even during hectic times. Last but not least, we would also like to thank Dr. Peter Schildhauer for translating the abstracts into English, the EDP support of our faculty (Martin Schmitz), the conference office of the ZiF (Trixi Valentin) and Larissa Jagdschian, who helped editing the texts with great commitment.

For the final editing and proofreading of the automated translation of this volume into English we were able to enlist Liam Rennekamp for our project, who we all thank very much.

Bielefeld, Germany
December 2021

Petra Josting
Marlene Antonia Illies
Matthias Preis
Annemarie Weber

Contents

Introduction: Concepts, Corpus and Strategies of Media Network Research.. 1
Petra Josting, Marlene Antonia Illies, Matthias Preis, and Annemarie Weber
Recording Criteria of Children's and Youth Film...................... 2
Recording Criteria for Children's and Youth Radio Programmes.......... 5
Recording Criteria for Children's and Youth Theatre................... 7
Recording Criteria for Print Media, Vinyl, and Advertising Material 9
Media Networks: Theoretical Frameworks........................... 10
   Media as a Compact Concept According to Siegfried J. Schmidt 10
   Limits of Schmidt's Media System Model 11
   Popular Culture Network Models................................ 12
   Seriality Theories 14
   Network Discussion in Children's and Youth Literature Research........ 15
   Storytising as Brand Management 16
   Marketing Science Models 17
Media Networks from 1900 to 1945................................ 18
   Definition 18
   Spectrum of Media Networks................................... 20
References... 33

Project Horizons: Introduction and Overview   39

Children's and Youth Radio from 1924 to 1945..................... 41
Annemarie Weber
Current State of Research and Desiderata 41
Political and Economic Framework of Early Radio Broadcasting......... 42
Technical Requirements of the Reception 46
Programme Press 47
Offers for Children and Young People in the Radio of the Weimar Republic   47
   Funk-Stunde AG 47

Nordische Rundfunk AG (Norag).................................. 49
Südwestdeutscher Rundfunkdienst AG (SWR) 50
Süddeutsche Rundfunk A. G. (Sürag)............................. 51
Deutsche Stunde in Bayern GmbH................................ 53
Ostmarken-Rundfunk AG (Orag) 54
Schlesische Funkstunde AG 55
Mitteldeutsche Rundfunk AG (Mirag) 56
Westdeutsche Funkstunde AG (Wefag): Westdeutsche Rundfunk
   AG (Werag).. 58
Deutsche Welle GmbH 60
Children's and Youth Broadcasts from Austria and Switzerland 61
Children's and Youth Broadcasts from 1933 and until the End of the War .. 61
Summary... 64
References.. 65

Children's and Youth Films from 1900 to 1945 71
Marlene Antonia Illies
State of Research and Desiderata 71
Children's and Youth Film in the Empire 73
Children's and Youth Film in the Weimar Republic 78
Children's and Youth Film During the National Socialist Era 83
Summary and Outlook 88
References.. 89

Children's and Youth Theatre from 1900 to 1945 97
Marlene Antonia Illies
References.. 100

Digital Explorations of Historical Media Networks 101
Matthias Preis and Friedrich Summann
Introduction.. 101
Goals and Challenges 102
From Theory to Metadata Structure 103
   Conceptual Considerations 103
   Technical Realisation 106
Search Engine Environment and Visualisation........................ 108
   Conceptual Considerations 108
   Technical Realisation 113
Application Scenarios.. 117
   (Un)conventional Search Queries............................... 118
   Double Perspectives with Timeline and Navigator.................. 119
   Media Networks in Profile 120
Summary... 121
References.. 122

Pioneers Take Over the New Types of Media — 125

From Children's Theatre to Film — 127
Petra Anders
- Introduction — 127
- Historical Framework — 128
- Genschow's Productions — 129
  - Stage and Film in the 1930s — 129
  - With the Children's Theatre Through Germany (1934) — 130
  - Genschow's *Studio des Jugendfilms* — 133
  - *General Stift und seine Bande* (1937) — 135
- Contemporary Reception of Genschow's Work — 141
- Conclusion — 143
- References — 144

Mickey Mouse — 147
Johannes Krause
- Introduction and Preliminary Considerations — 147
- *Mickey Mouse* as a Brand in 1930s Germany — 149
- Disney's Animated Films in the German Trade Press: Typically *American!* — 154
- *Mickey Mouse* in the Comic Strips of German Daily Newspapers — 157
- The German *Counter-Propaganda* — 160
- Concluding Remarks — 162
- References — 163

Funkheinzelmann — 167
Annemarie Weber
- Preliminary Remarks — 167
- Funkheinzelmann: A Radio Figure Becomes a Brand — 168
- Event Marketing — 170
- Geographical Expansion and Programme Diversification — 172
- Brand Extensions — 175
- The Record — 176
- The Revue — 177
- The Fairy Tale Storybooks — 181
- Merchandising — 181
- *Funkheinzelmann*: The Children's Magazine — 182
- The Author as the Motor of Seriality — 187
- References — 189

Stage Children Migrate to Radio and/or Film — 197

To the Moon and Back — 199
Julia Benner
- Prehistory: Introduction — 199
- The Nursery: Starting Point — 201

The Starry Meadow: Author and Text	205
The Milky Way: Visual Design	207
The Castle of the Night Fairy: Sonority and Music	213
The Christmas Meadow: Consumer Orientation and Branding	214
The Moon: Time and Space	215
Back in the Nursery: Theoretical and Methodological Considerations or the Journey to the Media Network	216
References	219

In Never-Never Land 225
Ulrike Preußer

Introduction	225
A Novel for Adults and a Children's Book Consisting of Some of Its Chapters: *The Little White Bird* (1902) – *Kleiner weißer Vogel* (2010) and *Peter Pan in Kensington Gardens* (1906) – *Peter Pan im Waldpark* (1911)	226
James M. Barrie's *Peter Pan*: The English and the German Stage Play – *Peter Pan, or the Boy Who Would Not Grow Up* (1904/1928) – *Peter Gerneklein (Der Knabe welcher nicht gross werden wollte)* (1904/1910) – *Peter Pan, oder Das Märchen vom Jungen, der nicht groß werden wollte* (1952)	231
James M. Barrie's *Peter Pan*: Prose Versions or *Peter Pan* in Germany After 1945	239
The First Film Adaptation of *Peter Pan* (1924)	241
Conclusion	245
Literature	245

Urian's Travels Around the World 249
Gina Weinkauff

Away From the 'Miracle': Lisa Tetzner and the Hans Urian *Stoff*	249
The Hans Urian Project	251
The Literary Pretexts	253
The First Performance	255
Reception as a Laienspiel Play	257
From the Play to the Children's Novel	258
History of Translation and Editing	260
Continuations	261
The DEFA Hand Puppet Film	264
Is the Hans Urian Project a Medienverbund (*Media Network*)?	265
References	267

Fairy Tales in Film and Radio   273

"That Was a Wonderful Fairy Tale!" 275
Annika Behler

Introduction	275

The (Original) Fairy Tale *Der fliegende Koffer* ... 276
The Dissemination and Processing of the Fairy Tale in Books ... 278
Animated Films and Series Appearances: *Der fliegende Koffer* on Screen .. 279
Lotte Reiniger's *Der fliegende Koffer* (1921) ... 280
Der fliegende Koffer (1944): Hohnsteiner Puppenspiele ... 281
Recent Cartoons: *The Flying Trunk (Story)* (2003 and 2018) ... 282
Der fliegende Koffer and Its Television Appearances: *Sandmännchen*
and *Siebenstein* ... 283
Der fliegende Koffer Audio Book/Play: From the Radio of the Weimar
Republic to MP3 Files ... 284
Suitcase, Art, and Consumption: The Colourful Palette of Merchandising
Products ... 285
Conclusion on the Media Network ... 286
References ... 287

Mutabor! ... 295
Ingrid Tomkowiak
Retrospect ... 295
Hauff's Fairy Tales ... 297
Early Films of Hauff's Fairy Tales ... 299
   Der kleine Muck ... 299
   Kalif Storch ... 302
   Das kalte Herz ... 306
Final Thoughts ... 311
References ... 312

Classics in All Types of Media   317

Max und Moritz **Across Media** ... 319
Bernd Dolle-Weinkauff
Wilhelm Busch and the Genesis of the Bubenstreich-Erzählung ... 319
Max und Moritz as a Media Phenomenon (1865–1930) ... 322
   The "Buschiade" as a Follow-Up: Imitation – Adaptation – Parody ... 323
Max und Moritz on Stage ... 325
… and on the Screen ... 328
Max und Moritz as the Initial Spark of the Comic Strip ... 331
   The Beginnings of the "Katzenjammer Kids" by Rudolph Dirks ... 331
   Transdiegetic Narrative and Characteristic Figure Speech ... 332
   The Establishment of the "Kid Strip" and Its Transformations ... 335
Max und Moritz: A Media Network? ... 338
References ... 341

Robinsonades between 1900 and 1945 ... 347
Sebastian Schmideler
Theoretical Framework: On the Significance of Children's
and Youth Media ... 347

On the Systematics of Robinson Adaptations and Robinsonades for
Children and Adolescents 349
Historical Contextualisation I: On the Impact History of the Successful
Model of the Robinsonades 351
Historical Contextualisation II: On the History of Reception between
1900 and 1945... 355
Robinsonades in the Media Network 358
Film, Radio, Book: Robinson and Robinsonades in Individual Specific
Types of Media.. 360
    Movie Versions 360
    "Robinson" on the Radio 363
    Tendencies of Modernisation in the Book Reception of the Robinsonades 365
Conclusion: Reflections and Theses on the Media Network Discussion 367
Literature.. 368

School Stories in the Theatre, Book and on the Screen   373

Beyond Romy and Lilli.. 375
Gabriele von Glasenapp
Preliminary Considerations...................................... 375
History and Genre Traditions 376
Christa Winsloe's Boarding School Story in the Media Network
(1930–1936) 379
Transmedial Narrative Worlds Since the 1950s 384
Intertextual and -medial References Within the Drama, Film, and Novel
Version(s) 389
The Film *Mädchen in Uniform* as a *Brand* and Reference Text 393
Conclusion 398
References.. 398

Traumulus 403
Petra Josting
Introduction.. 403
The "Production Community" Between Arno Holz and Oskar Jerschke 404
Traumulus: Pupil Drama and Pupil Suicide in the Wilhelminian Era........ 405
Traumulus' Reception on Stage 408
The Film Sector of the National Socialist Era 411
Traumulus (1935): Rated as *State-Political and as an Artistically
Especially Valuable Film*...................................... 413
Reception and Distribution of the Film Version *Traumulus* 420
Conclusion and *Traumulus* Today................................ 423
References.. 425

"Da stelle ma uns mal janz dumm"............................. 429
Heidi Nenoff
Introduction: Surveying the Current Situation 429

The Media Compact Concept as an Instrument of Analysis for the Media Network System *Feuerzangenbowle*	433
The Novel *Die Feuerzangenbowle* (1933)	437
The Film Versions from the Years 1934, 1944 and 1970	444
Summary	450
References	452

Crime and the Scandalous on the Big Screen — 455

Emotionalisation Between Sexuality, Generational Conflict, and Discourse on Power — 457
Marlene Antonia Illies

Introduction	457
The *Steglitzer Schülertragödie* as a Media Network?	458
The Press as a Medium of Documentation and Emotionalisation	461
Transmedial Extensions of the *Stoff*: Sexuality, Generational Conflict	463
Discourse on Power in the Media Network	464
The Student Drama as a Literary Reference System	466
The *Steglitzer Schülertragödie* in the Film Media System	468
Revolte im Erziehungshaus	475
Concluding Remarks	476
References	477

The Commercial Genre Supersystem of Early Cinema Screen Detectives — 481
Tobias Kurwinkel

Preliminary Remarks	481
The Beginnings of the Detective Film: Sherlock Holmes	483
Detective Movies in Series: Sherlock Holmes, Nat Pinkerton and Especially Nick Carter	485
Kinoschund and Trivialisation, Censorship: And How Children Got into the Cinema	489
The Detective Film of the War Years: Stuart Webbs and Joe Deebs	491
The Genre System of the Early Screen Detectives	493
References	495

"Donnerwetter, das ist famos" — 499
Caroline Roeder

The Girls' Book *Was tun, Sibylle?*	502
Lines of Tradition and References of the Novel	503
The Film as an Educator or *Die kleinen Ladenmädchen gehen ins Kino*	506
The Film Version *Was tun, Sibylle?*	508
The Ideal of Women in National Socialism as Measured by the Reading *Stoff* of the Class	509
Social Situation	510
Design of the Film with Attributes of *Modernity*	511

Racial-Propagandistic Iconography 512
Theft: *Volksgemeinschaft* 513
School and Educational Maxims 514
Conclusion and Outlook 515
References 516

Politics Conquer Book and Film 519

Pacifist Anti-War Films of the Pre-Fascist Era 521
Ricarda Freudenberg
Introduction 521
Im Westen nichts Neues (*All Quiet on the Western Front*) (USA 1930) 522
Novel and Film Adaptation (*Post Processing*): A Comparison from a
Narratological Perspective 523
The Production of the Film from a Media-Aesthetic Perspective 527
Distribution: Posters and Advertisements 529
Reception: Political Debates and Censorship 532
Post Processing: Reactions and Debates in the Feature Pages of the
Daily Press and in Film Magazines 534
The Media Network Around *Im Westen nichts Neues* from a Synchronous
Perspective: *Niemandsland* and the *Westfront 1918* 537
Niemandsland from a Production Perspective 538
On the Reception of *Niemandsland* in the Mirror of Post Processing 540
Reception and Post Processing of *Im Westen nichts Neues* (*All Quiet
on the Western Front*) in Comparison with *Westfront 1918* 542
The Media Network around *Im Westen nichts Neues* from a Diachronic
Perspective 543
Im Westen nichts Neues: *Eine Graphic Novel* (2014) 543
Conclusion 545
References 545

Boyish Romance in a Timeless Idyll? 549
Winfred Kaminski
Preliminary Note 549
Career Steps 550
Upright and Down to Earth 552
Fight and Play 554
Defensible Bodies 556
Bold Realism or a Trendy Film? 557
Director and Composer 560
Instruction, Probation, Conversion 563
References 564

Notes on Contributors

Petra Anders is a university lecturer for German language and literature teaching at primary school level at Humboldt University, Berlin. *Main research interests*: Film didactics, digital media, inclusive German teaching, poetry slam.

Annika Behler was most recently a research assistant at the University of Bielefeld in the DFG project *German-language children's and youth literature in the media network 1900–1945* (focus: films) and works as a freelance editor and elearning content manager.

Julia Benner is a university lecturer of Modern German Literature/Children's and Youth Literature and Media at the Institute of German Literature at Humboldt-University in Berlin. *Main research interests*: Political aspects of children's and youth media, exile literature, conceptions of childhood, and literary theory.

Bernd Dolle-Weinkauff was Akademischer Oberrat and Kustos at the Institute for Children's and Young Adult Literature Research at the Goethe University Frankfurt. He is an honorary professor at the JNE University of Kecskemét (Hungary). *Main research interests*: History and theory of children's and youth literature and its media, historical children's and youth literature, fairy tales, pictorial stories and comics.

Ricarda Freudenberg is a university lecturer for German literature and its didactics at the Faculty II/German at the PH Weingarten. *Main research interests*: Acquisition of literary competences, aesthetic experience and text reception, children's and youth literature and its didactics, media in literature teaching.

Marlene Antonia Illies is a research assistant at Bielefeld University, Faculty of Linguistics and Literary Studies/German Studies. Her dissertation project deals with Wilhelm Speyer's *Kampf der Tertia* in the media network. *Research interests*: Film, historical children's and youth literature, and children's literary media networks.

Petra Josting is a university lecturer of German Children's and Youth Literature and Media at Bielefeld University, Faculty of Linguistics and Literary Studies. *Main research interests*: Children's and youth literature research, literature and media didactics.

Winfred Kaminski was a university lecturer at the TH Köln, from 2004 to 2015 managing director of the Institute for Media Research and Media Education. *Main research interests*: Children's and youth literature as well as children's and youth media, most recently in the field of digital media, especially computer games (co-founder of the international computer games conference *Clash of Realities,* since 2006).

Johannes Krause has been a lecturer for special tasks (LfbA) at Bielefeld University, Faculty of Linguistics and Literary Studies/German Studies in the Department of Children's and Youth Literature, Literature and Media Didactics since 2018. *Research interests*: dystopian children's and youth literature (in the media network), reading socialisation, new media.

Tobias Kurwinkel is a university lecturer in literary studies and didactics at the University of Duisburg-Essen and editor-in-chief of KinderundJugendmedien.de. *Main research interests*: Literature and media didactics, children's and youth media (especially picture books and film), theory of the media network, intermediality and transmediality.

Heidi Nenoff was a teacher in Leipzig until 2017; since then research assistant at the University of Leipzig in the area of elementary school didactics German for entrants to the job from different fields. PhD 2015 on natural law and religion discourse in a novel utopia of the early modern period. *Research interests*: Children's and youth literature.

Matthias Preis is university lecturer (Akademischer Rat) at the Faculty of Linguistics and Literary Studies/German Studies at Bielefeld University. *Main research interests*: Digital children's and youth literature research, aesthetic education, literature and media didactics (especially audio media).

Ulrike Preußer is a university lecturer for literature didactics at the Faculty of Linguistics and Literary Studies at Bielefeld University. Her *research interests* include literary-aesthetic learning processes and children's and youth literature (especially text-image media such as picture books and comics).

Caroline Roeder is a university lecturer at the Institute for Languages, Department of German, at the PH Ludwigsburg, where she is head of the Center for Didactics of Literature Children Youth Media. *Main research interests*: Children's and youth literature and its media in historical (especially GDR) as well as cultural studies perspectives (especially topography research), literary criticism, political issues in children's and youth literature.

Notes on Contributors xvii

Sebastian Schmideler is a research associate for children's and youth literature at the Faculty of Education/Elementary School German Didactics, University of Leipzig. Main research interests: History and theory of children's and youth literature from the eighteenth century to the present, transmission of knowledge, popularisation of knowledge, image-text analysis.

Friedrich Summann works at Bielefeld University Library and is head of the LibTec department. *Current fields of work*: Digital Information Services, Search Engine Technology, Metadata Processing, Publication Services, ORCID Support, Digital Humanities, Data Science, Monitoring Tools, Visualisation Techniques.

Ingrid Tomkowiak is a university lecturer at the Institute for Social Anthropology and Empirical Cultural Studies (ISEK), Dept. of Popular Cultures at the University of Zurich. *Main research interests*: Popular literatures and media with a focus on children's and youth media.

Gabriele von Glasenapp is a university lecturer in literature and literature didactics with a focus on children's and youth literature studies at the University of Cologne, as well as the director of the Arbeitsstelle für Kinder- und Jugendmedienforschung (ALEKI). *Main research interests*: Children's and youth literature (and media), German-language Jewish (children's and youth) literature, didactics of children's and youth literature.

Annemarie Weber was a research associate in the DFG project *German-language children's and youth literature in the media network 1900-1945* at Bielefeld University, Faculty of Linguistics and Literary Studies/German Studies. *Research interests*: Romanian-German literature and cultural history, history of children's and youth literature, media theories.

Gina Weinkauff has been active in university teaching in various functions and employment since 1995. Among other things, she was a research associate at the Heidelberg University of Education for over 20 years and held visiting and substitute professorships at the universities of Vienna, Leipzig and Bielefeld as well as at the Free University of Berlin. *Research interests*: Children's and youth literature under poetological, historical and didactic aspects.

List of Figures

Introduction: Concepts, Corpus and Strategies of Media Network Research

Fig. 1　　Media system according to Schmidt (2008a, 149) 11

Digital Explorations of Historical Media Networks

Fig. 1　　Systematics of the developed metadata set 104
Fig. 2　　Analogy of perspectives: *Google Street View* and *media network navigator* (Map data © 2020 Google and © 2020 Geo-Basis-DE/BKG) 109
Fig. 3　　Text box with record display (partial view) and media network navigator 110
Fig. 4　　Timeline representation using the example of *Robinsonades* 111
Fig. 5　　Media network profile in the donut diagram 112
Fig. 6　　Ranking of the media networks (excerpt) 112
Fig. 7　　Chronological network list for *Quax, der Bruchpilot* (excerpt) 113
Fig. 8　　Data flow from acquisition to visualisation 114
Fig. 9　　Technical infrastructure and requirement areas 115
Fig. 10　Advanced search and cursory network view 118
Fig. 11　Media network of *Schneewittchen* in the timeline view 119

From Children's Theatre to Film

Fig. 1　　Theatre bus in *Mit dem Kindertheater durch Deutschland* (1934) (03:57) 131
Fig. 2　　Free play in *Mit dem Kindertheater durch Deutschland* (1934) 132
Fig. 3　　Oversight of the battle of the children's gangs in *Der Kampf um den Stiefen Ast* 136
Fig. 4　　Guards in *Der Kampf um den Stiefen Ast* (from Genschow 1937, 48) 138

Mickey Mouse

Fig. 1   *Frühling an der Donau* (1931), from: *Film-Kurier* 17 (1931) 125, 2 148

Fig. 2   Mickey Mouse as an advertising figure. *Paradies der Hölle* (1930), from: *Kinematograph* 24 (1930) 270 of 18.11., 6 152

Fig. 3   Mickey Mouse (1942), from: *Kladderadatsch* 95 (1942) 40 of 04.10., 7 f., https://digi.ub.uni-heidelberg.de/diglit/kla (25.03.2020) 161

Funkheinzelmann

Fig. 1   Timeline of the Funkheinzelmann media network 168

Fig. 2   Hans Bodenstedt and his fairy-tale characters. Above, close to the microphone Funkheinzelmann. Source: *Die Funk-Stunde* (1926) 11, 253 (© bpk/Staatsbibliothek zu Berlin/Dietmar Katz) 171

Fig. 3   Cover of the children's magazine *Funkheinzelmann:* It advertises the Funkheinzelmann revue at Berlin Großes Schauspielhaus (© bpk/Staatsbibliothek zu Berlin/Dietmar Katz) 178

Fig. 4   Advertisement for Funkheinzelmann chocolate in the children's magazine *Funkheinzelmann* (© bpk/Staatsbibliothek zu Berlin/Dietmar Katz) 183

To the Moon and Back

Fig. 1   Hans Baluschek: *Peterchens Mondfahrt,* 13.12.1913. Watercolour, opaque white, pencil; 65.50 cm × 69.00 cm. Inv. no.: TA 99/2054.3 Hz (© Stiftung Stadtmuseum Berlin. Reproduction: Oliver Ziebe, Berlin) 208

Fig. 2   Illustration from: Bassewitz, Gerdt von/Baluschek, Hans: *Peterchens Mondfahrt – Ein Märchen.* Berlin-Grunewald: Hermann Klemm ³[1917], 79 (Kinder- und Jugendbuchabteilung der Staatsbibliothek zu Berlin, BIV, BIV 2b, 875 <3>) 209

Fig. 3   (**a**) Cover of the "Märchenspiel" version of 1912 and (**b**) Fairy tale picture book version [c. 1917] 210

Fig. 4   Cover by John Jon-And: *Lille Petters resa till Månen* (von Bassewitz © Bonniers: Stockholm, 1930) 211

In Never-Never Land

Fig. 1   Announcement of the stage play *Peter Gerneklein (Der Knabe welcher nicht gross werden wollte).* Playbill Mog: 2°/43, 1905/1906, in the possession of the Libraries of the City of Mainz – Wissenschaftliche Stadtbibliothek 232

List of Figures

Fig. 2 From left to right: Mary Brian as Wendy Darling, Betty Bronson as Peter Pan, Esther Ralston as Mrs. Darling (© 1924 Paramount Pictures), https://www.britannica.com/topic/Peter-Pan-play-by-Barrie (24.02.2020).. 243

Urian's Travels Around the World

Fig. 1 (**a**) Cover of the original edition of *Hans Urian. Die Geschichte einer Weltreise* and (**b**) of the Dutch and (**c**) Spanish translations (cf. The bibliography at the end of this article for the titles of the covers) 261

Fig. 2 *Hans Urian. The story of a journey around the world* (Tetzner © Reinbek: Rowohlt, 1975) 262

Fig. 3 *Hans Urian holt Brot.* Hand puppet film (DEFA 1961)...................... 264

"That Was a Wonderful Fairy Tale!"

Fig. 1 Illustration of the fairy tale *Der fliegende Koffer* by Vilhelm Pedersen, https://upload.wikimedia.org/wikipedia/en/9/9b/Flying_Trunk_01.jpg (25.03.2020) 279

Mutabor!

Fig. 1 (**a**) Peter finds refuge with a family in the countryside. Karl Ulrich Schnabel/Raff Fluri, *Das kalte Herz* (1933/2016), screenshot (© 2016 Ann Mottier-Schnabel/Raff Fluri), (**b**) Peter dreams of Holländer-Michel. Karl Ulrich Schnabel/Raff Fluri, *The Cold Heart* (1933/2016), screenshot (© 2016 Ann Mottier-Schnabel/Raff Fluri) 310

Fig. 2 (**a**) Holländer-Michel pursues Peter in the forest. Karl Ulrich Schnabel/Raff Fluri, *Das kalte Herz* (1933/2016), screenshot (© 2016 Ann Mottier-Schnabel/Raff Fluri), (**b**) Lisbeth considers whether to help the old man. Karl Ulrich Schnabel/Raff Fluri, *Das kalte Herz* (1933/2016), screenshot (© 2016 Ann Mottier-Schnabel/Raff Fluri) 310

Max und Moritz Across Media

Fig. 1 First edition of *Max und Moritz*, cover and prologue (© Munich: Braun & Schneider, 1865) 320

Fig. 2 The Buschiade as war satire: *Max und Moritz im Felde* (© Berlin: Schneider, [1915]) 326

Fig. 3 *Max und Moritz* in the paper theatre. Play by Ernst Siewert (© Eßlingen: Schreiber, 1887) 328

Fig. 4 Advertisement of a *Max und Moritz* film produced by the International Cinematograph and Light Effects Society, Berlin (© *Der Kinematograph* (1907), issue 17)... 330

Fig. 5   Rudolph Dirks' Wilhelm Busch-inspired series *The Katzenjammer Kids* was the first to develop the complete semiotic inventory of comics. – Episode from December 29, 1901 (© *New York Journal*) 334

Robinsonades Between 1900 and 1945

Fig. 1   Cover of the brochure *Was liest unsere Jugend?* (Siemering/ Barschak/Gensch © Berlin: R. von Decker, 1930) 357
Fig. 2   Front cover of *Radio-Robinson. A modern Robinsonade for the young* (Ziegler © Reutlingen: Bardtenschlager, 1924) 366
Fig. 3   Title page and frontispiece of *Radio-Robinson. A modern Robinsonade for the young* (Ziegler © Reutlingen: Bardtenschlager, 1924) 367

Beyond Romy and Lilli

Fig. 1   Cover *Das Mädchen Manuela. The novel to the film "Mädchen in Uniform"* (Winsloe © Berlin: Krug & Schadenberg, 2012) 387

Traumulus

Fig. 1   Cover *Traumulus* (Holz/Jerschke © Munich: Piper, 1905) 406
Fig. 2   Emil Jannings in *Traumulus* (1935) (© Beta Film GmbH, DFF – Deutsches Filminstitut & Filmmuseum/KINEOS Collection) 414
Fig. 3   Poster by B. Arndt for the re-release of *Traumulus* from 1949 (© DFF – Deutsches Filminstitut & Filmmuseum) 424

„Da stelle ma uns mal janz dumm"

Fig. 1   Cover *Die Feuerzangenbowle* (Spoerl © Reprint [1933], with an addendum by Joseph A. Kruse, 2008) 430
Fig. 2   Cover of *Die Feuerzangenbowle* (© Kinowelt Home Edition GmbH, 2009) 432

Emotionalisation Between Sexuality, Generational Conflict, and Discourse on Power

Fig. 1   Ad for *Entgleiste Jugend*, from: *Film-Kurier* 10 (1928) 36 of 10.02., 4 470
Fig. 2   Ad for *Primanerliebe* (D 1927a), from: *Film-Kurier* 10 (1928) 41 from 16.02., Beibl. 2 470
Fig. 3   Advertisement for *Die Siebzehnjährigen* (D 1929a), from: *Der Kinematograph* 23 (1929) 10 from 13.01., 3 474

The Commercial Genre Supersystem of Early Cinema Screen Detectives

Fig. 1 *Sherlock Holmes Baffled* (1900), https://www.youtube.com/watch?v=KmffCrlgY-c (24.01.2020) 484

Fig. 2 Movie poster of the first *Nick Carter episode Le Guet-Apens* (1908b), https://en.wikipedia.org/wiki/File:Nick-Carter-b.jpg (24.01.2020) 487

Fig. 3 Film poster of the first *Zigomar film* (1911), https://ru.wikipedia.org/wiki/%D0%97%D0%B8%D0%B3%D0%BE%D0%BC%D0%B0%D1%80#/media/%D0%A4%D0%B0%D0%B9%D0%BB:Zigomar.jpg (24.01.2020) 489

"Donnerwetter, das ist famos"

Fig. 1 Sibylle absorbedly contemplating the female figures. Film still (© Bundesarchiv Berlin, 18821_3) 509

Fig. 2 Sibyl at home. Film still (© Bundesarchiv Berlin, 18821_2) 510

Fig. 3 Accident scene with Lene. Film still (© Bundesarchiv Berlin, 18821_7) 512

Fig. 4 In the card room. Film still (© Bundesarchiv Berlin, 18821_6) 512

Fig. 5 Theatrical scene *Wallenstein's* Camp. Film still (© Bundesarchiv Berlin, 18821_5) 513

Pacifist Anti-War Films of the Pre-Fascist Era

Fig. 1 *Im Westen nichts Neues (All Quiet on the Western Front)*, bomb crater scene (1:15:46) 528

Fig. 2 *Im Westen nichts Neues* [ad] (1930), from: *Kinematograph* 24 (1930) 279 of 29.11., 5 530

Fig. 3 *Niemandsland* (00:54:04) 539

Boyish Romance in a Timeless Idyll?

Fig. 1 Dust jacket of the young adult novel *Jakko* (Weidenmann © Stuttgart: Loewe, 1939) 551

Fig. 2 Cover of the youth non-fiction book *Junges Europa* (© Stuttgart: Loewe, 1940) 553

Fig. 3 Cover page of the *Illustrierter Film-Kurier* (1941) on the occasion of the film release of *Jakko* with the two main actors Norbert Rohringer as Jakko and Eugen Klöpfer as his fatherly friend Anton Weber 559

Introduction: Concepts, Corpus and Strategies of Media Network Research

Petra Josting, Marlene Antonia Illies, Matthias Preis, and Annemarie Weber

The study of children's and young people's literature and its media networks in the period 1900 to 1945 is an attempt to make an innovative contribution to the historiography of children's and young people's literature, which until now has concentrated mainly on the medium of the book and thus often neglected inter- and transmedial aspects as well as the view of those involved in the so-called system of action in children's and young people's literature, i.e. the producers, mediators, recipients and processors.

The first aim of the research project was to record films and radio broadcasts that were produced for children and young people and/or selected for them and/or received by them in the period from 1900 to 1945 as completely as possible. Secondly, based on these two new forms of media, the aim was to record media compilations as comprehensively as possible, mainly including epic but also dramatic literature; i.e. not only novels, stories, picture stories or picture books were included, but also stage manuscripts and theatre performances. Thirdly, those discourses, pronouncements, announcements, etc. were recorded that refer to the individual medium as well as to the persons and/or institutions involved in the production, mediation, reception and processing of the respective media offer.

Parallel to this work, a metadata concept was developed in cooperation with Bielefeld University Library in order to build an online portal on this basis, in which both linked metadata and digital copies can be stored. Only the linking of metadata

P. Josting (✉) • M. A. Illies • M. Preis
Faculty of Linguistics and Literary Studies, German Studies, Bielefeld University, Bielefeld, Germany
e-mail: petra.josting@uni-bielefeld.de; marlene.illies@uni-bielefeld.de; matthias.preis@uni-bielefeld.de

A. Weber
Bielefeld, Germany

enables a comprehensive view of the development and constitution of media networks and at the same time generates new perspectives on the corpus of children's and youth literature.

In the following, the recording criteria of children's and youth film, children's and youth radio, children's and youth theatre as well as print media, records and advertising material are first outlined here in the introduction. This is followed by the theoretical framework of the project and an overview of the media networks of the period under investigation, including a brief description of the range of contributions presented in this volume. The orienting introductory chapter contains three overview articles in which Annemarie Weber presents the findings on children's and youth radio and Marlene Antonia Illies describes the development of children's and youth film as well as children's and youth theatre. Finally, Matthias Preis and Friedrich Summann in their contribution *Digital explorations of historical media networks. Outlines of portal development from an interdisciplinary perspective* display the potential of such an endeavour by describing how the database was conceived and constructed, and what kinds of presentation, visualisation, and research possibilities it offers.[1] In the following, the volume brings together thematically grouped essays on specific media networks from the period under investigation, most of which go back to the Bielefeld project conference *Lichtspiel – Hörspiel – Schauspiel* in September 2017.

Recording Criteria of Children's and Youth Film

Film and radio are the two main forms of media recorded in the database and form most of the corpus. The technical dispositives, the communication instruments and modalities, the institutional framings of the individual types of media had to be taken into account in the recording. In the case of film, these are mostly elaborate productions, usually well documented on filmstrips, because films were stored and duplicated, which enabled a spatially broad and temporally persistent distribution. However, it is precisely the early productions that puzzle researchers today, as the source material is often not preserved; around 80% of all silent films are considered lost and thus lost forever. The reason for this is the sensitivity of the nitrate film used until around 1951, which is highly flammable (numerous cinemas, storage rooms and entire film archives burned down) and decomposes if it is not stored at the right temperature and humidity. Therefore, only reports and messages from contemporaries can provide information about the content and production of the films that are no longer available. Sometimes extensive paratexts of production and reception provide insights, sometimes, especially in the early years of cinema, only a single advertisement testifies to the existence of a film.

---

[1] http://medienverbundportal.kjl.uni-bielefeld.de

The film industry was privately organised, and politics and society attempted to control the production and publication or consumption of films by children and young people by means of binding rules, censorship, overt or covert subsidies or obstructions. During the period under study, film censorship went through eight different sets of regulations – from an absence of any censorship to recommendations of veritable acts of war (awarded the rating of *jugendwert*) for minors. Regardless of this, contemporary studies (cf. Auer 1911; Dinse 1932; Kimmins 1919) and the discussions in film and daily newspapers prove that children found their way into the cinemas even if a film had not explicitly been intended to be viewed by them.

These components constituting the media system of *film* helped determine the rules of recording. The recording is based both on clear decisions at the distribution level – such as youth releases, screening in children's/youth performances or the predicate *jugendwert* – as well as on indications that point directly to reception on the part of children and young people, for example when fairy tale films or drama adaptations were shown in school performances (cf. theatre), or when films deal with youth issues and/or are about young people.

In order to indicate where a reception by children and young people on the part of the distribution is intended or factually proven by sources or not, the individual films were keyworded according to the categories common in the discourse surrounding children and young people's literature. The keyword *KJ-spezifischer Film* refers to all films that were potentially and from the outset made for children and/or young people; the keyword *KJ-intendierter Film* refers to those that were addressed to children and young people at the distribution level (via censorship, advertising, screening in children's/youth performances). The frequently used phrase *For Young and Old* in advertisements is indicative of deliberately attracting adults (who can pay for the cinema) to the cinema via their children (who want to see the film). In addition, school screenings and films that were shown in the National Socialist *Jugendfilmstunde* were also marked as *KJ-intendiert*, since here political authorities judged the films to be suitable for children/young people or even forced them to attend. The keyword *faktische KJ-Nutzung* was chosen for all films that appeared neither intended nor specifically suitable for children and adolescents, whose reception, however, is assured on the basis of sources. For those productions for which the availability of sources does not yet allow for a clear statement, the keyword *KJ-Nutzung unsicher* is used. In this way, doubtful cases did not have to be left out, and it was possible to collect a large corpus that forms the basis for further research. Of course, misinterpretations cannot be ruled out.

To develop media networks, new adaptations of *literarische Stoffe*[2] or remakes were also included, i.e. films produced after 1945. Based on the changing censorship measures of the period under investigation as well as changing attitudes towards what is suitable for children and young people, such *Stoffe* were also

---

[2] See Schulz (2011) on pp. 16 for a more detailed definition: He defines *literarische Stoffe* "as the main default for the plot of a narrative work (in literature, radio play, drama, film, comic, etc.)".

comprehensively considered that were given a youth release at least once and possibly only after 1945 as a cinematic adaptation. Moreover, not only film adaptations of *literarischer Stoffe* were included, but also independent specific and intended children's and youth films, in order to cover the entire spectrum of production for this audience. Films were then, and still are today, dominant forms of media that often entail further processing; in the simplest case, the film is followed by film criticism, but often the screening of films was preceded by detailed reports on the production, and sometimes the so-called book to the film already followed in the period under investigation; this is also how media networks are formed.

A particular film forms one dataset at a time. The film critics, reviews, censorship decisions, various evidence of reception in different spaces and contexts (usually *Print (sekundär)*), and advertisements (*Werbematerial*) are linked to this dataset.

The main sources for the survey were the film magazines *Der Kinematograph* (1907–1934) and *Film-Kurier* (1919–1945). They are among the most widely distributed film periodicals of their time, cover the majority of the period under investigation, and had different target audiences. *Der Kinematograph* was a film trade journal that saw itself as representing the interests of the German film industry. The various specialist editorial departments served the areas of film politics, legal advice and technology, film criticism and international film reporting. The *Film-Kurier* however, focused on current news regarding the film industry, film reviews and schedules of Berlin cinemas. The paper, which was published daily at times, was addressed to a broader audience, the potential visitors of the cinemas.

In addition, the relevant research literature was evaluated. Reference was made to relevant encyclopaedias (Schäfer 1998), almanacs (Klaus 1988–2006; Lamprecht 1969), chronicles (Birett 1980; Estermann 1965; Hembus/Brennicke 1983), film histories (Faulstich/Korte 1994; Kreimeier 2012; Toeplitz 1975) and overviews (Faulstich 2005; Jacobsen/Kaes/Prinzler 2004; Schäfer/Wegener 2009). Informative insights into the viewing habits of and film production for children and young people can be found in period-, theme-, or genre-centered contributions on the cinema of the Kaiserreich (e.g., Müller 2008; Maase 2008; Töteberg 2008; Elsaesser 2002), the Weimar Republic (e.g., Räder 2009; Stiglegger 2003; Crăciun 2018; Nowak 2018; Marzolph 2008), the Nazi period (e.g. Hobsch 2009; Strobel 2009; Belling/Schütze 1975; Brücher 1995; Sander 1944/1984; Stelzner-Large 1996), fairy tale film (e.g. Höfig 2008; Pecher 2017; Schäfer 2017; Hartmann/Nölle 2017; Tomkowiak 2017; Schlesinger 2017) or on censorship (e.g. Kopf 2003; Loiperdinger 2004; Kanzog 1994). With the help of research literature on popular culture and trivial literature (e.g. Maase 2001; Kerlen/Rath/Marci-Boehncke 2005), a significant corpus of de facto children's and youth films was able to be recorded.

Recording Criteria for Children's and Youth Radio Programmes

Radio, unlike the film industry, was tightly framed by state institutions.[3] After a short phase of controllable auditorium screenings reception became public and generally accessible – if one owned an appropriate radio set and, in the best scenario, also paid the radio licence fee. Consequently, there was already pre-ordered censorship in the production phase. Offensive broadcasts were not produced in the first place, radio was therefore *per se* appropriate for minors. As a rule, the audience was addressed by means of programmes produced especially for the respective target group, their age-appropriate placement in the course of the day and their corresponding announcement in the programme guide.

Another difference to film lies in the production and distribution technology: Programmes were transmitted live in the early years of radio and archived only in exceptional cases until 1929, which did not include those addressed to children and young people. Even from the period thereafter, vanishingly few recordings survived (cf. Elfert 1985, 11 and 57). The records of this project are therefore almost exclusively based on the information in the programme guides, which were systematically evaluated. As a rule, at least two publications were examined in parallel for the period of recording, in order to be able to check programme details and to find as many different commentaries, reviews, references to programmes and special pages for children and young people as possible.

In contrast to film, radio production can only be documented in the sparse programme information. Another essential difference between film and radio lies in the form of publication of the two media, which led to different recording modalities. While a film is a completed work and was screened as such, thus receiving an entry in the database, individual radio broadcasts are often hybrid forms. If, for example, a literary part of a programme was followed by instructions for handicrafts or if several fairy tales were told, the entry in the database was not made for the entire programme, but for the literary part of it for each individual fairy tale, whereby the entire programme of the respective broadcast is recorded completely in the data record for contextualisation. This is the only way to compare the processing of the respective *Stoff* in film and radio on the one hand and to establish *Stoff*-based media networks with printed works, recordings, theatre performances, etc. on the other. A concrete reference to the *Stoff* of the respective contribution was a prerequisite for its recording. Programmes with general information such as *fables, sagas, fairy tales* or similar were generally not taken into account.

The corpus in the field of radio broadcasting thus represents the programmes or programme segments with a literary-entertaining claim addressed to children and young people, which were produced and broadcast by the publicly licenced German-language radio stations, including Austria and – as far as published in the German programme press – the Swiss stations Bern, Basel and Zurich, from the

---

[3] Cf. the article *Children's and youth radio from 1924 to 1945* by Annemarie Weber in this volume.

beginnings in 1924 up to and including 1944. No relevant broadcasts could be proven for the last months of the war.

Programmes were taken into account which were either identified as being addressed to children or young people or which could clearly be assumed to be (also) addressed to children or young people on the basis of other characteristics (indications). There had to be at least two indications in order for the programme to be considered: The title (ambiguous as to whether it was addressed to children or adults) and the time of broadcast (before the evening programme). Programmes from the early evening were also included, which were broadcast mainly during the Christmas period for an undefined group of listeners and were addressed to *adults and children, large and small children, the whole family*, and the like. This category includes programmes that (also) recommend books received by children and young people, but which are aimed at an adult (buying) audience.

When recording according to circumstantial evidence, there is a greater margin of discretion, which may well lead to misjudgements of the programmes recorded or not recorded. For example, not all of the broadcasters' fairy tale programmes were included, and indeed not those which were broadcast in the evening, for an adult audience only, often in combination with classical songs. Programmes that were recorded on the basis of circumstantial evidence and not on the basis of target group addressability are marked as *nicht als KJ-Sendung ausgewiesen* (not designated as programmes for children and young people). Programmes which have been identified at least once as being addressed to a target group are considered to be addressed to a target group overall and are generally not marked with the remark above. Programmes whose reception by children and/or young people is attested to in contemporary documents have been included. The comedy *Flachsmann als Erzieher* is one example, which was broadcast as a radio play by Funk-Stunde Berlin on February 11, 1927 from 20:30. It was followed with great interest by the pupils of a reformatory – according to a report by their director – on the radio in the common room (cf. Rake 1927).

In the case of mixed spoken word and music broadcasts, only the spoken word contributions were created as separate data records. Pure song or music broadcasts (including opera, operetta, etc.) were not recorded, except for so-called *school operas*. Programmes produced to support teaching were also taken into account, provided they met the above-mentioned recording criteria in terms of subject matter and genre – as a rule, they were identified as *Schulfunk*.

Programmes exclusively devoted to factual topics (hygiene advice, handicrafts, questions of etiquette, etc.) were not included. If literary forms – such as the fairy tale or the saga – served to convey educational content or questions of knowledge, the broadcasts were included, such as the Funk-Stunde Berlin series *Onkel Doktor als Märchenerzähler* or the naturalistic educational plays by Erna Moser produced by Mirag. Target group specific broadcasts addressing film and radio were included for contextualisation, even if they were not focused on literary content.

Accordingly, not all programmes addressed to children and young people are included, but only those which meet the criteria and restrictions listed. Programmes without content details in the programme guides were only taken into account in exceptional cases, such as the project focuses on *Funkheinzelmann* and *Kasperliaden*; on the other hand, the Stuttgart series' *Gretle von Strümpfelbach erzählt* was not recorded, despite numerous broadcast episodes, because no details about its content can be found in the programme guides. Despite all the limitations, this project is the first comprehensive collection of sources on children's and youth radio of the first half of the twentieth century in the German-speaking world.

To capture the broadcasts, the programme notes/indications were transcribed. These programme notes are *paratexts* according to a term by Genette modified to electronic media by Stanitzek (2005). In Ellerström's (2017) sense, the transcriptions of the paratexts into the database are *transmedial representations* of the radio programmes. In the media network constructed and represented by the database, they assume the role of placeholders for the broadcasts they represent. Paratexts that refer to the radio programmes, such as (short) reviews, reports, teasers, synopses and illustrations, e.g. on the target group-oriented special pages of the programme guides – *miscellanies* in Stanitzek's sense – are created as separate data sets, marked as *print* or *Bild* (image) and linked to the radio programme to which they refer. In the media network, they thus take the place of independent *media offers* in the sense of *process results* from the interaction of the four action domains of the media system identified by Schmidt: production, distribution, reception and post processing (cf. Schmidt 2008a, 148).

The main source of data collection was the national and oldest programme guide *Der Deutsche Rundfunk* (Berlin), which was published from 1923 onwards. In addition, individual volumes or numbers of the following magazines were consulted: *Die Funk-Stunde, Funk-Woche, Die Sendung* (all Berlin), *Die Funkwelt* and *Die Norag* (both Hamburg), *Die Mirag* (Leipzig), *Die Werag* (Cologne), *Die Sürag* (Stuttgart), *Radio Wien* (Vienna). For the period from 1 June 1941, when the programme guides had to cease publication (cf. Bauer 1993, 209), the daily newspaper *Völkischer Beobachter* (Berlin) was included. In 1941–1942 it published the radio programme only occasionally so that no contributions are recorded for 1942. It was not until 1943 and 1944 that there was a daily radio section, but the limited information (approximately 10 lines) no longer contains any target group addressing. The few contributions selected from this period are based exclusively on indications – as a rule, they are fairy tale radio plays or readings.

Recording Criteria for Children's and Youth Theatre

Children's and youth theatre is understood to cover the entire range of staged performances of *literarische Stoffe* for children and young people (puppet and figure theatre, *Singspiel*, professional stage performance, *Laienspiel*, school theatre, etc.). During the period under study, private associations and pedagogical committees in all large cities aimed to create theatrical performances suitable for schoolchildren, and some professional theatres founded their own youth departments.

Although the focus of the project is on adaptations in radio and film, the theatre could not be left out, since large interconnected fields developed during the period under investigation in which the media of film, theatre and radio were interwoven in a variety of ways – e.g. in radio adaptations of classical dramatic *Stoffe* for youth radio or in the outstanding role played by *Kasperle* stemming fom the puppet theatre in radio, in numerous film adaptations of dramas as well as in the commitment of the Genschow-Stobrawa Children's Theatre to film.

The field of theatre was recorded in two forms: Stage manuscripts and plays regularly available in bookstores were created as *Print (primär)* and tagged with the keyword *Theater* for attribution purposes. In addition to plays whose performances for children and young people are mentioned by contemporary sources, the directory *Für Fest und Feier* (NSLB 1935) was evaluated and the recommended plays recorded. This builds on the *Verzeichnis wertvoller Spiele für die Schul- und Jugendbühne* (VDP 1932) and, compared to the previous one, has been expanded primarily to include the sections *Sprechchor, Musik* and *Spiel und Bewegung*, as well as new publications that conform to the National Socialism. Since the majority of the plays in this list correspond to the older list (including the annotations), it was possible to build up a text corpus of recommended plays for children and young people that is valid for the Weimar Republic and the Nazi period.

Performances were created as a dataset *Theater.* An individual production can be recorded with varying degrees of accuracy depending on the source situation. Sometimes the underlying stage manuscript including the author is known and preserved, press releases and archived playbills reveal the names of the directors, actors and other persons involved in the production. In other cases, only a brief announcement is found: For example, *Snow White* was performed in a particular theatre as a Christmas fairy tale for children. Where further research was unsuccessful, these productions were recorded despite and with the limited information. The same keywording as for film was used to further identify the target audience: *KJ-spezifisch, KJ-intendiert, faktische KJ-Nutzung* and *KJ-Nutzung unsicher.*

In addition to *Für Fest und Feier*, contemporary monographies (e.g. Röttger 1922; Stahl 1911; Kalk 1926) on the subject have been evaluated. The statistics on school performances in various cities over a long period (from 1900) in Friedrich Bonn's *Jugend und Theater* (1939) proved particularly helpful. They made it possible to record numerous, mainly classical plays that were performed for children and young people or whose respective productions were at least recommended for them – in addition to *Minna von Barnhelm, Götz von Berlichingen, Die Räuber* and *Die Jungfrau von Orleans, Wilhelm Tell* occupies a prominent position throughout the entire period under investigation.

The trade journals *Das Puppentheater* (1923–1931) and *Der Puppenspieler* (1931–1933) were systematically evaluated and provided information on the development of puppet theatre in Germany. The theatre magazine *Die Schaubühne* was also examined, which from 1905 to 1918 was a good source for premieres and the general development of the German theatre industry, and always contained information about fairy tale plays, school performances, and children's and youth theatre in general. From April 4, 1918, the magazine was published under the new name *Die Weltbühne*, thus taking into account a development that can be observed since 1913: It was no longer a pure theatre magazine, but more and more turned towards economic and political topics. Nevertheless, it was studied until the last issue in 1933, as important references from the world of theatre, literature, film and radio could still be found. The aforementioned film and radio magazines also enriched the theatre corpus: The *Film-Kurier* had its own theatre section, which occasionally reported and reviewed plays for children and young people; on the radio, theatre performances were occasionally broadcast live.

Recording Criteria for Print Media, Vinyl, and Advertising Material

Books that were recommended or read on air in the radio broadcasts are recorded as separate records in the edition used (if reconstructible) and linked to the respective radio record. The same applies to printed works that were used as models for films, radio plays, theatre performances or other media adaptations. In the case of general information on the literature used (such as the Brothers Grimm's *Kinder- und Hausmärchen*),[4] we have attempted to include the first edition. In addition to these printed works marked primary literature, all secondary literature used in the project was also included in the database and linked to the corresponding *Stoff*, media and persons involved. Secondary literature primarily comprised scholarly discussions of specific (primary) works, but also included other contributions, discourses, and announcements, as long as they could not be assigned to the field of advertising texts. Contemporary sources from the period under investigation as well as research literature before and after 1945 were included. The online catalogues of the public libraries via the central network of the Gemeinsamen Bibliotheksverbund (GBV/VZG) or the Karlsruher Virtueller Katalog (KVK) were used to secure the bibliographical data.

The search for vinyl records was found to be difficult due to the lack of cataloguing of the medium. However, references to this storage medium, which was relatively new at the time, were found in the radio magazines evaluated, as recordings were also broadcast on radio for children and young people, and these are listed as independent records in the online portal. The corpus is rather narrow with just under 130 records and consists predominantly of fairy tale narratives, fairy tale radio plays, *Kasperle*-plays and *Funkheinzelmann* stories, but characters such as Mickey Mouse and those from *Struwwelpeter* also made their way onto vinyl records. According to Elfert (1985, 110), these were not original productions of the record companies, but successful contributions that had previously been broadcast on radio

---

[4] An index of the primary literature and films cited here in the introduction is omitted.

and subsequently recycled on disc records. Pigorsch (2001) however, in the case of the *Funkheinzelmann* disc records, assumes that they were produced directly for the new storage medium.

Advertising materials were mainly present in printed form during the period under study. The majority of the records recorded here (1793 in total) are advertisements that were primarily placed for films and were a natural part of the industry press. Film and theatre posters and star postcards also fall into this category. The emerging interest of the toy industry can be seen in dolls of famous media personalities, such as the Funkheinzelmann or the child star Shirley Temple, board games for the films *Emil und die Detektive* (1931) and *F. P. 1 antwortet nicht* (1932) or a card game for Lotte Reiniger's *Doktor Dolittle films* (1928).

Media Networks: Theoretical Frameworks

Media as a Compact Concept According to Siegfried J. Schmidt

The project *German-language children's and youth literature in the media network 1900–1945* was structured around Siegfried J. Schmidt's *media compact concept* (*Medienkompaktbegriff* – cf. Schmidt/Zurstiege 2000; Schmidt 2008a; cf. also Schmidt 1993, 2000, 2008b, 2012). Schmidt does not start from single forms of media, but designs a complex media system structured by four interrelated components, which in turn interact in four action domains. These components are (1) the communication instruments, (2) the technological devices or media techniques for the production, dissemination or reception of individual media offers, (3) the institutions for the production, financing, representation, etc. of the media offers, and finally, (4) the media offers themselves, which emerge from the interaction of the various components. The four components interact in four action domains: production, distribution, reception and post processing (Fig. 1).[5]

The term *post processing* is in need of explanation, when used "all processes [are to be understood] in which media offers are made the object of new media offers" (Schmidt 2012, 148), i.e. this includes both the diverse forms of media criticism (reviews, recommendations, etc.) and all forms of what classical intermediality research calls media change (Rajewsky 2002) – e.g. the film adaptation of a novel or, beyond that, merchandising articles. The basic structure of the media system allows for a differentiated observation of individual subsystems, such as radio or film. It also allows for the observation of different action roles in the different action domains (such as production and reception) and also the description of their hybridisation and mixing in the so-called media convergence (*Medienkonvergenz*, cf. Josting 2014).

---

[5] For the English version of Schmidt's theory of media as a compact concept see *Media Philosophy – A Reasonable Programme?* (2008b).

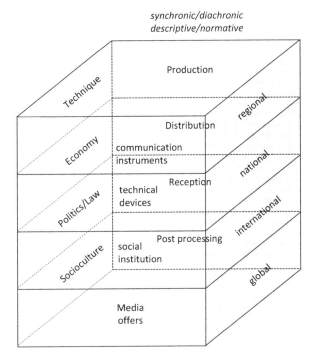

Fig. 1 Media system according to Schmidt (2008a, 149)

Schmidt later expanded his media theory to include the concept of *emotions* (cf. Schmidt 2014, 134–147; cf. also Schmidt 2005). This was unavoidable when dealing with visual media. His cube remains unchanged (cf. Schmidt 2014, 161), even though he now places it in a larger cuboid, which he refers to as *media culture* (the cube within it as *media system*). Four "folders or attractors" are involved in the interrelationship of emotions and media, he argues: "Cognition, emotion, morality (normative orientation), and empraxis (assessment of life-practical relevance)" (Schmidt 2005, 18). Particularly when observing early film and its reception by guardians and the adolescent audience, the analytical extension of the media system to include the concept of emotion is purposeful.

Limits of Schmidt's Media System Model

Compared to simpler models, Schmidt's system-oriented theoretical approach has the advantage that it considers actors, roles, social frameworks, cultural practices, technologies and dispositives along with the individual media products. The heuristic separation of, for example, the action roles of production, publication, distribution and usage should not lead to the erroneous conclusion that there are no transitions and forms of hybridisation between them – especially in the digital space (cf. Schmidt 2008a, 148). Schmidt, however, focuses less on the increasingly colourful interplay of media convergence: What are the videos of a so-called influencer? Product advertising or home story? Entertainment or business? What is an influencer? A fan, an advertising model or an actor in a reality soap? More like all of the above. In addition, he/she mixes and combines in his/her person the roles of producer and author with that of the performer and the portrayed character. Influencers who promote media events or products can themselves create events and become media stars. Roles and levels of action, it seems, have become interchangeable in many places. And even the communication genres that Schmidt still clearly distinguished (e.g. advertising, literature, journalism) often merge into mixed genres.

Schmidt's model allows for a structured view of the overall media system but does not resolve it finely enough if the dynamics of media networks are to be described. What led from the show to the series? Why did a character become popular, dominate the media market and disappear again sooner or later? Therefore it is worthwhile to also look at models that focus on other aspects of media developments. Above all, models based on the concept of *popular culture* moved into the research focus of the project work, including the well-known works by Henry Jenkins and Marc Steinberg, but also lesser-known works that deal critically with the aforementioned.

Popular Culture Network Models

The popular culture media models are, similar to the system-oriented models, holistically conceived, i.e. they integrate media in the narrower sense with their social, political and economic interactions. However, they tilt Schmidt's cube, so to speak, so that the reception and usage of media products takes precedence over their production. Thus the users of media products are at the top of the hierarchy, and they are also endowed with producer properties. The media industry – according to John Fiske (2011) – only provides the raw material with the product; it is the users who endow it with meaning and significance through its use. Popularity is generated through intensive use. The most excessive users are the *fans*. The self-creative practice of media users is strengthened in this model. Some critics of cultural studies see this as a "normative privileging of the fan or user perspective" (Kelleter/Stein 2012, 262). Intense usage, extensive exploitation and excessive fan culture are elements that have a dynamic effect on the development of media networks.

The Media Convergence Model by Henry Jenkins

Henry Jenkins, probably the best-known theorist of popular culture, is to be thanked for an interconnected model that under the name of *Medienkonvergenz* has also become popular in the German academic discourse. Jenkins (2006) describes the contemporary media economy as a *convergence culture*. In this model, media content migrates and multiplies on different platforms. Old and new technologies converge in the process. Authorised producers and users (fans) jointly contribute to a story that is told transmedial and synergetically.

And what fuels this process? In the case of *The Matrix*, a network that Jenkins describes as exemplary, the technological-semantic innovation thrust that aroused the interest of users was a decisive factor: For the first time the Wachowski siblings had designed a film as a completely fictional world and had it realised in collaboration with many creative people in a diverse product and media offer (Jenkins speaks of *the Matrix universe; the Matrix world*). In this way, different markets and audiences were served at different times via different communication channels (media) (film, TV, books, comics, games market, fan communication via the Internet, etc.). Jenkins explicitly mentions tangible economic interests of media companies and the market instruments for their realisation (keywords: *franchising, licensing*), without, however, paying analytical attention to them.

Jenkins' Critical Reception

Jenkins' *storyworld* has been widely received, often criticised, but also used as a research model by many authors, some of whom have developed their own models based on it. A summary (especially of the blog reception) is provided by Hanns Christian Schmidt (2014). In his study of American TV series, Jason Mittell (2014), for example, describes Jenkins' transmedial *storyworld* as one of several possible narrative strategies of a media network. Mittell calls it a *canonical integration strategy*. All participants respect the diegesis; a coherent story emerges whose individual narratives relate to each other like puzzle pieces. Heinz Hengst coins the term *script* for this composite strategy. The *script* is both "prescriptive and formable" (Hengst 2014, 152), it guarantees coherence on the object side, enables creativity on the subject side, and serves as a guide to action for all participants.

In contrast, some extensions do not stick to the *script*, but develop alternatives, side and counter stories, imagining the characters in completely new contexts of action. Jason Mittell speaks of *What if?* versus *What is strategies*, performative role-playing versus coordinated work on the canon (cf. Mittell 2014). *What if?* strategies would rather characterise fan culture, *What is* rather licensed *franchising*.

In the aforementioned popular cultural models, convergence, transmedial, synergetic *storytelling*, canonical and subversive narration, in short means and methods of narration, are highlighted as extension strategies of media networks.[6] When the proliferation and integration of media networks is to be described, the acting characters in some scholarly works move into a central position. Heinz Hengst describes the *character* in media networks, which is examined in the English-language literature, as an unrivalled key concept.

---

[6] Transmedial narration as an analytical model for media networks was a prominent topic in the project group's theory workshop on June 15, 2018 (cf. Meier 2020).

Marc Steinberg's Character-Centred Media Networks

Characters are made a key concept in a major study by Marc Steinberg, whom Heinz Hengst (2014) acknowledges accordingly in the aforementioned essay. In *Anime's Media Mix*, Steinberg (2012) describes how the characters of a Japanese comic book, through their usage on television as an anime series, became catalysing elements of integration as part of a large media network; he calls these media networks, driven and held together by characters, *character driven media environment* or *character driven media mix*.

According to Steinberg, it was the technically innovative conversion of Japanese comic characters into a TV format and its unique aesthetics that made these characters adaptable for other forms of media. A third element added to the connectivity was a market-based input. Osamu Tezuka, the producer, had sold his series *Tetsuwan Atomu* to the television company deeply under-priced, so to cover his expenses, he struck an advertising deal with a chocolate manufacturer. To better promote their chocolate, the company produced stickers (adhesive pictures) featuring the characters from the anime series, which they added to the packaging. With the stickers, the anime characters entered the lives of children and became omnipresent. Soon, chocolate became less and less important, people bought them to collect the characters. A cartoon character thus became the constitutive and nodal element of a communicative network, the *character network*. Steinberg compares Tezuka with Walt Disney, who was the first to engage in *character merchandising*.

Large media networks clearly don't grow without good marketing. Steinberg devotes an entire chapter to the *character business*. In the case of the *Matrix network* analysed by Jenkins, art and commerce created a successful combination too, the *storyworld* was marketed professionally. The profit expectations of the companies involved and their activities to maximise profits are strong drivers for the development and expansion of the media networks.

Seriality Theories

Another noteworthy approach to modelling the dynamics of media networks is offered by seriality theories. For some of its theorists, seriality is considered to be the momentum of popular culture par excellence. According to Kelleter/Stein (2012, 263), "there is no central management in the field of popular productions and receptions". Serial proliferation is a process of (narrative) proliferation that is inscribed with self-serialisation and the ability to generate variations through authorial reflection. The model of the momentum of series is fascinating, however it rather describes how popularity works (namely via self-serialisation), but not how a media product becomes popular or serialisable in the first place, or why its popularity (the momentum of its serialisation) eventually dries up. This model cannot explain the beginning and the end of seriality.

The works collected in Kelleter's volume *Populäre Serialität* (2012) represent different, partly contradictory approaches. Sabine Sielke, for example, in her contribution arguing at the edge of cognitive and cultural studies (cf. Sielke 2012), differentiates between seriality on the one hand and network on the other (which Kelleter/Stein think together). Seriality allows for the description of processes based on repetition and difference, while the network relies on inclusion. Sielke contrasts the spatial structure of the network with the temporal dynamics of echo, mimicry and adaptation.

Serial narration is examined from various perspectives. Hoppeler/Rippl operationalise the concept of *continuity* (cf. Hoppeler/Rippl 2012) in order to describe the connection and the tension between the individual episodes of a series that encourage continuation. Ganz-Blättler analyses a reality show under the concept of *cumulative storytelling* (cf. Ganz-Blättler 2012). Denson/Mayer take up the concept of *storytelling engines* coined by Michael Chabon (2008) in order to highlight the "dynamic of incessant continuality and re-enactability" (Denson/Mayer 2012, 187) of popular series.

Several works focus on *serial figures*. Denson/Mayer construct two different types of persons for the media of the nineteenth and twentieth centuries: *Serial characters* and *serial figures*. While the characters in a linear or episodic narrative develop a biography and thus complexity and depth, serial figures are basically flat, striking, without psychological depth and biographical continuity. This is, in fact, the basis of their success. This is the only way they can be used in ever new contexts and media. They are liminal figures, border crossers between worlds and media. Their "de-characterised flatness" allows them to change mediums "light-footedly" as soon as "the boundaries of a certain format have been explored" (ibid., 194). Denson and Mayer's *serial figures* are thus related to Steinberg's *characters*.

Network Discussion in Children's and Youth Literature Research

Ute Dettmar (2016) and Markus Raith (2016), among others, have dealt with the findings on the seriality of popular culture narratives published in Kelleter (2012). The relevant specialist discourse in children's and youth literature research likes to focus on structural-typological aspects, but the models are also frequently discussed in didactic contexts (cf. Krumschlies/Kurwinkel 2019).

From a historical perspective, Heinz Hengst – following Steinberg – outlines a historical development in German children's and youth literature from early hierarchical-vertical media networks to today's dynamic networks that integrate media and non-media elements. This modelling is taken up by Tobias Kurwinkel (2017). Furthermore, Kurwinkel analytically separates media networks on the one hand and product networks on the other, and adds the image of rhizomatic proliferations to his model, following Deleuze and Guattari (1977). Birgit Schlachter (2016) also refers to the image of the rhizome and links it to Umberto Eco's model of seriality (1989).

For Deleuze and Guattari, the rhizome is a complexly conceived philosophical category whose exemplary nature for media networks has been asserted many times, but which remains to be analytically proven. The metaphor of the rhizome, applied to the proliferation of media networks, suggests an organic, natural proliferation and growth, which for a phenomenon framed by legal regulations, by market forces, by social and political institutions, and taking place on man-made communication platforms, can conceal rather than reveal complexity.

Aren't the large media networks of the Internet age to be seen more like social networks such as Facebook or Google? For these, scientists have calculated growth curves and found mathematical formulas. One of them – called *preferential attachment* according to a theory by Barabási/Albert (1999) – states that new connections are most likely to emerge where there are already many other links. Overall, the larger a network, the more attractive it is to other potential users. Above a critical mass, its growth accelerates, the growth curve goes steeply upwards. Translated into media language: The more popular a media network, the higher its chances of becoming even more popular faster. This growth pattern has been called the *Facebook curve* (cf. Heuser 2018).

Storytising as Brand Management

Concepts such as *brand* and *merchandising* are an integral part of any form analysis of media networks today. But how does the interplay between fictional storytelling and the advertising industry work so that popular products are produced, consumed and new offers made, i.e. media networks are created? These questions are left unanswered by most literature and media studies. Therefore, a closer look at economics seems unavoidable.

A model of thought that links fiction and the connected emotional experience with the facts of the economy can be found in a book entitled *Dream society* from 1999. Its author, the futurologist Rolf Jensen, parallels the reality of companies with the reality of human experience, which is characterised equally by rationally recognisable stable structures and by emotional ups and downs. According to Jensen, management or marketing that wants to react adequately to the needs of market participants must shift to emotionalisation, to *storytelling*. Georgios Simoudis (2004) developed Jensen's theory further and identified *story-centered brand communication* as a central value-creation instrument of the post-industrial information age. Simoudis coined the term *Storytising* (the title of his book) for brand management. The story is the focal point, while advertising is more or less incidental. Jensen had developed his theoretical concept for a prosperous information society in the future. Simoudis shows that *storytising* was also successful with older brands (e.g. *Lurchi*).

From another direction, semiotic literary theory, Scolari (2009) argues very similarly: *Transmedia storytelling* – the title of the essay around Jenkin's concept of information-based media networks – has brought about a veritable mutation in the advertising-based media industry: It is no longer a matter of embedding a commercial brand in a fictional offer through advertising, but this (the transmedially told story) is itself built up as a brand (cf. ibid., 599). Although Scolari addresses the parallelism of the media industry to the advertising industry, he does not go further to show the actual strategies that both industries use to develop brands. He is analytically content to record a cartography of expansion, which he applies radially: A core narrative is enriched by micro, parallel, edge as well as user-generated stories from the inside out. The distinguishing features of the brand are the characters, the motifs and the aesthetic style of the fictional world, which can be transported transmedially.

Marketing Science Models

How brands function, are designed and developed is answered by specialised economic theories, e.g. the concept of *identity-based brand management* (cf. Meffert/ Burmann/Koers 2005). The so-called *emotional branding* (cf. Burmann/Nitschke 2005) provides information on the fact that and how brands are strategically emotionalised. It shows how the emotionalising power of events, fans and so-called endorsers is used in a market-oriented way.

The *story worlds* and their *characters* can also be found in economic studies. *Storytelling* (Jensen 1999) and *Storytising* (Simoudis 2004) refer to narrative strategies from the perspective of the advertising industry that are intended to make a brand attractive; *brand fiction* is a marketing buzzword that has also been addressed in media studies (e.g. Scolari 2009). Whether the story is generated by an entertainment medium or the advertising industry is ultimately irrelevant from a market perspective. What is important is the function of the story, which is to make the brand strong, to endorse it with genuine character and personality.

Under the title *Character-Oriented Franchise*, Jason Scott (2009) analyses the early media networks of the American entertainment industry and shows how their central figures (including the comic characters Felix the Cat, Mickey Mouse, or Woody Woodpecker) proliferated medially according to free-market criteria (according to the principle of franchising), whereby serialisation and merchandising are viewed as equally important instruments for profit maximisation. Mickey Mouse and Felix the Cat were already popular in the Weimar Republic. The early American media industry was a great economic model for German media entrepreneurs. The modern market and advertising mechanisms were well known in Germany in the 1920s, and they were also already the subject of scientific research (cf. König 1924).

The theoretical models outlined above were presented to the contributors of this volume in a workshop in June 2018 as a stimulus and put up for discussion. We were particularly interested in the dynamic models that show how media networks function, expand and diversify. In doing so, we looked at systems theory, popular culture theory, and economic theory. The contributions to this volume critically engage with some of the models on offer, while others are used to reinterpret the corpus.

Media Networks from 1900 to 1945

Definition

According to previous findings, the term *media network* (*Medienverbund*) was first used in 1972 in a paper on the subject of the *public sphere and experience* by Negt/ Kluge (1972), to which Hengst drew attention (cf. Hengst 2014, 144). In line with leftist currents of the time, the authors were largely concerned with "setting a framework for a discussion that opens up the analytical terms of political economy downwards, towards people's real experiences" (Negt/Kluge 1972, 16) and thus with the dialectic of bourgeois and proletarian public spheres. To simplify their account, they focus "on two newer mass media, the media network and television" (ibid.). And as was common in discourse contexts of the *Frankfurter Schule* and the *Critical Theory* it represented at the time, the theorists are keen to expose the so-called consciousness industry (cf. ibid., Chap. 5). They differentiate these into two groups: On the one hand, "traditional media", such as "press, publishing, film, adult education, radio, television"; on the other hand, "advanced, predominantly privately organised media", under which "[the] cassette industry, videodisk, wire radio, satellite radio, database, media network" (ibid., 232 f.) are subsumed. When such "new technical-organisational developments" lead to a "change in the form of the company", i.e. to the concentration of groups that use both traditional and new media, Negt/Kluge use the term "media network" (ibid., 233). They see a great danger in the fact that the companies of a media network influence the individual "on all channels and from all sides through entertainment, news, educational programmes" (ibid., 250).

It is well known that the *consciousness industry* has multiplied many times over in the meantime, as has its influence, even though media effects research in recent decades has been able to show that recipients are self-determined subjects who can actively deal with media or actively appropriate media content. Nevertheless, it is becoming increasingly apparent that many people are not in a position to do this, especially adolescents, who need to be introduced to questions of media ethics and media criticism, especially in educational institutions. However, here is not the place to discuss this problem in greater detail. Despite this is important to be aware of the original meaning of the term *media network*, which, as outlined, initially refers in abbreviated form to the economic level and therefore, following Schmidt's *media compact model* (2008a, 149), should also be considered in its broader dimensions. It refers to the entire media offer, thus also to production, distribution, reception and processing. An expansion of the understanding of the term, albeit without an exact definition, can be found a good 20 years later in Werner Faulstich's *Grundwissen Medien*, which first appeared in 1994. In the context of the factual article on *media economics*, Faulstich speaks both of the "media network on the provider side" and the "multimedia networked intensive media use" (Faulstich 2000, 51). And in the discussion of *media history*, he uses the term to describe changes at the time of the Reformation and the invention of printing technology, when the "new media leaflet, pamphlet/booklet and book [...] came onto the market in a media network with human media such as the singer and preacher" (ibid., 35).

Hengst, who has been working on questions of media networks in the German-speaking world for about 25 years, focuses on *children's* media culture and the analysis of media networks for children from the 1970s onwards. His search for translations of the term *media network* in the English-speaking world led to the terms "commercial supersystem, meta-media, or children's global multi-media" (Hengst 2007, 23; see also Hengst 2014, 144). While each of these placed a particular emphasis, they were useful insofar as they "refer to identity-creating (structural) features" (Hengst 2007, 23). Like many other theorists, Hengst thus focuses on economic and global aspects of the media network that have been observable for a long time, but also considers the level of the recipients. In this context, as noted above in the theoretical framings, he introduces the notion of the "script", which includes "details of plots or narrative elements, protagonists/actors, stages, sets, and props", all of which allowed for a certain "openness" or "formability" (Hengst 2007, 23). In the script, a kind of screenplay, he thus sees the unifying phenomenon of a network. For the analysis of media networks for children and adolescents in the period 1900 to 1945, this approach seems useful, but the openness and formability of a script are always limited, as Hengst himself notes. Instead, we prefer – as a heuristic and, in terms of data entry, pragmatic point of reference – the broader concept of *Stoff* in order to distinguish diverse compositions of media networks.[7] The following is understood when using the term *Stoff*

> as the main default for the plot of a narrative work (in literature, radio play, drama, film, comic, etc.). This default is not invented by the author himself, but found elsewhere: [...] As a pre-formed set of characters who have certain characteristics, their relationships and the sum of certain actions, a S. can be grasped relatively concretely, often also in its spatial and temporal situatedness. [...]. One does not encounter S. in a neutral 'basic form', but always only depending on the design conventions of the genre in which they have been found. In this respect, 'S.', even if the term seems very representational, does not denote anything real: To speak of the 'S.' of an artistic utterance is to undertake a modelling by which the level of content and action of this utterance is reduced to the extent to which it can be regarded as dependent on the level of content and action of its 'source'. (Schulz 2011, 312)

The core element *Stoff*, as can be read above, refers to the dependence of the "design conventions of the genre" (ibid.) and thus also of the individual form of media, whose respective aesthetic components play a central role, as Jutta Wermke already drew attention to (cf. Wermke 1997, 100). In concrete terms, we can thus assume the following regarding media networks: Namely that they "[...] assemble an aesthetically identifiable ensemble of media products under a lead medium." (Ibid.) And it is not relevant here whether a successful literary product in the form of the medium of a book, film, radio contribution, magazine article, etc. is followed by a second, third or multiple usages "or whether a 'package' is brought to market from the onset

---

[7] This is not to deny that – as explained above – other central influencing factors such as *character, brand*, etc. may not also be of importance in media networks.

with high expectations of success." (Cf. ibid., 67) Accordingly, we already use the term media network if there is a second usage, and it is likewise irrelevant whether the media network is on the market within a relatively short, manageable period of time so that it is available to recipients in its entirety.

The examination of approximately 3000 *Stoffe* in the period under investigation shows that it is not possible, and would be cutting it short, to clearly identify a limited number of media network types. Concerning current media networks, such an approach, as currently found (cf. Krumschlies/Kurwinkel 2019), is even more questionable, as such attempts at systematisation are based on a far too small empirical basis. Nevertheless, polarities can be identified that could serve as an orienting description and – if sufficiently valid – at least an approximate classification. These include antinomic constellations such as *synchronous* vs. *asynchronous* emergence, *national* vs. *international* branching, *Stoff-centered-* vs. *character-centeredness*, *serial* vs. *non-serial* continuation, *target group consistency* vs. *target group variance, centrist* vs. *rhizomatic* expansion, *leitmedial* vs. *plurimedial* constitution, *pre-industrial* vs. *culture-industrial* provenance, *high-cultural* vs. *popular-cultural* domain, *aesthetic* vs. *economic* impetus, etc. It must be taken into account that quite a few of the (heuristic) poles have the potential to hybridise or replace each other, i.e. are also conceivable in transitional and mixed forms. Against this complex background, it seems sensible to point out dynamic hotspots in the context of media networks, which is possible by using the visualisation of bibliographic data (Digital Humanities). Hotspots mean the accumulation of a *Stoff* on the level of one or more forms of media representation in a manageable period of several years, and equally includes the level of reception and processing.

Spectrum of Media Networks

Given the limited research time, the material indexed within the framework of the project cannot and does not claim to be complete, as outlined above in the description of the research procedure with regard to film and radio data. Nevertheless, the conception and establishment of the online database[8] has created the prerequisite for supplementing the existing material in the future and thus expanding the current state of research. At present, the diverse visualisation possibilities of the data offer, on the one hand, preliminary, but on the other hand, already meaningful findings and thus possibilities for analysis.

In the following, therefore, an attempt will be made to outline the spectrum of media networks and to show developmental dynamics. In general, it can be stated that the *Stoffe* in the media networks refer to a broad range of common genres and themes in children's and young people's literature – to series such as penny dreadfuls, but also to adult literature that was received primarily by adults as drama on the

---

[8] Cf. the contribution by Matthias Preis and Friedrich Summann in this volume.

stage, classics, bestsellers or new publications, but was then also accessible to a younger audience, especially in the course of film adaptations, because the censors either did not impose any age restrictions on them or provided for releases, e.g. from the age of 14. For children and young people, the media networks that played a central role in the period under investigation were those whose *Stoff*, mostly in printed form, had been part of the classic repertoire of children's and young people's literature since the nineteenth century, such as fairy tales, legends, Robinsonades and Kasperle[9] shows.

Since the second half of the nineteenth century, Kasper has been one of the most famous figures in puppet theatre; Franz von Pocci's *Neues Kasperl-Theater* (1855) is considered the founder of Kasperle comedy as an independent genre of children's literature. Most Kasperle plays are initially based on the fairground tradition in terms of *Stoff* and dramaturgy and are set in an adult milieu. It was only later that the typical arsenal of characters with a policeman, robber chief and crocodile established itself, as it is still known today (cf. Brunken 2008, 258 ff.) and delights both children and adults. Hotspots of the *Kasperle theme* appear in the period under study from 1924 to 1941: New Kasperle plays were published almost annually, and in parallel the character began to appear on the radio, often in the form of radio plays, but also in readings; in 1927, for example, there were 56, and in 1938 52 broadcasts. At the same time, a series of animated films appeared in the 1930s and up to 1944. The various representations are accompanied by paratexts such as commentaries on radio broadcasts or reviews of films, as well as instructions for crafting puppets such as the *Kasperle-Bastelbuch* (1934).

Fairy tales became increasingly important in children's and youth literature in the second half of the nineteenth century, as they were recommended as private reading and included in the curricula of elementary schools. To a greater extent, they also appeared in dramatic form as so-called fairy tale plays, predominantly written for the public stage. Another special feature is that, due to their comparatively short text length, they appear not only in fairy tale collections, but also in yearbooks, calendars and anthologies, as well as in fairy tale picture books. In this respect, it is a genre that developed as a media network early. The most important representatives are the Brothers Grimm with their *Kinder- und Hausmärchen* (1812/1814), but Ludwig Bechstein, Wilhelm Hauff and Hans Christian Andersen are also important. The significance of Grimm's work in the period under study is especially demonstrated by the fact that silent and sound film as well as radio broadcasting made equal use of the fairy tale *Stoff*.[10] Around 50 film versions of the Children's and Household Tales have been found and they are represented in almost 1300 radio broadcasts, especially in the early years; for example, in 1929 with 162 broadcasts. In the context of radio and fairy tales, the writer Lisa Tetzner deserves special highlighting. During the Weimar Republic, she toured the country as a

---

[9] German comedic Punch and Judy shows accompanied by puppetry with a certain set of stock characters.

[10] Both film and radio, however, only linked to a Grimm original if there was clear evidence of it; otherwise, only to the fairy tale material, since numerous adaptations could be the basis.

storyteller, published collections of fairy tales, became the director of the Berlin Children's Hour in 1927, and thus regularly told or read fairy tales, among other things; a total of 116 of her radio broadcasts have been identified.

Ancient and Norse-Germanic sagas of gods and heroes as well as local and regional folk tales had firmly established themselves in the canon of (not only) children's and young people's reading in the nineteenth century. It is therefore not surprising that the new types of media film and radio also liked to reference this genre, albeit to a lesser extent than fairy tales; a preference on the part of radio can also be clearly seen. Here there were regular programmes about sagas, many of them regionally linked, which were usually broadcast by the radio station of the corresponding broadcasting area. The *Nibelungen saga* stands out among the many sagas, with its hero Siegfried, the avenger Kriemhild, the proud Brunhild, and the battle-hardened Hagen, which has been adapted epically and dramatically for adults, but of which there have also been many adaptations for young people since the last third of the nineteenth century (cf. Krienke 2008). Representations in books, dramas and on stage were joined in 1924 by two films by Fritz Lang titled *Siegfrieds Tod* and *Kriemhilds Rache*, which were met with great success, as can be seen from reviews. Hotspots on the radio can be identified within youth radio between 1926 and 1929 with almost 20 broadcasts, but the Nibelungen continued to be present in the 1930s. Parallel to this *Stoff*, Münchausen[11] also experienced an increase in popularity in children's and youth literature since the 1870s, which was noticeable in prose adaptations, picture sheets, and picture books, but also in merchandising products such as "advertising collector's stamps, card game[s], glossy picture[s], and postcard series" (Wiebel 2008, 756 f.), thus marking the beginning of a large media network for adolescents. The *Stoff* grew immensely with ten films between 1920 and 1944 and around 50 contributions to radio (1926–1940).

If one looks at the *Stoffe* in the database and focuses on the largest number of linked records (ranking), which in turn refer to various types of media, in addition to those mentioned further media networks become evident. These for example refer to: Serial characters who amazed audiences as heroes of penny dreadfuls and subsequently thrilled audiences in silent films, or vice versa (e.g. Harry Piel or Nat Pinkerton); adult literature, which – as mentioned above – was subsequently filmed and attracted young people to the cinema, including boarding school stories with the motif of student suicide, which had been famous in epic and dramatic poetry since the turn of the century; classics such as James Fenimore Cooper's *Lederstrumpf series* or Heinrich Hoffmann's *Struwwelpeter* from the first half of the nineteenth century; contemporary children's literature. Contemporary children's literature such as Erich Kästner's *Emil und die Detektive* or historical figures such as Otto von Bismarck and Fridericus Rex.

Harry Piel is currently the media network with the most extensive record. He is considered a media pioneer who made his first film in 1912 and from then on was

---

[11] In the research literature, Münchhausen is assigned to different genres, the humorous or the swan and lie poetry, the picaresque literature or the fairy tales, fables or sagas (cf. Wiebel 2008, 756).

active in the film industry as a director, actor and producer, with detective, adventure and sensational films that had audiences at the edges of their seats. Between 1918 and 1933 alone he appeared with at least three movies a year, in 1919 even nine *Harry Piel* movies were released. Due to this spectacular success, the Leipzig-based Speka-Verlag, known for its booklet literature with heroes such as Sherlock Holmes or Buffalo Bill, published the *Schundliteratur* series *Harry Piel – der tollkühne Detektiv* (cf. Bleckman 1992, 91 f.) from 1920 onwards. The booklets, like the films also loved by children and young people, were initially based on old *Harry Piel films*, but these soon no longer sufficed as a model, so that further *Harry Piel stories* were invented according to a familiar pattern (cf. ibid., 91 ff.). Hotspots over a long period of time in the field of film, in which Piel was continuously active beyond 1945, are accompanied by an extensive production of booklets, especially in the first half of the 1920s. Hotspots in the field of reception, no less extensive, range from 1924 to 1942. Similar fame in the two aforementioned media, albeit with fewer film adaptations, but present instead with productions in the theatre and radio of the Weimar Republic, was achieved only by Sherlock Holmes, which has continued to this day. Nevertheless, detectives such as Nick Carter or Nat Pinkerton and adventure heroes such as Buffalo Bill were also penny dreadful and silent film characters who kept their age-spanning audiences in suspense at the beginning of the twentieth century.

The character of Lederstrumpf, created by James Fenimore Cooper, ties in well with the heroes last mentioned here in that he too took over the penny dreadful in the early 1920s and has long been one of the classics of children's and young adult literature. Like Daniel Defoe's *Robinson*, Cooper had written his five *Lederstrumpf novels* (1823–1841) for adults. They the plot centres around the trapper Natty Bumpoo, also known as Lederstrumpf, who mediates between settlers and Indians on the prairie. As adventure literature for young people became more popular in Germany in the second half of the nineteenth century, abridged versions for young people increasingly appeared on the market here as well. By 1900, there is evidence of more than 90 adaptations (cf. Pellatz-Graf 2008, 633), some of which were reprinted until 1944, for even the NS-*Schrifttumswalter* were full of praise for Lederstrumpf. For example, the prize-winning youth writer Fritz Steuben [i.e. Erhard Wittek], himself the author of Indian novels, wrote that a "National Socialist, German attitude" (ibid., 70) could also be discerned in Cooper's novels, that "two races" fought fatefully "for their right to live" (Steuben 1938, 70 f.), thus illustrating once again how literature was appropriated during the Nazi era. As far as the media network of this *Stoff* in the period under investigation is concerned, the series *Der neue Lederstrumpf* (*The New Leatherstocking*), comprising several hundred booklets, stands out alongside the many adaptations; furthermore, several silent and live films as well as numerous radio broadcasts from 1926 to 1936 in the form of readings, children's performances, biographical information about the author, and radio plays.

One of the best-known classics of children's and youth literature is Heinrich Hoffmann's *Struwwelpeter* (1845), the picture book written in humorous verse and a caricaturesque illustration style with its ambiguous and subversive stories of naughty and wicked children (cf. Friese 1995). This brief description also addresses what was innovative about Hoffmann's picture book at the time, which also has intermedial references to the new optical media of the time, such as photography and the magic disc. The popularity of the book, which – then as now – was met with both positive and negative criticism, can be seen in the 132 adaptations that appeared up to 1900 alone (cf. Wilkending 2008, 30), i.e. *Struwwelpeter* called upon many authors to imitate it, a trend that continues to present day with the publication of *Struwwelpetriad* books. For example, the *Kriegs-Struwwelpeter* was published in 1915, and the *Rundfunk-Struwwelpeter* and the *Struwwelhannes* in 1926. Parallel to these and other Struwwelpetriads as well as new editions of the original, the *Stoff* also caught the film industry's interest. It was the actor, director and screenwriter Fritz Genschow who made no less than five films in 1935, silent films with the written addition "for home cinema": (1) *Der Struwwelpeter*, (2) *Der Suppenkaspar*, (3) *Der Daumenlutscher*, (4) *Der Zappelphilipp*, (5) *Hans guck in die Luft*. Another *Struwwelpeter film* was made in 1938 by Hubert Schonger, who was known for his nature films. Hotspots can be seen in radio, which initially broadcast only readings from 1925 to 1940, but later also radio plays and musical comedies.

During the period under investigation, a whole series of films were made that were based on plays or novels for adults; some of these were historical and socially critical films, boarding school stories were also popular. As stated above (cf. Recording criteria of children's and youth film), these and others were intended children's and youth films. With the introduction of censorship, many were declared *jugendfrei* (*PG-rated*) or given the notation *für Jugendliche ab 14 Jahren (for age 14 and above)*. Often they could not only be received in the cinema but, as in the case of special state awards during the Nazi era, were compulsory viewing, so to speak, because they were screened in the so-called HJ youth film hours, such as the school story *Traumulus* (1935). Many novels were written about the Hohenzollern Frederick the Great, also known as *Fridericus Rex* or popularly as *Alter Fritz*, for adults and young people. Books printed as early as the Weimar Republic, such as *Friedrich der Große. Unser Held und Führer* (1936) by Oskar Fritsch were reprinted under National Socialism and recommended for young people. There are also numerous silent and sound films dealing with this particular German ruler: The *Fridericus Rex films* made in the early 1920s were hugely successful, as were those produced in the 1930s/40s by well-known directors as Hans Steinhoff with *Der alte und der junge König* (1935) and Veit Harlan with *Der große König* (1942).

This volume deliberately refrained from including contributions on media networks around classics such as *Emil und die Detektive* or *Heidi*, which are often referred to in literary studies as well as literature didactics regarding media networks. Instead, the focus is on media networks that have received little or no attention to date. The contributions collected in this volume take up individual genres and topics of the outlined spectrum of media networks, in part they expand it, and are briefly presented in the following, sorted into seven categories: *Pioneers Take over New Types of Media – Stage Children Migrate to Radio and/or Film – Fairy Tales in Film and Radio – Classics in All Types of Media – School Stories in the*

Theatre, Book and on the Screen – Crime and the Scandalous on the Big Screen – Politics Take over Book and Film.

Petra Anders, Johannes Krause and Annemarie Weber deal with pioneers who took over the new forms of media in the period under investigation in their unique way – the actor, director, producer and screenwriter Fritz Genschow, the Disney character *Mickey Mouse* and the radio character *Funkheinzelmann* from created by the radio director Hans Bodenstedt.

Petra Anders discusses *Media Convergence in the Early Work of Fritz Genschow and Renée Stobrawa.* Among other things, she discusses Genschow's feature film *Der Kampf um den Stiefen Ast*, which was influenced by his experiences with children's theatre and resulted in the book version *General Stift und seine Bande.* Furthermore, it fundamentally elaborates how the Genschow/Stobrawa couple developed a concept of the youth film studio that held together the story world of their diverse, convergent, and transfictional media network. What becomes clear from the perspective of the *Stoff* is that *General Stift und seine Bande* almost simultaneously appeared as a film and book in 1937, with the latter following as a children's novel with film images. In addition, the play *Kinderraub in Sevilla*, published a few years earlier, also flowed into the story. The motif of the gang of children thus migrated from theatre to film, or from film to book. Instead of fictional entities or narrative links, it is above all Genschow/Stobrawa's pedagogical concept that ensures the recognisability of the making of the narrated *Stoff*. Hotspots around *General Stift* can only be found in 1937 in the area of reception parallel to the publication of the book and film.

In his article *Mickey Mouse – an All-American Character in 1930s Germany* Johannes Krause deals with the still famous Mickey Mouse character by Walt Disney, who was also built up from an animated film character into a successful brand in 1930s Germany. In contemporary reception, in the course of great admiration for the films, there is a conspicuously frequent reference to Mickey Mouse as a typically American character. What is to be understood by this and how this understanding affected the reception of Disney's works or the productive handling of them is the subject of this article. The findings form the basis for the analysis of two productive realisations of the *Mickey Mouse* brand: The first is the comic strip *Mickey's Rosenmontag,* the second is a comic strip from the time of the Second World War that turns the mouse into a symbol of the American enemy. Hotspots of the *Stoff* in Germany can be found in the years 1930 to 1933 in books, films and above all radio; worthy of mention are the two records from 1930, *Micky Maus beim Hochzeitsschmaus* and *Micky Maus auf Wanderschaft.* An intensive examination of the character and the Disney empire, however, did not begin until 1935 and lasted until 1940.

Annemarie Weber analyses the *Funkheinzelmann – the Multimedia Career of a Radio Character* who was invented in 1924 as a fairy tale character for the children's programmes of Norag (Nordische Rundfunk AG) in Hamburg by the station's director Hans Bodenstedt and quickly became a brand name for the station. Bodenstedt developed the character for the new medium of broadcasting on the basis of stories which he largely wrote, directed and also spoke himself for the broadcasts. Funkheinzelmann's name and stories combined the classic fairy tale (*Heinzelmann*) with modern transmission technology (*radio*) and the current zeitgeist. The character quickly became popular, taking over even the largest theatrical stages for several years at Christmas time, being used in books, pressed onto records, and even a children's magazine of the same name and *Funkheinzelmann chocolate* appeared for fans. None of the *Stoffe* analysed in the volume feature as many hotspots as *Funkheinzelmann*, spanning the years 1924 to 1931.

A whole series of media networks originated on stage with successful theatrical productions because their protagonists thrilled the audience, be it the maybug Sumsemann, the *eternal* child Peter Pan or Hans with the rabbit Trillewipp. They began their triumphal march from the stage and conquered radio and/or film in their own specific way, as Julia Benner, Ulrike Preußer and Gina Weinkauff show.

In her contribution on *Peterchens Mondfahrt and his Journey Through Media*, Julia Benner deals with one of the best-known German-language stage plays and examines the different transformations in the period from 1911 to 1945. She concludes that one must distinguish between direct and indirect as well as retrospective and prospective media networks. If one considers the *Stoff* she uses as well as her findings from the perspective of the *Stoff*, a media network emerges whose beginnings lie in the Romantic period and which, especially with a recent film adaptation, extends into the present. The publication of the fairy tale play in 1912 was followed by several other publications and parallel theatrical performances until 1942 in Berlin. The numerous broadcasts on the radio up to 1936 should be emphasised, whereby for the year 1925 no less than seven could be proven, the majority of which were broadcast by the Breslau radio station. *Peterchens Mondfahrt* was either told by Kitty Seifert as a children's *fairy tale*, staged as a *Märchenspiel in sieben Bildern*, or presented to listeners in excerpts just before Christmas. Hotspots of the *Stoff* can be found in the mid-1920s, primarily in the field of radio.

Ulrike Preußer examines *Never-Never Land* and thus the history of the creation and dissemination of *Peter Pan, the eternal child,* up to the present day. While the popularity of the fantastic figure was immense in the Anglo-American world from the very beginning, it took much longer in Germany. Until 1945, it was primarily the play translated into German, an American film adaptation, and the translation of a few chapters spun off from a novel that were published under the title *Peter Pan im Waldpark* and made the story popular. This article is devoted to the creation and development of the literary character Peter Pan as a *transworld identity in a* text-oriented manner. Peter Pan first appears in the adult novel *The Little White Bird* (Barrie 1902). Some excerpted chapters appear in German translation under the title *Peter Pan im Waldpark* (Barrie 1911). However, the *Stoff* is more readily available to German audiences as the stage play *Peter Gerneklein* (1910), which appears in an altered version under the title *Peter Pan oder das Märchen vom Jungen, der nicht groß werden wollte* 1943. *Peter Pan* was released as a silent film in America in 1924 and German cinemas in 1925 under the title *Peter Pan, der Traumelf,* where it was well-received by critics. The *Stoff* did not arouse much interest among broadcasters: Only in March 1930 excerpts from the book read were on the Königsberg and

Danzig stations. In the period under investigation, therefore, there is a media network, and no hotspots can be found.

Gina Weinkauff examines *Urian's Travels Around the World* and thus the *Hans Urian Stoff*. Under the title *Hans Urian geht nach Brot. Eine Kindermärchenkomödie von heute* (Béla Balász and Lisa Tetzner), a successful children's theatre production appeared in Berlin in 1929 about a hungry working-class boy who travels around the world accompanied by a talking and flying rabbit, gaining elementary insights into the political economy of capitalism. Its success is also evident in numerous adaptations and sequels, the most notable of which is the novel version *Hans Urian. Die Geschichte einer Weltreise* by Lisa Tetzner, which has been repeatedly published and translated into many languages. A large number of radio stations discussed the novel in 1931/1932, and in 1932 the author herself even read from her book on a Swiss radio station, which must not have been difficult for her as an experienced storyteller and her extensive experience as head of the children's hour on Berlin radio. In addition – until 1933 and then again after 1945 – further narrative children's books were produced which varied the plot, as well as an animated film by DEFA. The article sheds light on the development of the *Stoff* since 1929, but also deals with its prehistory by revealing various pre-text references. The fact that no larger media network was initially able to develop around this *Stoff* during the period under investigation, and thus no hotspots are discernible, is related to the persecution of Lisa Tetzner and her husband Kurt Held, both of whom emigrated to Switzerland in 1933.

It has already been mentioned that since the nineteenth century fairy tales have often appeared as so-called fairy tale plays and not only in collections, but also in yearbooks, calendars, anthologies and fairy tale picture books. In their research, Annika Behler and Ingrid Tomkowiak show how fairy tales quickly conquered the new media of film and radio and how large media networks were created.

Annika Behler demonstrates in her article "*That was a Wonderful Fairy Tale!*" – *Der fliegende Koffer von H. C. Andersen in the Media Network* demonstrates that the fairy tale *Der fliegende Koffer* by the Danish writer Hans Christian Andersen is part of an extensive media network by looking at the *Stoff* from the beginning of its publication to the present. The story of a man's failure due to his own vanity and the motif of the flying suitcase with which he travels still has unbroken popularity, both nationally and internationally. There is a great variance in aspects such as motifs, topography, characters, target groups or even readings of the fairy tale. The common constant or essence of the media network is the memorable image of the flying suitcase, but there is no clear chronological development of the *Stoff*. Several printed editions, numerous radio broadcasts and two films were found for the period of the project. The first media adaptation was Lotte Reiniger's silhouette film of the same name from 1921, and interest in this fairy tale was also shown during the Nazi era, when it was produced as a Kasperle film by the Hohnstein Puppet Theatre as late as 1944. The radio was particularly interested in this *Stoff*, with a total of 17 broadcasts, especially in the Weimar Republic, e.g. as part of the broadcasts *Die Rundfunkprinzessin erzählt* or *Die Stunde der Jugend* and as a *Märchenhörspiel mit*

Musik. In addition, radio plays of the same name were still broadcast until the beginning of the Second World War. Hotspots lie in radio between 1924 and 1939.

Ingrid Tomkowiak deals with the *Kunstmärchen by* Wilhelm Hauff in the medial transfer, which are among the best known in the German-speaking world. Initially discredited as trivial literature, some of Hauff's fairy tales were soon canonised as children's literature and, from the early twentieth century onwards, were mostly filmed as such. This article presents early film adaptations of Hauff's fairy tales *Die Geschichte von dem kleinen Muck, Die Geschichte von Kalif Storch* and *Das kalte Herz* and sheds light on their contemporary setting. Depending on the sources, different aspects of production, distribution and reception are included. The films adapt the originals in their own specific way – historicising, updating, ideologising, aestheticising, psychologising – and thus contribute through expansion, modification and transposition to their transformation or to the innovative continuation, differentiation and diversification of the respective source text and its levels of meaning. Both Hauff's fairy tales themselves and some of the early film adaptations are attested to have been much more daring productions than the more recent ones are – on an aesthetic, technical or even content/society-related level. Concerning *Die Geschichte von dem kleinen Muck*, for example, there are hotspots in radio from 1925 to 1937, framed as they were by the 1912 and 1944 film versions and also accompanied by theatrical productions. The same is true for *Das Kalte Herz* and *Kalif Storch,* although in the case of the latter the film versions are more numerous.

Classics of children's and youth literature express basic human needs and conflicts in a simple form. Their narrative scheme often follows the pattern of *exodus, struggle, probation and return home.* There are clear oppositions of good and evil, happiness and misfortune, the preferred places are unlimited fantasy worlds such as caves, forests, gardens or islands, and their protagonists always invite admiration or compassion. As the history of children's and youth literature shows, such heroes have not only conquered the hearts of many generations but have also passed through all types of media. Bernd Dolle-Weinkauff and Sebastian Schmideler show this with the example of the characters Max and Moritz and Robinson.

In his study "*Max und Moritz*" *across Media – And a Closer Look at the Comic Strip* Bernd Dolle-Weinkauff works out that numerous follow-up products developed from the prank story *Max and Moritz* by Wilhelm Busch up to present day. In addition to the theatre, the new types of media film and radio, which emerged after the turn of the century, are also involved. The core and mainstay of development, however, is the print media – the picture book and the illustrated stories distributed in booklets or periodicals – which, in addition to the large number of original editions distributed in numerous languages, with the so-called *Buschiads,* set certain forms of adaptation and parody to which the productions in all other forms of media are oriented. He, therefore, describes the history of *Max und Moritz*'s impact as a rudimentary media network phenomenon, characterised by a persistent dominance of the original medium and the *Stoff* presented in it. In addition to continuous editions of books during the period under investigation, there is evidence of no less than 20 films made up to 1941, the majority of which were animated films, but also silent and live-action films. However, *Max and Moritz* were very present on the radio from 1925 to 1941: Hotspots in the years 1928 to 1934, in the initial phase of this new medium more as readings, but overall mainly as radio plays, and so-called Singspiele and children's performances can also be found.

Sebastian Schmideler examines *Robinsonades between 1900 and 1945 – from Silent Film Classic to Radio-Robinson* and thus devotes himself to the *Robinson Stoff*, which thematises the insular seclusion of a person and goes back to Daniel Defoe's novel *Robinson Crusoe* from 1719. Due to the presence of *Robinson Crusoe*'s *Stoff* in adult literature and the broad reception of the Robinsonades in the field of children's and youth literature, *Robinson* has been very present since the nineteenth century, both as private and family reading and as a subject of instruction and school reading *Stoff*. The article deals with numerous individual types of media, highlights different media networks and comes to the conclusion that the modernisation process of the years 1900 to 1945 can be seen in the affinity to the thematisation of innovative technology such as telegraphy, radio, aircraft construction, war technology in literary book-centred Robinsonades such as *Radio Robinson* and *Flieger Robinson,* but also in US film parodies such as *Mr Robinson Crusoe.* The development of traditional book-media Robinsonades (adventure type, non-fiction type) is quantitatively and qualitatively more far-reaching than their qualitative degree of innovation in exploitation in the media network, despite the radio and film adaptations being open to the new mass media. If we assume that the *Stoff* was always present in printed media, hotspots appear in the combination of book and film in the years 1913 to 1924, and the combination of book and radio in the first half of the 1930s.

Within the school stories, boarding school story constituted itself as a genre of youth literature in the second half of the nineteenth century, and since about 1900 a new, an independent literary genre was added with the motif of pupil suicide. Sometimes the motif is first found on the stage, but often also in novels, migrating from there to the screen. How media networks developed around this motif and within the genre of school history is the subject of the contributions by Gabriele von Glasenapp, Petra Josting and Heidi Nenoff.

In her article *Beyond Romy and Lilli* Gabriele von Glasenapp examines Christa Winsloe's story, written in the early 1930s and marketed under the title *Mädchen in Uniform,* with regard to its media network qualities and also in relation to other media networks. In terms of the subject matter, it deals with schoolgirl suicide at boarding schools and school and social criticism; in terms of genre, it is a Backfisch or boarding school story. The article analyses the media network spanning the years 1930 to 1936, the transmedial narrative worlds since the 1950s as well as intertextual and intermedial references within the drama, film and novel versions. It becomes clear, among other things, that the *Stoff*, which was written in the final phase of the Weimar Republic *and* initially appeared as a stage play under the title *Gestern und Heute* and thus in the theatre, only achieved its breakthrough with the film version of 1931, which bears the title *Mädchen in Uniform* and became the guiding light for subsequent media adaptations; this also applies to the author's novel *Das Mädchen Manuel. Der Roman von Mädchen in Uniform,* which was published in 1933 and translated into numerous languages. While the screening of the film, produced by

Carl Froelich, continued to be allowed in Germany and was highly successful both within and outside of Europe, Winsloe's works were on the *Liste des schädlichen und unerwünschten Schrifttums* from the mid-1930s. Consequently, the hotspots of this first media network were put to an end by the Nazi regime.

In her contribution *"Traumulus" – From Naturalistic Drama to National Socialist Film Adaptation*, Petra Josting devotes herself to the media network centred around *Traumulus*. The drama by Arno Holz and Oskar Jerschke, published in 1905, was one of the most successful productions on German-language stages in the first half of the twentieth century. Almost 800 performances were recorded in the 1904/05 season alone. The play was enthusiastically performed well into the 1940s and was also staged in West Germany. The subject matter is student suicide in a boarding school and school and social criticism of the Wilhelminian era. This criticism was taken up by the Nazi rulers and re-functionalised for their great goal, the building of a *new empire*. The National Socialist elite took part in the production of the film of the same name, which was released in 1936, e.g. the producer and director Carl Froelich as well as the actor Emil Jannings. Both received high awards for this movie which was awarded with the rating of *staatspolitisch und künstlerisch besonders wertvoll* (*state-political and artistic especially valuable*) in the same year and was also shown to teenagers from the age of 14. The film was also met with an enthusiastic audience abroad and was even broadcast by the Paul Nipkow television station in Berlin-Witzleben on April 5, 1937. Hotspots of this *Stoff* first appear with the extensive coverage of the filming in the fall of 1935, which extends into 1942, because up to this point the film was still being shown and the drama was also being staged.

In her contribution *"Da stelle ma uns mal janz dumm"*, Heidi Nenoff analyses the media network *Die Feuerzangenbowle,* a story about high school students in the Wilhelminian era with the typical, comedy-producing schoolboy pranks, interwoven with a love story. At least this is how the *Stoff* and genre are still anchored in cultural memory today, and the 1944 film version of the same name starring Heinz Rühmann still is an integral part of popular culture. The beginnings of its mass circulation date back to 1933, when the first part of the novel was printed in the liberal daily *Der Mittag* from April to May. The first film version – also starring Heinz Rühmann – appeared a year later under the title *So ein Flegel,* the second as *Die Feuerzangenbowle* towards the end of the Second World War, and the third in 1970. This article concentrates on the analysis of the novel and a comparative examination of the three film versions, taking a close look at the respective historical contexts, content, and sound and image levels. A characteristic feature of this media network is its enduring popularity, both before and after 1945. Radio did not play a significant role in this during the Nazi period, for only once, on April 2, 1934, did Leipzig radio broadcast a reading under the title *Lausbubengeschichten aus der 'Feuerzangenbowle'*. Even then, the first film version was decisive, with sales of the novel rising to over half a million copies, and during the war there were even Wehrmacht editions. Thus one can speak of a stable presence of book and film throughout the Nazi period, accompanied throughout by hotspots on the reception level.

Murder and other crimes, commissioners, and detectives – older literature, unfortunately, does not know any women in these functions – have always fascinated readers of different age groups and milieus. The majority of German literary studies turned away or turn away rather contemptuously. In children's and youth literature, crime stories first appeared in the village stories of the nineteenth century. With the advent of booklet and colportage literature, addressed to adults but devoured by adolescents as well, heroes such as Sherlock Holmes appear on the scene, quickly succeeding in film. In the 1920s and 1930s, these detectives were joined by other groups of characters, for example from real life or girls' literature, as the contributions by Marlene Antonia Illies, Tobias Kurwinkel and Caroline Roeder show.

Under the title *Emotionalisation between Sexuality, Generational Conflict, and Discourse on Power,* Marlene Antonia Illies deals with the *Steglitzer Schülertragödie* as a media network, the starting point of which is a criminal case: A 19-year-old shoots his sister's boyfriend and then himself. A fellow pupil of the suicidal murderer is accused of complicity, spends eight months in custody, stands trial and is acquitted. The subject matter is thus student suicide, which has appeared in German literature in large numbers since 1900. The article shows how this case was narrated, processed and exploited. The multitude of medial manifestations as well as the intermedial references are considered, which also refer to further media networks; medial (re)processing still exists after the turn of the millennium. The focus of this article, however, is on the level of contemporary adaptations in the years 1927 to 1929. The *Stoff* left its mark above all in the film industry; on the one hand, it aroused interest among production companies, and on the other hand, a number of films were advertised with reference to this *Stoff*. For example, *Primanerliebe, Frühlings Erwachen* or *Die Siebzehnjährigen,* but this *Stoff* was also present on the stage. Hotspots can be found in 1927, directly after the crime, as well as in 1928 in the course of the trial coverage in the press, furthermore in 1928/1929 with reports on plans to film the *Stoff,* its actual production and finally at a great scale with the publication of the film reviews.

Tobias Kurwinkel is dedicated to the *Genre Supersystem of the Early Cinema Screen Detectives* and traces the history of early detective films on the basis of selected protagonists such as Sherlock Holmes, Nick Carter, Stuart Webbs and Joe Deebs as media networks of a genre system. He works out that with the beginnings of the detective film in 1900, the media network around the character Sherlock Holmes is characterised by intra- and intermedial references between the media offers. Furthermore, he takes a look at cinematic serial narration for the period up to the end of the Second World War and shows that the so-called penny dreadfuls in particular formed the basis for film series of the genre in terms of structure, content and dramaturgy. In the print and film sector, the media network shows hotspots for *Sherlock Holmes* in the years 1910 to 1917, and for *Nick Carter* in the years 1913 to 1932. In the case of *Sherlock Holmes,* three theatre productions were also found for the year 1906, one in the Bürgertheater in Vienna and two in Hamburg, one in the Thalia Theater, the other in the Deutsches Schauspielhaus, which illustrates the interest of bourgeois circles in the detective story genre and the *Stoff* of *crime.*

Under the title *Donnerwetter, das ist famos*, Caroline Roeder analyses the media network surrounding *Was tun, Sibylle?* The literary model for the film for young people was the girls' book by the author Sofie Schieker-Ebe, which was published in 1930 and has the same title. The central setting is the school, where a theft has to be solved. The article focuses on the representation of the construction and shaping of girl characters in the medial context in order to relate the image of the girl created in the book to the contemporary figure drawings of women and girls, which have found their way into literary and art research on the Neue Sachlichkeit under the catchwords *New Woman* and *New Girl*. Furthermore, the film version of 1938 will be compared with the novel in order to show changes that are not only due to the media adaptation, but also possible shifts in the evaluation of gender images and arrangements – the latter being related to the revanchist image of women under National Socialism. Other ideological inscriptions, *modernisations,* questions of pedagogy and dramaturgy are also examined. The book was reprinted several times during the Nazi period up to 1943 (as it was in the FRG), and the film was shown in occupied foreign countries, such as Slovakia. Hotspots of the *Stoff* can only be identified in a few years after 1938.

Two, at first glance, completely contradictory *Stoffe* stand at the end of the volume. One is about anti-war films and Remarque's still famous book *Im Westen nichts Neues* (*All Quiet on the Western Front*), the other about a book for young people by the Nazi author Alfred Weidenmann and its film adaptation. What they have in common, however, is the political, albeit of course in a completely contrary form.

Under the title *Pacifist Anti-War Films of the Pre-Fascist Era,* Ricarda Freudenberg reconstructs the media network surrounding Erich Maria Remarque's anti-war novel *Im Westen nichts Neues*. The focus is on the novel and the American film adaptation *All Quiet on the Western Front,* which appeared a short time later. The analysis focuses on theme, dramaturgy and narrative perspective, but also includes questions of distribution, reception and processing in detail. The synchronic perspective of the media network is expanded by adding two German anti-war films produced almost simultaneously – *Westfront 1918* and *Niemandsland*. In a diachronic perspective, it becomes clear that media adaptations and transformations are still being marketed today. By way of comparison, the graphic novel of the same name published a few years ago will be drawn from this group, which refers to the American film. All in all, it becomes apparent that the film adaptation became the starting point of a media network that departs from the novel at least in parts in terms of content. Since pacifism did not fit into the concept of the Nazi dictatorship, it is not surprising that this *Stoff* was banned in all forms of media at the beginning of the Nazi rule; its wide distribution, which began in 1929, does not extend beyond 1933, so there are no hotspots.

Under the title *Boyish Romance in a Timeless Idyll?,* Winfred Kaminski looks at the writer, director and screenwriter Alfred Weidenmann and his media network surrounding *Jakko*. The novel was published in 1939 (the film adaptation of the same name in 1941), and its background ideology can be summed up by the saying "frangar, non flectar". For the film version, Weidenmann collaborated with the director Fritz Peter Buch, who was also successful during the Nazi era, and the film composer Otto Borgmann. The film, which the censors awarded in 1941 with the ratings *staatspolitisch wertvoll* (*valuable for state politics*), *volkstümlich wertvoll* (*valuable for* the *people*) and *jugendwert* (*valuable for young people*), shows, like the novel, a story of friendship and a circus; both types of media are not free of racism. The film was or is often compared with the *Hitlerjunge Quex* (1933), based on the novel of the same name by Karl Aloys Schenzinger, because the protagonist Jakko also ultimately turns to the Hitler Youth. Hotspots can be identified from 1940 to 1942, especially on the level of reception, because the film was already being actively covered by the press.

References

Auer, Fritz: Das Zeitalter des Films. Eine Kino-Umfrage. In: Der Kinematograph 5 (1911), 5–6.
Barabási, Albert-László/Albert, Réka: Emergence of Scaling in Random Networks. In: Science (15.10.1999), https://science.sciencemag.org/content/286/5439/509 (07.01.2020).
Bauer, Thomas: Deutsche Programmpresse 1923 bis 1941. Entstehung, Entwicklung und Kontinuität der Rundfunkzeitschriften. München 1993 (Rundfunkstudien; 6).
Belling, Curt/Schütze, Alfred: Die Filmarbeit der Hitler-Jugend. In: Bredow, Wilfried von/Zurek, Rolf (Hg.): Film und Gesellschaft in Deutschland. Dokumente und Materialien. Hamburg 1975, 199–205.
Birett, Herbert: Verzeichnis in Deutschland gelaufener Filme. 1911–1920. Entscheidungen der Filmzensur. München [u. a.] 1980.
Bleckman, Matias: Harry Piel. Ein Kino-Mythos und seine Zeit. Düsseldorf 1992.
Bonn, Friedrich: Jugend und Theater. Emsdetten 1939 (Die Schaubühne; Quellen und Forschung zur Theatergeschichte; 39).
Brücher, Bodo: Der Film als Mittel der Massenkommunikation in der NS-Jugenderziehung. In: Lauffer, Jürgen/Volkmer, Ingrid (Hg.): Kommunikative Kompetenz in einer sich verändernden Medienwelt. Opladen 1995 (Schriftenreihe der Gesellschaft für Medien und Kommunikationskultur in der Bundesrepublik e. V.; 9), 17–27.
Brunken, Otto: Theater für Kinder und Jugendliche. In: Brunken, Otto/Hurrelmann, Bettina/Michels-Kohlhage, Maria/Wilkending, Gisela: Handbuch zur Kinder- und Jugendliteratur. Von 1850 bis 1900. Stuttgart 2008, 233–278.
Burmann, Christoph/Nitschke, Axel: Profilierung von Marken mit Sponsoring und Events. In: Meffert, Heribert/Burmann, Christoph/Koers, Martin (Hg.): Markenmanagement. Identitätsorientierte Markenführung und praktische Umsetzung mit Best-practice-Fallstudien. Wiesbaden ²2005, 387–409.
Chabon, Michael. Fan Fictions. On Sherlock Holmes. In: Maps and Legends. Reading and Writing along the Borderlands. San Francisco 2008, 35–57.
Crăciun, Ioana: „Möchte doch wissen, wozu wir eigentlich auf der Welt sind!" Zur Inszenierung von Kindheit und Jugend im Weimarer Kino. In: Herbst-Meßlinger, Karin/Rother, Rainer/Schaefer, Annika (Hg.): Weimarer Kino neu gesehen. Berlin 2018, 120–143.
Deleuze, Gilles/Guattari, Félix: Rhizom. Berlin 1977.
Denson, Shane/Mayer, Ruth: Grenzgänger. Serielle Figuren im Medienwechsel. In: Kelleter, Frank (Hg.): Populäre Serialität. Narration – Evolution – Distinktion. Zum seriellen Erzählen seit dem 19. Jahrhundert. Zum seriellen Erzählen seit dem 19. Jahrhundert Bielefeld 2012, 185–203.

Dettmar, Ute: Fortgesetztes Erzählen. Kinder- und Jugendliteratur im Netz von Populär- und Medienkulturen. In: Anders, Petra/Staiger, Michael (Hg.): Serialität in Literatur und Medien, Bd. 1: Theorie und Didaktik. Baltmannsweiler 2016, [115]-126.

Dinse, Robert: Das Freizeitleben der Großstadtjugend: 5000 Jungen und Mädchen berichten. Eberswalde-Berlin 1932.

Eco, Umberto: Serialität im Universum der Kunst und der Massenmedien. In: Ders. (Hg.): Im Labyrinth der Vernunft. Texte über Kunst und Zeichen. Leipzig 1989, 301–324.

Elfert, Brunhild: Die Entstehung und Entwicklung des Kinder- und Jugendfunks in Deutschland von 1924 bis 1933 am Beispiel der Berliner Funk-Stunde AG. Frankfurt a. M. [u. a.] 1985 (Europäische Hochschulschriften; Reihe 40: Kommunikationswissenschaft und Publizistik; 3).

Elleström, Lars: Transfer of media characteristics among dissimilar media. in: Palabra Clave, 20 (2017) 3, 663–685, http://www.scielo.org.co/pdf/pacla/v20n3/0122-8285-pacla-20-03-00663. pdf (01.03.2020).

Elsaesser, Thomas: Kino der Kaiserzeit. Einleitung. In: Ders./Wedel, Michael: Kino der Kaiserzeit. Zwischen Tradition und Moderne. München 2002, 11–42.

Estermann, Alfred: Die Verfilmung literarischer Werke. Bonn 1965.

Faulstich, Werner (Hg.): Grundwissen Medien. München ^{4}2000.

Faulstich, Werner: Filmgeschichte. Tübingen 2005.

Faulstich, Werner/Korte, Helmut: Fischer Filmgeschichte: Von den Anfängen bis zum etablierten Medium. 1895–1924. Frankfurt a. M. 1994.

Fiske, John (Hg.): Understanding popular culture. London [u. a.] ^{2}2011.

Friese, Inka: Ein Klassiker am Ausgang seiner Epoche. Heinrich Hoffmanns „Struwwelpeter". In: Hurrelmann, Bettina (Hg.): Klassiker der Kinder- und Jugendliteratur. Frankfurt a. M. 1995, 358–378.

Ganz-Blättler, Ursula: DSDS als Reality-Serie: Kumulatives Storytelling „on the go". In: Kelleter, Frank (Hg.): Populäre Serialität. Narration – Evolution – Distinktion. Zum seriellen Erzählen seit dem 19. Jahrhundert. Bielefeld 2012, 123–141.

Hartmann, Andrea/Nölle, Michel: „Scissors on a screen". Lotte Reinigers Silhouetten-Märchenfilme. In: Dettmar, Ute/Pecher, Claudia Maria/Schlesinger, Ron (Hg.): Märchen im Medienwechsel. Zur Geschichte und Gegenwart des Märchenfilms. Stuttgart 2017, 85–100.

Hembus, Joe/Brennicke, Ilona (Hg.): Klassiker des Deutschen Stummfilms 1910–1930. Mit Bildern aus Kopien von Gerhard Ullmann und einem Vorwort von Xaver Schwarzenberger. München 1983.

Hengst, Heinz: „Buy us all – don't break up the family". Stichwort Medienverbund – Im Zirkel des Populären. In: Josting, Petra/Maiwald, Klaus (Hg.): Kinder- und Jugendliteratur im Medienverbund. Grundlagen, Beispiele und Ansätze für den Deutschunterricht. München 2007 (kjl&m 07.extra), 22–34.

Hengst, Heinz: Am Anfang war die Biene Maja. Medienverbund und Japanisierung der kommerziellen Kultur. In: Weiss, Harald (Hg.): 100 Jahre Biene Maja – vom Kinderbuch zum Kassenschlager. Heidelberg 2014 (Studien zur europäischen Kinder- und Jugendliteratur; 1), [143]–165.

Heuser, Uwe Jean: Die Facebook-Kurve. Ist ein Digitalkonzern erst mal in Führung, wächst sein Geschäft immer schneller. Woran liegt das? In: DIE ZEIT (2018) 17, vom 20.04. https://www.zeit.de/2018/17/netzwerkeffekt-internet-konzerne-facebook-groesse (07.01.2020).

Hoppeler, Stephanie/Rippl, Gabriele: Continuity, Fandom und Serialität in anglo-amerikanischen Comic Books. In: Kelleter, Frank (Hg.): Populäre Serialität. Narration – Evolution – Distinktion. Zum seriellen Erzählen seit dem 19. Jahrhundert. Bielefeld 2012, 367–379.

Hobsch, Manfred: Ideologie für Kopf und Herz der Jugend. In: Schäfer, Horst/Wegener, Claudia (Hg.): Kindheit und Film. Geschichte, Themen und Perspektiven des Kinderfilms in Deutschland. Konstanz 2009 (Alltag, Medien und Kultur; 5), 39–55.

Höfig, Willi: Die stumme Märchenfrau. Märchen und Sage im Stummfilm. Beispiele und theoretische Überlegungen der Zeit. In: Schmitt, Christoph (Hg.): Erzählkulturen im Medienwandel. Münster [u. a.] 2008, 87–108.

Jacobsen, Wolfgang/Kaes, Anton/Prinzler, Hans Helmut (Hg.): Geschichte des deutschen Films. Akt. und erw. Aufl. Stuttgart [u. a.] ²2004.
Jenkins, Henry: Convergence Culture. Where Old and New Media Collide. New York 2006.
Jensen, Rolf: Dream society. How the coming shift from information to imagination will transform your business. New York 1999.
Josting, Petra: Medienkonvergenz im aktuellen Handlungssystem der Kinder- und Jugendliteratur. In: Weinkauff, Gina/Dettmar, Ute/Möbius, Thomas/Tomkowiak, Ingrid (Hg.): Kinder- und Jugendliteratur in Medienkontexten. Adaption, Hybridisierung, Intermedialität, Konvergenz. (Kinder- und Jugendkultur, -literatur und -medien. Theorie – Geschichte – Didaktik; 89) Frankfurt a. M. 2014, 233–252.
Kalk, Otto: Theorie und Praxis der Jugendbühne. Osterwieck am Harz 1926 (Die Jugendbühne. Arbeitsgemeinschaft von Lehrern und Lehrerinnen; 2. u. 3.).
Kanzog, Klaus: „Staatspolitisch besonders wertvoll". Ein Handbuch zu 30 deutschen Spielfilmen der Jahre 1934 bis 1945. München 1994.
Kelleter, Frank (Hg.): Populäre Serialität: Narration – Evolution – Distinktion. Zum seriellen Erzählen seit dem 19. Jahrhundert. Bielefeld 2012.
Kelleter, Frank/Stein, Daniel: Autorisierungspraktiken seriellen Erzählens. Zur Gattungsentwicklung von Superheldencomics. In: Ders. (Hg.): Populäre Serialität: Narration – Evolution – Distinktion. Zum seriellen Erzählen seit dem 19. Jahrhundert. Bielefeld 2012, 259–290.
Kerlen, Dietrich: Jugend und Medien in Deutschland. Eine kulturhistorische Studie. Hg. v. Rath, Matthias/Marci-Boehncke, Gudrun. Weinheim [u. a.] 2005.
Kimmins: Der Film und die Kinder. In: Film-Kurier 1 (1919), 3.
Klaus, Ulrich J.: Deutsche Tonfilme. Lexikon der abendfüllenden deutschsprachigen Spielfilme (1929–1945), chronologisch geordnet nach den Daten der Uraufführungen in Deutschland, sowie der in Deutschland produzierten, jedoch nicht zur öffentlichen Vorführung gelangten Spielfilme. Berlin 1988–2006.
König, Theodor: Reklame-Psychologie, ihr gegenwärtiger Stand – ihre praktische Bedeutung. München [u. a.] ²1924.
Kopf, Christine: „Der Schein der Neutralität" – Institutionelle Filmzensur in der Weimarer Republik. In: Koebner, Thomas (Hg.): Diesseits der „Dämonischen Leinwand". Neue Perspektiven auf das späte Weimarer Kino. München 2003, 451–466.
Kreimeier, Klaus: Traum und Exzess: Die Kulturgeschichte des frühen Kinos. Bonn 2012.
Krienke, Jutta: Werkprofil: Die Rezeption des Nibelungenstoffes in der Kinder- und Jugendliteratur. In: Brunken, Otto/Hurrelmann, Bettina/Michels-Kohlhage, Maria/Wilkending, Gisela (Hg.): Handbuch zur Kinder- und Jugendliteratur. Von 1850 bis 1900. Stuttgart 2008, 743–755.
Krumschlies, Kirsten/Kurwinkel, Tobias: Transmediale Lektüre. Medienverbünde im Deutschunterricht der Primarstufe. In: kjl&m 72 (2019) 4, 78–85.
Kurwinkel, Tobias: Zur Theorie von Medien- und Produktverbünden und ihren Sammlungen am Beispiel von Bibi und Tina. In: kjl&m 69 (2017) 2, 14–21.
Lamprecht, Gerhard: Deutsche Stummfilme: 1903–1912. Berlin 1969.
Loiperdinger, Martin: Filmzensur und Selbstkontrolle. Politische Reifeprüfung. In: Jacobsen, Wolfgang/Kaes, Anton/Prinzler, Hans Helmut (Hg.): Geschichte des deutschen Films. Akt. und erw. Aufl. Stuttgart [u. a.] ²2004, 525–544.
Maase, Kaspar: Schundkampf und Demokratie. In: Ders. (Hg.): Prädikat wertlos. Der lange Streit um Schmutz und Schund. Tübingen 2001, 8–17.
Maase, Kaspar: Kinderkino. Halbwüchsige, Öffentlichkeiten und kommerzielle Populärkultur im deutschen Kaiserreich. In: Müller, Corinna/Segeberg, Harro (Hg.): Kinoöffentlichkeit (1895–1920). Entstehung, Etablierung, Differenzierung/Cinema's Publics Sphere (1895–1920). Emergence, Settlement, Differentiation. Marburg 2008, 126–148.
Marzolph, Ulrich: Der orientalistische Märchenfilm. Vom „Dieb von Bagdad" bis „Aladdin". In: Schmitt, Christoph (Hg.): Erzählkulturen im Medienwandel. Münster [u. a.] 2008, 127–138.

Meffert, Heribert/Burmann, Christoph/Koers, Martin (Hg.): Markenmanagement: Identitätsorientierte Markenführung und praktische Umsetzung mit Best-practice-Fallstudien. Wiesbaden ²2005.
Meier, Jan-Niklas: Im narrativen Verbund. Transmediale Perspektiven auf Medienverbünde. In: kjl&m 73 (2020) 1, 74–86.
Mittell, Jason (2014): Strategies of Storytelling and Transmedia Television. In: Ryan, Marie-Laure/Thon, Jan-Noël (Hg.):Storyworlds across media. Toward a media-conscious narratology. Nebraska-London 2014, 253–277.
Müller, Corinna: Kinoöffentlichkeit in Hamburg um 1913. In: Dies./Segeberg, Harro (Hg.): Kinoöffentlichkeit (1895–1920). Entstehung, Etablierung, Differenzierung/Cinema's Publics Sphere (1895–1920). Emergence, Settlement, Differentiation. Marburg 2008, 105–125.
Negt, Oskar/Kluge, Alexander: Öffentlichkeit und Erfahrung. Zur Organisationsanalyse von bürgerlicher und proletarischer Öffentlichkeit. Frankfurt a. M. 1972.
Nowak, Kai: Umkämpfte Filme. Skandal und Zensur im Kino der Weimarer Republik. In: Herbst-Meßlinger, Karin/Rother, Rainer/Schaefer, Annika (Hg.): Weimarer Kino neu gesehen. Berlin 2018, 214–237.
NSLB (Reichsamtsleitung des Nationalsozialistischen Lehrerbundes) (Hg.): Für Fest und Feier. Wertvolle Spiele für die Schul- und Jugendbühne. München 1935.
Pecher, Claudia Maria: Georges Méliès (1861–1938) – Pionier des Märchenfilms. In: Dettmar, Ute/Pecher, Claudia Maria/Schlesinger, Ron (Hg.): Märchen im Medienwechsel. Zur Geschichte und Gegenwart des Märchenfilms. Stuttgart 2017, 13–37.
Pellatz-Graf, Susanne: Abenteuer- und Reiseromane und -erzählungen für die Jugend. In: Brunken, Otto/Hurrelmann, Bettina/Michels-Kohlhage, Maria/Wilkending, Gisela (Hg.): Handbuch zur Kinder- und Jugendliteratur. Von 1850 bis 1900. Stuttgart 2008, 616–665.
Pigorsch, Enrico: Der Funkheinzelmann erzählt. Hans Bodenstedt und seine Märchen auf Homocord-Platten. In: Der Schalltrichter 17 (2001), 1–11.
Raith, Markus: Infotainment als Form seriellen Erzählens? Zur narrativen Dimension von Text-Bild-Kombinationen. In: Anders, Petra/Staiger, Michael (Hg.): Serialität in Literatur und Medien, Bd. 1: Theorie und Didaktik. Baltmannsweiler 2016, 188–200.
Räder, Andy: Der Kinderfilm in der Weimarer Republik. In: Schäfer, Horst/Wegener, Claudia (Hg.): Kindheit und Film. Geschichte, Themen und Perspektiven des Kinderfilms in Deutschland. Konstanz 2009 (Alltag, Medien und Kultur; 5), 21–38.
Rake, August: Rundfunk im Erziehungsheim. In: Der Deutsche Rundfunk 5 (1927) 13, 886–887
Rajewsky, Irina O.: Intermedialität. Tübingen 2002 (UTB für Wissenschaft Medien- und Kommunikationswissenschaft; 2261).
Röttger, Karl: Das Kindertheater. Frankfurt a. M. 1922.
Sander, Anneliese U.: Jugendfilm im Nationalsozialismus. Dokumentation und Kommentar. Nach der Sonderveröffentlichung Nr. 6 der Zeitschrift „Das junge Deutschland" (1944). Hg. von Hartmut Reese. Münster 1984.
Schäfer, Horst: Lexikon des Kinder- und Jugendfilms im Kino, im Fernsehen und auf Video. Erg.-Lfg. Meitingen 1998.
Schäfer, Horst/Wegener, Claudia (Hg.): Kindheit und Film. Geschichte, Themen und Perspektiven des Kinderfilms in Deutschland. Konstanz 2009.
Schäfer, Horst: Verkannt, vergessen, verschollen. Märchen-Stummfilme in Deutschland. In: Dettmar, Ute/Pecher, Claudia Maria/Schlesinger, Ron (Hg.): Märchen im Medienwechsel. Zur Geschichte und Gegenwart des Märchenfilms. Stuttgart 2017, 59–84.
Schlachter, Birgit: Syntagmatische und paradigmatische Serialität in der populären Jugendliteratur. In: Anders, Petra/Staiger, Michael (Hg.): Serialität in Literatur und Medien. Baltmannsweiler 2016, 100–114.
Schlesinger, Ron: Märchenfilm im „Dritten Reich". In: Dettmar, Ute/Pecher, Claudia Maria/Schlesinger, Ron (Hg.): Märchen im Medienwechsel. Zur Geschichte und Gegenwart des Märchenfilms. Stuttgart 2017, 143–177.

Schmidt, Hanns Christian: Origami Unicorn Revisited. ‚Transmediales Erzählen' und ‚transmediales Worldbuilding' im The Walking Dead-Franchise. In: Image 20 (2014), 5–24, http://www.gib.uni-tuebingen.de/own/journal/upload/b27370c83184f977128295b7bcc54d8c.pdf (08.01.2020).
Schmidt, Siegfried J.: Literaturwissenschaft und Systemtheorie. Positionen, Kontroversen, Perspektiven. Opladen 1993.
Schmidt, Siegfried J.: Kalte Faszination. Medien, Kultur, Wissenschaft in der Mediengesellschaft. Weilerswist 2000.
Schmidt, Siegfried J.: Medien und Emotionen: Zum Management von Bezugnahmen. In: Ders. (Hg.): Medien und Emotionen. Münster 2005 (Medien; 11), 11–39.
Schmidt, Siegfried J.: Der Medienkompaktbegriff. In: Münker, Stefan/Roesler, Alexander (Hg.): Was ist ein Medium? Frankfurt a. M. 2008a, 144–157.
Schmidt, Siegfried J.: Media Philosophy – A Reasonable Programme? In: Hrachovec, Herbert/Pichler, Alois (Hg.): Philosophy of the Information. Society Proceedings of the 30th International Ludwig Wittgenstein-Symposium, Kirchberg am Wechsel, Austria 2007. Volume 2. Frankfurt a. M. [u. a.] 2008b (Publications of the Austrian Ludwig Wittgenstein Society – New Series; 7), 89–105.
Schmidt, Siegfried J.: Rekurrenzen der Mediengeschichte. Ein Versuch. Weilerswist 2012.
Schmidt, Siegfried J.: Kulturbeschreibung ÷ Beschreibungskultur. Umrisse einer Prozessorientierten Kulturtheorie. Weilerswist 2014.
Schmidt, Siegfried J./Zurstiege, Guido: Orientierung Kommunikationswissenschaft. Was sie kann, was sie will. Reinbek bei Hamburg 2000.
Schulz, Armin: Stoff. In: Lauer, Gerhard/Ruhrberg, Christine (Hg.): Lexikon Literaturwissenschaft. Hundert Grundbegriffe. Stuttgart 2011, 312–315.
Scolari, Carlos Alberto: Transmedia Storytelling. Implicit Consumers, Narrative Worlds, and Branding in Contemporary Media Production. In: International Journal of Communication 3 (2009), 586–606, https://ijoc.org/index.php/ijoc/article/view/477/336 (08.01.2020).
Scott, Jason: The Character-Oriented Franchise: Promotion and Exploitation of pre-sold characters in American film, 1913–1950. In: Robert, Iain Smith (Hg.): Cultural Borrowings. Appropriation, Reworking, Transformation. Scope 2009, 34–55, https://iedimagen.files.wordpress.com/2012/01/cult_borr_ebook.pdf (08.01.2020).
Sielke, Sabine: Joy in Repetition. Acht Thesen zum Konzept der Serialität und zum Prinzip der Serie. In: Kelleter, Frank (Hg.): Populäre Serialität: Narration – Evolution – Distinktion. Zum seriellen Erzählen seit dem 19. Jahrhundert. Bielefeld 2012, 383–398.
Simoudis, Georgios: Storytising: Geschichten als Instrument erfolgreicher Markenführung. Groß-Umstadt 2004.
Stahl, Ernst Leopold: Der Hebbelverein in Heidelberg. Die Geschichter einer literarischen Gesellschaft. Ein Rückblick auf seine Tätigkeit von 1902 bis 1908. Heidelberg 1911.
Stelzner-Large, Barbara: „Der Jugend zur Freude"? Untersuchungen zum propagandistischen Jugendspielfilm im Dritten Reich. Weimar 1996.
Steuben, Fritz: Das Abenteuerbuch. In: Jugendschriften-Warte 43 (1938), 69–71.
Stanitzek, Georg: Texts and Paratexts in Media. In: Critical Inquiry 32 (2005) 1, 27–42, https://www.jstor.org/stable/10.1086/498002 (01.03.2020).
Steinberg, Marc: Anime's Media Mix. Franchising Toys and Characters in Japan. Minneapolis [u. a.] 2012.
Stiglegger, Marcus: Zwischen Revolte und Diktatur. Jugendfilme der Weimarer Republik. In: Koebner, Thomas (Hg.): Diesseits der „Dämonischen Leinwand". Neue Perspektiven auf das späte Weimarer Kino. München 2003, 311–326.
Strobel, Heidi: Formung der Gefühle – Kinderfilm in NS-Diktatur und früher Nachkriegszeit. In: Schäfer, Horst/Wegener, Claudia (Hg.): Kindheit und Film. Geschichte, Themen und Perspektiven des Kinderfilms in Deutschland. Konstanz 2009, 57–71.
Toeplitz, Jerzy: Geschichte des Films. 1895–1928. München 1975.

Tomkowiak, Ingrid: Capture the Imagination – 100 Jahre Disney-Märchenanimationsfilme. In: Dettmar, Ute/Pecher, Claudia Maria/Schlesinger, Ron (Hg.): Märchen im Medienwechsel. Zur Geschichte und Gegenwart des Märchenfilms. Stuttgart 2017, 121–142.

Töteberg, Michael: Neben dem Operetten-Theater und vis-à-vis Schauspielhaus. Eine Kino-Topographie von Hamburg 1896–1912. In: Müller, Corinna/Segeberg, Harro (Hg.): Kinoöffentlichkeit (1895–1920). Entstehung, Etablierung, Differenzierung/Cinema's Publics Sphere (1895–1920). Emergence, Settlement, Differentiation. Marburg 2008, 87–104.

VDP (Vereinigte Deutsche Prüfungsausschüsse für Jugendschriften) (Hg.): Verzeichnis wertvoller Spiele für die Schul- und Jugendbühne. Hamburg ^{5}1932.

Wermke, Jutta: Integrierte Medienerziehung im Fachunterricht. Schwerpunkt: Deutsch. München 1997.

Wiebel, Bernhard: Werkprofil: Münchhausen. In: Brunken, Otto/Hurrelmann, Bettina/Michels-Kohlhage, Maria/Wilkending, Gisela (Hg.): Handbuch zur Kinder- und Jugendliteratur. Von 1850 bis 1900. Stuttgart 2008, 755–759.

Wilkending, Gisela: Die Kinder- und Jugendliteratur im kulturellen und literarischen Prozess. In: Brunken, Otto/Hurrelmann, Bettina/Michels-Kohlhage, Maria/Wilkending, Gisela (Hg.): Handbuch zur Kinder- und Jugendliteratur. Von 1850 bis 1900. Stuttgart 2008, 23–48.

Project Horizons: Introduction and Overview

Children's and Youth Radio from 1924 to 1945

Annemarie Weber

Current State of Research and Desiderata

Early radio for children and young people (1923–1945) has hardly been researched to date, and overviews of the period under investigation are still completely lacking. The comprehensive *Programmgeschichte des Hörfunks in der Weimarer Republik* (Leonhard 1997) omits children's and youth hours "since separate presentation of these programme segments were originally planned" (ibid., 997, f.n. 3) and mentions them only sporadically in various contexts, including *Schulfunk*, the school supporting broadcast. Konrad Dussel's *Deutsche Rundfunkgeschichte* (Dussel 2010) provides a good overview of the institutional development of radio broadcasting, and the programme structure is also examined in more detail with regard to the entertainment function of radio. Children's programming, however, is not considered. The only systematic study on the emergence and development of children's and youth radio was presented by Brunhild Elfert (1985). Although her data collection includes all stations of the Weimar Republic, she solely focuses on the Funk-Stunde Berlin. In the case of all other stations, she only takes into account the dramatic form addressed to the target group (referred to as children's and youth plays). A comprehensive bibliography of radio plays (Strzolka 2010) is limited to the same period of investigation and only considers radio drama. The well-documented overview of writers' radio appearances by Wittenbrink (2006) only records the self-spoken broadcast dates of the listed authors and also does not go beyond 1932. Moreover, Wittenbrink's selection seems restrictive, since names such as Ingeborg Faber Du Faur (Munich), Rudolf Simon (Cologne), Ursula Scherz (Deutsche Welle) or Marion Lindt (Königsberg) are missing.

A. Weber (✉)
Bielefeld, Germany

Studies are available on some of the most notable personalities of early radio: Walter Benjamin's work for radio (including that addressed to children) is the subject of several studies (cf. among others Schiller-Lerg 1984, Steinbach 2010, Nowak 2017). Günter Eich's broadcasted radio plays are documented by Wagner (1999), but without own source research and thus incomplete. A carefully researched work on Hermann Kasack's radio works, including those addressed to children and young people, was published by Fromhold (1990; cf. also Besch 1992). Lisa Tetzner as a storyteller (also in radio) is the subject of Messerli's (2008) study; Bolius (1997) presented a rather conventional biography of Tetzner, based, however, on partly unpublished letters and other sources. Complete radiography of Max Ophüls (including his children's radio plays) is contained in the biography by Asper (1998).

There is, however, virtually no research literature on many prominent personalities of early children's and youth radio. Hans Bodenstedt, one of the co-founders of the Hamburg station – the inventor, author and speaker of the *Funkheinzelmann* format – has so far been honoured with a single small study dealing with the surviving records (cf. Pigorsch 2001). Completely forgotten are authors of Weimar children's radio such as Alice Fliegel or the director of children's radio in Cologne, Els Vordemberge (a first victim of the purges in 1933; cf. Schütte 1971, 135), the team of Dresden youth radio, consisting of Erna Moser (née Schirokauer, cf. Heinze 1991), Herbert Roth and Kurt Arnold Findeisen (whose radio work is hardly known), or the Munich protagonists of children's radio Ewis Borkmann, Otto Willner, Maria Devera and Teresa Roth. Ilse Obrig's work for Weimar, and later Nazi radio, is also known only in outline (cf. Elfert 1985, 220; Münkel 1998, 88).

The Austrian and Swiss radio stations have also been neglected by research so far, although they provided a rich programme offer for children and young people. The research project cannot close all these gaps, but with its database for the first time it provides a comprehensive collection of sources aiming at completeness. The contributions collected in this volume deal analytically with individual phenomena based on the new source material. They are the first and hopefully not the last studies to make use of the database. The systematic indexing of the press addressed to children and adolescents remains as a desideratum, in particular the special pages in programme guides produced in connection with radio and the children's magazines that accompanied popular radio formats.

Political and Economic Framework of Early Radio Broadcasting

The founding of so-called entertainment broadcasting in Germany coincided with the last major crisis of the Weimar Republic. Separatist unrest threatened to destabilise the country and inflation was almost out of control (cf. Großmann-Vendrey et al. 1986). In this critical situation, broadcasting was established under state control with private capital. The preparations were made by functionaries of the Reich Postal Ministry (RPM), bypassing the parliaments. The opening happened "head over heels" (ibid., 12 f.), without a programme concept. The declared aim of the founders was to help radio, as a mass entertainment medium already successful abroad, to achieve a breakthrough as quickly as possible despite chaotic economic and political conditions in Germany, and at the same time to prevent political instrumentalisation of the new technology (cf. Bredow 1956, vol. 2, 209 and 214). Rather, the new medium was intended to make the "enjoyment of intellectual goods and entertainment" available to broad sections of the population, including the poorer ones, i.e. "the German people" (ibid., 217). In defence of the initially controversial institution, radio was loaded with extensive symbolic capital: It was supposed to be a cultural factor of national rank, moreover, it was supposed to increase the people's enjoyment of work through diversion and relaxation, as well as become a significant economic factor and create jobs (cf. ibid.). Großmann-Vendrey et al. (1986, 13) describe the neutrality imposed from above as a handicap of the new medium, because it prevented politically committed journalists from having their say and political debates and even current affairs were tabooed. They also criticise the initially high reception costs and a bourgeois-oriented programme structure, which made it difficult for workers to access the new medium or ignored their needs (cf. ibid., 14).

According to Hans Bredow, the State Secretary in the RPM responsible for the development of the broadcasting network, the regionalisation of broadcasting in Germany was promoted by the state of Bavaria, which rejected the planned sonication from Berlin, so that in 1922 an independent programme company was founded in Munich named *Deutsche Stunde in Bayern* (cf. Bredow 1956, vol. 2, 203). Subsequently, the planned radio network was divided into nine broadcasting districts with their own broadcasting centres. In Berlin, the *Radiostunde AG* (spelling according to Bredow 1956, vol. 2, 221) was founded at the end of September 1923, which broadcast the first programme on October 29, but was not registered in the commercial register until March 29, 1924 under the name *Funk-Stunde AG* (cf. Elfert 1985, 54). According to their organisational model, eight other stations started broadcasting in 1924 (start of broadcasting according to Giesecke 1929, 35): *Mitteldeutsche Rundfunk AG* in Leipzig – *Mirag* (March 1, 1924), *Südwestdeutscher Rundfunk AG – SWR* in Frankfurt am Main (March 30, 1924), *Deutsche Stunde in Bayern GmbH* in Munich (March 30, 1924), *Nordische Rundfunk AG – Norag* in Hamburg (May 2, 1924), *Süddeutscher Rundfunk AG – Sürag* in Stuttgart (May 10, 1924),[1] *Schlesische Funkstunde AG* in Breslau (May 26, 1924), *Ostmarken-Rundfunk AG – Orag* in Königsberg (June 14, 1924), *Westdeutsche Funkstunde AG – Wefag* in Münster (October 10, 1924), from 1926 with headquarters in Cologne. The Prussian broadcasters founded a tenth, central broadcasting company (cf. Giesecke 1929, 35), *Deutsche Welle GmbH* with headquarters in Berlin, which was also called *Deutschlandsender* after the type designation of German long-wave transmitter used (cf. Halefeldt 1997, 127) and is also listed as *Königswusterhausen* in the programme guides after the transmitter location (start of broadcasting: January 7, 1926).

---

[1] May 11, 1924 according to Grube 1973, 20.

The decentralised broadcasters were set up as public limited companies with private investors under a model contract drawn up by the RPM, which retained 51% of the shares and thus control over the broadcasters. In return, it allowed the private shareholders to generate profits through subsidiary companies – for example, by selling equipment or publishing programme guides (cf. Halefeldt 1997, 28 f.; Bauer 1993, 47). The RPM issued the broadcasting licenses, provided the broadcasting facilities and passed on two-thirds of the broadcasting fees collected to the broadcasting companies. The latter committed themselves to a daily radio programme of at least two hours, for which they were granted a monopoly in their broadcasting district (cf. Halefeldt 1997, 28 f.).

In order to be able to implement necessary technical developments more quickly and to better represent their common interests, Mirag, Norag, SWR, Schlesische Funkstunde and Orag joined forces in 1925 to form an umbrella organisation proposed by the RPM, the *Reichs-Rundfunk-Gesellschaft* (RRG), which Funk-Stunde, Wefag and Sürag also joined in the course of the year (cf. Halefeldt 1997, 138 f.). In 1926, the *Deutsche Reichspost* (DRP) took over 51% of the RRG shares, thus strengthening its power to control and steer the stations (cf. Bauer 1993, 50). Deutsche Stunde in Munich did not join the RRG. For the listeners, the association paid off. Lindemann (1980, 48) considers the live transmissions of outstanding broadcasts and the stimulating effect of the station competition thus made possible to be particularly beneficial.

In mid-1926, the broadcasting companies founded a joint programme council – *Programmrat*, later called *Programmausschuss* (cf. Bredow 1956, vol. 2, 270), in which the directors of Vienna and Danzig were also represented as guests. The aim was the necessary exchange of experience and the coordination of joint planning (cf. Lindemann 1980, 48 f.). A political monitoring committee – *Überwachungsausschuss*, consisting of one representative of the federal government (*Reichsregierung*) and two of the respective state government (*Landesregierung*), was supposed to ensure non-partisanship at the broadcasters, but led to party-political influence (cf. Bredow 1956, vol. 2, 263 f.). A cultural advisory board – *Kulturbeirat*, appointed by the state government "in consultation with the Reich Ministry of the Interior" (Rieck 1927, 3246; cf. also Giesecke 1929, 87), was to ensure quality assurance in the artistic, scientific and popular education fields (cf. Richtlinien über die Regelung des Rundfunks 1927) but was controversial among the directors (cf. Dichtung und Rundfunk 1930, 110).

In 1932, during government negotiations with Franz von Papen, Hitler explicitly demanded access to radio (which had previously been barred to the National Socialists and the Communists). A first consequence was the establishment of *Stunde der Reichsregierung,* a daily propaganda broadcast that was obligatory for all broadcasters (cf. Lindemann 1980, 50). For the indoctrination of youth, *Stunde der Nation* (Hour of the nation) was introduced, renamed *Stunde der jungen Generation* (Hour of the young generation) in 1935 (cf. Stüven 1981, 42). In 1933, the newly established Reich Ministry *Reichsministerium für Volksaufklärung und*

Propaganda (RMVP) took over all shares and stakes in the broadcasting companies, which were thus eliminated as independent enterprises (cf. Bredow 1956, vol. 2, 267; Bauer 1993, 213). The RRG was also taken over by the RMVP and restructured. The *Reichssendeleitung* was established as its political management body. The decentralisation of programme operations was ended and the stations were also reorganised according to the model of the RRG based on the *Führer principle* (cf. Schütte 1971, 129). Beginning with Easter Monday 1934 (April 2), they were renamed *Reichssender* (cf. Hadamowsky 1934a). After that, there were nine *Reichssender*: Berlin, Breslau, Frankfurt, Hamburg, Cologne, Königsberg, Leipzig, Munich and Stuttgart. Deutsche Welle had already been transformed into *Deutschlandsender* at the beginning of 1933 (cf. Der neue Deutschlandsender 1932). Later, in the course of territorial changes and annexations during the war, further broadcasting stations were added: In 1935 the *Reichssender Saarbrücken*, in 1937 the *Landessender Danzig* (from 1939 also *Reichssender*). In 1938, the Radio-Verkehrs-AG (Ravag) in Vienna was dissolved and the Viennese broadcasting station was subordinated to the RMVP as *Reichssender Wien*. In 1939, the radio station Praha II (Prague) was annexed and declared *Reichssender Böhmen*. Further war-related restructuring followed.

After the National Socialists came to power, a massive purge took place. From April to July 1933, the new rulers replaced all but one of the directors, as well as the broadcasting staff on a large scale. Those who remained were forced to become members of the *Reichsrundfunkkammer* (RRK), which was also subordinate to the RMVP (cf. Schütte 1971, 125). In addition, the Nazis also exerted influence on broadcasting through the party structures. *Funkwarte*, radio watchdogs, were empowered to ensure the so-called closeness of radio programmes to the people (cf. ibid., 129 f.; Bauer 1993, 179). As Bredow (1956, vol. 2, 315) reports, their actual task was to spy on the broadcasting directors. In 1939, some of the aforementioned structures for steering and monitoring radio were dismantled, the RRK was dissolved, its assets were assigned to the RRG, and its members were distributed among the other chambers (cf. Schütte 1971, 180).

Under the National Socialists, youth radio was upgraded and expanded considerably at the individual stations, both in terms of personnel and in terms of broadcasting times and programme offers. As early as 1934, there was a youth radio department at every radio station, which was massively influenced by the broadcasting office of the Nazi youth organisation *Hitlerjugend* (HJ) through personnel mergers and a variety of measures (cf. Münkel 1998, 117–124). The programming of youth radio was expanded thematically and temporally and was given age- and gender-specific sections – following the model of the political Nazi organisations: *Funk für das Jungvolk* (radio for young people from ages 10 to 14), *HJ-Funk* (14–18), *Jungmädelfunk* (aimed at girls from ages 10 to 14), and *BDM-Funk* (aimed at girls from ages 14 to 21). A part of the programmes was provided by *Rundfunkspielscharen*, radio drama groups of the HJ and the BDM (cf. ibid., 119).

Technical Requirements of the Reception

At the beginning, the transmitters had small ranges and, due to the lack of amplifier antennas, could only be satisfactorily received in the respective large cities.[2] Noise interference and technically immature receivers, which were also relatively expensive, initially made radio a hobby for hobbyists or a privilege for people who could afford it (cf. Sch. 1924). However, the new entertainment medium was accompanied by an immense fascination, so that the illegal listening took on enormous proportions (cf. Großmann-Vendrey et al. 1986, 14). The DRP therefore reduced the user fee from 5 to 2 marks at the beginning of April 1924, so that the number of users increased significantly (cf. Bredow 1956, vol. 2, 250), and at the same time made investments in improving broadcasting technology. Thanks to series production, the receivers could be manufactured increasingly cheaper (cf. Breßler 2007, 54).

In 1926, thanks to powerful antennas and cable connections, broadcasters were already exchanging programmes between the stations and their auxiliary transmitters but receiving multiple stations with one device was still technically difficult (cf. Magnus 1929, 143). In 1927 and 1928, the main power supply connection for radios was made possible; before that, the device had to be operated with three different batteries (cf. Rundfunk-Jahrbuch 1929, 264). The loudspeaker was still described as an alternative, not as standard; the equipment manufacturers offered the loudspeaker as an additional device (cf. ibid., 337).[3]

At the end of 1928, about 2.5 million radio sets were licensed in Germany (cf. W. H. F. 1929). The ratio of radio listeners to inhabitants in Germany was 4.1% (cf. Rundfunk-Jahrbuch 1929, 332) with varying geographical distribution. Most areas had a saturation level of 1–3%, Berlin 13%, Hamburg, Düsseldorf, Cologne, Leipzig, Frankfurt, Dortmund and Munich above five and below 13%. By the end of 1933, the number of radio subscribers had doubled to 5 million (cf. Stüven 1981, 105). In May, mass production of a cheap radio, the *Volksempfänger,* began, which, together with accompanying measures (such as instalment payments), was to make radio a mass medium in Germany (cf. ibid., 6–11; Breßler 2007, 197–208). It was always possible to receive foreign stations in Germany, to which the national programme magazines responded as early as September 1924 by printing programme information for Prague, England, and later also Zurich, Vienna, and others. With the start of the war, listening to foreign stations became a punishable offence, and the magazines stopped printing their programmes.

---

[2] On the milieu-dependent different use of radio, cf. Lenk 1997, 27–28.
[3] On the development of broadcasting technology and radio sets, cf. Grau/Keil 2005; Lenk 1997, 86–119.

Programme Press

The regional broadcasting companies acquired their own programme guides through so-called subsidiary companies, in which often the same people sat in the management positions as in the broadcasting companies themselves (cf. Ohse 1971, 312–319; Bauer 1993, 48–54). In this way, the programme guides turned into profitable commercial enterprises; on the newspaper market, they generated the highest advertising revenues. The advantages for the advertising industry were their high circulation, the appealing layout, the homogeneous target group (the radio listeners) and the relatively long period of use – the papers were available for at least a week (cf. Bauer 1993, 297). In addition to the advertising revenues, there was also the more or less hidden subsidisation on the part of the radio companies. The latter provided their 'official' organs, whose titles already indicated their affiliation to a particular station, with programme flags free of charge, as well as image and text material that was in the broad interest of the station. From these "sideline activities" the executives earned "considerable income" (ibid., 87). The reading section of the programme guides sometimes included special offers (special pages or sections) for children and young people. They were used to varying degrees by radio producers to promote their programmes with synopses, illustrations and small text teasers and to interact with their target audience through storytelling competitions, letters to the editor, and prize competitions.

Offers for Children and Young People in the Radio of the Weimar Republic

Funk-Stunde AG

From the very beginning, German radio stations also included programmes in their schedule which were explicitly or implicitly addressed to children and young people. The first of these was Funk-Stunde AG Berlin,[4] which initially broadcast 30-minute programmes produced by Ullstein publishing house several times a week (cf. Elfert 1985, 65). The first programme offers were determined by the proximity to the book market (fairy tale lectures) or also to school theatre (classical dramas, adapted for young people). Furthermore, the reform efforts in youth education, youth literature, art education, and performance plays since the turn of the century (*Jugendbewegung, Jugendschriftenbewegung, Kunsterziehungsbewegung, Laienspielbewegung*) had a formative effect on the programming (cf. ibid., 18–22). The first announcements of a youth designated programme in the Berlin programme

---

[4] For an overview of the individual broadcasting formats and contents of the first broadcasting years, cf. Pinthus [1926], 37–39 and [1928], 197–208. On children's and youth radio, cf. Elfert 1985.

guide *Der Deutsche Rundfunk* dates from March 23, 1924. The programme description does not reveal any specific content or *Stoffe* at the beginning, but only contains vague information about the genres: Inventors and inventions (April 9, 1924), Fairy tales and purrs (May 11, 1924), Little poems and stories (April 13, 1924), From crafting and building (March 26, 1924), Exotic stories (April 6, 1924).

From September 24, 1924, the station produced the children's programmes itself and introduced a fairy tale format spoken by Adele Proesler called *Die Funkprinzessin erzählt* (The radio princess tells), which was broadcast twice a week (Sunday and Wednesday) from October (cf. ibid., 185). Every second Wednesday, the programme was aimed at a target group described in the programme announcement as "our youngest listeners" (cf. Fr. 1925), and by Proesler herself as the group of 6 (or 5) to 10-year-olds (cf. Proesler 1925b and 1925d, 1506). In the station-related illustrated magazine *Die Funk-Stunde,* Proesler was given the opportunity to announce the programmes in relative detail and to interact with the target audience via questions and suggestions about the fairy tale narratives. For example, before a reading of Thea Harbou fairy tales, she invited children to follow the action on the radio with "drawing pencil or paintbrush" (Proesler 1925c); or she asked "why on the 100th anniversary of the death of Sleeping Beauty's magic sleep the briar hedge was covered all over with roses" (Proesler 1925b), whereupon she received a multitude of fan letters which she read aloud on the station (cf. Fr. 1925). But there soon was a rift with the station management. Proesler complained publicly that she had only been able to give performances without music in her broadcasts "to the exclusion of all music and acoustic clown jokes" because the "directorate for fairy tale recitations" had decided against funding musical support suitable for broadcasting (Proesler 1925d, 1505). At the end of April (after only seven months), Proesler's broadcasts were terminated, and she was given her notice (cf. Proesler 1925a, 1199). The name of the broadcast series was still used until mid-1928 for fairy tales and children's stories by changing authors and narrators (cf. Elfert 1985, 95).

In March 1925, Alfred Braun introduced a series of broadcasts under the title *Jugend-Bühne*, the content of which was classical dramas in an (age-appropriate) adaptation. The beginning was made with Schiller's *Die Räuber* (March 28, 1925). This was followed by *Wilhelm Tell* (April 4, 1925), *Prinz Friedrich von Homburg* (April 18, 1925) and *Der zerbrochene Krug* by Kleist (April 25, 1925), dramas by Goethe (*Die Geschwister* and *Iphigenie auf Tauris),* Lessing *(Philotas* and *Nathan der Weise),* Körner, Freytag, Gutzkow and others. These broadcasts were drastically cut back in 1928. Pinthus saw one reason for this in the fact that they were simple "lectures of plays with distributed roles" (Pinthus 1928, 208), without the technical possibilities (background noise, music) already used at that time in radio adaptations for the evening programme. In 1926 and 1927, *Die Funkprinzessin erzählt* broadcasts also appeared in the programme guides under the heading *Jugendbühne (Unterhaltungsstunde).*

From October 30, 1927, Alfred Braun as *Kapitän Funk* accompanied by his dog Crambambuli (Buli) appeared on Sunday afternoons in front of the microphone to tell adventure stories to children. Following the example of Hamburg's *Funkheinzelmann,* the Berlin theatre Großes Schauspielhaus turned the show into a revue, which was performed on several dates in December 1927 and was also broadcast on the radio on December 4, by the Funk-Stunde. In the summer months, instead of the regular children's programme Berlin broadcast a format named *Kinderfest*, which can also be traced back to Braun. According to Elfert (1985, 101) it was produced "with the participation of several children 'noisily', aurally with musical interludes, recitations and Kasperle shows". In July 1925, the series *Onkel Doktor als Märchenerzähler* was added to the programme and continued at irregular intervals until 1927. A Dr. med. E. Mosbacher presented hygiene and health topics in the form of fairy tales.

From 1929 on, Lisa Tetzner was responsible for the fairy tale broadcasts as a freelancer (cf. Elfert 1985, 172, 315). She enriched them with new, contemporary *Stoffe* and often involved children, which she also justified theoretically (cf. Tetzner 1930). Her formats included children as co-creators, which is already evident from the names of the broadcast series: *Kinder spielen für Kinder* (*Children play for children*), *Eine Geschichte ohne Ende, die die jungen Hörer und Hörerinnen zu einem guten Ende führen sollen* (*A story without an ending, which the young listeners should lead to a good ending*). The latter, with Tetzner's own texts, was also adopted by Frankfurt, Cologne, Munich and Zurich.

From October 1, 1929, the Berlin station also offered a daily youth designated programme (cf. Jeden Tag Jugendfunk 1929; Tasiemka 1929). The subject areas of technology, sports, and music were expanded, and a special format dedicated to the city of Berlin was developed, in which well-known personalities, including Alfred Döblin and Walter Benjamin, spoke about life in the metropolis, its history, originals, and special features.[5] Book reviews and recommendations were a frequent feature of the youth programme from 1929 onwards. Likewise, industrial records were broadcast, including radio plays by Otto Wollmann and Liesel Simon or fairy tale retellings by Adele Proesler or Grete Maria Markstein, among others. The names and contents had become known through radio, they were exploited by the record industry and returned to radio in post processing.

Nordische Rundfunk AG (Norag)

The Hamburg station Nordische Rundfunk AG – Norag for short – distinguished itself from others with *Funkheinzelmann*[6] but also with folk tales and popular poetry for children; occasionally there were also Low German fairy tale readings, often in combination with songs or instrumental pieces. The Bremen and Hanover satellite stations also offered children's programmes in the same mix (fairy tales and songs) in their broadcasting area. The puppet theatre Niederdeutsches Puppenspiel in Kiel sometimes gave guest performances at Norag with Kasperle shows. *Funkheinzelmann*,

---

[5] Benjamin's radio lectures for children in Berlin and Frankfurt were published in book form in 1985 (Benjamin/Tiedemann 1985), and Harald Wieser rerecorded a selection on CD (Aufklärung für Kinder 2003).

[6] Cf. the contribution by Annemarie Weber in this volume.

invented by the station's programme director Hans Bodenstedt and usually spoken in person, quickly rose to become one of the most popular formats of the new medium. As early as autumn 1925, *Funkheinzelmann* programmes were also broadcast on the Berlin Funk-Stunde; they were apparently produced alternately in Hamburg and Berlin and transmitted live to the other station. From May 1926, they were also transmitted to Stuttgart and to the Mirag transmitters (Leipzig and Dresden).

In 1924, Norag established a broadcast series by Alice Fliegel-Bodenstedt (the director's wife), who was a reciter and author of religiously and ecologically motivated literature: *Das musikalische Bilderbuch,* apparently a literary adaptation of the libretti of famous operas, "narrated for the youth". The programme moved to the evening on January 7, 1925, with *Margarethe* after Charles Gounod, the addition of "for the youth" dropped. For a short time, Fliegel also created a series of broadcasts specifically addressed to girls, *Funkheinzelmanns Mädchenstunde* (12 episodes from September to November 1926), with mainly her own stories in a musical setting.

In 1928, Norag added another target group format to its programme: *Deutsche Jugendstunde* on Monday afternoons with various offers, mostly readings of adventure and other stories, for children from about ten years of age. Here children were also heard with their own performances (mostly of a musical nature). A special feature of the Norag was the *Aufsatzstunde* by Wilhelm Lamszus, actually a creative writing workshop for schoolchildren, later broadcast under the heading *Kindertheater* as part of *Deutsche Jugendstunde.* Lamszus himself associated this not only with reformist pedagogical ideas (cf. Elfert 1985, 22), but also with the ambition to develop "something like a children's theatre from 'below'" and to "provide the radio with a productive new generation" (Lamszus 1930, 307).

Südwestdeutscher Rundfunkdienst AG (SWR)

The Frankfurt station Südwestdeutscher Rundfunkdienst AG (SWR)[7] started a Sunday afternoon programme for children on April 27, 1924 under the title *Der gute Märchenonkel,* replaced in May by *Kindernachmittag,* in each case without any specific content in the announcement. It was not until October 1925 that *Stunde der Jugend*, a programme dedicated to young people, was established in the Frankfurt studio on six days a week under the direction of freelancer Karl Wehrhan, principal of the Volta Middle School in Frankfurt and textbook author (cf. Diller 1975, 215). He was in charge of various thematic broadcasts, including one purely musical and one vocationally orientated per week, and from 1926 onwards also a quiz programme (cf. Wehrhan 1927). These were the only programmes with age recommendations in the entirety of German broadcasting during this period. The terms *youth* and *children* were used synonymously.

---

[7] On the structures and developments of Frankfurt radio, especially under the National Socialists, cf. Diller 1975.

Stunde der Jugend was addressed to children, the age range was from four to fourteen years.[8] Wehrhan's series of broadcasts were among the longest-lived in German radio (they can be traced back to May 1933).[9] *Aus dem deutschen Märchenborn* was aimed at children from the age of four and included the well-known fairy tales by Andersen, Bechstein, Grimm, Hauff, Reinheimer, but occasionally also modern *Stoffe* by contemporary authors such as the *Industriemärchen* (industrial fairy tales) by Heinrich Kautz or *Maschinenmärchen* (machine fairy tales) by Ella Iranyi. Lisa Tetzner also got a slot here with an interactive format, the (already mentioned) stories without an ending (but also at the broadcasting stations in Stuttgart, Cologne, Munich and Zurich). The children were asked to come up with an ending for each story and send it in to the station; the best submissions were read on air. The series *Aus dem Buch der Sage und Geschichte* opened up a wide spectrum of *Stoffe*, ranging from Münchhausen and Till Eulenspiegel to the legend of Faust, from Siegfried, the dragon slayer, to Gutenberg, the inventor of printing, from local Frankfurt legends to Friedrich Ebert, the first President of Germany (June 4, 1930). The series *Kasperlestunde* (Punch and Judy hour) was performed by a guest ensemble, namely by *Liesel Simon's Kasperltheater,* a small Frankfurt touring stage that toured throughout Germany. Liesel Simon was a regular guest at the Frankfurt station with adaptations of Pocci, Grimm or her own plays. Her popularity led to several recordings which were broadcast by all German radio stations.

From September 1924 to November 1927, SWR regularly broadcast a *Lesestunde* (reading hour) on Saturday afternoons for a target group referred to as *mature youth,* which was continued without addressing the target group until November 1929 (cf. Wittenbrink 1997, 998 f.). For example, *Das Wirtshaus im Spessart* by Hauff was read in eleven weeks in 1926/1927, *Der Oberhof* by Immermann in 17 episodes in 1927/1928, and *Ivanhoe* by Walter Scott for an entire year from January 1928 to January 1929.

Süddeutsche Rundfunk A. G. (Sürag)

The Stuttgart station Süddeutsche Rundfunk A. G. (Sürag)[10] began with an initially unspecified musically accompanied *Kindernachmittag* (Children's afternoon) on May 31, 1924. From the end of August 1924, the content of the broadcast was

---

[8] Other stations also used the two terms without distinguishing between ages. In 1927, for example, Bonsel's *Die Biene Maja* was first broadcast by Radio Zürich under the moniker *Kinderstunde*, and a few days later another chapter was read aloud in a *Jugendstunde*. Königsberg broadcast *fairy tales for the youngest youth* and *stories for the more mature youth* in 1925 and 1926.

[9] Wehrhan retired in 1933 because of a heart condition, according to the Lexikon westfälischer Autorinnen und Autoren (cf. https://www.lexikon-westfaelischer-autorinnen-und-autoren.de/autoren/wehrhan-karl/#biographie, 26.03.2020).

[10] On the political and structural history of the South German broadcasting group up to and including 1933, cf. Grube 1973.

usually specified as sagas, fairy tales, and fables. In January 1925, the narrator character *Gretle von Strümpfelbach* was introduced for a now regular Saturday broadcast. Who spoke this character was not stated. According to Elfert (1985, 299, f.n. 25), Sophie Tschorn was behind the artificial character, who created children's programmes under her own name, especially from 1933 onwards. As a rule, the programme information was happy with the title of the series, *'s Gretle von Strümpfelbach erzählt*. There is evidence that children were invited to the studio and occasionally recited their own contributions; fan mail and Swabian fairy tales were also read on air (cf. K. W. 1926). Other programmes documented by more detailed information, whith *aunt* Gretle as (co-)creator, were mixed formats, which could be summarised with Wittenbrink (1997) under the term *Hörfolge*: "a montage of literary quotations, music and reportage, held together by a thematic as well as scenic or acoustic framework" (ibid., 1033). The weighting between *fiction* and *faction* fluctuated. In a programme from the Cannstatt open-air swimming pool, for example, the reportage elements probably predominated (*Mutterle, darf i heut ens Schwemme?* July 17, 1930), while in a collage of "true stork stories" (*Storch-Storch-Schnibel-Schnabel*, July 17,1929) the fictional narration probably predominated. In the station's own presentation, this format was simply a *cheerful* or *colourful children's hour* or *children's afternoon*. A permanent member of *Gretle*'s staff was Georg Ott,[11] who himself was in charge of another of the Sürag series aimed at specific target groups, the *Kasperltheater* (Punch and Judy show). He adapted well-known plays by Pocci or fairy tales by Grimm, directed and voiced Kasperl. Ott is documented as a regular contributor to *Kinderstunde* until 1930 (he occasionally appears in 1935 and 1937 as well); Halefeldt (1997, 75), however, claims that Ott left the station as early as 1928.

For another weekly offer, *Jugendstunde,* only the names of the organizers – Elsa Pfeiffer and Karl Köstlin – are given, no information on the programme content. The fact that the radio orchestra regularly is mentioned in the programme information suggests a rather musical format. For a whole year (from May 1926 to May 1927), the Sürag took over from Norag Sunday *Funkheinzelmann,* which was transmitted via Berlin to several German stations (also Dresden, Leipzig, Stettin, Deutsche Welle). From the end of November 1926, further transmitters of Sürag were launched: Freiburg, Mannheim, Karlsruhe. These secondary stations also occasionally produced programmes addressed to children and young people. From 1929 onwards, thanks to a then agreed close partnership between SWR and Sürag, there were regular mutual takeovers of programmes (cf. Halefeldt 1997, 148).

---

[11] Pseudonym, civil name Eugen Essig.

Deutsche Stunde in Bayern GmbH

The first target group broadcast of the Munich station Deutsche Stunde in Bayern GmbH was announced on June 4, 1924 as "Cheerful children's poems and funny fairy tales". Other similar programmes, with no further specification of content, followed at greater intervals and with different speakers. From February 1925, the programme was called *Für unsere Kinder*, followed by a programme for parents and educators in the daytime programme. On September 15, 1926, the programme was renamed *Stunde der Jugend,* and from October 20, *Jugendstunde.* The denominations were used inclusively and did not refer to different age groups. The children's and youth broadcasts were extended to one and a half hours at the end of 1926, and up to two hours in the course of 1927. In contrast to all other stations Deutsche Stunde also indicated the broadcasting times of the individual items in the programme guides until the end of 1927.

Little is known about the programme makers. In a sympathetic article about *Frau und Kind im Münchener Rundfunk,* "uncle" Otto Willner is praised for his "warm-hearted way of chatting and drawing with the little ones", and the performance art of the storyteller Maria Devera (here erroneously as "auntie Denera") is emphasised as "inimitable" (R. Z. 1926). In 1929, the management of women's and children's department was entrusted to Ewis Borkmann, and from 1931 to Marie Buczkowska (cf. Elfert 1985, 316; Dinghaus 2002, 48). Borkmann had previously headed women's radio, and it is possible that the two target-group departments were merged in 1929. Under Borkmann's leadership, both programming divisions were expanded (cf. Dinghaus 2002, 230). On the occasion of Borkmann's takeover of the business – the director's wife, as the paper points out – *Der Deutsche Rundfunk* reported extensively on Munich children's radio (cf. Zoellner 1929). Its offers were diversified according to age groups and genres: The weekly broadcast began with *Kinderstunde,* followed by *Jugendstunde.* The *Kinderstunde,* in turn, was divided into broadcasting time "for the very young" and for children aged 7–12. The *Jugendstunde,* according to Zoellner, was intended for "the adolescent youth", i.e. 12 to 17-year-olds (cf. ibid.). The genres of the *Kinderstunde* are listed as: Counting rhymes, songs, fairy tale games (with participation of the "very young"), Kasperle games, classic fairy tales, but also stories that address everyday topics ("hygiene, decent behaviour, dangers of the street") and handicraft lessons. The *Jugendstunde* offered radio play adaptations of classic literature, readings from travel, adventure and animal stories, light classical music pieces, but also career advice. The article notes the abolition of gender segregation. Until October 1928 there was a chess programme for boys at the end of the *Jugendstunde,* and until mid-1928 there was also an occasional *Mädchenkränzchen* (Girls' get-together) – but a "modern girl" would have no interest in this today. The performances („little plays, songs and dance songs") by the pupils of a Munich girls' school, under the direction of their teacher Teresa Roth, are specially emphasised, as is the Kasperle show by Otto Willner and main teacher Neuhäusler (who gave several performances with children from the Schwind School) as well as the "sensitive" readings by Georg Gidalewitsch.

Three new series were announced, of which, however, only individual broadcasts are verifiable: *Helden von heute* (*Today's heroes*) with only one broadcast, on July 3, 1929; *Berühmte Menschen* (*Famous people*) – no evidence, the series *Aus dem Leben berühmter Männer* (variant: *erfolgreicher Männer)* already existed before 1929; the youth book series *Jugendbücherfunk* (one broadcast, May 29, 1929), in which (also) pupils were to have their say. The Nuremberg auxiliary station, which opened on August 8, 1925, also occasionally produced the Wednesday programmes, mostly with a local focus; they were also broadcast on the main station.

Ostmarken-Rundfunk AG (Orag)

Even before broadcasting began (June 14, 1924), Ostmarken-Rundfunk AG (Orag) Königsberg announced an afternoon programme with fairy tales, with the note "not daily" (Königsberger Vortragsfolgen 1924). The first verifiable fairy tale broadcast is in the programme on August 2, 1924. The further fairy tales readings were already addressed to the target group, with the wording alternating between *for our children, for our youth, for the more mature youth,* and *for the youngest youth* (by which children were meant in the usual sense). *Stoffe* or concrete contents were not yet communicated in the first year in the programme press. The first broadcasts were narrated by Joseph Christean, the station's director, alternating with Kurt Lesing, who was also a musician in the small initial ensemble (cf. Fünf Jahre Rundfunkleiter 1929). In 1926, Hedi Kettner (Christean's wife) frequently appeared as narrator, and from 1927 the literary director of the station Walther Ottendorf (cf. Halefeldt 1997, 79).

From August 1925, the Orag diversified its offer with an *Unterhaltungsstunde für die reifere Jugend* (*Entertainment hour for the more mature youth*). In 1927, this became *Jugendstunde* in which historical, animal and adventure stories (by Freytag, Seton, Löns, among others) were read on air (narrators: Michael Pichon, Robert Marlitz, Paul Lewitt). Often the alternative series title *Literarische Jugendstunde* was used. The broadcast series was expanded in 1929, including the small subseries *Der arbeitende Mensch in der erzählenden Literatur* (The working man in narrative literature). In 1930, this programme, originally addressed to the *more mature youth,* was also opened up to children of fairy-tale age, mainly through the speaker and author Marion Lindt, who also spoke in parallel on the Orag *Märchenfunk* or *Kinderfunk.*

The first radio plays were broadcast by the Orag in November 1925 (Grimm adaptations by Josef Bürkner). Cooperation with the Königsberg theatres was close, especially because Christean himself and his first employees came from the field of theatre (cf. Halefeldt 1997, 42). In December 1925, the radio artists performed Robert Bürkner's *Schneeweißchen und Rosenrot* first at the Komische Oper, and only then they adapted it for radio (December 27, 1925). At the beginning of 1926, three classical dramas were also broadcast under the series title *Jugendbühne* (without any indication of direction or narrator): Lessing's *Nathan der Weise* (January 12,

1926), Goethe's *Götz von Berlichingen* (March 4, 1926), and Grillparzer's *Sappho* (March 18, 1926). The radio play series was only tentatively continued in 1927, including two more fairy tale adaptations by Bürkner, then greatly expanded in 1928 and enriched with radio-specific themes: *Die abenteuerlichen Reisen des Freiherrn von Funkhausen* by Arthur Lokesch (October 17, 1928 and November 4, 1928). The most frequently performed author until 1932 was Otto Wollmann (with adaptations of Grimm, Busch, Andersen, Storm and others), and the most frequently directed was Kurt Lesing.

Since the "cultivation of the sense of homeland" was "one of the main tasks of the provincial station" (Kollatz 1925), the Orag regularly broadcast programmes (often of a humorous nature) in the respective local dialect; accordingly, children's programmes in East Prussian dialect and fairy tales by poets from the region (e.g. Manfred Kyber) were also read on air. At the end of September 1926, an Orag station was launched in Danzig (Gdańsk), which produced its own programmes two to three times a week, including a *Kinderstunde* or *Märchenstunde,* mainly by the *Märchenfrau* Elsa Faber von Bockelmann. In 1928 a *Jugendstunde* was also introduced (with travel, hunting and adventure stories), and in 1931 the *Bastelstunde für unsere Kleinen* (Handicrafts hour for our little ones) was added.

Schlesische Funkstunde AG

According to the programme announcement, Schlesische Funkstunde AG in Breslau (Wroclaw)[12] broadcast its first target group programme with fairy tales for children on Saturday, June 14, 1924. Further broadcasts of this kind followed at irregular intervals. The announcement continues to stick with the generic title and gives no programme details. From June to August 1925, the fairy tale programme, with Kitty Seiffert as narrator, ran under the title *Im Hasenwunderland.* Seiffert, like Ilse Obrig in Leipzig or Lisa Tetzner in Berlin, turned unilateral fairy tale telling into an interactive play, craft and fairy tale hour from 1929 onwards and gathered a crowd of children in the radio studio.

Other hosts and speakers of the fairy tale hour with frequent presence were Christa Niesel-Lessenthien (1926–1931), Margot Eckstein (late 1927 to 1932), the *fairy tale uncle* Friedrich Reinicke (1925–1938) and Ludwig Barg (1926–1927). In addition to the usual fairy tales, Lofting's *Doktor Dolittle* was performed on 16 dates in 1927 (read by Kitty Seiffert), *Kai in der Kiste* by Wolf Durian in 1928 (five dates, read by Friedrich Reinicke), Max Ophüls' *Fips und Stips auf Kinderwelle 325* in 1929, directed by Peer Lhot (ten dates; cf. also Asper 1998, 175–178, 687). From 1926 to 1931, Reinicke was in charge of the loosely produced series *Funkkasperles Kindernachmittag* (without content details in the programme guide).

---

[12] On the structure and development of the station from the perspective of the 1940s, cf. the dissertation by Elven 1945.

In December 1925, the broadcast format *Literarische Jugendstunde* was set up for 14- to 16-year-olds, and Fritz Wenzel[13] was brought in to lead it (cf. Elfert 1985, 316). Wenzel had scenes from popular works (including *Faust, Rübezahl, Till Eulenspiegel*, and Hans Sachs' *Schwänke*) performed by the station's own youth drama troupe and spoke introductory words. Classic school *Stoff* (including Gryphius, Lessing, Hölderlin, Fontane) was also performed. Radio plays were produced from December 1925 onwards, the first being *Peterchens Mondfahrt* by Bassewitz, which was first narrated on three broadcast dates in October and was on the programme as a fairy tale play directed by Friedrich Reinicke on three days from Christmas onwards.[14]

At the end of October 1926, the station announced a new programme structure in which the two target group programmes were also given a fixed broadcasting slot: every other Thursday the *Literarische Jugendstunde* and on Friday the *Kinderstunde* (cf. H. U. 1926). The target group programmes were later expanded to include new formats and characters and more broadcasting days. Margot Eckstein told *Geschichten vom Funkpurzel* from August 1928 to August 1931. From September 1929 to April 1931, there was a *Kinderzeitung* (Children's newspaper) on Fridays with the protagonists *Schnuffibus* and *Zeitungsonkel*, spoken by Peer Lhot and Ewald Fröhlich. The previews suggest reports on topics from the children's environment. On June 7, 1931, Funkpurzel took the children to the pencil factory, on April 30, 1931, through the ruins of historic Breslau, on January 8, 1931, to the nursery and on June 29, 1931, he received travel reports from the newspaper uncle; the latter in turn seems to have been interested in news from sport, theatre and film: On August 31, 1931, he visited a Kasperle workshop, on February 28, 1931, a six-day race in the sports arena and in October and November the focus was on *Mickey Mouse*. On November 15, 1925, the Gleiwitz branch station was opened. A first *Märchenstunde* addressed to children can be found only one year later in the programme of the Gleiwitz station (December 12, 1926). The author and studio manager Paul Kania appeared as its narrator most frequently.

Mitteldeutsche Rundfunk AG (Mirag)

Mitteldeutsche Rundfunk AG (Mirag) in Leipzig began its children's programme on Wednesday, July 9, 1924, with an unspecified *Märchennachmittag für Kinder* (Fairy tales afternoon for children). It was not until 1926 that more specific programme details were also given. In 1927, the fairy tale afternoons appear to have been pushed back in favour of a new broadcast format *Aus dem Schatzkästlein für die Jugend*

---

[13] Wenzel distinguished himself in Breslau primarily as a sports editor and reporter and headed the station's current affairs department from 1929 to 1935 (cf. Halefeldt 1997, 84 f.). In 1935 he was dismissed and returned to teaching. In his time he was considered "one of the best sports announcers and reportage directors of German radio" (Elven 1945, 28).

[14] Cf. the contribution by Julia Benner in this volume.

(From the treasure chest for youth). It was a mixed form, which Elfert describes as a thematically coherent "combination of various contributions, e.g., recitations, introductory, transitional or commentary lectures, short reports, dialogues, smaller play scenes, sound effects as well as music recordings" (Elfert 1985, 213). Some headings: *Von tapferen Jungens* (August 31, 1927), *Tiere und Menschen* (September 14, 1927), *Von kleinen Ausreißern* (June 1, 1927).

In 1929, the offers for children and youth were significantly expanded. A Saturday craft hour was added to the Wednesday broadcast in the spring, and a *Geschichten- und Liederstunde für die Jugend* (*Story and song hour for young people*) was introduced on Thursdays in autumn. The Wednesday programme was more often divided according to age into a first segment *for the younger,* followed by a second segment *for the older.* On Tuesdays, books for young people were presented and recommended to an adult target audience every two weeks, or weekly before holidays. From November 1929 onwards, this programme was no longer aimed at parents or guardians, but directly at young listeners as *Bücherstunde der Jugend* (*Youth book hour*). The schedule for the first six episodes of the series included the following genres: "November 12: New picture books. November 19: Christmas plays. November 26: Books for Boys. December 3: Fairy tales from around the world. December 10: Books dealing with Christmas. December 17: Books for Girls." (Achtung! Achtung! 1929). In mid-December, the station decided to establish another bi-weekly Saturday broadcast for its school holiday listeners, called *Stunde der Jugendlichen,* which primarily dealt with topics of young working adults (cf. Findeisen 1929a).

Parallel to the expansion of the broadcasting offer for children and young people, the station-related programme magazine *Die Mirag* introduced a special page at the beginning of October 1929 (issue 39) under the title *Jugend-Funk* (later: *Die Kleine Mirag,* from 1934 *Die junge Front*). References to the programme, short excerpts from well-known youth books, illustrations of the broadcasts, and a mailbox section were part of the page's profile. The lead article for the first issue was written by Kurt Arnold Findeisen (1929c), who also edited the children's page together with Herbert Roth.

Findeisen was the full-time literary director of the Dresden studio (cf. Halefeldt 1997, 79) and like Hans Bodenstedt, the artistic director of Norag in Hamburg, he was in charge of the children's and youth section. In his leading position, he succeeded at the Mirag in a similar way to Bodenstedt in Hamburg, namely the expansion of children's and youth radio in terms of time as well as genre and content, and its corresponding positioning in an accompanying print medium. His artistic demands as a writer and his pedagogical experience as an elementary school teacher also aided the broadcasts he supervised and in part created himself (radio plays, radio features, book recommendations, school radio lessons, etc.). As a writer, – like Bodenstedt – he used the full possibilities of both media. Findeisen read and adapted his books for radio (e.g. *Klaviergeschichten,* printed in 1920, several broadcasts in 1929 and 1930; *Der Sohn der Wälder,* printed in 1922 and 1925, readings on May 7, 1931, in Hamburg and on July 08, 1931, in Munich, as a series of episodes on February 28, 1932, in the Studio Dresden); conversely, he published his broadcasts in book form (*Volksliedgeschichten*, broadcast April 17, 1928, December 5, 1929, November 13, 1930, June 30, 1931, printed 1932). Findeisen also tried writing radio plays, especially out of disappointment with the radio plays offered by the stations. The genre was still too much stuck in the "traditional cloying, kitschy, at least romantic-sentimental style"; the radio play finally had to follow the development of youth literature and "consider the sporty, unromantic, activist attitude of today's youth" (Findeisen 1930). As a counter-proposal, Findeisen wrote a modern *Schlaraffenlandspiel* (*Cockaigne play*), which he presented on the children's page *Jugend-Funk der Mirag* with the rhetorical question of whether it would not be more desirable for young people today if "instead of a salted pig, there were a snappy four-cylinder Opel car" and "instead of roasted pigeons, airplanes and zeppelins would buzz through the air". And wouldn't "a solid wire fence around a tennis court or a playground [...] be worth at least as much as a fence of fried sausages?" (Findeisen 1929b). *Das Schlaraffenlandspiel* was premiered by the Mirag on November 13, 1929, directed by Josef Krahé, repeated on January 22, 1930, also played by the Viennese station on 26 April 1930 and broadcast by the Norag as a pupil performance on October 26, 1931.

With radio play adaptations for a young audience and often as a director, Hans Peter Schmiedel, the literary director of the Mirag main studio Leipzig, was also in the programme. A special feature of Mirag offers were the nature educational radio plays by Erna Moser (1929–1931), who regularly presented and promoted her topics (migratory birds, spiders, life in ice and snow, the Amazon) on the children's page of the programme guide. Ilse Obrig, who worked for the Mirag from 1928 (cf. Halefeldt 1997, 310), developed the interactive format *Spielstunde für Kinder* in which she chatted live with children in the studio about books, did gymnastics, handicrafts, and sang. Some of the programmes were conceived as impromptu games, their protagonists were the numerous members of the *Familie Fröhlich* (*Happy family*), whose experiences at the zoo, the circus, the doll school and the doll wedding, building a dwarf city or travelling the world in the living room, etc. were developed and produced on the basis of suggestions from the target group and with the participation of children (cf. Obrig 1930).

Westdeutsche Funkstunde AG (Wefag): Westdeutsche Rundfunk AG (Werag)

On October 10, 1924, Westdeutsche Funkstunde AG (Wefag) in Münster became the last German regional radio station to go on air.[15] As early as November 5, it added a regular children's (fairy tale) broadcast to its programme. In September

---

[15] On the institutional development of Wefag and Werag, cf. the contributions collected in Först 1974, especially that by Bierbach; on the interweavings of the broadcaster with the programme press, cf. Bauer 1993, 116–132, passim.

1925, the Wefag studios in Dortmund and Elberfeld added their own programmes. Starting in October 1925, the Elberfeld studio began broadcasting *Funkheinzelmann* programmes with its own narrators (Carl Weinlein, later Rudolf Rauher); the *Funkheinzelmann orchestra* often played in addition. Marta (Martha) Walter, who was also present in the programme with fairy tale readings and other recitations, was responsible for an unspecified girls addressed *Mädchenkränzchen* on Sundays. In August 1926, Wefag's headquarters were moved from Münster to Cologne, where a so-called large transmitter was built and opened in early 1927. At the same time, the Elberfeld transmitter was closed. Wefag was renamed Werag (Westdeutsche Rundfunk AG) (cf. Bierbach 1974).

In January 1927, the pedagogue Rudolf Simon (lecturer for speech training at the Cologne Central Institute for Education and Instruction) took over the weekly children's hour of the Cologne station. He explained his concept and the structure of the broadcasting programme in detail in the station's programme magazine. His credo, reminiscent of Wolgast's demand for children's books, was that the programme "must be of literary and artistic quality and value in terms of content and form" (Simon 1927). Simon categorically rejected a childish adaptation of the *Stoff*: "The youth lesson should bring *pure joy*" (ibid., emphasis in the original underlined). The limited broadcasting time of only one hour on Sunday afternoons was divided into *Kinderfunk* for the so-called fairy tale age (up to about the age of 10) and *Jugendfunk* (up to the age of 15), each with half an hour of broadcasting time. In order to diversify the range of programmes, fairy tales alternated with stories in children's section and adventure reading with sagas and poetry portraits in youth section. The corresponding programmes were conceived as series from the very beginning. Every second Sunday was reserved for music for both age groups.

At the beginning of 1929, Cologne introduced another (daily) *Kinderspielstunde*, led by Els Vordemberge. It was aimed primarily at younger children and offered mainly games, songs, handicrafts, drawing, chats on various factual topics and also occasional children's stories and fairy tales. The popular Cologne Hänneschen Theater (a hand puppet stage) occasionally gave guest performances on their programme, which can be traced to 1937 even after Vordemberge's dismissal from broadcasting in 1933 (cf. Schütte 1971, 135).

Schulfunk, school supporting broadcast, took up more space in Werag programming than in the other regional stations, because it was also permitted by an exemption to supply secondary schools with teaching support programmes, for which Deutsche Welle was otherwise responsible (cf. Bierbach 1974, 210 f.). Literature from the school canon was presented and read in *Deutschkundlicher Schulfunk* in a way that was addressed to specific target groups and usually sorted thematically, for example: The animal in poetry, (June 20, 1931), industry in art and poetry (December 6, 1930), sports as poetic motif, (April 23, 1932), the image of Napoleon in German Poetry (November 22, 1930), in each case prepared for the intermediate level of higher educational establishments. Regional themes were also taken up, for example the Cologne dialect (July 4, 1931 – for the upper school) or the Rhenish landscape, "painted by the poet" (September 24, 1932 – for the middle school).

Deutsche Welle GmbH

In December 1927, Deutsche Welle[16] (indicated in the programme press as Königswusterhausen, according to the location of the broadcasting facility) also established a children's programme, which was offered six times a week (from Monday to Saturday) at the same time (14:20) as an almost half-hour programme. Three days of the week were devoted to literary themes – on Monday fairy tales for the smaller listeners, Wednesday radio plays for the same target group and Thursday adventure and travel stories for the older children. Nature, handicrafts and music were the subject areas of the other broadcasts (cf. Stiemer 1927; Ein Kinderfunk der „Deutsche Welle" 1927).

Deutsche Welle distinguished itself in the field of radio plays with the fairy tale adaptations of its freelancer Otto Wollmann, directed by the in-house director Konrad Dürre, often with music by Lilly Dürre. Konrad Dürre was responsible for children's radio and artistic-literary programmes at Deutsche Welle (cf. Halefeldt 1997, 131). Highly esteemed by critics (cf. Günther 1931), these radio plays also were popular amongst other broadcasters. Wollmann himself was convinced that radio theatre was "something great and serious" for the child (Wollmann 1930). He preferred the classic fairy tales by Grimm, Hauff, Andersen, fairy tales from 1001 Nights and well-known sagas (*Rübezahl*, *Der Rattenfänger von Hameln*, *Reineke Fuchs*, *Loreley*) and other popular *Stoffe* from children's and youth literature (*Max und Moritz*, *Struwwelpeter*, *Pole Poppenspäler*, *Robinson Crusoe*). Six productions were recorded by Deutsche Grammophon (*Aschenbrödel*, *Rotkäppchen*, *Die Bremer Stadtmusikanten*, *Froschkönig*, *Schneewittchen*, *Deutsches Weihnachtsspiel*) and came back to radio via this medium.

In the *Jungmädchenstunde* (*Young girls' hour*) of Deutsche Welle (cf. Dinghaus 2002), Grete Maria Markstein presented the series *Was wir lesen* in 1930–1931, in which she dealt with the reading of young girls. Markstein was also represented on the station with fairy tale stories, either live or with her recordings (cf. also Elfert 1985, 110). The *Bastelstunden* (*Handicraft hours*) with *aunt* Ursula Scherz were extremely successful and were praised accordingly by the contemporary press (cf. Gomoll 1932). Scherz developed exciting stories about her handicrafts, which were commented on and continued by children. The resulting radio story about *Familie Tüchtig* (*the Hardworking family*) was also used by Scherz as a novel (Scherz et al. 1930), which in turn was presented on the radio (December 7, 1930, Deutsche Welle) and also reviewed by the programme press (cf. „Familie Tüchtig" 1930).

---

[16] On Deutsche Welle, cf. the comprehensive study by Rolfes 1990; cf. also Halefeldt 1997, 123–134.

Children's and Youth Broadcasts from Austria and Switzerland

The German-language programming for children and young people also included the relevant broadcasts of the radio stations in Vienna[17] and Zurich, and later also Graz and Bern. Their programme guides were printed extensively by the Berlin magazine *Der Deutsche Rundfunk*. At the beginning, Vienna regularly had two children's programmes per week, Zurich three. Especially the Zurich broadcasts were listed in detail in the early years, with the programme structure, the titles of the texts or songs presented, and the names of the people involved.

Radio Wien as the main station of Radio Verkehrs AG (Ravag) began with a half-hour biweekly *Märchenstunde* – also *Märchenstunde für Kinder* (cf. Ergert 1974, 70). In October 1926, *Jugendbühne* was introduced for a youthful target audience, with classics (*Don Juan und Faust* by Grabbe, December 2, 1926) and fairy tale adaptations (*Schneewittchen,* October 23, 1926). The repertoire was to include highbrow literature as well as "folk plays, the poetry of the homeland and world literature" (Die Jugendbühne von Radio Wien 1926, 2308). Hans Nüchtern, Hermann Wawra and Aurel Nowotny alternated as play directors. From 1927 onwards, a distinction was made between *Kinderstunde* (mostly fairy tales) and *Jugendstunde* (with i.a. adventure, technology, animal stories). Radio Graz as a regional station of Ravag was often present on the radio with radio play productions (also for a youth audience) of the Schauspielhaus under the direction of Anton Hamik and with musical accompaniment of the Hüttl band.

Radio Zürich had *Kinderstunden* and *Stunden für die Jugend* (target group 8–13 years) in the programme. Fairy tales for younger children, often in the regional idiom, were mainly told by *aunt* Marie Böschenstein, while Emilie Locher-Werling also appealed to older children with stories of her own and those of others. Radio Bern produced its own children's programme. Here *aunt* Röseli Gilomen spoke to the children (about unspecified topics) and was also represented in the programme with fairy tale adaptations (e.g. *Zwerg Nase*, December 31, 1932; *Rotkäppchen*, May 18, 1932).

Children's and Youth Broadcasts from 1933 and until the End of the War

Crucial for the medium, and especially for the broadcasts addressed to children and young people, was the order issued personally by the head of the *Reichssendeleitung*, Eugen Hadamowsky, to the broadcasting directors to above all produce entertainment, "no entertainment hype, but light, captivating and good entertainment"

---

[17] On Austrian broadcasting until 1938, cf. Ergert 1974.

(Hadamowsky 1934b; cf. Reiss 1979). Of the prominent authors who remained present on the radio after 1933, Otto Wollmann should be mentioned first and foremost, whose fairy tale radio plays, played by all stations, can be traced back until 1940. Günter Eich can be traced back until 1936. More of Eich's broadcasts have been recorded than was previously known (cf. Wagner 1999). Radio plays by Lisa Tetzner, who was forced to emigrate in 1933, were still being produced by the German Reich stations until the end of 1934. However, the dismissal of tried and tested authors from the editorial offices and the permanent staff of writers at the stations (including Hermann Kasack, Paul Kania, Alfred Braun and Hans Bodenstedt) soon made itself noticeable. From 1933 onwards, the radio programme for children and young people was increasingly expanded with broadcasts on historical personalities or events in contemporary history, the genre of which was often indicated as radio play. For example: *HJ auf Fahrt durch den Harz* (Leipzig, June 12, 1934) or *Der Hindenburgdamm wird gebaut* (Hamburg, June 15, 1934). These were presumably forms of presentation that would be called docudrama today.

In addition, designated as *HJ-Funk*, there were numerous broadcasts with topics such as sports, hiking, comradeship, so-called race studies, or in 1934 the series *Blut und Ehre* (Blood and honour), in which Nazi functionaries had their say. Literary personalities were also increasingly appropriated for party purposes. In the summer of 1934, a Schiller celebration (also known as *Schillersonnwendfeier*) was held with a Germany-wide relay to Marbach, where thousands of young people from all over Germany would bring "certificates" with "what German youth has to say to the spirit of the great poet" (Die deutsche Jugend huldigt Friedrich Schiller in Marbach 1934). Figures from the political children's and youth organisations of the time soon entered the radio plays.

From 1936, the stations increasingly relied on mutual programme exchange.[18] Especially in the morning, up to five stations took over a contribution; often only two programmes ran in parallel on all ten German broadcasting stations: *Die hilfreichen Heinzelmännchen*, for example, was also broadcast from Berlin to Breslau, Munich, Stuttgart, and Saarbrücken on June 22, 1936; at the same time (10:00 a.m.), Frankfurt, Hamburg, Cologne, and Königsberg broadcast *Das Spiel vom glücklichen Hans,* a radio play for elementary schools broadcast from Leipzig. The multiple use of contributions also increased noticeably. The Deutschlandsender often used the radio play from its afternoon series *Kinderfunkspiel* in the *Grundschulfunk*, a morning programme for primary school children (e.g. *Am Bahndamm entlang* – broadcast as *Kinderfunkspiel* on May 31, 1936 and in *Grundschulfunk* on July 6, 1936). Recordings apparently circulated frequently between stations, but this exchange was rarely indicated (e.g. *Der Kampf um den Froschweiher* was broadcast by Munich on June 20, 1936, by Breslau on July, 18, 1936, by Frankfurt on August 22, 1936).

---

[18] Halefeldt (1976, 22) cites a survey according to which the number of broadcasts fell from 2000 in 1933 to 800 in 1936 – with a simultaneous increase in performances from 230,000 to 500,000, which he places in the context of the broadcasters' exchange of programmes.

From 1937 onwards, there was a tendency to no longer address programmes for children and young people. With the exception of Hamburg, whose Sunday radio play programme was consistently announced under the series title *Kinder, hört zu!* (*Children, listen up!*) the other stations increasingly dispensed with target group-oriented attributions. In these cases, an implicit addressability can only be concluded from certain formulations (e.g. *a funny game*), the broadcasting slot (in the early afternoon) and not least from the *Stoffe* itself (well-known fairy tales, Heinzelmännchen Kasperle, etc.).

The programme information is usually more concise. It probably happened more often (than stated in the programme) that stations used a lot of archived recordings, or slightly reworked older broadcast manuscripts, or didn't rework them at all, and put them in the programme under new authors' names. Examples: *Schneewittchen und die sieben Zwerge* was broadcast by Breslau on April 21, 1935, as a radio play by Erich Colberg with music and directed by Heribert Grüger, and repeated on December 26, 1937, under the title *Schneewittchen* allegedly written by Hans Herrmann, but with the same name for music and direction. *Das tapfere Schneiderlein* was broadcast several times by Deutschlandsender in 1935 and 1936 as a radio play version by Otto Wollmann. For the same title on the same station, Wollmann is named as the director on February 13, 1938, but Charlotte Hundertmark is given as author.

With the beginning of the war (September 1939), radio was converted to the needs of warfare. The editor-in-chief of *Der Deutsche Rundfunk,* Hans von Heister, asserted that entertainment broadcasting would continue despite restrictions, because "especially in serious times, distraction and encouragement [are] of importance [and] not to be underestimated for the favourable influence on the mental attitude of the people" (Heister 1939). The radio magazines, meanwhile, henceforth printed greatly reduced programmes. The details are taciturn, rarely reveal any substance, and disclose virtually none of the people involved. Since listening to foreign stations was made a punishable offence, the magazines refrained from printing the foreign broadcast programmes (cf. Warum keine Programme? 1939).

As of June 9, 1940, the stations were all centralised (the phenomenon is known as *Gleichschaltung*), they all broadcast the same standard programme and their offers were drastically reduced – there was now only one so-called Reich programme, which was broadcast on all stations (cf. Schütte 1971, 180). In addition, there was a small proportion of own productions of the stations, children's programmes included the content of which, however, was only rarely published in the magazines. With the abolition of the programme press on June 1, 1941, the source landscape became extremely precarious. The programme information published from then on in the general press does not address target groups. However, fairy tale programmes remain demonstrably present on German radio up to and including 1944, presumably until the end of the war.

Summary

Radio broadcasting in Germany was organised regionally in the early 1920s according to a state plan with private capital. There were nine broadcasting companies, each of which was granted a monopoly for a self-produced radio programme in a geographically defined broadcasting district. In addition, there was the Deutsche Welle as a supra-regional broadcaster. The infrastructure was provided by the *Reichspost*, which also collected the broadcasting fees and distributed them proportionally to the stations. The broadcasters were obliged to be politically neutral or balanced and were to provide entertainment and education. From the beginning, the stations included offers for children and young people, initially primarily fairy tale readings and poetry recitations, which corresponded to the general orientation of early radio towards books (cf. Wittenbrink 1997, 996). Interactive formats that involved children in the script or let them improvise in the studio were successful, such as Lisa Tetzner's stories without an ending, Wilhelm Lamszus' essay lessons, or the handicraft game shows by Kitty Seiffert, Ilse Obrig, and Ursula Scherz. Creative personalities with decision-making power used the new medium for technical experiments and developed radio-specific forms of presentation, such as Hans Bodenstedt in Hamburg, who developed the first media-specific fairy tale format with its own character narrator– *Funkheinzelmann,* or Kurt Arnold Findeisen in Dresden, who advocated a contemporary radio play at Mirag and promoted, reflected and thus upgraded the children's and youth broadcasts with a special page in the station's programme magazine. Ambitious projects that were not also linked to a position of power at the station failed, such as *Funkprinzessin* by Adele Proesler in Berlin.

The broadcasters attempted to fulfil their educational mandate for the younger generation by teaching classical literature. On the one hand, the format of *Jugendbühne* was introduced to present dramas by Schiller, Goethe, Kleist and others, on the other hand, *Schulfunk* was often used to disseminate the literary canon of the textbooks in readings, analyses, summaries. In later years, the school radio broadcasts faded from their school-accompanying profile, and fairy tale radio plays were more often taken over from the afternoon programme (especially by Deutsche Welle).

The so-called folk tales were the safest and most productive source for early children's and youth radio, outlasting all economic fluctuations, even the shortage of broadcasting time caused by the war. Another popular and resistant broadcasting format were *Kasperlespiele* (Punch and Judy shows), which all stations had in their programmes, whether in their own productions or as guest performances by travelling puppet theatres. *Kasperle* was also the godfather of the development of new media-specific characters, such as *Funkkasperle* in Breslau. A constant feature of children's and youth radio in the 1920s were also regionally specific fairy tales, legends, stories, poems, which were spoken by authors from the region, often in dialect. In Stuttgart, Sophie Tschorn developed her own Swabian radio series and narrator character, *Gretle von Strümpfelbach*. In Hamburg, Low German fairy tales were regularly broadcast, in Königsberg East Prussian fairy tales, in Frankfurt and Cologne regional sagas and local stories were part of the repertoire. On Swiss radio, broadcasts in the regional language were standard. In the 1930s, German broadcasters increasingly replaced regionally influenced content with national German content.

With the seizure of power by the National Socialists and the reorganisation of German broadcasting, most of the directors were dismissed, as were many established leading personalities who were also relevant to children's and youth broadcasting, such as Alfred Braun in Berlin, Hans Bodenstedt in Hamburg (despite his over-adaptation to National Socialist programming policy) or Kurt Arnold Findeisen in Dresden (whose books, however, continued to be listed on the Nazi recommended reading lists; cf. Hopster et al. 2001, 294 f.). Less exposed radio employees however, who were willing to adapt were able to keep their broadcasts – among them many women, also because they were underrepresented in power-relevant leadership positions (cf. Münkel 1998, 88). Under the National Socialists, youth broadcasts were upgraded and politicised. The entertaining fairy tale narratives and fairy tale radio plays continued to be produced and exchanged among the stations.

Almost 16,600 radio programmes were included in the project database. The number of broadcasts recorded is lower because each individual part of the broadcast that can be linked to a specific *Stoff* was assigned its own record. The radio year 1930 proved to be the most productive (about 2000 entries), followed by 1931 (1980) and 1929 (1840). The National Socialist *Gleichschaltung* is clearly noticeable in that from about 1500 entries in 1932 the number of records drops to about 990 in 1933. In the war years 1940–1944, the number of recorded programmes remains below 100 in each year. About 5300 are explicitly youth-addressed (*Jugendstunde, Jugendfunk, Jugendbühne*, etc.), about 4750 children-addressed (*Kinderfunk, Kinderstunde, Für die Kinder*, etc.). In addition, 800 book recommendations were recorded. The ratio between the records tagged as readings or radio plays is about 1:2, about half of both forms of presentation are noted as fairy tales.

References

Primary Literature

Benjamin, Walter/Tiedemann, Rolf (Hg.): Aufklärung für Kinder. Rundfunkvorträge. Frankfurt a. M.: Suhrkamp, 1985.
Findeisen, Kurt Arnold: Der Sohn der Wälder. Leipzig, Zürich: Grethlein, 1922.
Findeisen, Kurt Arnold: Klaviergeschichten: Einführungen in ein volkstümliches Verständnis der Musik. Mit Bildschm. nach alten Stichen und nach Zeichnungen von Albrecht Dürer [u. a.]. Leipzig: Dürr, 1920.
Findeisen, Kurt Arnold/Rübner, Kurt (Ill.): Der Raubschütz: Eine Erzählung (vom Dichter nach seinem Roman „Der Sohn der Wälder" für die Jugend bearbeitet). Leipzig: Hegel & Schade, 1925.

Findeisen, Kurt Arnold: Volksliedgeschichten und Geschichten in Volksliedern. Langensalza [u. a.]: J. Beltz, 1932.
Scherz, Ursula/Biesenthal, Rose (Ill.)/Wauer, William (Ill.): Familie Tüchtig. Ein Abenteuer-Märchen- und Bastelbuch. Zürich [u. a.]: F. A. Perthes, 1930.

Audiography

Aschenbrödel [Schallplatte] [1929?]. Frei nach Grimm, dramatisch bearb. von Otto Wollmann. Kompositionen: Lilly Dürre. Ensemble des Kinder-Theaters der Deutschen Welle, Berlin. Regie: Konrad Dürre. Berlin: Grammophon (27052).
Aufklärung für Kinder. Von Zigeunern und Hunden, Kaspar Hauser und Pompeji – nicht nur für Kinder [Hörbuch] (2003). Lesung des gleichnamigen Buchs von Walter Benjamin. Sprecher: Harald Wieser. Regie Holger Rink. Hamburg: Hoffmann und Campe.
Bremer Stadtmusikanten [Schallplatte] (1929). Frei nach Grimm, dramatisch bearb. von Otto Wollmann. Kompositionen: Lilly Dürre. Ensemble des Kinder-Theaters der Deutschen Welle, Berlin. Regie: Konrad Dürre. Berlin: Grammophon (27054).
Rotkäppchen [2 Schallplatten] (1929). Ein Märchen der Brüder Grimm. Bearb. von Otto Wollmann. Kompositionen: Lilly Dürre. Märchenensemble des Kinderfunks Berlin. Berlin: Grammophon (27056; 27057).
Froschkönig [2 Schallplatten] (1929). Frei nach Grimm, dramatisch bearb. von Otto Wollmann, Kompositionen: Lilly Dürre; Regie: Konrad Dürre. Berlin: Polydor (27098; 27099).
Schneewittchen [Schallplatte] (1930). Frei nach Grimm, dramatisch bearb. von Otto Wollmann. Kompositionen: Lilly Dürre. Ensemble des Kinder-Theaters der Deutschen Welle, Berlin. Regie: Konrad Dürre. Berlin: Grammophon (27201).

Secondary Literature Before 1945

Achtung! Achtung! In: Die Mirag (1929) 45, 25 (Jugend-Funk).
Der neue Deutschlandsender. In: Der Deutsche Rundfunk 10 (1932) 50, 9–10.
Dichtung und Rundfunk. Reden und Gegenreden. Berlin 1930.
Die deutsche Jugend huldigt Friedrich Schiller in Marbach. „Sonnwendfeier 1934". „Stunde der Nation" aus Stuttgart. Was?+Wann?+Wo? In: Die Mirag (1934) 25, 45.
Die Jugendbühne von Radio-Wien. Zur Eröffnung am Samstag, den 2. Oktober. In: Radio-Wien 2 (1926) 52, 2307–2308.
Ein Kinderfunk der „Deutschen Welle". In: Funk (1927) 49, 402.
Elven, Gisela: Der schlesische Rundfunk 1924–1939 unter Berücksichtigung seiner politischen und volkstumspolitischen Aufgabe. Leipzig, Univ., Diss., 1945.
„Familie Tüchtig". Ein Abenteuer-, Märchen- und Bastelbuch von „Tante Ursula" der Deutschen Welle. In: Der Deutsche Rundfunk 8 (1930), 11.
Findeisen, Kurt Arnold: Achtung! Achtung! In: Die Mirag (1929a) 50, 25 (Jugend-Funk).
Findeisen, Kurt Arnold: Das Schlaraffenlandspiel. Eine schöne, alte Sage, für die Jugend erzählt von Arnold Findeisen. In: Die Mirag (1929b) 45, 25 (Jugend-Funk).
Findeisen, Kurt Arnold: Ein paar Worte zu meinem „Schlaraffenlandspiel" für die Jugend: Zur Aufführung im Mitteldeutschen Rundfunk am 22. Januar. In: Der Deutsche Rundfunk 8 (1930) 3, 13.
Findeisen, Kurt Arnold: Jugend-Funk. Ein paar Worte an die Rundfunk-Jugend. In: Die Mirag (1929c) 39, 23 (Jugend-Funk).
Fr.: Die Frage der Funkprinzessin. In: Der Deutsche Rundfunk 3 (1925) 9, 545.
Fünf Jahre Rundfunkleiter. In: Der Deutsche Rundfunk 7 (1929) 3, 97–98.

Giesecke, Heinrich: Die Organisation des deutschen Rundfunks. In: Rundfunk-Jahrbuch 1929. Berlin o. J., 29–42.
Gomoll, Wilhelm Conrad: „Tante Ursula" und ihre Welt. 5 Jahre Kinderbastelstunde der Deutschen Welle. In: Der Deutsche Rundfunk 10 (1932) 49, 9.
Günther, Johannes: Kindermärchen – Kinderfunk. In: Der Hochwart 1 (1931) 12, 337–338.
Heister, Hans S. von: Der Rundfunk im Krieg. In: Der Deutsche Rundfunk 17 (1939) 35, [2].
H. U.: Neue Tageseinteilung in den Programmen der Schlesischen Funkstunde. In: Der Deutsche Rundfunk 4 (1926) 44, 3113–3114.
Hadamowsky, Eugen: Reichssender. Reichssendeleiter Eugen Hadamowsky kündigt an. In: Die Mirag (1934a) 14, 10.
Hadamowsky, Eugen: Rundfunkwinter 1934/35. Reichs-Sendeleiter Hadamowsky kündigt vor der bayrischen Presse ein glanzvolles musikalisches Winterprogramm im deutschen Rundfunk an. In: Die Mirag (1934b) 42, 4 und 56.
Jeden Tag Jugendfunk. In: Der Deutsche Rundfunk 7 (1929) 39, 1251–1253.
Kollatz, C. W.: Der ostpreußische Humor bei der Orag. In: Der Deutsche Rundfunk 3 (1925) 16, 1014.
Königsberger Vortragsfolgen. In: Der Deutsche Rundfunk 2 (1924) 22, 1207.
K. W.: Vom Stuttgarter Rundfunk. In: Der Deutsche Rundfunk 4 (1926) 11, 738.
Lamszus, Wilhelm: Auf dem Wege zum Kinderhörspiel. Aufsatzstunden im Rundfunk. In: Der Schulfunk 4 (1930) 19, 303–307.
Magnus, Kurt: Niederschrift der Sitzung des Programmrats der deutschen Rundfunkgesellschaften zu Wiesbaden. In: Rundfunk-Jahrbuch 1929. Berlin o. J., 120–208.
Obrig, Ilse: Liebe Familie Fröhlich. Zur Jugenddarbietung am Montag, 13. Oktober, 14,15 Uhr. In: Die Mirag (1930) 41, 43 (Jugend-Funk).
Pinthus, Kurt: Die Dichtung. In: Drei Jahre Berliner Rundfunkdarbietungen. Ein Rückblick 1923–1926. Berlin [1926], 34–64.
Pinthus, Kurt: Die Dichtung. In: Fünf Jahre Berliner Rundfunk. Ein Rückblick 1923–1928. Berlin o. J. [1928], 92–208.
Proesler, Adele: Adele Proesler an die Rundfunkjugend. In: Der Deutsche Rundfunk 3 (1925a) 19, 1199.
Proesler, Adele: Brief der Funkprinzessin. Märchenland, am 11. Januar 1925. In: Die Funk-Stunde (1925b) 2, 23.
Proesler, Adele: Brief der Funkprinzessin. Märchenland, am 22. Januar 1925. In: Die Funk-Stunde (1925c) 4, 59.
Proesler, Adele: Märchen und Jugendstunden im Rundfunk. In: Der Deutsche Rundfunk 3 (1925d) 24, 1505–1508.
Richtlinien über die Regelung des Rundfunks. In: Der Deutsche Rundfunk 5 (1927) 1, 32.
Rieck, Max: Der Rundfunk im Geschäftsbericht 1926 der Deutschen Reichspost. In: Der Deutsche Rundfunk 5 (1927) 47, 3246–3247.
Rundfunk-Jahrbuch 1929. Berlin o. J.
R. Z.: Frau und Kind im Münchener Rundfunk. In Der Deutsche Rundfunk 4 (1926) 38, 2667.
Sch.: Freuden, Leiden und Wünsche der Außenseiter. Rostocker Brief. In: Der Deutsche Rundfunk 2 (1924) 17, 820–821.
Simon, Rudolf: Jugend und Rundfunk. In: Die Werag 2 (1927) 4, 5.
Stiemer, Felix: Kinderfunk der Deutschen Welle. In: Der Deutsche Rundfunk 5 (1927) 49, 3367.
Tasiemka, Hans: Dr. Flesch beginnt. Die Berliner Funk-Stunde wird umorganisiert. In: Der Deutsche Rundfunk 7 (1929) 27, 872.
Tetzner, Lisa: Die Mitarbeit der Kinder am Jugendrundfunk als nötige Grundlage des Programmaufbaus. In: Der Schulfunk 4 (1930) 11, 167–169.
Warum keine Programme? In: Der Deutsche Rundfunk 17 (1939) 43, [3].
Wehrhan, Karl: Jugend- und Elternstunden im Frankfurter Rundfunk. In: Der Deutsche Rundfunk 5 (1927) 51, 3521–3522.
W. H. F.: Von 1928 zu 1929. In: Der Deutsche Rundfunk 7 (1929) 1, [1].
Wollmann, Otto: Das Kindertheater im Rundfunk. In: Der Rundfunk-Hörer 7 (1930) 9, 1f.
Zoellner, R.: Die Münchener Kinder- und Jugendstunde. In: Der Deutsche Rundfunk 7 (1929) 30, 963.

Secondary Literature After 1945

Asper, Helmut G.: Max Ophüls. Eine Biographie mit zahlreichen Dokumenten, Texten und Bildern. Berlin 1998.
Bauer, Thomas: Deutsche Programmpresse 1923 bis 1941. Entstehung, Entwicklung und Kontinuität der Rundfunkzeitschriften. München 1993 (Rundfunkstudien; 6).
Besch, Heribert: Dichtung zwischen Vision und Wirklichkeit. Eine Analyse des Werkes von Hermann Kasack. St. Ingbert 1992. Zugl.: Saarbrücken, Univ., Diss., 1992.
Bierbach, Wolf: Von Wefag und Werag. Rückblick und Chronik I (1924–33). In: Walter Först (Hg.): Aus Köln in die Welt. Beiträge zur Rundfunk-Geschichte. Köln 1974 (Annalen des Westdeutschen Rundfunks; 2), 167–229.
Bolius, Gisela: Lisa Tetzner. Leben und Werk. Frankfurt a. M. 1997. Zugl.: Berlin, Univ., Diss., 1995.
Bredow, Hans: Im Banne der Ätherwellen. Funk im Ersten Weltkrieg. 2 Bde. Stuttgart 1956.
Breßler, Eva S.: Von der Experimentierbühne zum Propagandainstrument. Die Geschichte der Funkausstellung von 1924 bis 1939. Köln 2009. Zugl.: Mainz, Univ., Diss., 2007.
Diller, Ansgar: Der Frankfurter Rundfunk 1923–1945. Unter besonderer Berücksichtigung der Zeit des Nationalsozialismus. Frankfurt a. M., Univ., Diss., 1975.
Dinghaus, Angela: Frauenfunk und Jungmädchenstunde. Ein Beitrag zur Programmgeschichte des Weimarer Rundfunks. Hannover, Univ., Diss., 2002.
Döhl, Reinhard: Das Hörspiel zur NS-Zeit. Geschichte und Typologie des Hörspiels. Darmstadt 1992.
Dussel, Konrad: Deutsche Rundfunkgeschichte. Überarb. Aufl. Konstanz ³2010.
Elfert, Brunhild: Die Entstehung und Entwicklung des Kinder- und Jugendfunks in Deutschland von 1924 bis 1933 am Beispiel der Berliner Funk-Stunde AG. Frankfurt a. M. [u. a.] 1985 (Europäische Hochschulschriften; Reihe 40: Kommunikationswissenschaft und Publizistik; 3)
Ergert, Viktor: 50 Jahre Rundfunk in Österreich, Bd. I: 1924–1945. Wien 1974.
Först, Walter (Hg.): Aus Köln in die Welt. Beiträge zur Rundfunk-Geschichte. Köln 1974 (Annalen desWestdeutschen Rundfunks; 2).
Fromhold, Martina: Hermann Kasack und der Rundfunk der Weimarer Republik. Ein Beitrag zur Geschichte des Wechselverhältnisses zwischen Literatur und Rundfunk. Aachen 1990.
Grau, Oliver/Keil, Andreas: Mediale Emotionen. Zur Lenkung von Gefühlen durch Bild und Sound. Frankfurt a. M. 2005.
Großmann-Vendrey, Susanna/Schumacher, Renate/Halefeldt, Horst/Reese, Dietmar/Soppe, August: Auf der Suche nach sich selbst. Anfänge des Hörfunks in Deutschland – Oktober 1923 bis März 1925. In: Deutsches Rundfunkarchiv: Historisches Archiv der ARD (Hg.): Materialien zur Rundfunkgeschichte, Bd. 2. Frankfurt a. M. 1986, 11–26.
Grube, Sibylle: Rundfunkpolitik in Baden und Württemberg 1924–1933. Berlin 1976 (Beiträge, Dokumente, Protokolle zu Hörfunk und Fernsehen; 2). Zugl.: Hannover, Techn. Univ., Diss., 1973.
Halefeldt, Horst O.: Schul- und Bildungsfunk in Deutschland. Quellen 1923–1945. Frankfurt a. M. 1976 (Materialien zur Rundfunkgeschichte; 1)
Halefeldt, Horst O.: Sendegesellschaften und Rundfunkordnungen [Kapitel]. In: Joachim-Felix Leonhard (Hg.): Programmgeschichte des Hörfunks der Weimarer Republik, Bd. 1, München 1997, 23–352.
Heinze, Helmut: Faktographie romancée – ein erster Blick auf das literarische Werk Arno Schirokauers (1899–1954). In: Gerhard P. Knapp (Hg.): Autoren damals und heute. Literaturgeschichtliche Beispiele veränderter Wirkungshorizonte. Amsterdam [u. a.] 1991, 713–730.
Hopster, Norbert/Josting, Petra/Neuhaus, Joachim: Kinder- und Jugendliteratur 1933–1945. Stuttgart [u. a.], Bd. 1: Bibliographischer Teil mit Registern. 2001.

Kleinsteuber, Hans J. (Hg.): Radio – eine Einführung. Wiesbaden 2012.
Lenk, Carsten: Die Erscheinung des Rundfunks. Einführung und Nutzung eines neuen Mediums 1923–1932. Opladen 1997 (Konzeption empirische Literaturwissenschaft; 20).
Leonhard, Joachim-Felix (Hg.): Programmgeschichte des Hörfunks der Weimarer Republik. 2 Bde. München 1997.
Lerg, Winfried B./Schulte-Döinghaus, Ulrich: Der Rundfunk und die kommunistische Emigration. Zur Geschichte des „Deutschen Freiheitssenders" 1937–1939. In: Ders./Steiniger, Rolf (Hg.): Rundfunk und Politik 1923 bis 1973. Beiträge zur Rundfunkforschung. Berlin 1975, 179–214.
Lexikon westfälischer Autorinnen und Autoren 1750–1950, https://www.lexikon-westfaelischer-autorinnen-und-autoren.de/autoren/wehrhan-karl/#biographie (26.03.2020).
Lindemann, Elmar: Literatur und Rundfunk in Berlin 1923–1932. Studien und Quellen zum literarischen und literarisch-musikalischen Programm der „Funk-Stunde" AG Berlin in der Weimarer Republik, Bd. 1. Göttingen, Univ., Diss, 1980.
Messerli, Alfred: Vom Thüringer Wald zur Berliner Funk-Stunde. Die Märchenerzählerin Lisa Tetzner zwischen primärer und sekundärer Oralität. In: Schmitt, Christoph (Hg.): Erzählkulturen im Medienwandel. Münster [u. a.] 2008, 55–74.
Münkel, Daniela: Zielgruppenprogramme. Der nationalsozialistische Frauen- und Jugendfunk [Kapitel]. In: Saldern, Adelheid von/Marßolek, Inge (Hg.): Radio im Nationalsozialismus. Zwischen Lenkung und Ablenkung. Tübingen 1998, 105–125.
Nowak, Anja: Hör-Abenteuer. Walter Benjamins Rundfunkgeschichten für Kinder. In: Eming, Jutta/Schlechtweg Jahn, Ralf (Hg.): Aventiure und Eskapade. Narrative des Abenteuerlichen vom Mittelalter zur Moderne. Göttingen 2017, 201–216.
Ohse, R[obert]: Chronik vom wirtschaftlichen Aufbau des deutschen Rundfunks. Hg. von der Historischen Kommission der ARD. O. O. 1971.
Pigorsch, Enrico: Der Funkheinzelmann erzählt. Hans Bodenstedt und seine Märchen auf Homocord-Platten. In: Der Schalltrichter 17 (2001), 1–11.
Reiss, Erwin: „Wir senden Frohsinn". Fernsehen unterm Faschismus, das unbekannte Kapitel deutscher Mediengeschichte. Berlin 1979.
Rolfes, Gabriele: Die Deutsche Welle – ein politisches Neutrum im Weimarer Staat? Frankfurt a. M. [u. a.] 1992 (Europäische Hochschulschriften; Reihe 40: Kommunikationswissenschaft und Publizistik; 30). Zugl.: Marburg, Univ., Diss., 1990
Saldern, Adelheid von/Marßolek, Inge: Radio im Nationalsozialismus. Zwischen Lenkung und Ablenkung. Tübingen 1998 (Zuhören und Gehörtwerden; 1).
Schiller-Lerg, Sabine: Walter Benjamin und der Rundfunk. Programmarbeit zwischen Theorie und Praxis. München 1984 (Rundfunkstudien; 1). Zugl.: Karlsruhe, Univ., Diss., 1981.
Schütte, Wolfgang: Regionalität und Föderalismus im Rundfunk. Die geschichtliche Entwicklung in Deutschland 1923–1945. Frankfurt a. M. 1971 (Beiträge zur Geschichte des deutschen Rundfunks; 3).
Steinbach, Janina I.: „Auf ins Stimmland". Untersuchungen zur Rundfunkarbeit Walter Benjamins für Kinder und Jugendliche. Frankfurt a. M., Magisterarbeit 2010.
Strzolka, Rainer: Das Hörspiel der Weimarer Republik. Eine Geschichte aus den Quellen. 2 Bde. und 2 Halbbde, Bd. 3/2: Zusammenfassung, Materialien, vollst. veränd. und erw. Ausg. Hannover ²2010.
Stüven, Erwin: Volksempfänger. Rundfunk im Nationalsozialismus. Berlin, Freie Univ., Diplomarbeit, 1981.
Wagner, Hans-Ulrich: Günter Eich und der Rundfunk. Essay und Dokumentation. Potsdam 1999.
Wittenbrink, Theresa: Rundfunk und literarische Tradition [Kapitel]. In: Leonhard, Joachim Felix (Hg.): Programmgeschichte des Hörfunks der Weimarer Republik. München 1997, Bd. 2, 996–1097.
Wittenbrink, Theresa: Schriftsteller vor dem Mikrophon. Autorenauftritte im Rundfunk der Weimarer Republik 1924–1932. Berlin 2006 (Veröffentlichungen des Deutschen Rundfunkarchivs; 36).

Children's and Youth Films from 1900 to 1945

Marlene Antonia Illies

State of Research and Desiderata

At the beginning of the research project, there were plentiful sources regarding the development of German and international film as well as the history of cinema. The decisive milestones and turning points have already been recorded, elaborated and presented in various ways, as the following overview shows[1]: German cinema begins with the first performance of so-called *living pictures*, which Max and Emil Skladanowsky presented on November 1, 1895 in the Berlin *Wintergarten*. This is followed by the establishment of the cinematograph with the apparatus of the Lumière brothers, the development from travelling cinema to fixed cinema, the short side road of the no-longer-silent German film with Oskar Messter's *Tonbilder* (ca. 1907 to 1909, a purely German phenomenon), the change from the cinema of attractions to narrative cinema, from short to feature-length films, the expanding of the German cinema landscape during World War I, the founding of the Ufa (1917), the heyday of German cinema in the Weimar Republic, including the discussions about own film paths versus Americanisation, the technical adaptation to sound film (since 1927, in Germany 1928/1929), political instrumentalisation and the nationalisation of the film industry under the National Socialists, the slow emergence of television – in 1935, still in public places – and the incipient triumph of colour film

---

[1] The following remarks refer mainly to Elsaesser 2002, Garncarz 2008 and Jacobsen/Kaes/Prinzler 2004.

M. A. Illies (✉)
Faculty of Linguistics and Literary Studies, German Studies, Bielefeld University, Bielefeld, Germany
e-mail: marlene.illies@uni-bielefeld.de

© Springer-Verlag GmbH Germany, part of Springer Nature 2024
P. Josting et al. (eds.), *German-Language Children's and Youth Literature In The Media Network 1900–1945*, https://doi.org/10.1007/978-3-476-05892-8_3

from 1937.[2] Due to the already existing detailed accounts of these topics, political and economic framework conditions as well as technical developments are only included in this contribution where they are relevant for the film reception of children and adolescents.[3]

Children's and youth film from 1900 to 1945 has also been examined from various perspectives, with a focus on specific periods or political systems, genres, themes, pioneers of children's film (such as Lotte Reiniger and the Diehl brothers), as well as the debate that was constantly present at all times as to what children and young people were and are allowed to see in the cinema. What was missing was an overview of the entire period under investigation and a corpus that – regardless of the short or feature-length film, genre and technique, specific production for children and young people or actual use by the same – comprehensively covers these films. The disagreement among researchers as to what should be considered a children's or youth film manifests itself in the discussion of early fairy tale film. In silent film research, it is sometimes stated that this film was aimed at an adult audience (cf. Räder 2009), sometimes at a child audience (cf. Höfig 2008), or it is argued that it was not exclusively a children's film, but a family film (cf. Schmerling 2007). The truth, should it exist, probably lies somewhere in between. In order to face these questions with an open mind, a keyword system was used in the collection of data, thus unearthing a rich treasure trove of specific, intentional, and de facto children's and youth films.[4] Where tracing was possible, where paratexts on production or usage exist, *KJ-spezifische* documentaries and films that children produced themselves and which were subsequently published have also been recorded.

Goergen proposes to distinguish between two types of cinema, the visible and the invisible (or less visible), which he describes as follows:

> Here the few premiere cinemas in the center of Berlin, there the mass of small and micro cinemas. The larger cinemas in the districts are still financially strong enough to advertise in some newspapers, especially the district newspapers; the mass of the smallest cinemas, however, are dependent on advertising on their outside facades (supplemented by criers and paper distributors). While the programmes of the premiere cinemas can be recorded to a large extent, at least as far as the main film is concerned, the offer of the *Ladenkinos* around the corner can probably no longer be reconstructed. The reactions of the major daily newspapers to the film premieres were used by the film industry as highly welcome advertising material, both to promote the individual film and to highlight the social prestige of the medium. Thus, different cinema publics overlap on the same topic. A reconstruction of the public perception of cinema and film cannot avoid this complexity of multiple cinemas; it always has to argue in the plural. (Goergen 2008, 77)

The invisible cinema is invisible because it serves only a small public area, limited to a village or a district, for example. Even when these cinemas advertised their

---

[2] There were many earlier attempts and variations of colour film, starting with hand-coloured films in the late nineteenth century.

[3] The various regulations of censorship during the period under investigation are dealt with in the sections relating to the respective period. In this context, a youth release generally applied to children from 6 and adolescents up to (and including) 18 years of age.

[4] Cf. the introduction in this volume.

programmes and the press reported on their screenings, it was only in local publications. It was precisely this invisible cinema that was considered dangerous by the those who sought to reform cinema, i.e. the Kinoreformer (cf. ibid., 67): it took place in a relatively uncontrolled manner and is therefore of particular interest to this area of research, because it was primarily here that children and young people were able to see films that were not actually released for them. Visible cinema, on the other hand, was intensively perceived by the public; it was predominantly located in the centres of large cities, with premiere theatres, well-known programmes and prominent guests. Its programmes were reviewed, it placed large advertisements in newspapers and thus became an important producer of contemporary sources (cf. ibid.).

Children's and Youth Film in the Empire

Film was initially a mobile medium, and from 1896 projectionists from the Lumière brothers toured Germany. Impressed by their success, "a whole number of showmen shifted to the business of tent and travelling cinemas" (Elsaesser 2002, 18), so that film initially established itself as a fairground attraction. From 1905 onwards, permanent cinemas became established with great success: "They spread from the centres of the large cities to the periphery and from the large cities via the medium-sized towns to the small towns. Their number increased steadily; by 1911 there were already more than 2000 cinemas in Germany." (Garncarz 2008, 40) Once settled, cinema programmes had to be restructured, because unlike mobile cinemas, which were not allowed to take up too much of visitors' time in an environment that offered many entertaining attractions, permanent cinemas had to handle an evening of entertainment on their own. Instead of 15 to 20 min, the programme compilations now lasted 60 min or longer; a period that was easier to cover with longer films. Thus the development from short to long films took its course: from the original 2 to 3 min to 10 min (from about 1908), 30 min (from 1911) and more (cf. ibid., 38). The increasing length made other narrative styles possible, drama entered film (cf. ibid., 39).

Children and young people were part of the audience from the very beginning. They flocked to the travelling cinemas as well as to the permanent cinemas and saw everything that came before their eyes, regardless of film genres; there was not yet a specific children's/youth film production. A cinema screening around 1907 was still very different from what is perceived as typical cinema today. Programmes were based on vaudevillian culture and its "inherent sequence of attractions, which could range from gags and comic skits to sentimental duets, acrobatic interludes, and magic tricks to dances, revue numbers, and solo performances of well-known plays, operettas, and operas" (Elsaesser 2002, 22). With the short duration of screenings, complex stories could not yet be told, which is precisely why children's and young people's *literarische Stoffe* found their way onto the screen early on: fairy tales and well-known characters such as Sherlock Holmes or Max and Moritz could be portrayed on film, they had recognition value. The longer programmes offered a new spectrum of popular film themes: Opinions and current affairs – later: newsreels -, detective films and social dramas, family melodramas and historical epics, romantic comedies, etc. (cf. ibid., 19). It can be assumed that films of all kinds were also shown in front of children, because censorship, and thus also youth releases and youth bans of films, had to first be established with this new medium.

All previous cultural institutions "of an entertainment public operating with performances" (Müller 2008, 109) did not know any age-related exclusions of parts of the audience, so film censorship had no model. The legal basis in the German Kaiserreich was the Preußische Landrecht, and the respective local police was responsible for "maintaining public peace, security and order" (Loiperdinger 2004, 256). Initially, this worked through the procedure of post-censorship: constables visited the screenings of travelling exhibitors, and later also those of permanent cinemas, and checked the films shown to ensure that they were unobjectionable. Objectionable films and film scenes had to be removed from the programme, which was not yet a problem with the numbered programmes; individual films could be replaced at will (cf. ibid.). However, this post-censorship was chaotic and inconsistent, the police themselves were overburdened, decisions were regularly criticised in the trade press as well as in the daily press, and as early as 1907 the Kinoreformer were formed, who took up arms against *Schmutz- und Schundfilme*.[5] The greatest fear regarding the new, rapidly spreading medium was that the audience could be seduced into criminal or morally questionable actions by corresponding depictions on the screen. Already since 1905, that is, since the arrival of permanent cinemas in the cities, efforts can be observed to "restrict the attendance of children at the cinema, to direct it as pedagogically as possible, and in any case to supervise it strictly" (Maase 2008, 137). Especially in the afternoons, cinema theatres were practically in the hands of the children, and the massive and still uncontrolled film consumption led to conflicts between cinema and social interests. Although no empire-wide regulation emerged until the end of the First World War,[6] it was simply not possible due to the legal basis (cf. Müller 2008, 109), the various official ordinances that emerged around 1910 onwards essentially followed two models:

> One solution was that children were generally forbidden to go to the cinema; people up to the age of 14, 15, 16 (the most common case) or even 18 counted as children. The only possibility for them to see films were officially approved children's screenings. In some cases, the programmes were put together by communal committees in which teachers and priests set the tone. The more widespread solution was for cinema operators to submit programmes for children's screenings, which had to be approved by the local authorities, usually the

---

[5] Roughly translated: dirty and trashy films.

[6] A first effort in this direction was the preventive censorship introduced in Berlin on May 5, 1906: before the first screening of a film, permission had to be obtained from the police headquarters, where each flick was screened in advance. A centralisation of these still small-scale decisions took place through the decree of the Preußischen Minister des Innern of 16 December 1910, which ordered that films released for Berlin could be shown in all Prussian provinces as long as the local police had the Berlin permit card 24 hours before the screening. A decree of 7 December 1912 also ordered that own censorship decisions had to be reported to Berlin (cf. Loiperdinger 2004, 526 f.).

police. [...] The other approval model allowed children to attend cinemas accompanied by adults (only if the films were approved for their age, of course); both restrictions were frequently undermined or reduced to absurdity. (Maase 2008, 137 f.)

Since censorship of this kind was an absolute novelty, this circumstance cannot come as a surprise, especially since the restrictions on cinema attendance were still legally weakly established. For the most part, they could only be enacted for preschoolers and schoolchildren, which sometimes led to the paradoxical situation "that older high school students were not allowed to go to the cinema, while visitors of the same age or even younger who had already graduated from elementary school had free cinema access" (Müller 2008, 110). Moreover, the local police authorities, as the executive arm of the law, were unable to keep up with the situation; subsequently, the reception of films by minors remained a central topic of discourse in the cinema debate, and discussions took place everywhere. In daily newspapers and magazines, in brochures and books, authors and writers of letters to the editor spoke out, pastors in church, teachers in class, parliamentarians at all levels, people in the pub, on the street, in the hallway (cf. Maase 2008, 138).[7] The loud voices of the concerned, above all those of the so-called "trash fighters", are not surprising, because they always appear "when a new medium enters everyday life. The phenomenon can be traced from cinema to television and video technology to the Internet" (Kaiser/Maurer/Richter 2001, 6). The contemporary debates did not, of course, bypass those affected, the children and young people, and increased the appeal of cinema. For them it was a contested terrain, a semi-forbidden pleasure, a place of emancipation and rebellion. There are the most positive and the worst accounts of how they behaved there, the latter predominating. Each perception described, however, is always influenced by the profession and the goals of the authors. To sum up: "We have to imagine children's cinema in the early 20th century for the most part as a world of its own, set apart from adult control." (Maase 2008, 141)

In view of this chaotic starting position, it can be assumed that the entire spectrum of films produced at this time was also received by children and young people. However, since it is not very useful to record all the films that can be found, we looked for indications of intended and de facto films for children and young people that could also be found in contemporary film magazines. Helpful here were, on the one hand, the decisions of the Hamburger Lehrerkommission, which recommended films for children's screenings. In 1908 – the actual movement began in 1906 – Hamburg provided the earliest model for regulating young people's cinema consumption, an extremely liberal and – a rarity – positively sanctioned one. Here, from 1911 onwards, all films to be shown in Hamburg had to be presented to a commission of teachers, who selected suitable films for children's screenings and

---

[7] It was not until the First World War that the discussions were moderated, censorship moved to the jurisdiction of the army, but often continued to be exercised by police authorities (cf. Loiperdinger 2004, 527). From those years, advertisements transmit, from today's perspective, questionable releases and recommendations of veritable acts of war for children and youth, which was to be repeated in the Second World War.

recommended them (cf. Müller 2008, 111).[8] These lists were regularly printed in the *Kinematograph* and were thus available at least throughout Germany.[9] The procedure was praised as exemplary, but was considered untransferable to other regions; in Hamburg it was only possible because of "the legislative autonomy of the Hanseatic city and the initiative of its enterprising teachers' association" (ibid., 112 and 123). Children were allowed to attend the special Hamburg children's screenings without the accompaniment of adults; regular screenings were only permitted for children and schoolchildren in Hamburg if they were accompanied by adults. Despite the exemplary nature, Hamburg did not adhere to these regulations in all respects; unauthorised and even prohibited films were also shown in children's screenings, and children and young people also attended other screenings (cf. Maase 2008, 131 f.). Nevertheless, the importance of children's screenings for cinema owners should not be underestimated. Töteberg for example reports on the outraged letter from Eberhard Knopf, owner of *Knopfs Lichtspielhaus*,[10] regarding the withdrawal of his concession for children's screenings. In his letter of July 25, 1910 to the Oberschulbehörde, which worked closely with the police, he states that he cannot accept the decision because it would damage his cinema "financially and morally" (Töteberg 2008, 94). When the concession of several theatres was revoked in November 1911, the concerned owners also turned to the authorities, explaining that

> the loss suffered by the "loss of the children's entree" was twice as high "because children naturally made the best advertisement to their parents and other relatives": "On the basis of their revenue lists, they [the reprimanded theatre owners] can prove that not only the children's attendance, but also the attendance of adults has decreased significantly." (Ibid., 98)

The young audience was therefore relevant. They belonged to the regular audience of the district cinemas in particular – i.e. the *invisible* cinemas according to Goergen – and were indispensable for their operators, which in turn required them to cooperate with the authorities (cf. ibid., 97). Children's screenings were also evaluated in terms of marketing strategy, and some institutions even offered themselves as reliable care institutions:

> Obscene and episodes of realistic content are not presented. For this reason alone, parents may entrust me with their children. The little guests are in the best of care with me, as they are led to their seats by ladies specially employed for this purpose, whose further duty it is to see to it that the children behave in a well-behaved and civilized manner. (Quoted from ibid., 98)

---

[8] Cf. in detail also Maase 2008.

[9] From these lists, only those films were included in the database (http://medienverbundportal.kjl.uni-bielefeld.de) that refer to a piece of literature – mostly fairy tales – as these are to be placed in a larger media context. The Hamburger Lehrerkommission also recommended many documentaries of educational content. The tracks of these films are difficult or impossible to trace and had no relevance under the focus of the project.

[10] A Hamburg cinema that was located on the Spielbudenplatz entertainment mile, which was densely populated by cinema theatres (cf. Töteberg 2008, 94).

Even independently of such special screening formats, the youth rating of a film was recognised as having advertising value and was highlighted in corresponding advertisements by distribution and production companies, which formed a further source of distribution-intended and even specific children's and youth films that were advertised particularly around Christmastime.

In addition to the film adaptation of fairy tales and legends,[11] which were present from the beginning and experienced an aesthetic peak during the First World War with the feature-length films Paul Wegener's *Rübezahls Hochzeit* (1916), *Hans Trutz im Schlaraffenland* (1917) and *Der Rattenfänger* (1918), the detective and adventure (series) films of those years form a second important genre.[12] Indicative of these factual and negatively sanctioned children's and youth films is the contemporary *Schmutz- und Schunddebatte*, in the course of which complaints and outrage were regularly voiced about the consumption of such films by children and young people (cf. e.g. Hellwig 1975 [1911], Die Kinematographen und die Jugend 1907, Lemke 1907, Häfker 1908); the same applies to the reading of corresponding dime novels (cf. e.g. Bekämpfung der Schundliteratur 1911, Maase 2001, Maase 2008, Maurer 2001, Schiel 1917).[13] The consumption of both media was seen as a danger of immoralizing and criminalizing semi-adolescents; actual negative effects could never be proven. The jurist and trash fighter Albert Hellwig himself had to admit, after asking colleagues – district court judges and especially juvenile court judges – for information, that "only in the rarest cases it is possible to prove beyond doubt a causal connection between a certain crime and the showing of a trash film" (quoted from Maurer 2001, 22). Nevertheless, he and many others continued their fight against *trash*. The most popular opponents in both film and reading were detectives Nick Carter and Sherlock Holmes, as well as Joe Deebs, Nat Pinkerton, Stuart Webbs and Harry Higgs, all of whom were published in serial formats. Some of them survived the First World War and were discovered by a new generation of children and young people in the Weimar Republic.

---

[11] Due to the aforementioned discussions in silent film research, they were deliberately not generally tagged with *KJ-spezifisch* or *KJ-intendiert*, but only in the case of corresponding indications. Many fairy tale and saga adaptations of this time were therefore also given the label *KJ-Nutzung unsicher.*

[12] Cf. the contribution by Tobias Kurwinkel in this volume.

[13] Paratexts that address concerns about possible criminalisation, early sexualisation, or otherwise possible depravity of children/youth through cinema have been tagged in the database (http://medienverbundportal.kjl.uni-bielefeld.de) with the keyword *Entsittlichungsgefahr.* Other established keywords/expressions, which at the same time allow an impression of the discussions of the time, are: *Jugendverbot, Kinderverbot, Kinder im Kino, Kino-Theater-Konkurrenz, Kinoreformbewegung, Kinosteuer, Märchenfilme, Schmutz und Schund, Zensur.*

Children's and Youth Film in the Weimar Republic

Looking at censorship instances, the film industry of the Weimar Republic began with a ticket to a free ride: After the abolition of all censorship on November 12, 1918,[14] it was only the passing of the Reichslichtspielgesetz on May 12, 1920, that brought nationwide access control for children and young people to film screenings. Before being shown to the public, films now had to be approved everywhere by a central screening office.[15] The legal restrictions for a youth release said:

> Filmstrips which are to be shown to juveniles under the age of eighteen [require] special approval. Apart from those prohibited under § 1 para. 2, all filmstrips that are likely to have a harmful effect on the moral, mental or health development or to overstimulate the imagination of minors are to be excluded from being shown to minors. (Quoted in Räder 2009, 24)

The cinema owners had to present the issued censorship cards to the local police authority before the respective screenings, but municipalities were also allowed to set their own regulations for the protection of children and young people.[16] Children under the age of 6 were in general forbidden to visit a movie theatre, and films without a youth clearance could only be viewed from the age of 18 – a censorship regulation which thus provided for the same films for 6 to 17 year-olds and which today seems like a farce.[17] Children and young people of compulsory school age could either see afternoon screenings of films released for them in the company of an adult, go to closed educational and feature-length film screenings organised by schools and associations, or go to children's and youth screenings.

Despite these now binding measures, the (children's) cinema debate continued. Politicians, educators and parents called for caution due to the possible negative side effects of the medium, which was still perceived as new (cf. ibid., 21). As the pivotal point of the discourse, the danger of debauchery was replaced by "concerns about a harmful effect of film images on the mental development of adolescents" (ibid.). There was further criticism that there were no films suitable for children, and as long as the silent film was in charge, people were bothered by the intertitles, since young people allegedly could not grasp the inserted written panels quickly enough (cf. ibid., 22 f.).

Since children and young people paid half-price admission to the cinema, specific screenings for this target group were only worthwhile if the halls were sold out,

---

[14] Regionally and locally, however, film censorship by decree or police intervention remained possible (cf. Loiperdinger 2004, 527).

[15] These were established in the production centres of the German film industry, Berlin and Munich (cf. Räder 2009, 23; on the staffing of the film review boards, cf. Loiperdinger 2004, 528).

[16] In Munich, this led to an increase in the minimum age for cinema attendance from 6 to 14 years (cf. Räder 2009, 24).

[17] The film industry also reacted in a huff; in June 1920 there was a large protest meeting of filmmakers, the well-known actress and singer Lotte Neumann arguing, "I was 15 years old when I acted in my first film, and I suffered no moral damage. Why should the film now endanger the morals of 16- and 17-year-olds?" (Quoted in Bleckman 1993, 91)

which is why "primarily adventure stories of popular heroes [were] shown. Detective and Wild West films from America were extremely popular, especially with boys" (ibid., 23) – the youthful trend genres from the Kaiserreich thus continued. They had a steady audience base among adolescents, with some cinemas opening as early as 10 am and showing only the popular film series. The low ticket prices enabled young viewers to visit the cinema several times a week (cf. ibid., 25).

It was the time of American heroes like Buffalo Bill and Tom Mix, German produced *Stuart Webbs* series was successful, and yet another German representative continued his brilliant film career that had already begun in the Kaiserreich: Harry Piel. He serves as a good example to mirror the actual enforcement of the harsh censorship guidelines. Harry Piel was a busy actor in the film business since 1912, as a director, actor and producer in one person. Between 1918 and 1933 he was represented with at least three movies a year, even four or five were not uncommon, the peak was the year 1919 with seven *Harry Piel* movies. The Speka publishing house knew how to take advantage of this media attention, publishing dime novels from 1920 onwards with the series title *Harry Piel – der tollkühne Detektiv* (cf. Bleckman 1993, 91 f.).[18] The plot of the trivial stories was initially based on old Piel films, whose titles the individual booklets also bore. Since no more scripts existed, the Speka authors[19] had to watch film after film and note down scene after scene in order to then reproduce them in the appropriate colportage style (cf. ibid., 92 f.). The booklets sold so briskly that the titles of the old Piel films were soon exhausted and freely invented stories were published.[20] They were considered *trash literature* and were loved by children, as documented by the personal campaign against Harry Piel by the journalist Egon Jacobsohn (from 1920 on editor of the pamphlet *Die Filmhölle*). Jacobsohn reported in the *Film-Kurier* on May 9, 1921:

> My attacks against Harry Piel began in February 1921, when I first saw a number of socalled 'Groschenschmöker' in the hands of a twelve-year-old. [...] At first I thought it was a joke, because I had no idea that a serious actor [...] could lend his name to such trash literature. I learned that this book series was unleashed on the youth (freed from Sherlock Holmes trash literature after a long struggle) with the explicit permission of Mr. Harry Piel. At that time I bought all the volumes and read them: [...] Each of these trashy books, written in wretched German, contained a never-ending hymn of praise to the personal courage of the movie detective Harry Piel. (Jacobsohn 1921)

By this time, Jacobsohn's outrage had already developed into a public debate, with Piel and his defenders on one side, Jacobsohn and a number of morality societies

---

[18] The Leipzig company was already successful with series of adventures of more or less classical heroes, such as Sherlock Holmes, Buffalo Bill, Klaus Störtebeker or John Kling (cf. Bleckman 1993, 91 f.).

[19] Apparently, these are exclusively men. Bleckman lists Alfred Bienengräber, Karl Lütge, Lothar Knud Frederik and Victor Abel, the latter two also wrote scripts for Piel from 1921/22 (Bleckman 1993, 92 f.).

[20] Harry Piel was able to publish a second series with Speka-Verlag, *Harry Piel – der Abenteuer-König und Verächter des Todes*, which appeared in 18 volumes from 1920–1921 and was continued from 1922–1926 under the series title *Harry Piel Abenteuer*. This is devoted, according to Bleckman, to the retelling of his new films (cf. Bleckman 1993, 93).

and their representatives on the other; however, it was not to damage Piel's reputation. Thematically, Piel reinvented himself at the beginning of the 1920s, switching from the detective to the adventure genre. All five films released by and with him in 1921 were banned for young people; this censorship decision for his productions lasted until 1929, when *Sein bester Freund* became the first Piel film to receive a youth release. However, in view of the intensive consumption of the Groschenschmöker series by children and the presence of the multi-talent as a media figure, his fans did not let any guardian of virtue or measure stop them, on the contrary:

> Despite all the marketing of the "legend" Harry Piel, who has almost become a cult figure, the films themselves are still the main attraction, and they find new fans year after year; for when a boy reaches a "certain" age (7 or 8), it becomes a must for him to see Harry Piel films – if only to be able to talk to his friends and classmates. The opportunity for this is offered by the reenactment theatres and suburban cinemas, whose owners care little about the official ban on Piel films for young people. Why should they, since they have little to fear from controls and the old Harry Peel [sic!] and Unus films[21] are still doing well at low rental fees in the afternoon showings. Thus, old Piel films continue to be exploited for years until the copy wears out, and the projectionists soon have the "delivery joke" going around: "Here's the copy, Maxe, you'll get the perforation delivered later." (Bleckman 1993, 169 f.)

That Piel had already been a hero to children and young people before then is proven by Georg Herzberg's review of the Piel film *Panik* (1928), in which he writes in transfigured memory of "our Harry Piel, whom we worshipped at the school desk like a demigod" (Herzberg 1928). After the turn to talkies, Piel profited from his old silent productions, which circulated in many smaller cinemas and especially in youth screenings (cf. Bleckman 1993, 224), and even after 1933 he remained successful,[22] attendance at his films was no longer negatively sanctioned. In a speech celebrating his 100th film, *Artisten* (1935, *jugendfrei ab 14 Jahre*), there is even talk of the "educational value" (ibid., 270 f.) of his productions. Piel's films influenced several generations at once; the film *Der Dschungel ruft* (1936, *jugendfrei*) was celebrated by many boys and girls whose parents had already raved about Harry Piel as children (cf. ibid., 279).[23] After 1945, Piel succeeded in bringing his old productions back to the cinema, in small theatres and again largely in youth screenings (cf. ibid., 354 f.). In a 1956 radio interview, he even declares his films to be intended for young people; the interviewer then formulates the wish that "Piel's work may provide the impetus for producers to create a new German youth film" (quoted in ibid., 361). Piel's films thus form an impressive example of initially de facto children's and youth films that develop into those intended at the distribution level and are perceived in retrospect as specifically produced.

---

[21] Both Harry Piel's film series.

[22] Piel quickly subordinated himself to the new system, though his Groschenschmöker were on the index.

[23] Piel was also internationally successful. In Russia, there was even a show trial in 1928 because of his films, which were to be banned "because they corrupted the youth, aroused antisocial feelings," and were based on an "anarchist worldview" – the defenders included "representatives of the youth" who pleaded for their idol (Bleckman 1993, 206).

After this digression, back to the program of children's and youth screenings of the Weimar Republic. American comedies were popular, short slapstick films by Buster Keaton, Harold Lloyd and Laurel and Hardy, as well as Charlie Chaplin, who was revered in every age group. With the latter's celebrated film *The Kid* (1921, not released in Germany until 1923), child star Jackie Coogan also became popular in Germany. Films featuring him – including some adaptations of literature such as *Oliver Twist* (1922), *Little Robinson Crusoe* (1924), *Tom Sawyer* (1930) – were not only usually given a youth release, they were also warmly recommended for children by reviewers. A now-forgotten child star of this period was *Baby Peggy* (actually Peggy-Jean Montgomery, born 1918), who was also an internationally popular figure in the film business between 1921 and 1926. She appeared in numerous (short) films, including fairy tale adaptations that were also successful in Germany and were released to young people.[24]

The fairy tale film also remained popular, although those film adaptations temporarily broke away from the children's label. Especially in the early years of the Weimar Republic, the real film adaptations show many early expressionist elements (cf. Räder 2009, 26), and with Ludwig Berger's *Der verlorene Schuh* (1923), a fairy tale film was deliberately staged that was also intended to appeal to an adult audience. This cross-age perception of the target audience dissolved at the latest when "many time aesthetic traditions were broken by the introduction of the sound film" (ibid., 26), after which the fairy tale film was only pursued as a specific children's film production. In terms of aesthetics and variety, there was a great development at this time. The silhouette artist Lotte Reiniger, who gave the fairy tales of the Orient, the Brothers Grimm or Wilhelm Hauff a completely new form with her silhouette films, contributed significantly to this development.[25] Probably under this influence, the first work of the brothers Paul, Hermann and Ferdinand Diehl – the later pioneers of the animated puppet film – was also a silhouette film: *Kalif Storch* (1930/1931).[26]

Historical and socially critical films did not establish themselves as specific, however as intended children's and youth films; they were regularly declared as suitable for minors by the censors. This was true of the popular films in the *Fridericus Rex* series (first starring Otto Gebühr as Friedrich der Große in 1920–1923, with many more films following at irregular intervals) as well as the two-part saga adaptation *Die Nibelungen* (1922–1924). Georg Wilhelm Pabst's *Kameradschaft* (1931), in which war and hatred of nations are overcome by solidarity between miners in Germany and France after the First World War, was also used for screenings to schoolchildren (cf. ibid., 31). Also mentioned in the list of children's and youth films of this period is *Die Unehelichen* (1926), which in its indictment of society was directed more towards an adult audience, but whose sensitive depiction of the

---

[24] Of the 24 German film titles found, only about half could be assigned to the corresponding original titles.

[25] Cf. the contribution by Annika Behler in this volume.

[26] Cf. the contribution by Ingrid Tomkowiak in this volume.

milieu and three child protagonists (between the ages of 6 and 13) "by no means exclude[d] young viewers" (ibid.).[27] Apart from the rating *"volksbildend"*,[28] no censorship decision has yet been found for this film.

The youth film is a phenomenon that is particularly difficult to grasp. As late as the Weimar Republic, Stiglegger notes that productions served only two markets: the family with children and the adult audience, which was almost certainly related to the censorship conditions that positioned children and youth together. "Youth was present as a paying mass, but decades later was hardly ever explicitly taken seriously or perceived as an audience." (Stiglegger 2003, 312) Nevertheless, there were definitely youth films in the Weimar Republic, or films that had adolescent protagonists and dealt with the problems and issues of youth. The youth films mostly deal with groups of pupils and emphasize the right of the young to rebel against the old generation (cf. Kracauer 1984, 169). The themes and theatres of struggle are quite diverse: The pupils in *Der Kampf der Tertia* (1928, based on the novel of the same name by Wilhelm Speyer, *jugendfrei*) fight for the lives of endangered animals; in *Die Räuberbande* (1928, based on the novel of the same name by Leonhard Frank, *jugendfrei*) a gang of 14-year-old pupils and apprentices rebels against sadistic teachers, exploitative instructors, parents – ultimately against the world of adults per se. The conflict between the generations is often combined with a critique of the parental and school education system, as in *Primanerliebe* (1927), *Der Kampf des Donald Westhof* (1927) or *Frühlings Erwachen* (based on Frank Wedekind's play of the same name, adapted twice in the Weimar Republic: 1923 and 1929). Melodramatic films about the love troubles of adolescents – sometimes qualitatively successful, sometimes bordering on colportage – such as *Der Geiger von Florenz* (1926), *Die Siebzehnjährigen* (1929, based on Max Dreyer's play of the same name) and *Ariane* (1931, based on Claude Anet's novel of the same name) stand alongside serious socially critical films such as *Tagebuch einer Verlorenen* (1929, based on Margarethe Böhme's novel of the same name), *Mädchen in Uniform* (1931, based on the play *Gestern und Heute/Ritter Nérestan* by Christa Winsloe),[29] *Revolte im Erziehungshaus* (1930, based on Peter Martin Lampel's play of the same name) or the American film adaptation of Erich Maria Remarque's *Im Westen nichts Neues* (1929) with the original (film) title *All Quiet on the Western Front* (1930).[30]

These films, which were often not approved for young people or even, like the last two examples, were burdened by high censorship requirements and constantly

---

[27] *"Die Unehelichen* [functions] as a veritable social drama: there the incisive father-son conflict prevails, which in the proletarian milieu expands into an often brutal generational struggle." (Stiglegger 2003, 313)

[28] Roughly translated: educational to the public.

[29] Cf. the contribution by Gabriele von Glasenapp in this volume.

[30] In her study on youth film under National Socialism, Sander comments on film attendance by young people before 1933 as follows: "The left-wing political and likewise the national youth groups, on the other hand, limited themselves essentially to attending films of the tendencies that suited them ('Im Westen nichts Neues' for one, 'Fridericus Rex' or 'Die Nibelungen' for another)" (Sander 1944/1984, 23). Cf. also the contribution by Ricarda Freudenberg in this volume.

fluctuated between approval and prohibition, and deal with themes that conservative thinkers would have liked to keep away from young people, but which were self-evident components of youthful life: Love and sexuality, rebellion and revolt against injustice and educational institutions, and, of course, the First World War and its aftermath.[31]

Even in this brief list of some youth films of the time, it is noticeable that many of them adapt novels and plays. For children's films, such tendencies can also be observed beyond fairy tale adaptations, such as *Die Biene Maja und ihre Abenteuer* (1926, based on the children's book of the same name by Waldemar Bonsels), Lotte Reiniger's *Doktor Dolittle* films (1928, based on Hugh Lofting's children's book *The Story of Doctor Dolittle,* which was first translated into German by Edith Jacobsohn in 1926) and, of course, the film adaptation of Erich Kästner's *Emil und die Detektive* (1931).

The film review of the *Baby Peggy* film *My Darling,* which appeared in the *Film-Kurier* on November 22, 1924 (Jackie Coogan's *Oliver Twist* is reviewed on the same page), still states:

> The general director of "Universalfilm" recently declared in an American trade journal that we Germans lack the universal recipe for the right audience success, while America possesses this universal recipe. So let me define it briefly: dramaturgically, this film is made according to the American universal recipe "children's film". (H. 1924)

While children's and youth screenings benefited enormously from American productions at the beginning of the Weimar Republic, which continued to be received gladly and intensively as long as it was permitted, a specific German children's and youth film production slowly developed in those years. The reception channels of minors were definitely noticed and listened to.

Children's and Youth Film During the National Socialist Era

The National Socialist regime knew how to use film for its own purposes. Hobsch even states that during the Nazi era "no other medium [...] practiced such efficient indoctrination and thus reached and for a long time also shaped so many people as film" (Hobsch 2009, 39). Immediately after Hitler's appointment as Reichskanzler on January 30, 1933, influences on the film industry were felt. The later so-called *Filmminister* Joseph Goebbels endeavoured to quickly *Aryanise* the entire business, the German film industry was *protected* from the import of foreign films, numerous films that were disliked for various reasons – from pacifist or communist works to the involvement of a single Jewish person – were banned in purges (cf. Loiperdinger 2004, 534 ff.).

---

[31] In this regard, Loiperdinger's observation must be emphasized that "the censors of the film review boards [of the Weimar Republic] were blind on the right eye, but all the more sharp-sighted on the left" (Loiperdinger 2004, 530). Glorification of the Prussian king Friedrich II in the numerous *Fridericus Rex* films did not pose a problem, whereas pacifist and socialist films did (cf. ibid.).

Little changed at the Film-Oberprüfstellen; the top film censors had "proven themselves in the past, even by National Socialist standards, and [remained] in office" (ibid., 536). The Reichslichtspielgesetz of 16 February 1934 also did not initially bring about any major changes: Films that were to be shown in front of young people had to be subjected to special scrutiny, promotion by ratings, which had begun in the Weimar Republic, was cemented within the law, and the most important innovation was "the introduction of preliminary censorship by the office of the Reichsfilmdramaturgen, to whom the scripts of all feature-length films must be submitted for review (§ 1, 2, 3 LSpG)" (ibid., 537). As film production was more and more in the hands of the state, the film review offices gradually became irrelevant, "from the beginning of 1942 [the] Reichsfilmintendant [was] responsible for the entire production policy and for the acceptance of the finished films" (ibid., 357).

According to Hobsch, between 20 and 30% of German production was found to be youth-friendly, but this statement again refers only to feature-length films. Even at that time, it was debated whether *jugendfrei* also meant *suitable for young people* – the special rating *jugendwert,* which was used from November 1938, was intended to fill this gap (cf. Hobsch 2009, 40). Since films that did not receive this rating were also used in *Jugendfilmstunden*, the regime took its own standards ad absurdum. Reese notes that only about 12 to 15 feature-length films were produced for youth during these years (cf. Reese 1984, I), an extremely small number of specific children's and youth (feature-length) films, then, considering the immense importance of youth in Nazi ideology. The number of films received by children and young people, and also the number of films they were exposed to, is far greater. On the one hand, there are numerous short films to be taken into account that are not counted in the usual long-film calculations, as well as the films listed in the Jugendfilmstunden, which – it should be emphasized once again at this point – are listed in the project database as *KJ-intendierte Filme.*

First, we will take a look at the "educational films" (Hobsch 2009, 43) of those years, which were aimed directly at children and young people and were intended to convey National Socialist ideology to them on film. The most prominent flick of this kind is certainly the adaptation of Karl Aloys Schenzinger's novel *Hitlerjunge Quex* (1933), but it is far from the only one to focus on the National Socialists' youth organisation, the Hitlerjugend (HJ). The film *Die Bande vom Hoheneck* (1934) was still shot with Boy Scouts, and the ending was changed under pressure to conform so that the actors now appear in HJ uniforms (cf. ibid., 41). In *Kopf hoch, Johannes!* (1941), *Jakko* (1941)[32] and *Jungens* (1941) the HJ takes a central role. The youthful protagonists of *Jungens* were even played exclusively by pupils of the Adolf Hitler School in Sonthofen; they were also present at the premiere and at first performances in different cities to talk about their life at the school (cf. ibid., 41). Of these three films, only *Jakko* received ratings – including *jugendwert.* In order to mobilize female youth, *Ich für Dich – Du für mich,* a film about female labor service, appeared as early as 1934, pure propaganda. The film *Zwei Welten* (1940) is

---

[32] Cf. the contribution by Winfred Kaminski in this volume.

about the so-called Erntehilfe,[33] the film *Hände hoch!* (1942) is dedicated to the Kinderlandverschickung, *Junge Adler* (1944) is a homage to Göring's Fliegerjugend[34] and promoted the armaments industry, *Himmelhunde* (1942) was already dedicated to flying. *Bravo, kleiner Thomas* (1945) wraps moral indoctrination about community values, comradeship, sports training, sacrifice and heroism in a football story – this film also received FSK clearance *Jugendgeeignet/Jugendfördernd* on September 3, 1954.[35]

School films are another popular genre of the time. Among them are *Reifende Jugend* (1933), based on Max Dreyer's play *Die Reifeprüfung* (1929), which is supposed to be about youth, but focuses primarily on authority and leadership (cf. ibid., 45). Nevertheless, this film also enjoyed success in London and was even compared to *Mädchen in Uniform* (cf. London meldet 1936). In *Traumulus* (1935), based on Arno Holz' and Oskar Jerschke's tragic comedy of the same name (1905), the belief in a new youth and a new age is propagated at the end.[36] Also worthy of mention are *So ein Flegel* (1934), *Die Feuerzangenbowle* (1944)[37] and *Was tun, Sibylle?* (1938).[38]

Comedies were popular in children's screenings, for example, the Danish comedy duo Pat and Patachon, who had been providing laughter since 1921. Their German-produced films *Mädchenräuber* and *Blinde Passagiere* premiered in 1936.

Since the German fairy tale was understood as a cultural asset, the fairy tale film continued to play a major role. Alf Zengerling, who began his career in the Weimar Republic, delivered nature-based actor's films, Hubert Schonger produced around 40 children's films with his Naturfilmproduktion studio in addition to fairy tale and Kasperle films, which he brought to the screen in collaboration with the Hohnsteiner Puppenspiele (cf. Hobsch 2009, 48). The Diehl brothers contributed animated puppet films, were even considered the pioneers of puppet film, and also provided numerous productions for educational purposes in school lessons. Fritz Genschow, who produced with children for children, not only created numerous other fairy tale films in addition to *Rotkäppchen und der Wolf* (1937), but also a whole series of children's films that do appear in the usual feature-length film lists due to their brevity. These short films, such as *Die Mühle von Werbellin* (1937) and *Die Sänger von der Waterkant* (1936), some of which, like *Jungjäger* (1938), are also documentaries, are among the specific children's films of the period.[39]

Despite clear restrictions on film imports, it was not exclusively German films that ran across the screen. The Italian film *Vecchia Guardia* (1935) is still reviewed disparagingly after its premiere in Rome: The best thing about the film would be the

---

[33] Roughly translated: harvest help.
[34] Roughly translated: aviation youth.
[35] Cf. https://www.filmportal.de/film/bravo-kleiner-thomas_0175530d166a48bda9d43e2027e36d47 (01.04.2020).
[36] Cf. the contribution by Petra Josting in this volume.
[37] Cf. the contribution by Heidi Nenoff in this volume.
[38] Cf. the contribution by Caroline Roeder in this volume.
[39] Cf. the contribution by Petra Anders in this volume.

performance of Franco Brambilla, who "plays an enthusiastic little fascist," but whose death scene seemed "staged and unnatural" (Vecchia Guardia 1935). Although the film was "met with great acclaim," it would hardly be considered for Germany, since "we know a Hans Westmar film" with which *Vecchia Guardia* could not compete (ibid.). It was not until 1937 that this Italian equivalent of *Hitlerjunge Quex* was released in German cinemas – the criticism was forgotten, it was rated *jugendfrei* and received the ratings of *staatspolitsch wertvoll* and *künstlerisch wertvoll* (cf. Zensierte Filme 1937). The American child star Shirley Temple is represented in the programmes from 1934 to 1939 with a total of 16 films; the attempt to counter her with a German (actually: Austrian) counterpart in the form of little Traudl Stark seems modest in comparison: The girl makes a total of ten films, four of which (*Seine Tochter ist der Peter* (1937),[40] *Peter im Schnee* (1937), *Liebling der Matrosen* (1937) and *Prinzessin Sissy* (1938)) received a youth release.

Film consumption and attendance were clearly directed during the Nazi era. Beginning with sound film vans, which were provided by the Reichspropagandaleitung in order to provide films even in villages without cinemas, to the state-run school film events from October 1933, to the introduction of the *Jugendfilmstunden des Deutschen Reiches*. Youth participation in these was considered "youth service" (Hobsch 2009, 53).[41] This involved

> large-scale propaganda events and "compulsory assemblies", which were supposed to help influence the young people in an emotional way and thus make the film screenings a communal experience. [...] The precisely thought-out sequence of Jugendfilmstunden and state-political school events in flag-draped cinema halls was subject to a fixed set of regulations, which included the closed march-in, singing, etc. (Ibid., 54)

Mandatory films for the youth is an apt phrase for this institution. Here Hitlerjungen, BDM girls, and so called Pimpfe came together and saw films that, while often not intended for them in the first instance, were shown consciously and not only intentionally, but obligatorily to them. Reese also points out that it was precisely the youth from rural areas and places without cinemas who sought out the Jugendfilmstunde – regardless of whether the films shown there interested them or not – because there was no other way for them to see a film (cf. Reese 1984, XXII). The ideas of the National Socialist world and life view were to be planted in young people. For example, the propagandistic military film *Pour le Mérite* (1938) received the rating *jugendwert* in 1939 and was used in Jugendfilmstunden. The Reichsfilmkammer, "in agreement with the Reichspropagandaleitung for Film," requested that those film theatres that had a copy of the film report "immediately" to the "responsible Gaufilmstelle to determine the Jugendfilmstunde" (Einsatz des jugendwerten Films "Pour le Mérite" 1939). The anti-Semitic propaganda film

---

[40] This film only received the release *Jugendfrei ab 14 Jahre*, all other mentioned were simply *jugendfrei*.

[41] "All young people up to the age of 18, but also the older members of the HJ, were to take part in these events. Furthermore, the following took part: the young people of the Napola and teacher training colleges, the air force and navy helpers from the ranks of the HJ. Millions of boys and girls were led to the movie theatres through the Jugendfilmstunden." (Hobsch 2009, 53)

Jud Süß (1940) was initially *only* given the ratings *staatspolitisch wertvoll* and *künstlerisch wertvoll* by the censors (cf. Zensiert 1940), but 14 days later it was also given the rating *jugendwert* (cf. "Jud Süß" ebenfalls jugendwert 1940) and was of course shown in the Jugendfilmstunden. In Anneliese Sanders' survey among leaders of the HJ and BDM, it nevertheless ranked only 33rd (cf. Reese 1984, IX).[42] The new season of the Jugendfilmstunden was ceremoniously opened by the Reichspropagandaminister Joseph Goebbels, in the fall of each year, and detailed articles explain which films were selected and why (cf. e.g. Die Eröffnung der Jugendfilmstunden 1942/1943 1942).

A look at the top ten films deemed good according to Sanders' study explains the spectrum of what young people were shown: 1. *Der große König* (1942, *Fridericus Rex* film, *jugendwert*), 2. *Bismarck* (1940), 3. *Die Entlassung* (1942, *jugendwert*), 4. *Friedrich Schiller* (1940, *jugendwert*), 5. *Heimkehr* (1941, *jugendwert*), 6. *Ohm Krüger* (1941, *jugendwert*), 7. ... *reitet für Deutschland* (1941), 8. *Andreas Schlüter* (1942, *jugendwert*), 9. *Stukas* (1941, *jugendwert)*, 10. *Kadetten* (1941) (cf. Reese 1984, XXII). Thematically, historical (war) films are mentioned for the most part, often revolving around the (National Socialist) interpretation of historical figures; many films were awarded the rating *jugendwert*, and all of them ran in the Jugendfilmstunden. In order to consider the actual film reception of children and young people during the Nazi era, such statements are relevant, even if these films no longer represent suitable children's and youth films from today's perspective. Reese states with regard to this top 10 list: "What does this list [...] say about youthful film attendance and youthful desires for film? It probably says nothing more than that adolescents basically consume the films that the general cinema program offers." (Ibid.) It is also important to note that the specific Nazi youth film does not have a special place in the overall results; it does not even appear among the best rankings. Films that were originally banned for young people were also recommended for the events, e.g. *Der Rebell* (1932) and *Morgenrot* (1933).

Also to be considered are documentaries with a feature story, which Sander counts among the "report films" in which "to a large extent [...] something like a political commissioned production can be discerned" (ibid., VII). Sander in turn distinguishes three categories, a) the reportage-like filming of specific events from the lives of youth, b) newsreel-like overviews of the work of youth, and c) cultural, instructional, or research film representations (cf. Sander 1944/1984, 17). Report films in the first category were included in the database, for example, *Jungbann 2* (1936), which is both a literary adaptation (based on the series *Jungen im Dienst* (1936–1938) by Alfred Weidenmann) and a documentary; the production company is the Hitlerjugend, Gebietsführung 20, Referat Film. By no means all report films, however, have a featured storyline; one can consider, for example, *Der Marsch zum Führer* (1940), *Glaube und Schönheit* (1940), and *Soldaten von morgen* (1941) as pure documentary and propaganda films, but they are specific children's and youth

---

[42] Hartmut Reese analysed Anneliese Sander's study (published in 1944) in 1984 and re-edited it with a critical commentary.

films, were produced for and in part with youth (cf. Reese 1984, VIII), and must accordingly be considered in the corpus. Sander's study, although ideological and tendentious, is also still instructive today, distinguishing between the *children's* feature-length film, "primarily for the under-teens" (Sander 1944/1984, 17), and the *youth* feature-length film, which could be paralleled in the form to the adult feature-length film, but could never be "entertainment only" (ibid., 18). This corresponds to the censorship practice during the Nazi regime, which also knew the release option *Jugendfrei ab 14 Jahre.* However, this provision was broken within the last years of the war insofar as, due to a special provision, certain films with this release were released for Jugendfilmstunden of the Hitlerjugend from the age of 10 (cf. ibid., 20).

Summary and Outlook

In the area of film, the aim was to open up the view for children's and youth films, taking into account previous research results, and to record film adaptations of children's and youth literature as well as films actually received by this target group, based on the contemporary specialist press. Among other things, it was found that the silent film era was strongly influenced by film adaptations of fairy tales and legends, but that the beginning of detective and adventure films and series can also be located here, which were considered in the survey. The contemporary discussion on the subject of *children and cinema* makes it clear time and time again that it was precisely these films that attracted a young audience. These productions, which were condemned as *trash films,* show very different relationships to literature. There were films that adapted literary models (e.g. *Sherlock Holmes*), those that led to book publications (e.g. *Joe Jenkins*) and others that inspired dime novel series (e.g. *Harry Piel*). With the help of research literature on popular culture and light fiction, a significant corpus of films actually received by children and adolescents could be recorded. In the course of the 1920s, the interest of minors in such *Stoffe* was gradually rewarded on the distribution level, and German productions of this kind were increasingly given a youth release alongside American productions. In addition, numerous (attempts at) film adaptations of dramatic *Stoffe* were published during the Kaiserreich, which were included in the database on the basis of knowledge gained through school performances about the intended reception of classical dramas by children and young people, but the actual use by minors is mostly unsecured at this point.

The adaptations of *literarische* and dramatic *Stoffe* in the Weimar Republic are more numerous than previously documented; in addition to comedies and American children's stars, the birth of the German youth film can be located in this period, which – despite ideological imprinting and questionable productions – constituted itself in distribution under National Socialism; young people were perceived as a separate audience to be distinguished from children. The fairy tale film, like all German film production, developed during this period and became a specific children's film genre with the turn to sound film. Animated films and cartoons were introduced to German cinemas by Walt Disney[43] towards the end of the 1920s. German film production went its own way with silhouette films thanks to the silhouette artist Lotte Reiniger. The animated puppet film – a specific children's film genre – did not become established until the 1930s, mainly with the productions of the Diehl brothers and Hubert Schonger.

The Nazi regime profited from the experimental years of the Weimar Republic, which led to an increase in the quality not only of German film in general, but also of specific and intended children's and youth film production, which, despite all tendencies and ideology, at least brought aesthetically and technically successful productions to the market and thus influenced contemporary youth. The National Socialists were very aware of the power of film.

With the help of the various sources, it was possible to create a corpus comprising over 1759 titles, thus enormously expanding the previous state of research. 331 films during the Kaiserreich, 818 during the Weimar Republic and 532 during National Socialism; 1000 silent films, 532 sound films. In the course of examining the film journals mentioned above, a wealth of material was discovered and evaluated as paratexts relevant to the media network: Film descriptions (Kaiserreich), film reviews (Weimar Republic) and observations (Nazi era), advertisements, announcements, notes and accompanying articles on film productions, recommendations for children's screenings, cinema programmes, portraits of actors as well as contemporary discussions on the subject of *children and cinema*. 1132 feature-length films and 590 short films were recorded, which have so far been left out of most research on this topic, but which form a large corpus, especially for young audiences. 1046 real films are contrasted with 219 animated films (133 of which are cartoons, 21 silhouettes and 30 puppet films).

150 specific children's and youth films are contrasted by 228 de facto and 778 intended children's and youth films, which form the largest group. There are question marks behind 558 recorded films whose reception by minors could not yet be ascertained.

References

Filmography

... reitet für Deutschland (D 1941) [Spielfilm]. Regie: Arthur Maria Rabenalt, Drehbuch: Fritz Reck-Malleczewen/Richard Riedel/Josef Maria Frank, Musik: Alois Melichar, Ufa.
All Quiet on the Western Front (USA 1930) [Spielfilm]. Regie: Lewis Milestone, Drehbuch: Maxwell Anderson/Del Andrews/George Abbott, Universal Pictures. Nach dem Roman *Im Westen nichts Neues* von Erich Maria Remarque [EA 1929].

---

[43] Cf. the contribution by Johannes Krause in this volume.

Andreas Schlüter (D 1942) [Spielfilm]. Regie: Herbert Maisch, Drehbuch: Helmut Brandis/Herbert Maisch, Musik: Wolfgang Zeller, Terra-Filmkunst GmbH. Nach dem Roman *Der Münzturm* [EA 1936] von Alfons von Czibulka.

Ariane (D 1931) [Spielfilm]. Regie: Paul Czinner, Drehbuch: Paul Czinner/Carl Mayer, Musik: Leo Witt, Nero-Film AG. Nach dem gleichnamigen Roman von Claude Anet [EA 1924].

Artisten (D 1935) [Spielfilm]. Regie: Harry Piel, Drehbuch: Max W. Kimmich/Harry Piel, Musik: Fritz Wenneis, Ariel Film GmbH.

Bismarck (D 1940) [Spielfilm]. Regie: Wolfgang Liebeneiner, Drehbuch: Rolf Lauckner/Wolfgang Liebeneiner, Musik: Norbert Schultze, Tobis-Filmkunst GmbH.

Blinde Passagiere (D 1936) [Spielfilm]. Regie: Fred Sauer, Drehbuch: Max Wallner/Georg Zoch, Musik: Walter Espe, Majestic-Film GmbH.

Bravor, kleiner Thomas! (D 1945) [Spielfilm]. Regie: Jan Fethke, Drehbuch: Odo Krohmann, Musik: Oskar Wagner, Bavaria Filmkunst GmbH.

Der Dschungel ruft (D 1936) [Spielfilm]. Regie: Harry Piel, Drehbuch: Georg Mühlen-Schulte/ Harry Piel, Musik: Fritz Wenneis, Ariel-Film GmbH. Nach dem Roman *Die Buschhexe* [EA 1930] von Georg Mühlen-Schulte.

Der Geiger von Florenz (D 1926) [Stummfilm]. Regie und Drehbuch: Paul Czinner, Musik: Giuseppe Becce, Ufa.

Der große König (D 1942) [Spielfilm]. Regie und Drehbuch: Veit Harlan, Musik: Hans-Otto Borgmann, Tobis-Filmkunst GmbH.

Der Kampf der Tertia (D 1928) [Stummfilm]. Regie: Max Mack, Drehbuch: Max Mack/Axel Eggebrecht, Musik: Giuseppe Becce, Terra-Film AG. Nach dem gleichnamigen Roman von Wilhelm Speyer [EA 1927].

Der Kampf des Donald Westhof (D 1927) [Stummfilm]. Regie und Drehbuch: Fritz Wendhausen, Musik: Artur Guttmann, Ufa.

Der Marsch zum Führer (D 1940) [Dokumentarfilm]. Deutsche Filmherstellungs- und Verwertungs-GmbH.

Der Rattenfänger (D 1918) [Stummfilm]. Regie und Drehbuch: Paul Wegener, Projektions-AG Union (PAGU).

Der Rebell. Die Feuer rufen (D 1932) [Spielfilm]. Regie: Kurt Bernhardt/Luis Trenker, Drehbuch: Robert A. Stemmle/Walter Schmidkunz/Henry Kosterlitz, Musik: Giuseppe Becce, Deutsche Universal-Film AG.

Der verlorene Schuh (D 1923) [Stummfilm]. Regie und Drehbuch: Ludwig Berger, Musik: Guido Bagier, Decla-Bioscop AG.

Die Bande vom Hoheneck (D 1934) [Spielfilm]. Regie und Drehbuch: Hans F. Wilhelm, Musik: Hans Ailbout, Czerny-Produktion GmbH.

Die Biene Maja und ihre Abenteuer (D 1926) [Stummfilm]. Regie: Wolfram Junghans, Drehbuch: Curt Thomalla, Kulturfilm AG. Nach dem gleichnamigen Roman von Waldemar Bonsels [EA 1912].

Die Entlassung (D 1942) [Spielfilm]. Regie: Wolfgang Liebeneiner, Drehbuch: Curt J. Braun, Felix von Eckardt, Musik: Herbert Windt, Tobis-Filmkunst GmbH.

Die Feuerzangenbowle. Ein heiterer Film (D 1944) [Spielfilm]. Regie: Helmut Weiss, Drehbuch: Heinrich Spoerl, Musik: Werner Bochmann. Terra-Film. Nach dem gleichnamigen Roman von Heinrich Spoerl [EA 1933].

Die Mühle von Werbellin (D 1937) [Kurz-Spielfilm]. Regie und Drehbuch: Fritz Genschow, Tobis-Melofilm GmbH.

Die Nibelungen (D 1922–1924) [Stummfilm]. Regie: Fritz Lang, Drehbuch: Thea von Harbou, Decla-Bioscop AG. In zwei Teilen, 1. Siegfried/Siegfrieds Tod, 2. Kriemhilds Rache.

Die Räuberbande (D 1928) [Stummfilm]. Regie: Hans Behrendt, Drehbuch: Leonhard Frank/Franz Schulz/Hans Behrendt, Felsom-Film GmbH. Nach dem gleichnamigen Roman von Leonhard Frank [EA 1914].

Die Sänger von der Waterkant (D 1936) [Kurz-Spielfilm]. Regie und Drehbuch: Fritz Genschow, Musik: Walter Ulfig, Fritz Genschow-Filmproduktion/Tobis-Melofilm GmbH.

Die Siebzehnjährigen [Stummfilm] (D 1929). Regie: Georg Asagaroff, Drehbuch: Fritz Falkenstein, Musik: Guiseppe Becce, Terra-Film AG. Nach dem Theaterstück *Die Siebzehnjährige* [EA 1904] von Max Dreyer.

Die Unehelichen (D 1926) [Stummfilm]. Regie: Gerhard Lamprecht, Drehbuch: Luise Heilborn-Körbitz/Gerhard Lamprecht, Gerhard-Lamprecht-Film Produktion.

Doktor Dolittle und seine Tiere (D 1928) [Silhouetten-Animationsfilm]. Regie: Lotte Reiniger, Comenius-Film GmbH/I. G. Farbenindustrie AG. Nach dem Kinderbuch *The Story of Doctor Dolittle* [EA 1920] von Hugh Lofting.

Emil und die Detektive (D 1931) [Spielfilm]. Regie: Gerhard Lamprecht, Drehbuch: Billy Wilder, Musik: Allan Gray. Nach dem gleichnamigen Roman von Erich Kästner [EA 1929].

Friedrich Schiller (D 1940) [Spielfilm]. Regie: Herbert Maisch, Drehbuch: Walter Wassermann/Lotte Neumann, Musik: Herbert Windt, Tobis-Filmkunst GmbH.

Frühlings Erwachen [Stummfilm] (D 1923). Regie: Jakob Fleck/L. Kolm, Drehbuch: Jakob Fleck/Adolf Lantz, Wiener Kunstfilm. Nach dem Bühnenstück *Frühlings Erwachen* [EV: 1891, EA: 1906] von Frank Wedekind. 1928 vertrieben unter dem Titel *Frühreife Jugend*.

Frühlings Erwachen. Eine Kindertragödie [Stummfilm] (D 1929). Regie: Richard Oswald, Drehbuch: Friedrich Raff/Herbert Rosenfeld, Musik: Walter Ulfig, Hegewald-Film. Nach dem Bühnenstück *Frühlings Erwachen* [EV: 1891, EA: 1906] von Frank Wedekind.

Glaube und Schönheit (D 1940) [Kurz-Dokumentarfilm]. Regie: Hans Ertl, Deutsche Filmherstellungs- und Verwertungs-GmbH (DFG).

Hände hoch! (D 1942) [Spielfilm]. Regie und Drehbuch: Alfred Weidenmann, Musik: Horst Hanns Sieber; Deutsche Filmherstellungs- und Verwertungs-GmbH.

Hans Trutz im Schlaraffenland (D 1917) [Stummfilm]. Regie und Drehbuch: Paul Wegener, Projektions-AG Union (PAGU).

Heimkehr (D 1941) [Spielfilm]. Regie: Gustav Ucicky, Drehbuch: Gerhard Menzel, Musik: Willy Schmidt-Gentner, Wien-Film GmbH.

Himmelhunde (D 1942) [Spielfilm]. Regie: Roger von Norman, Drehbuch: Philipp Lothar Mayring, Musik: Werner Bochmann, Terra-Filmkunst GmbH.

Hitlerjunge Quex. Ein Film vom Opfergeist der deutschen Jugend (D 1933) [Spielfilm]. Regie: Hans Steinhoff, Drehbuch: Bobby E. Lüthge, Musik: Hans-Otto Borgmann, Ufa. Nach dem gleichnamigen Roman von Karl Aloys Schenzinger [EA 1932].

Ich für Dich – Du für mich (D 1934) [Spielfilm]. Regie: Carl Froelich, Drehbuch: Hans Gustl Kernmayr, Musik: Hansom Milde-Meißner, Froelich-Film GmbH.

Jakko (D 1941) [Spielfilm]. Regie: Fritz P. Buch, Musik: Hans O. Borgmann, Tobis-Filmkunst GmbH.

Jud Süß (D 1940) [Spielfilm] Regie: Veit Harlan, Drehbuch: Veit Harlan/Eberhard Wolfgang Möller/Ludwig Metzger, Musik: Wolfgang Zeller, Terra-Filmkunst GmbH.

Jungbann 2 (D 1936) [Stummfilm]. Regie und Drehbuch: Alfred Weidenmann, HJ, Gebietsführung 20, Referat Film, Stuttgart. Basierend auf der Trilogie *Jungen im Dienst* [EA: 1936–1938] von Alfred Weidenmann.

Junge Adler (D 1943/44) [Spielfilm]. Regie: Alfred Weidenmann, Drehbuch: Alfred Weidenmann/Herbert Reinecker, Musik: Hans O. Borgmann, Ufa-Filmkunst GmbH.

Jungens (D 1941) [Spielfilm]. Regie: Robert A. Stemmle, Drehbuch: Otto Bernhard Wendler/Horst Kerutt/Robert A. Stemmle, Musik: Werner Egk, Ufa. Nach dem Roman *Die 13 Jungens von Dünendorf* [EA 1941] von Hans Kerutt.

Jungjäger (D 1938) [Kurz-Dokumentarfilm]. Regie und Drehbuch: Fritz Genschow, Musik: Walter Ulfig, Tobis-Filmkunst GmbH.

Kalif Storch (D 1930/31) [Silhouetten-Animationsfilm]. Regie: Ferdinand Diehl, Gebrüder Diehl-Filmproduktion.

Kadetten (D 1941) [Spielfilm]. Regie: Karl Ritter, Drehbuch: Felix Lützkendorf/Karl Ritter, Musik: Herbert Windt, Ufa.

Kameradschaft (D/F 1931) [Spielfilm]. Regie: G. W. Pabst, Drehbuch: Peter Martin Lampel/Ladislaus Vajda/Gerbert Rappaport/Karl Otten, Musik: G. von Rigelius, Nero-Film AG/Gaumont-Franco-Film Aubert.

Kopf hoch, Johannes! (D 1941) [Spielfilm]. Regie: Viktor de Kowa, Drehbuch: Toni Huppertz/ Wilhelm Krug/Felix von Eckardt, Musik: Harald Böhmelt, Majestic-Film GmbH.

Liebling der Matrosen (AT 1937) [Spielfilm]. Regie: Hans Hinrich, Drehbuch: Karl Peter Gillmann/ Detlef Sierck, Musik: Willy Schmidt-Gentner, Mondial Internationale Filmindustrie AG.

Little Robinson Crusoe (USA 1924) [Stummfilm]. Regie: Edward F. Cline, Drehbuch: Willard Mack, Jackie Coogan Productions. Nach Motiven des Romans *Robinson Crusoe* [EA 1719] von Daniel Defoe.

Mädchen in Uniform (D 1931) [Spielfilm]. Regie: Leontine Sagan, Drehbuch: Christa Winsloe/F. D. Andam, Musik: Hansom Milde-Meißner, Deutsche Film-Gemeinschaft GmbH. Nach dem Theaterstück *Gestern und Heute/Ritter Nérestan* [EA und EV 1930] von Christa Winsloe.

Mädchenräuber (D 1936) [Spielfilm]. Regie: Fred Sauer, Drehbuch: Max Wallner, Musik: Walter Ulfig, Majestic-Film GmbH.

Morgenrot (D 1933) [Spielfilm]. Regie: Gustav Ucicky, Drehbuch: Gerhard Menzel, Musik: Herbert Windt, Ufa.

The Darling of New York (USA 1923) [Stummfilm]. Regie: King Baggot, Drehbuch: King Baggot/ Adrian Johnson/Raymond L. Schrock, Universal Pictures.

Ohm Krüger (D 1941) [Spielfilm]. Regie: Hans Steinhoff, Drehbuch: Harald Bratt/Kurt Heuser, Musik: Theo Mackeben, Tobis-Filmkunst GmbH. Nach dem Roman *Ein Mann ohne Volk* [EA 1934] von Arnold Krieger.

Oliver Twist (USA 1922) [Stummfilm]. Regie: Frank Lloyd, Drehbuch: Frank Lloyd/Harry Weil, Jackie Coogan Productions. Nach dem gleichnamigen Roman von Charles Dickens [EA 1837–1839].

Panik (D 1928) [Stummfilm]. Regie: Harry Piel, Drehbuch: Herbert Nossen/Harry Piel, Ring-Film AG.

Peter im Schnee (AT 1937) [Spielfilm]. Regie: Carl Lamač, Drehbuch: Paul Hörbiger/Carl Lamač, Musik: Willy Schmidt-Gentner, Mondial Internationale Filmindustrie AG.

Pour le Mérite (D 1938) [Spielfilm]. Regie: Karl Ritter, Drehbuch: Fred Hildebrandt/Karl Ritter, Musik: Herbert Windt, Ufa.

Primanerliebe (D 1927) [Stummfilm]. Regie: Robert Land, Drehbuch: Alfred Schirokauer/Curt Wesse, Musik: Walter Ulfig, Domo-Strauß-Film GmbH.

Prinzessin Sissy (D 1938) [Spielfilm]. Regie: Fritz Thiery, Drehbuch: Friedrich Forster/Rudolf Brettschneider, Musik: Willy Schmidt-Gentner, Mondial Internationale Filmindustrie AG.

Reifende Jugend (D 1933) [Spielfilm]. Regie: Carl Froelich, Drehbuch: Robert A. Stemmle/ Walter Supper, Musik: Walter Gronostay, Froelich-Film GmbH. Nach dem Theaterstück *Die Reifeprüfung* [EA 1929] von Max Dreyer.

Revolte im Erziehungshaus (D 1929) [Stummfilm]. Regie: Georg Asagaroff, Drehbuch: W. Solsky/ Herbert Rosenfeld, Musik: Werner Schmidt-Boelcke, Grohnert-Film-Produktion. Nach dem gleichnamigen Bühnenstück von Peter Martin Lampel [EA: 1928, EV: 1929].

Rotkäppchen und der Wolf (D 1937) [Spielfilm]. Regie und Drehbuch: Fritz Genschow/Renée Stobrawa, Musik: Kurt Heuser, Tobis-Melofilm GmbH.

Rübezahls Hochzeit (D 1916) [Stummfilm]. Regie und Drehbuch: Paul Wegener, Projektions-AG Union (PAGU).

Sein bester Freund. Ein Abenteuer mit 15 Hunden (D 1929) [Stummfilm]. Regie: Harry Piel, Drehbuch: Hans Rameau/Harry Piel, Ariel-Film GmbH.

Seine Tochter ist der Peter (AT 1937) [Spielfilm]. Regie: Heinz Helbig, Drehbuch: Erich Ebermayer, Musik: Willy Schmidt-Gentner, Mondial Internationale Filmindustrie AG. Nach dem Roman *Und seine Tochter ist der Peter* [EA 1935] von Edith Zellweker.

So ein Flegel (D 1934) [Spielfilm]. Regie: Robert Adolf Stemmle, Drehbuch: Hans Reimann, Musik: Harald Böhmelt, Cicero-Film GmbH. Nach dem Roman *Die Feuerzangenbowle* [EA 1933] von Heinrich Spoerl.

Soldaten von morgen (D 1941) [Kurzfilm]. Regie und Drehbuch: Alfred Weidenmann, Musik: Horst Hanns Sieber, Deutsche Filmherstellungs- und Verwertungs-GmbH (DFG).

Stukas (D 1941) [Spielfilm]. Regie: Karl Ritter, Drehbuch: Karl Ritter/Felix Lützkendorf, Musik: Herbert Windt, Ufa.

Tagebuch einer Verlorenen (D 1929) [Stummfilm]. Regie: G. W. Pabst, Drehbuch: Rudolf Leonhard, Musik: Otto Stenzeel, Hom-Film AG/Pabst-Film GmbH. Nach dem gleichnamigen Roman von Margarete Böhme [EA 1905].

The Kid (USA 1921) [Stummfilm]. Regie, Drehbuch und Musik: Charlie Chaplin, Charles Chaplin Productions.

Tom Sawyer (USA 1930) [Spielfilm]. Regie: John Cromwell, Drehbuch: Grover Jones/William Slavens McNutt/Sam Mintz, Musik: John Leipold/Ralph Rainger, Paramount Pictures. Nach dem Roman *The Adventures of Tom Sawyer* [EA 1876] von Mark Twain.

Traumulus (D 1935) [Spielfilm]. Regie: Carl Froelich, Drehbuch: Robert A. Stemmle/Erich Ebermayer, Musik: Hansom Milde-Meißner, Froelich-Film GmbH. Nach dem gleichnamigen Bühnenstück von Arno Holz und Oskar Jerschke [EA 1905].

Vecchia Guardia (I 1935) [Spielfilm]. Regie: Alessandro Blasetti, Drehbuch: Alessandro Blasetti/Livio Apolloni, Musik: Umberto Mancini, Fauno Film.

Was tun, Sibylle (D 1938) [Spielfilm]. Regie: Peter Paul Brauer, Drehbuch: Wolf Neumeister/Heinz Bierkowski, Produktion: Ufa. Nach dem gleichnamigen Roman von Sophie Schieker-Ebe [EA 1930].

Zwei Welten (D 1940) [Spielfilm]. Regie: Gustaf Gründgens, Drehbuch: Felix Lützkendorf, Musik: Michael Jary, Terra-Filmkunst GmbH.

Secondary Literature Before 1945

„Jud Süß" auch jugendwert. In: Film-Kurier 22 (1940) 228 vom 28.09., 3.

Bekämpfung der Schundliteratur mit einer Zusammenstellung der bisher getroffenen Maßnahmen. Berlin 1911.

Die Eröffnung der Jugendfilmstunden 1942/43. Ansprachen von Reichsminister Dr. Goebbels und Reichsjugendführer Axmann. In: Film-Kurier 24 (1942) 251 vom 26.10., 1–2.

Die Kinematographen und die Jugend. In: Der Kinematograph 1 (1907) 36 vom 04.09., 3–4.

Einsatz des jugendwerten Films „Pour le mérite" in den Jugendfilmstunden der Hitlerjugend (HJ). In: Film-Kurier 21 (1939) 3 vom 04.01., Mitteilungsbl. 1.

H.: My Darling (Filmkritik). In: Film-Kurier 6 (1924) 276 vom 22.11., 2.

Häfker, Hermann: Für Kinder! In: Der Kinematograph 2 (1908) 72 vom 13.05., 5–6.

Herzberg, Georg: Panik (Filmkritik). In: Film-Kurier 10 (1928) 48 vom 24.02., 2.

Jacobsohn, Egon: Mein Kampf gegen Harry Piel. In: Film-Kurier 3 (1921) 107 vom 09.05., 3.

Lemke, Hermann: Die Kinematographische Reformpartei, ihre Aufgaben und Ziele. In: Der Kinematograph 1 (1907) 42 vom 16.10., 3–5.

London meldet: „Reifende Jugend" erfolgreich. In: Film-Kurier 18 (1936) 18 vom 22.01., 3.

Schiel, Adelbert: Im Kampf gegen Schmutz und Schund in der Jugendliteratur. Halle 1917.

Vecchia Guardia (Alte Garde). In: Film-Kurier 17 (1935) 22 vom 26.01., 3.

Zensiert. In: Film-Kurier 22 (1940) 216 vom 14.09., 3.

Zensierte Filme vom 5. bis einschließlich 10. April 1937. In: Film-Kurier 19 (1937) 96 vom 26.04., 4.

Secondary Literature After 1945

Birett, Herbert: Verzeichnis in Deutschland gelaufener Filme. 1911–1920. Entscheidungen der Filmzensur. München [u. a.] 1980.

Bleckman, Matias: Harry Piel. Ein Kino-Mythos und seine Zeit. Düsseldorf 1993.

Elsaesser, Thomas: Kino der Kaiserzeit. Einleitung. In: Ders./Wedel, Michael: Kino der Kaiserzeit. Zwischen Tradition und Moderne. München 2002, 11–42.

Garncarz, Joseph: Öffentliche Räume für Filme. Zur Etablierung des Kinos in Deutschland. In: Müller, Corinna/Segeberg, Harro (Hg.): Kinoöffentlichkeit (1895–1920). Entstehung, Etablierung, Differenzierung/Cinema's Publics Sphere (1895–1920). Emergence, Settlement, Differentiation. Marburg 2008, 32–43.

Goergen, Jeanpaul: Cinema in the Spotlight. The *Lichtspiel*-Theaters and the Newspapers in Berlin, September 1913. A Case Study. In: Müller, Corinna/Segeberg, Harro (Hg.): Kinoöffentlichkeit (1895–1920). Entstehung, Etablierung, Differenzierung/Cinema's Publics Sphere (1895–1920). Emergence, Settlement, Differentiation. Marburg 2008, 66–86.

Hellwig, Albert: Die Schundfilme, ihr Wesen, ihre Gefahren und ihre Bekämpfung [1911]. In: Bredow, Wilfried von/Zurek, Rolf: Film und Gesellschaft in Deutschland. Dokumente und Materialien. Hamburg 1975, 60–66.

Hobsch, Manfred: Ideologie für Kopf und Herz der Jugend. In: Schäfer, Horst/Wegener, Claudia (Hg.): Kindheit und Film. Geschichte, Themen und Perspektiven des Kinderfilms in Deutschland. Konstanz 2009 (Alltag, Medien und Kultur; 5), 39–55.

Höfig, Willi: Die stumme Märchenfrau. Märchen und Sage im Stummfilm. Beispiele und theoretische Überlegungen der Zeit. In: Schmitt, Christoph (Hg.): Erzählkulturen im Medienwandel. Münster [u. a.] 2008, 87–108.

Jacobsen, Wolfgang/Kaes, Anton/Prinzler, Hans Helmut (Hg.): Geschichte des deutschen Films. Akt. und erw. Aufl. Stuttgart [u. a.] ²2004.

Kaiser, Alexandra/Maurer, Dietrich/Richter, Ulrike: Vorwort. In: Maase, Kaspar (Hg.): Prädikat wertlos. Der lange Streit um Schmutz und Schund. Tübingen 2001, 5–7.

Kracauer, Siegfried: Von Caligari zu Hitler. Eine psychologische Geschichte des deutschen Films. Frankfurt a. M. 1984 [1947].

Loiperdinger, Martin: Filmzensur und Selbstkontrolle. Politische Reifeprüfung. In: Jacobsen, Wolfgang/Kaes, Anton/Prinzler, Hans Helmut(Hg.): Geschichte des deutschen Films. Akt. und erw. Aufl. Stuttgart [u. a.] ²2004, 525–544.

Loiperdinger, Martin: Akzente des Lokalen im frühen Kino am Beispiel Trier. In: Müller, Corinna/Segeberg, Harro (Hg.): Kinoöffentlichkeit (1895–1920). Entstehung, Etablierung, Differenzierung/Cinema's Publics Sphere (1895–1920). Emergence, Settlement, Differentiation. Marburg 2008, 236–245.

Maase, Kaspar: Schundkampf und Demokratie. In: Ders. (Hg.): Prädikat wertlos. Der lange Streit um Schmutz und Schund. Tübingen 2001, 8–17.

Maase, Kaspar: Kinderkino. Halbwüchsige, Öffentlichkeiten und kommerzielle Populärkultur im deutschen Kaiserreich. In: Müller, Corinna/Segeberg, Harro (Hg.): Kinoöffentlichkeit (1895–1920). Entstehung, Etablierung, Differenzierung/Cinema's Publics Sphere (1895–1920). Emergence, Settlement, Differentiation. Marburg 2008, 126–148.

Maurer, Dietrich: Schundkonsum als Kriminalitätsursache. Zum pädagogischen Diskurs vor 1933. In: Maase, Kaspar (Hg.): Prädikat wertlos. Der lange Streit um Schmutz und Schund. Tübingen 2001, 18–28.

Müller, Corinna: Kinoöffentlichkeit in Hamburg um 1913. In: Dies./Segeberg, Harro (Hg.): Kinoöffentlichkeit (1895–1920). Entstehung, Etablierung, Differenzierung/Cinema's Publics Sphere (1895–1920). Emergence, Settlement, Differentiation. Marburg 2008, 105–125.

Räder, Andy: Der Kinderfilm in der Weimarer Republik. In: Schäfer, Horst/Wegener, Claudia (Hg.): Kindheit und Film. Geschichte, Themen und Perspektiven des Kinderfilms in Deutschland. Konstanz 2009 (Alltag, Medien und Kultur; 5), 21–38.

Reese, Hartmut: Jugendfilm im Nationalsozialismus (Einleitung). In: Sander, Anneliese U.: Jugendfilm im Nationalsozialismus. Dokumentation und Kommentar. Nach der Sonderveröffentlichung Nr. 6 der Zeitschrift „Das junge Deutschland" (1944) hg. von Hartmut Reese. Münster 1984, I–IXXX.

Sander, Anneliese U.: Jugendfilm im Nationalsozialismus. Dokumentation und Kommentar. Nach der Sonderveröffentlichung Nr. 6 der Zeitschrift „Das junge Deutschland" (1944) hg. von Hartmut Reese. Münster 1984.

Schmerling, Alice: Kind, Kino und Kinderliteratur. Eine Untersuchung zum Medienumbruch in der Kinderkultur der Kaiserzeit und der Weimarer Republik. Köln 2007.

Stiglegger, Marcus: Zwischen Revolte und Diktatur. Jugendfilme der Weimarer Republik. In: Koebner, Thomas: Diesseits der „Dämonischen Leinwand". Neue Perspektiven auf das späte Weimarer Kino. München 2003, 311–326.

Töteberg, Michael: Neben dem Operetten-Theater und vis-à-vis Schauspielhaus. Eine Kino-Topographie von Hamburg 1896–1912. In: Müller, Corinna/Segeberg, Harro (Hg.): Kinoöffentlichkeit (1895–1920). Entstehung, Etablierung, Differenzierung/Cinema's Publics Sphere (1895–1920). Emergence, Settlement, Differentiation. Marburg 2008, 87–104.

Wanjek, Peter: Der deutsche Heftroman. Ein Handbuch der zwischen 1900 und 1945 im Deutschen Reich erschienenen Romanhefte. Wilfersdorf 1994.

Children's and Youth Theatre from 1900 to 1945

Marlene Antonia Illies

The printed play is a medium that transcends space and time. It is staged, interpreted and processed anew again and again; it comes to life on public stages or even school stages, moves into films and radio plays, into picture books and graphic novels. Classical dramas such as Goethe's *Faust* have been part of school reading for generations, a timelessly popular children's play such as *Peterchens Mondfahrt* by Bassewitz has been performed regularly at Christmas time since it was written more than 100 years ago.[1]

A single production, however, is fleeting and cannot be preserved. A camera that follows the actors on stage or a microphone that records and stores every spoken word can only capture a part of this experience, however, cannot capture the immediate view of the audience from their respective, mostly static seats on stage, cannot capture the dynamic chemistry between audience and actors. Because

> theatre takes place in public, yet a performance without an audience is not theatre, and has a transitory character, i.e. it is always present and is only constituted in performance – a theatre performance is unique, unrepeatable, and not preservable, the "theatrical image shows itself as a fleeting entity that takes place before the eyes and ears of the spectator and vanishes again the moment it appears". A theatrical performance instigates "a temporary social community […] that can be heterogeneously or homogeneously structured," so that also "the experiences of spectators are part of the performance, and not only those that correspond to the supposed intentions of a director." (Steiner 2011, 146 f.)

Theatrical performances are a live experience, even with a carefully dramaturgically developed production, each individual performance differs a little from the other.

---

[1] Cf. the contribution by Julia Benner in this volume.

M. A. Illies (✉)
Faculty of Linguistics and Literary Studies, German Studies, Bielefeld University, Bielefeld, Germany
e-mail: marlene.illies@uni-bielefeld.de

© Springer-Verlag GmbH Germany, part of Springer Nature 2024
P. Josting et al. (eds.), *German-Language Children's and Youth Literature In The Media Network 1900–1945*, https://doi.org/10.1007/978-3-476-05892-8_4

The differences between productions in varying places and at different times are even greater. That is why it was important to record not only stage manuscripts but also individual productions, in other words continuity and variation, which was done in the database (http://medienverbundportal.kjl.uni-bielefeld.de) by anchoring the printed plays in the medium of print and the productions in the medium of theatre.

The relationship between stage and film has always been competitive. Before cinema settled down, it was a fairground attraction, ousting the long-established Kasperle show from the fairgrounds. Technical innovations in film production regularly prompted dystopian predictions of the death of theatre. Instead however, the apparent competition developed into a mutually beneficial coexistence for those involved. Plays written for the theatre provided film material, actors and directors moved from the stage to the set and vice versa. This was similar to radio, which was initially also suspected of wanting to kill off the stage. Later, radio and theatre competed for the best voice actors. Many popular silent film actors were also recruited by radio, but disappointed because their voices did not meet the requirements of the new medium.

Large composite fields, in which the media of film/cinema, theatre and radio are interwoven in a variety of ways, develop the *literarische Stoffe* constituted via pedagogical-didactic discourses. Classical dramas taught in schools were among the first film adaptations and were present in early radio. While the film versions hardly aroused the interest of teachers, at best a rather critical one (cf. Schmerling 2007), radio established series of broadcasts early on, such as the *Jugend-Bühne*, where the dramatic subject matter of literature lessons was worked on in radio play form over a period of years. Alfred Braun, the initiator and director of this series on Berlin's Funk-Stunde, placed it in the tradition of the classic performances of the Berlin Schiller-Theater (cf. Braun 1968), a claim that was taken seriously and critically questioned by contemporaries (e.g. by Hermann Kasack in Dichtung und Rundfunk 1930). From statistics of the Schillertheater-AG (cf. Bonn 1939), the Hamburger list of recommendations such as the *Verzeichnis wertvoller Spiele für die Schul- und Jugendbühne* (VDP 1932) etc., a corpus of classics considered suitable for pupils or adapted for them could be determined. In addition to *Minna von Barnhelm* (14 productions, 7 radio records and one film, to which the majority of the 76 paratexts as well as the 8 advertising materials and 7 images refer), *Götz von Berlichingen* (7 performances, 5 radio records, 2 films), *Die Räuber* (8 performances, 5 radio records and 3 films, to which the majority of the 83 paratexts as well as the 29 advertising materials and 3 pictures refer) and *Faust (*21 radio records, 12 performances and 10 film adaptations, mostly of individual motifs), *Wilhelm Tell* (25 performances, 20 radio records, 52 paratexts, 9 film adaptations, 9 print data sets and one disc record) in particular occupies an outstanding position in the entire period under investigation.

The children's theatre Genschow-Stobrawa exemplifies and well illustrates how closely the actors and institutions of radio, film and theatre were often connected: Renée Stobrawa was a speaker of children's broadcasts on Berlin radio in the 1920s.

Her later partner Fritz Genschow was an actor at the Volksbühne and the Theater am Schiffbauerdamm, among other places; in the 1930s he appeared in numerous Ufa film productions and worked as a screenwriter, director, and producer. Stobrawa and Genschow began their collaboration in 1929 at the Theater am Schiffbauerdamm with the adaptation of an Andersen fairy tale *(Der große und der kleine Klaus)* adapted by Lisa Tetzner. Tetzner also worked for the Berliner Funk-Stunde in the 1920s, reading fairy tales and producing broadcasts for and with children. Together with Stobrawa, Genschow brought current children's literature to the stage alongside the typical fairy tale material (*Hänsel und Gretel* 1933; *Schneewittchen* 1935) at their children's theatre, which was institutionalised in Berlin in 1930. Just like Tetzner, they had children play for children, which in turn attracted the attention of the film industry. Incidentally, the best-known film by Stobrawa and Genschow is *Rotkäppchen und der Wolf* from 1937. In this case, as in numerous others, the manifold connections on the personal, institutional, *stoffliche* and media levels only become apparent when the stage is taken into account.

The shift of focus to the medium of theatre was forced by two genres, which produced large *Stoff* networks primarily in the children's broadcasts of radio during the researched period: the puppet theatre and the Kasperle show. At this point, the Cologne Hänneschen Theatre should be mentioned; a Cologne institution, a puppet theatre that played for children during the day and adults in the evening (cf. Lindner-Leuschner 1930) and which was also present in the children's programs of the Werag at the end of the 1920s. The radio contributions only become comprehensible and their wealth of material can only be understood if their original medium – the stage – is included in the research. The articles in the professional journals *Das Puppentheater* (1923–1931) and *Der Puppenspieler* (1931–1933), which were systematically evaluated, provide information on this.

A prominent figure in puppet theatre since the nineteenth century has been Kasperl or Kasperle. So it is not surprising that the new medium of radio also took up this *Stoff* and produced Kasperle shows. A very productive director and narrator of Kasperle shows was Liesel Simon (1887–1958), who founded the *Erstes Münchner Kasperltheater* in her Frankfurt apartment, following Pocci's tradition. Later she staged her own plays and toured Germany with them. Her productions were given a permanent slot on the Südwestdeutscher Rundfunk in Frankfurt and Deutsche Grammophon recorded 16 Kasperle plays on shellac records. The radio contributions of the authoress, who was forced out of the public eye from 1933 and went into exile in 1941, are completely unknown today, as is the connection between stage, radio and record production. Linked to the *Stoff* Kasperliaden are 44 other *Stoffe* (based on individual Kasperl stories by Pocci and others), 89 print adaptations, 18 films, 11 shellac records, 9 performances and impressive 740 radio records.

The small corpus of plays (237) and stagings (637) is far from complete, nor can it be. Above all, texts and performances that have characteristics of a media network were considered for this text. Here we were able to make a first attempt at recording, however this seems to only be possible in more detail in cooperation with theatres and small-scale research in various – also local – daily newspapers.

References

Bonn, Friedrich: Jugend und Theater. Emsdetten 1939 (Die Schaubühne; Quellen und Forschung zur Theatergeschichte; 39).
Braun, Alfred: Achtung, Achtung, hier ist Berlin! Aus der Geschichte des Deutschen Rundfunks in Berlin 1923–1932. Berlin 1968.
Dichtung und Rundfunk: Reden und Gegenreden, Verhandlungsniederschrift der Arbeitstagung „Dichtung und Rundfunk" in Kassel-Wilhelmshöhe am 30. September und 1. Oktober 1929. Berlin 1930.
Lindner-Leuschner, Hedda: Vom Wesen des Puppenspiels: Zur Wiedergeburt des Kölner Hänneschen-Theaters. In: Das Puppentheater (1930), 181–183.
Schmerling, Alice: Kind, Kino und Kinderliteratur. Eine Untersuchung zum Medienumbruch in der Kinderkultur der Kaiserzeit und der Weimarer Republik. Köln 2007.
Steiner, Anne: Klassenzimmertheater – Chance oder Hindernis für den Erwerb theatraler Rezeptionskompetenz? In: Bönninghausen, Marion/Paule, Gabriele (Hg.): Wege ins Theater: Spielen, Zuschauen, Urteilen. Berlin 2011 (Forum SpielTheaterPädagogik; 4), 141–166.
Vereinigte Deutsche Prüfungsausschüsse für Jugendschrifte (VDP) (Hg.): Verzeichnis wertvoller Spiele für die Schul- und Jugendbühne. Hamburg ^{5}1932.

Digital Explorations of Historical Media Networks

Outlines of Portal Development from an Interdisciplinary Perspective

Matthias Preis and Friedrich Summann

Introduction

There is a substantial academic dispute about a digital (re)accentuation of literary studies that shakes the conceptual foundations of familiar subject areas and methods (cf. Lauer 2019). An expansion or transformation of the philologies in the sense of Digital Humanities requires changing subject-specific basic knowledge, a considerably increased interdisciplinary openness, and last but not least: explorative courage beyond stable and proven research paths. The textual practices of *close* and *distant reading* in particular are often appropriated for less constructive polarisations in this context, whereas the gain of computational methodology undoubtedly lies in the strategic interweaving of both perspectives (cf. Schwandt 2018, 134; Weitin 2017). In a project that focuses on exceedingly complex network structures, it is obvious that conventional (analogue) methods remain limited in their scope, if only because of the sheer volume of data that needs to be handled. New strategies of investigation in the digital domain are required here.

This article describes the methodological path taken within the framework of the DFG project *Deutschsprachige Kinder- und Jugendliteratur im Medienverbund 1900–1945*, from the development of an initial metadata concept to the structural

---

M. Preis (✉)
Faculty of Linguistics and Literary Studies, German Studies, Bielefeld University, Bielefeld, Germany
e-mail: matthias.preis@uni-bielefeld.de

F. Summann
LibTec, Bielefeld University Library, Bielefeld, Germany
e-mail: friedrich.summann@uni-bielefeld.de

design of an online portal,[1] whereby, in retrospect, implementation problems that arose and corresponding approaches to solving them are also discussed. The wishes, ideas and requirements of literary studies are followed by the technical answers in the main part, which is organised as an interdisciplinary dialogue. This is followed by a discussion of concrete application scenarios which exemplarily demonstrate the methodological expansion of the field by integrating innovative and traditional perspectives. The article ends with an interdisciplinary conclusion to the project work, which was conceived as a cooperation between the German Studies of Bielefeld University and its University Library.

Goals and Challenges

The processing of historical network phenomena in the digital domain is linked to a multitude of theoretical, material-specific, and technological requirements that shape the field of conditions. Early decisions about the granularity with which data were to be recorded set the course for later observation and analysis. In this sense, they certainly constitute "an initial hermeneutic act" (Scheuermann 2016, 61), which has an impact on the procedural sequence of data *collection, processing,* and *analysis* (cf. Reiche/Becker/Bender/Munson/Schmunk/Schöch 2014, 6). A central goal of the project with regard to *data collection* is the definition of a metadata structure that meets the bibliographic requirements of the different media types on the one hand, and the complexity of their intermedial references on the other. At the same time, these structures must remain consistent with the theoretical underpinnings of the project by S. J. Schmidt.[2] Furthermore, it is necessary to enrich captured metadata sets with existing digital copies to make them publicly accessible later on, if allowed by copyright. The *preparation* of the data should allow on the one hand to feed a defined search engine environment and on the other hand to create systematics that can be connected to variable forms of visualisation. The linking of a more or less conventional catalogue search with further project-specific analysis options may be regarded as a central challenge. Finally, the *analysis* of the data should make it possible to profile media networks in their constitution, i.e. to depict multimedia expressions of a *literarischer Stoff* including all the actors involved. The simultaneous expansion of a network across diverse media forms, but also its chronological development in the chosen period of investigation 1900–1945 (as well as in individual cases beyond that) is to be made accessible. For the data pool, visualisation strategies should be pursued that allow comparisons of media networks on a quantitative and qualitative level and thus contribute, among other things, to the further development of the media network theories, which have hardly been founded

---

[1] The online portal for the project can be accessed via: http://medienverbundportal.kjl.uni-bielefeld. de (01.08.2020).
[2] Cf. the introduction to this volume.

more systematically so far. Functionally, options of an *explorative analysis* are in the foreground, which searches for "latent structures, patterns, trends, singularities or other conspicuous features" (Jannidis/Kohle/Rehbein 2017, 332) and – not least – initiates new entries into close literary hermeneutic horizons of interpretation.

From Theory to Metadata Structure

Conceptual Considerations

At the beginning of each database, the specific structural requirements are determined, which logically result from (a) the theoretical embedding of the leading research interest and (b) the expectations of the subsequent analysis possibilities including the presentation layer (search engine; visualisation). In addition, in order to ensure the best possible reusability of the data, it should be committed to basic library standards – such as the *Resource Description and Access* (RDA) rules – at least as far as the core bibliographic elements of the data sets are concerned. Furthermore, the *relational* level of the database model, which must allow the assignment of multifaceted attributes for record links, is central to media network research. Each dataset should also have the possibility to link corresponding digital copies (PDFs, TIFs, AVIs, MP3s, etc.) and to reference external URLs.

Unlike research projects that only focus on *one* type of media (e.g. print literature, images, etc.), the particular challenge in the case of the media network project is to define individual data structures for different forms of media representation. The following were distinguished as *media offers* in the sense of S. J. Schmidt (2008a, 2012): *Primary literature, secondary literature, film, radio, theatre, image, record, TV* and *advertising material*.[3] The unifying core element is the *literarische Stoff*, which as a purely schematic reference point does not itself contain any media-specific characteristics. The various actors in the media systems were arranged as the object type *person,* institutions or organisations (broadcasters, distributors, etc.) as *corporate bodies.*

The sometimes very different media-specific modes of *production, distribution, reception,* and *post processing*[4] require a metadata structure that does justice to these characteristics without losing a minimum of descriptive conformity. Therefore, basic *publication* data were to be included across all media (Fig. 1, item 1), such as title, subtitle, overall title, origin or publication details (e.g. place, publisher, date), edition notes and the count of consecutive publications. In addition, information on

---

[3] For a more detailed profile, see the introduction as well as the preceding contributions by Illies and Weber in this volume.

[4] S. J. Schmidt defines *post processing* as "all processes in which media offers are transposed into new media offers, e. g. screen adaptations of novels, the scientific analysis of daily soaps or all kinds of media critique" (Schmidt 2008b, 103).

Fig. 1 Systematics of the developed metadata set

the intended target group was provided, as far as this could be reconstructed. Furthermore, the action domains *production* and *distribution* (Fig. 1, Item 2/3) were to be depicted as nuanced as possible using suitable categories. A cross-media specification could not be taken as a basis here, since the production and distribution channels diverge greatly between film, radio, print literature, etc. as can be shown by this example: While key categories such as sales channels, censorship, etc. were to be differentiated for the distribution of films, completely different ways of distribution played a role in radio broadcasting, for example in the form of parallel broadcasts across several radio stations or other patterns of multiple exploitation. The granularity of the data in the area of *publication* was also naturally divergent: Whereas in the case of radio broadcasting, detailed broadcasting data of the first publication (date/time/duration of broadcasting) were available via programme booklet, in the case of *print* or *film,* it was generally necessary to operate much more blurrily at the level of the *year of publication*. The heterogeneity of the data generated in this way was to necessitate various abstraction and normalisation processes in data preparation at a later stage (cf. the function of the timeline in the section *Search Engine Environment and Visualisation*).

Extended descriptive metadata were collected for the *content-related* and *formal characteristics* of a media offer by means of the *description* section (Fig. 1, Item 4): On the content level, a genre classification, a meaningful keywording and an optional content description should be considered here. As far as available in programme booklets, announcements, or similar, detailed programme information – more so in the case of radio – was also transcribed verbatim. The *formal characteristics* supplement the descriptive data set with information on the technical nature of the media offers; they range from information on the audio and image technology to the material nature (film duration, font size, image dimensions, etc.).

In contrast, the rubric for the relational dimensioning of the data structure, the category *network*, can be thought of as homogeneous across media (Fig. 1, Item 5): The link to the *literarischer Stoff* as the neuralgic point of each media network was initially constitutive here. A further field serves the free linking to any data record or object type, whereby the relation can be provided with an attribute and, if necessary, specified with regard to concrete reference points (e.g. page numbers). The attributes used to identify relations – e.g. original *literary source, review,* etc. – should initially be bidirectionally differentiated, i.e. distinguished between outward and return directions (also terminologically). However, this concept could not be implemented consistently in view of the volume and complexity of the network data, so that preference was given to simple relationing. The *persons* involved in a media offer also belong to the category *network*, whose roles were to be identified by means of a flexibly expandable taxonomy (author, director, illustrator, etc.). The same applies to the related *corporate bodies*, whereby the spectrum of possible institutional functions (theatre, broadcaster, publisher, etc.) had to be tailored to the different media offers or object types.

Schmidt's domain of *reception* was conceptually integrated into a free *commentary* field (Fig. 1, Item 6); thematically relevant documents of the time were also addressed via literature references or linked digital copies in the *references* section. In addition to the possibility of linking relevant titles of *secondary literature*, the latter contains an option for comprehensive *source citation*. Furthermore, *external links* with title and URL can be entered. The *media library*, which is also integrated here, offers the possibility of storing unlimited image, text, and sound documents in various formats (Fig. 1, Item 7). The copyright status of any written documents, film excerpts and sound recordings can be documented via a description field available for each file. For subsequent public or internal access to the portal, such administrative markings proved to be indispensable due to any copyrights that may still be in force.

An important requirement for the software implementation was the flexible handling of taxonomies, i.e. the lists of terms for roles, functions, relationships, etc., which were to be supplemented and modified by the academic project staff as needed during data entry. For many fields, the option of making multiple entries in the form of repeat fields was also desired, for example with regard to persons involved, source information and comments, but especially links to other media or object types. In this context, automatic backlinking played an important role in regarding the density of intermedial references. If, for example, a novel was identified as a *literary model* inspiring a film adaptation, this should automatically be evident not only in the data record of the novel, but also of the film, in order to exclude double referencing in the input process. A special feature with regard to the area of *print* (primary and secondary) was the requirement to implement a basic import function in order to transfer existing records from catalog data via *Citavi* (CSV or BibTex format) individually or grouped into the project pool.

A further tool that turned out to be indispensable for the input environment was a search function with freely configurable facets. This was intended to enable targeted access to entered data along the lines of titles, *literarischer Stoff*, media types, publication dates, etc., but also with regard to administrative framework data such as creation date, modification date or last editor(s) of a data record. With the increasing complexity of the data pool, the need to set up an automated duplicate check became apparent – conversely, the option of duplicating any data sets in order to speed up the entry of related issues/broadcasts, serial formats, etc. was also taken into account.

The outlined metadata structure was a priori fully assembled for all media and object types. Nevertheless, countless modifications and additions only found their way in the course of computational implementation. The close interlocking of literary and information science perspectives turned out to be interdisciplinarily challenging and laborious, but also very fruitful. Even at the level of data entry, sufficient space had to be given to a constant process of equilibration between desirability and feasibility, as an insight into the software implementation strategy illustrates.

Technical Realisation

In the early conceptual phase of the project, several potential system environments for the technical implementation were discussed and examined in more detail. An important aspect of this evaluation was that the resources for the technical infrastructure were calculated in a comparatively manageable way, partly because existing system components were to be used. This work package is the responsibility of the University Library, which has built up broad expertise in the area of digital tools and applications in the context of various projects and undertakings – certainly related to the topic of Digital Humanities. In particular this includes the areas of *digitisation of bibliographic objects, search technologies, research data management* as well as *data preparation* and *presentation*. In the conceptual and start-up phase, the UB's digitisation platform (based on the *Goobi* software used for this purpose)[5] was envisaged as the technical environment, providing a presentation interface for digital media based on a comprehensive bibliographic metadata format (MODS) and also allowing configurable data capture. On closer examination, however, it did not seem realistic to map the rapidly evolving metadata format requirements within a reasonable scope. In addition to the digitisation platform, the UB's publication management system[6] was also examined – especially since this application was developed in an international development partnership (with the Lund and Ghent University Libraries) and thus appropriate know-how for flexible adaptations is available. This option was also discarded, as the requirements for restructuring the interface for data capture and the underlying metadata format would have meant considerable development effort over and above the configuration. Taking these preliminary considerations into account, the *Drupal* system[7] was then considered in more detail, which the Bielefeld University Library uses in Digital Humanities projects (in the fields of sociology and history) for similar requirements. In this context, technical system knowledge and the necessary experience for configuration, operation and adaptations have been built up, which can be re-used. In the end, the free definition of the acquisition schema and the broad spectrum of configuration and extension possibilities were decisive for the decision in favour of *Drupal*. Regarding the technical infrastructure, *Drupal* was used along a wide range of functions:

---

[5] Cf. https://www.intranda.com/digiverso/goobi (20.03.2020).
[6] Cf. https://pub.uni-bielefeld.de (20.03.2020).
[7] Cf. https://www.drupal.org (20.03.2020).

- Web-based data collection
- Design of the database structure (relational *MySQL* database in the background)
- Definition of media and object types and their attribute structure, including flexibly adaptable conceptual taxonomies
- Design of the input interface (to support the data entry process)
- Implementation of numerous *Drupal* add-on modules to meet the complex requirements of the project

The wide range of optional modules that can be installed proved to be particularly important here. These modules can be used to process special requirements and came into focus as needed during the course of the project. These include the additions of *Search, Biblio, Taxonomy, Backlinks, Entity Reference, Autocomplete, Feed Import, Multifield, Node Clone, Unique Field,* and a variety of other solutions for specific tasks. Throughout the course of the project, additional installations were made due to the literary research team's desire to expand the application options. For example, the *Biblio* module handles the collection of bibliographic metadata, while *Backlinks* allows display and retrieval of backlinks. *Node Clone* supports copying of existing records for efficient re-recording of similar sentence contents and *Unique Field* allows duplicate checking based on defined fields.

Both the *Drupal* base system and the add-on modules require extensive configuration activities. The adaptations of the *Autocomplete* module, which offers relevant data records for linking during input via automatic completion – whereby further attributes for distinguishing similar target records should be displayed in addition to the suggested key term – proved to be particularly complex. Support for the automatic import of metadata on radio broadcasts, which had initially been entered using a literature management program (*Citavi*) in the initial phase of the project, also required considerable time resources. A comparatively complex solution had to be developed for the highly diverse data schema of this object type in particular: *Citavi* export records were imported by means of a programmed script simulating the manual input and thus the complex data structure in *Drupal*. Since the complete HTML form structure and the *Drupal* access control had to be taken into account, the implementation was not trivial. A fundamental configuration problem that also had to be overcome was the web limitations for the parameter transfer of form data – in view of the sometimes very extensive description data, e.g. in the case of film data sets, the system sometimes reached its limits here.

As described, the core functionality of the *Drupal* system consists in the collection of data; special attention to detail is paid to the existing relations between the media network objects. With the help of web-based input forms, the design of which has been defined with *Drupal*, the project staff manually record the metadata of the media network objects. These are stored and are thus available for internal and external further processing. A database dump (relational backend: *PostgreSQL*) serves as the endpoint of the data collection based on *Drupal*, which makes the collected metadata available for further processing. The dump is generated early in the morning by a daily cronjob, and the file is transferred to the search engine environment with a subsequent copy process to serve as the basis for all further requirements of the final presentation layer (interface for research, analysis, etc.).

Search Engine Environment and Visualisation

Conceptual Considerations

In the course of the project, it turned out that the conceptual work on a scientifically goal-oriented user interface was more resource-intensive than originally assumed. It was possible to draw on the library's proven expertise, especially in the area of the search engine environment. One challenge, however, was not only to adapt existing approaches, but also to develop completely new ones, especially in the area of network visualisation, with quite limited personnel resources. The ritualised interdisciplinary exchange between the project participants proved to be an experimental process that repeatedly opened up new perspectives on the data material, even though it was undoubtedly necessary to accept erroneous paths.

From the perspective of literary studies, a basic search engine environment that enables text research within the framework of a conventional OPAC functionality was essential. This includes a global full-text search as well as a focused search for titles, persons, and years of publication. In addition to the media type (incl. *literarischer Stoff*), further specifics had to be addressable as selectable criteria (e.g.: film technique, genre, etc.), so that the search results could be focused on specific typed of media if required. New research horizons were opened up by the subsequently implemented option of searching not only for manifest records, but also for their specific relation. Furthermore, the generated result list of short titles should be able to be limited via faceting, whereby, among other things, the numerical distribution of the search results to publication years and different media types appears to be relevant. Clicking on a selected short title provides insight into the full record – including external references, digital attachments from the media library, and other references or comments that accompany each record entered via *Drupal*. A simple navigation function for the short display (forward, back, start, end) allows cursory browsing of more extensive result lists.

The described metadata search functions are sufficient as long as only the typical RDA core elements, i.e. basic descriptive data in short or individual view, are to be displayed. Person- and corporate bodies-related links can also be integrated and displayed without any problems. However, when it comes to the representation of the often complex intermedial network structures, the mere text representation – also in the form of conceivable hypertexts – reaches its limits. Therefore, a visualisation strategy had to be developed that combines textual information and graphical elements in such a way that users can switch as easily as possible between the big picture of the entire network and the insight into more detailed individual title information.

First drafts quickly revealed the core problem of this project: Unlike visualisations of network data, such as those presented in the research of correspondence networks (cf. Biehl/Lorenz/Osierenski 2015), the social network analysis of literary figures (cf. Dimpel 2018), or the representation of intertextual references (cf. Schubert 2018) in the Digital Humanities, the particular challenge was to accommodate a relatively large amount of text in graphic elements (ellipses, circles, etc.). As an example, it was essential to provide the complete title or the names of the persons – especially in the case of film productions, this was made more difficult by the fact that the number of persons involved (actors etc.) could quickly move into the higher double-digit range. A hybrid display of text and image elements inevitably reaches its limits here, even with sophisticated zoom functionality.

The approach ultimately pursued resulted from a change of perspective, as is known in a related way from the functionality of the online map service *Google Maps*: Instead of looking at the network from an Olympic position – as known from topography – this specific strategy was developed in order to enter the network, so to speak. *Google Maps* allows the analogous procedure by placing the so-called *Yellow Man* on the map and thus switching to the subjective view of the *Street View*. The next streets or connections are now visible from the first-person perspective, as it were, but no longer the network in its complex entirety (Fig. 2).

The *media network navigator* designed in this way acts from any starting point and displays all entries linked to this centre, grouped according to different object or media types.[8] The central circle and the facets in the periphery provide sufficient

Fig. 2 Analogy of perspectives: *Google Street View* and *media network navigator* (Map data © 2020 Google and © 2020 Geo-Basis-DE/BKG)

---

[8] Each object type has been assigned a color that is used consistently in the different display modes of the portal: Stoff (light orange); Film (light green); Theatre (dark green); TV (aquamarine); Image (light blue); Corporate bodies (dark blue); Print primary (orange); Print secondary (dark orange); Radio (red); Record (dark red); Advertising material (light purple); Person (purple).

(text) space to display meaningful bibliographical information (title, publication date, author, etc.). The view is complemented by a text box placed on the side, which displays further details of the respective central data set. Analogous to the street network in *Google Street View*, it is now possible to flexibly navigate within the media network: If, for example, one is interested in the corresponding film productions based on a certain *literarischer Stoff*, one first selects the corresponding (light green) group facet *Film* (Fig. 2), whereupon all relevant films are listed in the periphery. If one now clicks on the facet of a concrete film dataset, it moves to the center and the periphery instantly adapts to the selected film title – i.e., it shows media types, persons, etc. that are linked to this dataset; the information in the text box also updates. The specific relation between the center and the periphery, for example between a film and a linked secondary text, is displayed on the fly as one moves the mouse over the individual facets (e.g. as a *review, scientific essay, reference,* etc.; Fig. 3).

The media network navigator thus combines a vertical and a horizontal movement logic: Vertically, the periphery switches between the grouped overview view (i.e. the 'drawers' for linked media types, persons, corporate bodies, etc.) and the listing of concrete data records for a selected type (corresponding to an 'open drawer', e.g. all data records in the *Theatre* tab) while the centre remains constant. Horizontally, if there is a large number of links of the same object type, it is possible to scroll through the results using the dark grey navigation arrows. Since the display of the navigator only offers twelve facets, automatic subgroups have also been implemented here in the case of very high numbers of links – for example, sorting by year, alphabet, or person roles.

With the chosen strategy, the high complexity of the media network structures could be reduced, and an intuitive, targeted development of the individual networks was made possible. This was achieved at the cost of an orienting overall perspective, for example with regard to the very important temporal-historical development dynamics. Consequently, the navigator had to be extended by a kind of timeline that depicts complex temporal progression structures – variable characteristics of the

Fig. 3 Text box with record display (partial view) and media network navigator

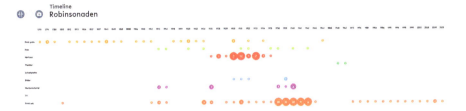

Fig. 4 Timeline representation using the example of *Robinsonades*

different media types should be comprehensible at a glance. From the multitude of possible timeline tools and visualisation techniques, the choice fell on a *bubble chart,* which differentiates on the Y-axis according to media types and along the X-axis unfolds the period under investigation in annual numbers (Fig. 4). The radius of the plotted circles reflects the number of media offers per year. Publication frequencies can thus be seen very vividly across all types of media and also over longer development periods. If the publication dates of relevant publications lie beyond the period under investigation – think of the Grimm's fairy tales as a popular reference point – the years in question are appended directly to the left or right. A *fold function* optionally ensures that years without any medial manifestation of a *literarischer Stoff* disappear from the timeline, i.e., a folding or compression of the timeline takes place. Intermedial development dynamics with larger temporal gaps (latency periods) thus become much easier to understand in terms of pattern analysis. On the software side, a graphical *snapshot option* was also desired: once timelines had been created for a *literarischer Stoff*, it should be possible to download and archive them as a high-resolution PNG file.

The timeline function is necessarily *centred* towards the *literarischer Stoff*, i.e. it can only be called up from the navigator if a selected *Stoff* is the focus. An integration of the perspectives – i.e. the *spatial aspect* (navigator) and the *temporal aspect* (timeline) – is provided by the individual *bubbles* in the timeline view: If one selects one of the colour circles via mouse click, the display switches back to the navigator, which now shows all manifestations of the *literarischer Stoff* for the selected coordinates of *publication year* and *media type* in the periphery. In the case of the advertising materials, a special mouse-over function is also integrated, which takes into account the media heterogeneity of this object type: If the mouse touches one of the purple-colored circle shapes, the internal distribution across different advertising materials (print, film, fan articles, etc.) is displayed in the form of a small pie chart. In this way, the field of advertising remains distinguished from genuine adaptations such as film or radio play versions but does not lose its media diversity.

In addition to the explorative core elements described above, further statistical, and bibliographic functions were developed for the portal that shed light on other (partial) aspects of the media networks. A kind of network-specific footprint could be vividly realised by means of *Stoff*-related *donut diagrams* (Fig. 5). Here, the medial spectrum of a media network is illustrated in colour in terms of percentage distribution – in addition, the absolute figures are given in brackets behind each

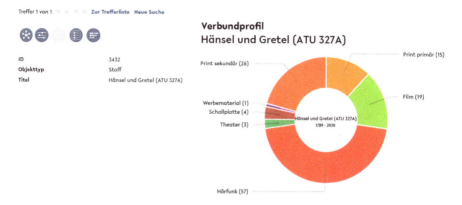

Fig. 5 Media network profile in the donut diagram

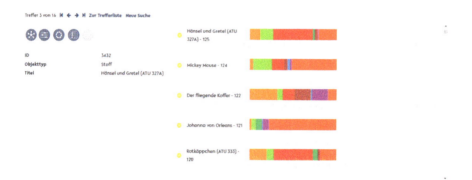

Fig. 6 Ranking of the media networks (excerpt)

media type, whereby all manifestations (if applicable, also beyond the focused period of investigation 1900–1945) are taken into account. A second global perspective is provided by a *ranking of the media networks* (Fig. 6): All included *Stoffe* are sorted here according to the total number of links (excluding persons and corporate bodies). The multicoloured bars indicate, in a laterally staggered form, the shares of the different media types in the network. The individual relations as well as their media-specific facets can be addressed directly from the list or examined more closely via a link using the navigator.

Another additional function relates exclusively to the area of persons, which, like corporate bodies, was not considered in detail in the primarily media-oriented statistics: For each person registered in the database, a *list of publications* can be automatically output, which appears to be faceted according to media type and also lists the respective role of the person (author, producer, etc.). Here, too, there is a direct link to the navigator from each individual data record, i.e. the specified individual publications can be easily classified in the context of their intermedial connections.

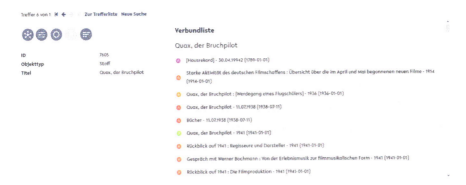

Fig. 7 Chronological network list for *Quax, der Bruchpilot* (excerpt)

One specific variant of this list function is the chronological output of all publications that have been published across all media on a particular *Stoff*. Due to the different granularity of the data (cf. above; year of publication vs. date/time of broadcast), the accuracy of the order is limited here. Nevertheless, on the basis of the existing data, the successive development of a media network is documented very systematically (Fig. 7). As is generally the case on all visualisation levels, the individual entries are colour-coded at the beginning, which allows for quick assignment to the different media types even in cursory reading.

The combined access of the display modes *navigator, timeline,* as well as the different list and overview functions, allow a research practice that versatily switches between micro and macro perspective. In this context, the explored intermedial references are per se initially no *more* than intermediate results that enter into the overall process of *scalable reading* (cf. Mueller 2012; Weitin 2017), i.e. illustrate complex connections, reveal (un)expected dynamics, indicate a need for further specification, in short: trigger new ways and processes of knowledge via fruitful irritations (cf. Schwandt 2018, 125). Some possible *application scenarios* for media network research will be outlined in this sense in the section of the same name. First, however, the information technology background of the search engine environment and the visualisation concept should be examined in more detail.

Technical Realisation

The data collection by means of the *Drupal* system and its differentiated configuration options have already been explained in detail above. The database dump listed there as the endpoint of the *Drupal* domain serves as the basis for all further processing and preparation processes. First, it is used to transfer the data from the SQL export format to the JSON file required for indexing with the help of a crosswalk script. For the flat field structures and the taxonomy values, the implementation using a mapping table is comparatively simple. The processing of the complex

Fig. 8 Data flow from acquisition to visualisation

network fields with hierarchical structures is more challenging, as they have to be converted into a suitable format in preparation for indexing with respect to the index structure. At this point, it is also advisable to think about the data structures required for the display at record level and to implement an efficient delivery of the data records in the presentation layer. A concrete example of this is the internal list of link records, which is supplemented with relevant field contents of the target record (title, record ID, media type, link type, publication date) for each entry; conversely, the corresponding backward links must also be taken into account here. In addition, steps are already taken in the script at this stage to support complex individual aspects of the later data visualisation. For example, the timeline data matrix is calculated from the linkage information of media type and publication year and stored with the record for efficient visualisation. Also a list of link frequencies of media types finds its early form here to generate the mentioned network profile as a donut diagram from it. The aim of this strategy is to keep the necessary data complete at the record level, if possible, and thus to largely avoid data supplementation by reloading from the index.

In concrete terms, the data flow from the *Drupal* system to the visual presentation of the data runs via a multi-stage combination of search index and JavaScript framework (Fig. 8): The collected data are exported from the *Drupal* environment as a database dump and prepared for indexing via script. The *Catmandu* framework employed by the Bielefeld University Library is then used to produce a *Lucene* index from the extracted metadata, which serves as the entry point for using the database and thus provides a web-based search and navigation environment. The display of search results (for list and single hits) is flexibly defined via HTML templates. For the single record display, in addition to the textual output of the metadata, a JavaScript framework for data presentation (*D3.js = Data-Driven Documents*)[9] is also integrated at this point, which controls the dynamic visual animations in the browser.

The entire provision of the technical infrastructure makes use of the expertise that has been built up over a longer period of time in the Bielefeld University Library

---

[9] Cf. https://d3js.org (20.03.2020).

in the fields of *bibliographic search environments* and *research data management*, and which will be reused in this environment. The three pillars of the implementation, *Drupal* (data acquisition), *Catmandu* framework (data preparation and search technology) and the *D3.js* framework (especially with a focus on visualisation) have already been used in other project contexts at the Bielefeld University Library. Therefore, a solid basis of expertise was available for the numerous necessary additions and adaptations. Figure 9 shows the individual layers of the technical infrastructure (column 1), the techniques used (column 2) and the requirements for the technical effort required by the Bielefeld University Library (column 3); the type of expertise required for the individual steps can be seen directly with this.

For the *search index* and the web-based search environment, the University Library uses the *Catmandu* framework. This is a program library based on *Lucene* and *Elasticsearch*, which has been further developed by Bielefeld University Library in cooperation with Lund and Ghent University Libraries since 2010. In particular, the *Catmandu* API is used as a programming interface for the flexible configuration and creation of a search engine index. At the same time, it served the goal of creating a universal production and presentation environment with the help of which individually adapted search environments for text-oriented databases can be set up. On the one hand, the tool makes it possible to define a suitable index structure from the data format generated during data transfer and thus to load existing metadata into the index. On the other hand, the framework conditions of an end user interface for the KJL media network database are specified. For this purpose, the predefined data format is used to display the field contents via template. Thereby the index data for the result records are provided in a complex record structure and can be used in combination with control statements and HTML definitions. The *BES* search environment provides a mixture of search mask, short title, and single record display with navigation support, which also offers additional functions such as sorting, faceting, marking of records, export, and citation engine integration. In previous usage scenarios, only text-based, bibliographic databases were created

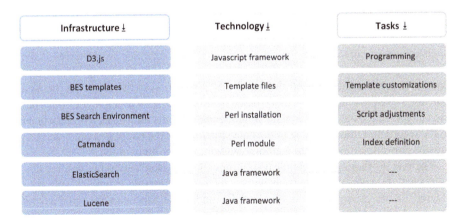

Fig. 9 Technical infrastructure and requirement areas

with this database environment. In the case of the KJL media network data, however, it became apparent early on that, in addition to these basic functions, an extension in the direction of a multi-layered visualisation of network structures, including a navigation environment, would have to be created. Visualisation techniques played a role in various IT contexts of the University Library, mostly to perform and present evaluations for infrastructures. After various preliminary tasks in the past with different software packages, in recent years work has been executed with *D3.js* in particular, so extensive expertise could be built up for this technology. *D3.js* is a widely used open-source JavaScript framework that provides numerous functions and countless, well-documented, reusable application examples for the use of SVG resources in the HTML5 context.

The user interface was created on the basis of this technical infrastructure. The text-based search options are implemented via two search masks: on the one hand, a simple search slot for a search across all fields and, on the other hand, an advanced search mask that addresses selected index fields (title, author, year of publication, media type, relation, etc.; cf. above) separately. Vocabulary-based fields such as the media type or the relation (i.e. the link attribute) are supported for use via a drop-down menu. The transition between the basic *search* functions, including *results display*, and *navigation* is triggered from the single hit display. The field contents from the index for the respective record are provided internally in their entirety during the template call and are thus available for text box output as well as for the labelling of graphical elements, for example. The bibliographic text information (title, authors, year of publication, etc.) is generated as static HTML code via template and output as a result list in the left sub-block. The result display is supplemented by the selection of facets of individual index fields, which are used for targeted result filtering (*search refinement*).

For the detailed single record display, the bibliographic description takes place in the left block (text box) in the form of a list output of the relevant fields. For the right block, which contains in particular the visualization elements such as navigator and timeline display (Fig. 3), the JavaScript source code is defined in the template. This controls the graphical display and also implements the dynamic actions in the browser, such as changing sections of the timeline display including the *fold/unfold* function, or the mouse-over technique used. For the implementation, numerous open-source examples were reused and adapted, for example in the case of the donut diagrams for the display of network-specific distributions (Fig. 5). As outlined above, the database from the search index prepared in the course of the data transfer is used to output the number-based information, such as number of links per media type, in the navigator or in the timeline matrix. This information is predefined in the record and thus available in the data structure for the template output and can thus be converted directly into a graphic without further preparation.

There is no shortage of technical solutions for the visualisation of complex networks based on very different frameworks and tools. Numerous examples were considered in the project context – especially under the aspect of resource-saving derivation of a mature solution that should meet the requirements to a high degree. A important premise was that the respective implementation had to be in line with the given technical infrastructure and the existing expertise. From a technical point of view, the preferred implementation is therefore primarily pragmatic and functionally conceived. For example, standard graphic elements such as circles, circle sections or rectangles are used to illustrate the navigation universe. The number of link levels shown in each case is limited to two (center vs. periphery in Fig. 2), and further connections are opened up by the navigation function realised via link, which makes use of link information stored at record level and thus is directly available. Standard techniques such as mouse-over and tooltips are used to display and hide additional information for the viewer on the fly. In the case of the list of works and the list of media networks (Figs. 6 and 7), the record level is not sufficient. Therefore, additional index queries have to be used to collect the required information, evaluate it, and then add it to the output. The media network ranking list analyses all records of the object type *literarischer Stoff* in the database – as this step takes some (computing) time, an up-to-date list is generated daily early in the morning for performance reasons, which can then be displayed on a daily basis.

From the implementation perspective, an extensive system environment emerged in the course of the project, which was permanently further developed based on existing expertise. While at the beginning the focus was on the requirements for the data structure and its implementation in the input forms during data entry, the discussions shifted towards the presentation layer in the course of development. Especially in the crucial area of data visualisation, the chosen mixture of search technology and JavaScript applications has resulted in a flexible implementation environment that allows far-reaching possibilities for subsequent use. The expertise gathered will, and this is also a strong motivation for the University Library's commitment, have a positive impact on other digital services and can support future offerings (not only) in the Digital Humanities. Finally, some application-oriented scope is outlined by means of three highlight-like usage scenarios in the portal environment.

Application Scenarios

The tools provided by the portal for the exploration of media networks open up a wide spectrum of analysis and search strategies. Often, a well thought out combination of the different access methods is required in order to set up the search in a target-oriented way or simply to roam through the network(s) unsystematically (according to the serendipity principle). Typical application patterns that have proven themselves in the course of this project work as well as portal development include:

(Un)conventional Search Queries

In the most common case, the search function is used to quickly find specific *literarische Stoffe*, media offers, persons, or corporate bodies. By faceting the results, even extensive lists can be quickly narrowed down and focused, for example with regard to selected years of publication, individual types of media, etc. (cf. above). However, it can also be informative to search *without* entering any specific titles, persons, or years of publication: if one leaves all text fields blank and select only one object type from the drop-down menu – for example, *film* – the list of results shows all film entries in the database, whereby the distribution across the different years of publication is directly visible. If you decide on a specific record, the display switches to the navigator view and shows the corresponding film title in its network structure. The hit list of the original search is always stored and can be addressed in the background. This results in the option of moving along the search results directly in the navigator view by means of superordinate arrow keys: Visually, this is very impressive in that the outer, colourful facets of the navigator display show changing activation patterns depending on the film title and the degree of media networking (Fig. 10). It goes without saying that result lists for *Stoffe*, primary literature, radio broadcasts etc. can be explored in an analogous way. The guiding principle here is the roaming view of network-specific distribution patterns – with a simultaneous view of the complete title data and the possibility of going into individual networks in greater depth via the navigator as required.

A special feature of the search function is that it not only searches for manifest data records of various object types, but also brings the *relations* between these data records into play. If, for example, one searches for all *literary film adaptations* in the period under investigation, one obtains the corresponding overview via the combination of *object type/film* and *relation/literary original*. This procedure can easily be transferred to other questions and enables very interesting, sometimes quite unusual perspectives on the plurimedial corpus. Conceivable combinations would be, for example, all *reviews* of *radio programmes,* all recorded *illustrators* for *print literature,* all *announcements* for *films,* etc. A flexible restriction of the search via additional information in individual text fields (title etc.) is of course possible. – It

Fig. 10 Advanced search and cursory network view

becomes apparent in such a flexibilisation of the search function that it is not only suitable for answering existing questions via research, but also for generating *new* questions for the corpus.

Double Perspectives with Timeline and Navigator

The presentation modes of the online portal have different strengths and weaknesses and should therefore be thought of as complementary in their application. The *navigator* shows intermedial links quasi up close, offers the complete information of all data sets and also shows the individual relations in the network – but it is hardly able to adequately depict temporal dynamics. The *timeline* cannot offer complex relations and nuanced data set information, but it does profile intermedial expansion movements, agglomerations, latency times of a network, and much more. If we look at the timeline for the media network of *Schneewittchen* (Fig. 11) as an example, we can understand how such dynamic network profiles are to be read and – much more importantly - what analytical search movements they trigger:

Of course, the timeline is readable in a media-specific way, i.e. line by line. In the case of the very popular fairy tale *Stoff*, for example, the large number of printed editions from the early editions at the beginning of the nineteenth century, initially still under the title *Sneewittchen* or *Schneeweißchen* (1812), through various illustrated editions to dramatised versions, becomes recognisable. The frequencies for theatrical or film performances of the fairy tale can also be quickly surveyed, as far as they were accessible to research. In the case of radio, it is very clear that the *literarischer Stoff* found its way onto the radio almost immediately after the start of German broadcasting in October 1923 and remained prominently represented there for the next few years with remarkable consistency. In the years 1934–1939, with a slight decline in radio presence, numerous film and theatre performances were added; the print sector also continued to be active, and sporadic advertising materials were recorded. The most striking aspect is certainly the immense increase in references from the area of *secondary literature,* which in a broader sense includes announcements, reviews in relevant (programme) magazines, but also in daily newspapers, for example. The navigator provides very concrete information on the media offers discussed; at the same time, however, in many cases it also makes it

Fig. 11 Media network of *Schneewittchen* in the timeline view

possible to view corresponding documents directly as digital copies by means of internal and external links (holdings of the Bielefeld University Library, DNB, etc.). The reason for the activity from the mid-1930s onwards quickly becomes apparent: a Walt Disney film of 2 million Marks is announced in the *Film-Kurier* of 2 December 1936 for the following year, and the length of the film is also already known: "about 2200 m" (Ein Walt Disney-Film für 2 Mio. Mark 1936, 3). In the following year, the year of release, one comes across the corrected and supplemented key data for the film: There is now talk of "3 million Marks" production costs, of "570 draftsmen", "230,000 drawings" and a numinous consumption of paper sheets "in a total length of 556 English miles" ("Schneewittchen" in Hollywood aus der Taufe aufgehoben 1937, 3). A few weeks later Klaus Mann will have his say from Hollywood and report on the "delightful perspectives" of Disney's aesthetic, on "effects of a completely undreamed-of kind": "What landscapes there are [...] to discover: grotesque, haunting, wild, enchanted landscapes: E. T. A. Hoffmann landscapes, Kubin landscapes, surreal regions." (Mann 1938, 3)

With just three *clicks*, this example bridges the gap between *distant viewing* and *close reading* and allows us to explore (in a form that is at best only hinted at here) the overarching dynamics of media development, technical production conditions, and aesthetic effects in their interconnection. Visualisation functions primarily as a coordinate system or navigational instrument that supports a targeted *zoom-in* or *zoom-out* and thus opens up new perspectives on the literary action system.

Media Networks in Profile

With regard to a systematisation of theory building, there is still a lot to be done in media network research. In the meantime, various approaches of very different provenance are available, which are dedicated to the development dynamics and/or typologisation of media networks.[10] Up to now, there has been a lack of possibilities to compare a larger number of networks with each other in order to gain new insights into media distribution mechanisms – beyond the canonically used current examples from the *Matrix* to *Harry Potter* to *Star Wars,* the *Pokémon, Superman* and *Maya the Bee.* The tools provided in the portal can facilitate this work, although they are no substitute for a detailed analysis of transmedial impact and transformation processes. The timeline representation already discussed in detail above enables pattern analyses in which the temporal expansion of media networks can be read. Dynamics of snowball-like growth (original medium, then successive transmedial dissemination) potentially become just as apparent as the concerted onset of transmedial network structures (simultaneous plurimedial origin; cf. Ryan 2013, 363). The granularity of the representation here cannot exceed the *annual* scaling due to the available publication data. However, if the also available network list in text form is added, the chronology of events – for example with regard to individual

---

[10] For an overview, see the introduction in this volume.

radio broadcasts, theatre performances, advertisements, etc. – can be further sharpened. In order to trace interactions in the network in a more nuanced way, however, the concrete relations must be researched in *each individual case* or reconstructed on the basis of available digital copies. Even in the case of a simple literary adaptation, this can – assuming several text versions of a *literarischer Stoff* exist – quickly require more extensive research work, which could at best be carried out on an exemplary basis during data entry. In this respect, the portal holds considerable transmedial treasures that still need to be exploited by the research community.

Another interesting perspective on overall networks is opened up by the portal's modes of presentation, which are by their very nature summative: the above-mentioned *ranking* not only provides (numerical) insight into the degree of interweaving of a media network, it also relates its quantitative and qualitative profile – on the one hand, in that neighbours of similar size serve as a historical comparative foil in the list, and on the other hand, in that the internal media structure of the networks is depicted in contrast by means of a stack diagram. While, for example, one of the front-runners, *Funkheinzelmann*, as an originally serial radio format, draws around two-thirds of its medial spectrum from this area and shows manifold references to theatre, print and advertising, an equally popular *Stoff* such as *Sherlock Holmes* relies primarily on print media manifestations, film, and numerous advertising texts. The comparison brings to light the complementary constitution of the networks here: the *Funheinzelmann* recognisably avoids the cinematic domain, *Sherlock Holmes* does not appear in the radio in the period under investigation – apart from a singular exception on 22 May 1929. Corresponding differences can also quite strikingly be seen in the footprint of the networks by means of a donut diagram (Fig. 5). It is obvious that a macro/meta analysis of corresponding distribution patterns enables new approaches for the typological differentiation of network phenomena. In these early forms, the focus is likely to be on the dynamics of different leading media, cross-media actors, advertising-strategic multiplication, and much more.

Summary

The interdisciplinary cooperation within the framework of the DFG project *Deutschsprachige Kinder- und Jugendliteratur im Medienverbund 1900–1945* was a challenging and constructive process in which a common vocabulary had to be found over time. The constant balancing of literary studies and information technology perspectives set limits, but at the same time expanded the horizons of both sides. The impact of digital forms of structuring and visualisation in literary studies is *not* limited to the (welcome) facilitation of quantifying procedures – rather, the explorative impulse of the project work contributes to the development of fundamentally different research questions than the established ones (cf. Herrmann/Lauer 2018, 131). The dynamics of the digital research process – similar to the sometimes intricate constitution of its object – tend to be branched and recursive rather than linear: if, for example, deficits in the metadata schema suddenly become apparent and thus meaningful at the level of visualisation, or if unexpected findings emerge in the data entry that run counter to the existing category system, the project coordinates may need to be readjusted quickly at several levels. Such a procedure demands flexibility and a high level of tolerance regarding frustration from all participants; however, one is rewarded with an increasingly accurate, valid, and multifaceted development of the subject field.

Perspectively, the preliminary work outlined in the article can be followed up in some respects: In the sense of the broadest possible reusability, an extensive export function of selected (partial) corpora would be desirable. The output of individual or combined media networks in a *GEPHI*-compatible format could also be implemented, thus providing a flexible visualisation functionality as an alternative to the timeline or navigator function, for example. The feeding in of publicly accessible digitised material is likely to be an ongoing task due to copyright issues. In the long term, the direct availability of preserved primary works (books and articles in full text, films, etc.) should be considered, so that the navigator can potentially be used for *close reading* of these texts and media. With regard to further research on media networks *after 1945,* the existing metadata scheme should be used as a central heuristic. The paradigmatically changing media practices in the twentieth century, especially with regard to television, the Internet, etc., promise to modulate the topography of network research once again.

What Felix Stalder identifies as one of the main characteristics of digitisation, the "multiplication of cultural possibilities" (Stalder 2016, 10), also applies to *scientific* possibilities and the Digital Humanities. The field is wide, the approach at times somewhat tentative, and it does not always seem predictable "how questions, methodology, and subject area relate to one another" (Herrmann/Lauer 2018, 148). This article hopes to have shown that this uncertainty can be a *productive* one – especially regarding the concern to continue the explorative spirit of the project in a larger research community with the public launch of the online portal.

References

Primary Literature

Grimm, Jacob/Grimm, Wilhelm: Sneewittchen (Schneeweißchen). In: Dies.: Kinder- und Haus-Märchen. Gesammelt durch die Brüder Grimm, Bd. 1. Berlin: Realschulbuchhandlung, 1812, 156–163.

Secondary Literature Before 1945

Ein Walt Disney-Film für 2 Millionen Mark. In: Film-Kurier 18 (1936) 282 vom 02.12., 3.
Mann, Klaus: Walt Disneys „Schneewittchen". In: Pariser Tageszeitung (1938) vom 16.01., 3.
„Schneewittchen" in Hollywood aus der Taufe gehoben. In: Film-Kurier 19 (1937) 300 vom 27.12., 3.

Secondary Literature After 1945

Biehl, Theresia/Lorenz, Anne/Osierenski, Dirk: Exilnetz33. Ein Forschungsportal als Such- und Visualisierungsinstrument. In: Baum, Constanze/Stäcker, Thomas (Hg.): Grenzen und Möglichkeiten der Digital Humanities (2015) (Zeitschrift für digitale Geisteswissenschaften; Sonderbd. 1), DOI: https://doi.org/10.17175/sb01 (20.03.2020).
D3.js. Data-Driven Documents (2020), https://d3js.org (20.03.2020).
Dimpel, Friedrich Michael: Narratologische Textauszeichnung in Märe und Novelle. In: Bernhard, Toni/Willand, Marcus/Richter, Sandra/Albrecht, Andrea (Hg.): Quantitative Ansätze in den Literatur- und Geisteswissenschaften. Systematische und historische Perspektiven. Berlin [u. a.] 2018, 121–147.
Drupal. Open Source CMS (2020), https://www.drupal.org (20.03.2020).
Goobi. Digital Library Modules (2020), https://www.intranda.com/digiverso/goobi (20.03.2020).
Herrmann, J. Berenike/Lauer, Gerhard: Korpusliteraturwissenschaft. Zur Konzeption und Praxis am Beispiel eines Korpus zur literarischen Moderne. In: Gessinger, Joachim/Redder, Angelika/Schmitz, Ulrich (Hg.): Korpuslinguistik. Duisburg 2018 (Osnabrücker Beiträge zur Sprachtheorie; 92), 127–156.
Jannidis, Fotis/Kohle, Hubertus/Rehbein, Malte (Hg.): Digital Humanities. Eine Einführung. Stuttgart 2017.
Lauer, Gerhard: Über den Wert der exakten Geisteswissenschaften. In: Joas, Hans/Noller, Jörg (Hg.): Geisteswissenschaft – was bleibt? Zwischen Theorie, Tradition und Transformation. Freiburg [u. a.] 2019, 152–173.
Mueller, Martin: Scalable Reading (2012), https://scalablereading.northwestern.edu/?page_id=22 (20.03.2020).
Portal für deutschsprachige Kinder- und Jugendliteratur im Medienverbund (2020), http://medienverbundportal.kjl.uni-bielefeld.de (01.08.2020).
PUB. Publikationen an der Universität Bielefeld (2020), https://pub.uni-bielefeld.de (20.03.2020).
Reiche, Ruth/Becker, Rainer/Bender, Michael/Munson, Matthew/Schmunk, Stefan/Schöch, Christof: Verfahren der Digital Humanities in den Geistes- und Kulturwissenschaften. In: DARIAH-DE Working Papers (2014) 4, PURL: http://resolver.sub.uni-goettingen.de/purl/?dariah-2014-2 (20.03.2020).
Ryan, Marie-Laure: Transmedial Storytelling and Transfictionality. In: Poetics Today 34 (2013) 3, 361–388.
Scheuermann, Leif: Die Abgrenzung der digitalen Geisteswissenschaften. In: Digital Classics Online, Bd. 2,1 (2016), DOI: https://doi.org/10.11588/dco.2016.1.22746 (20.03.2020).
Schmidt, Siegfried J.: Der Medienkompaktbegriff. In: Münker, Stefan/Roesler, Alexander (Hg.): Was ist ein Medium? Frankfurt a. M. 2008a, 144–157.
Schmidt, Siegfried J.: Media Philosophy – A Reasonable Programme? In: Hrachovec, Herbert/Pichler, Alois (Hg.): Philosophy of the Information. Society Proceedings of the 30th International Ludwig Wittgenstein-Symposium, Kirchberg am Wechsel, Austria 2007. Volume 2. Frankfurt a. M. [u. a.] 2008b (Publications of the Austrian Ludwig Wittgenstein Society – New Series; 7), 89–105.
Schmidt, Siegfried J.: Rekurrenzen der Mediengeschichte. Ein Versuch. Weilerswist 2012.
Schubert, Charlotte: Quellen zur Antike im Zeitalter der Digitalität: Kokkurrenzen, Graphen und Netzwerke. In: Huber, Martin/Krämer, Sybille (Hg.): Wie Digitalität die Geisteswissenschaften verändert: Neue Forschungsgegenstände und Methoden (2018) (Sonderband der Zeitschrift für digitale Geisteswissenschaften; 3), DOI: https://doi.org/10.17175/sb003_008 (20.03.2020).
Schwandt, Silke: Digitale Methoden für die Historische Semantik. Auf den Spuren von Begriffen in digitalen Korpora. In: Geschichte und Gesellschaft 44 (2018) 1, 107–134.
Stalder, Felix: Kultur der Digitalität. Berlin 2016.

Summann, Friedrich/Pfeiffer, Thies/Preis, Matthias: Kooperative Entwicklung digitaler Services an Hochschulbibliotheken. In: Bibliotheksdienst 52 (2018) 8, 595–609, DOI: https://doi.org/10.1515/bd-2018-0070 (20.03.2020).

Summann, Friedrich/Preis, Matthias: Bibliotheksdienstleistungen zur Unterstützung virtueller Forschungsumgebungen. Das DFG-Projekt *Deutschsprachige Kinder- und Jugendliteratur im Medienverbund 1900–1945* (2018), https://opus4.kobv.de/opus4-bib-info/files/3680/dbt_kjl_mpfs_textfassung.pdf (20.03.2020).

Weitin, Thomas: Scalable Reading. In: Zeitschrift für Literaturwissenschaft und Linguistik 47 (2017) 1, 1–6.

Pioneers Take Over the New Types of Media

From Children's Theatre to Film

Media Convergence in the Early Work of Fritz Genschow and Renée Stobrawa

Petra Anders

Introduction

Fritz Genschow (1905–1977) used a variety of media to express himself artistically. He was a theatre and film actor, directed plays, produced his own plays and films for children, young people and adults and was also active as the storyteller Uncle Tobias on the radio (RIAS Berlin). The present account looks primarily at the period of his work in the 1930s. The structure of the article follows Schmidt's (2008) media compact model: First, the historical framework of conditions for Genschow's work is traced, followed by the areas of production and distribution as well as reception related to his work. This structure makes it possible to proceed descriptively first and only at the end to compare one's own account with the state of research. However, this approach also revealed the limits of the media compact concept, because Genschow's work is characterised by dynamic processes:

> The biography of Fritz Genschow is a good example of the development from stage to cinema. In his films, he will always fall back on the methods of the theatre. Genschow may change the medium, but continuity emerges through the working method. He uses film less as a mediator of an artistic expression, but [...] as theatre with other means, [in order] to convey messages. (Scherer 2005, 26)

The important sphere of action of processing, which according to Schmidt also includes media changes, cannot be separated from the sphere of production (Chapter "Children's and Youth Films from 1900 to 1945") in view of this dynamic. On the contrary, Genschow's work is characterised by convergence of content. This can be seen in the play *Kinderraub in Sevilla* (1934) and the media network of *General Stift und seine Bande* (1936/1937). As will be seen below, Genschow's brand

P. Anders (✉)
Institute of Educational Sciences, Humboldt University Berlin, Berlin, Germany
e-mail: petra.anders@hu-berlin.de

essence runs through all the media he used for the production together with his wife Renate (Renée) Stobrawa in the 1930s. Renée Stobrawa (1897–1971) was an actress and scriptwriter and instrumental in all the productions mentioned below, e.g. as director of the children's theatre and actress.

In addition to Sigrid Scherer's well-founded exhibition catalogue (2005), the *Film-Kurier* proved to be a rich source for reconstructing Genschow's filmography. This politically and professionally not entirely unproblematic resource was the leading German film journal from 1919–1945, published daily. In addition to the film, it also reported on theatre, art, vaudeville, and radio. Among other things, the journal provided contemporaries with information on dates of cinema screenings and lines of development of German and international film, thus offering clues for the design of transitions between theatre and film as well as the differentiation of specific film genres.

Historical Framework

Since 1933, Germany was "similar to the USA, Great Britain, France and other industrial nations on the way to becoming a modern media society" (Zimmermann 2005a, 69). In 1937, there was a new attendance record in the cinemas in the large cities of Berlin and Munich (cf. G. H. 1937a). The press took this record as a sign that the movie theatres "have done everything to give the films that have come out worthy performance opportunities" and that "the production is quite capable of meeting the film tastes of the great masses" (ibid.).

Commercially proven entertainment for consumer satisfaction was far more important to the Nazis than nationalist propaganda (cf. Zimmermann 2005a, 69). Nevertheless, in 1933 Goebbels lamented the "lack of popular" and the "lack of realism" in German film (ibid., 70). Film under Goebbels was supposed to be a "contemporary tendency art from a National Socialist spirit" (ibid., 71). Since the Nazis were unable to achieve their goals "despite comprehensive control and steering measures in the capitalistically organised and profit-oriented film industry until 1937" (ibid.), Goebbels again pleaded in 1937 for the "*artistic* creation of contemporary problems from a National Socialist spirit" (ibid.). At the annual meeting of the Reichsfilmkammer on March 5, 1937, he announced that instead of crude propaganda films, propaganda should rather remain in the background as a "tendency, as a character, as an attitude" (Goebbels 1937; quoted in Albrecht 1979, 48). Various genres came into question for this purpose, but above all the cultural film, which had been stylized as the "medium of true German wesensschau and purpose creation" (Zimmermann/Hoffmann 2005c, 46).

An exact definition of the Kulturfilm can neither be (re)constructed for that time nor today. The cultural film was already "disputed territory" in the 1920s (Günther 1924, 42 f.); the term was usually "used as an umbrella term for the various documentary film forms" (Zimmermann/Hoffmann 2005b, 26). Before the First World War, documentary sub-genres such as actualities, travel pictures, industrial pictures were more committed to depiction. According to Gunning (1986), they did not so much want to tell the audience something as to show it something (cf. Zimmermann 2005b, 15). In 1932, Schmitt then distinguished the feature film as a "film with a plot" from the cultural film as a film "that pursues cultural, educational or economic purposes" (Schmitt 1932, 37), although the cultural film was increasingly embedded in action. While short educationally ambitious cultural films were shown as supporting films in the cinema in the 1930s, the production of longer cultural films seemed to decline. In the opinion of the *Film-Kurier,* the role of the cultural film as a supporting programme caused a devaluation of the cultural film. Therefore, in 1937, the Deutsche Gesellschaft für Ton und Film e. V. (Degeto for short) founded its own cultural film distribution company. This was intended to secure the economic existence of independent cultural film producers and to stimulate the production of feature-length cultural films (cf. Degeto starts with 17 films in 1937). The so-called large-scale cultural films were expected to reach a larger target group, i.e. people who were more enthusiastic about the "educational, pedagogical and entertaining values of the cultural film" (ibid.) and therefore went to the cinema. The time was favourable for this, since the "cultural film was currently the focus of public interest, of the audience as well as of theatre owners" (ibid.). In addition, it was hoped that the cultural film would stimulate feature film production: the cultural film had "not infrequently been the artistic pioneer of the feature film", and the "great pioneers of cinematic art" had emerged from the cultural film (ibid.).

In 1937, Degeto distributed 17 "major films from German and foreign production" that deserved "special attention" as cultural films because of their "artistic, cultural or generally human values" (ibid.). This included a wide variety of genres, including Murnau's adventure film *Tabu* (1929/1930) set in the South Seas, a mixture of feature film and ethnographic study, numerous expedition films and propaganda films. Genschow's films *Ikaruskinder* (1938) and *Rotkäppchen und der Wolf* (1937) also belonged to the Kinder-Kulturfilm series (cf. Degeto starts with 17 films in 1937).

Genschow's Productions

Stage and Film in the 1930s

Genschow lived in Berlin or, after 1945, in the later western part of the city. He began as a theatre actor, among others with Erwin Piscator (cf. Scherer 2005, 8). He was successful on stage as well as in film as early as 1928, receiving roles in over thirty films (cf. ibid., 15). For example, his "spirited" acting was convincing in the 1936 Berlin feature *Gleisdreieck,* which was set "in the immediate present" (Schwark 1937, 2). Among many other theatre roles, he appeared simultaneously in 1937 as a stage actor alongside Heinrich George at the Schiller Theater in the Alt-Berliner Posse *Ehrliche Arbeit* in the role of a "splendid" master baker (cf.

Schuhmacher 1937a). Parallel to his own acting, Genschow staged children's plays with his first wife Renée Stobrawa, such as a play by Lisa Tetzner at the Theater am Schiffbauerdamm in 1929 (cf. Scherer 2005, 10). From 1931/1932 they jointly ran their own children's theatre, which also included a children's theatre newspaper in which the children were the authors (cf. Ibid., 11). Genschow and Stobrawa were known for their fairy tale plays in Berlin. They performed German-language fairy tales at the Theater am Nollendorfplatz and the Komische Oper (especially in the pre-Christmas season) and offered a relevant children's program (cf. Bühnen-Notizen 1936), which, as the following review makes clear, also appealed to the actor and National Socialist General Director Eugen Klöpfer:

> The cheers and applause of the children were for the beautiful afternoon, for the artists who played so beautifully, and also for good uncle Eugen Klöpfer, who as general director must have said, "one should play something beautiful for the children!" (Schuhmacher 1936b)

Just as Genschow's own career was characterised by a coexistence of stage and film, a convergence emerges in Genschow's work in the field of children's media. According to a small note in *Film-Kurier*, the children's theatre Stobrawa had adapted the *Stoff* of Wolf Durian's serial *Kai aus der Kiste* (novel 1926) as a play, and the film recording of the play appeared in 1932 as an educational cultural film in a newsreel (cf. Kai aus der Kiste 1932). It is not known who made the film recording.

The connection between children's theatre and children's film is evident in 1934 with the short film *Mit dem Kindertheater durch Deutschland* (cf. section Kinder- und Jugendfilm im Kaiserreich). This was followed in 1935 by a "whole series of fairy tale films" for Agfa's narrow film distribution (cf. Schuhmacher 1936a, 1), which were seven twelve- to 30-minute black-and-white silent films based on fairy tales (*Rumpestilzchen, Schneewittchen, Prinzessin auf der Erbse, Hänsel und Gretel*) as well as six- to seven-minute films based on stories from the picture book *Der Struwwelpeter (Zappelphilipp, Der Suppenkaspar, Der Struwwelpeter)* (cf. Genschow-Film.de). These silent films are not recordings of theatrical performances that can be described as dramatic films (cf. Kepser 2012); rather, they were shot independently with a script.

With the Children's Theatre Through Germany (1934)

The short film *Mit dem Kindertheater durch Deutschland* (1934) is based on the play *Abenteuer deutscher Jungen im Ausland* (or: *Der Kinderraub von Sevilla*), which was self-published in 1934. In this play, Genschow "put into dramatic form" the "thoughts and ideas about German life abroad" of Dr. Karl König, the former director of the German School in Seville (Genschow/König 1934, supplement).

The play, as later in *General Stift,* is about child gangs, more precisely about a gang of child robbers called Mafa. It kidnaps a girl from a German school in Seville and is eventually convicted by the counter-gang with leader Jochen. His gang is organised in a strict hierarchy and names Jochen as a leader whom all must follow unconditionally. Many passages in the play demonstrate German nationalist disdain for the Treaty of Versailles and contain emotional statements about (former) territories and glorification of the Berlin-based Volksbund für das Deutschtum im Ausland (VDA). Genschow and König place praise for the Führer Adolf Hitler in the mouth of the director's character in particular.

> Direktor: Adolf Hitler ist nicht nur der Führer des neuen Deutschland. Sein Name war der Weckruf für das deutsche Volk. Sein Name ist dem neuen Deutschland ein Begriff wie eine Religion. Sein Name ist Kampf, Kampf für das Deutschtum in der ganzen Welt. Wißt ihr, was er selbst über Euch schreibt in seinem Buch „Mein Kampf"?: Nur wer selber am eigenen Leibe fühlt, was es heißt, Deutscher zu sein, ohne dem lieben Vaterlande angehören zu dürfen, nur der vermag die tiefe Sehnsucht zu ermessen, die zu allen Zeiten im Herzen der vom Mutterlande getrennten Kinder brennt. (Genschow/König 1934, 77)
>
> (Director: Adolf Hitler is not only the leader of the new Germany. His name was the wake-up call for the German people. His name is a concept like a religion to the new Germany. His name is struggle, struggle for Germanness throughout the world. Do you know what he himself wrote about you in his book "Mein Kampf"? "Only he who feels in his own body what it means to be German without being allowed to belong to the dear Fatherland, only he is able to gauge the deep longing that burns at all times in the hearts of children separated from the Motherland. (Genschow/König 1934, 77)

In addition, the director gives persuasive speeches for the children to take up a fight for Germany. In this context, homage is also paid to the German mother tongue, which the director sees in danger. The play also lists numerous places in Germany (cf. ibid., 79). The happy ending consists of plans being made for a trip to Germany: The German children living abroad (Seville) should thereby get to know or see their homeland again. Genschow and Renée Stobrawa put a trip to Germany similar to this fiction into practice in the same year, i.e. 1934: The VDA sent them on a bus with 24 people, including twelve children, across Germany to 70 cities; a teacher accompanied the group and gave school lessons on the way (Schuhmacher 1936a) (Fig. 1). The play advertises that it features actors who are already known from *Hitlerjunge Quex* (cf. Genschow/König 1934, supplement).

Fig. 1 Theatre bus in *Mit dem Kindertheater durch Deutschland* (1934) (03:57)

The theatre group performs the "romantic youth play" *Der Kinderraub in Sevilla*, just outlined in the film. In the course of this tour, a programme magazine *Der Theaterautobus* is produced with children's essays and an exchange of letters between the players and the young theatregoers (cf. Schuhmacher 1936a, 1). The 11-minute silent film *Mit dem Kindertheater durch Deutschland* (Agfa Film) documents the journey. It is not clear from the film material whether Genschow himself was the director.

The film briefly shows recruitment scenes for the children's theatre project at the beginning. A written panel shows the question: "Who wants to come along?" It not only subtitles the film clip, but indirectly addresses this question to the potential audience members. In the film, the children find out about the theatre project in the *Rolands-Blätter* – the NS-affiliated youth magazine of the VDA. This is followed by rehearsal scenes, all played by boys. The child actor Waldemar Kupczyk (stage name Drops, Fig. 2, third from right) apparently joins the acting group as a new actor in this film and is also shown later in the film as a crowd favorite. He already played the role of Gerold in Lamprecht's *Emil und die Detektive* (1931) and can also be seen in Genschow's *Ikaruskinder* (1938) as well as *Drops wird Flieger* (1937/38).

While the acting of the boys in the rehearsals seems quite free, the few short scene images from the play then performed in front of the audience rather show equipment and costume theatre. They take up only 30 seconds of the total film. City and landscape shots predominate, including the Dresden Zwinger, Hamburg harbour, Cologne Cathedral and Aachen Cathedral. Overall, the film presents the trip as a particularly positive event: The teenagers are shown as fun-loving boys who have an exceedingly good time traveling through Germany, are very well fed by billeting parents, are active in sports, and are "greeted joyfully everywhere" (07:21) aboard the theatre bus. Scripture panels in the film emphasise the warm welcome the children's theatre received in the cities: "The schools march united with their teachers to the performance." (08:44) The young actors were celebrated in the streets. However, there is no perspectivisation from the children's point of view. The film

Fig. 2 Free play in *Mit dem Kindertheater durch Deutschland* (1934)

remains zero-focused, meaning that the viewer has a knowledge advantage over the youthful protagonists through the written panels.

Overall, this short film oscillates between educational cultural film and the city film popular at the time. The tenor of the underlying play, the VDA as a sponsor, and the title plate *Propagandafahrt in einer Rheinstadt* indicate that this is a film with propagandistic intent. On the one hand, the film promotes the company's own children's theatre, but on the other hand it also promotes the VDA and "beautiful Germany" (cf. plaque at the end of the film, 10:59).

Genschow's Studio des Jugendfilms

Another indication of how film and theatre work symbiotically for Genschow is the founding of his so-called Arbeitsgemeinschaft Film und Theater, the *Studio des Jugendfilms*. With this, he found his own answer to the so-called authors' debate that the *Film-Kurier* was conducting in view of the shortage of film authors. With the title *Fördern? Fördern!* Horst Feldt, a budding film author, suggested that all those involved in film production could, as it were, switch from one medium to another – except the film author:

> Every other filmmaker brings with him a firm foundation of artistic or technical skill on which he can now build and consolidate his cinematic activity. Whether this is the actor, the director, composer, operator, architect, lighting technician or projectionist, they all more or less only need to adapt and expand their knowledge to work appropriate for film. And yet for each of them opportunities for special further training are necessary – and also available. Only the film author, with whom all threads of the most versatile film design should and must run together, remains dependent on his literary abilities, and now it is a matter of completely mastering the acting and technical means of the film! (Feldt 1937)

For further training, Heldt demands more practical experience for film authors with the new medium of film, which functions according to its own laws:

> Perhaps through a "connection" he also comes to the studio from time to time and sees and hears some things there that are useful to him. Does he thus master the expressive means of film?
>
> Almost a year ago, the new generation made very clearly specified demands in this place: Give him the opportunity to see noteworthy and exemplary films for free (and preferably several times).
>
> Let him volunteer at a suitable place in the production, so that he gets to know and master the special laws and means of film on the spot.
>
> Let the new generation collaborate on the script of the much-maligned short film. (The latter could make up for a lot with this.) Bring together the new generation, as far as they have decided to work predominantly in the cinematic field, in a working group and let appointed forces speak to them.
>
> As I said, these demands are not new; they were made a year ago. What has happened in the meantime? Nothing! Only the call for talented young authors will not be silenced. But where much is demanded, something must be offered! (Ibid.)

With his concept of a studio of youth film, Fritz Genschow implemented such a working community and working method and productively combined theatre and film:

> There are still people – says Fritz Genschow – who want to separate theatre and film on their artistic basis as it were in a hostile way – what for? Is not theatre the mother of film from the marriage with the giant technique? (Schuhmacher 1936a, 1)

The term studio is derived from Italian and means work, effort, zeal. It can stand for an artist's workshop or experimental stage, or a recording space for audiovisual media. As a studio, the Children's Theatre was to constantly engage in collaborative practical training work with film in the areas of directing, acting and poetry (cf. ibid., 2). One feature of the studio was that Genschow worked with a permanent group of child actors whom he presumably took from the Children's Theatre into film; there is talk of a "saucy tribe of Genschow boys' films" (Schuhmacher 1937b). Genschow did not call the children by their real names, but introduced nicknames, e.g. Kleiner Drops, Kai Tüte, Semmel, Spitzmaus, Brille, Strammer Hund, Mungo (cf. ibid.), because it was not his intention to create a star cult (cf. Scherer 2005, 12). The stage name Drops also appears as the name of one of the protagonists in the novel *General Stift und seine Bande*; it is the youngest in the fictional gang, to whom a separate chapter is even dedicated; in 1938, Genschow's major film *Drops wird Flieger* even bears the name in its title.

Another feature of Genschow's productions is the work with the same film crew, among others in the films *Sänger von der Waterkant, Die Pfennigschlacht, Die Mühle von Werbellin, Ikaruskinder* and probably also in *Der Kampf um den Stiefen Ast*. They were the cameraman Fred Fuglsang, also called Mister Fu, and the sound engineer Walter Ulfig. Renée Stobrawa was also always involved in the filming: She did the film editing or was seen in the female lead of the adults. The male lead of the adults was usually played by Fritz Genschow himself. Genschow described the approach of his film production in 1936 in *Der deutsche Film* as follows:

> For him, there is nothing better than playing with children. For films with children, he looks for those that show an untamed will to live. In film or theatre work, he wants to respond to the personal feelings of the children. His theatre should not be a training school, not a theatre school; the children should not bring with them the professional goal of acting, rather he is looking for natural talents. One of his methods for finding this out was the *Zirkus Knorke*: here every boy was allowed to be the director for a change and to guide and present other children (Genschow 1936; quoted in Hobsch 2009, 50 f.).

It was hoped that Genschow's concept would provide "significant stimuli – indeed the opening up of entirely new areas of Stoff" (Schuhmacher 1936a, 2) for the youth film: "Room for the youth film! The German fairy tale on the screen" (ibid., 1). Not only the youth film, but also the fairy tale film was to be designed by Genschow in such a way that it would stand out from Disney fairy tale films. In 1937, Genschow made *Rotkäppchen und der Wolf* (1089 m) with Renée Stobrawa as the "first German colour fairy tale sound film" (Lydor 1937). In this film they experimented with colour film in such a way that they used it – even before the US film *Wizard of Oz* (1939) – in a meaningful way as a clear contrast to black and white film. Genschow explains:

> In order to gradually accustom the viewer to the colours, we have created a modern frame story shot in black and white. From the real, present-day events, the image gradually fades to the unreal, colourful fairy-tale world and then returns to the harsh, colourless reality. (Ibid.)

However, Genschow did not intensively continue fairy tale film production until 1953 (cf. Wiedemann 2017 for further details). From 1936 to 1938 he devoted himself intensively to youth films: he shot *Die Sänger von der Waterkant* (1936), *Die Mühle von Werbellin* (1937, 624 m), *Die Pfennigschlacht* (1937, 916 m) (cf. Zensierte Filme 1937), *Die Schlacht am Stiefen Ast* (1937). The *Film-Kurier* announced further film projects by Fritz Genschow as early as May 1937: *Ikaruskinder,* then films about "International Children's Exchange", about "Professional Education" and about the "Love for animals of Children" (cf. Die Filmschaffenden 1937). The movies *Drops wird Flieger* (995 m) and the shorter version *Ikaruskinder* were realised by Genschow in 1938. In the same year the movie *Wilderer im Jagen 161* (1164 m) followed. All movies got the required predicates, that means they passed the censorship of the National Socialists successfully. However, his activity as a producer of children's and youth films during the Nazi era ended in 1938. Genschow's estate contains a statement in which he states that he refused to produce a commissioned film entitled *Marsch der H. J. zum Führer* (Scherer 2005, 20).

General Stift und seine Bande (1937)

The *Stoff General Stift und seine Bande* (1937) is available as a film and a book. It is divided into a first part, *Der Kampf um den Stiefen Ast,* and a second part, *Die Pfennigschlacht.* The entire film, which then bears the title *Der Kampf um den Stiefen Ast* is Genschow's longest and best-known film, with a length of 1633 metres. It contains both parts (i.e. also *Die Pfennigschlacht*) and was released in December 1937. The only short, half-hour film *Die Pfennigschlacht* was shot in the summer of 1936 and went through censorship as early as April 1937 (cf. Scherer 2005, 63). The book edition was published in 1937 under the title *General Stift und seine Bande* and the indication: "Based on the film of the same name, which was awarded the title *volksbildend,* with many photos from the film". Consequently, this is a book about the film, published after the film. It partly deviates from the film plot. It is aimed at boys and girls from the age of eight. Fritz Genschow was the author of the book and the screenplay, and he directed both the short and the feature film, while also playing the adult protagonist in the film. In a telephone interview Renée Stobrawa (mistakenly called "Ilse" in the interview) did with the *Film-Kurier* (Am Telefon 1937), she speaks of *Pfennigschlacht* as a film in "two versions, the feature-length film and the short film." She also played in both films, in the role of the sister Inge Beyer (cf. Filmportal.de).

The first part of the film, shot in Berlin-Grunewald in the summer of 1937 (cf. Scherer 2005, 63), is about the struggle for a ruin with the strange name *Der Stiefe*

Ast. The sound film begins with a strong musical score, presumably harking back to the musical film comedies that were booming internationally. Boys aged about eight to ten sing Berlin songs or folk songs together, e.g. *Als unser Mops ein Möpschen war* and *Die Eisenbahn in Tempelhof* – similar to the Tempelhoflied by Alexander Flessburg. The insert *Gehört den Rüben* is emblazoned on the old factory building. From the book one learns that the name of the ruin, *Stiefer Ast,* sprang from the child's mouth of the youngest of the gang, Drops, and is supposed to mean something like crooked, abandoned branch. This branch runs through this very derelict factory building, possibly as a symbol of a new beginning. The film uses the motif of the abandoned place as a significant place for the boys, which also appears in numerous later novels and films about children and young people and symbolises possibilities for children to act and shape their lives: That which other generations no longer use can become important for their own development and place in life.

The boys are often shot from a slight frog perspective. This makes them look bigger and brings them to the fore as actors; the viewer perceives them as significant. However, the children's perspective does not come into focus throughout. There are, to be sure, some passages of internal focalisation in which the viewer knows only what the boys know, and thus their perspective is reinforced. For example, a scout watches the scene through binoculars; the viewers are also only allowed to see the scene through the binocular perspective of the scouting boy due to this effect, allowing for a brief moment of internal focalisation. However, there are a majority of scenes with zero focalisation, the dominant form of narrative storytelling in feature films (cf. Kuhn 2013, 133). The camera as the narrator observes the characters, keeps an eye on everything and already knows more than the youthful protagonists. For example, when the boys' play turns into battle scenes: the folk songs change to mocking songs; one of the two gangs attacks, the boys camouflage themselves in the grass, barricades are set up. Water and mud battles develop, which can be seen from above and take up the whole picture (Fig. 3).

The battles are accompanied by howling and music (including pan flute). The supervision is replaced by a long shot, which above all illustrates the large number of boys as a group. In the film, an old tank enters the picture quite abruptly at film

Fig. 3 Oversight of the battle of the children's gangs in *Der Kampf um den Stiefen Ast*

metre 240. In the book, this scene is prepared in great detail: The children of one gang want to use the tank to take the factory building of the other children in a surprise attack.

Parallel to this film plot, an adult motorcycle race occurs in this first part of the film. Rudi Meißner, played by Fritz Genschow, is established as the hero in the role of the motorcycle racer. The two storylines then intertwine: the boys' tank moves into the battle of the children with loud musical accompaniment. Rudi Meißner races off on his motorcycle. Two boys from the gang that is attacked by the tank run to Inge Beyer, the big sister of one of the gang members, and secretly organise a clothesline. A neighbour lectures the boys not to splash the expensive water. Here we get the first hint that the film's action takes place more in a milieu where money and resources are scarce. The two boys stretch the line across the road, as they intend to use it to stop the tank. Instead of the tank, however, a loud engine noise announces the motorcycle, which drives right into the boys' barrier. After this nasty accident, there is silence for the first time in the film. The motorcycle burns out.

This incident, as a driving moment of the film plot, has two historical references: First, it alludes to the subject of motor racing, which was significant at the time. Motorways, car racing and motor sport were very popular subjects of the cultural film – the historian Uwe Day even speaks of an "automotive wave" that rolled towards the cinema audience (cf. Day 2005, 266). Bob Stoll of TOBIS-Kulturfilmproduktion, for example, worked on the "big sports film about all international car races in 1937" (*Spannung in Sekunden* 1937), with which "the racing cars of the most modern type [...] become racing film stars that bear witness in all countries of the world to German sporting spirit, German commitment and German technology" (ibid.). To this end, a film crew was to record races on the then new Roosevelt track in New York (G. H. 1937b, 2). Genschow's *Kampf um den Stiefen Ast* is less about the technology, which fails anyway due to Rudi's accident, and more about the "audience's desire for speed, spatial and mental liberation, and national edification" (Day 2005, 266) that cinema was able to fulfil on the virtual experience level. Rudi only rises professionally and rehabilitates himself as a hero when his motorcycle is repaired.

On the other hand, during the period from 1934 to 1938, there was a criminal gang – the Götze brothers – who were up to mischief in Berlin through street robbery by means of car traps. In Grunewald, where Fritz Genschow lived (Königsallee 35, Berlin-Grunewald) and where he shot the film in the summer of 1937, they found their first victims; victims came forward almost daily. The Götze brothers built barriers for motorised vehicles, mainly by stretching cords and cables across roads, sometimes decapitating their victims. Goebbels forbade the media from reporting on this so as not to damage Berlin's reputation before the Olympic Games were held. The Götze brothers were eventually charged with 157 counts of robbery, had 16 counts of aggravated assault and two counts of murder to answer for. Their actions gave rise to the Reichsautofallengesetz of June 22, 1938, which retroactively led to the imposition of the death penalty on the Götze brothers and was enforced by Roland Freisler and others. The law disregarded the rule of law principle that criminal laws may not be retroactive and went down in criminal history as the Lex Götze.

This National Socialist penal law against street robbery by means of car traps still applies today with some changes: According to the StGB, a minimum sentence of five years is threatened for a "predatory attack on motorists".

For Genschow and the film audience, these criminal cases were probably very present. The processing of these incidents in the film contributed to the everyday relevance of German (cultural) films demanded by Goebbels and the local colour of the youth film. The reactions to the motorcycle incident staged in the film are different: the sister Inge Beyer does punish the boys by slapping one of them in the face, insulting them with "You lazy bums" and making them feel guilty by blaming them: "You have destroyed a position in life". She already knows that Rudi was a courier at a company before a test drive. Now the vehicle is burned out and the chance for the permanent position is forfeited. Fritz Genschow, who plays the role of Rudi Meißner himself, stages himself as a child lover and pedagogue. He cuddles the head of the leader, General Stift. "We were all unlucky – I should have driven more carefully" is his comment on the accident. The adult viewer suspects that Rudi was lucky in his misfortune: Inge Beyer and Rudi Meißner seem to fall in love; the mis-en-scène at the end of the film finally creates the image of a harmonious extended family.

The accident causes the boys to rethink: instead of fighting each other as gangs, they now want to join forces to help and raise money for the complete repair of the motorcycle under their own steam, i.e. through auxiliary work. The battle for the Stiefer Ast factory ruin turns into the so-called penny battle. This is the beginning of the second part of the film and the novel.

When the children develop the idea for the penny battle, the spectator is deliberately kept on the outside – he "waits" with the two guards in front of the factory building until the idea becomes public (Fig. 4).

Here, the zero focus and internal focus briefly dissolve in favour of an external focus. This supports the effect that the boys have come up with the penny battle themselves. It comes, as it were, entirely originally from them, with no outside influence. So instead of the boys conquering a territory in wild battle (over the *Stiefe Ast*), they think about effective organisational structures (the *Pfennigschlacht*) for economic success. Despite complete decay (Leaning Branch) and destruction

Fig. 4 Guards in *Der Kampf um den Stiefen Ast* (from Genschow 1937, 48)

(Motorcycle), a new beginning is dared. If one wants to interpret the film and novel plot politically, the following parallels suggest themselves: After Germany supposedly had to accept losses due to the Treaty of Versailles, a systematically organised new beginning is suggested with National Socialism. The ideals – in the film as in the society of the time – are the cohesion of the group of boys, innovative ideas for making money and precise cooperation. A scene on film metre 248 clearly shows signs of community pressure: all the boys bawl approvingly when General Stift asks, "Who's with me?" The only boy to voice criticism is Knieß. He is excluded from the boys' group in the book edition and is only readmitted much later by the boy named General Stift.

The general shines through his organisational skills: Cinematically, the penny battle is realised in a serial arrangement of unskilled labour. 22 short scenes, each about six metres of film, show the boys' ideas of earning quick money: Looking after bicycles at the post office (metres 271–277), pumping water (metres 277–283), walking the dog (metres 283–290), carrying a bag, shopping, helping with sightseeing ("Hello Mr. Foreigner, How do you do?"), collecting earthworms for fishing, repairing scooters, leading sightseeing tours of the *Stiefe Ast,* turning cow pats into fertiliser, watching out for belongings on the beach, lending umbrellas, selling newspapers, trading stickers, selling sausages, standing in the theatre line for others, rat hunting, painting fonts, calling out advertisements for the Union Theater, giving physical education lessons, singing folk songs *(Am Brunnen vor dem Tore)*, and finally, trading firewood for potato peels.

When the money is not enough, the boys involve some girls in the penny-pinching. However, the girls are not given any background information in the film, i.e., they are shown with a lot of commitment without knowing what they are working for in the first place. Their tasks seem rather stereotypical: Picking berries, washing cups, babysitting, darning stockings, selling flowers. While the boys also speak during their work, the girls' passages are without words, silent, merely accompanied by music. At the end of the film, Rudi Meißner is finally able to take his repaired motorcycle, paid for by the boys, for a test drive. In the crowd, only the boys can be seen rooting for him. The girls – except for Inge Beyer – no longer play a role.

The scenes of *Pfennigschlacht* are closely linked to everyday life in Berlin. Berlin-Köpenick is given as the official filming location (cf. Scherer 2005, 63). In fact, other locations can be seen. At some, the camera takes its time to show the viewer a sight more extensively: at the Strandbad Müggelsee, at the Oberbaumbrücke, at the Olympic Stadium, and at a theatre (not further identifiable) where the boys are queueing for other people. Here the camera catches swastika flags in the area. The film seems to want to show contemporary Berlin life; the proximity to the culture film is clear.

Die Pfennigschlacht went through censorship as early as April 1937. The film stood on its own without the pre- and post-film narration and was released, presumably as a cultural film, from January 1938 as a supplementary programme to *Petermann ist dagegen* (Director: Wisbar 1938) (ibid.). The two parts of the film differ in their target audience: while *Kampf um den Stiefen Ast* deals with boys' play, *Die Pfennigschlacht* is more focused on everyday life of adults in Berlin. The love story that unfolds between Rudi and Inge also addresses an adult audience – the film seems to have been a multi-addressed family film by today's standards.

The book edition, which was published after the film, largely coincides with the film plot of the complete film. The main themes already outlined for the film are intensified in the 30 chapters in total: Like the film, the novel is characterised by zero focus: The narrator, who has everything in view, thinks ahead and sometimes comments precociously and politically questionably, knows more than the characters and also fleshes out the regional reference. Thus, in addition to the Berlin locations chosen in the film, Alexanderplatz (Genschow 1937, 62) and Molkenplatz (ibid., 105) are explicitly named as locations in the text. Furthermore, the Berlin dialect contributes to the local colour, e.g. "Ei wei wie" (ibid., 13), "Aus dem ff" (ibid., 13), "Kieke" (ibid., 20). From today's perspective, the language seems strange at the point where the mutual soiling of the boys in the mud fight is described as "turning them into negroes" (ibid., 26).

Author Genschow clearly distinguishes the portrayal of the girls from that of the boys by marking the separation of the sexes with dash lines in the running text. The narrator, in turn, refers to the girls as "Gummipuppen" with "langhaarigem Verstand" (ibid., 99) and comments: "Das schönste für ein Mädel ist, helfen zu können" (ibid., 103). While in the film Rudi Meißner's reflections on honour and masculinity are put into his mouth, in the book the narrator takes over these remarks on masculinity (ibid., 75), we also learn from him political statements packaged as wisdom about the boy's game, which seem to catch the reader of the time: "Was nützt es, etwas aufzubauen, wenn das durch Feinde bedroht ist" (ibid., 15). The novel compares the activities of the youth gang to an "Ameisenhaufen" and pays homage to the "Staatsrad" (ibid., 61); the boys are "kleine Rädchen im großen Getriebe" (ibid., 61), people excluded from it, on the other hand, are "schädlich" (ibid., 62).

The war theme is even more evident in the book than in the film: the narrator compares the boys' gang fight to the Battle of Waterloo (ibid., 96), refers to the tank as a Trojan horse (Ibid., 29); overall, the transitions between play and war action are fluid: "Zum Kriegführen gehört Material, besonders im Zeitalter der Technik" (ibid., 23). The cult surrounding the leader is unmistakably invested in the following utterances: "Es ist nicht schwer, alles nachzurufen, was der Redner spricht" (ibid., 16); "Sie fragen nicht lange, ob es gut ist, was der General sagt" (ibid., 22).

The author also resorts to the above-mentioned dash lines in the depiction of the battle in order to montage actions as in the film: Thus, the fronts are marked by dash lines (ibid., 12 f.) and parallel actions are delimited by dash lines (ibid., 50). One could say that the author here in the novel narrates with cinematic elements. Also, zero focalisation, which is more typical of narrative fiction, is dominant in both media, film and book. Contemporary references are found in intertextual allusions: For example, the author links to the popular Danish comedian duo Pat and Patachon, known from the film (ibid., 87), mentions Robinson Crusoe (ibid., 24) and draws on famous personalities from sport, theatre, and film as a comparison: 'Max Schmeling würde auch nicht gegen Heinz Rühmann boxen' (ibid., 21).

Compared to the film, the plot in the book unfolds much more comprehensibly and seems coherent and probably quite exciting for adolescents at the time. The film, on the other hand, seems rather incoherent, especially in the beginning when the gang fights are depicted. Without reading the book beforehand, the first passages of the film are hardly comprehensible. One gets the impression that Genschow, as a filmmaker, wanted to capture the free play of the boys rather than tell a structured story. At the end of the book, however, the reader finds a surprising twist: instead of ending with the harmonious image of Rudi, Inge and the group of children, as the film does, the narrator in the book has his gang of children build up the so-called homeland under the leadership of General Stift: "Wir haben Arbeit genug. Meldet Euch bald. Wir können jeden gebrauchen" (Genschow 1937, 144). The end of the book thus supports the above-mentioned thesis that the film plot presents a downplayed picture of Germany's political situation in the 1930s.

Contemporary Reception of Genschow's Work

Genschow's film *Der Kampf um den Stiefen Ast* went through the censorship usual for the time at the beginning of November 1937 (G. H. 1937a). Only a few days later, on November 9, 1937, the *Film-Kurier* (cf. Ganz kurz 1937) announced the successful awarding of a rating, but the film title was written incorrectly. The newspaper therefore repeated this news on the 11th of November 1937, spelling the film's title correctly. The predicate *volksbildend* awarded to the film (in addition to the predicates *künstlerisch* and *Lehrfilm*) was already common in the Weimar Republic, when directors applied for such a predicate in order to have the film exempted from entertainment tax in whole (predicate *künstlerisch*) or in part (predicate *volksbildend*), which promised that cinemas would be more willing to include these films in their program. With the Lichtspielgesetz of February 16, 1934, the awarding of the predicates was not done on a voluntary basis but was part of the censorship process that was taking place anyway. The Filmprüfstelle, as the censorship authority, took over the predicating. At that time, the predicate *volksbildend* meant that the films promised to enrich the viewers' knowledge "in an impeccable manner". This predicate does not testify to any particular National Socialist tinge. The film was distributed by Degeto in 1937 as a Tobis Kulturfilm production and was received as a cultural film. It is not clear from the *Film-Kurier* announcements when the film had its premiere. It was shown on Christmas Day in the afternoon screening of the Regina-Kino Spandau (cf. Was spielt Berlin? 1937).

Contemporary reviews in the *Film-Kurier* consistently emphasise Genschow's children's theatre in a positive light and his films for young people that his choice of themes was closely related to the lives of young people and that he had a special skill in dealing with child actors. Genschow and Stobrawa knew how to lead children and to put "educational-ethical weight" into the children's play (Schuhmacher 1936 as well as Schuhmacher 1937c on *Die Mühle von Werbellin;* Schuhmacher 1937d on *Ikaruskinder*). This characterisation can be described as the brand essence of Genschow's and Stobrawa's productions. It pervades both theatre and film productions.

Film aesthetic aspects were not explicitly mentioned in any review of the *Film-Kurier*. However, it was always emphasised that the camera played along well. This is already a judgmental statement, because in terms of film technology it was difficult to capture everyday life: The cameras were heavy and needed a tripod; the film material was not very sensitive to light, so that filming was only possible on sunny days (Zimmermann/Hoffmann 2005b, 28). The fact that children or young people in Genschow's *Der Kampf um den Stiefen Ast* acted naturally in front of the camera, almost like in a documentary film, can therefore also be seen as a special film-aesthetic feature. It probably also helped the children that they worked in a fixed acting group and film crew.

In 1938, Dr. Eckhardt of Degeto judges Genschow's youth films in a detailed article in *Film-Kurier* as those that actually touched youth (Eckardt 1938). The approach that children played children and that Genschow's films corresponded to the imaginary world of children is not, however, viewed in terms of the promotion of creativity or personality development, but rather instrumentalised politically:

> Such youth films can bring many a state-political educational task closer to the youth, which in no other way would become such a vivid experience for them. For this reason, the German youth leadership is also keenly interested in the development of this new branch of German filmmaking. (Ibid.)

The Bannführer Alfred Schütze, head of the Youth Film Head Office in the Reichspropagandaleitung of the NSDAP, on the other hand, devalued Genschow's films in his article on the role of the Hitler Youth (HJ) four days later:

> Without wishing to oppose free artistic initiative in the least, we must note that the boys who confront us, for example, in *Kampf um den Stiefen Ast* no longer exist in Germany today. The boys who want to let off steam have better opportunities in the tent camps of the HJ and on the trips than to play in the street mud and organise street fights after the pattern of the well-known American youth film *No more glory*. We are also of the opinion that youth films must grow out of the youth and should not be created from a bureaucratic position. For this very reason we may well allow ourselves to ask whether one believes, for example, that the film *Drops wird Flieger-General* will be correctly understood by the many thousands of Hitlerjugend who serve German aviation in the flying squads of the Hitlerjugend, using their youth? For this kind of youth film it may suffice to say that the Hitlerjugend recognises the good will shown, but without agreeing with these films. (Schütze 1938, 2)

Schütze was concerned with the content-related co-determination of the Hitlerjugend. In his contribution, he did emphasise the special importance of the medium of film for the Hitlerjugend: "Through the Hitlerjugend, the German youth has committed itself to filmmaking as one of the most beautiful and strongest forms of expression of contemporary art" (ibid., 1). As Bannführer, however, he insists on the influence of the HJ:

> It may therefore be emphasised most emphatically at this point that the direction of march taken by the youth film is determined exclusively by the Hitlerjugend, for 90 percent of the boys and girls for whom these films are made march in the ranks of the Hitlerjugend today. (Ibid., 1)

The National Socialist propaganda film served Schütze as a benchmark for the youth film; according to him, the HJ "knew only one youth film after the seizure of power: The *Hitlerjunge Quex*" (Ibid.). According to Schütze, another "prime example of a youth film" was the documentary Schmalfilm *Feindliche Ufer* (1938, 715 m, cf. Bundesarchiv), which was made "out of the formations of the HJ" in the camp of the Bremen Jungvolk. This film was "new and peculiar": It depicted the tent camp, i.e. a "Stoff that became the template for a hundred similar Schmalfilme"; thus "entirely from the sensibilities of the youth" (Schütze 1938, 2).

Conclusion

With regard to Genschow, Scherer raises the question of why progressive tendencies in children's culture, which had long existed at that time in rudimentary form and also in the period before 1933, were not able to assert themselves (Scherer 2005, 7). For her, Genschow is a "man possessed of a great gift for improvisation, a doer and a tireless one" who had a "great pedagogical sense of mission" (ibid.). At the same time, she criticises:

> When observing the characters on stage or in the film, the children should adopt the norms and values presented. They do not turn against the adults, do not attack their authority, but fill the space that the adults mark out for the children. (Ibid., 41)

Schneider pointed out as early as 1982 that the aesthetic space Genschow created in his youth films certainly satisfied "the ideological requirements in their Hitler realism" (cf. Schneider 1982, 22). Brill (2011) even counts Genschow's book *General Stift und seine Bande* among the reading books with ideologically shaped *Stoff* and an adventurous-seeming story that would have served to educate so-called auxiliary pupils, i.e. pupils with special needs, to be ready for military service under National Socialism.

The above analyses show that Genschow's works selected for this article corresponded to the requirements of Goebbels' cultural film on the level of content. The written works corresponding with the films – the play *Kinderraub in Sevilla* and the novel *General Stift und seine Bande* – are thereby also committed to National Socialist thinking. The above-mentioned criticism by Scherer is confirmed by the analyses presented here: The narrative modes in the media network on *General Stift und seine Bande* clearly show that hardly any narrative is told from a genuinely childlike perspective. Nevertheless, from the perspective of the National Socialists, Genschow's work is considered a "free artistic initiative" (Schütze 1938, 2) and is therefore rejected. As part of the "film work" (ibid.) of the Hitlerjugend, films such as *Feindliche Ufer* were shot by the "formations of the Hitlerjugend" (ibid.) with cine cameras – presumably even with the smooth-running 8 mm amateur cameras such as the Agfa Berlin: Movex 8, which came onto the market in 1937; however, it cannot be assumed that the adolescents had freedom of content and aesthetic design in this respect.

Genschow as well as his partner and colleague Renée Stobrawa can be called pioneers in the respect that they created an innovative way of working with the studio of youth film and in the 1930s created a media network with their work that can be characterised by convergence: Free children's play, which is documented in the opening scenes of the short film *Mit dem Kindertheater durch Deutschland* (1934) and which was a feature of the Genschow-Stobrawa Children's Theatre, becomes the starting point of the studio of youth film and can also be seen in film scenes in *Der Kampf um den Stiefen Ast* (1937); content from the Children's Theatre, which already existed as print products, can be found in short films (*Kai aus der Kiste* 1932, *Mit dem Kindertheater durch Deutschland* 1934); So-called large-scale films are based on fairy tale *Stoff* (Fairy Tale Films since 1935) and the *Stoff* about *General Stift und seine Bande* is processed simultaneously as a short film (*Die Pfennigschlacht* 1936/1937), a large-scale film *Der Kampf um den Stiefen Ast* 1937) and a children's novel with film images (*General Stift und seine Bande* 1937). As so-called cultural films, *Mit dem Kindertheater durch Deutschland* and *Der Kampf um den Stiefen Ast* also make explicit use of regional references (e.g. sights, everyday life in Berlin, the Götze criminal case), with which the storyworld is expanded. With the phenomenon of *Drops,* Genschow and Stobrawa create a kind of transfiction: the stage name Drops of one of the child actors introduced as a supposed new actor in *Mit dem Kindertheater durch Deutschland* appears in the credits of the film *Der Kampf um den Stiefen Ast* and becomes a fictional character in the children's novel *General Stift und seine Bande* as well as the titular main character of Genschow's short film *Drops wird Flieger* (1937/1938). In Genschow's and Stobrawa's work, the media content, e.g. the motif of the children's gang, migrated from theatre to film and from film to book. They created media networks that were held together by the Genschow and Stobrawa brand core outlined above, which has been invoked repeatedly in contemporary reviews. In addition to fictional entities and narrative links, a pedagogical concept (theatre rehearsals, studio of youth film) in particular ensures a high recognition value in the early work of Genschow/Stobrawa.

References

Primary Literature

Genschow, Fritz: General Stift und seine Bande. Berlin: Schneider, 1937.

Filmography

Feindliche Ufer [Kurzfilm] (Bremen 1938), https://www.bundesarchiv.de (20.02.2020).
Der Kampf um den Stiefen Ast [Spielfilm] (D 1936/37). Regie: Fritz Genschow, Tobis-Melofilm GmbH Berlin.

Die Pfennigschlacht [Kurz-Spielfilm] (D 1937). Regie: Fritz Genschow, Tobis-Melofilm GmbH Berlin.
Mit dem Kindertheater durch Deutschland [Kurzfilm] (D 1934). Regie: Fritz Genschow, Agfa Film.

Theatrography

Genschow, Fritz/König, Karl: Abenteuer deutscher Jungens im Ausland (Kinderraub in Sevilla). Stück für die Jugend. Romantisches Schauspiel in vier Akten. Berlin: Selbstverlag, 1934 (79 Seiten mit Beiblatt *Mit dem VDA durch Deutschland*).

Secondary Literature Before 1945

Am Telefon: Ilse Stobrawa im Wintergarten. In: Film-Kurier 19 (1937) 122 vom 29.05., 2.
Günther, Walther: Kulturfilm und Jugend. In: Beyfuss, Edgar/Kossowsky, Arthur (Hg.): Das Kulturfilmbuch. Berlin 1924, 42–59.
Bühnen-Notizen. In: Film-Kurier 18 (1936) 255 vom 30.10., 2.
Degeto startet mit 17 Filmen. In: Film-Kurier 19 (1937) 235 vom 09.10., Beibl. 1.
Eckardt, Dr.: Filme für die Jugend. In: Film-Kurier 20 (1938) 35 vom 11.02., 1–2.
Die Filmschaffenden. In: Film-Kurier 19 (1937) 106 vom 10.05., 2.
Feldt, Hans: Fördern? Fördern! In: Film-Kurier 19 (1937) 78 vom 05.04., 3.
G. H.: Berliner Zahlen für September. In: Film-Kurier 19 (1937a) 255 vom 02.11., 1.
G. H.: Filmkameras auf der Avus. In: Film-Kurier 19 (1937b) 122 vom 29.05., 1–2.
Ganz kurz. In: Film-Kurier 19 (1937) 261 vom 09.11., 2
Jugend und Film gehören zusammen. In: Film-Kurier 23 (1941) 54 vom 05.03., 2.
Kai aus der Kiste. In: Kinematograph 26 (1932) 39 vom 25.02., 3.
Lydor, Waldemar: Rotkäppchen bunt in schwarz-weißem Rahmen. In: Film-Kurier 19 (1937) 280 vom 02.12., 2.
Schmitt, Walter: Das Filmwesen und seine Wechselbeziehungen zur Gesellschaft. Versuch einer Soziologie des Filmwesens. Freudenstadt 1932.
Schütze, Alfred: HJ. bestimmt Marschrichtung des Jugendfilms. In: Film-Kurier 20 (1938) 39 vom 16.02., 1–2.
Schuhmacher, Hans: Platz für den Jugendfilm! Das deutsche Märchen auf der Leinwand. In: Film-Kurier 18 (1936a) 51 vom 29.02., 1–2.
Schuhmacher, Hans: Theater am Nollendorfplatz (Volksbühne). „Rumpelstilzchen". In: Film-Kurier 18 (1936b) 287 vom 08.12.1936, 2.
Schuhmacher, Hans: Alt-Berliner Posse im Schiller-Theater. „Ehrliche Arbeit". In: Film-Kurier 19 (1937a) 78 vom 05.04., 3.
Schuhmacher, Hans: Ikaruskinder am Teufelssee. Genschow dreht Jungens-Film im Grunewald. In: Film-Kurier 19 (1937b) 131 vom 09.06., 3.
Schuhmacher, Hans: Neue Tobis-Kulturfilme. In: Film-Kurier 19 (1937c) 82 vom 09.04., 4.
Schuhmacher, Hans: Ikaruskinder am Teufelssee. Genschow dreht Jungens-Film im Grunewald. In: Film-Kurier 19 (1937d) 131 vom 09.06., 3.
Schuhmacher, Hans: Sieben Tobis-Beifilme. In: Film-Kurier 18 (1936) 291 vom 12.12., 2.
Schwark, Günther: „Gleisdreieck"/Ufa-Palast am Zoo. In: Film-Kurier 19 (1937) 23 vom 28.01., 2.
Spannung in Sekunden. Vom Werden eines internationalen Autorennsport-Films. In: Film-Kurier 19 (1937) 210 vom 09.09., 3.
Was spielt Berlin? In: Film-Kurier 19 (1937) 299 vom 24.12., 3.
Zensierte Filme. In: Film-Kurier 19 (1937) 96 vom 26.04., 4.

Secondary Literature After 1945

Albrecht, Gerd: Film im Dritten Reich. Eine Dokumentation. Karlsruhe 1979.
Brill, Werner: Pädagogik der Abgrenzung. Die Implementierung der Rassenhygiene im Nationalsozialismus durch die Sonderpädagogik. Leipzig 2011.
Day, Uwe: ‚Stoßtrupp der Motorisierung': Rennsport und Massenmotorisierung. In: Zimmermann, Peter/Hoffmann, Kay (Hg.): Geschichte des dokumentarischen Films in Deutschland, Bd. 3, Stuttgart 2005, 266–275.
Filmportal.de, Die Pfennigschlacht, https://www.filmportal.de/film/die-pfennigschlacht_65a4b1 c23a534c80882a502581bebef7 (20.02.2020).
Genschow-Film.de, https://www.genschow-film.de (20.02.2020).
Hobsch, Manfred: Ideologie für Kopf und Herz der Jugend. In: Schäfer, Horst/Wegener, Claudia (Hg:): Kindheit und Film. Geschichte, Themen und Perspektiven des Kinderfilms in Deutschland. Tübingen 2009, 39–55.
Kepser, Matthis: Der Dramenfilm. Eine Typologie der Filmformen dramatischer Texte. In: Bathrick, Davis/Preußer, Heinz-Peter (Hg.): Literatur inter- und transmedial. Inter- and Transmedial Literature. Amsterdam [u. a.] 2012 (Amsterdamer Beiträge zur neueren Germanistik; 82), 361–382.
Kuhn, Markus: Filmnarratologie. Ein erzähltheoretisches Analysemodell. Berlin [u. a.] 2013.
Scherer, Sigrid: Märchenwelten. Der Schauspieler, Regisseur und Produzent Fritz Genschow. Ausstellungskatalog. Deutsches Filmmuseum. Frankfurt a. M. 2005.
Schmidt, Siegfried J.: Der Medienkompaktbegriff. In: Münker, Stefan/Roesler, Alexander (Hg.): Was ist ein Medium? Frankfurt a. M. 2008, 144–157.
Schneider, Wolfgang: Stationen des deutschen Kinderfilms. In: Ders. (Hg.): Aufbruch zum neuen bundesdeutschen Kinderfilm. Themen, Macher und Projekte. Eulenhof 1982, 8–33.
Wiedemann, Dieter: Es war einmal … Märchenfilme in der Bundesrepublik und in der DDR. In: Dettmar, Ute/Pecher, Claudia Maria/Schlesinger, Ron (Hg.): Märchen im Medienwechsel. Zur Geschichte und Gegenwart des Märchenfilms. Stuttgart 2017, 179–228.
Zimmermann, Peter: Ziele der Filmpolitik. ‚Zeitnahe Tendenzkunst' und dokumentarischer ‚Wirklichkeitsbericht' in ‚nationalsozialistischem Geiste'. In: Ders./Hoffmann, Kay (Hg.): Geschichte des dokumentarischen Films in Deutschland, Bd. 3. Stuttgart 2005a, 69–74.
Zimmermann, Peter: Vorwort. In: Ders./Hoffmann, Kay (Hg.): Geschichte des dokumentarischen Films in Deutschland, Bd. 3. Stuttgart 2005b, 13–16.
Zimmermann, Peter/Hoffmann, Kay (Hg.): Geschichte des dokumentarischen Films in Deutschland, Bd. 3. Stuttgart 2005a.
Zimmermann, Peter/Hoffmann, Kay: Die Kulturfilm-Debatte zur Zeit des Nationalsozialismus und die Rechtfertigungsliteratur nach 1945. In: Ders./Hoffmann, Kay (Hg.): Geschichte des dokumentarischen Films in Deutschland, Bd. 3. Stuttgart 2005b, 26–32.
Zimmermann, Peter/Hoffmann, Kay: Von der Gleichschaltungs- und Propaganda-These zur differenzierten Erforschung dokumentarischer Genres. In: Ders./Hoffmann, Kay (Hg.): Geschichte des dokumentarischen Films in Deutschland, Bd. 3. Stuttgart 2005c, 45–56.

Mickey Mouse

An All-American Character in 1930s Germany

Johannes Krause

Introduction and Preliminary Considerations

To call Disney one of, if not the biggest player in the entertainment industry of our time is hardly an exaggeration. At the latest with the acquisition of *21st Century Fox* as well as the rights to the *Star Wars universe* with its components from the film, book and merchandising area, an intermediate peak of Disney's market power was reached. The foundation for the omnipresence was laid in the early days of the Disney company by the activity of its founder because Walter Elias Disney recognised early the possible potential of cross-media marketing of his *Stoffe*. The classic Disney *characters* of the 1920s/1930s each founded their own small *marketing empires,* which on the one hand steadily increased the popularity of the *characters* and on the other hand these were able to profit from it in return. With the growing success of the company, the number of characters and *Stoffe* also increased, around with an endless smorgasbord of realisations in the most diverse media and also marketing strategies ever formed. At the end of the 1920s and beginning of the 1930s, Disney's enthusiasm spread from the American continent to Europe with the establishment of Mickey Mouse and was eagerly received by the German population. The mouse was perceived and celebrated as the company's trademark in Germany as well. This enthusiasm led to the development of a separate media network around the little mouse and his friends. In addition, Disney liked to use German

J. Krause (✉)
Faculty of Linguistics and Literary Studies, German Studies, Bielefeld University, Bielefeld, Germany
e-mail: johannes.krause@uni-bielefeld.de

fairy tales, especially in the early days, in order to make them usable for its animated films. Both in the field of short films and feature-length films – e.g. *Snow White and the Seven Dwarfs* (1937) – it was especially the fairy tales of the Brothers Grimm that offered this still rather young studio a vast pool of stories to develop and implement as new film material.

Thus, even a superficial examination reveals that Disney's works made an impactful impression on its German audience and that German culture, as a result of this, clearly left visible traces within the Disney conglomerate. These traces will be briefly followed and the reception of Disney's works in Germany before 1945 will be examined more closely. In addition to this, the contemporary film magazines digitised as part of the DFG project *Kinder- und Jugendliteratur im Medienverbund 1900–1945* at Bielefeld University will be examined. This material will be supplemented by various comic strips, merchandising catalogues and sources from the period. Written testimonies from the (trade) press of the time as well as various realisations of Mickey Mouse for the German market will be included and evaluated in the study. A volume accompanying an exhibition at the Filmmuseum Potsdam (Storm/Dreßler 1991), which summarises the reception of Mickey and other characters in countless media forms, is particularly useful for this purpose.

It is striking, even from a mere skimming of the material, that many of the film magazines of this period examined reveal – at first often in passing remarks – a longing for a similarly successful German animated film production to that of the Disney studios. In this context, there is repeated mention of typically American characteristics or an "American shaping" (Frühling an der Donau 1935, Fig. 1) of certain *Stoffe*. Therefore, the focus will be on the question of what this *American character* of the Disney figures, frequently named in the German media landscape of the 1930s, consists of and how it was perceived and used in the German press. In line with media network research, the article deals with this question on both the reception and production levels in order to give as broad a picture as possible. Therefore, in addition to presenting the reception of Disney and especially Mickey Mouse films in the film magazines reviewed between 1930 and 1942, two contrasting examples of productive engagements with the film character of Mickey Mouse are also examined. As examples, forms of representation of Mickey Mouse for entertainment as well as (counter-)propaganda purposes during the National Socialist regime are used.

Before the production and reception levels of the Mickey Mouse media network are discussed, it should first be exemplified what is understood and subsumed under

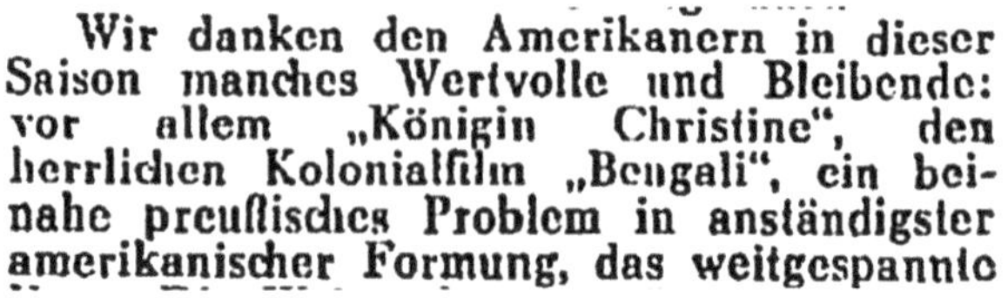

Fig. 1 *Frühling an der Donau* (1931), from: *Film-Kurier* 17 (1931) 125, 2

Wir danken den Amerikanern in dieser Saison manches Wertvolle und Bleibende: vor allem „Königin Christine", den herrlichen Kolonialfilm „Bengali", ein beinahe preußisches Problem in anständigster amerikanischer Formung, das weitgespannte

a media network in the following explanations. In line with the general understanding, a media network is first considered as a phenomenon in which "one and the same content appears in different media, whereby each medium retains its specific function" and has an economic orientation that aims at "the longest possible marketing chain", (Möbius 2014, 224; cf. also Frederking/Josting 2005, 8; Hengst 2014, 144; Josting 2018, 392). Research in the media composite field comprises both a purely receptive and a productive area, on the basis of which the recipient's interaction with the composite can be described. The *Stoff* is the element that forms the *tertium comparationis,* so to speak, and holds the media network together. The investigation of the Mickey Mouse composite also includes the theories of *brands* and *characters* in order to describe a media composite as such *tertia comparationis*. Both terms denote figures that can be at the center of a media network. A *character* is a figure that "has a face and a body" and "always stand[s] in close relation to the narrative" (Steinberg 2012, 191; quoted in Hengst 2014, 153). That is, the character of a *character* manifests itself within the action, the story, a narrative. *Brands,* on the other hand, are more abstract characters that work more through "signs" and "logos" (ibid., 2014, 153), that is, as the translation suggests, more like a trademark that no longer stands for and embodies a single, concrete character, but a specific *brand* idea. Both terms can establish and hold together a media network.

Based on these basic theoretical ideas, this study is divided into three steps. The first step is to define what the contemporary German press used to define what was *typically* American about the characters. Afterward, this will also be examined on the productive side by the means of two examples. The three complexes of meaning are intended to shed light on how Disney's American style was received in Germany. Guiding are the following questions: (1) How is the concept of *American shaping* defined and evaluated in the German contemporary film press? (2) To what extent was the *character* of Mickey Mouse adapted for German entertainment? (3) How was Mickey Mouse as a *brand* used for German *counter-propaganda* during the war? Since Mickey's reception by the cinema audience as well as his popularity among the German population are already quite extensively known and researched (cf. among others Fuchs 1998a; Koebner 2002; Platthaus 2001; Sackmann 2015b; Seßlen 1998; Tomkowiak 2017), the focus here will be explicitly on the reception by the trade press and the prolific artists.

Mickey Mouse as a Brand in 1930s Germany

Mickey Mouse is more than a mere cartoon character; he is rather a "real" symbol, "supra-temporal religious invention, but completely profaned" (*Mickey Mouse wird 70* 1998). The skill in building such iconic *characters*[1] was (and is) one of the guarantors of Disney's enduring prosperity, while also paving the way for innovative

---

[1] In addition to Mickey Mouse, Donald Duck is especially noteworthy here.

film projects (cf. Koebner 2002, 656; Tomkowiak 2017, 123). However, it took five years to get there: From the founding of Disney Studios on October 16, 1923, to the establishment of Mickey Mouse as the *face* of the Disney world. Walt Disney always met changes from the outside with his characteristic flexibility in order to constantly expand his company and, above all, the characters that ensured his success: *Oswald the Lucky Rabbit* – himself very much inspired by *Felix the Cat* – thus became, after a copyright dispute with the distribution company, a "mouse modelled in simple strokes, walking upright and equipped with four-fingered grasping hands, with round ears and a winningly cheeky grin" (Seßlen 1998, 211). Disney gave it the name Mortimer Mouse, but quickly changed it to Micky (short for Michael) at the suggestion of his wife: Mickey Mouse was born on March 10, 1928 (cf. Fuchs 1998a, 219 f.). The film career of the anthropomorphised mouse began with the short film *Steamboat Willie* (1928), which was released on November 18, 1928 and quickly became a classic,[2] the third film with Mickey Mouse to be shot but the first to be broadcast, which began its triumphal march across the USA (cf. Platthaus 2001; Seßlen 1998; Fuchs 1995, 1998a; Tomkowiak 2017). Mickey Mouse is – alongside Donald Duck as another iconic Disney *character* – arguably the company's biggest *brand* and at the same time the *face* of the Disney empire to this day, because within the collective global memory he represents the central figure of the Disney universe as a supposed *founding member.*

In the area of marketing Disney also learned from the experiences with earlier figures, and then reached a certain perfection in the days of Mickey Mouse. Already with Oswald, the entrepreneur recognised the potential of a full-scale figure marketing, because he used Oswald as an advertising medium in many different areas. For the first time, merchandising products such as figurines or licensed everyday objects were also used; be it to promote an already released or soon to be completed film in advance, or to lend further popularity to the *character* of the Lucky Rabbit in general (cf. Platthaus 2001, 37). Fuchs (1998a, 223) doubts whether Disney already at this early stage had in mind the establishment of an entire empire, which was to extend to the opening of huge amusement parks,[3] based on one (*brand*) character – whether it was called Oswald or Mickey. The man from Chicago could be trusted, however, if one considers his genius that was always as far-sighted as it was risk-taking.

It remains undisputed, however, that the figure of Oswald was the first *attempt* to enter the terrain of further marketing and money acquisition outside of cinematic and narrative realisations. Little by little, Disney added more and more facets to the concept of a cult of *characters* that spanned the media and also *escaped* the original medium. To even begin to describe Disney's merchandising empire, which even in the early days was sprawling, would go beyond the scope of this article. In addition

---

[2] Disney and Iwerks shot the Mickey films parallel to the Oswald productions that continued to appear, for the most part in the evenings in their free time, in order to comply with the existing contract, but also to have a secure source of income and at the same time to set themselves up for the future (cf. Fuchs 1998a, 219 f.).

[3] On the emergence of theme parks, cf. Fuchs 1998a, 223.

to Mickey, Disney's other *regular characters* such as Pluto, Donald and Co, "i.e. the individualistic cartoons based on characters that had been developed to perfection in the meantime [...] provided enormous additional income in the licensing business" (Platthaus 2001, 103). Disney's flair for far-reaching marketing opportunities was evident in his creativity in all areas of business. For example, starting in 1937, he even sold the seemingly worthless cels – celluloids used to animate the characters for the animated films – first to employees after realising that they could not be recycled for further films, and then to fans of the films. Later, he created a small department of his own, which he had produce artificial image cels for the film shoots after the cels lost their relevance for media production, which were then sold to fans as part of the production.

This wave of success, on which Mickey Mouse was also able to move seemingly playfully, was not limited to the United States from the beginning, but initially spilled over to the Old Continent through the Mickey Mouse cartoons. Here, as in America, the new technology of the "sound film miracle[s]" (Sackmann 2015b, 65) and the weakness of the economy, "in which people were looking for diversion [...]" (Fuchs 1998a, 220 f.), played a decisive role in the mass enthusiasm that the animated films triggered among German cinema audiences.

The structure of the figure Mickey itself also contributed to its massive worldwide success. Georg Seßlen describes Mickey as a figure that can be understood without a "cultural code" (Seßlen 1998, 211). That is to say, it functions the same way outside its origins in American culture: "Everywhere Mickey is, he is different and at the same time the same; across times and countries he transforms himself in order to remain himself." (Ibid.) This is largely true, at least for the central European cultural sphere, and thus also for the early 1930s. Mickey became an icon of (pop) culture, deftly moving between different cultures and systems and able to find his place in almost any situation. The figure not only vagabonds between media and markets, but also between cultures and systems, is embedded in diverse contexts due to its mutability (cf. ibid.). Over time, it has taken on the most diverse roles and adapted the most diverse *Stoffe*; it has been placed in a new context without losing its *brand's essence,* its abstract meaning (cf. Palme 1998, 204). Viewers knew what to expect when they saw a new film with Disney's mouse.

Mickey also quickly and easily crossed media boundaries in Germany as an already successful film character, and various products spread among the German population. In pre-war Germany, enthusiasm for the character was "a breeding ground for all sorts of derivatives such as postcards and knick-knacks." (Sackmann 2015b, 65). It is interesting to observe the interaction that ensured that a separate media network emerged within Germany with the character of Mickey at its centre. In response to the resounding box office success in Germany, enterprising German filmmakers produced their own versions of Mickey Mouse films, which they released unlicensed, i.e. as plagiarised, films in German cinemas (cf. ibid.). The network also extends from comic book adaptations in German daily newspapers to merchandising products and the propaganda machinery of the late 1930s and 1940s, which in Germany produced a very unique – – and also ambivalent – approach to Disney *characters* in general and Mickey Mouse in particular (Fig. 2).

Fig. 2 Mickey Mouse as an advertising figure. *Paradies der Hölle* (1930), from: *Kinematograph* 24 (1930) 270 of 18.11., 6

The spread can be traced back to the large-scale marketing strategies and settings. Disney had several marketing centres in Europe, which are comparable to today's merchandise shops. There were T-shirts, figurines and many other fan products, for example, 230,000 Mickey locomotives in the Christmas trade. This created an interaction between fans, products, and animated films, which cross-fertilised each other (cf. Koebner 2002, 656 f.). However, Disney also had an interest in importing merchandising products developed in Europe and distributing them in America. Licenses for Disney products were distributed in Europe at the time by the agencies George Borgfeldt & Co. and William Banks Levy. After only a quarter of a year of cooperation, 28 licenses were available in Germany, including toothbrushes, candles, postcards, calendars, figurines, porcelain articles, soap models, handkerchiefs, wallpaper and books. Every company wanted a slice of the cake. However, this form of licensing business only lasted for a little less than a year. Problems arose because of the lack of coordination between Borgfeldt and Levy, but also because many of the work samples sent to the Disney brothers did not meet their high quality standards and were therefore rejected. Many producers drew profit from this confusion and produced their own products without applying for licenses (cf. Storm/Dreßler 1991, 172 ff.). Therefore, Disney began early on to enforce its rights to royalties in court. In Germany there were proverbial masses of court cases due to the permissive handling of copyright regulations, which due to their size had to be partly outsourced to cinemas and theatres. This harshness in license protection shows the importance Walt Disney placed on this form of marketing for the success of his business. However, even the legal measures did nothing to diminish the popularity of Disney in general and Mickey Mouse in particular (cf. Fuchs 1998a, 221).

The German companies that had the pleasure of being granted original licenses by Disney advertised them extensively. They came from the most diverse areas of production, and the spectrum of non-film products already alluded to above was correspondingly diverse, adding many pieces to the media network in Germany. From advertisements in toy brochures it can be concluded that various figures and toy dolls were produced. The Heinz & Kühn company, for example, sold Mickey and Minnie costumes for carnival parties. Well-known companies such as Südfilm AG produced brooches and clasps, Steiff and Schuco also participated in the lucrative business with the mice. Uncounted are also the porcelain products such as plates, cups, egg cups or salt shakers. These are just a few examples from the extensive portfolio, which cannot be listed here in its entirety.[4] Some daily newspapers also used Mickey Mouse as an advertising figure, as the well-known *brand* promised to increase sales figures (cf. Sackmann 2015b, 72). In Germany, the star in the shape of a mouse sometimes went so far that Mickey Mouse addressed personal Christmas greetings to the readership, for example. A newspaper from Gera included a board game at Christmas 1930, advertised with the sentence "like Mickey Mouse coming to Gera in person." (ibid., 72 f.).

In the German film press there are some interesting perspectives on the course of merchandising both in Germany and abroad. As an example, an article from the *Film-Kurier* of September 23, 1936, traces the course of Disney's licensing worldwide with both admiration and astonishment, and then states that "a product only becomes a bestseller [...] by being given the name 'Mickey Mouse pocket watch', for example." (Dies und Das 1936, 3) The market that Disney's works have tapped so far is simply impossible to survey. Attempting to list it one would hardly come to an end (cf. ibid.).

The figure or the *brand* of Mickey Mouse thus also functioned in Germany without the context of a specific narrative. It unfolds its effect here by letting its face shine from "wrapping paper, boxes, [...] china, boxing gloves, dollhouses, toys, from the smallest to the largest" (ibid.). The comprehensive penetration of really all areas of life by a cartoon character seems to have been new, at least to this extent. Even "diapers (!)" (ibid.), notes the *Film-Kurier*, expressing its astonishment at this

---

[4] A very large collection of merchandising items, including extensive visual material, can be found in the volume accompanying an exhibition at the Filmmuseum Potsdam (cf. Storm/Dreßler 1991, 152–206).

curiosity with an exclamation mark, were available for purchase with a Mickey Mouse image.

From these two components – the factual quantity of merchandising products available in contemporary Germany and the admiring enumeration of the manifold products in the *Film-Kurier* – it can be concluded that Mickey Mouse had also managed to become a trademark, a *brand,* in Germany. This is the reason for his great relevance for the film world in the Weimar Republic up to the Nazi era, in which the *character* of Mickey Mouse was able to reach and also influence a large number of people.

Disney's Animated Films in the German Trade Press: Typically *American!*

In the following, we will examine what the various print media see as the repeatedly mentioned American attitude in the Disney works with Mickey as a representative *character* and why this aspect is repeatedly mentioned in the reviews of individual films. American humor in particular is the focus of the authors' consideration, as it was a large part of the *brand's* success. The motivation for these reflections is described vicariously in a 1935 article in the *Film-Kurier*: "When the talk turns to drawn film, the immediate response is, 'Yeah, we can't do that as well as the Americans – they're way ahead of us.'" (Edmund Smith schafft einen ernsten Trickfilm 1935, 1). This sense of inferiority pervades almost all of the news coverage of the 1930s. Many articles speak of American humor or "American shaping" (Frühling an der Donau 1935), but without specifying this in more detail (cf. also Film-Kabarett in Hamburg 1938, 3).

Interesting are some articles in film magazines from the year 1935, which deal with the development of the German animated film, among others with the example of the animator Edmund Smith, or the analysis of the weakness of the German animated film industry in comparison with the Disney films. In doing so, the *Film-Kurier* compares, at least immanently, the working methods of the German animated film with those of the American. Two terms are juxtaposed to illustrate the fundamental differences between German and American animated films: Differentiation is made between the "ernsthafte[n] Zeichenfilm" on the one hand and the "grotesque" on the other (Ernsthafter Zeichenfilm 1935). Edmund Smith is credited with finally having made an animated film that sets itself apart from the cheerful mood of Disney productions (cf. ibid.). Lotte Reiniger, who is still known today as the producer of famous silhouette films of the Weimar Republic, also commented on this. In addition to the economic distance to American productions, which was the reason why "America's Mickey Mouse is better known," she sees a " difference in mentality" between the German and American animated films; while the German one is more serious and deeper in feeling, the American one depicts the "natural boyishness of this American," in other words, it is altogether more cheerful and softer, while German humor is considered more melancholy, but also more profound (Lotte Reiniger sprach über ihre Arbeit 1935, 3). References to this discussion can also be found alongside the announcement of the film *Snow White and the seven dwarfs* (Walt Disney filmed *Snow White* in 1935) in an issue of the *Film-Kurier* from 1935, which speaks of "typical American humor" concerning American military propaganda films, saying that it is "biting", rarely "cynical", but never "anti-state" (USA-Spielfilm als Werber 1935, 1).[5]

As for Disney's artistic quality, it is always highlighted and explicitly praised. In a review of the *Merry Menagerie,* a compilation of seven Disney films traditionally shown at Christmastime on one evening at the cinema, there first is praise of the quality of the product and also reference to the positive reaction of the audience. This is followed by another reference to the wish for a German equivalent, in this case a menagerie of short films and sketches by the German comedian Karl Valentin, which would certainly be very successful (cf. "Lustige Menagerie" – Sieben Disney-Filme in der "Kurbel" 1936). However, above all the economic conditions of animated film production in Germany are criticised. Like Lotte Reiniger, other connoisseurs of the scene are also of the opinion that in comparison to the Americans, Germany lacks finances in the field of animated film, which diminishes its quality. This was also the case with the animator Kurt Wolfes in a lecture at the Berlin Hochschule in the spring of 1937, reported by the *Film-Kurier*. Because of the American superiority, Wolfes demanded a separation from the big brother from the USA. Technical equivalence could not be achieved because of the economic difference, but this was not necessary. One should concentrate on the further development of content (cf. Wirkliche Unwirklichkeit 1937).

With the increasing influence of the National Socialists on the film industry, the discussion changed in the following years. In an article about German film in Bucharest, there are remarks about the decline in audience interest in German productions in Romania. It is explained primarily by the "invasion" of the Romanian market by American films; the tendency is to say that German films are "more carefully elaborated" and "better thought out", i.e. of higher artistic quality overall (Deutscher Film in Bukarest 1937). In addition, the American films, due to their lack of depth, better met the taste of the rather undemanding audience in Romania, the more profound German films "would find little understanding here" (ibid.). Anti-Semitism is also blatantly revealed when the alleged density of Jewish employees in the Romanian distribution system and the hatred of Germany attributed to them are held responsible for the boycott of German films.

Another example is the feature-length film *Snow White and the Seven Dwarfs,* released in 1937, which became the subject of intense debate in the German trade press, not only because the Grimm fairy tales were claimed to be so-called German cultural assets. Walt Disney was fascinated by the Grimm brothers' fairy tales from

---

[5] More by chance, but quite significantly, one comes across an article in the same newspaper directed *Gegen alte Filme mit nichtarischen Darstellern* (1935). The showing of such films, especially those with proven emigrants in the leading roles, would be forbidden. This indicates a development that will also become increasingly visible in the reception of Disney films.

the very beginning (cf. Platthaus 2001, 29). He already chose *Rotkäppchen* as a model for his very first work within the *Laugh-o-grams*[6] (*Little Red Riding Hood* 1922). He had recognised the relevance of the genre for the European market and consequently planned it as an important factor. So what could be more obvious than to use popular fairy tale *Stoffe* to bind the audience more closely to the animation studio through the already familiar.[7] With his first feature-length film, Disney continued the concept of using fairy tales, which had become almost a tradition. *Snow White and the Seven Dwarfs* was a resounding success that was to establish the triumphant advance of feature-length films from Disney (cf. Fuchs 1998a, 223). The extremely short original fairy tale *Stoff* was extended to the length of a feature-length film by enriching the *Stoff* with typical Hollywood elements such as melodrama or slapstick, but the characters also changed. In the case of *Snow White and the Seven* Dwarfs, the dwarfs were each given their own character traits, which made them the secret stars of the film (cf. Tomkowiak 2017, 124). In this way, Disney increasingly adapted the characters and plot to American viewing habits: "individualism, work ethic, optimism, innocence, the pursuit of happiness", but also "romantic love and the victory of good over evil, all of this, mind you, within the rules of a hierarchically structured society" (ibid., 130) can be found in the film.

Although the fairy tales of the Brothers Grimm were highly regarded in Nazi Germany, the Disney adaptation of Snow White more or less failed with contemporary critics and was not allowed to be shown (cf. Schlesinger 2017, 147 f.).[8] It was doubted whether the German fairy tale *Stoff* was actually suitable to provide the plot for an animated film designed for humour, and one was glad to have alternatives with German animated fairy tale films (cf. Ein kleiner gemalter Märchenfilm 1938). A central accusation was that Snow White had been "entgruselt" (*Schneewittchen entgruselt* 1937). Examples were used to show how particularly gruesome scenes had been removed, and the "optimistic relaxation" (ibid.) instead of the gloomy ending was also criticised, which would make the American approach clear, namely the bypassing of gloomy themes.[9] "Our" Snow White must now "pay [...] tribute" to this "optimism at all costs" (ibid.). Other authors also described this film adaptation as a "banal touching play" (Tomkowiak 2017, 126) that inadequately portrayed the sublimity of the source material. The contemporary reviews cited present a relatively uniform picture of *Snow White's reception*: Too little creepiness, too much optimism. It is therefore not surprising that Mickey Mouse films were also changed, with song interludes being partially cut "for good luck" (Filmtheater in East Africa

---

[6] For a complete overview, see Tomkowiak 2017, 122 f.

[7] This continues consistently in the choice of material in the years that followed, with *The Four Musicians of Bremen* (1922), which Disney began immediately after completing *Little Red Riding Hood*. After two American stories - *Jack and the Beanstalk* (1922), and *Goldie Locks and the Three Bears* (1922) - Disney turned back to classic European fairy tale material with *Puss in Boots* (1922) and *Cinderella* (1950) (cf. Platthaus 2001, 28 f.).

[8] For an extensive censorship list of Disney films, see Storm/Dreßler 1991, 148–151.

[9] In England, interestingly enough, the film was not released until the age of 16 due to cruelty (cf. *Man hört und liest* 1938).

1937). What critics found good or bad often did not coincide with audience taste. Optimism and cheerfulness, which met or meet in the character or rather the brand Mickey Mouse, universally appeal to the audience.

Mickey Mouse in the Comic Strips of German Daily Newspapers

The question of the influence of the Mickey Mouse brand on the German cultural landscape will be explored not only at the level of reception in a narrower sense, but also in the area of productive interaction with the media network. Two examples have been chosen that are diametrically opposed to each other and illustrate the opposition described above between the adoration of the mouse on the one hand and its reception as a trivial and *typically* American cultural asset on the other. Using the implementation of the *character* in comic strips in Germany as an example at the beginning of the 1930s the following section focuses on this level of production.

In the USA, the mouse had just made the leap from cartooning to comics and thus onto the magazine shelf under the auspices of cartoonist Floyd Gottfredson (cf. Seßlen 1998, 213), when German publishers began sending their cartoonists to the USA for study visits to observe the latest developments and gain inspiration (cf. Scholz 2014, 67). While in the rest of (Western) Europe the form of comic strips[10] slowly took a firm place in newspaper publishing, only a few papers in Germany wanted to jump on this bandwagon, as the German public was rather skeptical about serial forms of publication (cf. ibid.). This may come as a surprise, because contrary to popular belief, the comic culture that emerged in the USA did not only reach the German cultural sphere through the American occupation forces after the end of the Second World War. As early as the German Revolution of 1848/1849, "cartoonish, narrative picture stories" are known to have been the "forerunners of the comic in Germany" (Fuchs 1998b, 249). Nevertheless, one has to look more closely in order to find a transfer of the extremely successful comic strips in America to the German newspaper system (cf. ibid., 65).[11]

"The *Arbeiter Illustrierte Zeitung* (1930) can take credit for having published the first 'Mickey Mouse' newspaper strip in Germany in mid-1930." (Sackmann 2015b, 65; cf. also Scholz 2014, 67 f.) The first strips appeared irregularly and with large intervals between them. Already here, the pattern of adapting American comic strips and simply reproducing them with German text, which was also practiced later in other newspapers, becomes apparent. Despite the Maus's fame in Germany, the newspaper strips were not exactly a great success, which is attributed, among other

---

[10] Short, sketch-like comic series consisting of a few sequences of images.
[11] Eckart Sackmann's surveys in the context of *Deutsche Comicforschung,* on which this presentation is largely based, offer a detailed insight into this topic, although Sackmann admits that research into comic strips is difficult to carry out and, at the same time, is to a large extent shaped by chance.

things, to the fact that the scheme of serial comics was not yet widespread in Germany, as mentioned above (cf. Sackmann 2015b, 65). It is also possible that the intervals between the individual episodes in the *AIZ*, which was only published weekly, were too long to do justice to the serial format and retain readers. On the German market, daily newspapers were more likely to be the medium of choice for this form of publication. The *Erfurter Allgemeine Zeitung (Thüringer Zeitung)* dared to take this step and also published an episode of an original comic strip series in 1930. In this case, this did not mean a mere translation into German, but also an adaptation of the comic strips, which appeared every two days in different parts of the newspaper, as familiar with the German readership. Since speech bubbles were not yet common in Germany, the texts were placed in a continuous text below the picture (cf. ibid., 69 f.). However, at the end of 1930 the implementation of speech bubbles changed. While they were initially removed, they were later filled with exclamation and question marks, as well as being used for spoken language along the lines with the American originals. Thus, in a sense, there was a renewed Americanisation of the Germanised, originally American medium. Sackmann additionally interestingly notes that the language in German was far less "elaborate" (ibid., 70) and assumes as reasons either a different addressee reference (children) or consideration for the unfamiliar literary form, which was not supposed to overwhelm German readers (cf. ibid., 70 f.). The second daily newspaper Sackmann identifies as a medium for the dissemination of Mickey comic strips is the *Kölnische Illustrierte Zeitung*. Beginning on December 27, 1930, it published original American strips in German adaptations in regular intervals. The fidelity to the original went so far as to retain Walt Disney's original signature (cf. Scholz 2014, 67).

When advertising the comic strips, the *Kölnische Illustrierte Zeitung* focused on Mickey's success in the cinema and used this to also advertise the printed version: "Now a 'reflection of their black-and-white existence on the big screen' should also appear on newsprint." (Ibid.) The newspaper itself thematised Mickey Mouse's rumored change of media in its advertising copy. It goes on to say:

> Here, too, her mercurial, truly mouse-like agility, her fantastic play with reality, is bustling; here, too, the heroic battles take place that she, a little David with mouse ears, fights out against the Goliath powers of men and machines and the big bad animals, and the great dances that the ingenious pencil of her creator Walt Disney and his twelve collaborators improvise for her. [...] Mickey makes all the peoples of the earth laugh. If there were a Nobel Prize for the world's jokers, Mickey Mouse would have to have it. (quoted from Storm/Dreßler 1991, 196)

In doing so, the daily newspaper demonstrated a comprehensive awareness of the character's already-acquired notoriety, but also of the hurdles that German readers could face. The cover of the newspaper showed a large Mickey in front of a photograph of a crowd streaming into a cinema auditorium. In addition to the comic strip, the first issue included an explanatory text on American comics in order to educate the German audience about the still little-known medium and to socialise readers towards reading comics (cf. Sackmann 2015b, 66). But even these publications were only a brief success, as no more comic strips appeared after a good year (cf. ibid., 72). In 1931, a total of 24 strips found their way into the *Kölnische Illustrierte*

Zeitung. The series ended with the onset of the banking crisis and the resulting financial problems in the newspaper sector (cf. Scholz 2014, 68). However, an innovation can also be found during this short publication period: for the first – and at the same time for the last time (cf. Storm/Dreßler 1991, 196 f.) – not only the original comic strips were used, but an own creation by a German illustrator, in this case Frank Behmaks, was published. The strip[12] consists of eight individual pictures showing Mickey Mouse attending a carnival party. In the first picture, the mouse stands at the entrance to the dance palace and says with his characteristic cheerfulness, "Ich gehe in meinem Originalkostüm. Das macht mir keiner nach." The fact that he is not in disguise when he says this, and is wearing only his *mouse costume*, gives the scene its *characteristic* Mickey Mouse mischievous wit. However, when he enters the hall (Fig. 2), this cheeky idea is reversed and surprises the mouse itself. Everyone at the party is dressed as Mickey or Minnie Mouse, the original simply indistinguishable. Mickey therefore tries to prove his uniqueness with a dance trick – he ties his legs together and then quickly twirls around – (pictures 3–6). Finally, he is thrown out by the guardian, Puss Karlo, to the thunderous laughter of the others, not without passing a casual remark (pictures 7–8).

While the plot was moved into the Weimar Republic, the *American* character of the comic is also clearly recognisable: Behmak created a symbiosis of the American original and his German adaptation, not only by imitating Disney's style, but also by adapting the caption "freely adapted from Walt Disney" to the original. He also used the classic speech bubbles early on, which shows the closeness to the *American*. He also was formally inspired by the original American strips, adopting the style and character drawing of Mickey Mouse, yet adapting the content to the German audience: the strip is about Rosenmontag with Mickey Mouse (cf. Lettkemann 2011, 61 f.). Mickey has retained his familiar appearance, as he also notes himself, and speaks with his characteristic cheerfulness. At this point, the two spheres mix: The resourceful prankster circumvents the German tradition of compulsory disguise on Rosenmontag by employing his uniqueness and appealing to it with his alleged disguise. However, he is thwarted by his own notoriety, symbolised by all the guests' disguises as Mickey Mouse, and eventually ends up on the street. In Mickey Mouse's unprovable originality, a caricature of the many imitators is evident who visually match the real Mickey Mouse, but in no way possess his abilities – only the original can perform the special comical dance. The overabundance of Mickey Mouse in the cinemas of the Weimar Republic is also certainly recognisable here, the auditorium overflowing with Mickey Mice. The happy ending, on the other hand – Mickey is not discouraged and disappointed, but rather makes another cheeky remark as soon as he hits the pavement – is in keeping with the American optimism noted above. In this comic strip, then, the employment of Mickey Mouse for German cultural purposes can be traced. On the one hand, popularity is used to increase circulation, and on the other, the familiar American form of the optimistic and positive yet cheerful figure of Mickey Mouse is used to please readers in times of economic recession.

---

[12] Reprinted in Storm/Dreßler 1991, 197.

The *character* was – here representative of many other products[13] – adapted to German needs, thus offering a familiar amusement in a *German guise*. His American *characteristics* survived the change to the new cultural environment and, in a sense, fuse with the German parts of the comic strip.

At this point, however, the inclusion of Mickey Mouse in German daily newspapers of the time comes to an end. Eckhart Sackmann currently knows of no further publication of Mickey Mouse adventure strips in German-language daily newspapers, which "does not necessarily mean that there was no such thing" (ibid., 73). Storm/Dreßler (1991), however, were able to locate at least a few magazines that still printed Mickey Mouse comic strips in the mid-1930s (cf. ibid., 197 f.).[14] With the ever-increasing control that National Socialism exerted on people's lives restrictions came against American comics. Although the National Socialists did not reject American comics per se, American humour was becoming less and less suited to the "German essence" (Scholz 2014, 76) and publications probably petered out because of this.

The German *Counter-Propaganda*

When the political as well as social situation in Germany changed drastically in the course of the Nazi seizure of power, Mickey Mouse was misused together with other Disney *characters* for (counter-)propaganda purposes. Interestingly, the Nazi rulers initially tried to use Disney for their own purposes by referring to his alleged German ancestry, but later they claimed that he was of Jewish heritage (cf. Fuchs 1995, 376). The love for Mickey Mouse continued, however, among the public in Germany, and Hitler as well as Goebbels and Mussolini adored Disney's mouse, had Mickey Mouse films brought to them from the occupied territories,[15] even though German propaganda had long since discredited Disney as an example of a "Jewish Ungeist" (Platthaus 2001, 177).

It is not surprising that the National Socialist government instrumentalised comics for its propagandistic purposes. At the latest since the First World War, comics and caricatures had been used in the American sphere as a tried and tested means for propaganda purposes (cf. Sackmann 2015a, 56). This technique was taken up again by the USA with its entry into the war (cf. Scholz 2014, 83). In addition to the widely known American propaganda films and comics against the German enemy[16]

---

[13] Examples include the film *Das Micky-Maus-Girl* from 1930 (cf. *Deutscher Tonfilmerfolg in Wien* 1930) or the rival product *Krazy Kat* (cf. *Paradies der Hölle* 1930).

[14] Only the places of appearance are mentioned, no further information is provided. A listing shall therefore be omitted at this point.

[15] See also Koop 2015 for a comprehensive list of the film tastes of the ruling elite in the *Third Reich*. There are quite a few Disney films to be found in it, even during later wartime.

[16] One rumour has it that the Disney film *Victory Through Air Power* (1943) even persuaded Churchill to support the Americans in the air war (cf. Platthaus 2001, 176 f.).

(cf. ibid., 77), Disney *characters* were also used on the German side to influence their own population. In 1941, under the impression of a highly successful propaganda film for the Canadians, the American leadership commissioned a film of its own to convince citizens of the need for a new tax to finance the war. The *characters* appeared in U.S. films "geared to the specifically American wartime (and later postwar) interest" (ibid.). The resounding success of these propaganda measures gave the final go-ahead in Germany for the link with the person Walt Disney and American culture (cf. Platthaus 2001, 178 f.). When the Americans then began to use Disney *characters* as mascots for their fighter planes, the tide finally turned. For their part, the Germans launched a kind of 'counter-propaganda' (ibid., 177), so that Mickey became more and more the target of German polemics (cf. Fuchs 1998a, 220). Many German cartoonists had spent time in the USA before the Second World War and were familiar with Disney's drawings and comics. At the beginning of the war, they used the knowledge they had acquired to support the propaganda of German interests, making use of Walt Disney's well-known repertoire of *characters*. Now, contrary to their other global impact, the characters, which included Mickey, were again reduced to their function as signifiers of the American cultural community and thus to their American *brand* role. In their comic strips, the various authors depicted the Disney *character* Mickey, as well as Donald, Goofy and Pluto, as bomb-throwers who bombed German cities (Fig. 3).

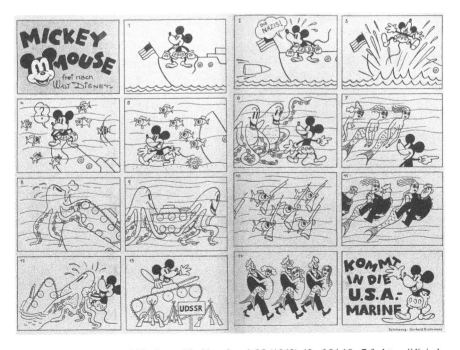

Fig. 3 Mickey Mouse (1942), from: *Kladderadatsch* 95 (1942) 40 of 04.10., 7 f., https://digi.ub.uni-heidelberg.de/diglit/kla (25.03.2020)

An impressive example of this *counter-propaganda* can be found in the magazine *Kladaradatsch* from 1942, which had a nationalist orientation since the late 1930s and for which the illustrator Gerhard Brinkmann worked (cf. Sackmann 2016, 84; on Brinkmann's biography, cf. Sackmann 2011). Mickey Mouse is happily sitting on an American military boat that is destroyed by an incoming German shell and lands in the sea. Briefly confused (question mark in picture 4), he quickly comes to a solution in his typical manner. Picture by picture, he recruits the sea creatures as soldiers to help the US in the war against Germany. They answer his call and bring weapons like tanks and guns to the front. The mermaids rescue the shipwrecked sailors and are eventually carried by them like wives. Brinkmann here utilises the aforementioned look of the American Mickey comic strips. Micky is, as usual, a cheerful character, always has a smile on his lips and never resigns. In this respect, he corresponds to Behmak's Micky at the Rosenmontag party, who also doesn't let his expulsion stop his cheerfulness. He also shines with unconventional ideas, getting the anthropomorphised (also typical of Disney) sea creatures to help him gather forces. The comic book here is returned to its original American form. Even the sailors look like decals from an American propaganda film for the Navy but are ridiculed because the mermaids carry them first and not the other way around. Through this, Brinkmann takes aim at the appropriation of Disney *characters* by US propaganda. Ridiculousness, lack of logic and also inappropriateness of the American recruitment comics are highlighted by the author. In comparison to Behmak, Mickey is not cast positively here but inappropriately cheerful, although he possesses similar characteristics. German interests are served not only by merging with but also by distinguishing him from the typical American *character*. Again, Mickey is active as the *brand* he represents: He represents the America hated by the Nazis, which must be fought. With the help of a comic mouse, both sides thus attempted to mobilise their respective addressees.

Concluding Remarks

So what is the typically *American character* of Mickey Mouse, which is received and productively implemented in various ways by the media examined here? First of all, it should be noted that in the German film magazines examined here, the typically *American character* of Disney products in general and of the – also German – Mickey Mouse *brand* in particular can be found primarily in the cheerful but naïve optimism inherent in Disney's animated films and other forms of expression. This peculiarity was at first neutrally described in film magazines *as American,* but then, as the influence of the National Socialists increased, it was more or less explicitly evaluated negatively. The superiority of German cinematic taste was increasingly emphasised, but without seriously questioning the quality of Disney films.

This ambivalent reception of American cartoon culture could also be traced and expanded on the basis of the two examples on the productive level of dealing with the media network. The comic strip *Mickys Rosenmontag*, which was adapted to

German needs, made use of the Mickey Mouse *brand*, which was also successful in Germany, by picking up on its well-known skills and pranks as well as its popularity in Germany, but placing it in a new context. The American *character* merged, so to speak, with the German history of the comic strip. A very different sentiment is found in the employment of Mickey for Nazi *counter-propaganda*. Disney's *characters*, in this case Mickey Mouse, are thrown back on another aspect of their *brand in* the Brinkmann's example examined: their cheerful wit and optimism now represent the prototypical American enemy, whose (lack of) culture was far removed from the supposed *spiritual depth of* the German people. In an ironic way, it became possible to play with the familiar Mickey Mouse comic clichés, to discredit the American enemy.

Overall, a very versatile reception of the American side of the Disney *character* Mickey can be found. The *American element* found its way into German culture in various forms and was used for German interests in the various manifestations of the *brand*. This brief insight into the implementation is in no way to be regarded as complete but can only offer a glimpse of a topic area within media network research on Mickey Mouse and other Disney products that still needs to be dealt with more extensively. In the context of this article, the focus was only on the trade press and the artists. It therefore goes without saying that in the everyday life of the German population this image of Mickey Mouse did not have to correspond to reality. Simply because of the ever-increasing pressure from the National Socialists, the press had to appear more in line with the system than was perhaps necessary in all sections of the population, especially in the entertainment market. Restrictions increased in this area, but Mickey Mouse was still successfully represented in German cinemas until the early 1940s (cf. Der Januar in Hamburg 1941) or was used for educational films (cf. Polizeifilme werben 1942). In the children's rooms things may have also been ambivalent. Mickey Mouse had played his way into the hearts of (not only) children, and therefore it was certainly not unusual for young people who were enthusiastic about National Socialism to have Mickey Mouse accessories in their rooms (cf. Platthaus 2001, 177.). The mouse was used for propaganda, but ultimately even a fascist state with bans could not completely break the enthusiasm for the *most quintessentially American* and at the same time most transformable of all cartoon characters.

References

Primary Literature

Behmak, Frank: Mickys Rosenmontag. In: Kölnische Illustrierte Zeitung 6 (1931) 7 vom 14.02.
Brinkmann, Gerhard: Micky Maus. In: Kladderadatsch 95 (1942) 40 vom 04.10., 7f., htttps://digi.ub.uni-heidelberg.de/diglit/kla (25.03.2020).
Reingefallen. In: Arbeiter Illustrierte Zeitung (1930) 24 vom 27.12.1930.

Filmography

Goldie Locks and the Three Bears (USA 1922). Regie: Walt Disney, https://www.youtube.com/watch?v=DK3M1oLze2U (25.03.2020).
Jack and the Beanstalk (USA 1922). Regie: Walt Disney, https://www.youtube.com/watch?v=v1hLr5oeUog (25.03.2020).
Little Red Riding Hood (USA 1922). Regie: Walt Disney, https://www.youtube.com/watch?v=mAwb2bxk6Eo (25.03.2020).
Das Micky-Maus-Girl (alternative title: Die vom Rummelplatz) (D 1930). Regie: Carl Lamac, Ondra-Lamac-Film (DVD).
Puss in Boots (USA 1922). Regie: Walt Disney, https://www.youtube.com/watch?v=H9n4Jb1kFns (25.03.2020).
Snow White and the Seven Dwarfs (USA 1937). Regie: David Hand, Wilfred Jackson, Ben Sharpsteen, Larry Morey, William Cottrell, Perce Pearce, Disney (DVD).
Steamboat Willie (USA 1928). Regie: Ub Iwerks, Walt Disney, https://www.youtube.com/watch?v=BBgghnQF6E4 (25.03.2020).
The Four Musicians of Bremen (USA 1922). Regie: Walt Disney, https://www.youtube.com/watch?v=1_3sI9WW6_A (25.03.2020).
Victory Through Air Power (USA 1943). Regie: Frank Thomas, Clyde Geronimi, Jack Kinney, James Algar, Perce Pearce, Fred Moore, H. C. Potter, Roach, Hal Roach, https://www.youtube.com/watch?v=tUeKeN9bXSE (25.03.2020).

Secondary Literature Before 1945

Der Januar in Hamburg. In: Film-Kurier 23 (1941) 35 vom 11.02., 1.
Deutscher Film in Bukarest. Die Ursachen der rückläufigen Entwicklung. In: Film-Kurier 19 (1937) 74 vom 31.03., 1–2.
Deutscher Tonfilmerfolg in Wien. In: Kinematograph 24 (1930) 230 vom 02.10., 5.
Dies und Das. In: Film-Kurier 18 (1936) 223 vom 23.09., 3.
Edmund Smith schafft einen ernsten Trickfilm. In: Film-Kurier 17 (1935) 178 vom 02.08., 1–2.
Ein kleiner gemalter Märchenfilm. In: Film-Kurier 20 (1938) 286 vom 07.12., 2.
Ernsthafter Zeichenfilm. In: Film-Kurier 17 (1935) 137 vom 15.06., Beiblatt, 2.
Film-Kabarett in Hamburg. In: Film-Kurier 20 (1938) 303 vom 28.12., 3.
Filmtheater in Ostafrika. Reiseeindrücke vom Roten Meer bis Kapstadt. Kinos in Kenya. In: Film-Kurier 19 (1937) 100, Beibl. 1–2.
Frühling an der Donau. In: Film-Kurier 17 (1935) 125 vom 31.05., 2.
Gegen alte Filme mit nichtarischen Darstellern. In: Film-Kurier 17 (1935) 136 vom 14.06., 1.
Lotte Reiniger sprach über ihre Arbeit. In: Film-Kurier 17 (1935) 68 vom 21.03, 3–4.
„Lustige Menagerie" – Sieben Disney-Filme in der „Kurbel". In: Film-Kurier 18 (1936) 279 vom 28.11., 2.
Man hört und liest. In: Film-Kurier 20 (1938) 32 vom 08.02., 3.
Paradies der Hölle [Anzeige]. In: Kinematograph 24 (1930) 270 vom 18.11., 6.
Polizeifilme werben. In: Film-Kurier 24 (1942) 42 vom 19.02., 3.
Schneewittchen entgruselt. In: Film-Kurier 19 (1937) 232 vom 06.10., 3.
USA-Spielfilm als Werber In: Film-Kurier 17 (1935) 136 vom 14.06., 1–2.
Walt Disney verfilmt „Schneewittchen". In: Film-Kurier 17 (1935) 136 vom 14.06., 1.
Wirkliche Unwirklichkeit. Filmkunst des Tricks. In: Film-Kurier 19 (1937) 59 vom 11.03., 1 und 4.

Secondary Literature After 1945

Frederking, Volker/Josting, Petra: Der Vielfalt eine Chance... In: Dies. (Hg.): Medienintegration und Medienverbund im Deutschunterricht. Baltmannsweiler 2005 (Diskussionsforum Deutsch, 18), 1–15.
Fuchs, Wolfgang J.: Der Erfinder der Micky Maus. In: Medien und Erziehung 39 (1995) 6, 375–376.
Fuchs, Wolfgang J.: Das Disney-Imperium. Wie ein Name zum Markenzeichen wurde. In: Medien und Erziehung 42 (1998a) 4, 219–225.
Fuchs, Wolfgang J.: Die illustrierte Aufklärung? Unterweisung mit Bilderbüchern und Comics. In: Medien und Erziehung 42 (1998b) 4, 249.
Hengst, Heinz: Am Anfang war die Biene Maja. Medienverbund und Japanisierung der kommerziellen Kultur. In: Weiß, Harald (Hg.): 100 Jahre Biene Maja – Vom Kinderbuch zum Kassenschlager. Heidelberg 2014 (Studien zur europäischen Kinder- und Jugendliteratur/ Studies in European Children's and Young Adult Literature; 1), 143–165.
Josting, Petra: Kinder- und Jugendliteratur im Medienverbund. In: Lange, Günter (Hg.): Kinder- und Jugendliteratur der Gegenwart. Ein Handbuch. Grundlagen, Gattungen, Medien, Lesesozialisation und Didaktik. Unter Mitarbeit von Hannelore Daubert. Unveränd. Aufl. Baltmannsweiler ⁴2018, 391–420.
Koebner, Thomas (Hg.): Reclams Sachlexikon des Films. Stuttgart 2002.
Koop, Volker: Warum Hitler King Kong liebte, aber den Deutschen Micky Maus verbot. Die geheimen Lieblingsfilme der Nazi-Elite. Berlin-Brandenburg 2015.
Lettkemann, Bernd: Frank Behmak. In: Sackmann, Eckart (Hg.): Deutsche Comicforschung 2012 (2011) 8, 56–63.
Möbius, Thomas: Adaption – Verbund – Produsage: Implikationen des Begriffs Medienkonvergenz. In: Weinkauff, Gina/Dettmar, Ute/Möbius, Thomas/Tomkowiak, Ingrid (Hg.): Kinder- und Jugendliteratur in Medienkontexten. Adaption – Hybridisierung – Intermedialität – Konvergenz. Frankfurt a. M. 2014 (Kinder- und Jugendkultur, -literatur und -medien; 89), 219–232.
Mickey Mouse wird 70. In: Medien und Erziehung 42 (1998) 4, 210.
Palme, Hans-Jürgen: Mickey Mouse hat Geburtstag. In: Medien und Erziehung 42 (1998) 4, 204.
Platthaus, Andreas: Von Mann & Maus. Die Welt des Walt Disney. Berlin 2001.
Sackmann, Eckart: G. Bri – Gerhard Brinkmann. In: Ders. (Hg.): Deutsche Comicforschung 2012 (2011) 8, 64–78.
Sackmann, Eckart: Big and Little Willie – und Max und Moritz noch dazu. In: Ders. (Hg.): Deutsche Comicforschung 2016 (2015a) 12, 56–63.
Sackmann, Eckart: Frühe „Micky Maus" – Zeitungsstrips in Deutschland. In: Ders. (Hg.): Deutsche Comicforschung 2016 (2015b) 12, 64–73.
Sackmann, Eckart: Gerhard Brinkmann: *Mickey Mouse* von 1942. In: Ders. (Hg.): Deutsche Comicforschung 2017 (2016) 13, 84–85.
Schlesinger, Ron: Märchenfilm im „Dritten Reich". In: Dettmar, Ute/Pecher, Claudia/Schlesinger, Ron (Hg.): Märchen im Medienwechsel. Zur Geschichte und Gegenwart des Märchenfilms. Stuttgart 2017, 143–177.
Scholz, Michael F.: „Comics" in der deutschen Zeitungsforschung vor 1945. In: Eckart Sackmann (Hg.): Deutsche Comicforschung 2015 (2014) 11, 59–84.
Seßlen, Georg: Die Maus als Anarchist und als Angepaßter. Mickey Mouse zum siebzigsten Geburtstag. In: Medien und Erziehung 42 (1998) 4, 211–218.
Steinberg, Marc: Anime's media mix. Franchising Toys and characters in Japan. Minneapolis [u. a.] 2012.
Storm, J. P./Dreßler, Mario: Im Reiche der Micky Maus. Walt Disney in Deutschland 1927 – zur Ausstellung in Filmmuseum Potsdam. Berlin 1991.
Tomkowiak, Ingrid: Capture the Imagination – 100 Jahre Disney-Märchenanimationsfilme. In: Dettmar, Ute/Pecher, Claudia/Schlesinger, Ron (Hg.): Märchen im Medienwechsel. Zur Geschichte und Gegenwart des Märchenfilms. Stuttgart 2017, 121–141.

Funkheinzelmann

The Multimedia Career of a Radio Character

Annemarie Weber

Preliminary Remarks

Funkheinzelmann was a character invented for the children's programmes on young German radio in 1924 and soon became one of the most popular heroes of German popular culture. With Old Shatterhand and Felix the Cat, Funkheinzelmann conquered the Berlin revue theatre and became the cover character of a children's magazine. The fairy tales created with and for Funkheinzelmann were pressed onto records and published in books, Funkheinzelmann became an identification figure for young peer groups and an advertising brand for German radio. After about four years, the productivity of the character, who is now forgotten, died out.[1]

The multimedia process that allowed Funkheinzelmann to grow into a large media network (Fig. 1) can be described in its ascending and descending dynamics, its becoming and passing away with the concept of seriality, as modelled for popular culture in a variety of ways, for example, by the authors of the anthology edited by Frank Kelleter (2012b). The seriality from which the popularity of Funkheinzelmann was fed and multiplied took place in commercial and semi-commercial contexts that mutually dynamised each other for a certain period of time, with the "narrative proliferation" (Kelleter 2012a, 31) of the figure mainly taking place on the free

---

[1] The database of the research project lists well over 900 records on the subject of Funkheinzelmann, including around 700 radio items.

A. Weber (✉)
Bielefeld, Germany

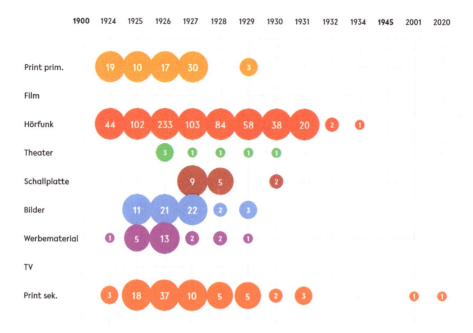

Fig. 1 Timeline of the Funkheinzelmann media network

market under the competitive conditions that prevailed here. It is therefore obvious to also use the insights of brand marketing and advertising communication to describe the serial proliferation of Funkheinzelmann.

How advertising works was broadly known at the beginning of the twentieth century. In 1924, the most important German advertising psychologist at the time, Theodor König, was already able to summarise numerous relevant experimental studies (cf. König 1924), which testify to a pronounced professionalisation of the American, but also already of the German advertising industry. The development of a brand, the positioning of a product in the market, and customer loyalty were strategies that were mastered by the successful players in the media market and in some cases used with virtuosity.

Funkheinzelmann: A Radio Figure Becomes a Brand

As early as May 4, 1924, two days after the Nordische Rundfunk AG (Norag) went on air for the first time in Hamburg, *Funkheinzelmann der Norag* appears in the programme. Both the name (from June onwards without the addition of „der Norag") and the broadcasting slot are later retained unchanged, which suggests long-term planning. In the first two months, the programme is created with changing authors and speakers, and the content does not yet reveal a uniform concept. Songs and fairy tales from well-known fairy tale literature are played, mostly without reference to a character or a narrator called Funkheinzelmann, and apparently also texts written especially for the radio, for example by Alice Fliegel, the wife and collaborator of Hans Bodenstedt.

From July 6, 1924 Hans Bodenstedt appears as the author of Funkheinzelmann. Funkheinzelmann is introduced as a fictional narrator who also experiences the stories he performs himself. Bodenstedt was one of the two directors of the Norag broadcasting company, as well as the artistic and scientific director of the programme, and also one of the two editors of the station's programme magazine, *Die Norag*. Funkheinzelmann thus had the greatest possible capital at his disposal from the very beginning: All the technical and programming possibilities as well as the symbolic capital of its inventor. After only two months, the Funkheinzelmann brand was found and its personality already contoured: Funkheinzelmann was simultaneously a programme for children, a narrator and a fairy tale character. At that time, Norag's programme magazine already published the first fan mail to Funkheinzelmann (cf. Ein Lob dem Funkheinzelmann 1924).[2]

According to the identity-based brand theory of Burmann/Meffert (2005), essential attributes of a strong brand are: individuality, consistency, continuity and the so-called reciprocity, in short the image of a brand. Funkheinzelmann got its unmistakable individuality through its narrator and author Hans Bodenstedt and his leading position in the station, which was reinforced by listener letters and survey results[3] with a corresponding image and ensured a certain consistency. The fixed broadcasting slot, the relative regularity of the broadcast dates and not least the seriality of the programme and the listener feedback ensured the necessary continuity.

The reciprocity of the brand (its image) was specifically modelled by the broadcaster. In April 1925, Norag addressed a competition to its young audience and asked for drawings for the Funkheinzelmann broadcast. The success was surprising, even for the station. A lot of mail (with drawings, but also fan fiction) arrived from all over the reception area (cf. St. 1925b). For Norag's first birthday on May 2, 1925, countless fan articles, artistic handicrafts – from blankets and suits to baskets and aeroplanes – had been sent to the station (cf. St. 1925c, 1264). Identity-based branding distinguishes between *brand generated content* and *user generated content* (cf. Burmann/Halaszovich/Schade/Piehler 2018, 222). Norag knew how to use both forms in the sense of consistent brand communication within the framework of the relatively limited possibilities at that time compared to today.

---

[2] Further letters were published in volumes 14 (An den Funkheinzelmann 1924) and 16 (Funkheinzelmann 1924).

[3] On April 10, 1925, Norag published the interim results of a survey on its programming. After evaluating the first thousand entries, the results were positive, with Funkheinzelmann being mentioned "in almost every entry". Funkheinzelmann had not only thrilled the children, but had also "brought more relaxation from the week's work to those in practical life than all the dance tournament bands," an audience member from Hanover was quoted saying (Unsere Vertrauensfrage an die Hörer 1925, 1 f.).

The Funkheinzelmann broadcast format was developed as a mixed genre of fairy tales and everyday life stories, prose, poetry and drama, spoken text with background noise and music. The broadcasts were – as far as can be concluded from the programme information and the recordings handed down (no broadcast recordings have survived) – composed like stage performances; the format made use of all the sensual and emotional possibilities of the medium. As Bodenstedt reports in an essay on the methods of musical illustration and onomatopoeia in radio in 1925, he had also used the children's programme as an experimental laboratory for the evening programme. The experiences with Funkheinzelmann had benefited the productions of Goethe's *Faust* and Ibsen's *Peer Gynt,* among others (cf. Bodenstedt 1925a; Wochenvorschau der Norag 1925).

Funkheinzelmann, the adventurer and improviser, also became the symbolic figure of the new medium of radio, which was still in its infancy but was developing rapidly and experimentally. The character's impact was by no means limited to a child audience; he also enlivened the imagination of an adult audience and apparently also fascinated the radio staff. In a short commentary, a Norag author discusses his stage fright in front of the microphone and quotes "Direktor Bodenstedt, de[n] Funkheinzelmann" (Müller-Förster 1925) with some encouraging words. A *Heinz Funkemal* addresses a joking poem to Funkheinzelmann, asking to ship him "by radio" to Vienna or London "at a reasonable price" (A. M. F. 1925). A *Wellenmann* (presumably an insider at the station) complains to Funkheinzelmann about the gnomes and elves who are up to mischief in the broadcasting room (cf. Lieber Funkheinzelmann! 1925). This type of fan fiction thematises the fairy-tale character in the contexts of the adult world, using him here, as in fairy-tale fiction, to solve problems – stage fright, money shortages, the station's susceptibility to interference – or to project dreams and desires.

Funkheinzelmann was initially a media product of broadcasting, shaped by its technological devices (recording technology, transmitters, receivers), its institutional framings (weekly broadcasting time, state-subsidised and controlled production conditions), its communication instruments (spoken language, music, sounds) and finally by the broadcast content itself (modeling according to Schmidt 2000, 94 f.). The radio Funkheinzelmann was developed serially in periodically broadcast stories. What held the series together was the innovative figure of the invisible, only audible narrator and the personality of Hans Bodenstedt (Fig. 2), who told the stories on the radio.

Event Marketing

The leading heads of Norag, above all Hans Bodenstedt, early began to popularise radio, to build emotional bonds with listeners, whether through live broadcasts of open-air events or adventure trips with a select fan community and press to unusual places (to the Brocken in the Harz mountains or the seabed by the islands of Helgoland), or by staging large listener festivals – events in today's sense. Within

Fig. 2 Hans Bodenstedt and his fairy-tale characters. Above, close to the microphone Funkheinzelmann. Source: *Die Funk-Stunde* (1926) 11, 253 (© bpk/Staatsbibliothek zu Berlin/ Dietmar Katz)

identity-based brand theory, event communication is an important factor for emotionalising the brand and increasing its symbolic benefit: The "experience of brand values and brand personality at an event" causes „a strong identification of the demanders with the brand", at the same time "an image transfer from the event to the brand takes place" (Burmann/Nitschke 2005, 394). Norag's first listener festival documented in its programme magazine was an open-air event on June 27, 1925 at Hamburg Zoo. The number of participants was estimated at around 60,000 (cf. Siegeslauf des „Funkheinzelmann" 1925). Funkheinzelmann appeared in the role of the lottery fairy. Portrayed by an actor in an appropriate costume, the voice Funkheinzelmann became a physical figure (cf. St. 1925d). In the Hamburg Zoo, Funkheinzelmann thus made a decisive change of media: The radio figure moved from radio to the medium of theatrical representation. From the point of view of market strategy, Norag had thus undertaken a brand expansion, the extension of its

Funkheinzelmann brand to include a further product. Burmann/Meffert (2005, 83 f.) describe four variants of brand expansion strategies: *Geographic expansion*, *brand extension*, (*line extension*), and *category extension*. The latter refers to expansion into new, unrelated product categories.

The success of the listener festival in Hamburg led to its repetition on August 1, in Harburg. In the advance notice, Funkheinzelmann occupies a central place, and programme details are given about his appearance – a region-specific „Heide- und Haake"-Funkheinzelmann fairy tale is to be performed, with the participation "of all Norag artists" (Die Norag geht nach Harburg 1925; Noragfest in Harburg 1925). In a later issue of the programme guide, the item with Funkheinzelmann is then noted as a pantomime by Hans Bodenstedt (cf. Die Norag in der Goldenen Wiege 1925) – without broadcasting, of course. From the brief programme information it can be concluded that it was either a completely silent performance or a more body-focused performance facing the live audience, unsuitable for voice recording.

On the occasion of the Harburg Festival in 1925, the Hamburg programme magazine reports on a "community" of Norag listeners whom the first "folk festival" in Hamburg has supposedly welded together in the "strive to deepen and ennoble life". The expected Norag artists are announced as "our dear friends", first among them Funkheinzelmann, who will tell fairy tales to "his circle of friends". Director Bodenstedt has promised to come to Harburg "with all of his own", where a "very large following" awaits them (Noragfest in Harburg 1925). With the expansion of radio into the event sector, Norag expanded and strengthened its fan base and at the same time intensified the emotionalisation of the Funkheinzelmann brand.

Geographical Expansion and Programme Diversification

The geographical expansion of the Funkheinzelmann broadcast product began with the takeover of the format and content by Westdeutsche Funkstunde AG (Wefag) in Münster. According to the programme press, a total of eleven programmes were broadcast from December 21, 1924 to July 26, 1925, under the heading *Der Hamburger Funkheinzelmann erzählt*, most of which were spoken by actor Heinz Halban. Later, the Wefag regional studios in Elberfeld[4] and Dortmund[5] included Funkheinzelmann broadcasts in their programming. Elberfeld built up the director and speaker Carl Weinlein as Funkheinzelmann, the Dortmund one does not appear by name, it was Hermann Probst according to the programme press (W. V. 1926).

A further geographical expansion of the Funkheinzelmann brand was planned in August and September 1925 and prepared by appropriate marketing. This involves expansion into the largest and most important German media market: Berlin. Just in

---

[4] From September 30, 1925 until the station was shut down at the end of 1926, 51 broadcasts could be traced in the programme press.
[5] Between December 6, 1925 and July 7, 1927, 56 broadcasts could be traced in the programme press.

time for the start of a series of Funkheinzelmann broadcasts on Funk-Stunde, the radio station with the largest audience in the Reich at the time, the Berlin station's programme guide[6] printed an artfully composed studio photo showing Bodenstedt as a jovial gentleman with round-glass spectacles together with a Funkheinzelmann doll (cf. Funkheinzelmann begegnet dem Märchendichter Hans Bodenstedt 1925). Further similar photos are printed in subsequent issues. In addition, there is a full-page presentation in text and pictures of the fairy tale fountain in Berlin's park Friedrichshain, a spacious complex with sculptures of the well-known Grimm fairy tale figures, to which Bodenstedt pays reverence in his first Berlin broadcast: Funkheinzelmann undertakes a "a moon trip" to the fairy tale fountain, according to the programme text. The Hamburg director and Funkheinzelmann author, who was already famous throughout the German Reich, was to personally design and speak in the broadcasts in the Reich capital and is presented by the Berlin station with the appropriate advertising effort. According to Elfert (1984), Bodenstedt personally spoke Funkheinzelmann on the Berlin station every Sunday from October 4, 1925 to March 27, 1927. I was not able to verify this assumption, but some indications speak for it.

As of December 6, 1925, the Funkheinzelmann broadcasts on the Hamburg and Berlin stations ran simultaneously (each Sunday, starting at 3:30 p.m.). In Hamburg, there is no precise programme information, so that one could conclude that a takeover from one station to the other took place. From January 1926 onwards, there are also programme details for Hamburg, and they differ from those for Berlin. If Bodenstedt spoke the Berlin programme, he could not speak the Hamburg programme at the same time. Were sound recordings used?

As early as August 1925, an electromagnetic recording process had been developed in the USA for the record industry. This made it possible to produce high-quality recordings on discs with a playing time of up to 40 minutes at a low cost. *Phonographische Zeitschrift* in Berlin reported on this immediately, although still skeptically (cf. Eisler 1925). The American consortium promoted its technology aggressively in Germany and tried to interest the broadcasting executives in it by means of special advertising measures (cf. K. W. 1926). In early 1928, the radio station Südwestdeutscher Rundfunk (SWR) experimented with the Tri-Ergon process (sound recordings on film) and, according to contemporary reports, achieved recordings of extraordinary quality (cf. dr. H. B. 1928; Bagier 1928). This method was used not only in Frankfurt, but also in Stuttgart and Hamburg (cf. Mühl-Benninghaus 1999, 69). It is possible, but not provable, that Funkheinzelmann broadcasts were recorded and circulated in this way. Also conceivable is the early use of wax plates or electromagnetic storage on tape. These two methods were also known early on. Starting in 1927, the radio organisation Reichs-Rundfunk-Gesellschaft (RRG) had them tested for their practicality (cf. Führer 1997).

At the beginning of 1926, the Funkheinzelmann broadcasts of Norag and Funk-Stunde were increasingly also transmitted by other broadcasters. In March 1926, the

---

[6] 375,481 radio subscribers were registered in the Berlin broadcasting area on October 1, 1925 (cf. Übersicht über die Zahl der Rundfunkteilnehmer nach dem Stand am 1. Oktober 1925).

Norag estimated the regular audience of Funkheinzelmann at around 750,000 families (cf. Übersicht über die Tätigkeit der Nordischen Rundfunk Aktiengesellschaft 08.03.1926). It probably overestimated this figure,[7] however this is evidence of the *perceived* popularity of the format within the Norag.[8] In Berlin, Funkheinzelmann also profited from indirect comparative advertising with the so-called *Funkprinzessin* of Funk-Stunde, which had been devalued in the critical press with reference to the allegedly better Hamburg model.[9] Funkprinzessin was limited to recitation, with no music or soundscape, which the performer Adele Proesler blamed on the management's disdain for the format (cf. Proesler 1925). After only seven months, the Proesler's format was replaced by a profile-less fairy tale hour in which alternating speakers had their say. Most stations invested less in their children's programmes than Norag. Only the Sürag in Stuttgart tried to establish its own narrator figure with *Gretle from Strümpfelbach*, although this was restricted to the region.[10]

In mid-1926, the stations' mutual programme takeovers were given an institutional framework by the programme council of RRG, which was headed by Friedrich Georg Knöpfke, the director of Funk-Stunde Berlin, and Hans Bodenstedt, the director of the Norag. There is no question that their experience and success in coordinating, among other things, the Funkheinzelmann broadcasts not only encouraged them in their further cooperation, but also secured the necessary trust from the other broadcasters for larger projects. In addition to the popular sports broadcasts,[11] Funkheinzelmann was, in a way, a pilot project for comprehensive networking of German broadcasters.

---

[7] At the beginning of 1926, 1,022,299 radio subscribers were registered throughout Germany (cf. Braun 1968, 81).

[8] As an example of how "popular" the broadcast was, the Norag reporter of *Der Deutsche Rundfunk* cites the fact that pupils from the Bremen Cathedral School write letters to the Funkheinzelmann as an essay exercise (St. 1925a).

[9] "The 'Funkprinzessin' is a very unnatural daughter of the Hamburg Funkheinzelmann, and no thinking person is able to guess why the storyteller was made a princess" (J. L. 1924). When the spokeswoman for the Funkprinzessin Adele Proesler had to leave the station in mid-1925 and the format was discontinued, there was once again criticism of the "cloying and kitschy pointed brand" (J. L. 1925). In the programme magazine *Der Deutsche Rundfunk*, on the other hand, Proesler was always praised in the highest terms (cf. Berliner Bericht 1925a, b).

[10] According to Elfert (1984, 229, f.n. 25), the writer and Sürag employee Sophie Tschorn, who in 1927 also published the children's magazine *Hallo! Gretle von Strümpfelbach erzählt*, which flanked the broadcast, was discontinued after only 19 issues.

[11] On June 27, 1926, Norag broadcast a horse race from the Hamburg racecourse. Twelve other German broadcasters were connected live. The broadcast was celebrated in the Berlin programme press as a technically flawless, entertaining event (cf. Egl. 1926).

Brand Extensions

Around Whitsun 1925, the Sunday schedule of Funkheinzelmann was supplemented with a small Wednesday series: *Die Blumenmärchen vom Funkheinzelmann* – four episodes, broadcast only by and for Norag. From January to March 1926, the eight-part series *Goldhärchen und Funkheinzelmann* was broadcast on Sundays by Funk-Stunde and Norag; on the same day, at the same time, but not the same episode was broadcast (according to the programme announcement) in Berlin and in Hamburg. In October, the miniseries *Funkheinzelmanns Schöpfungsgeschichte*, inspired by the biblical creation story, followed – the same day, the same time and the same programme in Hamburg and in Berlin (six episodes until November 7, 1926). Was it produced in Hamburg or in Berlin? On Wednesday, January 13, 1926, a new format was introduced in Hamburg – with transmission also to the SWR and Mirag: *Funkheinzelmanns Kindertheater.* Funkheinzelmann is now no longer just narrated but also performed as a radio play with distributed roles. Up to 15 narrators are used per broadcast. Spoken and sung texts alternated, the composer of the songs was Carl Krüger. The seven *Bilder* (scenes) of the series can be found with almost identical titles as seven *Märchen* (fairy tales) in the textbook of the Rufu publishing house (cf. Bodenstedt/Krüger 1926). This is presumably the first radio adaptation of an original that was already being discussed for stage performances at the end of 1925 (cf. rb. 1925). After four episodes, the format *Funkheinzelmanns Kindertheater* was continued with further content (plays by Görner, Pocci, a total of 38 episodes).

At the beginning of 1928, Bodenstedt launched a new radio series in Berlin, this time also thematically tied to Berlin and the discourse of the time.[12] *Funkheinzelmanns Großstadtmärchen* (14 broadcasts in all) were devoted – as can be cautiously inferred from the sparse programme information – to the infrastructure of a modern metropolis: tram traffic, electricity, lighting.[13] In July, an ocean crossing is thematised for a current occasion. It was the time of great shipbuilding in the shipyards of Hamburg and Bremen.[14] The *Großstadtmärchen* were also broadcast sometimes from Hamburg, sometimes from Berlin, and were usually picked up by other stations as well.

Further extensions of the Funkheinzelmann brand are no longer directly tied to the name Hans Bodenstedt, such as *Funkheinzelmanns Mädchenstunde* (12

---

[12] In 1927, two films that dealt with the theme of the big city in different ways, Fritz Lang's *Metropolis* and Walther Ruttmann's *Berlin, die Symphonie der Großstadt*, were released, and reflected in various media. Images from *Metropolis* were also used in the magazine *Funkheinzelmann* without mentioning the film (cf. Weber 2017).

[13] Modern lighting technology was a major topic of the time. In October 1928, a *light festival* was held in the shopping streets of Berlin for three nights to showcase all the technical possibilities of the modern lighting industry (cf. Dominik 1928).

[14] A few weeks later, Bodenstedt and his team broadcast sensational reports from the launching of the Europa and Bremen, two of the largest passenger steamships of the time. The broadcasts are taken over by Werag, Sürag (Stuttgart and Freiburg) and Orag (cf. Aktuelle Hamburger Woche 1928).

episodes from September to November 1926). The centerpiece of the programme, framed with songs and instrumental pieces, is the story *Die Zwillinge der Försterin* by Alice Fliegel (1926a, b), which had previously appeared in eleven episodes in the magazine *Funkheinzelmann* and was read aloud by the author herself in five broadcast episodes. *Funkheinzelmanns literarische Jugendstunde* introduces individual writers with a biography and a selection of texts. The broadcast date on Saturday afternoons and the musical setting indicate a certain educational claim (eight broadcast dates from October 1926 to February 1927). From October 1927, fairy tales by various authors (not by Bodenstedt) were broadcast in radio play format or as readings under the title *Funkheinzelmanns Märchenstunde*. Hans Freundt directed most of the broadcasts. The new formats differed from the regular programme (fairy tales by and with Bodenstedt) and were aimed in part at other target groups. But these expansions cannot dilute the brand, because its carrier and endorser Bodenstedt continued to be present on the radio with its own formats.

The Record

Between 1927 and 1930, the Homocord record label released a total of seven Funkheinzelmann records. In the pre-Christmas period of 1929, one of these recordings is explicitly featured in the radio programme for the first time (on December 13, *Ein Weihnachtstraum* on the Berlin Funk-Stunde). Given the large number of Funkheinzelmann broadcasts, of which there are no detailed programme listings, it cannot be ruled out that the recordings were also used unannounced by the stations.

Pigorsch (2001) assumes that the aesthetically relatively elaborate records were produced specifically and were not adaptations of the radio broadcasts. However, one did not exclude the other. Homocord enabled a media expansion of the radio stories, which should not be confused with a secondary usage (the same content in a different media form). Not the broadcast, but its seriality was reproduced in the medium of record: Funkheinzelmann, Ticketick, gnomes, fairies, mermaids, Rübezahl, the "Christkind" – the characteres the three- to four-minute episodes tell a story about also populated the broadcasts, they originated for the most part from popular fairy-tale culture and were constantly changed and iterated anew by Bodenstedt as narrative set pieces. Funkheinzelmann and Co. were typical serial characters (cf. Denson/Mayer 2012), able to produce stories on the run, though none had to be, or were allowed to be, particularly original. Rather, to function as a series, the stories had to reproduce their own pattern in changing productions. In addition to the narration, essential components of the radio Funkheinzelmann were Bodenstedt's voice (and personality) with its musicality and specific singsong, the alternation of rhythmic speaking, music and sound effects, the playful, humorous mix of traditional motifs and their modern interpretation, the tension between old fairy tale motifs and new technology.

The Revue

Parallel to the radio figure, the stage figure Funkheinzelmann also expanded in Berlin. Together with one of the most successful entertainment directors of the time, Erik Charell,[15] Hans Bodenstedt developed a so-called revue in the autumn of 1925 at the largest theatre in the capital (and Germany) at the time, the Großes Schauspielhaus.[16] The revue genre, with its loosely strung together numbers, was extremely popular in the 1920s in Berlin, then a city of four million people – the opulent productions attracted up to 11,000 spectators a day (cf. Lethen 1986). Charell's and Bodenstedt's Funkheinzelmann revue is linked to the best event date of the year: Christmas. *Funkheinzelmanns Weihnachtsmarkt* is announced for a total of 15 performances (from November 14, to December 30). The official programme magazine of Funk-Stunde advertises the performances with full- and half-page, partly illustrated ads. The connection to Berlin radio was secured by a strong endorser: Alfred Braun. The probably most popular speaker, furthermore main director and head of the radio play department as well as initiator and head of the so-called *Jugend-Bühne* of the station, a radio play series for a young audience, played Santa Claus in the revue (Fig. 3). In the advertisements, his name is boldly highlighted in a frame with the note: „With the personal assistance of Alfred Braun" (Ich, der Funkheinzelmann 1925).

The revue was divided into six *Bilder* (scenes), which allowed for a varied sequence of different themes and settings. The headings speak for themselves: *Heiligabend, Funkheinzelmann, Im Theater, Im Kino, Im Circus, Unterm Christbaum* (cf. ibid.). This names some of the most attractive places and themes of the time for children and their adult companions. The cinema was one of them.

As soon as November 20, after only two performances, Norag takes stock of "Funkheinzelmann's victory run" in Berlin (rb. 1925).[17] It reports on sold-out performances and quotes the Berlin press, which had raved about the "jubilant" small audience and had even gone so far as to claim that Funkheinzelmann was as well known to children today as Rübezahl or Rumpelstilzchen had been in the past.[18]

At the same time, however, the modernity of the character is emphasised. Funkheinzelmann is "endowed with all the qualities that the child of our time demands of a being who can transfigure everyday life into a fairy-tale", and also enables it to "master the tempo of things". Funkheinzelmann makes "the technical achievements of the nineteenth and twentieth centuries ripe for fairy tales": "Telephones and railways, airships and steam cranes wandered into the fantastic world and filled it with new life" (Siegeslauf des „Funkheinzelmann" 1925). *Tempo,*

---

[15] On Charell and the Berlin revue theatres cf. Jansen/Laade 1987.
[16] On Großes Schauspielhaus Berlin cf. Dömeland 2004; Hostetter 2003; Buzwan 2012, 175-190.
[17] The success report is reprinted by *Deutscher Rundfunk* (cf. Siegeslauf des „Funkheinzelmann" 1925).
[18] Critical reviews remain unmentioned. The *Vossische Zeitung* wrote distantly: "A parody of a parody of a revue. Children want to cheer, the applause imitated by the clever adults alone is no cheer" (erle 18.11. 1925).

Fig. 3 Cover of the children's magazine *Funkheinzelmann:* It advertises the Funkheinzelmann revue at Berlin Großes Schauspielhaus (© bpk/Staatsbibliothek zu Berlin/Dietmar Katz)

a buzzword of the time, and technology are highlighted here as necessary and important forms of access to the modern world for the child of the 1920s.

The box office success at the Berlin Schauspielhaus inevitably led to a further expansion – a geographical one – of the Funkheinzelmann revue. Several provincial theatres wanted to stage the play in their own productions and adaptations (in Bremerhaven, the Christmas play was planned as an Easter play). Charell's revue, written especially for the Berlin Großes Schauspielhaus, could not be exported to the provincial theatres, but its original was: The "actual fairy tale of the Funkheinzelmann, dramatised by Hans Bodenstedt, to which Carl Krüger wrote the music" (rb. 1925), had been acquired by the municipal theatres in Stettin, Altona and Bremerhaven, as *Norag* reports. The Rufu publishing house published the textbook (Bodenstedt/Krüger 1926) as a cheap booklet, presumably before the middle of 1926 – it also contains an advertisement for the magazine *Funkheinzelmann* together with an order form for the year 1926.[19] And of course the dramatisation was also used on the radio. As a Wednesday series (*Funkheinzelmanns Kindertheater*), the scenes of the fairy tale play went on air from January 13, 1926 on Norag. Revue, textbook and radio play – in just a few months the Funkheinzelmann brand had undergone a triple brand extension.

The revue by Charell and Bodenstedt was restaged a year later in Berlin under the title *Funkheinzelmanns Märchenreise*. This time Funkheinzelmann was played by the actress Alexa Porembski.[20] However, Alfred Braun was also announced as the main actor this time, who leads through the episodes as the magician Merlin. In an advertising review in the magazine *Der Deutsche Rundfunk* („Funkheinzelmanns Märchenreise" 1926), two other apparently popular characters are mentioned in addition to Funkheinzelmann, the magician Merlin and Santa Claus: The Karl May-hero Old Shatterhand as well as Felix the Cat, who "in the interlude [...] performs his funny pranks on the flickering screen." The American film hero Felix the Cat,[21] already known in Germany, was used as an endorser – in two scenes of the revue he is the main character. Furthermore, with Felix, his original medium, the (silent) animated film, seems to have been integrated into the revue. A surprising multimediality. However, it was not a rarity, but rather the rule in the theatres and cinema palaces of the time (cf. Berg 1989). The heterogeneity of the themes and performances (artistry, pantomime, music, film) was experienced by the audience as a *sensation*. The sensual theatre experience also included small gifts, such as tea and biscuits during the breaks or small gift figurines of popular performers. There is a possibility that Funkheinzelmann chocolate was distributed to the audience in the Christmas revue. There is evidence that it was made. More about that below.

Märchenspiel vom Funkheinzelmann was premiered simultaneously in Hamburg-Altona and Hannover, i.e. in Norag's broadcasting area, at the beginning of December 1926. The advertising for the play was placed in both Norag-related print media, the program guide of the same name and the children's magazine *Funkheinzelmann*, in parallel and in a target-group-specific manner. All forms of press work that are successful in terms of brand strategy were used: Pictorial advertising (photos of the leading actress), information (on ticket sales), storytelling – the preview of the stage show (cf. Esmarch 1926a), the review of the premiere (cf. Esmarch 1926b), selected press quotations (cf. Was sagt die Presse zum Funkheinzelmann 1926). On December 20, the performance in Altona was broadcast on the radio. The *Norag* brought a detailed programme announcement with a list of all the plot chapters, all the roles and their performers. The pluri-medial usage of the dramatised *Funkheinzelmann* had been realised in Hamburg just as skilfully in terms of brand strategy as it had

---

[19] The only traceable copy of the textbook is in the possession of the Deutsches Rundfunkarchiv in Frankfurt am Main, a digital copy was kindly made available to us.

[20] Also spelled Porembsky.

[21] Felix the Cat was already so popular in the early 1920s in the USA that the character caused a merchandise craze: there were Felix towels, Felix toys, Felix porcelain. And finally, Felix was also marketed as a comic strip in newspapers by his cartoonist Otto Messmer (cf. Scott 2009). Felix cartoons were also shown in Germany.

been a year earlier in Berlin: Christmas was again chosen as the time, and once again the brand communication in the press, on the radio and on stage was differentiated, focused on the target group and perfectly coordinated.

In 1927 (by the Carl-Schultz-Theater in Hamburg) and 1928 (in Berlin) Funkheinzelmann was also marketed as a revue during the Christmas season. While the Hamburg production drew on the familiar fairy tale (Funkheinzelmanns Bilderbuch 1927), the Berlin revue a year later showed clear tendencies towards updating. The medium of film features prominently in the title of the show, which was staged at Berlin's Capitol: *Funkheinzelmann filmt!* The character Brennecke, newly introduced into the Funkheinzelmann shows at the time, appeared on stage alongside the obligatory Santa Claus, and "an excellent Indian troupe" also made an appearance and was stormily celebrated by the child audience – as the in-house critic of *Der Deutsche Rundfunk,* Hans Tasiemka, enthusiastically reports. The house management distributed the usual small gifts among the audience, which the reviewer mentions in passing: "The little boys and girls were immensely proud of the Indian feathers that the Capitol management gave them as a present. They would probably rather have had the chocolate taken away than the colorful pretty feathers" (Tasiemka 1928).

Additionally, the latest technical innovations were also celebrated in the show. The sensation of 1928 – the first American flight of the airship Graf Zeppelin on October 11, 1928 – had only been a month and a half ago and Bodenstedt was already incorporating it into the revue as the story of a stowaway. The venue was a Berlin cinema – the location suited the title of the revue and suited the young audience's enthusiasm for the film. In the detailed chronicle of *Vossische Zeitung* of December 3, 1928, the versatility and thus the broad connectivity of Funkheinzelmann becomes clear (cf. Funkheinzelmann films 1928). He is not only a fairy-tale figure with fantastic abilities, but he also acts in the children's environment and fulfils for them – at least in fiction – the consumer promises of the modern world: An overseas flight in a zeppelin and their personal American dream of prosperity. Bodenstedt also reworked this revue into a radio play, which was broadcast by Norag on January 4, 1929.

For the Christmas season of 1929, the Funkheinzelmann fairy tale *Die wunderschöne Goldenhaar* is staged by Alfred Maak at Hamburg's Theater des Westens. The presumed premiere on November 17, is broadcast live on the radio by Norag. Produced for the first time in 1926, the *Funkheinzelmann-Märchenspiel* with music by Carl Krüger was again adapted for radio in 1928 and 1929 during Advent and Christmas, respectively. In 1931, both plays were restaged and broadcast by Norag – on November 1, i.e. outside the Christmas season, *Märchenspiel* and on December 18, *Goldenhaar.*

The Fairy Tale Storybooks

Starting in mid-October 1924, *Die Norag* announced the Sunday Funkheinzelmann hour as a broadcast *Aus dem Märchenbuch des Funkheinzelmanns*. The publication of the storybook was announced for Christmas. The advertisement for the book as a Christmas present now accompanied – with updated text in each case – every announcement of the Sunday Funkheinzelmann broadcast, which was presented as a radio series of the book chapters. Even before the print version appeared (Bodenstedt 1924a, b, c), the processing of the book texts into broadcasts began. In terms of brand strategy, the Norag company prepared the line extension of the Funkheinzelmann brand into the print market by updating the broadcast, thus strengthening the core brand at the same time. The following year, the apparently successful book-to-broadcast-to-book strategy was repeated. The first broadcast from "Funkheinzelmann's new storybook", *Funkheinzelmann der Wanderbursch* (Bodenstedt 1925b), is announced for November 29, 1925 – this time in the Berlin programme guide *Die Funk-Stunde*. In the run-up to Christmas, sales advertisements are placed for both Funkheinzelmann storybooks; at the same time, the Funkheinzelmann revue at the Großes Schauspielhaus is advertised in full-page ads. The Berlin programme guide is thus used as an advertising medium for the prospering Funkheinzelmann media network, and in turn profits from the success of its plurimedial exploitation and distribution.

In 1929 Hans Bodenstedt uses the *Goldhärchen* radio series of the year 1926 in another book: *Funkheinzelmanns Harz-Märchen* (Bodenstedt 1929a), which is published by the "Funkheinzelmann publishing house" Karl Welchert in Thale (Harz). It is illustrated with photo montages by H. Haas. One shows Bodenstedt surrounded by children with headphones. Most of the photos use a Funkheinzelmann sculpture (brightly polished, possibly bronze), which appears placed in front of different scenery (nature, big city). The same sculpture had also been featured in the children's magazine *Funkheinzelmann* (cf. Funkheinzelmann-Rademacher Preis 1926) as a prize for best performance in swimming (named after the popular sports swimmer Erich Rademacher). Book, broadcast, revue, text advertising, drawings and photos complemented and reinforced each other and all together formed the Funkheinzelmann brand.

Merchandising

Bekmeyer-Feuerhahn (2013) defines merchandising as "secondary marketing of popular phenomena" for the purpose of emotionalisation and customer loyalty. She observes merchandising in correlation to event marketing. Accordingly, the merchandising or fan items are objects that refresh the experience of the brand event as mementos, suggest social relevance for consumers (belonging to a group of trendsetters) and reduce the advertising costs for the actual product.

The first known merchandising of the Funkheinzelmann brand is the Funkheinzelmann doll mentioned above. It seems to have been a by-product of Bodenstedt's publicity shots for his Berlin broadcasts. A doll costumed in the studio and shot by the photographer interacting with its author Hans Bodenstedt. Barely two months after its Berlin debut, on November 20, Norag already announced that the Funkheinzelmann doll could soon be purchased in all toy stores (cf. Siegeslauf des „Funkheinzelmann" 1925). Another facet of the brand's merchandising was the aforementioned figurine (Rademacher prize, later used as book illustration). Who designed and created it and for what original purpose or occasion I could not find out.

The chocolate with Funkheinzelmann motifs, on the other hand, was Norag's own product, which it promoted vigorously. At the end of March 1926, it published an advertisement in a programme guide aimed at retailers. It offered them Funkheinzelmann chocolate "with the pictures from the Funkheinzelmann fairy tales and large bonuses for industrious collectors".[22] "Free advertising for retailers" is this chocolate, it says (Gratisreklame für Detaillisten 1926). Admittedly, the business model probably favoured the Norag, whose sales strategy relied on the emotional attachment of fans to the brand (brand involvement) and attempted to stimulate buying propensity and increase sales of the merchandising chocolate by means of collectible pictures.

The chocolate was advertised in the children's magazine from the very first issue (end of April 1926) until it was discontinued (Fig. 4). The accompanying text refers in bold letters to the "serial pictures" and to the "Funkheinzelmann chocolate collector's album" which can be purchased "for only 30 pfennigs". A collector's premium is promised (cf. Funkheinzelmann-Schokolade ist die beste! 1926). In the 3rd issue the magazine reports that Funkheinzelmann gave away „a whole lot" of Funkheinzelmann chocolate at a Berlin children's festival (Eine frohe Mitteilung! 1926).[23] However, Funkheinzelmann chocolate was not able to establish itself on the market as an independent product (cf. Elfert 1984, 108, f.n. 12) and thus failed as a category extension of the Funkheinzelmann brand.

Funkheinzelmann: The Children's Magazine

A second category extension that was launched almost simultaneously with the chocolate was the magazine *Funkheinzelmann*. It was published by an obscure Berlin publishing house, Filmbücherei GmbH. The editor in charge was Artur

---

[22] The Exqisit chocolate factory in Berlin-Weißensee is given as the manufacturer. Cf. Gratisreklame für Detaillisten 1926.

[23] The chocolate advertisement appears in eleven of the 43 issues of the children's magazine. Ads for Funkheinzelmann chocolate also appear in *Die Funk-Stunde* in May and June 1926.

Fig. 4 Advertisement for Funkheinzelmann chocolate in the children's magazine *Funkheinzelmann* (© bpk/Staatsbibliothek zu Berlin/Dietmar Katz)

Lokesch.[24] Its announcement in *Die Norag* (cf. Funkheinzelmann-Bund 1926) makes it clear that it was conceived as a members' magazine, a newsletter for the brand community. It was intended to be the mouthpiece of the *Funkheinzelmann-Bund*. The *Jugendbünde* (youth alliances) were a fashionable fad of the time. They fulfilled a similar role to today's internet communities: Cultivating a strong sense of community and creating a social identity for members, as well as sharply delineating and distinguishing themselves from outsiders. In *Norag*'s justification for the journal's appearance, the Funkheinzelmann community is described with ethical-social arguments (inclusive) and with emblematic features (distinctive):

> The friends of the Funkheinzelmann have founded a federation, to which everyone can belong. It wants to cultivate the readiness to help and to promote politeness. Each covenant brother or sister receives a badge. The members of the covenant in all cities greet and help each other as far as they can. (Ibid.)

---

[24] The publishing house is not listed in the publishing register of Sperling's *Zeitschriften- und Zeitungsadressbuch* in 1927 or 1928, so it did not publish any other periodicals. The Berlin trade register (1931) lists 1926 as the year the publishing house was founded, and Gustav Karstädt as managing director (cf. Berliner Handelsregister 1931, B, 659). In the Berlin address book, the company does not appear as a publishing bookshop until 1927 and is no longer listed in 1932 (cf. Berliner Adreßbuch 1927, IV, 688; 1932, IV, 581). Film-Bücherei GmbH appeared as a book publisher with apparently only one publication, the textbook of a Ufa educational film (cf. Thomalla 1926). At the same address at this time was the Eigenbrödler publishing house, whose managing director in 1921 was the same Artur Lokesch.

The community of values suggested here was, from a market perspective, a brand community, that is characterised by the close ties of its members to the brand. This results in two side effects that are valuable in terms of brand strategy: Firstly, direct and personal contact with the target group and secondly, the (positive) influence of the group itself on consumer behaviour (cf. Burmann/Halaszovich/Schade/ Piehler 2018).

The willingness to help inscribed in the Funkheinzelmann-Bund with its founding is expanded into larger fundraising campaigns and benefit events. At the beginning of 1927, a major fundraising campaign in aid of urban children in need took place in the name of Funkheinzelmann; the magazine publishes long lists of donors in four successive issues. The Christmas revues of 1926 and 1928 were also associated with charity (children's aid, artists in need).

In the logic of the markets, fundraising is not a disinterested charity event, but always also an instrument of relationship marketing, which serves to cultivate the relationship with the target group, to consolidate its trust in the brand (cf. Bruhn 2016, esp. 393–401). Contact with the target group was already established in the run-up to the magazine's foundation. At the end of 1925, a Christmas wish of Funkheinzelmann had appeared in *Die Norag*: "He wishes for nothing but a photograph of each of his little listeners [...] so that he knows to whom he is telling his fairy tales" (Funkheinzelmanns Weihnachtswunsch 1925). The photograph was to include the name and age. The aim of the campaign, which was elaborate for the group of people addressed and also not cost-neutral (photos were taken by/at the photographer, the parents had to pay for the photo and postal expenses), was obviously a community measure that served to cultivate fans. The magazine makers immediately used the submissions for a personalised customer approach: A listener portrait (boys only) is printed on the cover of the children's magazine in each of the first eleven issues.

Other strategies used in the transfer of the radio character Funkheinzelmann to the magazine market also read like something out of the advertising industry textbook. In the standard work by Kroeber-Riel/Esch (2015, 139) it says: "Brand name and brand mark must be unmistakably presented to the consumer. [...] For this reason, it is most important to stage the brand itself in a lively and entertaining way". Integrated into the title font of the children's magazine is a Pierrot-like figure in a black doublet with a white ruff and legless harem panties, his feet in red ballet slippers, his long-sleeved cap like a waving handkerchief in his outstretched hand. Androgynous and of indeterminate age, the title figure opens herself up to ambiguity and connectable indeterminacy – typical characteristics of serial figures (cf. Denson/Mayer 2012, 194).

The magazine market in the mid-1920s was dominated by the popular children's magazine segment *Der heitere Fridolin,* published by Ullstein, also in Berlin. The colorful *Fridolin* was placed in the *dirt and trash* corner by the influential educators of the time, condescendingly criticised and largely ignored,[25] which did not diminish its success with the young readership. *Funkheinzelmann* copied the *Fridolin*'s recipe for success in many respects and tried to outdo the model with instruments typical of the market. First of all, the price can be mentioned: 15 pfennigs was the price of an issue of *Fridolin*, 10 pfennigs was the introductory price of *Funkheinzelmann*. Several protagonists and formats of the new magazine show clear similarities to *Fridolin*. The comic couple Laatsch and Bommel from *Fridolin* presumably provided the foil for Plumm and Plautz in *Funkheinzelmann*, the comic dog Schlupp (*Fridolin*) for the comic dog Fox (*Funkheinzelmann*), puzzle uncle Ben (*Funkheinzelmann*) is reminiscent of inventor uncle Otto (*Fridolin*). Even the drawn title fonts of *Funkheinzelmann* show stylistic similarities to *Fridolin*. *Fridolin* also practiced the multiple use of the brand. For Christmas 1926, for example, the *Fridolin* picture books illustrated by Walter Trier are recommended, as well as the *Fridolin* tear-off calendar for 1927, which was also accompanied by an ink box. Repetition and adaptation to the model (*Fridolin*) are strategies that can be observed today, but they were not exhibited in the development of the *Funkheinzelmann* product; rather, distinguishing features were overemphasised: *die erste Funk- und Film-Jugend-Zeitung der Welt* (thus the subtitle) laid claim to uniqueness and particularity. By means of the format (double page size) and the elaborate layout (drawn title fonts, graphically sophisticated layout and sparing colour printing – one, later two colours), the editors attempted to free the magazine from the shadow of the cheap boulevard, thus orienting themselves towards other pre-images existing on the market – namely the periodicals recommended as *valuable* (cf. Thalhofer 1924; Thalhofer/Antz 1925). The identification figure of Fridolin was copied in the new title by that of Funkheinzelmann on the one hand, and surpassed on the other. Funkheinzelmann was not only a fictional figure of the print medium, but already both a fictional and a real plurimedial figure (the narrator Bodenstedt on the radio, the writer Bodenstedt, the actor Hans Thiemig as Funkheinzelmann in the Großes Schauspielhaus Berlin, etc.). The Funkheinzelmann brand benefited from its seriality on the radio when it was introduced to the print market. Its popularity had increased by leaps and bounds, especially in recent months, as a result of the Funkheinzelmann fairy tales broadcast live by the Berlin radio station.

Hans Bodenstedt was Norag's leading personality. He began his professional career as a journalist and publisher.[26] He therefore mastered the medium of print and

---

[25] "What is offered here to the young as wit and humour is at times so hanebolically stupid that even the young readers notice it and are amused by the cartoonists and writers who are acting foolishly for their amusement" (Fronemann 1925, 80). John Fiske, to whom cultural studies owes the objectifying view of pop and tabloid, in 1992 describes the effect of tabloid journalism in words similar to Fronemann's in 1925, but without its negative valuation: "One of its most characteristic tones of voice is that of a sceptical laughter which offers the pleasures of disbelief, the pleasures of not being taken in." (Fiske 1992, 49).

[26] Hans Bodenstedt (born October 25, 1887 in Magdeburg) had already had an impressive journalistic career before his career in radio. He started at the *Harzer Kurier* in 1905, then went to Berlin, where he worked as an editor at *Zeit im Bild* and *Berliner Illustrirte Zeitung*, among others, and after World War I at the *Deutsche Allgemeine Zeitung*. He came to work in the radio industry via

may well have been interested in a magazine of the same name on the wave of success of his radio character Funkheinzelmann. It is unclear to what extent he was actually involved in the publication and the profits of the magazine. Circumstantial evidence suggests that he was. Pigorsch's (2001, 9) statement that Bodenstedt's involvement in the journal was "if at all, only discernible in the first volumes", however, must be expressly contradicted. Up to and including issue 15, the series *Die Abenteuer des Funkheinzelmann* appeared under Bodenstedt's authorship. In the following issues, Bodenstedt's private address is even given as the postal address of *Funkheinzelmann*: Heimhuderstraße 80 in Hamburg (cf. Hamburger Adreßbuch 1927, II, 94).

The involvement of the Rufu publishing house, which published the programme guide *Die Norag* from 1926 onwards, can be regarded as certain: The appearance of the respective issue of the children's magazine is regularly announced and advertised in *Die Norag* (from No. 3 with the print of the newspaper head). But it was not until October 15, (issue no. 12) that *Funkheinzelmann* was officially published by Rufu-Verlag (cf. Unseren kleinen Freunden 1926). In issue 13, Binderstraße 28 in Hamburg is given as the address for fan mail. According to the Hamburg address book of 1926 (Hamburger Adreßbuch 1926, IV, 100), this is where the Chief post office and the editorial office were located (house numbers 26–30). It can be assumed that the editorial staff of the *Funkheinzelmann* was allowed to use the *Norag* premises rent-free and that some other *Norag* employees also benefited from the institutional links. Alice Fliegel, Kurt Esmarch and Rudolf Damm also or mainly worked for the broadcaster, published in the programme guide and were also present in the children's magazine. The children's magazine thus appears as a by-product of the programme guide. As Bauer convincingly demonstrates (1993, 88 f.), Bodenstedt had a 15% share in its net profit. The programme guide was generously financed by the broadcasting company; even the salary of its editor was paid by the broadcaster. *Die Norag* or the publishing house could keep most of the surpluses, only 10% of which went back to the broadcaster.

Advertisements for the children's magazine were also placed in *Die Werag* (cf. Funkheinzelmann – Diese reich illustrierte Kinderzeitung 1927). The programme guide of Westdeutscher Rundfunk also belonged to Rufu-Verlag (cf. Bauer 1993, 117). A geographical expansion of the children's magazine had thus been initiated and, according to the publisher's plans, was to be extended "to the whole of Germany".[27] The magazine *Funkheinzelmann* was discontinued at the end of 1927

---

the newspaper *Hamburger Nachrichten,* where he edited the first radio supplement in 1923 (cf. Sie 29.11.1930).

[27] In an unsigned and undated *Exposé* to the Rufu-Verlagsgesellschaft m.b.H., presumably written at the beginning of 1927, which is in the holdings of the Staatsarchiv Hamburg, the publication of the *Funkheinzelmann* magazine is justified by the popularity of the character and presented as an advertising measure for German radio in general: "The character of the 'Funkheinzelmann' created at the Hamburg station for the children's world of radio, has constantly brought an enormous number of letters. In order to promote this interest in radio among the next generation, a children's magazine, the 'Funkheinzelmann', has been created, which is probably the most beautiful magazine in this field today. [...] It is of particular importance that this children's magazine is to be

after only 43 issues. Possibly the publisher had miscalculated and was unable to cover the costs of the elaborate layout and color printing through sales.

Die Norag attempted a tentative revival in 1933. *Funkheinzelmanns Kinder-Norag* was established as a weekly children's special page in the programme magazine. The main feature of the page is a comic strip drawn by A. W. Oldage with droll rhymes in the style of Wilhelm Busch, from whose stories some of the characters are also borrowed (Fips the monkey, the raven, who is called Johnny here). There are hardly any references to radio. From issue 13 onwards, the magazine appears only every two weeks. From issue 26 onwards, the name Funkheinzelmann is dropped from the title. The fate of Funkheinzelmann founder and director Hans Bodenstedt was already sealed at this point: He was forced to resign and leave broadcasting.

The Author as the Motor of Seriality

Hans Bodenstedt developed his show as author, director and producer and became its identification figure as speaker/actor. The success on the radio was, as already shown, the motor for more and more new episodes and series. This was followed by the exploitation of the show on the book market and the recycling of the books in the show. Bodenstedt exported the Hamburg broadcast format to Berlin. Here his brand expanded into the revue market. Stage Funkheinzelmann then also experienced geographical expansion. Finally, Funkheinzelmann also expanded into the magazine market, where the content from the show, books, and revue was once again processed and used to cultivate and expand the fan base.

Skillful marketing, high productivity, clever brand expansion, the activity and public position of its creator were important factors contributing to the popularity of the Funkheinzelmann brand. Meanwhile, in the non-public discourses of the time, the radio format was quite controversial. On the one hand in 1927, in the political monitoring committee of the Norag, the Kiel District Administrator Adler praised Funkheinzelmann for knowing how to "chat with the smallest children in such a whimsical, cheerful manner", in sharp contrast to "tendentious" fairy tales that criticise certain social classes in a one-sided manner (Bedenken gegenüber einseitig „proletarischen" Märchen 14.-18.07.1927).[28] On the other hand, the broadcasting committee of the Hamburg Youth Welfare Office flatly demanded the removal of the "completely inartistic Funkheinzelmann shows" from Norag's programming. The Funkheinzelmann fairy tale hours would deal "throughout with such fairy tales

---

distributed throughout Germany and is already being distributed in part, so that the advertising material contained in the magazine will benefit the whole of German radio." (Exposé über die Rufu-Verlagsgesellschaft m.b.H., Hamburg 1927).

[28] This mainly referred to fairy tales by the Hungarian author Maria Szucsich, which were to be broadcast by Norag at a children's camp but were removed from the programme by Bodenstedt due to Adler's intervention.

which we must reject today from the point of view of spiritual youth care; but which are at least presented in such a way that they are not to be judged as youth educational" (Vorschläge des Rundfunk-Ausschusses beim Jugendamt Hamburg 15.12.1927).

Although the broadcast polarised, Bodenstedt was identified with it. The Nazi newspaper *Völkischer Beobachter,* which was concerned about political conditions at Norag at the end of 1931, also explained Bodenstedt's identity to its readers with the parenthesis: "known throughout Germany as 'Funkheinzelmann'" (In Funkheinzelmanns Reich 01.12.1931). By this time, Bodenstedt had long since stopped investing in the development of his brand, as had Norag. As early as 1930, the Sunday Funkheinzelmann broadcasts were often cancelled without replacement; more space (also in Norag's programme guide) was taken up by the *Deutsche Jugendstunde* on Mondays (with different programming and programmers); the name Bodenstedt no longer appeared in the programme press in connection with the Funkheinzelmann broadcasts as of 1930.

The broadcast format *Funkheinzelmann* was abandoned, the series was abandoned. Thus it met the same fate as all popular series:

> Popular series often do not end at all in the demanding sense of the word, but simply disappear. In this, they show themselves for what they are according to their materiality: mass-reproduced industrial goods whose production is no longer worthwhile after a certain point or becomes impossible for other reasons. (Kelleter 2012a, 27)

When the *Funkheinzelmann-Märchenspiel,* once successful throughout the German Reich, was once again included in the Norag programme during the (pre-)Christmas season of 1931, there was only derisive criticism. Funkheinzelmann had "soon worn himself out through his all-too-frequent participation" and "then lost himself in embarrassing sentimentalities and naive banalities," wrote *Der Deutsche Rundfunk* (K. Tgt. 1931). The devaluation of the character by the Berlin programme magazine does not stop at the broadcasting format, however, but also dismantles the person of the author and artistic director Bodenstedt. His new productions during the Christmas season are not only devalued as being of a low standard, he is also accused of running a quasi-family clique at the station "with his wife Alice Fliegel" to the detriment of quality. Yet Alice Fliegel was not involved in any of these broadcasts.

Bodenstedt attempted another comeback in 1933. With his unerring sense for the *zeitgeist*, he was the first radio director in the German Reich to recognize and exploit the potential of the National Socialist turn in 1933. As early as April 4, he put a collage under the title *Das Hakenkreuz. Eine deutsche Passion* in the evening programme. On the eve of May 1, which shortly before had been elevated to a state holiday by the National Socialists as National Labor Day, Bodenstedt introduced a *Stunde der Hitler-Jugend,* whose leadership he shared with *Reichsjugendführer* Baldur von Schirach. Despite over-adaptation, however, he not only had to give up his post as director at the end of June, but also had to leave the station (cf. Intendant Bodenstedt ausgeschieden 28.06.1933).[29]

In 1984, the Hamburg press recalled Norag, which had gone on air 60 years ago. The popular children's show was also mentioned, but its identification figure had already faded so much into the memory of contemporaries that the newspaper reported on the "Funkheinzelmännchen" (Wauschkuhn 28./29.04.1984) and quite unembarrassedly left out the alleged announcement of the first show from the storybook of 1925. The myth had finally replaced the story.

References

Primary Literature

A. M. F.: Heinz Funkemal an Funkheinzelmann. Aus der Serie der groben Unfunklieder auf der mit der Antennenlitze bespannten Gitarre zu singen [Fanfiction]. In: Die Norag (1925) 20, 12.
Bodenstedt, Hans: Funkheinzelmann der Wanderbursch. Neue Märchen. Berlin: Springborn, 1925d.
Bodenstedt, Hans/Krüger, Carl: Funkheinzelmanns Kinderlieder. Hamburg: Libellen [1927].
Bodenstedt, Hans: Die Abenteuer des Funkheinzelmann. In: Funkheinzelmann 1 (1926a), 1–15, [o. S.].
Bodenstedt, Hans: Funkheinzelmanns Harz-Märchen. Ein Buch von Freude und Sonne für klein und groß. Thale (Harz): K. Welchert, 1929a.
Bodenstedt, Hans: Märchen vom Funkheinzelmann. Hamburg: Walther von Danckelman, 1924a.
Der heitere Fridolin. Halbmonatsschrift für Sport, Spiel, Spass und Abenteuer. Berlin 1921–1928.
Fliegel, Alice: Die Zwillinge der Försterin. Erinnerungen eines Wickelkindes. In: Funkheinzelmann 1 (1926a) 1–11, [o. S.].
Funkheinzelmann. Erste Funk- u. Film-Kinderzeitung der Welt, [ab Nr. 2:] Erste Funk- u. Film-Jugendzeitung der Welt! Berlin 1926 (1–11); Hamburg 1926 (12–17) und 1927 (1–26).

Audiography

Bodenstedt, Hans: Aus dem Märchenbuch des Funkheinzelmanns. Für die Kinder erzählt, die es noch nicht gehört haben. I. Die Glockenblumenkönigin. Musikalische Illustration durch das Norag-Orchester. Norag Hamburg 19.10.1924b, 16:30. Quelle: Die Norag 1924, 23, 2. Weitere Folgen: Funkheinzelmann im Vogelland, 26.10.1924; Funkheinzelmann im Riesenreich, 02.11.1924; Funkheinzelmann im Riesenland, 09.11.1924; Funkheinzelmann im Schlaraffenland, 16.11.1924; Funkheinzelmann im Nixenreich, 23.11.1924; Funkheinzelmann in Indien, 21.12.1924.

---

[29] From 1933 Bodenstedt worked for various publishing houses in Berlin and during the war moved to what was then Sudetenland, now the Czech Republic. In 1945 he returned to Hamburg, where he again worked for radio and the printed press. Among other things, he wrote for the children's magazine *Der Knattermax*. He died in 1958 in Bavaria, where he spent the last five years of his life together with his second wife Hanna (cf. Bodenstedt 13.02.1966).

Bodenstedt, Hans: Das Funkheinzelmann-Märchenspiel. Musik von Carl Krüger. Norag Hamburg, 16.12.1928, 14:00. Quelle: Die Norag 5 (1928a) 50, 2.
Bodenstedt, Hans: Das Funkheinzelmann-Märchenspiel. Musik von Carl Krüger. Musikalische Leitung: Fritz Gartz. Norag Hamburg, 25.12.1929, 14:30. Quelle: Die Norag 6 (1929b) 51, 8.
Bodenstedt, Hans: Das Funkheinzelmann-Märchenspiel. Musik von Carl Krüger. Musikalische Leitung: Fritz Gartz. Regie: Hans Freundt. Norag Hamburg, 01.11.1931, 16:50. Quelle: Die Norag 8 (1931a) 44, 16.
Bodenstedt, Hans: Das Hakenkreuz. Eine deutsche Passion. Funkbuch von Hans Bodenstedt. Deutsche Hymne: Horst Platen. Norag Hamburg, 04.04.1933, 20:00. Quelle: Die Norag 10 (1933) 14, 27.
Bodenstedt, Hans: Die Blumenmärchen vom Funkheinzelmann. I. Die Rose. Norag Hamburg 13.05.1925, 18:00. Quelle: Die Norag (1925a) 19, 4. Weitere Folgen: Die Tulpe, 20.05.1925; Das Veilchen, 27.05.1925; Das Vergißmeinnicht, 03.06.1925.
Bodenstedt, Hans: Die wunderschöne Goldenhaar. Ein Funkheinzelmann-Märchen in fünf Bildern. Musik und musikalische Leitung: Horst Platen. Regie: Hans Freundt. Norag Hamburg, 18.12.1931, 17:00. Quelle: Die Norag 8 (1931b) 50, 39.
Bodenstedt, Hans: Die wunderschöne Goldenhaar. Märchen. Musik von Horst Platen. Musikalische Leitung: Erwin von Clarmann. Regie: Alfred Maak. Übertragung aus dem Theater des Westens. Norag Hamburg, 17.11.1929, 16:00. Quelle: Die Norag 6 (1929c) 46, 2.
Bodenstedt, Hans: Ein Weihnachtstraum, erzählt vom Funkheinzelmann Hans Bodenstedt. [Programmpunkt in der Sendung:] Um Weihnachten herum (Stunde für Kinder, Schallplatten). Funk-Stunde Berlin, 13.12.1929, 14:00. Quelle: Der Deutsche Rundfunk 7 (1929d) 49, [o. S.].
Bodenstedt, Hans: Funkheinzelmann begegnet dem Märchendichter Hans Bodenstedt, der ihn den Berliner Kindern zum ersten Male vorstellt. Er erzählt: „Funkheinzelmann am Märchenbrunnen". Eine Mondfahrt durch den Friedrichshain. Funk-Stunde Berlin, 04.10.1925, 15:30. Quelle: Der Deutsche Rundfunk 3 (1925b) 40, 2576.
Bodenstedt, Hans: Funkheinzelmann filmt! Ein Filmfunkfabelspiel in 15 Bildern. Musik von Hermann Erdlen. Norag Hamburg, 04.01.1929, 16:15. Quelle: Die Norag 5 (1928b) 52, 12.
Bodenstedt, Hans: Funkheinzelmann im Vogelland. Ein fröhliches Märchen. Musikalische Illustrationen von Paul Hagemann. Norag Hamburg, 06.07.1924, 17:00. Quelle: Die Norag (1924c) 8, [1].
Bodenstedt, Hans: Funkheinzelmann, der Wanderbursche. Aus dem neuen Märchenbuch des Funkheinzelmanns von Hans Bodenstedt. Funk-Stunde Berlin, 29.11.1925c, 15:30. Quelle: Die Funk-Stunde (1925) 48, 1001.
Bodenstedt, Hans: Funkheinzelmann. Märchenspiel. Musik von Carl Krüger. Musikalische Leitung: Fritz Gartz. Norag Hamburg, 20.12.1926, 16:00. Quelle: Die Norag 3 (1926b) 51, 4.
Bodenstedt, Hans: Funkheinzelmanns Kindertheater. Lieder von Carl Krüger. 1. Bild: Die Glockenblumenkönigin. Norag Hamburg, 13.01.1926, 17:00. Quelle: Die Norag 3 (1926c) 2, 5; Übertragung auch auf Frankfurt, Kassel, Leipzig und Dresden. Quelle: Der Deutsche Rundfunk 4 (1926) 2, 120–122. 2. Bild: Ein Kind fällt vom Himmel, 20.01.1926; 3. Bild: Frau Holle, 4. Bild: Im Riesenland, 5. Bild: Im Schlaraffenland, 27.01.1926; 6. Bild: Die Quellnymphe, 7. Bild: Im Märchenland, 03.02.1926.
Bodenstedt, Hans: Funkheinzelmanns Schöpfungsgeschichte: Als Gott das Licht schuf. Norag Hamburg, 03.10.1926, 15:30. Quelle: Die Norag 3 (1926) 39, 11; u. d. T.: Als Gott das Reich schuf. Funk-Stunde Berlin, 03.10.1926, 15:30. Quelle: Die Funk-Stunde (1926) 40, 1053. Übertragung auch auf Leipzig und Dresden „von Hamburg über Berlin". Quelle: Die Mirag 3 (1926) 40, 3. Weitere Folgen (gleiches Programm in Hamburg und Berlin, mit Übertragung auch auf Deutsche Welle, Mirag und Sürag): Als Gott Himmel und Erde schuf, 10.10.1926; Als Gott die Bäume und Blumen schuf, 17.10.1926; Sonne, Mond und Sterne, 24.10.1926; Adam und Eva, Als Gott die Tiere schuf, 31.10.1926; Das Engelfest im Paradies, 07.11.1926d.
Bodenstedt, Hans: Goldhärchen und der Ticketick. Funk-Stunde Berlin, 10.01.1926, 15:30. Quelle: Die Funk-Stunde (1926e) 2, 31 – Norag Hamburg, 17.01.1926. Quelle: Die Norag 3 (1926) 2, 8. Weitere Folgen: Prinz Wassertröpfchen trägt das Glück. Berlin, 17.01.1926 – Hamburg, 24.01.1926; Goldhärchen in der großen Stadt. Berlin, 24.01.1926 – Hamburg, 31.01.1926;

Korinthchen und Rosinchen. Berlin, 31.01.1926 – Hamburg, 07.02.1926; Schutzengleins Schloß am Abendstern. Berlin, 07.02.1926 – Hamburg, 14.02.1926; Holper, Stolper, Pürzelchen. Berlin, 14.02.1926 – Hamburg, 21.02.1926; Goldhärchen und Goldkäferchen. Nur Hamburg, 28.02.1926; Goldhärchens Hochzeit. Berlin, 28.02.1926 – Hamburg, 07.03.1926.

Bodenstedt, Hans: Funkheinzelmanns Großstadtmärchen: Brennicke beschwört den Maschinenkarl. Funk-Stunde Berlin, 05.02.1928, 15:30. Quelle: Der Deutsche Rundfunk 6 (1928c) 6, 374; Übertragung auch auf Stettin und Deutsche Welle (ebd., 375). Weitere Folgen (mit Übertragung auf die gleichen Sender): Der Straßenbahnschaffner fängt den Funkenpuck, 12.02.1928; Haus im Licht, 26.02.1926; (u. d. Serientitel) Funkheinzelmanns Großstadtmärchen: 11.03.1928; 26.03.1928; 22.04.1928; 29.04.1928; 06.05.1928; 13.05.1928; 14.10.1928; von Hamburg aus mit Übertragung auch auf die Funk-Stunde, Deutsche Welle und die Sürag: Brennecke fährt nach Amerika, 22.07.1928; Brennecke flieht zu den Tieren, 19.08.1928; Brennecke entdeckt Berlin, 02.09.1928; Brennecke und der Erdgeist, 16.09.1928.

Fliegel, Alice: Funkheinzelmanns Mädchenstunde: Die Zwillinge der Försterin. Gelesen von der Dichterin. Norag Hamburg, 29.09.1926, 17:15. Quelle: Die Norag 3 (1926b) 39, 6; [fortgesetzt am 06.10., 13.10., 20.10. und 29.10.1926].

Funkheinzelmann der Norag [erste angekündigter Sendung]. 1. Funkheinzelmann erzählt. 2. Kinderlied (Hans Bodenstedt), Engelbert Humperdinck. Aus dem Manuskript gesungen von Fräulein Falck. 3. Hänsel und Gretel, aus dem Hausmärchen der Brüder Grimm, mit Motiven aus Engelbert Humperdincks Oper. Erzählt von Lotte Klein. Gesungen von Fräulein Helene Falck und Frau Aida Gotthart-Montes. Norag Hamburg, 04.05.1924, 17:00. Quelle: Die Funkwelt (1924) 4, [o. S.].

Stunde der Hitler-Jugend. Erster Nachmittag: Vater und Sohn. Leitung: Baldur von Schirach und Hans Bodenstedt. Norag Hamburg, 30.04.1933, 15:00. Quelle: Die Norag 10 (1933) 18, 15.

Übertragung der Glocken der St. Michaelis-Kirche in Hamburg. Choral der Turmbläser des Norag-Orchesters. Funkheinzelmann hebt das neue Jahr aus der Taufe. Norag Hamburg, 31.12.1924; 24:00. Quelle: Die Norag (1924) 33, 6.

Discography

Das Abenteuer des kleinen „E" [Schallplatte] (1928). Funkheinzelmann-Märchen. Musik. Illustr. von A. Bortz, erzählt vom Funkheinzelmann Hans Bodenstedt. Berlin: Homocord (4-2663, Seite B).

Das gefangene Lied [Schallplatte] (1928). Funkheinzelmann-Märchen, erzählt vom Funkheinzelmann Hans Bodenstedt. Berlin: Homocord (4-2661, Seite B).

Der Grillengeiger [Schallplatte] (1928). Funkheinzelmann-Märchen, erzählt vom Funkheinzelmann Hans Bodenstedt. Berlin: Homocord (4-2662, Seite A).

Der singende Baum [Schallplatte] (1927). Funkheinzelmann-Märchen, erzählt vom Funkheinzelmann Hans Bodenstedt, mit Gesang von Kurt Rodeck. Berlin: Homocord (4-2362, Seite B).

Der Singepuck [Schallplatte] (1928). Funkheinzelmann-Märchen, erzählt vom Funkheinzelmann Hans Bodenstedt. Berlin: Homocord (4-2662, Seite B).

Der Vogelpeter [Schallplatte] (1928). Funkheinzelmann-Märchen, erzählt vom Funkheinzelmann Hans Bodenstedt. Berlin: Homocord (4-2661, Seite A).

Die güldene Trompete [Schallplatte] (1927). Funkheinzelmann-Märchen, erzählt vom Funkheinzelmann Hans Bodenstedt. Mus. Ill. Fritz Gartz. Berlin: Homocord (4-2361, Seite A).

Ein Weihnachtstraum. [Schallplatte] (1928). Funkheinzelmann-Märchen, erzählt vom Funkheinzelmann Hans Bodenstedt. Berlin: Homocord (4-2663, Seite A).

Funkheinzelmann beim Ticketick [Schallplatte] (1927). Funkheinzelmann-Märchen, erzählt vom Funkheinzelmann Hans Bodenstedt. Mus. Ill. Fritz Gartz. Berlin: Homocord (4-2360, Seite B).

Funkheinzelmann im Glockenland [Schallplatte] (1927). Funkheinzelmann-Märchen, erzählt vom Funkheinzelmann Hans Bodenstedt. Mus. Ill. Fritz Gartz. Berlin: Homocord (4-2361, Seite B).
Funkheinzelmann stellt sich vor [Schallplatte] (1927). Funkheinzelmann-Märchen, erzählt vom Funkheinzelmann Hans Bodenstedt. Mus. Ill. Fritz Gartz. Berlin: Homocord (4-2360, Seite A).
Johannismännchen [Schallplatte] (1930). Erzählt vom Funkheinzelmann [Hans Bodenstedt]. Homocord-Orchester und Kinderchor. Berlin: Homocord (H-62836).
Johannisnacht – ein neues Fest [Schallplatte] (1930). Erzählt vom Funkheinzelmann [Hans Bodenstedt]. Homocord-Orchester und Kinderchor. Berlin: Homocord (H-62837).
Wenn das Fräulein Violine Hochzeit macht [Schallplatte] (1927). Funkheinzelmann-Märchen, erzählt vom Funkheinzelmann Hans Bodenstedt. Mus. Ill. Fritz Gartz. Berlin: Homocord (4-2362, Seite A).

Theatrography

Bodenstedt, Hans/Krüger, Carl: Das Funkheinzelmann-Märchenspiel. Musik von Carl Krüger. Hamburg: Rufu 1926.
Die wunderschöne Goldenhaar (Uraufführung?). Regie: Alfred Maak. Theater des Westens Hamburg 17.11.1929.
Funkheinzelmann filmt! (Uraufführung). Regie: Luis Gutmann. Capitol Berlin. 01.12.1928.
Funkheinzelmanns Bilderbuch (Uraufführung). Carl-Schultze-Theater Hamburg, 08.12.1927.
Funkheinzelmanns Märchenreise (Uraufführung). Regie: Eric Charell. Großes Schauspielhaus Berlin. 06.11.1926.
Funkheinzelmanns Märchenspiel (Erstaufführung). Regie: Martin Gien. Deutsches Theater Hannover. Anfang Dezember 1926a.
Funkheinzelmanns Märchenspiel (Erstaufführung). Regie: Robert Bürkner. Stadttheater Altona. 05.12.1926b.
Funkheinzelmanns Weihnachtsmarkt (Uraufführung). Regie: Eric Charell. Großes Schauspielhaus Berlin. 14.11.1925.

Secondary Literature Before 1945

[Bedenken gegenüber einseitig „proletarischen" Märchen. Schriftverkehr zwischen dem preußischen Landrat Adler, der Bedenken gegen eine geplante Märchensendung der Norag im Kinderlager Seekamp äußert, und dem Vorsitzenden Senatsrat Zinn, der den Hamburger Regierungsrat Stoltz informiert (insgesamt 5 Briefe); Beschluss des Überwachungsausschusses, die Sendung nicht zu beanstanden (Auszug aus dem Sitzungsprotokoll)]. Kiel und Hamburg 14.–18.07.1927, Staatsarchiv Hamburg, Signatur 542/135-1_I-IV_542.
„Funkheinzelmanns Märchenreise". Eine Weihnachtsrevue im Berliner Großen Schauspielhaus. In: Der Deutsche Rundfunk 4 (1926) 46, 3248.
Aktuelle Hamburger Woche. In: Der Deutsche Rundfunk 6 (1928) 35, 2329–2330.
An den Funkheinzelmann [Fanpost]. In: Die Norag (1924) 14, 5.
Bagier, Guido: Der akustische Film. Zu der am Berliner Sender stattgefundenen Veranstaltung am 26.06.28. In: Die Sendung 5 (1928) 27, 327–328.
Berliner Adreßbuch. Unter Benutzung amtlicher Quellen. Berlin. 1926, 1927, 1932.
Berliner Bericht. Ein Abend bei Frau Stein. Der lustige Beethoven. In: Der Deutsche Rundfunk 3 (1925a) 7, 411–413.
Berliner Bericht. Melodramen-, Brahms- und Haydn-Abend – die neue Woche. In: Der Deutsche Rundfunk 3 (1925b) 2, 149–151.

Berliner Handels-Register. Verzeichnis der in den Amtsgerichtsbezirken Berlin-Mitte, Charlottenburg, Köpenick [...] wohnenden eingetragenen Einzelfirmen, Gesellschaften und Genossenschaften. Berlin 1931.

Bodenstedt, Hans: Funkdramatische Erfahrungen. Hinter den Geräuschkulissen der Hamburger Sendebühne. In: Die Norag (1925) 14, 8.

Börsenverein der Deutschen Buchhändler (Hg.): Sperlings Zeitschriften- und Zeitungsadressbuch. Handbuch der deutschen Presse. Leipzig 1926–1947.

Die Norag geht nach Harburg. In: Die Norag (1925) 28, 1.

Die Norag in der Goldenen Wiege. In: Die Norag (1925) 31, 1.

Dominik, Hans: Berlin im Licht. In: Die Sendung 5 (1928) 42, 538–539.

dr. H. B.: Hörspiel aus der Konservenbüchse. Die erste Tonfilmübertragung in Frankfurt a. M. In: Funk 5 (1928) 10, 80.

Egl.: Das deutsche Derby im Rundfunk. In: Der Deutsche Rundfunk 4 (1926) 27, 1918.

Ein Lob dem Funkheinzelmann. Grüße unserer Funkfreunde. In: Die Norag (1924) 7, 1. Beil.

Eine frohe Mitteilung! Berlin, 12. Juni 1926. In: Funkheinzelmann 1 (1926) 3, [1].

Eisler, Max: Ein neues grammophonisches Aufnahmeverfahren. In: Phonographische Zeitschrift 26 (1925) 18, 768.

erle: Funkheinzelmanns Weihnachtsmarkt. In: Vossische Zeitung/Das Unterhaltungsblatt der Vossischen Zeitung (1925) 546 vom 18.11., 3.

Esmarch, Kurt [u. d. Pseud. Kurt-Ernst Gustav]: Funkheinzelmanns Märchenspiel. In: Funkheinzelmann 1 (1926a) 16, [5] f. und 17, [10].

Esmarch, Kurt [u. d. Pseud. Kurt-Ernst Gustav]: Funkheinzelmann ist da! In: Die Norag 3 (1926b) 50, 17

Exposé über die Rufu-Verlagsgesellschaft m.b.H., Hamburg [1927], Staatsarchiv Hamburg, Signatur 135–1 I–IV_589.

Funkheinzelmann begegnet dem Märchendichter Hans Bodenstedt [Bildtext]. In: Die Funk-Stunde (1925) 40, 803.

Fronemann, Wilhelm: Neue Jugend-Zeitschriften. Kritische Bosheiten. In: Jugendschriften-Warte 30 (1925) 9/10, 78–80.

Funkheinzelmann [Fanpost]. In: Die Norag (1924) 16, 13.

Funkheinzelmann – Diese reich illustrierte Kinderzeitung. In: Die Werag 2 (1927) 4, 18.

Funkheinzelmann filmt. Im Capitol. In: Vossische Zeitung (1928) vom 3.12, Beilage Sport, Spiel und Turnen, 2.

Funkheinzelmann-Bund. In: Die Norag 3 (1926) 18, 1.

Funkheinzelmann-Rademacher-Preis. In: Funkheinzelmann 1 (1926) 5, [1].

Funkheinzelmanns Bilderbuch. In: Die Norag 4 (1927) 49, [1].

Funkheinzelmanns Weihnachtswunsch. Neue Märchenfahrten des Funkheinzelmanns. In: Die Norag (1925) 52, 2.

Funkheinzelmann-Schokolade ist die beste! [Werbe-Anzeige]. In: Funkheinzelmann 1 (1926) 2, [o. S.].

Gratisreklame für Detaillisten. In: Die Norag 3 (1926) 13, 14.

Hamburger Adreßbuch. Hamburg. 1926, 1927.

Ich, der Funkheinzelmann [ganzseitige Anzeige der Revue „Funkheinzelmanns Weihnachtsmarkt" im Großen Schauspielhaus Berlin]. In: Die Funk-Stunde (1925) 46, 966.

In Funkheinzelmanns Reich. In: Völkischer Beobachter (1931) vom 1.12.

Intendant Bodenstedt ausgeschieden. In: Hamburger Nachrichten (1933) vom 28.06.

J. L.: „Zwischensender" Berlin? In: Funk 1 (1924) 29, 444.

J. L.: Die Berliner Funkstunde und ihre Funkprinzessin. Kleines Beschwerdebuch. In: Die Sendung 2 (1925) 19, 8.

K. Tgt.: Die Märchenstunde der Norag. Kritik. In: Der Deutsche Rundfunk 9 (1931) 52, 68.

K. W.: Vom Stuttgarter Sender. Die deutschen Rundfunkgrüße an Amerika – Schweizer Gäste – Musikalisches – Vorträge. In: Der Deutsche Rundfunk 4 (1926) 3, 157–158.

König, Theodor: Reklame-Psychologie, ihr gegenwärtiger Stand – ihre praktische Bedeutung. München [u. a.] ²1924.

Lieber Funkheinzelmann! Hamburg, Mai 1925. In: Die Norag (1925) 21, 9.
Müller-Förster, Alfred: Lampenfunkenfieber oder Funklampenfieber. Ein Geständnis von Alfred Müller-Förster. In: Die Norag (1925) 18, 18.
Noragfest in Harburg. In: Die Norag (1925) 30, 2.
Proesler, Adele: Märchen und Jugendstunden im Rundfunk. In: Der Deutsche Rundfunk 3 (1925) 24, 1505–1508.
rb.: Der Siegeslauf des „Funk-Heinzelmanns". In: Der Deutsche Rundfunk 3 (1925) 48, 3189.
Sie: 25jähriges Berufsjubiläum des Intendanten Hans Bodenstedt. In: Hamburger 8-Uhr-Abendblatt (1930) vom 29.11.
Siegeslauf des „Funkheinzelmann". In: Die Norag (1925) 47, [1].
St.: Die fünfzigste Neueinstudierung für die Norag-Funkbühne. In: Der Deutsche Rundfunk 3 (1925a) 4, 219–220.
St.: Die Rundfunktypen der Norag. In: Der Deutsche Rundfunk 3 (1925b) 15, 1009–1011.
St.: Ein Rundfunksendespiel auf der Alster. Das erste Freiluftsendespiel der Welt. In: Der Deutsche Rundfunk 3 (1925c) 20, 1264–1265.
St.: Hörerschau im Hamburger Zoo. In: Der Deutsche Rundfunk 3 (1925d) 28, 1765–1766.
Tasiemka, Hans [u. d. Kürzel H. Ta.]: Die Funkheinzelmann-Revue im Berliner Capitol. In: Der Deutsche Rundfunk 6 (1928) 50, 3388.
Thalhofer, Franz X./Antz, Joseph: Die Jugendlektüre. Geschichtliches und Grundsätzliches. mit ausführlichen Verzeichnissen empfehlenswerter Bücher, Zeitschriften und Bühnenwerke für die Jugend. Paderborn ²1925.
Thalhofer, Franz X.: Die Jugendlektüre. Geschichtliches und Grundsätzliches. Mit ausführlichen Verzeichnissen empfehlenswerter Bücher, Zeitschriften und Bühnenwerke für die Jugend. Paderborn 1924.
Thomalla, Curt: Falsche Scham. [Populär-medizin. Darstellg]. Berlin/Leipzig 1926.
Übersicht über die Tätigkeit der Nordischen Rundfunk Aktiengesellschaft. [Anschreiben an den Direktor der Staatlichen Pressestelle Hamburg A. Zinn]. Hamburg 08.03.1926, Staatsarchiv Hamburg, Signatur 135–1 I-IV_529.
Übersicht über die Zahl der Rundfunkteilnehmer nach dem Stand am 1. Oktober. In: Der Deutsche Rundfunk 3 (1925) 43, 2807.
Unsere Vertrauensfrage an die Hörer. Sichtung der ersten tausend Zuschriften. In: Die Norag (1925) 15, 1–2.
Unseren kleinen Freunden. In: Die Norag 3 (1926) 42, 1.
Vorschläge des Rundfunk-Ausschusses beim Jugendamt Hamburg zur Verbesserung des Sendeprogramms der [Norag]. Hamburg 15.12.1927, Staatsarchiv Hamburg, Signatur 135-1_I_IV_551.
W. V.: Erzählende Kunst im Dortmunder Sender. In: Der Deutsche Rundfunk 4 (1926) 16, 1100.
Was sagt die Presse zum Funkheinzelmann. In: Die Norag 3 (1926) 51, 30.
Wochenvorschau der Norag. Bizets „Djamileh". Kreutzers „Nachtlager". Fritz Reuter und Hans Friedrich Blunck. In: Die Norag (1925) 4, 1.

Secondary Literature After 1945

Bauer, Thomas: Deutsche Programmpresse 1923 bis 1941. Entstehung, Entwicklung und Kontinuität der Rundfunkzeitschriften. München 1993.
Bekmeyer-Feuerhahn, Sigrid: Erlebniswertorientierte Markenstrategien. In: Bruhn, Manfred (Hg.): Handbuch Markenführung: Kompendium zum erfolgreichen Markenmanagement. Strategien – Instrumente – Erfahrungen 2013, 879–902.
Berg, Jan: Die Bühnenschau – ein vergessenes Kapitel der Kinoprogrammgeschichte. In: Hickethier, Knut (Hg.): Filmgeschichte schreiben. Ansätze, Entwürfe und Methoden; Dokumentation der Tagung der GFF 1988. Berlin 1989, 25–40.

Bodenstedt, Hanna: Hans Bodenstedt [2 Seiten Masch.]. Feldafing Obb. 13.02.1966, Staatsarchiv Hamburg, Signatur 621-1/144_1257.
Braun, Alfred: Achtung, Achtung, hier ist Berlin! Aus der Geschichte des Deutschen Rundfunks in Berlin 1923–1932. Berlin 1968.
Bruhn, Manfred: Relationship Marketing. Das Management von Kundenbeziehungen. München ⁵2016 (Vahlens Handbücher der Wirtschafts- und Sozialwissenschaften).
Burmann, Christoph/Halaszovich, Tilo F./Schade, Michael/Piehler, Rico: Identitätsbasierte Markenführung: Grundlagen – Strategie – Umsetzung – Controlling. Wiesbaden ³2018.
Burmann, Christoph/Meffert, Heribert: Managementkonzept der identitätsorientierten Markenführung. In: Meffert, Heribert/Burmann, Christoph/Koers, Martin (Hg.): Markenmanagement. Identitätsorientierte Markenführung und praktische Umsetzung; mit Best-practice-Fallstudien. Wiesbaden ²2005, 74–114.
Burmann, Christoph/Nitschke, Axel: Profilierung von Marken mit Sponsoring und Events. In: Meffert, Heribert/Burmann, Christoph/Koers, Martin (Hg.): Markenmanagement. Identitätsorientierte Markenführung und praktische Umsetzung; mit Best-practice-Fallstudien. Wiesbaden ²2005, 387–409.
Buzwan, Josefine: Architektur – Stadt – Inszenierung. Theater in Berlin – vom Königlichen Opernhaus bis zur Schaubühne. Berlin 2013 (Schriftenreihe zur Baugeschichte und Architekturtheorie des Labors für Baugeschichte und Bauerhaltung; 7). Zugl.: Berlin, Hochsch. für Technik und Wirtschaft, Masterarbeit, 2012.
Denson, Shane/Mayer, Ruth: Grenzgänger. Serielle Figuren im Medienwechsel. In: Kelleter, Frank (Hg.): Populäre Serialität: Narration – Evolution – Distinktion. Bielefeld 2012, 185–203.
Dömeland, Janine: Grosses Schauspielhaus Berlin. Musiktheaterkonzepte in der Weimarer Republik. In: Grosch, Nils (Hg.): Aspekte des modernen Musiktheaters in der Weimarer Republik. Münster 2004, 139–158.
Elfert, Brunhild: Die Entstehung und Entwicklung des Kinder- und Jugendfunks in Deutschland von 1924 bis 1933 am Beispiel der Berliner Funk-Stunde-AG. Frankfurt a. M. [u. a.] 1985 (Europäische Hochschulschriften. Reihe 40, Kommunikationswissenschaften und Publizistik; 3). Zugl.: Münster (Westf.), Univ., Diss., 1984.
Fiske, John (Hg.): Understanding popular culture. London [u. a.] ²2011.
Fiske, John: Popularity and the Politics of Information. In: Dahlgren, Peter/Sparks, Colin (Hg.): Journalism and popular culture. London 1992, 45–63.
Führer, Christian: Aufzeichnungstechnik: Wachs- und Schwarzplatten. In: Leonhard, Joachim F. (Hg.): Programmgeschichte des Hörfunks. In der Weimarer Republik. München 1997, 710–711.
Hostetter, Anthony: Max Reinhardt's Großes Schauspielhaus. Its artistic goals, planning, and operation, 1910–1933. Lewiston [u. a.] 2003 (Studies in theatre arts; 20).
Jansen, Wolfgang/Laade, Wolfgang: Glanzrevuen der zwanziger Jahre. Berlin 1987 (Deutsche Vergangenheit; 25).
Kelleter, Frank: Populäre Serialität. Eine Einführung. In: Ders. (Hg.): Populäre Serialität: Narration – Evolution – Distinktion. Bielefeld 2012a, 11–46.
Kelleter, Frank (Hg.): Populäre Serialität: Narration – Evolution – Distinktion. Bielefeld 2012b.
Kroeber-Riel, Werner/Esch, Franz-Rudolf: Strategie und Technik der Werbung. Verhaltens- und neurowissenschaftliche Erkenntnisse. Stuttgart ⁸2015.
Lethen, Helmut: Chicago und Moskau. Berlins moderne Kultur der 20er Jahre zwischen Inflation und Weltwirtschaftskrise. In: Boberg, Jochen/Fichter, Tilman/Glaser, Hermann (Hg.): Die Metropole. Industriekultur in Berlin im 20. Jahrhundert. München 1986, 190–213.
Mühl-Benninghaus, Wolfgang: Das Ringen um den Tonfilm. Strategien der Elektro- und der Filmindustrie in den 20er und 30er Jahren. Düsseldorf 1999.
Pigorsch, Enrico: Der Funkheinzelmann erzählt. Hans Bodenstedt und seine Märchen auf Homocord-Platten. In: Der Schalltrichter 13 (2001) 17, 1–11.
Schmidt, Siegfried J.: Kalte Faszination. Medien, Kultur, Wissenschaft in der Mediengesellschaft. Weilerswist 2000.

Scott, Jason: The Character-Oriented Franchise. Promotion and Exploitation of pre-sold characters in American film, 1913–1950. In: Smith, Iain R. (Hg.): Cultural Borrowings. Appropriation, Reworking, Transformation. Nottingham 2009, 34–55.

Wauschkuhn, Franz: Mit Kabarett, Tanzmusik und Kinderfunk zum Pionier des Rundfunks. Vor 60 Jahren ging die Nordische Rundfunkaktiengesellschaft (NORAG) zum ersten Mal auf Sendung. In: Hamburger Abendblatt (1984) vom 28./29.04., 5.

Weber, Annemarie: Billy Tom rettet Metropolis. Marginalie zu einer ungewöhnlichen Verwertungsgeschichte der Filmstandbilder Horst von Harbous. In: Preußer, Heinz-Peter (Hg.): Späte Stummfilme. Ästhetische Innovation im Kino 1924–1930. Marburg 2017, 318–327.

Stage Children Migrate to Radio and/or Film

To the Moon and Back

Peterchens Mondfahrt and His Journey Through Media

Julia Benner

Prehistory: Introduction

Peterchens Mondfahrt is one of the best-known unknowns in the history of German-language children's literature, as Hans-Heino Ewers also notes when he writes: "Rarely has a popular success been so completely ignored by research and criticism" (Ewers 2006, 74).[1] All the more remarkable is the longevity of *Peterchens Mondfahrt,* which is still indispensable in children's rooms, playhouses, and on TV screens, and to which the various media transformations have undoubtedly significantly contributed.

The story of the romantic, fairytale like narrative *Peterchens Mondfahrt*[2] focuses on a chubby maybug called Herr Sumsemann, whose sixth leg together with the wicked woodcutter responsible for the loss of his leg has been banished to the moon by a fairy. Together with the siblings Peterchen and Anneliese, Herr Sumsemann sets out on an adventurous journey to the moon in order to regain his missing leg and embarks. However, this article embarks on the arduous journey to answer the

---

[1] In the 1970/1980s, the quantity of literary criticism regarding Peterchens Mondfahrt increased (cf. Schedler 1972; Jahnke 1977; Bauer 1980; cf. also Ewers 2008). Apart from the aforementioned contributions by Ewers, there has hardly been any research on *Peterchens Mondfahrt* in the twenty-first century (Steinlein 2008, for example, is an exception). However, the *literarische Stoff* is always mentioned in all relevant introductions as well as relevant handbooks and encyclopaedias.

[2] Gerdt von Bassewitz's second children's book *Pips der Pilz* (1916) is similar to *Peterchens Mondfahrt*. It also narrates a journey, employs a fairy, and contains the themes of nature and Christmas.

J. Benner (✉)
Department of German Literature, Humboldt-University Berlin, Berlin, Germany
e-mail: bennerju@hu-berlin.de

© Springer-Verlag GmbH Germany, part of Springer Nature 2024
P. Josting et al. (eds.), *German-Language Children's and Youth Literature In The Media Network 1900–1945*, https://doi.org/10.1007/978-3-476-05892-8_9

following interwoven questions: Beginning at the very understanding of a media network as a system of individual types of media interconnected within a single copyright (media mix/franchising/commercial supersystem, product network)[3] or even perceived together, it will be determined whether the material at hand is a media network. If neither is the case, it will be examined how this phenomenon can be described. It will also be clarified in which interdependent relationship the various individual types of media regarding *Peterchens Mondfahrten*[4] stand to each other, by which "internal[n] procedures" the individual texts "develop a relationship to other texts" (Meier 2020, 77) and whether they could potentially be received together contemporarily. In advance it should be revealed that the *Stoff* in question was already available in different media variants in the first half of the twentieth century, but at first glance it is not clear how these relate to one another, that is, what constitutes the strong connection between them.

In most versions, the moon journey of Peter, Anneliese and Herr Sumsemann – similar to this contribution – is divided into several stages, which also correspond to the number of maybug legs: six. The starting point of the story is Peter and Anneliese's nursery, where the siblings meet the unfortunate Herr Sumsemann. After that, the companions reach the starry meadow, where they meet the Sandman and the little stars, while in the second section I will address the aspects of authorship, text, and popularity. The journey continues to the Milky Way and consequently to visual design. Afterwards, nature spirits meet in the castle of the night fairy for a chat, while the corresponding section will focus on sonority, acoustics and music. Riding on the Great Bear, the children and the maybug arrive at the Christmas Meadow – that is, a place of seemingly endless materialistic consumption. Finally, Peterchen and Anneliese are shot to the moon with a cannon, where they must contend with the ravenous Moon Man to retrieve the sixth little leg. In this chapter I will cover the aspects of time and space. In the end, the travelers return home, while this paper will offer theoretical and methodological considerations, trying to answer the initial questions.

---

[3] Regarding the German-language research, see e.g. Kümmerling-Meibauer 2007; Frederking/Josting 2005; Hengst 1994; Josting/Maiwald 2007; Josting 2013; Kruse 2014; Maiwald 2007, 2010; Kurwinkel 2017; Meier 2020; Renner 2013. In this article I am not concerned with a detailed discussion of the term *media network* in general, which is why the research situation on the media network is not presented here in full detail, which also helps to avoid redundancies within the volume. Instead, the focus is on the question of the applicability of the term in relation to the specific material before me. Of further interest is the question of how and by what the individual elements are connected with each other.

[4] Since there are different types of media they will be referred to either as individual media or as *Peterchens Mondfahrten* in order to choose a name that is as neutral as possible.

The Nursery: Starting Point

Our journey begins ... where actually? Even to determine the starting point of this *Stoff* rich in varieties proves difficult. *Peterchens Mondfahrt* was initially known as a "fairy tale play",[5] which Ewers calls an "entertainment revue", a "Christmas fairy tale", a "children's play", a "humorous parody of the fairy tale tradition" (Ewers 2006, 74) and a "modern fairy tale revue" (Ewers 2008). It was extraordinarily popular with the public and, according to Taube, advanced to become the most frequently performed children's play of the twentieth century (cf. Taube 2000, 576).

Bassewitz wrote the text in 1911 during a stay at the famous Königstein sanatorium of Oskar Kohnstamm, whose children Peter and Anneliese are apparently immortalized in the eponymous main characters (Terhorst 2013). This form of speculation regarding the text's origins and authorship is almost prototypical for children's literature. Many books that are often referred to as *classics* were, according to their respective narratives, created from a play by and with children; one only needs to think of A. A. Milne's *Winnie the Pooh* or J. M. Barrie's *Peter Pan*. However, it is striking that these central characters (Christopher-Robin as well as Peter, George, John and Michael Nicholas) are also named after real-life persons.

Peterchens Mondfahrt was first published by Rowohlt in Leipzig as a stage manuscript consisting of four pictures in 1912. This early text by Bassewitz was largely written in a sugary and somewhat clumsy verse, which is why it is hardly surprising that the other works by Bassewitz, who actually wanted to establish himself as an author of adult literature, were almost unanimously reviled by critics (cf. Stupperich 2017, 1). While his other works proved to be slow sellers, *Peterchens Mondfahrt* was printed in five editions within the same year. From the fourth edition onwards, the now expanded text was published by the Munich publishing house Verlag der Weißen Bücher with the addition of *ein Märchenspiel in sieben Bildern*. The edition published around 1915 by Kurt Wolff, marked by the wartime economy, is also divided into seven acts, although the subsidiary texts are considerably more concise. Later versions are often divided into six acts. The text was thus changed several times, and there was no dominant or common variant in the period before 1945.

The date of the premiere at the Alte Stadttheater Leipzig on December 7, 1912, is already an indication that *Peterchens Mondfahrt* is primarily narrative *Stoff* in the context of bourgeois, pre-Christmas entertainment (cf. Schmidt 2017). Children from a ballet school performed dances and the performance was musically directed by Josef Achtélik. The Christmas revue, directed by Paul Prina, was very popular with audiences and was performed one hundred and eighty times in Leipzig alone (Kaiser 2014). However, its critical reception was not always gracious here either, although it was by and large more positive in bourgeois circles than in social democratic ones, for example (cf. Stupperich 2017, 13 f.). Without mentioning *Peterchens*

---

[5] This is how it reads in the notices and in the subtitles of the first publications.

Mondfahrt directly[6] the contemporary critic Jacob Löwenberg, who was obviously following the literary tradition of Heinrich Wolgast, was generally scathing about this art form in his article entitled *Das Elend unseres Weihnachtsmärchens* (January 1913), published shortly after the first performance. He concluded by describing the play as "better trash literature" (Löwenberg 1913, 155):

> All its [trash literature's; note JB] characteristics are found here: the addiction to the adventurous, the lust for sensation, for the impossible situations, the lack of any psychology, and a language that gives slaps in the face to any finer sensibilities. Only this I admit, one thing is perhaps lacking – the intention to affect the brute instincts, and so I mitigate my judgment and say they belong to the better trash literature. (Ibid.)

Löwenberg criticizes that the producers of Christmas fairy tales do not perceive children as a demanding audience and therefore do not try to create art. He believes that there is no appealing literary-aesthetic design here, but sees in the Christmas tales an eclectic jumble full of "stupid clown jokes unworthy of a good circus" (ibid., 150). Also, he is bothered by what he sees: The unnecessary allegories (which he deems incomprehensible to children) and the ballet:

> This degenerate child of dance, this hermaphrodite of anticulture and überculture! Nothing more unnatural, nothing more repulsive and unchildlike than a ballet in a fairy tale. [...] But in fairy tales everything dances: snowmen and nutcrackers, storks and ice crystals, and so that the nonsense reaches its boiling point, the freezing point dances a solo. (Ibid., 152)

Apart from the thoroughly amusing polemic words, it can be seen ascertained from these lines by Löwenberg that many parallels in terms of content (e.g. anthropomorphisation of natural phenomena) as well as design (e.g. ballet) can be drawn between *Peterchens Mondfahrt* and other Weihnachtsmärchen of that time. But unlike the other German-language plays, *Peterchens Mondfahrt* is still well-known, popular, and widely performed today. This leads to the question of what exactly is so special about it. Consequently, shortly after the successful premiere in Leipzig, numerous performances followed, with those in Berlin being particularly important. Bassewitz himself writes:

> The play was performed in Berlin at the Theater an der Weidendammer Brücke, which was empty at the time and had been rented for this purpose by friends of my work, with participation of actors from all the major Berlin stages and the orchestra of the royal opera house under Schmalstich's direction, who had written me some very pleasant accompanying music for the songs. The play was then taken over by the Künstlertheater (Nürnbergerstr.) under Grunwald's direction and performed at the Berlin Theater in the season 1913–14. (Bassewitz 1917, 8 f.)

This production, directed by Friedrich Zelnitz at the Weidendammer Brücke (13 December 1913), i.e. at the Deutsches Schauspielhaus in Berlin,[7] received much praise by the critics of the time. Clemens Schmalstich, who now composed the

---

[6] It can be assumed that Löwenberg, who apparently lived in Northern Germany, had not seen the play at the time.

[7] Today the Komische Oper.

music and took over the musical direction, was chorus repetiteur and Kapellmeister at the Royal Opera from 1919–1920 (cf. DBE 2008, 4). The set was designed by the artist Hans Baluschek, known primarily for his socially critical works of art and as a member of the Berlin Secession. In 1916,[8] the text was published in its prose version under the title *Peterchens Mondfahrt – Ein Märchen* in Berlin-Grunewald by the publishing house Hermann Klemm with illustrations by Hans Baluschek. This text is still available in stores today, partly with Baluschek's pictures, partly with other illustrations. The scores by Clemens Schmalstich are also found in some editions alongside the text.

During the reign of National Socialism, the success of Peterchens Mondfahrt did not fade away, although the name Hans Baluschek now receded somewhat into the background. Baluschek, whose pictures can also be found in the book editions published during the Nazi regime, was instrumental in the success of *Peterchens Mondfahrt* (see below), but was ostracized by the National Socialist regime as a Marxist – he was a Social Democrat – and associated with so-called *degenerate art*. In his place, Clemens Schmalstich, who had composed the music for the 1913 play, was now increasingly mentioned in reviews (cf. e.g. Herzberg 1937),[9] which is hardly surprising since he had been a member of the NSDAP since 1932 (cf. Klee 2007, 527).[10]

Even after the Second World War, there were many performances of the play, which continues its success story to this day; other media adaptations and transformations joined in. For example, the first *Peterchens Mondfahrt* film, a live-action television film in black and white, was released in 1959. It was directed by Gerhard F. Hering and Hein Heckroth. The opening sequence shows an elderly lady reading from a book of fairy tales in the wake of Perrault. Interestingly enough clearly referring not to the play but to the book of fairy tales. However, she is not holding the book with the prose text and Baluschek's pictures, but a prop made especially for the film. Since this is a live-action film, supernatural-wondrous elements – such as the anthropomorphized maybug – are produced primarily through elaborate costuming, painted screens as backgrounds, and mechanics,[11] which means that parallels to theatrical performances and the Christmas fairy tale aesthetic cannot be dismissed. Furthermore, the film is partly reminiscent of Géorge Méliès' *Le Voyage dans la Lune* (1902) due to this décor and the thematic affinity.

In 1990, moreover, an animated film directed by Wolfgang Urchs was released. Klaus Doldinger, known for his film music (e.g. *Das Boot, Tatort, Die unendliche*

---

[8] In the libraries 1915 is given here in square brackets – i.e. as an estimated year – but Bassewitz himself writes 1916.

[9] The popularity of Schmalstich's compositions at this time is also indicated by an appeal in an exile magazine. In 1946, Lydia Petrowa from Mexico asked in *Aufbau:* "Who can get me *Peterchens Mondfahrt* by Schmalstisch [sic!] for the purpose of staging it for Jewish relief purposes?" (Petrowa 1946).

[10] Schmalstich composed music for theatre, opera and, in the 1930s/1940s, for film, and was much in demand at this time; from 1933 to 1945 he was even a professor at the Berlin Musikhochschule (DBE 2008, 4).

[11] The polar bear, for example, is a puppet that has been attached to a rail.

Geschichte), arranged the music based on Schmalstich's compositions. The film, which is often the only more widely known variant of *Peterchens Mondfahrt* internationally, was shortly thereafter expanded by a few scenes and broadcast as a five-part TV series (1992).[12] In May 2019, the "modern variant of the fairy tale classic"[13] produced by Little Dream Entertainment (directed by Ali Samadi Ahadi) was also screened at the International Festival of Animated Film in Stuttgart.[14]

Games also exist: A board game from 1967 refers decidedly to "the fairy tale by Gerdt von Bassewitz", which is retold in the box text; Bassewitz's pictures were used for the visual design of the game board and cards. A card game set from Pestalozzi Verlag, on the other hand, consists of three newly produced pictures showing the children flying out of the window of their nursery together with the maybug. There is also a sleigh ride on the Milky Way and a visit to the Night Fairy. The characters are rounder and seem to be trivialized, but the influence of Baluschek can be clearly seen here as well, which is especially evident when looking at the Sleigh Ride picture.

It is already clear that *Peterchens Mondfahrten* is a subject with many question marks: It could be argued that the verses by Gerdt von Bassewitz, i.e. the original text, mark the starting point of *Peterchens Mondfahrt*'s journey through media. However, the question arises whether this would not inadmissibly privilege the text, since no variant of the *Stoff* subsequently refers directly to these verses. It could be argued that the performances in Leipzig are the starting point, but it could also be argued that it was the Berlin performances, in which Schmalstich and Baluschek were involved, that really popularised *Peterchens Mondfahrt*. Thus, as already indicated, the later transformations often refer to Baluschek's pictures and/or Schmalstich's music. But how can an unrecorded performance be understood at all, in this context and does it really lay the foundation for further media? Would it not then be consistent – and I would explicitly not argue for this – to take the play by Bassewitz and the children Peter and Anneliese Kohnstamm as the starting point? Moreover, it could be argued that the prose/picture book version is the most widespread variant overall from a temporal and spatial point of view, which especially later medial transformations seem to primarily refer to.

Thus, several starting points of the possible media connection present themselves. For the time being, *Peterchens Mondfahrten* seem to be describable as transmedial (cf. Meier 2020; Rajewski 2001, among others) and rhizomatic, in the sense that a "rhizome is an acentric, non-hierarchical and asignifying system without a general" (Deleuze/Guattari 1992, 36). This figure of thought introduced by Deleuze and Guattari forms a counter-model to hierarchical fixed models of relations and

---

[12] There are some exceptions, which are discussed further below.
[13] http://www.littledream-entertainment.com/filme/peterchens-mondfahrt/ (12.03.2019).
[14] https://www.itfs.de/event/neuerzaehlung-von-peterchens-mondfahrt/ (26.06.2019).

communication symbolised by a tree. Unlike the tree, there is no fixed form or order in the rhizome, but a polycentric and possibly subversive network.[15]

The determination of an original starting point can thus be considered obsolete. However it is still unclear whether and how these individual media units are linked to one another and whether a receptive network or system of this kind actually emerges. In the following and exactly for this purpose aspects will be examined that seem to be plausible as a connecting element and are frequently mentioned in literary research regarding media networks. Accordingly, it will now be a matter of determining the intricacies of the boundaries of the media network.

The Starry Meadow: Author and Text

The name of the author Gerdt von Bassewitz-Hohenluckow is known to only a few people today. However, one or the other may have encountered the surname in connection with the history of Germany, as Bassewitz comes from a noble family that was politically and culturally important in many respects and can be traced back to the Middle Ages.[16]

Biographical information about Gerdt von Bassewitz can mainly be gleaned from his self-report, which he wrote to the pedagogue Franz Brümmer, who compiled biographies of writers for encyclopedias (cf. Bassewitz 1917; see also Stupperich 2017). Compared with other sources, however, this self-report gives the impression of being slightly embellished. In any case, in accordance to his status, Bassewitz initially pursued a career as an officer; however, he was always drawn to the theater and – as he writes to Brümmer – to astronomy. This reveals an enthusiasm for the stars highlighted in *Peterchens Mondfahrt* (cf. ibid., 5). Bassewitz first worked as a theatre critic and was later employed as a "director and assistant artistic director" (ibid., 7) at the Kölner Schauspielhaus. He published a few plays and a volume comprised of poetry, but remained unsuccessful with them. He stayed in different sanatoriums and health resorts various times for medical reasons, which shows that his physical and/or psychological condition had been unstable. On February 6, 1923, Gerdt von Bassewitz committed suicide after reading from *Peterchens Mondfahrt* at an event in the Villa Siemens at the Wannsee; within sight of the place where the much-admired Heinrich von Kleist also took his own life in 1777. However, we can only speculate about the reasons for Bassewitz' suicide. Thus, Amrei Stupperich states in her encyclopedia entry:

---

[15] Today the term *rhizome* is mostly used to describe hypertextuality. Even though I will work with this term in the following, I would like to note that I am critical of it in two respects: On the one hand, from my point of view it is always problematic to use terms from biology to describe cultural aspects. Secondly, the term has meanwhile moved far away from its original use by Deleuze and Guattari, who used it primarily in the context of cognitive processes and knowledge systems.

[16] Parallels can be drawn here with the maybug family of the Sumsemanns (see also Ewers 2006).

Whether this was a consequence of the lack of recognition of his works in Germany during the Weimar period and thus of his continuing financial worries, which were certainly exacerbated during the inflation, or whether it was due to his unstable state of health, has not yet been researched. (Stupperich 2017, 8)

The particular staging of the author can contribute to the medial expansion of a work, especially if the writer advances to become a kind of cult figure, as happened, for example, with Edgar Allan Poe. Bassewitz was a man from a prominent family who took his own life quite spectacularly and who, according to contemporaries, must also have looked handsome, as evidenced by available testimonies by other authors such as by Franz Kafka and Otto Klemperer (cf. Kafka 1976, 407; Weissweiler 2010, 85 f.), thus there had been a certain potential for reception. However, the press reported virtually nothing about him, and even his suicide did not make it into the newspapers. A media spread about the reception of the author can therefore not be recorded.

Just as few media connections running through the main characters could be proven. There is neither a Sumsemann spin-off nor a maybug doll[17] in the period under investigation – and certainly no merchandise featuring the pale-drawn children Peterchen and Anneliese.[18] Although the maybug was also often regarded as a messenger of spring that was supposed to bring good luck, especially at Whitsun, and was already known to have a firm place in literature and culture – especially in children's literature – at that time, it was regarded as a pest and vermin on farms at the beginning of the twentieth century (cf. Zimmermann 2010, 157 ff.). Incidentally, Ewers recognizes in Mr. Sumsemann a parody of German nobility, which clearly lost popularity in the period after the publication of the fairy tale picture book, and in this course, reference can also be made to the Maikäferbund of 1848. The nobility of Mr. Sumsemann and Mr. Bassewitz may thus have stood in the way of their popularity. Overall, the historical situation can be held (partly) responsible for the lack of a "character-driven media environment" (Steinberg 2012, 19).

There is therefore neither an author-centered unifying feature as with Poe nor a character-centered one such as with Spongebob Squarepants (cf. Steinberg 2012; Bertetti 2014), nor a combination of both as with J. K. Rowling and *Harry Potter*. Rather, the story, which is popular in itself, or some of its narremes, have been adapted several times in different forms and variants. One of the reasons for their popularity seems to have been their connectivity to the pre-Christmas season and

---

[17] Not even the name Sumsemann is retained in all the individual texts.

[18] Peterchen and Anneliese are child characters shackled by gender stereotypes. The portrayal of their characters thus remains entrenched in clichés. As Peterchen sums up quite aptly:
„Anneliese träumt immer von Schafen,
Und ich viel lieber von Pferden und Grafen
Und von Prinzen und Soldaten
Und von Bonbons und Kuchen und Braten
Und von …"
(Bassewitz 1912, 9)
Which I think also clarifies why it is called *Peterchens Mondfahrt* and not *Peters and Annelieses Mondfahrt* or *Mr. Sumsemanns Mondfahrt*: Peter is dreaming here.

their inherent references to other forms of art (see below). In any case, the term transfictionality, which according to Marie-Laure Ryan appropriately describes "the 'migration' of fictional quantities through different texts" (Ryan 2013a, 92), is most applicable here (cf. also Ryan 2013b; Saint-Gelais 2005, 613).

The Milky Way: Visual Design

It can be assumed that the illustrator and stage designer Hans Baluschek was altogether more significant for the popularity and continuing reception of *Peterchens Mondfahrt* than the author, as illustrated, among other things, by the frequent use of the term *picture book* for the 1916 book version. Baluschek maintained close ties to the art and literary scene and was known for his socially critical urban art. He not only produced the illustrations for the book, but also the sets for the stage play performed at the Deutsches Schauspielhaus, as Lothar Schirmer (2000) has determined.[19] Some of the costume and stage designs are preserved in the Stadtmuseum Berlin and, when compared with the later book illustrations, make it clear that they were not created directly together, although some of the characters in the two versions are similar. The similarity of the Eismaxe depictions (stage design and book) is particularly remarkable. The clothing is almost identical and the milk bottle is also present in both versions. In the book, however, the polar bear has been added, while the Eismaxe on the stage design still holds a bell in his hand (Figs. 1 and 2).

Contemporary reviews praised the performance significantly, but were particularly taken away by Baluschek's set (Fig. 3a). The *Berliner Tageblatt,* for example, reported on a "refined[n] art of decoration" behind which "Gerdt von Bassewitz's undemanding but graceful poetry almost receded a little." (quoted after Schirmer 2000, 52) The *Tägliche Rundschau* also praised "Baluschek's colourful and cosy stage designs"; Bassewitz, on the other hand, is named solely as a "young poet" (in 1913 he was already 35 years old), the text cautiously described as "folksy" (Aus dem Kunstleben 1914).

Summarising what has been pointed out above, Baluschek did not only contribute to the success story of *Peterchens Mondfahrt* with the illustrations for the prose version, but was involved much earlier (cf. Schirmer 2000, 52), although it remains unclear how early he was actually involved. In any case, it is striking that Baluschek adopted the motif of the shadowy woodcutter in the moon from the cover of the first edition at Rowohlt for his cover illustration of the fairy tale picture book (Fig. 3b), which could be an indication that he was actually involved even before the Berlin performance.[20] The illustration is cleverly put together showing – depending on the angle of view – the face of the moon or the woodcutter that was banished there.[21]

---

[19] Baluschek also made the costumes for the stage version of Bassewitz's *Pips der Pilz* (1916).

[20] The later book illustrations are clearly different from the stage designs and therefore were not created together.

[21] In any case, the illustrator of the early cover design is not listed.

Fig. 1 Hans Baluschek: *Peterchens Mondfahrt*, 13.12.1913. Watercolour, opaque white, pencil; 65.50 cm × 69.00 cm. Inv. no.: TA 99/2054.3 Hz (© Stiftung Stadtmuseum Berlin. Reproduction: Oliver Ziebe, Berlin)

Like the narrative, the picture thus alludes to traditional fairy tales in which a wood thief is banished to the moon as punishment and thus becomes the man in the moon (cf. Uther 2000, 77; Goldberg 1999).[22]

In contrast to the text, which was often reviewed somewhat disparagingly, the critics again found only praise for Baluschek's pictures in the prose version. The illustrations were even exhibited in their original form in 1924 at the Große Berliner Kunstaustellung, which Baluschek directed from 1929 to 1933. This is all the more

---

[22] A corresponding fairy tale with the title *Das Märchen vom Mann im Monde* can be found in Ludwig Bechstein's *Deutsches Märchenbuch*. Johann Peter Hebel's *Der Mann im Mond* can also be cited here.

Die Ankunft der Kinder im Schloß der Nachtfee

Fig. 2 Illustration from: Bassewitz, Gerdt von/Baluschek, Hans: *Peterchens Mondfahrt – Ein Märchen*. Berlin-Grunewald: Hermann Klemm ³[1917], 79 (Kinder- und Jugendbuchabteilung der Staatsbibliothek zu Berlin, BIV, BIV 2b, 875 <3>)

astonishing since there were eight years between the first publication and the exhibition, which indicates that these pictures were received as artistically outstanding.[23]

Although exhibitions play a major role in the dissemination and reception of media or individual *Stoffe*, which is evident, for example, in view of the *Harry Potter exhibition*, they have so far been neglected in the research literature on media

---

[23] The publishing house Hermann Klemm had its own station at the exhibition in the section *Das illustrierte Buch* (the illustrated book), where, in addition to Baluschek's pictures, illustrations by Otto Engel for *Grüner Heinrich*, Walter Klemm for *Don Quixot* and *Ekkehard*, and others were on display (Grosse Berliner Ausstellung 1924, 86). Baluschek was also in the room *Filmkunst. Entwürfe und Modelle* and with his picture *Großstadt* in the section *Verein Berliner Künstler*. The film is likely to be the Zille film *Mutter Krausens Fahrt ins Glück* (1929), which was under the protectorate of Käthe Kollwitz and Hans Baluschek (cf. Gandert 1993). Baluschek was a co-founder of the Bund für proletarische Literatur (League for Proletarian Literature) and on the film review committee.

Fig. 3 (**a**) Cover of the "Märchenspiel" version of 1912 and (**b**) Fairy tale picture book version [c. 1917]

networks and transmediality.[24] Similar to games, exhibitions encourage visitors to engage with art and, especially today, to actively participate and try things out, thus expanding the narrative cosmos.

After Hans Baluschek, various artists tried to visually translate *Peterchens Mondfahrt*, many of them taking their cue from the pictures of the well-known painter. In this respect, theatre posters are particularly relevant in the period before 1945 in Germany. They were often produced by artists such as Ingrid Wullenweber (1937)[25] and Remigius Geyling (1926).[26, 27] In addition, some translations are truly revealing, as they were always accompanied by additional illustrations. The important traditional Stockholm publisher Bonniers published the book in 1930 with illustrations by John Jon-And (Fig. 4) and later again in Swedish in 1955 in a translation by Ellinor von Goette and illustrations by Torsten Århem.

---

[24] This is especially true for children's and youth literature research, while museum didactics publications are available (see, for example: Mateos-Rusillo/Gifreu-Castells 2018).

[25] http://www.bildindex.de/document/obj04040932?part=0&medium=kg3219023, Stöges (bunte Litographie, Süterlin, 1924. http://www.bildindex.de/document/obj14031054?part=0&medium=kb4357_050) (12.03.2019).

[26] Litographie, http://www.bildindex.de/document/obj16304377?part=0&medium=on2560097 (12.03.2019).

[27] http://www.bildindex.de/document/obj16304377?part=0&medium=on2560097 (12.03.2019).

Fig. 4 Cover by John Jon-And: *Lille Petters resa till Månen* (von Bassewitz © Bonniers: Stockholm, 1930)

Interestingly, the illustrator John Jon-And, who was influenced by Cubism and Kandinsky in particular, was also a scenographer at the Kungliga Operan (Royal Opera) where the play was performed in 1934. In 1956 there was also a notably unusual Icelandic edition with illustrations by Freysteinn Gunnarsson, featuring photographs of a performance.[28] In addition, in 1930–1933 a group of artists led by Madge Atkinson performed *Peterchens Mondfahrt* at the Prince's Theatre and Milton Hall in Deansgate (both in Manchester). Through the material kept within the Natural Movement Archive at the National Resource Centre for Dance Archive at the University of Surrey, it can be understood that the play *Peter and Anneli's Journey to the Moon* is loosely based on the book published by Klemm and

---

[28] In addition to the Swedish editions, two English (2007, 2008) and one each of Chinese (2016), Korean (2001), Dutch (2004), and Georgian (2014) editions could be identified after 1945, although it is unclear why the book was suddenly translated multiple times and into very different languages in the twenty-first century.

illustrated by Baluschek. According to the programme, it was "freely adapted" by Madge Atkinson from the "German by Gert [sic!] von Bassewitz", although other sources were also used (NM/E/4/4). However, it is rather questionable whether the historical audience could make references to the text by Bassewitz, since a book in English was only published in 2007. The *Stoff* of *Peterchens Mondfahrt* can therefore not be assumed to have been known.

The group around the choreographer Atkinson created special costumes for this production, which were to form a symbiosis with the dance art. The artists were looking for new ways to express themselves and wanted to create art that was close to nature in the sense of the Natural Movement. In order to achieve this they also took up ideas from the Arts and Crafts movement, i.e. they endeavoured to bring crafts and art into harmony. This resulted in works that combined choreography, natural philosophy, pottery, and fashion. The dancing was done in nature and in clothing that was based on natural materials and patterns, through which the inner being was to be found in the dancing body (cf. Fensham 2015, 355). The corresponding music came from different artists, but not from Achtélik or Schmalstieg.[29] Without the title, however, the photos of Atkinson and her troupe's performance would not indicate that it was an adaptation/transformation of *Peterchens Mondfahrt*; it could just as easily be another fairy tale of the sun, moon, and stars. Also, in addition to Peter, Ann, and the so-named Mr. Beetle, there are numerous other characters such as butterflies. However, the programme booklet makes it clear that the structure is based on Bassewitz's text and that some of the stages (bedroom, starry meadow, castle of the night fairy, moon) have been adopted.

Additionally as already noted, *Peterchens Mondfahrt* was performed at the Royal Opera in Stockholm as a dance piece in 1934. Therefore before 1945, many of the performances were particularly movement-intensive, which is not only rooted in the tradition of the bourgeois Christmas fairy tale revue, but also corresponds with the fantastic travel motif. Different artists obviously enjoyed meeting the challenges posed by the text in terms of visual realisation and experimented with different styles and forms. The visual design of *Peterchens Mondfahrten* was therefore by no means uniform, but adapted to various trends and currents. It is also interesting that the Mondfahrten elements in Germany – with the exception of the Berlin exhibition – are all aimed at children and are perceived as being specific to children. However, this does not always seem to be the case with the foreign media elements, resulting in not only a spatial expansion, but also one of the target groups.

---

[29] Carroll, Mendelssohn, Grieg, Swinstead, Heller, Tyrer, and Howell. Manchester, December 3, 1932. http://www.dance-archives.ac.uk/media/1088 (10.03.2018) "Peter and Ann's Journey to the Moon" (1930), Natural Movement: NRCD. URL: [29.08.2017] http://www.dance-archives.ac.uk/media/1088 (12.03.2019).

The Castle of the Night Fairy: Sonority and Music

As already indicated in the previous remarks, the acoustic-musical components play an important role in *Peterchens Mondfahrt* and its transformations. Almost all later versions make use of the fact that songs are present in the text and music exists for the stage version. In addition, not only are dance aspects emphasized in performances abroad, but the first performance also involved ballet. There is a lot of singing in all the later films, and there are currently a conspicuously large number of audio media and media networks of *Peterchens Mondfahrt* on the market, some of which are produced in media networks with certain films or series or adapt the narrative text as an audio book or radio play.

The music for the premiere was written by Josef Achtélik, but the musical notes were considered lost until a few years ago. As MDR reports, the composer's grandson discovered them in the attic, and thus MDR children's choir was able to perform the piece appropriately for the 100th anniversary in 2012 (cf. Terhorst 2013, 77). However, as mentioned, until 1945 Clemens Schmalstich's music was central and was also used for radio plays and films after 1945.

In addition, the onomatopoeic language of the moon's inhabitants is implemented in all available variants of the *Stoff*, which virtually tempts an adaptation in an acoustic medium. Thus, the Donnermann (thunder man) always says "Potz Donner", the Regenfritz (rain man) constantly lets the onomatopoeic "Drüppelü – tüp – tüp", the Blitzhexe's (lightning witch) "Sirrr, sirrr" and the storm giant's "Hu – hu" flow into the speech. In between the water sprite blubbers: "Putsch – patsch – blubber – quax!" (Bassewitz 1912, 69) and the military Eismaxe speaks German with a Berlin dialect. The direct speech of the elemental spirits is also found in the prose version in verse form. This onomatopoeia makes the text particularly attractive for reading aloud, which is why it is hardly surprising that *Peterchens Mondfahrt* was adapted for radio very early on, namely in 1925, when radio was just beginning to establish itself as a medium of entertainment. The broadcasts aired in 1925 were mainly fairy tale plays, sometimes including only parts of the whole play. At Nordischer Rundfunk AG (Norag), for example, *Die Weihnachtswiese* (Christmas meadow) from *Peterchens Mondfahrt* was performed as part of a *Weihnachts-Märchenstunde* (Christmas fairy tale hour), which included music as well as poems by Theodor Storm and Richard Dehmel. In addition Schlesischer Rundfunk, Silesian radio, for example, broadcast a continuation series of *Peterchens Mondfahrt*. Considering how few radio stations existed at the time and, moreover, how few children's radio programs were broadcasting at that time (cf. Wicke 2016), the fact that there were no less than three radio adaptations of *Peterchens Mondfahrt* in 1925 is rather impressive.[30]

Consequently, it can be stated that musical and visual components are significant for the various realizations. In terms of text, music, performance and illustrations,

---

[30] Cf. the online database of the DFG project *Deutschsprachige Kinder- und Jugendliteratur im Medienverbund 1900–1945* (http://medienverbundportal.kjl.uni-bielefeld.de).

there are more dominant variants, but the design changes very often. Moreover, both the play and the storybook, which is sometimes called a prose version and sometimes a picture book, can be seen as a network of media, as can all the other variants presented. Each individual *Peterchens Mondfahrt* thus has a particularly great potential to stimulate further media (networks).

The Christmas Meadow: Consumer Orientation and Branding

Overall, *Peterchens Mondfahrt* has a high consumer orientation. The very first lines of the stage version describe an upper middle-class child's room equipped with luxury goods of the time:

> Peterchens und Annelieses Schlafzimmer. In der Ecke links ein großes Bett mit bunten Vorhängen. Vorn links ein Spielzeugschrank, eine Puppenstube und ein Schaukelpferd. In der Mitte des Zimmers ein breiter, niedriger Kindertisch. Rechts vorn eine Tür hinter geblümten Vorhängen. Neben der Tür ein Kleiderschränkchen, Badewanne, Waschtischchen mit zwei Schüsselchen und eine bunte Kommode mit Bilderbüchern darauf. Im Hintergrunde breites Fenster mit Vorhängen und Blumen. (Bassewitz 1912, 7)

The journey takes the children through landscapes marked by abundance, reminiscent of the land of milk and honey: already in the first stage version, the Christmas meadow can be found, where the longed-for toys grow in abundance. The story also ends with a Christmas feast at which the children receive rich gifts. In later versions, there is also an Easter nest and a trip with the Sandman to the Night Fairy, which leads past milk trees with Milky Way honey, sky goats grazing on the moon spinach, a reservoir with will-o'-the-wisp fish, sky cows and moon calves, and a shooting star cloud from which shooting star snowballs can be made.[31] This reinforces the paradise motif, the sensual and exuberant.

However, the texts do not advertise other products from a *Peterchens Mondfahrt* series and so the works do not entice readers to buy other products or consume other media. Nonetheless, the publication of *Peterchens Mondfahrt* as an illustrated fairy tale book or fairy tale picture book certainly had not only artistic but also economic reasons. The Große Berliner Kunstaustellung can also be seen as an advertisement in the broader sense, since the pictures advertised the book. Apart from that, there do not seem to have been any further economic links – even reviews of the plays do not refer to the book, for example. Marketing with the characters or the illustrations, as is often done with Elsa Beskow's pictures, for example, is virtually non-existent to this day – or it refers to the 1990 film.[32]

---

[31] In addition, the ride with the big bear is described in more detail.
[32] For example, there is a sleeping pillow for this purpose: https://www.amazon.de/Kleines-Schlafkissen-Lavendel-f%C3%BCr-Kinder/dp/B06XV1JCJX/ref=sr_1_50?ie=UTF8&qid=1503473637&sr=8-50&keywords=%22peterchens+moonride%22 (12.03.2019).

An episodic and thus expansive character is most likely to be inherent in the story itself, which is subdivided into various pictures. Consequently, the play can be performed in several sets, the story read out in sections one after the other; and this in turn makes, for example, radio play productions in continuation particularly easy. Neither Achtélik's nor Schmalstieg's music, neither Bassewitz's nor John Jon-And's pictures aim at a trashy-commercial, if you will, *mass-cultural* marketing. Rather, they suggest, as does the text, that their target audience consists of commoners and aristocrats; that it is affluent and educated. Thus *Peterchens Mondfahrt* is, so to speak, the popular counter-programme to the Groschenheft (penny dreadful), even if Löwenberg attests to the Christmas tale's close affinity to these magazines, which have a reputation for being *trash*. *Peterchens Mondfahrt* emphasizes its artistic character and thus refuses – at least before 1945 – to be cheaply reproducible, which critics such as Benjamin and Adorno deplored.

Juxtaposed, for example, the prose edition with John Jon-And's paintings and Baluschek's stage decorations does not at first glance reveal any obvious connection. Associations with other art objects, paintings, narratives, etc. are no less obvious than those with Bassewitz's *Peterchens Mondfahrten*, which raises the question of whether they have been received as interrelated at all. What, then, distinguishes *Peterchens Mondfahrten* from Mickey Mouse media elements, which – I would argue – were also recognizable as interconnected before 1945?

Unlike other fictional children's literature animals such as Mickey Mouse, Mr. Sumsemann has never become a cultural icon. Like Douglas B. Holt, many scholars who deal with advertising strategies and branding assume that the reduction to a specific symbol and the connection of the product with a person or character with a concrete set of values is significant for becoming and being perceived as a cultural icon (cf. Holt 2004, 1). Above all, "that icons come to represent a particular kind of story – an identity myth – that their consumers use to address identity desires and anxieties" (ibid., 2). Literature (in a broad sense) is obviously ideally suited to spread identity myths and value systems and to appeal to emotions. In *Peterchens Mondfahrt,* these aspects are even highlighted in a particularly striking way. What the *Peterchens Mondfahrt Stoff* lacks, however, are "material markers" (ibid., 3) such as a logo and a certain acoustic and/or visual design that guarantee recognizability. Unlike in the case of many non-literary products, there is a story here, but no brand (cf. ibid., 3; see also Radkte 2014 and Szabo 2009). In this respect, the media spread of *Peterchens Mondfahrt* over a long time and a large space is all the more noteworthy.

The Moon: Time and Space

Time and space are central quantities for various systems, including literatures. Taken together, a considerable number of *Peterchens Mondfahrten* are available today, but there is often a great deal of time between the various elements, and in some cases also a great deal of space by the standards of the time, for which there are several reasons that are not only related to the sometimes longer production times during writing. But these historically determined difficulties play a major role for the temporal gaps between the individual *Peterchens Mondfahrten*: First of all, the First World War, and with it the war service as well as the breakdown of Gerdt von Bassewitz, prevented a quickly following further product/medium. Between the publication of the prose version and the Große Berliner Kunstaustellung there were again eight years, which could possibly be connected with the death of von Bassewitz or also with the decline of the Kaiserreich – the von Bassewitz family is, after all, so-called Old Nobility. Radio adaptations soon followed, and in 1930 the Swedish edition. Continuity in this period of investigation was provided by the prose or picture book as well as the play, but the latter is a very ephemeral variant, bound to place and time and no longer retrievable – after all, theatre performances were not recorded and certainly not put on the Internet. The same holds true for radio broadcasts. Thus it is difficult to imagine that more than two *Peterchens Mondfahrt* media elements were received by a significant number of people at the same time before 1945. At this point, the question arises as to whether this reception potential is sufficient to characterize *Peterchens Mondfahrten* as a media network.

As Holt points out, it is significant for the branding process that the story is received collectively: "what makes a brand powerful is the collective nature of these perceptions" (Holt 2004, 3). In other words, the experience of the product must be able to be shared and renewed. However, this requires it to be continuously available, which incidentally is not only important for cultural branding, which Holt sees as particularly successful, but is also true for other forms of branding. Continuous presence is thus fundamental to the fact that – depending on the branding model – a certain myth can be performed, a positive association or a deep emotional bond can be established, or simply mass attention can be generated for the product (cf. ibid., 14).

Back in the Nursery: Theoretical and Methodological Considerations or the Journey to the Media Network

As could be portrayed, there is no brand connection between the *Peterchens Mondfahrten* that existed before 1945 and thus no commercial media network. Although the author Bassewitz and the artist Baluschek are responsible for the first expansions, a brand identity is as lacking as a brand license, which leads to the existence of very different *Peterchens Mondfahrt* media variants. These however, are not necessarily immediately recognizable as such, but can instead be perceived as independent artistic products. Consequently, the question arises whether the "similarity relationship" (Meier 2020, 83) of the individual elements is strong enough as they do not come across as a series at all and not only the visual design, but also the title was partly changed (even the author's name was written differently). Moreover, there is sometimes such a long period of time between the individual elements that the target audience is unlikely to have received more than one medium: Anyone who saw the first performance as a six-year-old in 1912 might no longer be interested in the fairy-tale picture book in 1916 – that is, as a ten-year-old – and the likelihood that this person was waiting spellbound for the radio adaptation of this very *Stoff* at the age of nineteen is even smaller.

Thus, differences become obvious between *Peterchens Mondfahrten* and well-known major media networks/commercial supersystems produced by, for example, Marvel- or Disney (such as *Avengers, Star Wars*). Because these differences have glaring implications for reception, overall I think it makes sense to differentiate between licensed and non-licensed media networks, as well as direct and indirect media network relationships. This seems to be relevant beyond *Peterchens Mondfahrten* also with regard to imitations. It thus emerges that defining a media network through a copyright is the simplest and most pragmatic definition of the term. However, limiting the definition to the media elements linked by a copyright runs the risk of giving undue importance to the economic component and tending to relegate research to the economic domain. However, if the media elements are not connected by a copyright and it is also not clear to which *Mondfahrten* variant they refer, the question arises as to how a connection between the individual elements is generated. In this regard, it has been assessed that the various *Peterchens Mondfahrt* elements are primarily connected by individual and at the same time varying narremes. These connections are loose and unsystematic, and the individual elements cannot be hierarchized in the sense of a tree-order. Rather, it is initially obvious to describe the (dis)order as rhizomatic. This is also supported by the fact that individual *communication roots* can be cut and the system can nevertheless *continue to grow*. It seems to be advantageous for the continuity of *Peterchens Mondfahrt* in the period under investigation, which was marked by political, cultural and aesthetic upheavals, that artists of different social origins, aesthetic changes and political views were involved at the hinges of its realization. However, I would not go so far as to call the connections hierarchy-free. In the examined period, some variants are clearly more dominant and some artists' names much more present than others. In most of *Peterchens Mondfahrten* and the corresponding reviews, for example, the name Gerdt von Bassewitz appears, but other contributors – such as the make-up artists or the actors – remain unnamed. Moreover, in the historical situation, the general connectivity – and thus a general receptivity – of the individual elements does not seem to exist. According to Deleuze and Guattari, however, this "principle of connection and heterogeneity" constitutes a basic prerequisite of a rhizomatic model: "Any point of a rhizome can and must be connected to any other" (Deleuze/Guattari 1992, 11). From this point of view, a continuous and/or broad availability of the *Stoff* is required in order to be able to speak of a rhizomatic dissemination – and the *sixth leg*, so to speak, is also missing for the direct media network. The abundance of *Stoff* available from today's point of view quickly tempts one to subsequently assume close links as well as a broad system of reference. This however, could not be established in the historical situation because the individual elements were too far apart in time and place. This also makes the description of the *Stoff* as a media network questionable, because the term media network is used to characterize a system of several individual types of media, and it is aimed primarily at the reception of this system, whether in terms of consumption or didactics. However, a review of the *Stoff* on the various media transformations of *Peterchens Mondfahrt* has revealed that a coherent reception of several elements in the pre-1945 period is very unlikely. Although the various types of media can be subsequently taught within a media network, afterwards it is still hardly conceivable that they are or have been received together. The reason for this is not only the lack of a brand and thus the hope, linked from a marketing point of view, that after reading *Peterchens Mondfahrt* a child will insist on buying a suitable board game, or from a didactic point of view that a Christmas play will encourage the reading of the text. Above all factor of time, coupled with the factor of place. With regard to reception, the concept of *media network* would therefore have to be framed historically and spatially (retrospectively/prospectively).

Furthermore, the question arises as to which elements can still count as part of a media network. Where does the *Stoff* move so far away from preceding media and materialities that it should be excluded? Conversely, can a specific type of tea, for example, be part of a media network? Is it only if a corresponding text is printed on the package or can we assume that the tea *Peterchens Mondfahrt* of the company Tee-Maass is supposed to make the Christmas meadow a sensual experience from an olfactory and taste point of view?[33] If not, is this just a simple quotation used in a different context and therefore not worthy of further consideration? This example illustrates that from a methodological point of view it makes sense to ask oneself at the very beginning what is to be investigated and for what purpose. Otherwise, at best, phenomenologically oriented work alone will emerge and there is a stark risk of collecting diligently, however not having gained any insight at the end. Research on multimedia sensory experiences could possibly include the tea product, which at first seems rather far-fetched (cf. on this Slothower/Susina 2009). Systems are expandable and can be narrowed down. Therefore, a cannon is needed, so to speak, that shoots far enough and precisely enough at the same time. Consequently, it is important to define the framework of the field of investigation from the outset.

But how are elements as different in terms of media, design and content as the performance in Leipzig, the Icelandic narrative text and the radio broadcast in the Norag connected? It has been shown that the connections between the individual *Peterchens Mondfahrt* elements are no more concrete than the Milky Way is an actual path. We do not find solid lines of connection, but at best dashed lines. Nor are all of the elements presented here connected to each other underground or above ground as in a rhizome. Rather, to remain with nature's metaphors despite all skepticism about them, some seem to be fertilized by spores and thus resemble

---

[33] The website advertises the tea as follows: "BLACK TEA – PETERCHENS MONDFAHRT One of the most fantastic stories there is. Peterchens Mondfahrt fascinates and inspires everyone who picks up the book. This delicious black tea composition is dedicated to this beautiful story. A dreamlike blend with a cinnamon anise flavor." With this, the advertisement clearly points to a book version of *Peterchens Mondfahrt*. The black tea can also be associated with night, the spices with Christmas. Tee-Maas: Peterchens Mondfahrt: https://www.tee-maass.de/html/peterchensmondfahrt/item-1-21242.html (12.03.2019).

mushrooms. The individual texts are indeed descended from others, but it is not readily traceable from which. Moreover, only the outer bodies of fungi are usually noticed, which can form at different time intervals and in several places (e.g. witch rings), while the actual fungus spreads unnoticed underground. Here, then, there is no easily recognizable order, and there are no straight and precise lines leading from element A to element B (cf. Deleuze/Guattari 1992, 14). The elements recognizably refer to each other, but this eludes fleeting observation, which is crucial in terms of attention and thus the likelihood that a product will be purchased and received.

Furthermore, with reference to *Peterchens Mondfahrt*, it can be stated that there are recurring narremes across media and that the term transfictionality lends itself to describing the phenomena examined here. Moreover, the intermediality of the early media networks and the synaesthetic qualities of the text, its musical narrative forms and its figurative language mean that narremes can be well and easily transmedially disseminated and performed. Thus *Peterchens Mondfahrt* was comparatively quickly transposed into the new media of the first half of the twentieth century. In the various media networks, language, image and music enter into a symbiotic relationship, playing with different materials and forms of expression. It thus becomes clear that Bassewitz's text is designed to dissolve media boundaries. It is a sensual text in every respect, aiming at a multi-sensual reception and an intensive performance. The text mentions colours, forms, spaces, music, song, and dance, so that pompous realisations in pictures, dance, opera, ballet, and radio play are not surprising, but on the contrary are virtually demanded by the text. Moreover, what is particularly remarkable about *Peterchens Mondfahrt* is that the *Stoff* spread via various paths (roots and spores) and was thus able to survive political upheavals, trends and fashions as well as cultural and market-specific differences.

At the end of this lunar and media network journey, it can be stated that unfortunately due to the historically conditioned scarcity of material, many questions cannot be answered in a satisfactory manner. Thus, the path to the moon seems to be almost easier than the one to the media network, but perhaps it is also true here that many paths lead to the goal in the end.

References

Primary Literature

Bassewitz, Gerdt von/Baluschek, Hans (Ill.): Pips der Pilz. Ein Wald- und Weihnachtsmärchen. Berlin-Grunewald: Hans Klemm, 1920.
Bassewitz, Gerdt von/Baluschek, Hans: Peter and Anneli's Journey to The moon. A fairy tale. Übers. Marianne H. Luedeking. Great Barrington, MA: Bell Pond Books, 2007.
Bassewitz, Gerdt von/Baluschek, Hans: Peter, Anneliese and Mr Sumsemann Fly to The Moon. Übers. von Yvonne Stadler. West Hobart, Tas.: Y. Stadler, 2008.
Bassewitz, Gerdt von/Baluschek, Hans: Peterchens Mondfahrt und Prinzessin Huschewind. Berlin: Deutsche Buchgemeinschaft, 1932.

Bassewitz, Gerdt von: Lille Petters resa till Månen. Übers. Ellinor von Goette. Bearb. von Stig Kassman. Ill. John Jon-And. Stockholm: Bonniers, 1930.
Bassewitz, Gerdt von: Lille Petters resa till Månen. Übers. Ellinor von Goette. Bearb. von Stig Kassman. Umschlagillustration von Torsten Århem. Bonniers: Stockholm, 1955.
Bassewitz, Gerdt von/Baluschek, Hans: Peterchens Mondfahrt – Ein Märchen. Berlin-Grunewald: Hermann Klemm, [3][1917].
Bassewitz, Gerdt von: Ferþin til tunglsins. Übers. von Freysteinn Gunnarsson. Reykjavík: Ísafoldarprentsmiþja, 1954.
Kafka, Franz: Tagebücher 1910–1923. Hg. von Max Brod. Frankfurt a. M.: Fischer, 1976.
Uther, Hans-Jörg (Hg.): Die schönsten Märchen von Sonne, Mond und Sternen. München: Knaur, 2000.

Filmography

Le Voyage dans la Lune (dt. Die Reise zum Mond) (F 1902). Regie und Drehbuch: Géorge Méliès.
Peterchen's Mondfahrt (BRD 1959). Regie: Gerhard F. Hering, Drehbuch: Gerhard F. Hering und Hein Heckroth.
Peterchens Mondfahrt (TV-Serie): Regie und Drehbuch: Wolfgang Urchs. ZDF 25.12.1992–26.12.1992.
Peterchens Mondfahrt (D 1990). Regie und Drehbuch: Wolfgang Urchs.

Audiography

Bassewitz, Gerdt von: „Peterchens Mondfahrt". Kindermärchen, erzählt von Kitty Seiffert. Schlesische Funkstunde Breslau: 11.10.1925; 18.10.1925; 25.10.1925; Quelle: Der Deutsche Rundfunk 3 (1925) 41, 2644; Der Deutsche Rundfunk 3 (1925) 42, 2716; Der Deutsche Rundfunk 3 (1925) 43, 2788, Uhrzeit: 16:00–16:30.
Bassewitz, Gerdt von: Die Weihnachtswiese aus „Peterchens Mondfahrt". Weihnachts-Märchenstunde. Mitwirkende: Gertrud Stolzenbach und das Kammerorchester der Norag. Ernst Koedel. Norag-Orchester. Quelle: Die Norag (1925a) 51, 5, Uhrzeit: 16:15.
Bassewitz, Gerdt von: Peterchens Mondfahrt. Ein Märchenspiel in sieben Bildern. Spielleitung: Friedrich Reinicke Schlesische Funkstunde Breslau: 20.12.1925b; 25.12.1925; 31.12.1925; Quelle: Der Deutsche Rundfunk 3 (1925) 51, 3368; Der Deutsche Rundfunk 3 (1925) 51, 3388, Der Deutsche Rundfunk 3 (1925) 52, 464, Uhrzeit: 16:00.
Bassewitz, Gerdt von: Peterchens Mondfahrt. Ein Märchenspiel in 7 Bildern. Norag Hamburg für alle Noragsender: 26.12.1926. Musik von Clemens Schmalstich. Dirigent: Fritz Gartz. Regie: Hermann Beyer. Quelle: Die Norag (1926) 51, 11, Uhrzeit: 16:30.

Theatrography

Anna-Lisa i Lille Petters resa till månen (1934), http://www.dansportalen.se/111/-fler-artiklar/nyhetsarkiv/2010-09-17-ellen-rasch-jubilerar.html (03.02.2019).
Bassewitz, Gerdt von: Peterchens Mondfahrt. Ein Märchenspiel. Musik von Clemens Schmalstich. Leipzig: Rowohlt, 1912.

Bassewitz, Gerdt von: Peterchens Mondfahrt. Ein Märchenspiel. Musik von Clemens Schmalstich. Berlin: Drei Masken, 1916.
Peterchens Mondfahrt (Uraufführung). Regie: Paul Prina. Altes Theater (Leipzig). 07.12.1912.
Peterchens Mondfahrt (Erstaufführung). Regie: Friedrich Zelnitz. Theater an der Weidendammer Brücke. 13. Dezember 1913.

Other Media

Große Berliner Ausstellung: Katalog 1924, https://doi.org/10.11588/diglit.12825%230093 (03.02.2019).
Hof-/Staatstheater Stuttgart: Aufführungsakten 1922. Landesarchiv Baden-Württemberg, Abt. Staatsarchiv Ludwigsburg, E 18 VIII Hof-/Staatstheater, http://www.landesarchiv-bw.de/plink/?f=2-34750-1 (03.02.2019).
Kungliga Operan auf Facebook, https://www.facebook.com/KungligaOperan/videos/10153476927934818 (03.02.2019).
Kungliga Operan, http://www.dansportalen.se/111/-fler-artiklar/nyhetsarkiv/2010-09-17-ellen-rasch-jubilerar.html (03.02.2019).
Peterchens Mondfahrt – die aufregende Suche nach dem 6. Beinchen [Brettspiel]. Nürnberg: J. W. Spear Verlag 1967 (03.02.2019).
Peterchens Mondfahrt Pestalozzi Legespiel Nr. 6895. Fürth/Bay: Pestalozzi [o. J.], https://www.booklooker.de/Spiele/Peterchens-Mondfahrt-Pestalozzi-Legespiel-Nr-6895/id/A0015VTc41ZZZ (03.02.2019).
Peterchens Mondfahrt, Veranstaltungsplakat, Hg.: Operettentheater Leipzig. Leipzig, 11.1946, Deutsches Historisches Museum, Berlin, DG 90/4395.
Peterchens Mondfahrt: Inszenierung: Wilhelm Speidel, Bühnenbild: Eduard Schmidt, Kostüme: Ernst Pils. Laufzeit: 4. Dezember 1938. Stuttgart, Landesarchiv Baden-Württemberg, Abt. Staatsarchiv Ludwigsburg, [E 18 III Bü 318], https://www.deutsche-digitale-bibliothek.de/item/D4Z375KTPOQ7723SDXD7ANB2USPQKOUV?isThumbnailFiltered=true&query=peterchens+mondfahrt&rows=20&offset=120&_=1503063279601&reqType=ajax&viewType=list&firstHit=5YDT4MIYKOFWTN74UQPYCX3XZUZWLEWT&lastHit=lasthit&hitNumber=132 (03.02.2019).
Schlafkissen „Peterchens Mondfahrt", Amazon, https://www.amazon.de/Kleines-Schlafkissen-Lavendel-f%C3%BCr-Kinder/dp/B06XV1JCJX/ref=sr_1_50?ie=UTF8&qid=1503473637&sr=8-50&keywords=%22peterchens+mondfahrt%22 (03.02.2019).
Tee-Maas: Peterchens Mondfahrt, https://www.tee-maass.de/html/peterchens-mondfahrt/item-1-21242.html (03.02.2019).
Theaterzettel, Landesarchiv Thüringen – Hauptstaatsarchiv Weimar » Generalintendanz des Deutschen Nationaltheaters und der Staatskapelle Weimar, Signatur: 1913, Blatt:170, Verfilmungsnummer: 035696 und 035697.

Secondary Literature Before 1945

Aus dem Kunstleben. In: Tägliche Rundschau vom 03.12 1914, 4.
Bassewitz, Gerdt von an Franz Brümmer (Autobiographische Angaben) vom 10.03.1917. In: Nachlass Franz Brümmer. Staatliche Bibliothek zu Berlin; http://bruemmer.staatsbibliothek-berlin.de/nlbruemmer/autorenregister/transkription.php?id=11 (13.03.2019).

Herzberg, Georg: Berliner Bühnen: Kinderjubel im Admiralspalast. In: Film-Kurier 19 (1937) 283 vom 06.12, 4.
Löwenberg, Jacob: Das Elend unserer Weihnachtsmärchen. In: Neue Bahnen 24 (1913) 4, 145–157.

Secondary Literature After 1945

Bauer, Karl W.: Emanzipatorisches Kindertheater. Entstehungszusammenhänge, Zielsetzungen, dramaturgische Modelle. München 1980.
Bertetti, Paolo: Toward a typology of transmedia characters. (Transmedia Critical). In: International journal of communication 8 (2014), 2344–2361.
Bröhan, Margit: Hans Baluschek. 1870–1935; Maler, Zeichner, Illustrator. ³Berlin 2012.
Deleuze, Gilles/Guattari, Félix: Tausend Plateaus: Kapitalismus und Schizophrenie. Berlin 1992.
DBE (Deutsche Bibliographische Enzyklopädie). Hg. von Rudolf Vieraus, 2. Ausg., Bd. 9: Schlumberger-Thiersch. München 2008, 4.
Ewers, Hans-Heino: „Peterchens Mondfahrt" und der Feldzug gegen das Weihnachtsmärchen. Versuch einer Neubewertung des Kinderschauspiels von Gerdt von Bassewitz". In: Reiß, Gunter (Hg.): Kindertheater und populäre bürgerliche Musikkultur um 1900. Frankfurt a. M. 2008 (Kinder-und Jugendkultur, -literatur und -medien. Theorie – Geschichte – Didaktik; 55), 55–65.
Ewers, Hans-Heino: Zu unrecht verteufelt: „Peterchens Mondfahrt". Eine moderne Märchenrevue für Kinder. In: Franz, Kurt/Payrhuber, Franz-Josef (Hg.): Peterchen, Kai und andere Helden. Klassiker der Kinder- und Jugendliteratur. Baltmannsweiler 2006 (Schriftenreihe der Akademie für deutsche Kinder- und Jugendliteratur; 34), 74–78.
Fensham, Rachel: Designing for Movement: Dance Costumes, Art Schools and Natural Movement in the Early Twentieth Century. In: Journal of Design History 28 (2015) 4 vom 01.11., 348–367, https://doi.org/10.1093/jdh/epv017 (13.03.2019).
Frederking, Volker/Josting, Petra: Der Vielfalt eine Chance…: Medienintegration und Medienverbund im Deutschunterricht. In: Dies. (Hg.): Medienintegration und Medienverbund im Deutschunterricht. Baltmannsweiler 2005 (Diskussionsforum Deutsch; 18), 1–18.
Gandert, Gero (Hg.): Der Film der Weimarer Republik 1929. Ein Handbuch der deutschen Kritik. Im Auftrag der deutschen Kinemathek. Berlin [u. a.] 1993, 469–477.
Gnoth, Kirsten: Peterchens Mondfahrt, http://www.kinderundjugendmedien.de/index.php/filmkritiken/145-von-kirsten-gnoth (01.03.2019).
Goldberg, Christine: Art. Mann in Mond. In: Enzyklopädie des Märchens. Handwörterbuch zur historischen und vergleichenden Erzählforschung, Bd. 9, Berlin [u. a.] 1999, 183–187.
Hengst, Heinz: Der Medienverbund in der Kinderkultur. In: Hiegemann, Susanne (Hg.): Handbuch der Medienpädagogik. Theorieansätze, Traditionen, Praxisfelder, Forschungsperspektiven. Opladen 1994, 239–254.
Holt, Douglas B.: How Brands Become Icons. The Principles of Cultural Branding. Boston, Mass. 2004.
Jahnke, Manfred: Von der Komödie für Kinder zum Weihnachtsmärchen, Untersuchungen zu den dramatischen Modellen der Kindervorstellungen in Deutschland bis 1917. Meisenheim/Glan 1977.
Josting, Petra/Maiwald, Klaus: Einführung: Kinder- und Jugendliteratur im Medienverbund. In: Dies. (Hg.): Kinder- und Jugendliteratur im Medienverbund. Grundlagen, Beispiele und Ansätze für den Deutschunterricht. München 2007 (kjl&m7.extra), 7–9.
Josting, Petra: Medienkonvergenz im aktuellen Handlungssystem der Kinder- und Jugendliteratur. In: Weinkauff, Gina/Dettmar, Ute/Möbius, Thomas/Tomkowiak, Ingrid (Hg.): Kinder- und Jugendliteratur in Medienkontexten. Adaption – Hybridisierung – Intermedialität – Konvergenz. Frankfurt a. M. 2013 (Kinder- und Jugendkultur, -literatur und -medien. Theorie – Geschichte – Didaktik; 89), 233–252.

Kaiser, Ulrich: MDR Klassik über Josef Achtélik/Gerdt von Bassewitz Peterchens Mondfahrt (2014), http://www.rundfunkschaetze.de/mdr-klassik/08-peterchens-mondfahrt/#Dornr%C3%B6schen (03.02.2019).

Klee, Ernst: Das Kulturlexikon zum Dritten Reich. Wer war was vor und nach 1945. Frankfurt a. M. 2007, 527.

Kruse, Iris: Brauchen wir eine Medienverbunddidaktik? Zur Funktion kinderliterarischer Medienverbünde im Literaturunterricht der Primar- und frühen Sekundarstufe. In: Leseräume 1 (2014), http://leseräume.de/wp-content/uploads/2015/10/lr-2014-1-kruse.pdf (04.12.2019).

Kümmerling-Meibauer, Bettina: Überschreitung von Mediengrenzen: theoretische und historische Aspekte des Medienverbunds. In: Josting, Petra/Maiwald, Klaus (Hg.): Kinder- und Jugendliteratur im Medienverbund. Grundlagen, Beispiele und Ansätze für den Deutschunterricht. München 2007 (kjl&m7.extra), 11–20.

Kurwinkel, Tobias: Zur Theorie von Medien- und Produktverbänden und ihren Sammlungen am Beispiel von Bibi und Tina. In: kjl&m 69 (2017) 2, 14–21.

Maiwald, Klaus: Literatur im Medienverbund unterrichten. In: Rösch, Heidi (Hg.): Literarische Bildung im kompetenzorientierten Deutschunterricht. Freiburg/Br. 2010, 135–156.

Maiwald, Klaus: Ansätze zum Umgang mit dem Medienverbund im (Deutsch-)Unterricht. In: Josting, Petra/Maiwald, Klaus (Hg.): Kinder- und Jugendliteratur im Medienverbund. Grundlagen, Beispiele und Ansätze für den Deutschunterricht. München 2007 (kjl&m extra; 7), 35–48.

Mateos-Rusillo, Santos M./Gifreu-Castells, Arnau: Transmedia Storytelling and Its Natural Application in Museums. The Case of the Bosch Project at the Museo Nacional del Prado. In: Curator. The Museum Journal 61 (April 2018) 2, 301–313.

Meier, Jan-Niklas: Im narrativen Verbund. Transmediale Perspektiven auf Medienverbünde. In: kjl&m 72 (2020) 1, 76–86.

Petrowa, Lydia: „Wer hat „Peterchens Mondfahrt"? In: Aufbau 12 (1946) 30 vom 26.07, 14.

Radtke, Bernd: Markenidentitätsmodelle Analyse und Bewertung von Ansätzen zur Erfassung der Markenidentität. Wiesbaden 2014.

Rajewski, Irina O.: Intermedialität. Stuttgart 2001.

Renner, Karl. N. (Hg.): Medien – Erzählen – Gesellschaft. Transmediales Erzählen im Zeitalter der Medienkonvergenz. Berlin 2013.

Ryan, Marie-Laure: Transmediales Storytelling und Transfiktionalität. In: Medien – Erzählen – Gesellschaft. Transmediales Erzählen im Zeitalter der Medienkonvergenz. Berlin 2013a (Media Convergence/Medienkonvergenz; 2), 88–117.

Ryan, Marie-Laure: Transmedial Storytelling and Transfictionality. In: Poetics Today 34 (2013b) 3, 361–388.

Saint-Gelais, Richard: Transfictionality. In: Herman, David/Jahn, Manfred/Ryan, Marie-Laure (Hg.): Routledge Encyclopedia of Narrative Theory. New York 2005, 612–613.

Schedler, Melchior: Kindertheater. Geschichte, Modelle, Projekte. Frankfurt a. M. 1972.

Schirmer, Lothar: Hans Baluschek und „Peterchens Mondfahrt". Auf den Spuren der ersten Berliner Aufführung des Märchenspiels. Museums-Journal. Berlin 2000.

Schmidt, Laura: Weihnachtliches Theater. Zur Entstehung und Geschichte einer bürgerlichen Fest- und Theaterkultur. Bielefeld 2017.

Scolari, Carlos Alberto: Transmedia Storytelling: Implicit Consumers, Narrative Worlds, and Branding in Contemporary Media Production. In: International Journal of Communication 3 (2009), 586–606.

Slothower, Jodie/Susina, Jan: Delicious Supplements: Literary Cookbooks as Additives to Children's Texts. In: Keeling, Kara K./Pollard, Scott T. (Hg.): Critical Approaches to Food in Children's Literature. New York 2009, 21–40.

Spreckelsen, Tilmann: Fahren wir Schlitten auf der Milchstraße? 100 Jahre Peterchens Mondfahrt. FAZ 17. August 2017, http://www.faz.net/aktuell/feuilleton/buecher/autoren/100-jahre-peterchens-mondfahrt-von-bassewitz-14427872-S3.html (01.03.2019).

Steinberg, Marc: Anime's Media Mix. Franchising Toys and Characters in Japan. Minneapolis [u. a.] 2012.

Steinlein, Rüdiger: „eigentlich sind es nur Träume". Der Traum als Motiv und Narrativ in märchenhaft-phantastischer Kinderliteratur von E. T. A. Hoffmann bis Paul Maar. In: Zeitschrift für Germanistik. N. F. 18 (2008) 1, 72–86.

Stupperich, Amrei: Gerdt von Bassewitz. Fran, Kurt [u. a.] (Hg.): Kinder- und Jugendliteratur: Ein Lexikon, 64. Erg-Lfg. Meitingen 2017, 1–34.

Szabo, Sascha (Hg.): Brand Studies. Marken im Diskurs der Cultural Studies. Magdeburg 2009.

Taube, Gerd: Kinder- und Jugendtheater. In: Lange, Günter (Hg.): Taschenbuch der Kinder- und Jugendliteratur, Bd. 2, Baltmannsweiler 2000, 568–589.

Terhorst, Gaby: Anneliese, Peter, Gerdt, Oskar und die Mondfahrt. In: Königsteiner Burgfestbuch 2013, 700 Jahre Stadtrechte in Königstein Burgverein Königstein e. V., 77–78, http://www.burgverein-koenigstein.de/downloads/b10-2013.pdf (13.03.2019).

Weissweiler, Eva: Otto Klemperer – Ein deutsch-jüdisches Künstlerleben. Köln 2010.

Wicke, Andreas: Kinderhörspiel (2016), http://kinderundjugendmedien.de/index.php/begriffe-und-termini/1491-kinderhoerspiel (13.03.2019).

Zimmermann, Gisbert: Maikäfer in Deutschland. Geliebt und gehasst. Ein Beitrag zur Kulturgeschichte und Geschichte der Bekämpfung. In: Journal für Kulturpflanzen 62 (2010) 5, 157–172.

In Never-Never Land

How *Peter Pan* Made Book, Theatre, and Film History

Ulrike Preußer

Introduction

As well-known as the *literarischer Stoff* seems to be today – *Peter Pan* took a long time to gain a foothold in Germany. Until 1945, it was primarily the play translated into German, a film adaptation and the translation of a few chapters spun off from a novel that were published under the title *Peter Pan im Waldpark* (Barrie 1911) and found their way to the German public. A reason for this could be its extremely convoluted genesis, in which the medial transfer in the sense of "interliterary adaptations" (Schrackmann 2009, 30) is already inscribed and which will be traced in this article. In this regard, the following article aims not to adopt a biographically oriented perspective, but rather a text-oriented one, from which the creation and development of the literary figure Peter Pan as a "transworld identity" (Doležel 1998, 17) is repeatedly brought into view.

U. Preußer (✉)
Faculty of Linguistics and Literary Studies, German Studies, Bielefeld University, Bielefeld, Germany
e-mail: ulrike.preusser@uni-bielefeld.de

A Novel for Adults and a Children's Book Consisting of Some of Its Chapters: *The Little White Bird* (1902) – *Kleiner weißer Vogel* (2010) and *Peter Pan in Kensington Gardens* (1906) – *Peter Pan im Waldpark* (1911)

James M. Barrie had Peter Pan appear for the first time in a novel for adults – in *The Little White Bird* (1902). As *Kleiner weißer Vogel* (Barrie 2010), the novel was only made accessible to German-speaking readers over a hundred years later in a translation by Michael Klein and is now out of print, without a second edition having been published. In the novel, Peter Pan takes up only a small part of the narrated event, forming an episode that the first-person narrator Captain W. tells the little boy David, whom he wants to win over.

Captain W. is an observer, following the life of young Mary with fervor and at the same time geat ironic distance, who falls in love with an artist and has a child with him – little David – for whose company Captain W. henceforth always longs. They meet and eventually become friends, a friendship that is reflected in several small anecdotes in the novel. The unmistakable biographical imprint of the novel, which has striking parallels with Barrie's own acquaintance with the family of Baron Arthur Llewelyn Davies, who had many children himself, and – as is well known from the author – shows a great affinity for the young, their games and ways of thinking, will not be traced further here, as it has been sufficiently done elsewhere.[1]

Rather, Peter Pan's first appearance is to be brought into focus – here in the already mentioned translation by Michael Klein at the end of the thirteenth and at the beginning of the fourteenth chapter:

> Hier in der Nähe beginnt die Serpentine. Das ist ein hübscher See, und sein Grund besteht aus einem versunkenen Wald. Wenn du über den Rand schaust, siehst du all die Bäume verkehrt herum in die Tiefe wachsen, und man sagt, nachts seien darin auch ertrunkene Sterne zu sehen. Falls das so ist, sieht Peter Pan sie, wenn er mit seinem Drosselnest über den See segelt. Lediglich ein kleiner Teil der Serpentine liegt im Park, denn rasch verläuft sie unter einer Brücke hindurch in die Ferne, wo jene Insel liegt, auf der all die Vögel geboren werden, die mal kleine Jungs und Mädchen werden. Kein Mensch, abgesehen von Peter Pan (der ja nur zur Hälfte ein Mensch ist), gelangt zu dieser Insel, aber man darf auf ein Stück Papier schreiben, was man sich wünscht (Junge oder Mädchen, dunkel oder blond), es zu einem Schiffchen falten und es zu Wasser lassen, und nach Einbruch der Dunkelheit erreicht es Peter Pans Insel. [...]
>
> Wenn du deine Mutter fragst, ob sie als kleines Mädchen Peter Pan kannte, wird sie sagen: „Natürlich, Kind", und wenn du sie fragst, ob er damals auf einer Ziege geritten sei, antwortet sie: „Was für eine dumme Frage, selbstverständlich." Wenn du anschließend deine Großmutter fragst, ob sie als kleines Mädchen Peter Pan kannte, wird sie ebenfalls sagen: „Natürlich, Kind", wenn du sie jedoch fragst, ob er damals auf einer Ziege geritten sei, antwortet sie, von einer Ziege hätte sie nie etwas gehört. Mag sein, dass sie es vergessen hat, wie sie manchmal deinen Namen vergisst und dich Mildred nennt, wie deine Mutter heißt. Andererseits könnte sie schwer eine so bedeutsame Sache wie die Ziege vergessen.

---

[1] On biographical references, see, among others, Birkin 2003, 46–55; Grieser 1987, 54–57; Green 1954, 13–28.

Infolgedessen gab es keine Ziege, als deine Großmutter noch ein kleines Kind war. Das zeigt uns, dass es ziemlich töricht wäre, die Geschichte von Peter Pan mit der Ziege zu beginnen (wie es die meisten Leute tun), derart töricht, als zögen wir die Jacke vor dem Hemd an. Es zeigt uns auch, dass Peter Pan schon sehr alt ist, aber er hat stets dasselbe Alter, so dass das nicht im mindesten etwas ausmacht. Sein Alter ist unveränderlich eine Woche, und obwohl er bereits vor langer Zeit geboren wurde, hat er niemals einen Geburtstag erlebt, noch besteht die geringste Möglichkeit, dass er je einen erleben wird. Der Grund dafür ist, dass er vor dem Menschendasein flüchtete, als er sieben Tage alt war; er flüchtete durchs Fenster und flog zurück in den Kensington Park. (Barrie 2010, 99–102)

The characteristics that become apparent in this introduction of the literary figure are briefly summarised here. (1) *The speaking name*: Peter Pan's name attracts attention as an alliteration – and thus as an aspect of Verfremdung[2] – and can claim a high degree of memorability. The combination of a common, frequently used first name with the name of a god also represents an oxymoron. This contradiction already inherent in its name, its – one could call it – binary oppositional design, is also reflected in its essence, which will become significant in the course of the consideration of the various adaptations. The reference in the name to Pan, the god of the pastureland, who, in addition to his many other attributes (which will be listed at the appropriate place), entered ancient mythology as the protector (shepherd) of sheep and goats, and who, with his small horns and buck feet, shares striking external features with these animals (cf. Grant/Hazel 1995, 318), is made explicit by the mentioning of the goat on the surface of the text. Moreover, the direct reference to Peter Pan's half-humanity ("who is, after all, only half a man") also focuses on his supernatural, half-divine nature. (2) *Fairy-tale or fantastic*: after Peter Pan initially enters the plot directly, virtually like an old acquaintance, the focus on his story is made indirectly rather than directly, while in the process his existence is simultaneously authenticated and disavowed. The chapters that take Kensington Park as their subject are, like much of the novel, multi-authored and -addressed, for it is Captain W., established as a narrative figure, who addresses David (in the sense of a general narrative mediation concept). Additionally, a fictional author addresses a fictional reader, as is repeatedly clear from the isolated reading of the Peter Pan chapters in *Kleiner weißer Vogel*. By prompting the fictional reader (or to be precise David) to ask his mother or grandmother about Peter Pan, he becomes a character with tradition and history. However, the fact that Peter Pan has been known for generations leaves it unclear whether he has always been a fictional or a real (or real-fictional) figure in the cultural memory of the protagonists (or the readers?). Moreover, the fictional author's (or Captain W.'s) reasoning need not be believed, as he proves to be an unreliable narrator at many points in the text, and he admits to this when he states that the grandmother also could have forgotten the goat. While he ultimately explains the goat's presence or absence out of common sense or children's common sense, the varied transmission may also be due to the fact that the *Stoff* surrounding Peter Pan has always been a fairy tale whose survival is fed by different sources and

---

[2] Here and in the following, the terms *Verfremdung, Autofunktionalität* and the *Vorherschen der Konnotation* are used as well as semanalytic principles according to Link 2004.

thus by different hearsay. (3) *Origin and rejection of being human*: Peter Pan lives, as his first mention in the thirteenth chapter informs us, in Kensington Park on Serpentine Lake, which he can cross in a "thrush's nest" and with which he can visit the island of birds "who will one day become little boys and girls". Here it is already clear that little children, by their very nature, are not human beings but birds – a kinship that is deepened as the novel progresses. Peter Pan, according to his binary opposition, is not only human and divine, not only man and bird, but also young and old at the same time. He was "born long ago" but has "always the same age" of seven days, has "never known a birthday" and never will. The actual reason for his escape from "being a man", which is hinted at in the sequel, will also only be made explicit in the course of the further chapters. (4) *Mothers and their relationship with their children*: Interestingly, Captain W. (or rather the fictional author) exclusively recommends asking the female relatives about Peter Pan – the male ones find no mention. This already implicitly suggests (by omission) Peter Pan's relationship to girls and women – and to mothers in particular.

Peter Pan's story in the following chapters is told around the above four cornerstones: Because of its avian origin, the seven-day-old child's shoulders itch, it climbs onto the window ledge of its bedroom, and it flies back to Kensington Park. In doing so, it is firmly convinced that it is a bird, and only this conviction actually makes it fly:

> Es ist ein Segen, dass er es nicht begriff [dass er kein Vogel war; U. P.], denn sonst hätte er das Vertrauen in seine Fähigkeit zu fliegen verloren, und im selben Moment, in dem man daran zweifelt, fliegen zu können, hört man für alle Zeit auf, es zu können. Der Grund, warum Vögel fliegen können und wir nicht, ist schlicht der, dass sie völliges Vertrauen haben, und völliges Vertrauen verleiht Flügel. s. (Barrie 2010, 105 f.)

The narrator's mediation strategy is always oriented towards making Peter Pan – like everything supernatural – plausible: While a fairy-tale approach would presuppose that one is dealing with a self-contained secondary world in which nothing needs to be explained because such a world is subject to its own rules, Barrie has his narrator repeatedly make comparisons with the real-fictional, empirically comprehensible world that create a permeability between primary and secondary worlds.[3] The constant referencing of primary and secondary worlds thereby creates a resolution of the question of the fairy-tale-like or the fantastic in an allegorical-poetic view of everyday reality: perceiving with the senses of a child, everything is initially true that is conceivable in the sense of "wild thinking" (Lévi-Strauss) or also of "egocentricity" (Piaget) (Rank 2002, 102).[4]

---

[3] On the fantastic in *Peter Pan-Stoff* in general, see Schrackmann 2009, 12–20.

[4] Here, Bernhard Rank and his unifying view of the approaches of Gerhard Haas and Wolfgang Meißner is referenced: both based their definition of the fantastic in children's literature on an "extraliterary criterion". In Haas's case, this was Claude Lévi-Strauss's approach to mythical thinking, in Meißner's, Jean Piaget's specific view of the child's surrounding world (cf. Rank 2002, 102). Despite the resulting different definition of the fantastic, both approaches have in common that they assume a specifically childlike thinking as the driving force (and pattern) of the fantastic, which can be understood in Barrie's depiction of the Peter Pan figure.

After the elves in Kensington Park all flee from Peter Pan, he flies to Serpentine Island to Solomon Krächz, who reveals his true nature to him. As "ein Dazwischen-und-nichts-Richtiges-und-nichts-Ganzes" (Barrie 2010, 107) with the outward form of a man and the heart of a bird, Peter Pan can no longer fly after coming to this realisation, must come to terms with himself being a half-being, and settles on the thought of never being able to leave Serpentine Island. But since Solomon is willing to teach him everything birds know; he appropriates their carefree cheerfulness. The expression of his constant joy is singing – but since he has no voice like a bird, he makes himself a flute on which to express his lightheartedness. He does this with such fervour that all the animals on the island are virtually enchanted – similar to the way the god Pan knows how to enchant with his flute (cf. Grant/Hazel 1995, 318 f.).

Soon, however, Peter is struck by a great longing to play in Kensington Park. And indeed, with the help of a thrush's nest as a boat and his child's nightgown as a sail, he manages to leave the island. The two tools, which are an expression of his half-being between bird and man, also help him make friends with the fairies who rule Kensington Park at night – during closing hours. They are the female fairies who are full of pity for Peter and want to comfort him with their care as he is motherless despite his youth. As a result, Peter spends his days on the island and his nights in Kensington Park, as he is not allowed to be seen by humans as a half-being. Slowly, a new desire arises in Peter – he wants to visit his mother, whose unbreakable love he is always aware of. The elves help him make his wish a reality by flying him to his mother's bedroom window one night. Peter assumes that it is always open for him, as he is convinced that his mother misses him and is waiting for his return. This is indeed the case, but once at her house he leaves her asleep, unable to decide to stay with her for good. After returning to the park, he continues to put off the decision to live with his mother day after day, until one night he does feel ready. However, when he reaches her window, it is locked, "mit Eisengittern davor, und als er ins Innere spähte, sah er seine Mutter friedlich schlafen, und sie hatte ihren Arm um einen anderen kleinen Jungen gelegt." (Barrie 2010, 130).

Barrie lets readers through the agency of his narrator know, that Peter's experience holds a universal truth, namely that there is" keine zweite Chance [gibt], nicht für die meisten von uns. Wenn wir das Fenster erreichen, ist Schließzeit, und die eisernen Stäbe sind vor uns aufgestellt fürs Leben" (Barrie 2010, 130). For Peter, Barrie's or rather Captain W.'s protagonist, the certainty of his mother's unconditional love is lost through this experience. Worse, the mother betrays her son by turning to another child. It is Peter's evident loss that thus leaves a lasting mark on Peter's behavior. And this applies less to his further development in *Little White Bird* than to his reappearance in many subsequent adaptations (cf. Schrackmann 2009, 131–132).

In the seventeenth chapter, Peter Pan meets Maimie Mannering in Kensington Park, who in turn already knows the story of Peter Pan (cf. Barrie 2010, 133). Maimie has been forgotten in the park by her nanny and locked in and experiences an exciting night in the busy countryside until she has a conversation with Peter, from which his existence as "Dazwischen-und-nichts-Richtiges-und-nichts-Ganzes" (Barrie 2010, 147) clearly emerges in several aspects. He first uses this to explain his nakedness to Maimie, which seems strange and surprising to her. By introducing himself to her not as a boy but as the being that Solomon Krächz refers to him as, he first acknowledges his semi-beingness to her. It further becomes clear from the conversation that Peter possesses notions of human behavior, particularly human speech, and human play, that diverge greatly from the real-fictional world embodied by Maimie. Peter recognises toys for what they are, but he uses them in entirely different ways. Moreover, he does not know what to do with a handkerchief, and when Maimie finally wants to give him a kiss, he holds out his hand in anticipation of an object. In order not to hurt Peter, she hands him a thimble, which he immediately puts on – the later kisses exchanged between the two become thimbles as a result of this deliberate confusion. The de facto substitution and the reconstruction of the linguistic sign give the relationship between Peter and Maimie a special status. Among other things, they lead Peter to want to marry Maimie, even though it is not entirely clear to him exactly what that means. Maimie, however, cannot break away from her mother and therefore cannot accompany Peter to Serpentine Island – even after he enlightens her about the nature of traitorous mothers. And yet Maimie remains loyal to Peter, regularly giving him gifts, including a made-up goat that the fairies bring to life at night so Peter can ride it around the park. Maimie becomes a fascinating girl figure, replacing and exaggerating her mother, whom Peter always remembers. In her lies his fascination with the feminine; his encounter with her explains why only the female members of his family are asked about Peter Pan. Consequently, it is Maimie who shows Peter what the human world can be like, and at the same time becomes involved with him, and who also shows him the interest and care that he can no longer get from his lost (and treacherous) mother.

As early as 1906, after the play *Peter Pan* celebrated its great success in England (cf. Schrackmann 2009, 30), chapters 13 to 18 from *The Little White Bird* were published separately under the title *Peter Pan in Kensington Gardens* with only minor changes and accompanied by illustrations by Arthur Rackham. The edition was aimed – and this was new – decidedly at children. As early as 1911, the volume (in a free translation by Irmgard Funcke) was also published in Germany by Kiepenheuer Verlag. The edition, which was also aimed at children, contained not all of Rackham's illustrations, but 16 selected ones. It was not until 2011 that a new edition was published under the title *Peter Pan in Kensington Gardens* translated by Selma Urfer. In this edition there are 50 illustrations by Arthur Rackham (Barrie 2011).

These illustrations bring to mind what can be imaginatively visualised in the reader's mind when one reads Peter Pan's first introduction: He is, in outward appearance, a week-old infant, and Arthur Rackham depicts him in exactly the same way. This means that, when Peter is flying, he is depicted clad in a shirt – the shirt that will serve as his sail when he later crosses the Serpentine Lake – and, when he is in Kensington Garden, he is completely naked. This introduction and portrayal of Peter Pan changes radically with the stage play. But before moving on to it, a final brief mention must be made of another text which heavily influenced the further development of Peter Pan as a literary character.

It is entitled *The Boys Castaways of Black Lake Island* and was written by Barrie for children in 1901 while on holiday with the Llewellyn Davies family and printed in an edition of two copies (see Green 1954, 20–28). One copy was lost during a train journey in 1902, the other is held by the Beinecke Rare Books & Manuscript Library.[5] Although the text is designed without the literary character Peter Pan, and no elves appear in it, it feeds on motivic set pieces that become central in the later stage play: Pirates, Indians, desert islands, and ships and shipwrecks (cf. Green 1954, 20).

James M. Barrie's *Peter Pan*: The English and the German Stage Play – *Peter Pan, or the Boy Who Would Not Grow Up* (1904/1928) – *Peter Gerneklein (Der Knabe welcher nicht gross werden wollte)* (1904/1910) – *Peter Pan, oder Das Märchen vom Jungen, der nicht groß werden wollte* (1952)

The stage play *Peter Pan, or the Boy Who Would Not Grow Up* was first performed at the Duke of York's Theatre in London on December 27, 1904 (cf. Green 1954, 83), but was not published in written form for the first time until 1928 (cf. Schrackmann 2009, 31). While the translation of *The Little White Bird* into German took over a hundred years, the stage version of *Peter Pan* was translated into German much more quickly and – contrary to the widely varying information in German-speaking countries – premiered as early as December 23, 1905 (i.e. barely a year after the premiere in London) under the title *Peter Gerneklein (Der Knabe welcher nicht gross werden wollte)* at the Stadttheater Mainz.

As the playbill shows (Fig. 1), the translation by Berta Pogson was the basis of the performance. Under the deviating title *Peter Gerneklein's [sic] erster Christbaum. Weihnachtsmärchen mit Gesang und Tanz (Christmas Tale with Song and Dance)*, this translation was published by Felix Bloch around 1910, but no edition of this apparently first German-language translation is now available – the Berlin State Library reports the volume as lost during the war,[6] and the theatre publisher Felix Bloch Erben no longer has a version either. Even the change of title from *Peter Pan* to *Peter Gerneklein*, however, promises to provide a new insight into the reception of the text in the German-speaking world. After all, the speaking name

---

[5] Cf. https://beinecke.library.yale.edu/collections/highlights/jm-barries-boy-castaways (16.09.2019). The Beinecke Rare Books & Manuscript Library at Yale University's information for the story *The Boys Castaways of Black Lake Islands* thus differs from that given by Kümmerling-Meibauer (2004, 72) in *Klassiker der Kinder- und Jugendliteratur. Ein internationales Lexikon*.

[6] Cf. http://stabikat.de/DB=1/LNG=DU/CLK?IKT=12&TRM =443338787 (16.09.2019).

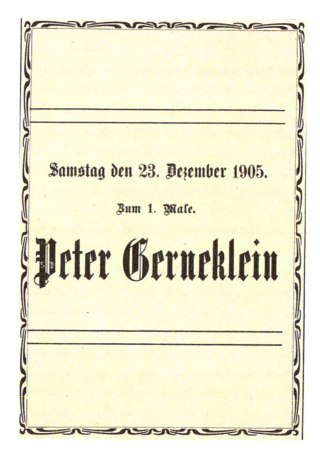

Fig. 1 Announcement of the stage play *Peter Gerneklein (Der Knabe welcher nicht gross werden wollte)*. Playbill Mog: 2°/43, 1905/1906, in the possession of the Libraries of the City of Mainz – Wissenschaftliche Stadtbibliothek

that Pogson uses emphasises Peter's flight from adulthood and at the same time obscures the view of the half-being of the character, which already plays such a central role in *The Little White Bird*. In terms of content, the stage play, which in England was in the tradition of the *Christmas pantomimes* and in German-speaking countries was and is often (even after 1945) performed as a Christmas fairy tale in large theatres, can be interpreted as oriented towards what Barrie considered to be children's dreams and fantasies, as Klaus Doderer concludes (cf. Doderer 1995, 139).

In German-speaking countries, the popularity of the stage play can be classified as rather moderate (cf. Günther 2006, 63). Currently, it appears from time to time on the repertoire of larger theatres (especially the flying numbers and the many, even silent roles require a well-equipped house and a large ensemble), but this circumstance does not lead to a prominent or even several different translations being readily available.[7]

The stage play, divided into five acts, is considered to be "trend-setting for the dramaturgy" der "Traum-Abenteuer-Spiele" (Doderer 1995, 139), as Manfred Jahnke (cf. Jahnke 1977, 169 f.) names plays for children of similar structure. The dream-adventure play replaces "a new dramatic type" (ibid., 169) the Christmas fairy tale on German stages. It differs from it essentially in that it consistently takes the child's perspective and is in this respect an expression of the reform pedagogical thinking that increasingly took hold at the beginning of the twentieth century (cf. ibid., 170).

The first act takes place in the house, mainly in the children's room, of the Darling family: the children Wendy, John and Michael are put to bed by their parents and the nanny Nana – a Newfoundland dog. While the parents attend a dinner party, Peter Pan secretly comes flying into the children's room to look for his shadow, which he had lost on a previous visit. As he bursts into tears, unable to reattach his shadow, Wendy wakes up. After the two have introduced themselves and Wendy learns in the ensuing conversation that Peter has no mother, she wants to hug him for comfort, but he refuses: "Du darfst mich nicht anfassen […]. Niemand darf mich anfassen" (Barrie 1969, 271). Peter himself does not know why he is *untouchable* – but this is a statement that, according to the stage direction, is actually to be implemented in the play and thus gives Peter an aura of the unapproachable, which is expressed, among other things, in his half-beingness.

Wendy knows a thing or two about shadows and is aware that Peter's will have to be sewn back on, since other methods of attachment won't work. By believing, both Peter and Wendy, in their capacity as children, not only in the autonomy and animacy of shadows (the adult Darlings are also convinced of this, at least in part), but in all the entities and connections that seem intuitively (rather than rationally-causally) true to them, they are able to suspend the rules of a rational world order. This allows "wild thinking" – in Haas's understanding of the Lévi-Straussian category (Haas 1978, 349–350) – to take its place. This is particularly evident when Peter Wendy explains why fairies exist and how they die:

> Das ist so, Wendy: Als das allererste Baby zum allerersten Male lachte, zersprang das Lachen in tausend Stücke. Sie hüpften auf und davon. Und seitdem gibt es Feen. Auch heute noch wird aus dem ersten Lachen jedes Babys eine Fee. So müßte es eigentlich für jeden Jungen und jedes Mädchen eine Fee geben. […] Aber nein. Die Kinder sind so gescheit! Sie glauben an keine Feen mehr, und jedesmal, wenn ein Kind sagt: „Ich glaube nicht an Feen", fällt irgendwo eine Fee tot um. (Barrie 1969, 272–273)

---

[7] When quoting from the German translation of the stage play in the following, the translation by Erich Kästner is followed, which was not written until 1952. Dieter Petzold refers to another translation from 1948, which originated from "K. Janecke and G. Blöcker", but is not accessible "as an unsellable stage manuscript" (Petzold 1994, 83). There is another German translation by Bernd Wilms. This edition is available as a school theatre text exclusively from the authors' publishing house in pdf format (cf. SCHULTHEATERTEXTE.DE, https://www.schultheatertexte.de/peter-pan-oder-der-junge-der-nicht-erwachsen-werden-wollte, 16.09.2019); it is abridged (especially in the secondary texts) and overall shows some deviations from the source text. Wilms takes a different approach to translation than Kästner, for example, he leaves the names in the original English and calls the land Nirgendwo (Never Land) "Niemalsland" (Barrie 2008, 10). A comparison of both translations is still pending and offers great potential for a deeper textual exegesis.

They are not yet aware that both have abilities that seem supernatural to the other, and at the beginning of the conversation this is only apparent from the incidental texts of the stage play. While Peter reacts incredulously to the fact that Wendy can produce light by flipping a switch – "Sie dreht am Schalter, und zu Peters Erstaunen wird es hell." (Barrie 1969, 271) – the zero-focalised narrative instance discernible from the corresponding stage direction indicates that Peter's ability to fly will, in turn, leave Wendy stunned: "Wahrscheinlich flöge er Wendy etwas vor, wenn er wüßte, daß Fliegen etwas Besonderes ist" (Barrie 1969, 271).[8]

The conversation between Wendy and Peter also reveals some background to Peter's circumstances and provides insights into his worldview: His motherlessness – self-chosen, as in *Kleiner weißer Vogel* – his association with fairies, and his untouchability have already been mentioned; moreover, it emerges from their dialogue that Peter lives with the "verlorene Jungens" (Barrie 1969, 274), who are among the children "die aus dem Kinderwagen fallen, weil das Kindermädchen nicht aufpaßt. Wenn sie nach einer Woche nicht abgeholt worden sind, werden sie ins Land Nirgendwo geschickt" (Barrie 1969, 274). Erich Kästner translates "Never Land" (Barrie 1928, 34), still referred to in this way by Barrie, into "das Land Nirgendwo" and in this transfer into German emphasises more strongly the place ("Land" and "-wo"), while the later more common translation "Nimmerland" is a composite that merges time and place. This later translation fits Peter's view of his self-chosen home much better: in response to Wendy's inquiry as to where he would live, he is able to describe how he would get there – linking space and time – but is unable to give a topologically correct location or even an address: "Second to the right and then straight on till morning" (Barrie 1928, 28) or "Die zweite rechts und dann geradeaus bis morgen" (Barrie 1969, 270).

Peter's companion, the fairy Tinker Bell, which Erich Kästner translates neologistically-reduplicatively as "Klingklang" and not yet, as in many later translations, as "Glöckchen", is almost inseparable from him, which is already marked by Mrs. Darling's first awareness:

> Der Junge war das *erste* Mal nicht allein. Mit ihm kam ein – ich weiß nicht, ob ich's dir beschreiben soll, – eine kleine leuchtende Kugel, nicht größer als meine Faust, aber sie bewegte sich im Zimmer wie ein Lebewesen. (Barrie 1969, 264)

It is Klingklang who brings jealousy into play and emotionally charges Peter and Wendy's first meeting in this regard. As in *Little White Bird,* Wendy in the stage play tries to kiss Peter, or rather to get Peter to kiss her, but she does not succeed:

---

[8] One striking feature of the stage play *Peter Pan* is the relationship of the main and secondary texts to each other and their special design, which will already have become clear to some extent from the passages quoted above. Klaus Doderer specifies this observation as follows: "What is striking about Barrie's play are the author's detailed stage directions, which go far beyond the usual scope of stage and costume introductions or factual notes on the performance and portrayal of the characters. The secondary text not only gives background information on the psychology and social situation of the characters, but serves primarily to colour the basic atmospheric mood in which the action is embedded." (Doderer 1995, 140).

PETER *einlenkend*: Was ist ein Fingerhut?
WENDY: Es geht so ... *Sie beugt sich vor, aber irgendetwas hindert ihre Gesichter daran, sich zu berühren.*
PETER *befriedigt*: Soll ich dir jetzt einen Fingerhut geben?
WENDY: Bitte sehr. *Ehe er ihr nahekommen kann, schreit sie auf.*
PETER: Was hast du?
WENDY: Mich hat wer an den Haaren gezogen!
PETER: Das muß Klingklang gewesen sein! So frech war sie noch nie! *Klingklang bimmelt. Sie steckt wieder in dem Krug.*
WENDY: Was hat sie gesagt?
PETER: Sie wird dich jedesmal, wenn ich dir einen Fingerhut geben will, an den Haaren ziehen.
WENDY: Warum denn?
PETER *ebenso ahnungslos*: Warum denn, Klingklang? *Sie klingelt, er übersetzt.* Sie sagt schon wieder „Dummkopf" zu mir. (Barrie 1969, 274 f.)

Wendy and Peter do not know why Klingklang pulls Wendy's hair, nor why she calls Peter a fool. The jealousy can be reconstructed from the situation insofar as Klingklang marks it as such with her behaviour. The children, or at least Peter, are unaware of this subliminally erotic aspect of their encounter. Wendy, however, who demands a kiss from Peter that is described as a thimble, reveals that she certainly has an interest in Peter that is oriented towards interpersonal proximity.

Peter and Wendy are fundamentally similar in terms of their animistic thinking, but differ in their oppositional experiences of the world, their constellation of characters resembles that of Peter and Maimie in *The Little White Bird* not only in terms of the moments and events adopted (such as the exchange of thimbles and kisses), but also structurally. The exchange of thimbles and kisses, but also structurally: although a different space of action is established in the stage play (including an interior instead of an exterior space), the equivalences and oppositions between the fantastic figure Peter and the girl he encounters, who is endowed with predominantly real-fictional qualities, remain the same.

Peter wants to hear stories with a tremendous urgency. This is why he regularly visits the Darlings as an undiscovered guest in the first place. These stories, in Peter's view, can only be told by females – either Wendy's mother or Wendy herself. For this reason, he wants to take her with him to the Land Nirgendwo. Peter doesn't care that Wendy wants to take her brothers with her – since she insists, he shows not only her, but Michael and John how to fly with the help of fairy dust and happy thoughts. Together they set off for the Land Nirgendwo, where Wendy is to become the mother of Peter and his lost boys.

While Peter in *Kleiner weißer Vogel* and *Peter Pan im Waldpark* is still portrayed as an infant and also lives such a secluded life that he never leaves his park, both of these characteristics have changed in the stage play. Peter Pan seeks out a house and kidnaps the children living in it – so he becomes active. Outwardly, he is only slightly smaller than twelve-year-old Wendy and is dressed in "Herbstblätter und Spinnweben" (Barrie 1969, 69). He is later said to be wearing a "Laubanzug" (ibid., 272). However, the character will only gain its more detailed appearance in the course of the numerous stage productions, which endows it with its high recognition value, and in the context of other media adaptations (cf. Klein 2010, 270) – essentially after 1945.

Finally, in the second act, the four arrive in the Land Nirgendwo, where Peter is already awaited by the six lost boys. While in the original English the lost boys are called "Toodles," "Slightley," "Curly," "Nibs," and "First Twin" and "Second Twin" (Barrie 1928, 47–48), Kästner renders them "Tütchen" (Toodles), "Bißchen" (Slightley), "Löckchen" (Curly), "Spitzchen" (Nibs) and "Zwilling I" and "Zwilling II" (Barrie 1969, 279–280). The six are in hiding when the pirate Captain Hook – rendered into German by Kästner with a name that speaks again as "Haken" (Barrie 1969, 281) – appears with his crew, always on the lookout for Peter to avenge the hand (complete with wristwatch) he cut off in battle, which a dangerous crocodile ate. The crocodile now constantly pursues Hook in order to eat him now whole and is always recognised by Hook through his ticking stomach contents. Hook and his crew take flight as soon as they become aware of the ticking crocodile. In their place, the beauty queen of the Indians, Tigerlilly, and her Rotzbubenstamm appear and shortly after depart. Meanwhile, Klingklang convinces the lost boys that Peter wishes them to shoot the approaching supposed white bird – it is Wendy – with a bow and arrow. Tütchen complies with the wish and Wendy falls to the ground. An acorn, given to her earlier by Peter in an exchange of thimbles and kisses, saves her life. Peter then banishes Klingklang for a week and asks the lost boys to build a house around the unconscious Wendy. When she awakens, she agrees to stay with them as their mother, with Peter taking on the father role.

Klingklang's scheming behaviour reinforces the aspect of jealousy from the first act. With Tigerlilly, another female character also appears who will vie for Peter's affection and whom everyone wants "zur Frau" (Barrie 1969, 285) – with the exception of Peter himself, to whom erotic feelings are completely strange. He longs – as do the adult pirates later in Act III – for a mother. In this desire, and in Wendy's willingness to act as one, even though she is "doch selber noch ein Kind ist" (Barrie 1969, 292), it is clear how "[t]he role of the lover and loving wife, the sexual partner, which is otherwise regarded at least as a natural intermediate stage between the role of girl and that of mother" (Petzold 1977, 18) is skipped in Barrie's play.

The third act takes place on "Nixensee" (Barrie 1969, 293) and essentially focuses on a skirmish between Captain Haken and his crew and Peter and the lost boys. After the pirates capture Tigerlilly and tie her to a rock "[on] which she is to drown as the tide rises" (Schrackmann 2009, 159), Peter frees her again by ordering the pirate crew to untie her, imitating Haken's voice. When the pirate captain figures out the plan, Peter further unsettles him from hiding by continuing to imitate Haken's voice until the latter no longer knows who he is. However, when he discovers Peter, a scuffle ensues, leaving Wendy and Peter on the rock where they are in danger of drowning. Wendy manages to save herself with the help of a paper kite, and Peter is able to escape in the nest of a large bird, reminiscent of his means of transportation in *The Little White Bird*.

Peter's adoption of Haken's identity by imitating his voice refers to the mirroring of both characters, which can also be seen in other passages of the text, as Schrackmann (2009, 50–52) already points out. Although both figures are binary oppositional (e.g. adult vs. child, tall vs. short, male vs. asexual), they also show clear equivalences, such as their not clearly positive or negative connotations. Moreover, they are mirrored in action when Peter climbs the rock at the same time as Haken – only coming from the opposite side: "*Haken klettert auf den Felsblock, um zu verschnaufen. Im gleichen Augenblick kommt, neben Wendy, Peter von der anderen Seite. […] Jetzt stehen sie einander Auge in Auge gegenüber.*" (Barrie 1969, 299) At the end of the stage play, after Haken dies by jumping into the crocodile's throat, Peter even appropriates his function as a pirate captain, his insignia and his attitude: "*Der Vorhang fällt und geht wieder auf, um Peter als Sieger zu zeigen. Er steht auf dem Achterdeck mit Hakens Hut und Doppel-Zigarre und – mit einer kleinen eisernen Klaue.*" (Ibid., 325).

Klingklang, Wendy and Tigerlilly – three female characters – ultimately vie for Peter's affection, while he – completely a child – does not notice any of this and remains in the realm of the asexual (cf. Schrackmann 2009, 48–49). At the same time, Peter at Wendy's side assumes the role of father to the lost boys: " JOHN: Darf ich auf Peters Stuhl sitzen? / WENDY: Auf Vatis Stuhl? Natürlich nicht!" (Barrie 1969, 303 f.) and thereby seems indirectly to claim both functions for himself after all – that of son and spouse. However, he has no idea of the assumed father role and must first learn it from the other children. A dialogue between the two at the beginning of the fourth act makes it clear that there is in fact no personal or even need-driven idea behind this on Peter's part, and that Wendy is rather the one who *also* wants to win Peter over as a partner (and less as a son):

> WENDY: […] *Wendy und Peter sind am Feuer allein. […] Sie liebt ihn zu sehr, um nicht zu wissen, daß er sie weniger liebt. Sie zögert wie jemand, der, ohne gefragt zu haben, die Antwort des anderen bereits kennt.* Was ist mit dir, Peter?
> PETER *beunruhigt*: Wir *tun* doch nur so, als sei ich der Vater?
> WENDY *enttäuscht*: Ja, ja.
> Er seufzt, ohne Rücksicht auf ihre Gefühle, erleichtert auf.
> WENDY: Und sie sind *doch* deine und meine Kinder!
> PETER *auf Tatsachen erpicht*: Aber nicht *richtig*!
> WENDY: Wenn du nicht magst, nein.
> PETER: Ich mag *nicht*!
> WENDY *weiß, daß sie es lassen sollte, aber etwas in ihr gibt keine Ruhe*: Und magst du *mich*, Peter?
> PETER *wie im Klassenzimmer*: Ja. Wie ein Kind seine Mutter.
> WENDY *wendet sich ab*: Das dachte ich mir!
> PETER: Ihr seid so komisch. Mit Tigerlilly ist es genauso. Die möchte auch immer irgendetwas von mir sein, sagt sie. Bloß nicht meine Mutter.
> WENDY *lebhaft*: Da hast du's!
> PETER: Aber was denn sonst?
> WENDY: Darüber spricht man als Frau nicht.
> Klingklangs Vorhang öffnet sich ein wenig. Sie hat zweifellos gelauscht, und nun lacht sie wütend.
> PETER *irritiert*: Vielleicht will *die* meine Mutter sein!
> *Klingklangs Antwort lautet: „Dummkopf!"* (Barrie 1969, 306 f.)

The excerpt shows, on the one hand, that all three female beings around Peter have at least some erotic feelings for him, and, on the other hand, that Peter has no idea at all what these might be: "Die möchte auch immer irgendetwas von mir sein [...] Bloß nicht meine Mutter." (Ibid., 306) At the same time, Wendy, by refusing to give Peter an explanation, shows that Peter, for his part, has to discover his feelings for her, because they are something unspeakable, perhaps indecent.

Finally, Wendy tells the lost boys and their brothers a story that turns out to be her own, and to that extent has the effect of a mise-en-abîme: It's about the Darlings, who have three children who one day fly off to the Land of Nirgendwo resulting in their parents at home deeply missing their daughter and two sons. Peter's only interjection is to point out something that the literary character in *Kleiner weißer Vogel* also has to experience:

> PETER: Aber was du über Mütter erzählt hast, ist falsch. Das mit dem Fenster, das glaubte ich auch einmal. Aber als ich nach vielen Monaten zurückgeflogen kam, war das Fenster zu. Meine Mutter hatte mich vergessen. Und in meinem Bett schlief ein anderer kleiner Junge. (Ibid., 309)

Wendy, moved by her own story and troubled by Peter's interjection, wants to leave immediately with her brothers and the lost boys to see if their mother is actually waiting for them with the window open. Everyone, except Peter, wants to come along and stay with the Darlings from now on. Peter seems unmoved and tells Klingklang to escort the children outside so they can make the return trip home. There, the Indians, and the pirates have a fierce battle, in which the Rotzbubenstamm is defeated. When the children leave the house, they are immediately captured by Haken and his crew. Peter, meanwhile, is asleep. Unnoticed by Peter, Haken manages to slip poison into his medicine left to him by Wendy, which Klingklang ultimately drinks to sacrifice himself. Peter then breaks the fourth wall of the stage by turning to the audience and asking them to express their belief in fairies so that Klingklang will not have to die. Both subsequently set out to save Wendy, her brothers, and the lost boys.

The fifth act is divided into two scenes. The first takes place on the Jolly Rogers, the pirates' ship to which Haken has retreated with his crew and the captured children. While Haken is still contemplating his unpopularity in relation to Peter's popularity, and he is pondering how to proceed with the children, Peter is already approaching from the air. After he has eliminated the pirate crew, there is a final fight with Haken, who, when he acknowledges his inferiority, voluntarily jumps into the maw of the crocodile already waiting for him.

The second scene of the fifth act is divided into two parts: The first part is set in the Darlings' home. After Peter initially tries to close the window so that Wendy cannot return home for good, he opens it again because he realises that Mrs. Darling deeply wants her children to return. The Darling children, as well as the lost boys, are welcomed with open arms. Wendy gets permission from Mrs. Darling to fly to the Land Nirgendwo once a year for spring cleaning to visit Peter. In the second part, the setting changes, but so does the perspective on it, as the incident text reveals: "Wir träumen, wir wären ein Jahr drauf wieder im Lande Nirgendwo." (Ibid., 332) In this final scene, it is clear that Wendy has grown older: "*Wendy sieht älter aus. Peter ist unverändert. [...] Und eine betrübliche Mitteilung wäre zu machen: sie fliegt in diesem Jahr schon so schlecht, daß sie dazu einen Besenstil [sic] braucht."* (Ibid., 333) In particular, her poor flying skills indicate that she will soon be unable to perceive Peter Pan and the Land Nirgendwo as she grows up. Peter, on the other hand, has already forgotten both the lost boys and Klingklang and seems to have few memories of his past with Wendy. Wendy notices his oblivion and realises that one day he will have forgotten her completely and replace her with another little girl.

There is another act that Barrie added in 1908 and that was not published for the first time until 1957. Erich Kästner could therefore not have been aware of it at the time of his translation (cf. Schrackmann 2009, 31). Petra Schrackmann emphasises for the English-speaking world that this additional act usually replaced the "Traum vom Land Nirgendwo" at the end of the second scene of Act Five in later theatrical performances.

When Wendy grew up: An afterthought (Barrie 1999, 155–165) begins several years later in the Darlings' nursery, where grown up Wendy is putting her daughter Jane to bed. She has already told her many stories of Peter Pan. After Jane falls asleep, Peter Pan comes into the room, sees that Wendy has grown up and now has a daughter of her own, and he feels the need to stab her. Instead, however, he bursts into desperate tears, from which Jane awakens. The two introduce themselves to each other, and what happens next provides information about how the circle opened in the first act will come full circle: Jane promises to be Peter's mother, and Wendy allows her to fly to Neverland once a year for spring-cleaning, as all generations of Darling girls will do from then on (cf. Barrie 1999).

Wie Wendy erwachsen wurde is only included in some German prose versions – in this or a similar way – as the heading of the last chapter.[9] Apart from Kästner's translation and the abridged translation by Bernd Wilms mentioned in footnote eight, which is accessible exclusively in pdf format, no other translations of the stage play into German are available even today. Until 1945, prose versions were generally only available in the form of the freely translated chapters from *Kleiner weißer Vogel,* i.e. as *Peter Pan im Waldpark.* Therefore, in the following we will only briefly discuss the diverse prose versions in German, which later gradually became established on the German market.

James M. Barrie's *Peter Pan*: Prose Versions or *Peter Pan* in Germany After 1945

The popularity of the play led to the desire for a prose version of *Peter Pan.* Barrie was not initially interested in such an adaptation, so he allowed various authors to adapt it (cf. Schrackmann 2009, 31). One of these retelling prose adaptations was by

---

[9] The title quoted above is found, for example, in the translation by Martin Karau (Barrie 1995, 180). In Adelheid Dormagen's translation, the chapter is called *Als Wendy erwachsen wurde* (Barrie 2009, 198), while Ursula von Wiese dispenses with chapter titles altogether (Barrie 1968).

May Byron, which became known in the German-speaking world primarily in connection with the 1939 illustrations by Sophie Scholl and in the translation by Hanspeter Nägele, but was not published until 1989 (Barrie 1989). Barrie wrote his own novel version in 1911 under the title *Peter and Wendy,* which was eventually renamed *Peter Pan and Wendy* and after 1987 was published only as *Peter Pan* (cf. Schrackmann 2009, 31 f.). However, Barrie's own prose version as well as those of various other authors have been and continue to be republished (cf. Barrie 1965, among others).

Whilst *Peter Pan im Waldpark* was only available in Germany as a prose version until 1945, the number of translations and new adaptations of the prose versions that followed the play increased steadily thereafter (cf. among others Barrie 1968, 1995, 2010, 2012, 2013, 2015 and 2017). In addition to these adaptations, some of which combine *Peter Pan in Kensington Gardens* and *Peter Pan and Wendy,* there are now also heavily edited, abridged versions prepared for first-time readers (see Barrie 2005, 2009, 2019, among others).

In the following, Peter's appearance during his first introduction will be briefly examined once again – and in the form in which it takes shape in various translations into German. Two different translations, based on Barrie's prose version, will be used as a basis.

Peter's first appearance in the prose version authorised by Barrie is somewhat different from that of the stage version. Here, too, he comes flying through the open window, but his target is explicitly Mrs. Darling, since he knows her from their childhood (as already indicated in the stage play, and more emphatically laid out through motifs in *Kleiner weißer Vogel*), but she has obviously forgotten him because she has grown up. In the translation by Bernd Wilms, Peter's first appearance is described as follows:

> Mit einem Schrei sprang sie auf und sah den Jungen, und irgendwie wusste sie sofort, dass es Peter Pan war. Wenn du oder ich oder Wendy es miterlebt hätten, dann hätten wir gesehen, dass er dem Kuss von Mrs. Darling glich. Er war ein hübscher Junge, mit Laub und Spinnweben bekleidet. Aber das Erstaunlichste an ihm war, dass er noch all seine ersten Zähne hatte. Als er sah, dass Mrs. Darling erwachsen war, knirschte er böse mit den kleinen Perlen. (Barrie 2017, 24)

Adelheid Dormagen translates the passage as follows:

> Sie fuhr mit einem Schrei hoch und sah den Jungen, und irgendwie wusste sie sofort, dass es Peter Pan war. Wären du oder ich oder Wendy dort gewesen, hätten wir bemerkt, dass er große Ähnlichkeit mit Mrs. Darlings Kuss hatte. Es war ein niedlicher Junge in einem Gewand aus Blattgerippe, mit Harz verklebt: das Reizendste an ihm aber war, dass er noch alle seine Milchzähne hatte. Als er erkannte, dass sie eine Erwachsene war, knirschte er mit den perlweißen Zähnchen. (Barrie [3] 2015, 22 f.)

Essentially, when comparing the two translations, it is noticeable that Dormagen portrays Peter Pan as clearly childlike and insofar harmless. This is achieved by the phrase "niedlicher Junge", the compound noun "Milchzähne" and by the diminutive "Zähnchen". At the same time, the "Milchzähne" make up "das Reizendste" thing about him, with *reizend* having equivalences with *niedlich*. Wilms chooses a different path by using the phrase "hübscher Junge", which – rather than *niedlich* can – suggest an erotic connotation. In Wilms' work, Peter also does not have "Milchzähne" but "noch all seine ersten Zähne", which cleverly avoids belittlement. His teeth are also not described as "das Reizendste", but as "das Erstaunlichste". In this way Wilms emphasises a special feature, but one that can be ambivalent in its effect. It is not immediately characterised as pleasant (and thus harmless), but as unusual and thus potentially unsettling, perhaps even dangerous. Finally, it all boils down to the last sentence. Dormagen writes Peter "knirschte [...] mit den perlweißen Zähnchen" and, by using the diminutive, removes any threat from Peter's grinding teeth. This is reinforced in Wilms by adding the adjective "böse". In summary, Dormagen's translation tends to portray Peter Pan as a one-dimensional positive character, while Wilms has in mind Peter Pan's ambiguity, which is demonstrable across all of Barrie's textual versions.

A differentiated, systematic comparison of the numerous translations into German, which can only be hinted at here by way of example, has yet to be carried out and could provide information about the transcription of the figures that goes hand in hand with the stylistic design.

The First Film Adaptation of *Peter Pan* (1924)

The first film adaptation of *Peter Pan* (1924), directed by Herbert Brenon, is an American silent film with superimposed text panels containing direct quotations from Barrie's stage play. The film version is heavily based on the play presented in detail above. Barrie himself collaborated on the film – among other things, in casting Peter Pan, he chose the then-unknown Betty Bronson, whose ballet training gave her the best qualifications to be convincing in the flying numbers (see Brenon 1924). Thus, the first film version continued a tradition that had already proven itself on stage: Peter is traditionally played by a girl (cf. Schrackmann 2009, 34).

In December 1925, the film was released in German cinemas under the title *Peter Pan, der Traumelf*.[10] The apposition added to the film's title in Germany gives rise to speculation about its purpose: Was it intended to give German audiences, most of whom were unfamiliar or only distantly familiar with the character of Peter Pan, a first impression of his nature and, to that extent, to evoke a more detailed expectation? Something similar can already be observed in the translation of the stage play text when Kästner transfers *Peter Pan, or the Boy Who Would Not Grow Up* into *Peter Pan, oder Das Märchen vom Jungen, der nicht groß werden wollte*. Whereas Barrie focuses on the boy and thus the protagonist, in Kästner's case it is the literary genre to which the *Stoff* can be assigned. If Barrie's stage play can perhaps still be declared a fairy tale (although even this is ultimately debatable), the composite term "*Traumelf*", on the other hand, is purely factually incorrect: Peter Pan is not an elf

---

[10] This version of the film is no longer available. The original English-language version, on the other hand, was restored and given a new orchestral score (cf. information in the filmography).

and will not turn out to be a dream character in the course of the film. In this respect, the term must have another function, perhaps that of once again locating the reception of the film (and thus of the character Peter) in the realm of the fantastic or the fairy-tale-like. The fact that the translation of film titles into German often produces inaccurate and even fundamentally distorting stylistic blossoms should only be mentioned here in passing.[11]

The response to the film can be gleaned from an issue of the film trade journal *Der Kinematograph*, in which the critics' opinions from various newspapers were compiled, unanimously praising the great acting performances, the excitingly staged plot and the family-friendly orientation of the film. Thus *Der Kinematograph* refers to the *8-Uhr Abendblatt vom 18.12.1925*: "Ein Wunderland tut sich auf ... Ein Wunderland, das die Kinder staunen macht, das die Großen aus dem Alltag der Komplikationen zu sich lockt." (Der Kinematograph 1925/983, 22 1925a) This brief commentary already clearly shows that the film was suitable for a wide range of audiences and that it was capable of inspiring young and old alike. In a further article, *Der Kinematograph* refers to the *Film-Kurier* of 18.12.1925, the *Berliner Morgenpost* of the same day, the *Montag-Morgen* of 21.12.1925 as well as the *Berliner-Tageblatt of* 20.12.1925, all of which comment on the naturalness of the performance of the leading actress Betty Bronson and on her persuasiveness, which lends credibility and authenticity to the fairy tale portrayed (cf. Der Kinematograph 1925/983, 22 1925a). The short introduction to the film printed by *Der Kinematograph* is also full of praise and emphasises both the fairytale-like quality and the natural acting of the child actors (cf. Der Kinematograph 1925/983, 28 1925b). The reception of the audience attending the performance is also indicated here: "Erstaufführung viel Beifall " (Ibid.). The reviewer, who remains unnamed, also refers to the lack of popularity of the *Peter Pan-Stoff* in Germany and thus provides contemporary evidence of the obvious assumption already expressed in several places:

> "Peter Pan" is a fairy tale of immense popularity in English-speaking countries. Despite the fact that we lack this prerequisite, what a delightful fairy-tale film this "Peter Pan" is, not only for the children, but also for the older ones, as far as they are not hopelessly dried up or rusty. (Der Kinematograph 1925/983, 28 1925b)

In film, the character of Peter Pan acquires a form that can be shared and communicated intersubjectively. Text versions without pictures leave the idea of the outer appearance of a character largely to individual imagination, as they are interspersed with points of indeterminacy. In illustrated versions – depending on the illustrator – there are different interpretations of the written text, and in stage versions the directors and actors change, so that (not only) the exterior and its staging are constantly changing. The first – and for a long time the only – film version by Herbert Brenon created an image of Peter Pan for the first time, which not only made the outer appearance widely receivable through the film screening itself, but also through the

---

[11] A good example of this – which could be joined by countless others – is certainly the transfer of the American film title *Finding Neverland* (2004) into *Wenn Träume fliegen lernen*. Schubert 2004, among others, has dealt with this phenomenon.

Fig. 2 From left to right: Mary Brian as Wendy Darling, Betty Bronson as Peter Pan, Esther Ralston as Mrs. Darling (© 1924 Paramount Pictures), https://www.britannica.com/topic/Peter-Pan-play-by-Barrie (24.02.2020)

dissemination of film posters and scene photos[12] in the public sphere, in newspapers and film magazines, and in this respect added it to the cultural memory as a common idea.

Peter Pan, as shown in the scene photo (Fig. 2), is about the same height as Wendy, has short dark curls and wears a tight-fitting little cap on his head. The short costume, which leaves the arms and legs bare, is decorated with a leaf pattern and is torn at the hem. Peter Pan is, moreover, barefoot. A white collar is visible at the neck, adding a middle-class accent to the nature-inspired costume. In the outward appearance, therefore, a binary opposition is expressed that stretches between the two aspects mentioned. Freedom, self-determination, and independence can thus be associated with Peter Pan's appearance, but at the same time also an – however pronounced – anchoring in the world of people. Peter Pan's appearance already reveals his oscillation between living out his youth, independence and irresponsibility and his longing for care and attention, which is symbolised by the mother figure.

---

[12] Here, the term scene photograph rather than film still is chosen to express the staging (and insofar the independent creation) of the photographs, which are received as supposedly frozen film moments (cf. Moser 2016).

However, the scene photo from *Peter Pan* shows something else that makes a marked change from the stage version clear: Peter Pan is not untouchable in the film. When – as shown here – Peter's farewell to Wendy and Mrs. Darling is depicted analogously to the second scene of the stage play's[13] fifth act, and Peter reaches out his hand to mother and daughter, this is just one example of many others in which Peter embraces, is embraced, kisses or gives and receives other physical touches. In this way, fascination and closeness between the acting characters is created on a visual level in the film.

The next film adaptation of the *Peter Pan-Stoff* did not occur until after 1945, in the form of Walt Disney's 1953 animated film *Walt Disney's Peter Pan*, which played in German cinemas that same year under the title *Peter Pans heitere Abenteuer* and continued to be distributed under the simple title *Peter Pan*.[14] Although this adaptation achieved great notoriety and remains closely aligned with Barrie's stage version on the plot level, it obscures the contradictory, binary-oppositional design of the characters, especially Peter Pan's (cf. inter alia Necknig 2006, 121).

As a result, countless film adaptations of the *Stoff* were made, most of which came to Germany from the Anglo-American world and sometimes worked closely with the original, but sometimes simply adopted motifs from the stage play, predecessor films and/or the prose version.[15] In the German-language versions, the practice of retaining the English names of the protagonists became increasingly common. In the case of Tinker Bell alone, there are repeated attempts at translation – e.g. Glöckchen (Geronimi et al. 1953), Glühweiße (Brenon 1924), Naseweis (Budd/Cook 2002).

Prequels and sequels[16] are also becoming increasingly popular. In 2002, for example, *Peter Pan 2: Neue Abenteuer im Nimmerland* (originally *Return to Neverland*) was released, a sequel to the Disney film in which Wendy's daughter Jane is kidnapped by Captain Hook and finally meets Peter Pan in Neverland.

An early German adaptation is *Peter Pan oder Das Märchen vom Jungen, der nicht groß werden wollte* (1962). Directed by Paul Verhoeven, the TV film is a version working with Erich Kästner's translation, now casting a boy (Fernando Möller) in the role of Peter Pan – a practice that has become common in film versions.

---

[13] The additional act *When Wendy Grew Up. An Afterthought has* not been realised in the film version.

[14] The Internet Movie Data Base lists the German premiere as Dec. 22, 1953, https://www.imdb.com/title/tt0046183/?ref_ =kw_li_tt (16.09.2019).

[15] For example, Peter *Pan* (1955), *Hook* (1991), *Peter Pan* (2003), *When Dreams Learn to Fly* (2004), *Peter & Wendy* (2015).

[16] For example, *Neverland. Der Anfang von Peter Pans Abenteuerreise* (2012), *Pan* (2015).

Conclusion

All in all, it can be said that interest in the *Peter Pan-Stoff* began much later – and more diffusely – in Germany than in England or America. The low presence of Peter Pan in the German media landscape until 1945 speaks for itself. Even in the period after 1945, adaptations hardly came from Germany, but mainly from the Anglo-American, and to some extent also from the French region, such as the comic series *Peter Pan* by Régis Loisel (cf. on this Schrackmann 2009). The films, but also the comic by Loisel (2014, 2015) or the Muppet Show special *Muppet Peter Pan* (Randolph/Mebberson 2011) are successfully marketed in Germany, but hardly inspire independent media processing of the *Stoff*. The most common examples are audiobook adaptations (also with music), such as the reading by Leander Haußmann, accompanied by Element of Crime from 2000 (Barrie/Haußmann 2000). Against this background, the immense number of different translations, adaptations, and editions of the prose version available in Germany, especially in modern times, is surprising. All in all, the convoluted history of the origins of the text and the manifold productions of the figure of Peter Pan show that, as Jacqueline Rose sums[17] it up, it represents a "cultural myth" (Rose 1993, xii) in which the idea of the eternal child has taken root and which, in this respect, represents less a childlike quality than the longing of adults for precisely this state (cf. Rose 1993, vii).

Literature

Primary Literature

Barrie, James M.: The Little White Bird [1902]. London: Hodder & Stoughton, 1930.
Barrie, James M.: Peter Pan in Kensington Gardens [1906]. London: Hodder & Stoughton, 1908.
Barrie, James M.: Peter Pan im Waldpark. Übers. von Irmgard Funcke. Weimar: Kiepenheuer 1911 und 1930.
Barrie, James M.: Peter Pan. Übers. von Ursula von Wiese. Mit Zeichnungen von Horst Lemke. Berlin [u. a.]: Deutsche Buchgemeinschaft, 1968.
Barrie, James M.: Peter Pan & Wendy. Für kleine Leute nacherzählt von May Byron. Ins Deutsche übertr. von Hanspeter Nägele. Mit Zeichn. von Sophie Scholl. Zweisprachige Ausg. München: Matthes & Seitz, 1989.
Barrie, James M.: Peter Pan. Übers. von Martin Karau. Mit Ill. von Barbara Schumann. Berlin [u. a.] Altberliner, 1995.
Barrie, James M.: Peter Pan. Neu erzählt von Wolfgang Knape. Mit Ill. von Christiane Hansen. Zwickau: Arena in Zusammenarb. mit Westermann, ⁵2005.
Barrie, James M.: Peter Pan. Nacherz. von Rüdiger Bertram. Mit Bildern von Rolf Bunse [Leserabe – Lesestufe 3]. Ravensburg: Ravensburger, 2009.

---

[17] Jacqueline Rose is also briefly referred to by Kümmerling-Meibauer (2004, 74) in her encyclopedia article.

Barrie, James M.: Kleiner weißer Vogel. Abenteuer im Kensington Park. Ill. von Arthur Rackham. Übers. a. d. Engl. von Michael Klein. Merzig: Gollenberg, 2010.
Barrie, James M.: Peter Pan. A. d. Engl. von Martin Rometsch. Mit Ill. von Robert Ingpen. München: Knesebeck, ⁴2010.
Barrie, James M.: Peter Pan in Kensington Gardens. Übers. von Selma Urfer. Mit Ill. von Arthur Rackham. Wien: Verlagshaus Mescheryakov, 2011.
Barrie, James M.: Peter Pan. Nacherz. von Sabine Rahn. Bilder von Andrea Offermann. Hamburg: Ellermann im Dressler, 2012.
Barrie, James M.: Peter Pan. A. d. Engl. von Kim Landgraf. Köln: Anaconda, 2013.
Barrie, James M.: Peter Pan. A. d. Engl. von Adelheid Dormagen. Berlin: Insel, ³2015.
Barrie, James M./Gréban, Quentin: Peter Pan. Gek. Nacherz. von Xavier Deutsch. Freiburg im Breisgau: Kizz bei Herder, 2019.
Barrie, James M.: Peter Pan. A. d. Engl. von Bernd Wilms. Mit Ill. von Minalima. Münster: Coppenrath, 2017.
Loisel, Régis: Peter Pan. [1991–1996]. Gesamtausg. 1. Übers. a. d. Franz. von Eckhart Sackmann. Köln: Egmont, 2014.
Loisel, Régis: Peter Pan. [1997–2005]. Gesamtausg. 2. Übers. a. d. Franz. von Eckhart Sackmann. Köln: Egmont, 2015.
Randolph, Grace/Mebberson, Amy: Muppet Peter Pan. Übers. a. d. Amerik. von Michael Bregel. Köln: Ehapa, 2011.

Filmography

Hook (USA 1991). Regie: Steven Spielberg, Musik: John Williams, Collector's Edition 2002 (DVD).
Neverland. Der Anfang von Peter Pans Abenteuerreise [TV Miniserie] (GB/USA 2011). Regie: Nick Willing, Musik: Ronan Hardiman, 2012 (DVD).
Pan (USA 2015). Regie: Joe Wright, Musik: John Powell, 2016 (DVD).
Peter Pan [Stummfilm] (USA 1924). Regie: Herbert Brenon, Musik: Philip C. Carli. From the play by James M. Barrie, Restaurierte Fassung 1999 (DVD).
[Walt Disney's] Peter Pan [Zeichentrickfilm] (USA 1953). Regie: Clyde Geronimi, Wilfred Jackson, Hamilton Luske, Jack Kinney, Musik: Oliver Wallace. Restaurierte Fassung 2002 (DVD).
Peter Pan oder Das Märchen vom Jungen, der nicht groß werden wollte [Fernsehfilm] (D 1962). Regie: Paul Verhoeven, Musik: Otto Erich Schilling, 2014 (DVD).
Peter Pan [Musical, Fernsehfilm] (USA 1955). Regie: Clark Jones, Musik: Jule Styne, Mark Charlap, Trude Rittmann, 2016 (DVD).
Peter Pan 2: Neue Abenteuer im Nimmerland [Zeichentrickfilm] (2002). Regie: Robin Budd, Donovan Cook, Musik: John Flansburgh, John Linnell (Songs), Joel McNeely (Score) 2003 (DVD).
Peter Pan (USA 2003). Regie: P. J. Hogan, Musik: James Newton Howard, 2004 (DVD).
Peter & Wendy [Fernsehfilm] (USA 2015). Regie: Diarmuid Lawrence, Musik: Maurizio Malagnini, 2016 (DVD).
Wenn Träume fliegen lernen (GB/USA 2004). Regie: Marc Forster, Musik: Jan A. P. Kaczmarek, 2005 (DVD).

Audiography

Peter Pan. Von James M. Barrie. (2000) Ungek. Lesung. Gelesen von Leander Haußmann. Mit Musik von Element of Crime. Tacheles: Roof Music [Vertrieb Buchhandel: Eichborn 2009].

Theatrography

Barrie, James M.: Peter Gerneklein's erster Christbaum. Weihnachtsmärchen mit Gesang und Tanz. Übers. von Berta Pogson. Berlin: Bloch [um 1910].
Barrie, James M.: Peter Pan or The Boy Who Would Not Grow Up. The Plays of J. M. Barrie. London: Hodder & Stoughton, ⁴1928.
Barrie, James M.: Peter Pan oder Das Märchen vom Jungen, der nicht groß werden wollte. Übers. von Erich Kästner. In: Erich Kästner: Gesammelte Schriften für Erwachsene, Bd. 5. Theater. Zürich: Atrium, 1969, 251–334.
Barrie, James M.: When Wendy Grew Up: An Afterthought. In: James M. Barrie: Peter Pan and other Plays. Oxford [u. a.]: Oxford University Press, 1999, 155–163.
Barrie, James M.: Peter Pan oder der Junge, der nicht groß werden wollte. Deutsch von Bernd Wilms. Frankfurt a. M.: Verlag der Autoren, 2008.

Secondary Literature Before 1945

Peter Pan, Paramount-Film der Ufa. In: Kinematograph 19 (1925a) 983/984 vom 25.12., 22.
Peter Pan [Rez.]. In: Kinematograph 19 (1925b) 983/984 vom 25.12., 28.
Filmprodukte der Verfallszeit. In: Film-Kurier 19 (1937) 264 vom 12.11., 2
Im Westen nichts Neues [Anzeige]. In: Kinematograph 23 (1929) 159 vom 11.7., 2
E. K.: Vom Film. „Im Westen nichts Neues" (Mozartsaal). In: Die Welt am Montag 36 (1930) vom 8.12.
„Niemandsland" [Rez.]. In: Kinematograph 25 (1931) 285 vom 10.12., 4
Pariser Notizen. In: Kinematograph 26 (1932) 44 vom 3.3., 4

Secondary Literature After 1945

Birkin, Andrew: J. M. Barrie and the Lost Boys. The real story behind Peter Pan [1979]. Yale 2003.
Doderer, Klaus: Geschichte des Kinder- und Jugendtheaters zwischen 1945 und 1970. Konzepte, Entwicklungen, Materialien. Frankfurt a. M. 1995 (Kinder-, Schul- und Jugendtheater; 7).
Doležel, Lubomír: Heterocosmica. Fiction and Possible Worlds. Baltimore, Md. 1998.
Grant, Michael/Hazel, John: Lexikon der antiken Mythen und Gestalten [1980]. München 1995.
Green, Roger Lancelyn: Fifty Years of Peter Pan. London 1954.
Grieser, Dietmar: Peter Pan oder: Sie waren fünf. James Barrie: „Peter Pan". In: Ders. (Hg.): Die kleinen Helden. Kinderbuchfiguren und ihre Vorbilder. München 1987, 47–60.
Günther, Wolfgang: Wege ins Wunderland. Von Peter Pan bis Harry Potter. Frankfurt a. M. 2006.
Haas, Gerhard: Struktur und Funktion der phantastischen Literatur. In: Wirkendes Wort 28 (1978) 5, 340–356.
Internet Movie Data Base: Peter Pans heitere Abenteuer (1953), https://www.imdb.com/title/tt0046183/?ref_=kw_li_tt (15.09.2019).
J. M. Barrie's Boy Castaways (2019), https://beinecke.library.yale.edu/collections/highlights/jm-barries-boy-castaways (15.09.2019).
Jahnke, Manfred: Von der Komödie für Kinder zum Weihnachtsmärchen. Bodenheim 1977.
Klein, Michael: Nachwort. In: Barrie, James M.: Kleiner weißer Vogel. Abenteuer im Kensington Park. Ill. von Arthur Rackham. Übers. a. d. Engl. von Michael Klein. Merzig 2010, 253–270.
Kümmerling-Meibauer, Bettina: Klassiker der Kinder- und Jugendliteratur. Ein internationales Lexikon. Sonderausg. Stuttgart [u. a.] 2004.

Link, Jürgen: Literatursemiotik. In: Brakert, Jörn/Stückrath, Jörn (Hg.): Literaturwissenschaft. Ein Grundkurs. Reinbek bei Hamburg ⁸2004 (Rowohlts Enzyklopädie; 55523), 15–29.

Moser, Walter (Hg.): Film-Stills. Fotografien zwischen Werbung, Kunst und Kino. Wien 2016.

Necknig, Andreas Thomas: Wie *Harry Potter, Peter Pan* und *Die unendliche Geschichte* auf die Leinwand gezaubert wurden. Literaturwissenschaftliche und didaktische Aspekte von Verfilmungen phantastischer Kinder- und Jugendliteratur. Frankfurt a. M. 2006.

Peter Gerneklein's erster Christbaum (o. A.), http://stabikat.de/DB=1/LNG=DU/CLK?IKT=12&TRM=443338787 (05.08.2019).

Petzold, Dieter: Der Traum vom verlorenen Paradies – Bemerkungen zu J. M. Barries *Peter Pan*. In: Diller, Hans Jürgen/Kohl, Stephan/Kornelius, Joachim/Otte, Erwing (Hg.): Anglistik und Englischunterricht, Bd. 2: Trivialliteratur. Trier 1977, 9–26.

Petzold, Dieter: Die Rezeption klassischer englischsprachiger Kinderbücher in Deutschland. In: Ewers, Hans-Heino/Lehnert, Gertrud/O'Sullivan, Emer (Hg.): Kinderliteratur im interkulturellen Prozess. Studien zur Allgemeinen und Vergleichenden Kinderliteraturwissenschaft. Stuttgart [u. a.] 1994, 78–91.

Rank, Bernhard: Phantastik im Spannungsfeld zwischen literarischer Moderne und Unterhaltung. Ein Überblick über die Forschungsgeschichte der 90er Jahre. In: Kinder- und Jugendliteraturforschung 2001/2002 (2002), 101–125.

Rose, Jacqueline: The Case of Peter Pan or The Impossibility of Children's Fiction [1984]. University of Pennsylvania Press 1993.

Schrackmann, Petra: „An Awfully Big Adventure!" J. M. Barries *Peter Pan* im medialen Transfer. Zürich 2009 (Populäre Literaturen und Medien; 2).

Schubert, Christoph: Die Appellwirkung englischer Filmtitel und ihrer deutschen Neutitel: Techniken interkulturellen Transfers. In: Arbeiten aus Anglistik und Amerikanistik 29 (2004) 2, 239–259.

Urian's Travels Around the World

History of Motifs and Media Adaptations

Gina Weinkauff

Away From the 'Miracle': Lisa Tetzner and the Hans Urian *Stoff*

> Hans Urian runs away from home without money and wants to buy bread. He meets a hungry hare on his way. Man and hare now travel around the world in a fantastic, adventurous way and experience – via town and country, farmer and factory – the social process of production: work – money, money – bread. These social realities in the form of a funny-childish comedy, almost grotesque seeming, interwoven with the clash of the hare's respectively animal philosophy and the civilization of man is the basic idea of the plot. (Tetzner 1929)

With these words, Lisa Tetzner accurately sketches the plot, themes, addressee design, reality model and genre contexts of the *Hans-Urian* story in its first publicized media version in a newspaper article published in 1929. It is a fantastic tale with adventurous and humorous elements that addresses social antagonisms as well as economic, ethical, and social issues in a form geared towards child addressees. Following the pattern of a fantastic world journey, the plot revolves around a child protagonist who, accompanied by a magical helper, sets out with the intention of procuring food for himself and his sick mother.

The article refers to the production, still in preparation at the time of its appearance, of the play *Hans Urian geht nach Brot,* co-written by Lisa Tetzner and Béla Balász, which premiered at the Lessing Theatre in Berlin on November 13, 1929. In addition, the short article is set in the context of a discussion about current children's theatre innovations that took up a full page in the paper. Lisa Tetzner's article is virtually framed by two passionate pleas for the interests of children as theatregoers. The author of the first is Fritz Gentschow, who was working as a director at

G. Weinkauff (✉)
Frankfurt, Germany

the same time at the Theater am Schiffbauerdamm on the production of another Tetzner play; the second author is Fritz Künkel, a Berlin psychiatrist influenced by Alfred Adler and appearing in many public debates, who pleaded here for psychological reasons for more realism in children's theatre.

The striking title of Lisa Tetzner's contribution *Fort vom 'Wunder'* seems to tend in the same direction, but at the same time it points beyond the realm of children's theatre to the artistic development of the authoress herself, from a fairy-tale teller inspired by the youth movement and the New Romantics to a significant representative of realism in Children's Literature. With the title *Fort vom 'Wunder'* Lisa Tetzner signals her departure from a conservative (kulturpessimistischen) perspective on fairy tales, as still expressed, for example, in the preface to the amateur play *Siebenschön,* published in 1926:

> This play is intended as an open-air play for village squares under the lime tree or in front of the church. [...] The plot is based on the German fairy tale, which seems to me to be the most German and best of all the German fairy tales after Grimm, and which belongs like hardly any other to a summery forest and meadow landscape. (Tetzner 1926, 3)

Lisa Tetzner herself reflected on her development in various contributions, for example in an account entitled *Meine Erfahrungen als Märchenerzählerin und meine Einstellung und Arbeit von 1918 bis heute,* which appeared in 1930 in the journal of the "Bund entschiedener Schulreformer" (Association of Decisive School Reformers). There she reports on encounters with her audience, which had changed so much during the years of the Weimar Republic that she felt compelled to switch from fairy tales to realistic, contemporary narrative *Stoff*:

> In the last 3 years I have observed even greater changes in the youth, especially the children of the big city and the proletariat. I began to have doubts about conventional storytelling to these children. [...] The child of today wants more and a different way of guidance. It does not want the refuge in wishful images that is a point of rest and enjoyment for us adults, but it wants to be enlightened about itself and the world. (Tetzner 1930, 21)

Lisa Tetzner registered the social, political and cultural aspects of social modernization very precisely and derived appropriate consequences for her literary work from these observations. However, this was done on the basis of a conception of the social mission of literature that was still shaped by the self-image of the traditional storyteller, which in turn was well compatible with the operative concepts of the proletarian revolutionary literary movement. When she wrote her contribution for Paul Oestreich's monthly *Neue Erziehung,* she herself moved into the environment of the Communist Party, also mediated by her partner Kurt Kläber.

Without mentioning the political contexts of her work during the Weimar period, Lisa Tetzner wrote a review of her beginnings as a children's book author in 1955. She concealed them probably for reasons of self-protection, because in the 1950s she and Kurt Kläber-Held were subjected to severe hostility from conservatives in the 1950s. Nevertheless, this version of events makes it clear that the socially committed storyteller always remained true to herself in a certain way, even as a socialist children's book author, that traditional and modern tendencies were closely linked in Lisa Tetzner's work:

In 1926 I attempted my first children's book. [...] 'Hans Urian, die Geschichte einer Weltreise'. Man and animal served as opposing parties. I took over the black-and-white painting from the fairy tale in order to make it easier for a child to feel moral sympathy. I made use of the limited childish vocabulary of 'here and there', 'he came', 'he went'. (The Pestalozzi-Fröbelhaus was now bearing its fruit.) As far as possible I told only in main sentences and said everything aloud to myself in thoughts of the child. Even then I lived in my Ticino home in the southern canton of Switzerland, which was my love, and I stayed there most of the year. Only the call of the Berlin radio hour to the leader of the fairy tale hour there inevitably led me back to Berlin again. There I found a Berlin play group, which I encouraged to play fairy tales and my own experiences in the youth hour. What was born came from impromptu play, the content of the children, the form from me. In this way the first four stories of the children from number 67 came into being. The children were my model. They eagerly worked with me. In 1933, my beloved flock flew off in all directions. I myself moved to Switzerland with my husband for good, and we still live there today. (Tetzner 1955, 16)

The *non-political* tone also includes the highly trivializing account of their escape from Germany – the Nazis had already imprisoned Kurt Kläber and put him on trial for alleged involvement in the Reichstag fire.

The text offers two more interesting references: to Lisa Tetzner's work in radio, which provides one of the background experiences for her development into realistic writing, and to the year 1926 as the date of the writing of a first book manuscript. This statement is almost unanimously doubted in the secondary literature. The book manuscript, if there was one, is untraceable, and there are many factors which speak against Lisa Tetzner giving the *Stoff* its first (epic) form as early as 1926. Nevertheless, she seems to have been the actual originator of the plot and numerous motifs that shaped it.

The Hans Urian Project[1]

Apparently Lisa Tetzner and Béla Balász wrote the play *Hans Urian geht nach Brot* together, but not necessarily in harmony. This emerges from the "clarification" reproduced here, which appeared in the KPD-affiliated *Welt am Abend* on the day of the premiere, November 13, 1929:

We learn the following about the origin of the fairy tale play 'Hans Urian geht nach Brot': Lisa Tetzner came up with the suggestion in a meeting to found a children's theatre. She herself remembered a poem by Claudius 'Herr Urians Reise um die Welt' and a French children's book by Vaillant Couturier 'Hans ohne Brot'. From this she developed the idea of how a proletarian child, out of need and hunger to find relief, leaves home, on his way meets a rabbit that has detachable ears that become propellers and give him the ability to fly

---

[1] This term was coined by Bernd Dolle-Weinkauff, who in his dissertation *Das Märchen in der proletarisch-revolutionären Kinder- und Jugendliteratur der Weimarer Republik von 1918–1933* elaborated fundamental points with regard to books and plays and their reception in the contemporary press (cf. Dolle-Weinkauff 1984, 130–143). The author of this text profited greatly from numerous suggestions and hints as well as the opportunity to use his extensive collection of sources.

like an airplane. Balasz agreed to write the play with Lisa Tetzner. He invented the political concept and created various adventurous developments of the plot. Lisa Tetzner wrote the first draft of the play, Balasz then wrote a new version and shaped the problem and dialogues in the form of a comedy.

We have described the genesis of the play because for some time now to our surprise we have observed that on posters, in newspaper announcements, when quotations are printed, etc., Balasz is cited as the sole author. We do not know why this is happening, nor do we know whose fault it is. Perhaps the "Gruppe junger Schauspieler" who are putting on the play under the direction of Hans Deppe are not clearly informed. We have therefore clarified these facts on the basis of letters from Lisa Tetzner and Bela Balasz. (Clarification 1929)

Ten years older than Lisa Tetzner, Béla Balász (i.e. Herbert Bauer) had already produced an extensive body of work as a writer, journalist and scholar in the late 1920s. An an author publishing in Hungarian, he had written a series of poems, a drama and libretti for two of Béla Bartók's operas when, having become a Communist under the impact of his wartime experiences, he was forced to flee to Vienna after the suppression of the Hungarian soviet republic. In German, Béla Balász appeared, among other things, as a critic, screenwriter, and film theorist, as well as the author of fairy tales for adults in the Symbolist tradition, and the author of the highly acclaimed fantastic tale for children *Das richtige Himmelblau* (1925). Since moving to Berlin, he was extremely present in the proletarian-revolutionary cultural scene and his works continued to reach a 'bourgeois' public far beyond the KPD environment.

Consequently, there is a major discrepancy between the two authors of the play *Hans Urian geht nach Brot*. This explains why Béla Balász and not, say, Lisa Tetzner, presented the theoretical-programmatic background of the Hans Urian project in the journal of the Arbeiter-Theater-Bund Deutschlands (cf. Balász 1929a), and it also explains the tone of his self-representation in the *Welt am Abend*. Here he and Fritz Gentschow were given the opportunity to comment on the two productions of the New Children's Theatre that premiered in October and November 1929 *(Der große und der kleine Klaus* and *Hans Urian geht nach Brot)*. Both leave Lisa Tetzner's part out. Béla Balász announces the production as an educational play in political economy created for children:

> In my fairy tale 'Hans Urian geht nach Brot', which will premiere on November 13 performed by a group of young actors, children are made aware of concepts such as *exploitation, profit, strikes, imperialism, organisation* and the *balance of power between the classes* within the framework of a journey around the world [emphasis added]; the form remains – as I said – cheerful and fantastic; animals are among the main characters. (Balász 1929b)

It can be imagined that Lisa Tetzner was not particularly pleased by the reduction of the play to the communication of political slogans, nor by the suppression of her share of authorship. Regarding her involvement in the project, she writes the following in the 1930 contribution cited earlier:

> I also collaborated on the play, since the basic outline of the journey around the world, in which the child is supposed to see the world as it is today, and the figure of the hare came from a children's book manuscript of mine, which I had in mind in the form of a Niels (sic!) Holgersson book, i.e. socio-economic realities of our time within a fairy tale Stoff. (Tetzner [1930], 23)

In any case, justice was done to her by the *Welt am Abend,* where the following article by Paul Friedländer appeared even before the premiere:

> Finally, a comment on, let us say, a particular *forgetfulness* [emphasis in original] that occurred to both Bela Balász and Gentschow. As far as I know Balász is not the sole author of 'Hans Urian', but co-author (if I am not mistaken, also initiator), is Lisa Tetzner. And Gentschow did not adapt *'Klaus'* as a drama, but Lisa Tetzner did likewise. This seems to me not unimportant to note, because here is a striking example of how a bourgeois fairy-tale writer develops into a proletarian one. (Friedländer 1929)

To reaffirm this, Paul Friedländer reminds us that Lisa Tetzner is a courted bourgeois intellectual who already sympathizes with the communist movement and who should not be snubbed by such rude behavior. Within the framework of the premiere critique, the detailed clarification reproduced at the beginning then follows.

The Literary Pretexts

The dispute over Lisa Tetzner's authorship provides three references to literary impulses that she incorporated into her version of the *Stoff* that preceded Béla Balász's stage version: Selma Lagerlöf's *Nils Holgersson,* a children's book by the French Communist Paul Vaillant-Couturier [i.e. Paul Charles Couturier], whose German translation was published in 1928 under the title *Hans ohne Brot* by the Verlag der Jugendinternationale, and Matthias Claudius's song *Urians Reise um die Welt,* written in 1786. The protagonist took his name from the latter. The motivic similarity between the stories of Lisa Tetzner and Béla Balász and the eighteenth-century satire critical of the Enlightenment is rather vague. Here the traveler has a mission to fulfil and in the end returns home with significant knowledge, there we encounter the boasts of a talkative busybody who in the end can only conclude the futility of all expeditions in the face of the omnipresence of human folly. There is, however, a link between the one and the other Urian in the form of the picture book by Irene von Richthofen-Winkel, who must have worked more or less simultaneously on the illustration of the *Negermärchen* published by Lisa Tetzner. The sequence of stations in Claudius' song, which also determines the dramaturgy of Tetzner's and Balász's play, is further underlined by Irene von Richthofen-Winkel's illustration.

Selma Lagerlöf's *Nils Holgersson* undoubtedly influenced various fantastic or fairy-tale travel stories in German children's literature of the early twentieth century. As in *Nils Holgersson,* the Hans-Urian stories portray an educational journey centered around a magical animal figure. And if one only looks for it, one can also extract connectable messages from the novel *Nils Holgersson* for a proletarian counterpart.[2]

---

[2] For example, in the form of the child hero's enthusiasm in the face of prosperity and justice in the Norwegian province of Medelpad: "Surely this is a wonderful country! Wherever I may come, there is something by which people can make a living." (Lagerlöf 1920, 372) Cf. "Det är ett märkvärdigt land, som vi har. Vart jag kommer, alltid finns det något för människorna att leva av." (Lagerlöf 1907, 528).

Lisa Tetzner drew even more and more direct inspiration from the parabolic fairy tale *Jean sans pain,* which stands in the Left Expressionist tradition, was originally published in 1921 and is strongly influenced by the illustrations of Jean Picart le Doux. These give the book a children's literary feel: through their intense color, the drawing style common in early twentieth-century children's book illustration, and to some extent through the choice of motifs. The viewer is reminded of illustrations by Gertrud Caspari and Elsa Beskow.

Jean sans Pain also sets out on his journey because of his hunger and in the company of a magical hare. His journey, however, does not take him to the wide world, but it lets him see behind the scenes of the class society that has already robbed him of his father and mother. Jean discovers the factory where his mother contracted her fatal lung disease, witnesses the splurges of wealthy warlords, and experiences his father's agonizing death on the battlefield. The picture book ends with an apotheosis on a better socialist future and with Jean joining the ranks of the fighting proletariat.

We encounter considerably more pathos in this literary pretext than in Lisa Tetzner's and Béla Balász's, yet essential elements of the *Hans-Urian Stoff* are already preformed: Here, similar to Tetzner's and Balász's text, the story is told of a poor boy who, in his distress, sets out on a journey accompanied by a hare that ultimately helps him find his proletarian class identity. The following excerpt from the German translation of *Jean sans Pain,* which describes the beginning of the journey, shows that the similarities go even further:

> Nun – denke mal! – schraubt der Hase seine Ohren ab, eines nach dem anderen, klebt sie zusammen, steckt sie einem Feldhuhn in den Schnabel, bläst darauf, hei, wie dreht sich der Propeller im Wind!
> [...]
> Hans lässt sich zwischen den Feldhühnern nieder. Freundlich rücken sie beiseite. Jedes hält ein Stäbchen im Schnabel und mitten auf den Stäbchen, die man zusammenfügt, sitzt Hans.
> [...]
> Als sie eine gewisse Höhe erreicht hatten, senkte Hans seine Nase – bisher hatte er sie in die Luft gestreckt. Er sucht die Feldhühner und findet – die Seitenwände eines Eindeckers.
> [...]
> Vor ihm – das ist gar kein Hase, sondern ein Steuermann, mit Pelz und Ledermütze. Der gibt acht auf Weisungen, die er bekommt und auf jedes Geräusch seines Motors. (Hans ohne Brot 1928, 13 ff.)[3]

---

[3] "Now – think! – the hare unscrews his ears, one by one, glues them together, sticks them in the beak of a partridge, blows on them, hey, how the propeller turns in the wind! [...] Hans settles down among the partridges. Friendly they move aside. Each one holds a little stick in its beak and in the middle of the sticks, which are joined together, sits Hans. [...] When they reached a certain height, Hans lowered his nose – until now he had stretched it in the air. He looks for the partridges and finds – the sides of a monoplane. [...] In front of him – that's not a rabbit at all, but a helmsman, with fur and a leather cap. He pays attention to the instructions he receives and to every sound his engine makes." (Hans ohne Brot 1928, 13 ff.)

So this hare also has detachable ears that it can use as a propeller. However, in Vaillant-Couturier's work we encounter a multiple metamorphosis of the fantastic vehicle, which Tetzner and Balázs have not adopted. It would have been difficult to portray on stage and would also contradict the reality model of the *Hans-Urian Stoff*, which is more influenced by the folk tale. Incidentally, Lisa Tetzner also came into contact with the original through a personal contact, she was friends with the illustrator of the German edition Maria Braun (cf. Dolle-Weinkauff 1984, 131). Lisa Tetzner took the name of the rabbit Trillewip from a fairy tale she edited, a Danish Rumpelstiltskin variant, while *Kagsaksuk, the poor orphan boy* comes from the Inuit fairy tale of the same name from this collection. Although this character does not appear in the play, he does play an essential role in Lisa Tetzner's children's novel published in 1931.

In view of her processing of the various influences, the idea suggests itself that Lisa Tetzner contributed a first (unpublished) version of the plot to the Hans Urian project in the form of an epic narrative or even in the form of a mere collection of *Stoffe*, which Béla Balász then politically and ideologically enriched and adapted for the stage.

The fact that a whole series of other works can be counted among the literary pretexts of the *Stoff*, whose direct use by the authors cannot be proven, should only be mentioned here in passing. For example, various fantastic world travel stories in picture book form, some of which also feature anthropomorphised rabbit figures (cf. Weinkauff/Dolle-Weinkauff 2005). Or – just as obvious – the motif of fantastic flight in children's theatre, which has enjoyed a certain popularity since the premiere of Gerdt von Bassewitz's Christmas fairy tale *Peterchens Mondfahrt* (1912). Almost at the same time as *Hans Urian geht nach Brot*, a play entitled *Fritzchens Flug zum Glück (Fritzchen's Flight to Happiness)* premiered in Berlin, which, according to the critics' descriptions, can almost be regarded as its infantilizing (kindertümelnder) bourgeois counterpart.[4]

The First Performance

Due to the great attention that the premiere of the play had received, certain elements of the staging can be reconstructed. The stage directions in the printed version are also indicative of the staging style. As is familiar from productions by

---

[4] "First of all in this 'fairy tale of today' we notice that the ultra-modern flight around the world is only partly made by means of a zeppelin at the end, while the actual start and record is completed on a stork's back. [...] Before his sportive trip around the world he quickly puts a little daughter into the cradle of the poor tailors, whereupon Fritzchen sits down on his back [...] and flies to Africa, where the [...] cannibal king Owambo lets himself be converted from evil human food to harmless calf's knuckle [...]. From the North Pole one then travels [...] to the car king Ford in America, who, because of the giant diamonds found in Africa, immediately engages in grandiose transactions with Fritzchen [...] and we sing a Christmas carol at the end in thanks for the giant diamond." (Diebold 1929)

Erwin Piscator, for example, the director used projection images, which were highlighted in various reviews as particular highlights of the production (cf. Milgr. 1929; Zavrel 1929). The stage directions provide for the use of banners in the flying scenes (with the silhouettes of the flying: Urian Brot, 16, 23, 38, 46). The backdrops are not meant to represent the settings of the play illusionistically, but merely to suggest them. Their signifying function is underlined by appropriate captions provided in the stage directions (e.g. "Hier wohnt Hans Urian mit seiner Mutter", ibid., 5). The stage design by Wolfgang Böttcher is praised in several reviews. In addition to the projection images, mention is made of the (two-dimensional) prop of a large steamer that was pulled across the playing surface (cf. Diebold 1929). In addition to these decidedly anti-illusionist, partly epic elements, several critics also emphasized the sporty, artistic performances of Rolf Müller in the role of Hans Urian (cf. e. b. 1929; Wilde 1929).

The printed version contains various humorous lazzi from the tradition of folk drama: slapstick, comedy of mistaken identity and Kasperly style linguistic comedy. The first meeting of Hans and the hare (Urian Brot, 13)[5] and that of the hare with the peasants (Urian Brot, 3rd picture, 17 ff.) has decidedly clownish features. In the scene with the "Negroes" the two colonial officers argue because they do not have a complete overview of the situation (Urian Brot, 9th picture, 47 ff.) and on arrival in New York a comic extempore by Hans rapidly turns into a telephone conversation with the hare (Urian Brot, 7th picture, 39 ff.).

In any case, the musical accompaniment by the jazz group of the Hungarian musician and composer Tibor Kasics, known from contemporary cabaret, added to the splendor of the production. The *Lexikon verfolgter Musiker* und *Musikerinnen der NS-Zeit* writes about the composer Wilhelm Grosz that he was "one of the most versatile talents that Central European musical life produced in the 1920s", that he was "equally successful as a composer, conductor, pianist and musicologist", and that his oeuvre encompassed "the genres of art song, opera, operetta, symphonic and chamber music, jazz, stage and film music, songs and Schlager" (Gayda 2010). He also collaborated with Béla Balász on another project: the dance grotesque *Baby in the Bar,* which premiered in Hanover in 1928 (Béla Balász was the librettist).

In addition, Erich Kästner had contributed two songs to the play, which, however, are not included in the printed version and unfortunately can only be reconstructed in fragments to this day. It is possible that there was even more singing in the premiere, as the reviews repeatedly mention couplets and choirs that encouraged the audience to sing along (cf. Wilde 1929; Bez-Mennicke 1930, 90). The critics' memorial quotations do not convey a flattering picture of the quality of the song lyrics; since they are always found in the context of politically motivated slurs, doubts about their authenticity are warranted: "Der Arbeiter, der gilt nichts auf der Welt / Die Reichen nur verdienen das Geld" (F. S. s. 1929) or "Der Arbeiter hat die Hölle auf Erden / Das muss anders werden" (Wilde 1929). The fact that the songs

---

[5] Short title for citation references from the play by Lisa Tetzner and Béla Balász *Hans Urian geht nach Brot* [EA 1929].

have disappeared is probably due to the reserved attitude Kästner took towards the Hans Urian project after its premiere. This is documented in one of his *letters to his mother:*

> Berlin, 14 Nov 29
> Dear, good mummy!
> Before I get down to work: a quick little letter to the very best. […] Yesterday was the premiere of the children's play 'Hans Urian geht nach Brot', for which I wrote a few children's songs. The first review I have read so far praised my work very much. Unfortunately, I didn't like my own songs very much. I heard them for the first time with music. Next time I will listen to them before the performance. […]
> Millions of greetings and kisses
> Your old boy
> (quoted in List 2010, 109)

In the printed version of the play there are three references to song interludes: at the first start of Hans and the Hare, at the return to his mother, and at the very end of the play (cf. Urian Brot 1929). Thus, two songs serve an important structuring function, marking the onset of the travel plot and formulating a political message appealing to the audience at the end. The memory quotations reproduced above probably document the impression that the final song left on critics. The first song may have contained the passage that Lisa Tetzner used as the motto of her novel:

> Er hatte keinen Reiseplan
> Und erst recht kein Geld für die Eisenbahn
> Wie die andern! Die andern!
> Doch von der Luft wird keines satt
> Und wer kein Brot im Hause hat
> Muß wandern! Muß wandern!
> (Urian Weltreise[6])

Reception as a Laienspiel Play

Although the play's premiere was so well received, it was not restaged in Germany on a professional scale until 1933. As far as is known, this did not happen in the 1968 period either, despite the interest in the left-wing children's theatre tradition that existed at the time. Only the blurb of the 1944 edition of the novel mentions a production of the play in Zurich around 1944.

However, there is an interesting indication of a contemporary reception of the play as an amateur play within the social-democratic workers' children's movement. The reference is noteworthy not only because it documents a shift from professional to amateur theatre and from communist to social democratic environments, but also because of the author's persona. In his autobiography, published in 1982, Willy Brandt recalls the following:

---

[6] Short title for citation references from the novel *Hans Urian. Die Geschichte einer Weltreise* by Lisa Tetzner [EA 1931]. Quoted according to the 1975 edition. English translation: He didn't have an itinerary / And certainly no money for the railroad/ Like the others! The others! / But no one gets enough of the air /And who has no bread in the house / Must hike! Must hike!

> In 1930, with 2500 participants, a Children's Republic was held at the Bay of Lübeck. The participants first visited the city and were all accommodated in private quarters. This was a remarkable achievement, but not unusual at the time. The festive opening in the Hansa Theatre with a play in which I played the leading role – 'Hans Urian geht nach Brot' – left me with a rather unpleasant memory: I had not learned my lines well. Without a capable prompter, this would have caused a medium-sized scandal. (Brandt 1982, 28)

Because the person in question resigned from the SPD much later due to local political disputes with the left-wing party youth in a way that attracted media attention, we also know who played the second leading role in 1930. Under the title *Parteiaustritt in Lübeck. Trillewipp verließ Urian* (*Party Resignation in Lübeck. Trillewipp left Urian*), the weekly *Die Zeit* reported on the incident. According to the report, Marga Krüger, a member of the Lübeck parliament, had already been a member of the *Rote Falken* in 1929 and had played the role of Hare in the performance of *Hans Urian geht nach Brot* alongside Willy Brandt (cf. Schönherr 1973). Even in the post-war period, namely in 1948 and 1956, two amateur play editions of the play identical to the first edition were still published by social democratic publishers.

From the Play to the Children's Novel

Lisa Tetzner's novel cannot be described as an adaptation of the 1929 play due to its of its complicated genesis. There is no doubt that the play already had an epic draft, most likely written by Lisa Tetzner, and the print version of the novel will be based on both this and the play or its drafts. In order not to drift too far into the realm of speculation, I would simply like to point out some significant differences between the two printed versions of the *Stoff* – the epic and the dramatic.

First of all, the plot of the novel is much more extensive, it includes two travel stops that are missing in the play (Greenland and the Soviet Union), and with the "Eskimo" boy Kagsagsuk and the American Bill, the Hans Urian of the novel gains two friends in the course of the plot who do not appear in the play. In general, the readers of the novel are offered different and more suggestive means of identification than the viewers of the play. The novel begins with an authorial exposition and is generally determined by an alternation of authorial and scenic-neutral narrative passages, as is also characteristic of Erich Kästner's children's literature, for example. In the play, the sparsely furnished stage space is transformed into a backdrop before the eyes of the audience, whereupon the action begins medias in res. In the novel, Hans Urian is initially frightened by the talking rabbit, who then knows how to reassure him by moralizing and psychologizing:

> ‚Guten Tag, Hase!' sagte Hans und freute sich, einen Hasen so nahe zu sehen.
> ‚Guten Tag, Hans Urian', antwortetet der Hase.
> Jetzt erschrak Hans noch mehr. 'Du kannst sprechen?' rief er. Das hatte er nicht erwartet. Er hatte noch nie gehört, daß ein Hase redet. 'Ja', sagte der Hase. 'Alle Hasen sprechen. Ihr Menschen wißt das nur nicht. Wir haben Angst vor euch, weil ihr uns jagt, und in der

Angst finden wir keine Worte. Aber du hast mich so freundlich wie deinesgleichen begrüßet. Das hat noch kein Mensch vor dir getan.' (Urian Weltreise, 11f.)[7]

In the play, both characters are less jumpy and considerably more belligerent (not only in the scene reproduced below), and Hans Urian's consternation in the face of the talking hare is acknowledged with a metafictional joke:

Hans: Wie kommt es, daß du sprechen kannst, wenn Du ein Hase bist? Das gibt es doch nicht. Kein Tier kann reden, wie der Mensch, nur der Papagei.
Hase: Ich bin aber kein gewöhnlicher Hase, ich bin ein Theaterhase und Theaterhasen können auch sprechen.
Hans: Theaterhasen? Hör mal, das ist ein Schwindel.
Hase: Was hast du zu reden? Du bist auch kein wirklicher Hans, sondern nur ein Theaterhans.
Hans: Das ist eigentlich wahr. Dann wollen wir nicht zanken. (Urian Brot, 13)[8]

In general, the encounter between man and animal in the novel tends to be the occasion for reflections critical of civilization, while the animal figures in the play tend to function as mouthpieces of political insights and experiences. At the beginning of the journey, Hans and the Hare encounter a talking horse, which in the play is eloquently agitated by the Hare (cf. Hans Urian geht nach Brot 1929, 19). In the novel, this episode is dealt with much more succinctly, as an encounter between wild animal and farm animal. While its owner, the farmer, confronts the two travellers with suspicion and has already set out to alert the local hunter, the good-natured horse invites them to share his meal. The following dialogue ensues:

‚Ich heiße Trillewipp', sagte der Hase und kam näher.
‚Ich heiße Liese', sagte das Pferd und stieß dem Hasen mit dem Huf den Hafer zu.
‚Puh, Liese ist ein Menschenname', sagte der Hase verächtlich.
‚Ja, leider', nickte das Pferd. ‚Mein Herr, der Bauer hat ihn mir gegeben.'
Der Hase war froh, daß er Hafer fressen konnte. Er knackte ihn zwischen den Zähnen und schluckte sehr. (Urian Weltreise, 21)[9]

The fact that Lisa Tetzner varied the motif of the cross-class friendship between children from Kästner's *Emil und die Detektive* in her novel was resented by left-wing critics, and several later adaptations of the *Stoff* use this motif to make it clear

---

[7] 'Good-day, Hare!' said Hans, delighted to see a hare so near. 'Good day, Hans Urian,' replies the hare. Now Hans was even more frightened. 'You can speak?' he cried. He had not expected that. He had never heard a hare talk before. 'Yes,' said the hare. 'All hares talk. You humans just don't know that. We are afraid of you because you hunt us, and in fear we cannot find words. But you greeted me as kindly as your kind. No man has ever done that before you.'
[8] Hans: How come you can talk when you are a rabbit? There is no such thing. No animal can talk like man, only the parrot. / Hare: But I am not an ordinary hare, I am a theatre hare and theatre hares can also talk. / Hans: Theatre hares? Listen, this is a fake. / Hare: What have you to talk about? You are not a real Hans either, but only a theatre Hans. / Hans: That's actually true. Let's not bicker then.
[9] "My name is Trillewipp," said the hare, coming closer. "My name is Liese," said the horse, nudging the hare's oats with his hoof. "Pooh, Liese is a human name," the hare said scornfully. "Yes, unfortunately," nodded the horse. "My lord, the farmer gave it to me." The hare was glad that he could eat oat. He cracked it between his teeth and swallowed very hard.

that such friendships are doomed to failure under capitalist conditions. In the play, there is only the friendship between Hans and the hare, which itself experiences a comparatively less emotional portrayal and is by no means the central theme of the play.

History of Translation and Editing

The first edition of the book was published in 1931 by Gundert in Stuttgart with illustrations by Bruno Fuck (i.e. Boris Dimitrow Angeluschew). It is highly probable that there was already a draft for a story by Lisa Tetzner before the play was printed and premiered, which formed the basis for Béla Balász's adaptation; the story was not published until 1931. Five further German-language editions or runs of the book could be identified in 1944, 1948, 1949 and 1975, all identical in text and all with illustrations by Bruno Fuck but partly altered typesetting and title design. In 1944 the book was published by Büchergilde Gutenberg in Zurich, with a blurb by Hermann Hesse taken from his review of the first edition. Lisa Tetzner's preface contains programmatic statements on the continuing topicality of the themes of her narrative and references to the numerous translations the work had undergone in the meantime. The importance of the former to her throughout her life is also documented by the name of the house in Ticino where she and her husband Kurt Kläber-Held had offered shelter to numerous exiled writers during the Nazi regime: Casa Pantrova, the House of Found Bread.

Most of the translations appeared in publishing houses that also published other translations by exiled German-language children's book authors. The first (into Italian), however, appeared as early as 1932 and the last (into Danish) in 1948. Bruno Fuck's illustrations were adopted in all translations, some adopting the complete design, including the title illustration, while others chose a different title design or cover illustrations more determined by children's literary conventions, making it clear that the book tells of a fantastic journey around the world that is also marked by entertaining exoticism (Fig. 1a, b, c).

A year before the translation, a German edition intended for school use was published in Poland in 1936, with Polish explanations and suggestions for a newly reformed oriented lesson with the book.

The publication of the 1949 German edition by Verlag Weiß was the subject of a dispute with the American censorship authorities, who initially banned the book in October 1949 and held out the prospect of printing permission in the event that the two chapters dealing with America and the Soviet Union were deleted. After a lively correspondence between Lisa Tetzner and the officer responsible for the matter in Berlin and public criticism in the fall of 1949, the book was finally allowed to appear unabridged, as the story goes (cf. Geus 1997, 192–195). However, the edition cannot be found in any library.

Fig. 1 (**a**) Cover of the original edition of *Hans Urian. Die Geschichte einer Weltreise* and (**b**) of the Dutch and (**c**) Spanish translations (cf. The bibliography at the end of this article for the titles of the covers)

The last German edition to date was published in 1975 as a Rotfuchs paperback – with the text unchanged, the illustrations by Bruno Fuck, a title illustration reminiscent of Nils Holgersson and a slightly nonsensical, whimsical land of milk and honey fantasy in Jan Schniebel's cover comic (Fig. 2).

Continuations

Lisa Tetzner's story of the starving working-class boy who, through his journey on the back of a hare endowed with magical powers, comes to see the world in a socialist light, however, has been carried on beyond the dramatization. Two of these continuations will be examined here: Fritz Rosenfeld's children's novel *Tirilin reist um die Welt* (EA 1931) and the illustrated story *Ulle Bam's wundersame Reise um die Erde* by Eva Maria Haasis and Georg Willroda with drawings by Kurt Rübner (1949).

Fritz Rosenfeld, who before the children's novel had already written two choral works and a novel set in the milieu of the film industry, and who worked as a feature editor for the social-democratic Wiener *Arbeiterzeitung*, was most likely in personal contact with Béla Balász. It is obvious that he drew impulses from the play *Hans Urian geht nach Brot*. After all, the Berlin premiere was a public event and the printed version was in the public domain. Tirilin, who unlike Hans Urian is an orphan, is also prompted to make his journey by hunger and need; he too travels in the company of a magical animal figure and eventually returns home with a consolidated class consciousness.

With few deviations, the course of the world journey is the same. First, events in the protagonists' immediate rural surroundings are depicted or narrated, highlighting the plot conflict and the story's model of reality. The subsequent fantastic

Fig. 2 *Hans Urian. The story of a journey around the world* (Tetzner © Reinbek: Rowohlt, 1975)

journey takes the protagonists across the ocean, where they experience class society in the microcosm of a large passenger ship. Other stations in all three texts are America, Africa and China, in Lisa Tetzner's novel also Greenland and the Soviet Union, and in Fritz Rosenfeld's a rather fairytale-like Orient. The fairy-tale elements in his novel, however, are part of an enlightened calculation on his part.

Unlike Lisa Tetzner and Béla Balász, Fritz Rosenfeld primarily tells a story of disillusionment. For Tirilin was looking for a fairy-tale land and believed himself to be understood in his longing for happiness, prosperity and justice by a friend of the same age who, however, is at home on the other side of class society. Such a figure does not appear in the play *Hans Urian geht nach Brot,* but he does in Lisa Tetzner's novel in the form of the American factory owner's son Bill.

This depiction of a child friendship that transcends class in the manner of Erich Kästner's children's novels must have seemed suspicious to left-wing critics of the novel (cf. Dolle-Weinkauff 1984, 133). It almost seems as if Fritz Rosenfeld, anticipating such criticism, had taken up the motif and changed it, for in contrast to the friendship of Hans Urian and Bill, that of Tirilin and Bob fails painfully because of class antagonism. And in the end Tirilin understands the fairy-tale land only as a metaphor for the socialist future, which the working people must create by their own efforts. It therefore seems highly probable that Fritz Rosenfeld knew not only the play but also a draft version by Lisa Tetzner.

With the magical animal figure, the ship's voyage, and the travel stops in America and China, Fritz Rosenfeld not only adopts the didactic intentionality but also essential parts of the content of his narrative from the literary pretexts. The novel is therefore far from being in the area of plagiarism, but rather an adaptation or, more precisely, a kind of counterfactual. Its originality lies exactly in its narrative style. Although, like Lisa Tetzner's story, it contains plenty of authorial elements in keeping with the children's literary tradition, and the characters are laid out in a planar rather than psychologically individualising manner, recipients are directed to a much lesser extent than in both *Hans Urian versions*. Instead, the narrative instance is limited to reproducing the protagonist's childlike naïve view of the world, which only proves illusory at the end.

In addition, unlike Hans Urian, Tirilin also travels in fairy-tale-like, fantastic spaces of action, which, staged in a parable-like manner, become the settings for enlightened, didactic symbolic actions. This model of reality determines the subsequent tale *Der Flug ins Karfunkelland* in toto, while *Der Regenbogen fährt nach Masagara* has no fantastic elements at all. The two works of the Exilliteratur share the enlightenment-didactic intentionality with *Tirilin reist um die Welt*, which is why they can also be seen in a broader sense as extensions of the narrative cosmos around Hans Urian. The many translations of *Tirilin reist um die Welt* also undoubtedly contributed to the continued existence of the *Stoff*/motif complex.

Following on from this, Eva Maria Haasis and Georg Willroda wrote their tale *Ulle Bam's wundersame Reise um die Erde,* which was determined by the misery of children in the post-war period, peace pathos, reformist pedagogical thinking and great sympathies for the socialist-communist world movement, and which was furnished by Kurt Rübner with double-page coloured maps and black-and-white illustrations framing the text. In the story, the character of Ulle Bam, a myth-enshrouded child friend, has taken the place of the magical animal figures. Ulle Bam also has a fantastic travel vehicle in the form of the feather on his pith helmet with the help of which he and the two children Finele and Marcel take to the skies. As in the other texts belonging to the *Stoff*-motif complex, hunger is the starting point and the acquisition of insights into the unjust distribution of wealth in the world is the actual goal of the journey. The book is a typical example of a trend in children's literature of the post-war period, equally found in East and West, which I call 'children's literature of international understanding' (cf. Weinkauff 2017, 222 ff.). The exaltation of the classic characters of international children's literature into ambassadors of peace fits in with this – an idea that Jella Lepman, Erich Kästner and Walter Trier also shaped at the same time in their famous children's literary peace parable *Die Konferenz der Tiere*. The second *Ulle Bam* episode (*Ulle Bam auf neuer Fahrt*), published in 1953, the year of Stalin's death, hardly shows any such intersections. The journey now takes us to the sites of the Soviet Union's major power diversion and dam projects, and gives the protagonists stirring encounters with North Korean war orphans. As it seems, censorship had its effects on this particular novel.

The DEFA Hand Puppet Film

As with several other contemporary productions by the DEFA animation studio in Dresden, we are dealing with a combination of hand puppet and animation techniques with partly painted, partly three-dimensional backdrops. Cast and crew were prominent: The director Gerda Hammer-Wallburg and the puppeteers (Walter Später, Werner Hammer, Johannes Walter, Hans Claus and Arnim Rüdiger) had already appeared in various productions. With Helmut Straßburger, Traute Richter, Rudolf Fleck and Ferdinand Felsko, well-known actors were involved in the production as narrators. The composer Hans Sandig had founded the Leipzig Radio Children's Choir in 1948, with its orchestra he recorded the theme tune for the GDR Sandman. He also produced the Christmas song *Sind die Lichter angezündet,* which was hardly less popular in the GDR. The puppets were created by the sculptor Dietrich Nitzsche, who had been working for DEFA since 1959.

The screenshot (Fig. 3) shows the hare flanked by a Soviet pioneer who welcomes the companions to the last of three countries they have visited. The fact that the film seems a little ponderous in comparison with other contemporary DEFA animated film productions is due to the authorial framing of the action by an off-screen voice, to external features such as the antiquated fractal script in the opening credits, but also to the overly simplistic political message.

The novel by Lisa Tetzner is less likely to have served as a model than the play, the filmmakers only used it as an idea. In other words, the plot was taken over in a reduced form, without Africa, a travel destination dominated by exoticism, and without China, which had become politically problematic in the meantime, so that DEFA's Hans Urian only travels to America, the North Pole and the Soviet Union. In America he meets the capitalist's son from Lisa Tetzner's novel, who, however, unlike the "Eskimo" boy Kagsagsuk, does not become his friend, but appears as an antagonist from the start. Because they witnessed the destruction of wheat in

Fig. 3 *Hans Urian holt Brot.* Hand puppet film (DEFA 1961)

America, the three travelling companions have to leave the continent in a hurry, only to experience all the more security in the motherland of all working people. Afterwards, Hans Urian returns to his mother with a Soviet loaf of bread in his hand, richer by many experiences, and recovers from the strains of the journey. The voice-over ends the film rhyming in the manner of the Sandman: "Nun Kinder, seid schön leise. / In seinem Traume loht ein herrliches Backofenfeuer. / Und Brote liegen dort bereit, / und die sind nicht zu teuer. / Er träumt von unserer Zeit."[10]

Worth mentioning is the music, which – similar to the 1929 play – fulfils both an emotionalising and a dramatising effect on as well as illustrative and structuring functions for the listener. In addition to atmospheric instrumental music, which has hints of jazz during the arrival in New York and echoes of Russian folk music during the arrival in the Soviet cornfield, there is a song in three verses, one of which is sung in each of the flight sequences: at the start of the world journey, after the "Eskimo" boy Kagsagsuk has joined them, and during the escape from America. It is not entirely improbable that some of the artists involved in the film knew the 1929 production from their own experience and that their memories of it were incorporated into the film production. The scenography of the film could also have been influenced by that of the play.

Is the Hans Urian Project a Medienverbund (*Media Network*)?

Although this contribution appears in an anthology on the history of children's and youth literature m*edia networks*, this term is avoided in it. It therefore makes sense to address the terminological problems explaining this reticence in the conclusion.

The term "Kindermedienverbund", which in English-language research can be translated as *commercial supersystem* or *children's global multimedia,* among others (cf. Kurwinkel 2017, 14), or as *children's media network*, as it is handled in this volume, has been widely used in the German-speaking world since the mid-1990s.[11] In cultural and media studies research, this term is usually aimed predominantly at the cross-media dissemination of popular culture *Stoffe*, and occasionally even the terms *media network* and *merchandising* are used synonymously.

Hans-Heino Ewers formulated a special position in his 2004 article *Die Göttersagen der Gegenwart. Die Medienverbundangebote sind die großen Narrationen unserer Zeit*: he assigns genre characteristics to the *media networks* and describes them as a "hypermedia genre in which the plurimedial staging is intended from the outset" (Ewers 2004, 5) and which for this reason cannot be approached with traditional literary categories such as the concept of adaptation. It

---

[10] "Now, children, be quiet. / In his dream a wonderful oven fire is blazing. / And loaves of bread lie ready there, / and they are not too expensive. / He dreams of our time."
[11] Cf. Hengst 1994, Wermke 1998 as well as Josting 2001 and – in summary – 2012.

seems to me that it is less the concept of genre that is relevant here than the differentiation of the *media network* from other potentially cross-media phenomena, such as that of adaptation. I myself would also describe cross-media literary offerings that do not belong to popular mass culture but are rather to be regarded as artistically sophisticated avant-garde products as *media networks*, insofar as the *Stoffe* in question are actually staged plurimedially and the cross-media production and distribution processes cannot be adequately described with the term adaptation (cf. Weinkauff/von Glasenapp 2017, 213 ff.).

However, I tend to define the term more narrowly than Petra Josting, who in her contribution to the Handbuch *Kinder- und Jugendliteratur der Gegenwart* proposes a concept of a *media network* for which "from a technological perspective" a *media network* can already be assumed to exist "when there is a second exploitation" (Josting 2012, 393), which is why she consequently considers C. A. Görner's Christmas fairy tale productions in the mid-nineteenth century, which adapt Grimm's fairy tale *Stoff*, to be *media network* phenomena.

Research on media development in the context of the history of children's and young adult literature in the eighteenth, nineteenth and early twentieth centuries is an important desideratum; in particular, far too little light has been shed on cross-media phenomena, and it makes absolute sense to search for terms that make it clear that we encounter such phenomena not only in the present. And, of course, concepts of media or media networks grounded in cultural studies or sociology are conceivable that are not primarily aimed at describing cross-media presentation and discourse of *Stoffe* or texts, but at phenomena of reception and impact in the broadest sense. The Werther fever of the late eighteenth century could also be described on such a theoretical basis, as suggested by the editors of this volume at the second project conference, as a *media network* phenomenon (cf. also Andree 2006). The question is whether such a broad concept of media makes sense for research in literary studies.

It also seems unclear to me whether it makes sense to speak of *media networks* even when there are large historical distances between the individual media versions or media-induced impact phenomena, or whether it is better to reserve the term for cases where the versions tend to be available simultaneously. In the first case, one would have to say, for example, that the dramatic work of Carlo Goldoni and the commedia dell'arte or the Children's and Household Tales of the Brothers Grimm and their written and oral models form *media networks*. For current research on children's and young people's literature and media, I see a need for conceptual differentiation, for example between national and international, popular-cultural and high-cultural, serial and non-serial media networks or those that are associated with simple or complex, static or dynamic concepts of addressees. A uniform labelling of the most diverse phenomena as *media networks*, however, does not necessarily contribute to differentiation.

In no way the complex of *Stoffe* and motifs surrounding Hans Urian is a media network in the same way as those surrounding the Heidi and Pinocchio anime from the late 1970s, Paul Maar's Sams or Princess Lillifee. Its genesis documents how, within the framework of certain discourses on children's culture in the environment of the political left, a *literarischer Stoff* is developed in various media versions and later also perpetuated. In this process, it seems, concepts of individual authorship were not so much transgressed as violated, and in attempting to reconstruct the shares of the various authors, it makes sense to examine the shaping of the two central media versions and also the updates by Fritz Rosenfeld and Georg Willroda as adaptation processes.

While the literary pretexts of these two versions can be located in different media contexts (a song, children's literary narrative texts and picture books, children's plays), the continuations take place preferably in the book medium, namely in the form of epic narratives. The DEFA hand puppet film is probably more of a late adaptation than a phenomenon of *media network* in the narrow sense, especially if one takes into account that Lisa Tetzner's novel was not even printed in the GDR and that the amateur play booklet from 1948 (in which her name is not mentioned) was certainly long out of print by the time the film was premiered. The film's recipients therefore did not have access to the earlier media versions of the *Stoff*.

There are undoubtedly other sources of influence for the genesis of this *Stoff* beyond the immediate literary pretexts, and the consideration that Lisa Tetzner's development into a realistic, left-wing author was influenced by her experiences working with a children's group in radio cannot be dismissed out of hand. It is also quite possible that Lisa Tetzner worked on parts of the *Stoff* of an early book manuscript in radio and that it could thus serve as a model for Fritz Rosenfeld.

Apart from this, the complex intertextual network surrounding Hans Urian is only partially cross-media in nature, and an exclusive focus on media aspects would narrow the view of the subject matter. Therefore, the instruments of a cross-media history of *Stoffe* and motifs, intertextuality research and the concept of media adaptation seemed to me to be more productive for the *Hans Urian project* than the concept of a *media network*.

References

Primary Literature

Original Versions Incl. Reprints and Translations

Balázs, Béla: Hans Urian geht nach Brot. Eine Kindermärchenkomodie von heute. Mit Verwendung einiger Ideen von Lisa Tetzner. Freiburg: Max Reichhard [1929]; weitere Ausgaben ohne Nennung Lisa Tetzners: Hamm: Hasselbeck, 1948 (Die Falkenbuhne; 5), Hannover: Schaffende Jugend, 1956 (Schriftenreihe Laienspiel; 5).

Tetzner, Lisa: Hans Urian. Die Geschichte einer Weltreise. Ill. Bruno Fuck [d. i. Boris Dimitrow Angeluschew]. Stuttgart: Gundert, 1931; Zürich: Büchergilde Gutenberg, 1944 und ²1948; Berlin: Weiss, [1949]; Jena: Arbeitsgemeinschaft thüring. Verleger, [1949]; Wien: Wiener Volksbuchverlag, 1948; Mainz: Bücherring, [1948]; Reinbek: Rowohlt, 1975.

Tetzner, Lisa: Hans gira il mondo. Übers. von Lucia Taparella. Mailand: Bompiani, 1932.

Tetzner, Lisa: Hans Urian. De Geschiedenis van een Wereldreis. Übers. von Bep van Eck. Den Haag: Van Goor Zonen, 1933.
Tetzner, Lisa: Masʿēj Hans ʾUrjān. Übers. von Ben-Chawwa, Isaak: Tel Aviv: Hōṣāʾat sefārim Mišpāh, 1934a.
Tetzner, Lisa: Kom med ut i världen. Illustrationen av Bruno Fuk. Übers. von Dan Byström. Stockholm: Homström, 1934b.
Tetzner, Lisa: Hans sees the world. Übers. von Margaret Goldsmitz. New York: Covici-Friede, 1934c.
Tetzner, Lisa: Hans Urian: die Geschichte einer Weltreise. Hg. von Edward Buczowski. Lemberg [u. a.]: Książnica Atlas, 1936.
Tetzner, Lisa: Podróż Janka naokoło świata. Übers. von Lila Friedländerowa. Krakau: Księgarnia Powszechna, 1937a.
Tetzner, Lisa: Hans y su liebre encantada. Historia de un viaje alrededor del mundo. Übers. von José María Quiroga Plá. Valencia: Estrella, 1937b.
Tetzner, Lisa: Hans Urian putuje oko sveta. Übers. von Lj. Gosić. Belgrad: Nolit, 1938.
Tetzner, Lisa: Hannun maailmanmatka. Übers. von Sivi Kortelainen. Helsinki: Kustannusosakeyhtiö Tammi, 1944.
Tetzner, Lisa: Trillevip rejser med Jorden rundt. Übers. von Baeklund og Mogens Hjort. Kopenhagen: Fremad, 1948.

Literary Pretexts

Bassewitz, Gerdt von: Peterchens Mondfahrt. UA Leipzig 1912; Peterchens Mondfahrt. Ein Märchenspiel in vier Bildern. Leipzig: Wolff, 1912; Peterchens Mondfahrt. Mit Bildern von Hans Baluschek. Berlin: Klemm, [1915].
Beskow, Elsa: Hänschen im Blaubeerenwald. Mit Reimen von Karsten Brandt. [Stuttgart: Loewe, 1903] [schwed. EA: Puttes äventyr i blåbärsskogen 1901].
Caspari, Gertrud: Kinderfriese und Kinderbilder. Leipzig: Voigtländer, [1904].
Claudius, Matthias: Urians Reise um die Welt. Mit Anmerkungen. Erstdruck im Vossischen Musenalmanach (1786), 166.
Claudius, Matthias: Urians Reise um die Welt. Mit Bildern von Irene von Richthofen-Winkel. Köln: Schaffstein, 1930.
Ginzkey, Franz Karl: Hatschi Bratschis Luftballon. Ill.: Mor von Sunnegg. Berlin: Seemann, 1904.
Kutzer, Ernst/Holst, Adolf: Der Osterhas auf Reisen. Stuttgart: Levy und Müller, 1917.
Lagerlöf, Selma: Die wunderbare Reise des kleinen Nils Holgersson mit den Wildgänsen. Übers. von Pauline Klaiber. Ill.: Wilhelm Schulz. München: Langen, 1920 [EA dieser Übers. 1907/1908; schwed. EA 1906].
Lagerlöf, Selma: Nils Holgerssons underbara resa genom Sverige. 2 Bde. Stockholm: Albert Bonniers, förlag 1906/1907.
Negermärchen. Für die Jugend. bearb. und hg. von Lisa Tetzner. Mit Federzeichnungen von Irene von Richthofen-Winkel. Köln: Schaffstein, [1931].
Rikli, Herbert: Hasen-Königs Weltreise. Fahrten und Abenteuer in Bildern und Versen Basel: Frobenius, 1918.
Tetzner, Lisa: Die schönsten Märchen der Welt für 365 und einen Tag. Mit 14 farbigen Tafeln und 123 Textabbildungen von Maria Braun. Jena: Diederichs, 1926.
Vaillant-Couturier, Paul: Hans-ohne-Brot (Dt. Ausg. von Anna Nussbaum). Berlin: Verl. d. Jugendinternationale, 1928.
Vaillant-Couturier, Paul: Jean sans pain. Histoire pour tous les enfants. Ill.: Picart le Doux. Paris: Éd. Clarté, 1921.

Continuations

Evmari [d. i. Eva Maria Haasis]/Willroda, Georg: Ulle Bams wundersame Reise um die Erde. Mit Zeichnungen von Kurt Rübner. Dresden: Dresdener Verlagsgesellschaft, 1949 und ²1950.

Feld, Friedrich [d. i. Fritz Rosenfeld]: Der Flug ins Karfunkelland: Eine fast wahre Geschichte voll seltsamer Abenteuer. Wien: Jungbrunnen, 1948 und ²1955.

Feld, Friedrich [d. i. Fritz Rosenfeld]: Der Regenbogen fährt nach Masagara. Ein Kinderbuch. Prag: Staatliche Verlagsanstalt, 1938 (Deutsche Jugendbücherei; 14); Wien: Jungbrunnen, 1950 und ³1961; Wien: Büchergilde Gutenberg, 1950; Neubearb. Ausg. Wien [u. a.]: Obelisk, 1971 (Stern-Taschenbücher; 18).

Hans Urian holt Brot. Handpuppenflm (DDR 1961). Regie: Gerda Hammer-Wallburg. Nach einre Idee von Lisa Tezner [Kopie bei der DEFA-Stiftung].

Kästner, Erich: Die Konferenz der Tiere. Nach einer Idee Jella Lepmans. Ill. von Walter Trier. Zürich: Europa, 1949.

Rosenfeld, Fritz: Tirilin reist um die Welt. Leipzig [u. a.]: Prager, 1931; Wien: Jungbrunnen, 1951.

Willroda, Georg: Ulle Bam auf neuer Fahrt. Bilder von Kurt Rübner. Berlin: Altberliner, 1953.

Filmography

Hans Urian holt Brot. Handpuppenfilm (DDR 1961). Regie: Gerda Hammer-Wallburg. Nach einer Idee von Lisa Tetzner [Kopie bei der DEFA-Stiftung].

Theatrography

Balázs, Béla: Hans Urian geht nach Brot. Eine Kindermärchenkomödie von heute. Mit Verwendung einiger Ideen von Lisa Tetzner. Freiburg: Max Reichhard [1929]; weitere Ausgaben ohne Nennung Lisa Tetzners: Hamm: Hasselbeck, 1948 (Die Falkenbühne; 5), Hannover: Schaffende Jugend, 1956 (Schriftenreihe Laienspiel; 5).

Bassewitz, Gerdt von: Peterchens Mondfahrt. UA Leipzig 1912; Peterchens Mondfahrt. Ein Märchenspiel in vier Bildern. Leipzig: Wolf, 1912; Peterchens Mondfahrt. Mit Bildern von Hans Baluschek. Berlin: Klemm, [1915].

Lustig, Ludwig [Ps.?]: Fritzchens Flug zum Glück. Nach einer Idee von Eugen Klöpfer. Musik von Eugen Klöpfer. UA Berlin: Dt. Volkstheater, 1929.

Secondary Literature Before 1945

Balász, Béla: Das Kindertheater. In: Arbeiterbühne 16 (1929a) 12, 1–2.

Balász, Béla: Das neue Kindertheater. Gespräch mit Bela Balasz [sic!] und Fritz Gentschow [sic!]. In: Welt am Abend (1929b) 248 vom 23.10.

Bez-Mennicke, Trude: Proletarisches Kindertheater. In: Neue Blätter für den Sozialismus 1 (1930) 2, 88–90.

e. b. [Ps.]: Hans Urian geht nach Brot. Lessing-Theater. In: Vorwärts 53 (1929) Spätausg. vom 14.11.

F. S. s. [Ps.]: Kommunistische Kindererziehung im Lessing-Theater. In: Berliner Lokal-Anzeiger 46 (1929) Morgenausg. vom 14.11.
Diebold, Bernhard: Kinder-Theater. In: Frankfurter Zeitung 74 (1929) vom 02.12., 898.
Friedländer, Paul: Das neue Kindertheater. Ein paar Bemerkungen. In: Welt am Abend 7 (1929) vom 28.10., 252.
Klarstellung. In: Die Welt am Abend 7 (1929) vom 13.11.
Milgr. [Ps.]: „Hans Urian geht nach Brot". Eine Kindermärchenkomödie? In: Berliner Zeitung am Mittag 25 (1929) vom 14.11.
Tetzner, Lisa: Fort vom ‚Wunder'. In: Berliner Tageblatt 57 (1929) vom 17.10.
Tetzner, Lisa: Meine Erfahrungen als Märchenerzählerin und meine Einstellung und Arbeit von 1918 bis heute. In: Die Neue Erziehung 12 (1930) 1, 20–24.
Tetzner, Lisa: Vorwort. In: Dies. (Hg.): Siebenschön. Ein sommerliches Liebesspiel. München: Kaiser, 1926 (Münchener Laienspiele; 22), 3.
Wilde, Richard: Politisiertes Kindertheater. „Hans Urian geht nach Brot" im Lessing-Theater. In: 3. Beiblatt des Achtuhr-Abendblattes der National-Zeitung 81 (1929) vom 14.11., 267.
Zavrel, Lotte: Hans Urian geht nach Brot. Lessing-Theater. In: Vossische Zeitung (1929) Morgen-Ausg. vom 14.11., 2018.

Secondary Literature After 1945

Andree, Martin: Wenn Texte töten. Über Werther, Medienwirkung und Mediengewalt. München 2006.
Bolius, Gisela: Lisa Tetzner. Leben und Werk. Frankfurt a. M. 1997. Zugl.: Berlin, TU, Diss, 1995.
Brandt, Willy: Links und frei. Mein Weg 1930–1950. Hamburg 1982.
Dolle-Weinkauff, Bernd: Das Märchen in der proletarisch-revolutionären Kinder- und Jugendliteratur der Weimarer Republik von 1918–1933. Frankfurt a. M. 1984 (Jugend und Medien; 8). Zugl.: Frankfurt a. M., Univ., Diss, 1983.
Ewers, Hans-Heino: Die Göttersagen der Gegenwart. Die Medienverbundangebote sind die großen Narrationen unserer Zeit. In: Tausend und ein Buch 18 (2004) 2, 1–10.
Gayda, Thomas: Wilhelm Grosz. In: Maurer Zenck, Claudia/Petersen, Peter (Hg.): Lexikon verfolgter Musiker und Musikerinnen der NS-Zeit. Hamburg 2010, https://www.lexm.uni-hamburg.de/object/lexm_lexmperson_00002583 (02.09.2020).
Geus, Elena: ‚Die Überzeugung ist das einzige, was nicht geopfert werden darf'. Lisa Tetzner (1894–1963). Lebensstationen – Arbeitsfelder. Frankfurt a. M., Univ., Diss, 1997.
Hengst, Heinz: Der Medienverbund in der Kinderkultur. Ensembles, Erfahrungen und Resistenzen im Mediengebrauch. In: Hiegemann, Susanne/Swoboda, Wolfgang H. (Hg.): Handbuch der Medienpädagogik. Theorieansätze, Traditionen, Praxisfelder, Forschungsperspektiven. Opladen 1994, 239–254.
Hoffmann, Ludwig/Pfützner, Klaus (Hg.): Theater der Kollektive, Bd. 1. Berlin 1980.
Josting, Petra: Medienverbund, Deutschunterricht und Medienkompetenz. In: Beiträge Jugendliteratur und Medien 53 (2001) 3, 174–185.
Josting, Petra: Kinder- und Jugendliteratur im Medienverbund. In: Lange, Günter (Hg.): Kinder- und Jugendliteratur der Gegenwart. Ein Handbuch. Baltmannsweiler: Schneider 2012, 391–420.
Karrenbrock, Helga: Märchenkinder – Zeitgenossen. Untersuchungen zur Kinderliteratur der Weimarer Republik. Stuttgart 1995. Zugl.: Osnabrück, Univ., Diss., 1993; ²2001.
Kurwinkel, Tobias.: Zur Theorie von Medien-und Produktverbünden. In: kjl&m 69 (2017) 2, 14–21.
List, Sylvia (Hg.): Meine Mutter zu Wasser und zu Lande. Geschichten, Gedichte, Briefe [von Erich Kästner]. Zürich 2010.

Lokatis, Siegfried: Ulle Bam unterwegs. In: Berliner Zeitung 58 (2003) vom 28.10., http://www.berliner-zeitung.de/15459724 (31.08.2017).
Merseburger, Peter: Willy Brandt 1913–1992. Visionär und Realist. München 2002.
Savoy, Sonja S.: Die Utopie des Märchenlands. Eine Wiederentdeckung des vergessenen Kinder- und Jugendbuchautors Friedrich Feld. Wien, Univ., Diss., 2014, http://othes.univie.ac.at/33614/1/2014-04-29_0103224.pdf (02.09.2020).
Schönherr, Hans: Parteiaustritt in Lübeck. Trillewipp verließ Urian. In: Die Zeit 28 (1973) vom 12.1., 3, http://www.zeit.de/1973/03/trillewipp-verliess-urian?print (02.09.2020).
Tetzner, Lisa: So kam ich zum Jugendbuch. In: Jugendliteratur 1 (1955) 1, 16.
Weber, Inge: Zum epischen Werk Lisa Tetzners für Kinder und Jugendliche. Zwickau, PH, Diss., 1986.
Weinkauff, Gina: Lisa Tetzner. Eine realistische Geschichtenerzählerin. In: Kinder- und Jugendliteraturforschung 1994/95 (1995), 47–53.
Weinkauff, Gina: ‚Verzähl Er doch weiter Herr Urian'. Phantastische Weltreisen in der Kinderliteratur. In: Härle, Gerhard/Weinkauff, Gina (Hg.): Am Anfang war das Staunen. Wirklichkeitsentwürfe in der Kinder- und Jugendliteratur. [Festschrift für Bernhard Rank]. Hohengehren 2005, 149–166.
Weinkauff, Gina: Bauen Kinderbücher Brücken? Kinder- und Jugendliteratur im Kulturtransfer. In: Dies./Glasenapp, Gabriele von (Hg.): Kinder- und Jugendliteratur (2010). Paderborn [u. a.] ³2017, 222–247.
Weinkauff, Gina/Dolle-Weinkauff, Bernd: Esterhazys Ahnen: Reisende Hasen im Kinderbuch der 20er und 30er Jahre. In: Josting, Petra/Fähnders, Walter (Hg.): ‚Laboratorium Vielseitigkeit'. Zur Literatur der Weimarer Republik. Festschrift für Helga Karrenbrock. Bielefeld 2005, 433–445.
Weinkauff, Gina/Glasenapp, Gabriele von: Die Medien der Kinder- und Jugendliteratur. In: Dies./Dies. (Hg.): Kinder- und Jugendliteratur (2010). Paderborn [u. a.] ³2017, 192–221.
Wermke, Jutta: Kinder- und Jugendliteratur in den Medien oder: Der Medienverbund als ästhetische Herausforderung. In: Rupp, Gerhard (Hg.): Ästhetik im Prozess. Opladen [u. a.] 1998, 179–218.
Zonneveld, Johan: Bibliographie Erich Kästner, Bd. 1., Primärliteratur und Zeittafel. Bielefeld 2011.

Fairy Tales in Film and Radio

"That Was a Wonderful Fairy Tale!"

Der fliegende Koffer by H. C. Andersen in the Media Network

Annika Behler

Introduction

Hans Christian Andersen's fairy tale *Der fliegende Koffer* (EA 1839), which as an original text represents the starting point of an extensive and multifaceted media network, crosses media boundaries to the same extent as centuries. To this day, the popularity of Andersen's fairy tales seems unbroken, and the stream of publications – whether in form of anthologies or as individual editions – never ceases. The continuing interest in the Danish author, albeit regularly increasing around the (pre-)Christmas season, also becomes clear when looking at the 'Google Trends' of the last fifteen years, which also reveal two short periods in which Andersen received particular attention on the Internet: Around his 200th birthday in April 2005, and five years later, when Google celebrated the poet with five *Thumbelina doodles* (see Doodle Archive, April 2, 2010). Also honored with a Google Doodle for her birthday was the silhouette artist Lotte Reiniger (cf. ibid., June 2, 2016). What these two artists have in common, however, is not limited to a virtual tribute to their life's work but goes far beyond that. In addition to their fascination with fairy tales, they also shared an enthusiasm for making silhouettes (see, e.g., Happ 2018; Buschhoff/Stein 2018). Furthermore, Lotte Reiniger repeatedly used Andersen's fairy tales as an inspiration for her silhouette films, including one of her own first animated films, *Der fliegende Koffer* (1921). In the following approach to the complex media network surrounding Andersen's fairy tale *Der fliegende Koffer*, a special focus will therefore be placed on the examination of Lotte Reiniger's cinematic adaptation. In addition to the primarily visual silent film, other cinematic and auditory media

---

A. Behler (✉)
Bielefeld, Germany
e-mail: abehler@fachworthaus.de

products will be considered – since the 1920s, several audiobooks of the fairy tale have been published. Furthermore, adaptations of the visual arts as well as the manifold merchandising products are taken into consideration.

The (Original) Fairy Tale *Der fliegende Koffer*

In his fairy tale, first published in 1839 under the title *Den flyvende kuffert*, Hans Christian Andersen tells a story of man's failure due to his own vanity against an oriental backdrop. He not only takes up this theme in the frame story, but also makes it appear in a sharpened form in embedded internal narratives. The framework of the tale is the story of a merchant's son who, after squandering his inheritance and losing his reputation, travels to the land of the Turks in a flying suitcase. There, the bon vivant learns of a princess, shielded high in the castle, who has been prophesied an ominous lover. With the help of his flying suitcase, he reaches the king's daughter, who believes him to be the Turk god, agrees to marry him and invites him to tea with her parents. As a bridal gift, the merchant's son is to tell the king and queen a fairy tale (cf. Andersen 1847a, 141 ff.). This embedded narrative (intradiegetic narrative) is a "Dingmärchen" (Stiasny 1996, 66): the merchant's son has all kinds of personified objects and utensils appear in his fairy tale situated in a kitchen. Some of these kitchen utensils, for example the sulphur woods or the iron pot, in turn tell their own stories from their lives (metadiegetic narrative). In a typically humorous and cutting Andersen manner (cf. ibid., 67 ff.), human characteristics and motifs such as vanity and self-interest are illuminated in the interactions of the anthropomorphised objects:

> "Ja, [lasst] uns davon sprechen, wer der Vornehmste ist!" sagten die Schwefelhölzer. „Nein, ich liebe es nicht, von mir selbst zu reden," wendete der Topf ein […]. Und der Topf fuhr zu erzählen fort, und das Ende war [ebenso] gut als der Anfang. Alle Teller klapperten vor Freude, und der Kehrbesen zog grüne Petersilie aus dem Sandloche und bekränzte den Topf, denn er [wusste], [dass] es die Andern ärgern würde. „Bekränze ich ihn heute," dachte er, „so bekränzt er mich morgen."[1] (Andersen 1847a, 145 f.)

That nothing of substance (certainly no self-knowledge) can be found behind all the arrogance and gentility is impressively illustrated by Andersen at the end of his embedded Dingmärchen:

> "Ja, [lasst] uns [Spektakel] machen!" sagten [alle]. Da ging die [Tür] auf. Es war das Dienstmädchen, und da standen sie stille. Keiner muckte; aber da war nicht ein einziger Topf, der nicht [gewusst] hätte, was er zu [tun] vermöge und wie vornehm er sei; „ja, wenn ich gewollt hätte," dachte jeder, „so hätte es ein recht lustiger Abend werden sollen!"

---

[1] "Yes, [let's] talk about who is the most distinguished!" said the sulphur woods. "No, I do not love to talk of myself," objected the pot […]. And the pot went on telling, and the end was [as] good as the beginning. All the plates rattled with joy, and the sweeper pulled green parsley out of the hole in the sand and garlanded the pot, for he [knew] it would annoy the others. "If I wreathe it today," he thought, "it will wreathe me tomorrow."

> Das Dienstmädchen nahm die Schwefelhölzer, machte Feuer damit – Gott bewahr' uns, wie sie sprühten und in Flammen [gerieten]! „Nun kann doch [jeder]," dachten sie, „sehen, [dass] wir die Ersten sind! [Welchen] Glanz haben wir! [Welches] Licht!" – und damit waren sie verbrannt.[2] (Ibid., 147 f.)

A similarly unhappy end also befalls the merchant's son in the frame story, who gains the favour of the king's parents through his fairy tale, but in the run-up to the wedding he loads the flying suitcase with fireworks and launches them over the town. While he mingles with the people to listen to their flattering reactions, the suitcase burns in the forest: "Ein Funken des Feuerwerks war zurückgeblieben, der hatte Feuer gefangen, und der Koffer lag in Asche. Er konnte nicht mehr fliegen, nicht mehr zu seiner Braut gelangen." (Ibid., 149).

The here briefly outlined encapsulated fairy tale text holds numerous interesting linguistic details in store for the attentive reader – parallels to other fairy tales by Andersen are also apparent: familiar objects or protagonists (e.g., lighter, matches or nightingale) as well as typical motifs such as social ascent/descent, unrequited love or man's lack of modesty also appear in *Der fliegende Koffer*. Considering media theory, the narrative structure (fairy tale within a fairy tale) as well as Andersen's specific narrative style seem particularly interesting. Heinrich Detering describes Andersen's fairy tales as "folk tales of the second power" and states: "Above all, their fictitious orality creates the pleasurable illusion of oral immediacy within a highly developed and here highly reflected written culture [...]" (Detering 2004, 7:45 ff.). This narrative practice can also be observed repeatedly in *Der fliegende Koffer*, for example through interpolations such as "Gott bewahre uns!" (Andersen 1847a, 142) or hints to the reader: "'Wollen Sie uns nun ein Märchen erzählen,' sagte die Königin [...] "Ja wohl!' erwiderte er und erzählte; da mu[ss] man nun gut aufpassen" (ibid., 144). According to Detering, this creates the impression of an "oral narrative without the detour of writing in the medium of writing" (Detering 2004, 8:35 ff.). Following Werner Wolf's terminology of intermediality forms, these impressions could already be identified as an intermedial phenomenon – keyword "intracompositional phenomenon" (Wolf 1999, 36). Regarding the dimension of the quality of intermediality, a concealed form (imitation) could be stated in this case (cf. ibid., 39 ff.). It is also possible that intertextual or intermedial references to orally transmitted or written models could be found for the fairy tale. Wegehaupt (1990, 12), for example, cites *Märchen aus Tausendundeiner Nacht* as a model for the fairy tale *Der fliegende Koffer*. It would not have been unusual for Hans Christian Andersen to adapt older sagas and fairy tales (cf. Stiasny 1996, 56). In the preface to a collected edition of his fairy tales from 1847, however, Andersen points out that *Der fliegende Koffer* belongs to the fairy tales that are "entirely his own invention" (Andersen 1847b, VI).

---

[2] "Yes, [let] us make [spectacles]!" said [all]. Then the [door] opened. It was the maid, and there they stood still. No one grumbled; but there was not a single pot that did not [know] what it was capable of [doing], and how genteel it was; "yes, if I had willed," thought everyone, "it should have been quite a merry evening!"

The maid took the sulfur sticks, made fire with them – God preserve us how they sprayed and [burst] into flames! "Now [everyone]," they thought, "can see [that] we are the first! [What] splendor we have! [What] light!" – and with that they were burned.

The Dissemination and Processing of the Fairy Tale in Books

In bibliographical compilations, such as that of the International Youth Library from 1994 (where only a Yugoslavian edition of the fairy tale from 1983 is listed), it is not clear how often *Der fliegende Koffer* has actually been published as a single edition (mostly as a picture book) over the course of time. In addition to international individual editions, e.g. from Japan (1959), Czechoslovakia (1962/1974) or Peru (2008), there is evidence of several separate publications of the fairy tale on the German-language book market.[3] Furthermore, *Der fliegende Koffer* has been reprinted in countless anthologies such as general fairy tale collections or anthologies specifically featuring Andersen's fairy tales. Sometimes the fairy tale even serves as title and cover inspiration (*Der fliegende Koffer. Das Buch der Märchen*, 2001).

Looking at a selection of different editions of the fairy tale (from the nineteenth, twentieth and twenty-first centuries), only minor differences, and in some cases also abridgements, are noticeable. One example is the figure of the pot (1847 version), which – probably in order to emphasize the difference to the iron pot – in other versions is also referred to as a clay pot (1933), clay jug (1990) or milk pot (2000), among others. Part of the linguistic variance in the texts is presumably due to different translations of the Danish original. For example, Stiasny states regarding Andersen's fairy tales: "Many turns of phrase are untranslatable, many jokes and puns are lost, some things fall into the sentimental [...]; numerous mediocre illustrations also create a false basic chord" (Stiasny 1996, 7). With regard to illustrations of *Der fliegende Koffer*, various nuances become apparent: In contrast to the text versions, which speak of the merchant's son, whose age – apart from the fact that he is marriageable – is not discussed in detail, a look at associated illustrations and cover designs for the fairy tale offers an interesting range of ages of the depicted protagonist. There are both depictions of the merchant's son that appear rather childlike (e.g. Andersen/Pohl 1964) and illustrations in which he is depicted with a beard (e.g. Andersen/Kubašta 1962) or wrinkled skin (e.g. Andersen/Hložník 1956). There are also some major differences in the colour of his hair, facial features, facial expressions, and equipment of the character. The different depictions of the merchant's son also reflect different target groups of the fairy tale editions. The issue of child appropriateness in the context of Andersen's fairy tales is one of complexity and has been the subject of controversy among critics. Ewers states with regard to Andersen criticism of the last century: "No matter how much their author may be regarded as a figurehead of children's literature, the suitability of Andersen's fairy tales as children's reading is anything but uncontroversial, even and especially in children's literature circles" (Ewers 2006, 47). Andersen himself had written his fairy tales – even though they were published at the beginning with the addition

---

[3] Hannover: Molling, [c. 1910]; Vienna [et al.]: Sesam, 1922; Winterberg: Steinbrener, 1941; Berlin: Kinderbuchverlag, 1955; Hamburg: Carlsen, [1960]; Fürth: Pestalozzi, [1968]; Waldkirchen: Dessart, 1989; Münster: Coppenrath, 2003 – to name just a few examples.

Fig. 1 Illustration of the fairy tale *Der fliegende Koffer* by Vilhelm Pedersen, https://upload.wikimedia.org/wikipedia/en/9/9b/Flying_Trunk_01.jpg (25.03.2020)

"fortalte for Børn" (Engl.: "told for children") – also for mixed age groups. Thus, he wrote in a letter, "I tell the children while I remember that father and mother often listen, and they must be given something for the mind" (Detering 2004, slide 7).

In 1847 Hans Christian Andersen chose the Danish artist Vilhelm Pedersen in consultation with his publisher Karl Berend Lorck for the task of illustrating his collected fairy tales – for both the German and Danish markets (cf. Wegehaupt 1990, 20 ff.). This early illustration by Pedersen directs the focus – fitting Andersen's chosen title – to a particular scene from the fairy tale's frame story (Fig. 1): the merchant's son sits in a flying suitcase and floats over an oriental-looking landscape with palm trees and buildings with domes and towers. As far as the medium of the book is concerned, it can be concluded regarding recent publications that, in addition to the usual internal combination of text and image in illustrated editions, external forms of media combinations are increasingly being published and marketed, for example by publishing an audio book version to go with the book (*Der fliegende Koffer. Das Buch der Märchen,* 2001 and *Der fliegende Koffer. Das HörBuch der Märchen,* 2003) or sold directly in combination (e.g., *Der fliegende Koffer,* 2004a as a book with audio book and fairy tale quiz on CD). Before focusing more closely on the area of audio media, however, we will first take a look at cinematic versions of the fairy tale.

Animated Films and Series Appearances: *Der fliegende Koffer* on Screen

Lotte Reiniger's silhouette animation film (1921) seems to be the first appearance of *Der fliegende Koffer* in the German-language medium of film. The silent film was followed in 1944 by an adaptation of the fairy tale as a Kasperle-Film by the Hohnsteiner Puppenspiele. Furthermore, a Japanese animated film from 1971 (German first broadcast in 1989), a DEFA animated film from the GDR entitled *Der*

Koffer (1981/1982) and more recent (English-language) animated films (2003 and 2018) can also be mentioned. In the case of the aforementioned films, according to Rajewsky's terminology, a change of media has taken place: a "transformation of a media-specifically fixed product or product-substrate" – in this case the literary original – "into another medium conventionally perceived as distinct", a film (Rajewsky 2002, 19). Furthermore, intermedial individual references (cf. ibid., 73) to the fairy tale can be found in German television, for example in the GDR's *Sandmännchen* or also in the series *Siebenstein* (2012).

Lotte Reiniger's *Der fliegende Koffer* (1921)

The silhouette film *Der fliegende Koffer* is described in the booklet accompanying the DVD edition (Absolut Medien, 2006) as "Lotte Reiniger's earliest surviving fairy tale film based on motifs from a fairy tale by Hans Christian Andersen". At the time of its premiere, which took place on the 14th of September 1921 at Berlin's Terra-Theater Motivhaus (cf. ibid.), its creator was just twenty-two years old. In the decades that followed, Lotte Reiniger, whose lifelong "work focuses: Silhouette, Shadow Theatre and Silhouette Film" (Kimmich 2011, 4), created another cinematic version respectively illustrations of Andersen's fairy tales such as *Thumbelina* (film: 1953/1954) or *The Little Mermaid* (book 1980) – "Lotte Reiniger loved Andersen's fairy tales all her life" (booklet accompanying the DVD 2006). When Stiglegger states that "it is precisely the oral form [that makes fairy tales] particularly suitable for adaptation in another medium such as film" (Stiglegger 2017, 3), this reference simultaneously underscores the challenge that comes with a change of media from a textual fairy tale to a purely visual silent film. Thus, against the backdrop of Andersen's literary model, some peculiarities can be identified in Reiniger's *Der fliegende Koffer*: The specific representational possibilities in Lotte Reiniger's silhouette silent film cannot take up the "orality"-suggesting narrative style of the original fairy tale, and the intertitles, which are limited in scope, can only be equipped with short descriptions and sentences in order to maintain the flow of the film. Accordingly, it does not seem surprising that in the short film, the embedded fairy tale narratives are left out, thus also breaking with the theme of (fairy) tale narration itself, which is extremely present in the original. In terms of the overall impression and especially with regard to the content of the story, Reiniger's version of the fairy tale deviates in large part from the literary original: In terms of content, the film is about the emperor's daughter Hsien-Yuyü, who – just like in Andersen's story – is prophesied a sorrowful love. Her father therefore "forbids her suitors, the great General Hu and the sublime sage Wei, to approach her!" (Intertitle, 01:12 ff.). As a precaution, he locks his daughter in a high pagoda. The two suitors fail in their attempt to get up there with the help of a catapult and a magic bean (02:55 ff.) – at this point an intermedial reference to the beanstalk from *Jack and the Beanstalk* becomes clear. There is also (as a variant of the merchant's son) poor Yen, who sees the princess, falls in love, and out of lovesickness plunges into the floods.

At the bottom of the sea, he rescues a sea creature (possibly the character represents an allusion to Andersen's sea witch from *The Little Mermaid*) and is given a flying suitcase in thanks, which he uses to get to the princess, to whom he introduces himself as the "god of butterflies" (05:22). "The flowers tell the butterflies about the deception" (06:43 ff.) – this scene with little people sitting in the flowers is again reminiscent of the fairy tale *Thumbelina* – and in the end a large flock of butterflies takes the suitcase away from Yen, who then stabs himself (07:55 ff.). Not only the added proper names and the equipment of the characters, but also the setting of the Reiniger film has an Asian feel. Topographically, there are also differences in comparison to Andersen's original fairy tale, which ultimately cause the fairy tale to be evaluated in a film review as follows: "A few too many titles interrupt the lightness of this Chinese fairy tale" (*Film-Kurier*, 15.09.1921, 2). All in all, in the medium of the silhouette silent film, a completely unique work of art is created with only one narrative level, which is reminiscent in basic features of the frame story of *Der fliegende Koffer*, but also works with further intermedial fairy tale references. An interesting parallel is revealed in the medial realisation of emotions in Reiniger's silhouette film: the character's heartbreak is made clear by a heart cut-out in the chest area, which bursts into flames (08:08 ff.) – the heart placed in the chest was also repeatedly used by Hans Christian Andersen in his own silhouettes (e.g. *Bogmærke, Christines Billedbog, opslag 55* or *Møllemand*, see Mylius/Andersen 2019).

Der fliegende Koffer (1944): Hohnsteiner Puppenspiele

The 27-minute puppet show film *Der fliegende Koffer* (directed by Curt A. Engel), released in 1944, is one of the "[f]ictional Kasperle-Film made by the Hohnstein puppeteers for the supporting programme in the Nazi cinema [...]" (Schlesinger 2017, 162). In these fairy tale adaptations, individual motifs and characters from literary models were arranged around the Kasper puppet and – in the case of *Der fliegende Koffer* – also Seppel (cf. ibid.). Known components from Andersen's original are only the flying suitcase as a magical object as well as the journey – in this case of Kasper and Seppel – to a foreign country. Regarding National Socialist propaganda in the film, some aspects should be addressed at this point: For example, the contrast between the frugal and home-loving Kasper and Seppel characters on the one hand and the rich, work-shy, and brutal Sultan and the greedy, parasitic robber chief on the other hand. The character design in the film thus fits the elements of the National Socialist worldview described by Schlesinger, which frequently appear in fairy tale films of the *Third Reich* (cf. ibid., 164 ff.). The German homeland is topographically juxtaposed with an Oriental-African foreign land. Kasper and Seppel treat the foreign culture with disrespect – they make fun of it with words and deeds. This ranges from a harmless, joking retort at the greeting ("Salam aleikum" – "Gummi arabicum", 12:29) and playful rudeness "Erhabene Sultanine [...]" (13:24) to barely concealed insults ("Kaffer", 12:46). The presentation of the foreign culture also makes such a superior point of view plausible to the viewer; for example, the dark-skinned slaves – particularly exaggerated in the character of a slave named Aladdin – are submissive to dim-witted characters. In addition, stereotypes such as polygamy (the sultan refers to his favourite wife) are invoked. Physiognomic stereotypes (cf. Schlesinger 2017, 171), however, are difficult to discern in the film, as the curved, long nose, for example, is also a typical characteristic of the Kasper character. In a censorship decision of August 14, 1944, the film *Der fliegende Koffer* was awarded the rating *volksbildend*. The exact reasons for this are unclear, Schlesinger states in reference to the fairy tale film production of the time:

> Whether the artistic and/or ideological implementation of the fairy tale templates influences the decision of the film review board or whether the state authority primarily wants to (financially) promote this film production with its predicates remains [...] open. (Ibid., 172)

In view of the aforementioned mode of representation and the language used in the film (terms such as "Mohrenland" or "Bimbo" are used), it seems questionable that the film can nowadays be viewed on YouTube without any indication of the time and context in which it was made.

Recent Cartoons: *The Flying Trunk (Story)* (2003 and 2018)

In the following, we will briefly look at the special features of the film adaptations of the fairy tale that were released after the turn of the millennium. The first is *The Flying Trunk* (2003), an animated film that appeared as part of a series of fairy tale adaptations of Andersen produced in a Danish-British-German collaboration (first German broadcast on 28.12.2003 on Super RTL). At the beginning of the film, a narrator figure visually reminiscent of Hans Christian Andersen appears – *Der fliegende Koffer* is thus given an additional setting, the author himself and his telling of the fairy tale become part of the story. The members of the audience in the film are children, and presumably they are also the target audience for this adaptation of the fairy tale in reality. This version is clearly based on the text of the fairy tale (for example, the embedded fairy tale narrative with the kitchen utensils is included – albeit in a shortened form), although there are also notable deviations and embellishments. For example, the father of the merchant's son in the film becomes a miserly character reminiscent of Dickens' Ebenezer Scrooge (01:20 ff.). In this film version, the merchant's son himself bears a proper name, Sven, and gains accessibility, personality, and depth for the recipients in comparison to the character from the fairy tale text. Thus, at the end of the fairy tale, there is also a form of self-awareness of the merchant's son: "I never loved money and princesses. I just loved the stories" (24:00 ff.). From an intermedial perspective, a scene at the market is particularly interesting: a merchant there sells small statues (presumably intended to represent clay figures) of the merchant's son on his suitcase – in the context of the film story, the flying suitcase is thus already abstracted as a motif and offered as a kind of merchandising product (15:53). From a gender perspective, this fairy tale film reveals another novelty: the princess does not appear as a naïve figure who is simply kissed awake and deceived by a stranger, but she shows herself to be unimpressed and sceptical towards the merchant's son. Finally, her analysis of the Dingmärchen being told is as follows: "She [the princess] finally understood the story of the matches in the kitchen, for just like the matches, who tried so hard to impress everybody, the angel had burned out" (24:45 ff.; note: the merchant's son pretends to be an angel in this version).

The fairy tale's moral already echoes a linguistic allusion to the condition of burnout, which appears even more explicitly in the English-language film *The Flying Trunk Story*, released in 2018 on the YouTube channel My Pingu Tv: "So, the moral is ... Never burn yourself out to impress those around you. Be yourself!" (12:21 ff.). The 2018 film seems to be fundamentally inspired by the 2003 film version (e.g., in terms of the princess character, the naming of the merchant's son, or the moral). Another similarity lies in the fairy tale film's address to a young target group, which is already marked in the title with "Stories for Kids". However, the user comments under the video make it clear that it is actually more likely to be a mixed audience.

For the two comparatively recent animated versions of *Der fliegende Koffer* – in contrast to their historical predecessors, which adapted rather isolated motifs from the fairy tale – a far closer proximity to the original text version of the fairy tale can be observed. In particular, the oral narrative style of the original is more strongly expressed in the films examined here. Moreover, the 2003 version conveys a new reading of the fairy tale by focusing on the theme of friendship/social standing and the merchant's son's passion for storytelling (his vocation). This focus is again adopted in the 2018 YouTube fairy tale film.

Der fliegende Koffer and Its Television Appearances: *Sandmännchen* and *Siebenstein*

At this point, attention should be briefly drawn to exemplary manifestations of *Der fliegende Koffer* on German television. For example, it was featured on GDR television in the popular programme *Unser Sandmännchen*. In the episode in question, the Sandman travels to an oriental castle in a flying suitcase. The suitcase can be similarly operated to the original text version of the fairy tale – "[s]obald man an das Schlo[ss] drückte, konnte der Koffer fliegen" (Andersen 1847a, 142). In other cinematic adaptations, the flight mechanism works via a key (e.g., 2003) or a magic spell (1944), and the suitcase even gets wings once (2018). The image of the Sandman sitting in the suitcase, however, is reminiscent of the original fairy tale and Pedersen's original illustration. In the castle, a princess is already waiting for the Sandman, to whom he performs the embedded bedtime story that is usual for the show, before he again flies away with the suitcase. The fact that this brief appearance of the Sandman in the flying suitcase has far-reaching consequences for the media network surrounding the GDR broadcast will be examined in more detail in the chapter on merchandising products.

As part of the ZDF series *Siebenstein*, an episode entitled *Der fliegende Koffer* was broadcast in 2012, in which the series characters open an ominous package containing an old oriental carpet. The talking suitcase (this character is a series regular) thinks he recognises something in the knotted pattern: "Vielleicht ist es ja eine [Märchen]-Figur aus *Tausendundeiner Nacht*" (06:08). Accordingly, the carpet turns out to be a flying carpet, which flies off together with the suitcase lying on it. The allusion to Andersen's fairy tale is supported by the choice of title; the intermedial reference unfolds primarily through the image of the flying suitcase that arises in combination with the magic carpet. On the basis of the appearances in *Sandmännchen* and *Siebenstein* described here, the possibilities of the reference can only be illuminated by way of example – how often there were further, possibly similar appearances of *Der fliegende Koffer* in German television programming remains questionable.

Der fliegende Koffer Audio Book/Play: From the Radio of the Weimar Republic to MP3 Files

The oldest entry on the fairy tale *Der fliegende Koffer* in radio broadcasting in the database of the DFG project *Deutschsprachige Kinder- und Jugendliteratur im Medienverbund 1900–1945* (http://medienverbundportal.kjl.uni-bielefeld.de) is a broadcast from September 24, 1924, in which the *radio princess* tells fairy tales by Andersen (see audiography). In the radio of the Weimar Republic there are further broadcasts of *Der fliegende Koffer* for children and young people (1924, 1926, 1927, 1928, 1929a, b), some of which are broadcast repeatedly, for example in the case of the fairy tale radio play by Hans Peter Schmiedel (1930, 1931). There is also evidence of adaptations of the fairy tale on the radio of the Nazi state in 1934, 1936 and 1937. Unfortunately, according to the German Radio Archive, no audio recordings of these early broadcasts have been archived. However, there are contributions to Hans Peter Schmiedel's radio play, among others, in sections of the *Mirag* programme magazine addressed to young people (Jugend-Funk 1930; Jugendfunk 1931), from which it can be seen that Schmiedel incorporated new plot lines and characters (with proper names) and provided the story with a novel happy ending – "young Klaus loses all his possessions, but at the end he not only has a lot of money again, but also a pretty wife" (Jugend-Funk 1930, 21). Also, the theme of false friends, which already existed in Andersen's original fairy tale, seems to be embellished (cf. ibid. as well as Jugendfunk 1931, 70). An article in *Die junge Front – Die Zeitung der Mirag-Jugend* from 1934, on the other hand, announces an audio play that – as far as the few sentences on the content reveal – is more strongly oriented towards Andersen's fairy tale text. The author of the article writes:

And with this I have now also revealed to you the moral of this fairy tale of the "flying suitcase": for we too possess the "flying suitcase", if only we want to: It is our [f]antasy that can take us over hills and valleys, over streams and seas to the farthest lands; however, we must be careful that the fireworks of our romantic ideas and feelings do not one day set the whole suitcase on fire and leave us at the end with only a heap of ashes, like a dull remnant of life. (Die junge Front 1934, 11)

This interpretation of the radio play, which the text suggests to the young recipients, already seems to contain a warning that conforms to National Socialist ideology – an excess of fantasy and feelings could undermine desirable Nazi virtues such as discipline, obedience, or fulfilment of duty (cf. Hobsch 2009, 39 ff.). The three aforementioned magazine articles on the radio broadcasts are also accompanied by illustrations – each time depicting the typical scene of the protagonist in the flying suitcase. The same scene can also be found on almost every cover of the audio media produced for the fairy tale in the following decades. All in all, a large number of records, cassettes, and CDs with the story of *Der fliegende Koffer* can be traced for the radio sector. Sometimes these are individual editions, sometimes the radio plays and books are part of larger albums – together with fairy tales by other authors or specifically as a compilation of Andersen's fairy tales. It also seems popular to publish the story in combination with other audio fairy tales that are also set in an oriental setting: e.g., the combination of *Der fliegende Koffer* and *Der kleine Muck* (2005; 2010). New audio books and plays continue to be produced to this day, and in some cases old versions are also reissued and distributed as CDs or online as MP3 versions, for example the fairy tale audio play *Tobias mit dem fliegenden Koffer* (1957/2013/2017) or *Der fliegende Koffer* (played and narrated by Aunt Ursula and Uncle Fritz with their funny dwarfs; 1964/2008). The large number of adaptations of the fairy tale in audio media could also be due, among other things, to the oral narrative style of the original; the theme of storytelling, the embedded fairy tales and the extensive dialogues seem to encourage recordings.

Suitcase, Art, and Consumption: The Colourful Palette of Merchandising Products

In addition to books, films and audio media, a considerable number of merchandising products and the like have been published for the fairy tale *Der fliegende Koffer*: The colourful palette ranges from an Annaberger puzzle from the GDR (it shows the flying suitcase above an oriental backdrop, with fireworks glowing in the background) to various collectible figurines and paintings to ornate kitchenware – silver egg cups, children's cutlery, sugar bowls, or even (wall) plates. While in the original fairy tale the story of the kitchen utensils is embedded in the frame story with the suitcase, the suitcase is now incorporated into real utensils and ornaments from the kitchen – for example, plates are also equipped with the original illustration by Vilhelm Pedersen. In addition, *Der fliegende Koffer* appears on postcards (GDR 1985), as a pewter figure, on Hans Christian Andersen stamps, or in a quartet game about his collected fairy tales (1987). Furthermore, the fairy tale appears in public and cultural life: In Odense, Andersen's birthplace, there is a sculpture by the sculptor Jens Flemming of the fairy tale *Der fliegende Koffer* (unveiled on May 4, 1991), along with other of his fairy tale sculptures. At the Sand Sculpture Festival in Søndervig, in the 200th year of Andersen's birthday, there was a detailed sculpture of the fairy tale – it not only depicted the suitcase, the merchant's son and the princess on the back, but also personified objects from the fairy tale (more precisely, a teapot and matches with human mouths). Less ephemeral is the attraction *Den flyvende kuffert* at Tivoli amusement park, a themed ride in which visitors sit in opened suitcases and are guided through Hans Christian Andersen's fairy tale world.

Finally, I would like to remind you of the television appearance of the Sandman in the flying suitcase, as a result of which a whole series of related merchandising articles was produced: In addition to various collectible figurines (among others in the series *Unser Sandmännchen Traummobile*), various postcards with the scene of the Sandman in the suitcase were also distributed. On the book market, the appearance was also accompanied by effects, probably for the first time in 1978 when the anthology *Gute-Nacht-Geschichten. Vom Sandmännchen erzählt für 365 Tage* was published, which also contained the fairy tale *Der fliegende Koffer* (further editions in 1981, 1983 and 1986). Finally, on the occasion of the Sandman's 50th birthday, even stamps with the suitcase motif were released. Andersen's fairy tale therefore obviously had a lasting influence on the *Sandmännchen* media network.

Conclusion on the Media Network

Regarding the aspects of characters, topography, motifs and varying readings of the fairy tale, the centuries-spanning pool of media products reveals a great variance, which could only be touched upon within this article (for example, the adaptation of the story in theatre would still be noted as a research desideratum). However, the following can be stated for the media studied: The image of the flying suitcase as a wondrous object always makes an appearance as an essence and also shapes the accompanying (cover) illustrations in particular. Accordingly, the media network does not profit from the exploitation and marketing of individual characters (the main character can easily be taken over by the Sandmännchen as well), but seems to be fuelled – even if the proximity to the original varies greatly depending on the intermedial reference – by the memorability of the miracle suitcase image as well as by the enduring popularity of its original author and his fairy tale as an overall work of art. A chronological (further) development of the fairy tale material can hardly be discerned; as was shown in the section on cinematic adaptations, it is the more recent productions, that are increasingly approaching Andersen's original again. In the age of the Internet, a complex juxtaposition of older and newer versions of the text, audio books/plays, films, etc. is opening up online around the fairy tale *Der fliegende Koffer* – there seems to be no end in sight to the media network story.

References

Primary Literature[4]

Andersen, Hans C.: Den flyvende kuffert. In: Ders.: Eventyr, fortalte for Børn. Ny Samling. Andet Hefte. Kopenhagen: Reitzel, 1839, [o. S.].

Andersen, Hans C.: Der fliegende Koffer. In: Gesammelte Märchen. Dritter Theil. Leipzig: Lorck, 1847a, 141–149 (H. C. Andersen's Gesammelte Werke; 14) Digitalisat unter: http://www.digitale-bibliothek-mv.de/viewer/resolver?urn=urn:nbn:de:gbv:9-g-4889612 (08.09.2019).

Andersen, Hans C./Pedersen, Vilhelm (Ill.): Gesammelte Märchen. Mit 112 Illustrationen nach Originalzeichnungen von V. Pedersen. In Holz geschn. von Ed. Kretzschmar. Leipzig: Lorck, 1849.

Andersen, Hans C.: Drei Märchen. 1. Das Feuerzeug. 2. Der fliegende Koffer. 3. Die roten Schuhe. Berlin: F. Schulze, 1905 (Schulbibliothek Stolze-Schrey; 4) [weitere Aufl.: [1924] und [1926]].

Andersen, Hans C./Anker, Hanns (Ill.): Der fliegende Koffer. Hannover: Molling, [um 1910].

Andersen, Hans C./May, Walo von (Ill.): Der Schatten. Der fliegende Koffer. Der Goldschatz. Tölpel-Hans. München: „Die Welt-Literatur", 1916 (Die Welt-Literatur; 51).

Andersen, Hans C.: Der fliegende Koffer. Wien [u. a.]: Sesam, 1922 (Bunte Sesam-Bücher; 48).

Andersen, Hans C./Cramer, Rie (Ill.): Der fliegende Koffer und andere Märchen. Leipzig: Anton & Co., 1928 (Märchen/Andersen; 6).

Andersen, Hans C./Nicolai, Walter (Ill.): Der fliegende Koffer. Der standhafte Zinnsoldat. Märchen für Schule und Haus. Breslau: Hirt, 1933 (Hirts deutsche Sammlung/Literarische Abteilung/Gruppe 3/Märchen; 32).

Andersen, Hans C./Müller, F. (Ill.): Märchen von H. Chr. Andersen. [Inhalt: Die wilden Schwäne. Der fliegende Koffer. Die Geschichte von einer Mutter]. [Reutlingen]: Ensslin & Laiblin, 1939.

Andersen, Hans C.: Der fliegende Koffer. Winterberg: Steinbrener, 1941.

Andersen, Hans C./Born, Gerda (Ill.): Der fliegende Koffer. Nach Hans Chr. Andersen. Wien: Waldheim-Eberle, 1950 (Die bunten Waldheim-Bücher/[Sechs Märchen nach Hans Christian Andersen/Born; 4]) [weitere Aufl.: 1953].

Andersen, Hans C.: Der fliegende Koffer. Viby J.: Nordische Papierwaren-Industrie, 1951 (Andersen, Hans Christian: Märchen; 5) [9 Bd. in Pp. Kassette in Schrankform].

Andersen, Hans C./Haller, Ruprecht (Ill.): Der fliegende Koffer. In: Berliner Lesebogen. Nr. 8: Andersens Märchen. Berlin: Kinderbuchverlag, 1955, 3–9.

Andersen, Hans C./Hložník, Vincent (Ill.): Andersen. Rozpravky. Bratislava: [Slovenské nakladatelstvo detskej knihy], 1956.

Andersen, Hans C.: Der fliegende Koffer. Übers. von S. Ohata. [Tokyo]: Daisan Shobo, 1959 (Märchen-Bücherei/Andersen; 5).

[Andersen, Hans C.]: Der fliegende Koffer. Hamburg: Carlsen, [1960].

Andersen, Hans C./Kubašta, Voitěch (Ill.): Der fliegende Koffer. [Aufstellbilderbuch]. [Prag]: Artia, 1962 [weitere Aufl.: 1974].

Andersen, Hans C./Pohl, Norbert (Ill.): Der fliegende Koffer. Märchen. Berlin: Kinderbuchverlag, 1964 (Robinsons billige Bücher; 112) [weitere Aufl.: 1965 und 1971].

Andersen, Hans C./Ridolfi (Ill.): Der fliegende Koffer und andere Märchen. Bearb. von Liselotte Julius. Stuttgart [u. a.]: Delphin, 1967 (Goldene Happy-Bücher; 29) [weitere Aufl.: 1973].

Andersen, Hans C./Röschl, Kurt (Ill.): Der fliegende Koffer. Fürth: Pestalozzi, 1968 (Pevau-Büchlein; 37) [weitere Ausg.: [1969]].

---

[4] The following information is not a complete list of media products related to the fairy tale *Der fliegende Koffer*. This would go beyond the scope of this section, since, for example, numerous other anthologies would have to be considered. This restriction applies in particular to the area of primary literature and audiography.

Andersen, Hans C./Svensson, Kamma (Ill.): Nattergalen. Den flyvende Kuffert. Kritisch editiert von Erik Dal. Kopenhagen: Nordlunde, 1973 (Udsendelse fra Nordlundes Bogtrykkeri, København; 42).

Andersen, Hans C./Vulcănescu, Petre (Ill.): Däumelinchen, der fliegende Koffer und andere Märchen. Bukarest: Kriterion, 1976 [Gemeinschaftsausg. mit dem Vollmer-Verl., Wiesbaden].

Andersen, Hans C.: Der fliegende Koffer. In: Barth, Doris (Hg.): Gute-Nacht-Geschichten. Vom Sandmännchen erzählt für 365 Tage. Erlangen: Pestalozzi, 1978, [o. S.] [weitere Aufl.: 1981, 1983, [1986] – teils u. d. T.: „Sandmännlein erzählt Geschichten für 365 Tage"].

Andersen, Hans C./Hechelmann, Friedrich (Ill.): Vier Andersen-Märchen. [Inhalt: Der fliegende Koffer, Die Prinzessin auf der Erbse, Die Großmutter, Der Schweinehirt]. Mönchaltorf/Hamburg: Nord-Süd, 1975 (Ein Nord-Süd-Taschenbuch) [weitere Aufl.: 1983, 1992].

Andersen, Hans C./Stupica, Marija Lucija (Ill.): Leteči kovček. Übers. von Janez Gradišnik. Ljubljana: Mladinska knjiga, 1983.

Andersen, Hans C./Hummel, Lore (Ill.): Der fliegende Koffer. Waldkirchen: Dessart, 1989 [weitere Aufl.: 1991].

Andersen, Hans C.: Der fliegende Koffer. In: Heinz Wegehaupt (Hg.): Hundert Illustrationen aus anderthalb Jahrhunderten zu Märchen von Hans Christian Andersen. Hanau: Dausien, 1990, 165–174.

Andersen, Hans C.: Der fliegende Koffer. In: Märchen. Stuttgart [u. a.]: Thienemann, 2000, 177–184 [EA 1991].

Andersen, Hans C./Hanke-Basfeld, Magdalene (Ill.): Der fliegende Koffer. Eine Erzählung. Leicht veränderte und modernisierte Fassung. Münster: Coppenrath, 2003 (Linos Reise-Märchen/Lino-Bücher; 25/Lino-Box; 5).

Andersen, Hans C.: Der fliegende Koffer. Teil: Buch. Köln: Paletti, 2004a [mit Hörbuch und Märchenquiz auf CD].

Andersen, Hans C.: Der fliegende Koffer. Nach einem Märchen von Hans Christian Andersen. Köln: Paletti, 2004b (Mein allererstes Märchenbuch).

Andersen, Hans C./Yachachin, Julio (Ill.)/Velayos, Juan (Ill.): El cofre volador. Adaptación y aplicación metodológica. Bearbeitet von Serafín Ipenza. San Borja (Lima, Perú): Editorial María Trinidad, 2008 [Buch und CD].

Andersen, Hans C./Gotzen-Beek, Betina (Ill.): Der fliegende Koffer. In: Dies.: Andersens Märchen. Ravensburg: Ravensburger, 2017, 78–87.

Andersen, Hans C./Reiniger, Lotte (Ill.): Die kleine Seejungfrau. Märchen. Dettenhausen: Evang. Kirchengemeinde, 1980.

Jacoby, Edmund (Hg.)/Seelig, Renate (Ill.): Der fliegende Koffer. Das Buch der Märchen. Hildesheim: Gerstenberg, 2001.

Audiography

Der fliegende Koffer. In: Die Funkprinzessin erzählt: Andersen-Märchen […]. Die Funkprinzessin: Adele Proesler. Funk-Stunde Berlin, 24.09.1924, 16:15 Uhr.

Der fliegende Koffer. In: Stunde der Jugend (Leitung Mittelschulrektor K. Wehrhan). Aus dem deutschen Märchenborn, vorgetragen von der Märchentante. Wunschnachmittag […]. SWR Frankfurt, SWR Kassel, 05.09.1926, 15:00–16:00 Uhr.

Der fliegende Koffer. In: Jugendbühne (Unterhaltungsstunde). Die Funkprinzessin erzählt […] Die Funkprinzessin: Erika Burgin. Funk-Stunde Berlin, Funk-Stunde Stettin, 04.05.1927, 16:30 Uhr.

Der fliegende Koffer. In: Märchen von H. Chr. Andersen. Erzählt von Dorothea Thieß […]. Norag Hannover, 02.05.1928, 16:15 Uhr.

Der fliegende Koffer. In: Rektor Simon [Rudolf Simon]: Jugendfunk […]. Werag Köln, Aachen, Münster, 18.01.1929a, 17:00 Uhr.

Der fliegende Koffer. In: Märchen. Erzählt von Johanna Meyer [...]. Funk-Stunde Berlin, Magdeburg, Stettin, Deutsche Welle, 14.07.1929b, 15:30 Uhr.
Der fliegende Koffer (nach Andersen). Ein Märchenhörspiel von Hans Peter Schmiedel. Musik: Erich Liebermann Roßwiese. In: Jugendfunk [...]. Mirag Leipzig, Dresden, 02.04.1930, 14:30 Uhr [Wiederholungen: am 28.05.1930, 14:30 Uhr, am 09.12.1931, 16:00 Uhr].
Kinderstunde. Vom fliegenden Koffer und andere Geschichten (Ida Mannersdorfer). Ravag Wien, 14.04.1931, 17:00 Uhr.
Jugendnachmittag. „Der fliegende Koffer" nach H. Chr. Andersen. Leipzig, 07.02.1934, 14:40 Uhr.
Kinderfunkspiel. Der fliegende Koffer. Frei nach Andersen für den Funk bearbeitet von Irmtraut Hugin. Spielleitung: Gert Randolf-Schmalnauer. Deutschlandsender, 01.03.1936, 14:00 Uhr [Wiederholungen: am 03.05.1936, 14:00 Uhr; Reichssender Breslau, 11.10.1936, 15:30 Uhr].
Kinder, hört zu! Wir spielen das Märchen: Der fliegende Koffer. Nach Andersen. Reichssender Hamburg, 17.10.1937, 14:00 Uhr.
Tobias mit dem fliegenden Koffer. Der Schatten des Herrn Alexander. Kinderhörspiele mit Ursula Langrock, Hans Bernhardt [u. a.]. Nach Hans Christian Andersen. SWR, 1956/1957 [weitere Ausg.: SWR Edition (Audible.de), 2013; Der Audio Verlag, 2017 (Album: Die Schneekönigin und weitere Märchen-Hörspiele)].
Der fliegende Koffer. Nach Hans Christian Andersen von Ingeborg Walther. 1 Schallplatte. Hamburg: Decca, [1960] (Tönende Bilderbücher).
Der fliegende Koffer. Teil 1 und 2. [Nach Hans Christian Andersen]. Gespielt und erzählt von Tante Ursula und Onkel Fritz mit ihren lustigen Zwergen. Vinyl/Single. Telefunken, 1964 [vermutlich weitere Ausg.: 1991 und 1994 – zuletzt: Bella Musica Edition, 2008].
Der fliegende Koffer. Das Feuerzeug. Hörspiele [nach] Hans Christian Andersen. Sprechplatte. Verfasser: Kurt Vethake. Erzähler: Peter Schiff. [Hamburg]: [Phonogram Tonges], [1970].
Der fliegende Koffer. Ein Märchen-Hörspiel nach Hans Christian Andersen. Musik: Peter I. Tschaikowsky. Tölpelhans. Ein Märchen-Hörspiel nach Hans Christian Andersen. Musik: Johann Sebastian Bach. Gesamtbearbeitung: Inge Famira. Hamburg: Metronome Records Ges., [1974].
Die Bremer Stadtmusikanten. Däumelinchen. Der fliegende Koffer. Tonkassette. [Köln]: Concord, [1977].
Schneewittchen. Der fliegende Koffer. Frau Holle. Rotkäppchen. Mit dem Ensemble des Süddt. Puppentheaters. Tonkassette. [Köln]: OPP, [1979] (Märchenland; 6).
Der fliegende Koffer und drei andere Märchen. Verfasser: Hans Christian Andersen. Tonkassette. Murrhardt: Schumm, 1981 (Schumm sprechende Bücher).
Die Bremer Stadtmusikanten. Der fliegende Koffer. Tonkassette. [Elbigenalp]: [Koch], 1982 (Märchenzauber).
Der fliegende Koffer. Das hässliche junge Entlein. Hörspielbearbeitung: Anke Stamm [u. a.]. Märchen nach H. C. Andersen. Tonkassette. Bella Musica, [1982] (Bunte Märchenwelt; 7).
Zwerg Nase [nach Wilhelm Hauff]. Der fliegende Koffer [nach Hans Christian Andersen]. Hörspielbearbeitung und Regie: Heikedine Körting. Tonkassette. Quickborn bei Hamburg: Miller-International-Schallplatten, [1983] (Die Märchenbox; 14).
Die Prinzessin und der Schweinehirt. Der fliegende Koffer. [Märchenhörspiele nach Hans Christian Andersen] von Kurt Vethake. Tonkassette. Hamburg: Gruner und Jahr, 1983 (Die schönsten Märchen).
Der fliegende Koffer. Hofhahn und Wetterhahn. Mutter Hollunder. Nach Hans Christian Andersen. Interpret: Manfred Steffen. Tonkassette. Hamburg: Polygram [u. a.], 1993 (Reihe: Hörfest).
Der fliegende Koffer. Das HörBuch der Märchen. Sprecher: Christian Brückner. Musik, Produktion und Regie: Ulrich Maske. 2 CDs. Hamburg: Jumbo, 2003a [weitere Aufl.: 2004; digitale Übertragung: Leipzig [u. a.]: Deutsche Nationalbibliothek, 2019].
Der fliegende Koffer. Teil: CD. Sprecher: Reinhart Firchow. Köln: Paletti, 2004 [in Bucheinbandtasche; digitale Übertragung: Leipzig [u. a.]: Deutsche Nationalbibliothek, 2019].
Der kleine Muck [Wilhelm Hauff]. Der fliegende Koffer [Hans Christian Andersen]. Ein Hörbuch für Kinder. Gelesen von Gerd Baltus [u. a.]. CD. München: [Terzio-Nortorf]: Lighthouse Home Entertainment, 2005 [Digitale Übertragung: Leipzig [u. a.]: Deutsche Nationalbibliothek, 2019].

[Andersens Märchen]. Des Kaisers neue Kleider – Das häßliche Entlein – Die Prinzessin auf der Erbse – Der fliegende Koffer. [Nach Hans Christian Andersen]. Erzähler: Klaus Brose, Regie: Oliver Potthast. Gekürzte Ausgabe. Online-Ressource (mp3). Korschenbroich: Power Station GmbH, 2007.
Der fliegende Koffer. Der standhafte Zinnsoldat. Der unartige Knabe. [Die schönsten Märchen von Hans Christian Andersen]. Erzähler: Wolfgang Müller. Gekürzte Lesung. Online-Ressource (mp3). München: cbj audio, 2010.
Der kleine Muck/Der fliegende Koffer. Online-Ressource (mp3). Kolibri, 2010.
Der fliegende Koffer. MärchenWelt. Von Sven Görtz. Online-Ressource (mp3). ZYX Music, 2011 [weitere Ausg. (teils auf CD): 2015, 2016, 2018].
Der fliegende Koffer. Erzähler/Produzent/Regie: Jürgen Fritsche. Gekürzte Ausgabe. Online-Ressource (mp3). Butzbach: BÄNG Management & Verlag, 2013 (Die schönsten Märchen von Hans Christian Andersen; 7) [weitere Ausg.: Masterpieces – Kids, 2014; BÄNG, 2015 (Album: Die schönsten Märchen aus 1001 Nacht: Der orientalische Märchenschatz)].
Der fliegende Koffer. [Hans Christian Andersen]. Sprecher: Gerald Pichowetz. Audio Media Digital, 2014 [weitere Ausg.: 2017, 2019].
Der fliegende Koffer. Das HörBuch der Märchen. Sprecher: Christian Brückner. Musik, Produktion und Regie: Ulrich Maske. 2 CDs. Hamburg: Jumbo, 2003b [weitere Aufl.: 2004; digitale Übertragung: Leipzig [u. a.]: Deutsche Nationalbibliothek, 2019].

Filmography

Der fliegende Koffer [Kurzfilm] (D 1921). Regie, Drehbuch und Animation: Lotte Reiniger, Kamera: Karl Koch, Institut für Kulturforschung e. V. Berlin [Prädikat 1922: Jugendfrei].
Der fliegende Koffer [Kurzfilm] (D 1944). Regie: Curt A. Engel, Boehner-Film Dresden [Prädikate 1944: Jugendfrei, Feiertagsverbot, anerkennenswert, volksbildend, https://www.youtube.com/watch?v=QhRcinjhV1o (16.09.2019)].
The Flying Bag/Der fliegende Koffer (JP 1971). Mushi Productions/Paramount Pictures (Andersen Monogatari/The Hans Christian Andersen Fairytales/Pixi im Wolkenkuckucksheim. Auf den Spuren von Hans Christian Andersen; Folge 16) [Deutsche Erstausstrahlung 1989 auf Sat1; Titelsong: https://www.youtube.com/watch?v=P80U-qQe-44 (10.09.2019)].
Der Koffer [Kurzfilm] (DDR 1981/1982). Regie und Drehbuch: [Kurt] Weiler, DEFA-Studio für Trickfilme [Prädikat 1981: besonders wertvoll].
[Unser Sandmännchen mit fliegendem Koffer – Folge mit Fuchs und Elster] (Originaltitel und Jahr unklar), https://www.youtube.com/watch?v=kFHZyc3sUpA (10.09.2019).
The Flying Trunk [Kurzfilm] (DK/GB/D [2003]). (The FairyTaler; Episode 14; dt. Reihentitel: WunderZunderFunkelZauber – Die Märchen von Hans Christian Andersen), https://www.youtube.com/watch?v=V1h2lqtP7Hs (10.09.2019).
Märchen und Fabeln. Die Klassiker von Lotte Reiniger [Kurzfilm-Sammlung] (D 2006). Absolut Medien, Berlin (absolut Medien; 784) [enthält u. a. Der fliegende Koffer und Däumelinchen].
Der fliegende Koffer (D 2012). Regie: Arend Agthe, ZDF tivi (Siebenstein), https://www.zdf.de/kinder/siebenstein/der-fliegende-koffer-102.html (10.09.2019).
The Flying Trunk Story. Stories for Kids [Kurzfilm] (IN 2018). My Pingu Tv, YouTube, https://www.youtube.com/watch?v=XQ7VQmfFx3w (20.09.2019).

Other Media/Products

Briefmarken Bund Michel Nr. 2453 postfrisch Hans Christian Andersen, https://www.briefmarken-klein.de/Bund-Mi-Nr-2453-postfrisch-Hans-Christian-Andersen_p9859.html (11.09.2019).

"That Was a Wonderful Fairy Tale!"

Briefmarken Bund Michel Nr. 2748–2751 postfrisch, 2009 – Für die Jugend: 50 Jahre Unser Sandmännchen, https://www.hausderbriefmarke.de/bund-michel-nr-2748-2751-postfrisch-fuer-die-jugend-50-jahre-unser-sandmaennchen.html (11.09.2019).

DDR-Puzzle – Der fliegende Koffer, Hersteller: Annaberger Puzzle, Teile: 500, [Jahr unbekannt], https://picclick.de/Der-fliegende-Koffer-DDR-Puzzle-Annaberger-Puzzle-500-1930 83030443.html (12.09.2019).

Eierbecher – Der fliegende Koffer, W&S Sorensen Horsens 830 [dänisches] Silber, [Jahr unbekannt], https://www.ebay.de/itm/W-S-Sorensen-Horsens-830-danisches-Silber-Der-Fliegende-Koffer-Eierbecher-/163452050127 (12.09.2019).

Figur – Der fliegende Koffer, Royal Copenhagen, Sammlerstück aus der Reihe der Hans Christian Andersen Figuren, https://www.dphtrading.de/produkte/figuren/1249228 (12.09.2019).

Figur – Sandmännchen im fliegenden Koffer, Sammlerfigur [1994], https://sandspielfiguren.de/media/image/ab/41/24/2964_600x600.jpg (12.09.2019).

Kinderbesteck, Sterlingsilber, mit Motiven von Ole Luköje (der Sandmann), Tölpel-Hans, Das Feuerzeug, Der Schweinehirt, Das kleine Mädchen mit den Schwefelhölzern, Der fliegende Koffer, Das hässliche Entlein und Die Hirtin und der Schornsteinfeger, https://www.antiknetz.de/antikkram/stort.asp?selbnr=92969 (12.09.2019).

Löffel – Der fliegende Koffer, Abenteuer des H. C. Andersen Kinderbesteck aus Silber, https://antiknetz.de/antikkram/stort.asp?selbnr=358825 (12.09.2019).

Märchenquartett – Andersens Märchen, [Der fliegende Koffer u. a.], Quartettspiel für Kinder von 8 Jahren an, Auswahl und Text: Erika Schröder, Bilder: Traude Schlegel, Altenburger Spielkartenfabrik/Verlag für Lehrmittel Pössneck, [1987], https://images-na.ssl-images-amazon.com/images/I/A1XhQX31EHL.jpg (12.09.2019).

Postkarte – Der fliegende Koffer, Erfurter Weihnachtsmarkt, [DDR 1985], https://www.antik-falkensee.de/catalog/product_info.php?products_id=266633&osCsid=c7f35103b2aef2fd7c9 bd922348f6d75 (11.09.2019).

Postkarte (s/w) – Unser Sandmännchen, fliegender Koffer, G 6762, https://static5.akpool.de/images/cards/219/2196121.jpg (12.09.2019a).

Postkarte (farbig) – Unser Sandmännchen, fliegender Koffer, Modern Times, A6, Nr. 111–310, https://www.amazon.de/Postkarte-SANDM%C3%84NNCHEN-FLIEGENDEN-KARTENKOMBINAT-TELEPOOL/dp/B00JFS727W (12.09.2019b).

Sammelbild – Der fliegende Koffer. Aus dem Sammelbuch „Deutsche Märchen", Bild Nr. 19, Gruppe 12. Gemalt von Paul Hey, http://www.ansichtskarten-center.de/webshop/shop/ProdukteBilder/70262/AK_40130591_gr_1.jpg (11.09.2019).

Sandskulptur „Den flyvende kuffert" in Søndervig 2005, https://www.hcandersen-homepage.dk/?page_id=47121 (11.09.2019).

Skulptur – Der fliegende Koffer. Adresse: Jernbanegade 8, 5000 Odense C, Künstler: Bildhauer Jens Flemming, enthüllt am 04.05.1991, https://www.visitodense.dk/den-flyvende-kuffert-gdk1077448 [Detail-Aufnahmen: http://www.visithcandersen.dk/skulptur_den_flyvende_kuff.html] (11.09.2019).

Stockmann Märchen-Sammelbilder – Der fliegende Koffer, Deutschland, Stockmann, [ab 1945/50er-Jahre], https://www.ebay.de/itm/Stockmann-Sammelbilder-Sammelkarten-Maerchen-Der-fliegende-Koffer-50er-Jahre-/282728858417 (07.09.2019).

Teller I, Motiv: Der fliegende Koffer, H. C. Andersen Märchenteller Nr. 4, Royal Copenhagen, Ausgabejahr: [1994–1999], https://www.dphtrading.de/produkte/sammelteller/1264822 (12.09.2019).

Teller II, Motiv: Der fliegende Koffer (Illustration von Vilhelm Pedersen), Hans Christian Andersen Teller, Bing & Grøndahl, https://www.dphtrading.de/produkte/sammelteller/bnr8844-628 (12.09.2019).

Teller III, Motiv: Der fliegende Koffer (Illustration von Vilhelm Pedersen), Hans Christian Andersen Wandteller, Bing & Grøndahl, https://www.dphtrading.de/produkte/sammelteller/bnr4516-620 (12.09.2019).

Unser Sandmännchen Traummobile, PU 387, Fliegender Koffer, https://webimg.secondhandapp.com/w-i-mgl/56b71253505a1f3d06b7edfa (12.09.2019).

Zinnfigur – Der fliegende Koffer. Zinnfiguren-Museum Goslar, Album: Märchenquiz 2011, https://www.facebook.com/Zinnfigurenmuseum/photos/a.175985082495737/17598 5192495726/?type=3&theater (11.09.2019).

Zuckerdose – Der fliegende Koffer, Lucia Service von Bing & Grøndahl, Royal Copenhagen, https://www.dphtrading.de/produkte/fuer-den-tisch/3740-302 (12.09.2019).

Secondary Literature Before 1945

Andersen, Hans Christian: Vorwort. In: Gesammelte Märchen. Erster Theil. Leipzig 1847b, 5–6 (H. C. Andersen's Gesammelte Werke; 12). Digitalisat unter: http://www.digitale-bibliothek-mv.de/viewer/resolver?urn=urn:nbn:de:gbv:9-g-4889568 (08.09.2019).

Bi – Ba – Bo: H. P. Schmiedel: „Der fliegende Koffer". (Zur Jugendarbietung am Mittwoch, 28. Mai, 14:30 Uhr). In: Jugend-Funk/Mirag (1930) 21, 21.

Der fliegende Koffer. Märchenspiel nach Andersen von H. P. Schmiedel. Musik von Erich Liebermann-Roßwiese. Regie: Josef Krahé. (9. Dez., 16 Uhr). In: Jugendfunk/Mirag (1931) 49, 70.

Hans Christian Andersen und sein Märchen vom „fliegenden Koffer". Zu dem Märchenspiel für Leipzig am Mittwoch, 7. Februar, 14,40 Uhr. In: Die junge Front – Die Zeitung der Mirag-Jugend (1934) 6, 11.

[p. m.]: Film-Kritik. „Der fliegende Koffer". In: Film-Kurier 3 (1921) vom 15.09.1921, 215, 2.

Secondary Literature After 1945

Begleitheft zur DVD: Märchen und Fabeln. Die Klassiker von Lotte Reiniger. Berlin 2006 (absolut Medien; 784).

Buschhoff, Anne/Stein, Detlef (Hg.): Hans Christian Andersen. Poet mit Feder und Schere. Köln 2018.

Detering, Heinrich: H. C. Andersen: Märchen. 04.05.2004. Klassiker der Kinderliteratur – Ringvorlesung, http://www.literaturwissenschaft-online.uni-kiel.de/ringvorlesungen/klassiker-der-kinderliteratur/ (20.09.2019).

Doodle-Archiv, 2. April 2010, https://www.google.com/doodles/hans-christian-andersens-205th-birthday (20.09.2019).

Doodle-Archiv, 2. Juni 2016, https://www.google.com/doodles/lotte-reinigers-117th-birthday (20.09.2019).

Ewers, Hans-Heino: Der „König aller Verfasser von Kinderbüchern"? Hans Christian Andersen und seine Märchen im kinderliterarischen Diskurs des 20. Jahrhunderts. In: Kinder- und Jugendliteraturforschung 2005/2006 (2006), 37–53.

Google Trends, Suchwort: Hans Christian Andersen, 2004–2019, https://trends.google.de/trends/explore?date=all&geo=DE&q=hans%20christian%20andersen (20.09.2019).

Happ, Alfred: Lotte Reiniger. Schöpferin einer neuen Silhouettenkunst. Tübingen 2018 (Tübinger Kataloge, 105).

Hobsch, Manfred: Ideologie für Kopf und Herz der Jugend. In: Horst Schäfer/Claudia Wegener (Hg.): Kindheit und Film. Geschichte, Themen und Perspektiven des Kinderfilms in Deutschland. Konstanz 2009 (Alltag, Medien und Kultur; 5), 39–55.

Illustration – Flying Trunk, von Vilhelm Pedersen, https://upload.wikimedia.org/wikipedia/en/9/9b/Flying_Trunk_01.jpg (20.09.2019).

Internationale Jugendbibliothek (Hg.): MärchenReise mit Hans Christian Andersen. Ein Streifzug durch 250 illustrierte Märchenausgaben aus 32 Ländern. München 1994.

Kimmich, Dorothee: Einleitung. In: Stadtmuseum Tübingen (Hg.): Lotte Reiniger im Kontext der europäischen Medienavantgarde. Tübingen 2011 (Lotte-Reiniger-Schriften; 1).

Mylius, Johan de/Andersen, Hans Christian: H. C. Andersen. 40 papirklip. 40 paper cuts. Kopenhagen 2019.

Rajewsky, Irina O.: Intermedialität. Tübingen [u. a.] 2002 (UTB; 2261).

Schlesinger, Ron: Märchenfilm im „Dritten Reich". In: Dettmar, Ute/Pecher, Claudia Maria/Schlesinger, Ron (Hg.): Märchen im Medienwechsel. Zur Geschichte und Gegenwart des Märchenfilms. Stuttgart 2017, 143–177.

Stiasny, Kurt: Was Andersens Märchen erzählen. Original und Deutung. Mit Scherenschnitten von Ute Stiasny. Schaffhausen 1996.

Stiglegger, Marcus: Märchenfilm und Filmmärchen. Der beschwerliche Weg zum Happyend. In: Dettmar, Ute/Pecher, Claudia Maria/Schlesinger, Ron (Hg.): Märchen im Medienwechsel. Zur Geschichte und Gegenwart des Märchenfilms. Stuttgart 2017, 1–12.

Wegehaupt, Heinz: Hundert Illustrationen aus anderthalb Jahrhunderten zu Märchen von Hans Christian Andersen. Hanau 1990.

Wolf, Werner: The Musicalization of Fiction. A Study in the Theory and History of Intermediality. Amsterdam [u. a.] 1999 (Internationale Forschungen zur Allgemeinen und Vergleichenden Literaturwissenschaft; 35).

Mutabor!

Fairy Tales by Wilhelm Hauff in Media Adaptations

Ingrid Tomkowiak

Retrospect

Those who, like me, were born in the 1950s, knew Wilhelm Hauff's fairy tales, apart from the written version, as a child above all from the illustrations by Ruth Koser-Michaëls, as they were represented for decades in the extremely widespread edition published by Knaur Verlag since 1939 by Karl Hobrecker (Hauff 1965). While critics were disturbed by "the anachronistic, Biedermeier character of the scenes and the tendency to overdo it" as well as "the uniformity of the forms of representation and expression" (Pforte 1977, 249), the generations of buyers apparently did not take offence: the fairy tale edition with the colourful watercolours by Koser-Michaëls was reprinted numerous times in large editions; the edition of my childhood, published by the Droemersche Verlagsanstalt Th. Knaur Nachf. (with the copyright note from 1939), recorded a "total circulation" of 151,000 units in 1965. In 2016, Knaur published a new complete edition – with the same illustrations.

For me as a child, this book was my introduction to the world of the *Orient*. The exoticizing illustrations of Hauff's fairy tales shaped my idea of life in the Middle East for a long time: deserts and oases, caravans and caravanserais, turbans, caftans, veils and slippers, bazaars, palaces and mosques, the rich and the poor and the extremely poor – slaves whose existence depended on the arbitrariness of those who ruled them. Orientalism in the sense of Edward Said (1978) can be identified not only within Koser-Michaël's illustrations, but is also assumed and discussed for Hauff's texts, as a play between the foreign and the own, for which the Orient served primarily as a scenery (cf. Kittstein 2002; Polaschegg 2005).

I. Tomkowiak (✉)
University of Zurich, Zurich, Switzerland
e-mail: ingrid.tomkowiak@uzh.ch

But in my childhood and youth there were also audiovisual impressions of Hauff's fairy tales. I can vividly recall films by the Augsburger Puppenkiste and these being broadcast on television (*Zwerg Nase* 1955; *Der kleine Muck* 1957; *Kalif Storch* 1971; *Das kalte Herz* 1978), radio plays on records and on the radio (*Kalif Storch* and *Zwerg Nase*, directed by Claudius Brac, narrated by Hans Paetsch, ca. 1966) as well as the live-action films *Das kalte Herz* (1950) by Paul Verhoeven, *Die Geschichte vom kleinen Muck* (1952) by Wolfgang Staudte and *Das Wirtshaus im Spessart* (1957) by Kurt Hoffmann, a musical comedy of errors starring Lieselotte Pulver. The first two films had initianally been produced by DEFA in the GDR, but they were also shown in West German cinemas. After the Berlin Wall was built, they were initially shown only on GDR television, and later on West German television as well.[1] Marc Silberman (2005)[2] has worked out how closely these films were linked to the German mentality of the 1950s. While the GDR productions *Das kalte Herz* and *Die Geschichte vom Kleinen Muck* sought to elaborate a message critical of capitalism and in favor of humanism and thus pleasantly distinguished themselves from the National Socialist entertainment film in terms of content, although aesthetically they remained bound to the well-worn patterns of the "Heimat" and adventure film; in the Federal Republic the tradition of mainly home-related, humorous, shallow fairy tale films was continued.

Although explicitly addressed to an adult audience, these films also reached children and adolescents from the very beginning (cf. ibid., 240 f., 245, 252 f. and pass.; Giera 2002a, 295–300; id. 2002b; Shen 2015, 45–82). Interestingly, the critic Ilse Kümpfel-Schliekmann, writing under the pseudonym Ponkie, attested in the magazine *Filmblätter* to the film *Zwerg Nase* (1952/53) by Francesco Stefani with Hans Clarin in the title role, which was addressed more to children, that the film was successful precisely because

> it satisfies the child's imagination with its "realistic plot", but it also satisfies the critically observant viewer with its beautiful care in the construction of the scenes, its efforts to create a charming photographic atmosphere and its pretty directorial ideas. It is also pleasant that the film avoids the infantile, teasing, kindergarten tone that is so easily associated with this genre of film. (Quoted in Hahn/Jansen/Stresau 1986, 589)

The imagery conveyed or imagined with these media products was so powerful that I cannot imagine Hauff's fairy tales any other way than associated with those images. It was, I am sure, precisely the renunciation of a child-specific design of the films, which is why I liked them so much and why they still remain within my memory. In the case of Verhoeven's *Das kalte Herz*, this is probably achieved by the use of different genre conventions; similar to Hauff's original, this film, enriched by animation technology, is a hybrid of "Heimat", fairy tale and horror film, social

---

[1] In 1961, the Federal Republic of Germany's ARD decided to stop broadcasting DEFA productions; after 1968, this was corrected to the effect that "artistically high-ranking and politically non-superficially tendentious feature films by DEFA" (quoted in Wiedemann 2017, 205) were allowed to be broadcast.

[2] The article also contains an appendix with two extensive lists of Hauff adaptations: Motion Pictures from 1916 to 1985 and Television Films from 1954 to 1985. Cf. Silberman 2005, 260 f.

critique and character study. Set in a rural, Biedermeier ambience, this first DEFA colour film delivers thrilling entertainment, offers identification that appeals to a sense of justice and has opulent visuals.

However, many film adaptations of Hauff's fairy tales already existed before this time. They were oriented towards contemporary media conditions, artistic conventions and political developments, told the fairy tales in new versions, in part created completely different images and addressed quite different audiences, often aimed at children and adults at the same time. However, before I discuss these films, which were made between 1921 and 1944, I would like to focus briefly on Hauff's texts.

Hauff's Fairy Tales

Wilhelm Hauff's fairy tales appeared in 1826, 1827, and 1828 in three editions of the *Märchen-Almanach* [...] *für die Söhne und Töchter gebildeter Stände* (edition used here: Hauff 2003), which was founded specifically for this purpose. Hauff wrote about the first volume in April 1825 to the publisher J. B. Metzler:

> It is for girls or boys of 12-15 years and gives 7 mostly Oriental fairy tales as they are suitable for this age; I have tried to make them as interesting as possible, have thereby always observed the strict moral without, however, letting the fairy tales amount to a useful application or "fabula docet" [...] the idea of such an almanac [is] new and perhaps not unwelcome, especially in higher classes. (Quoted from Rölleke 1990, 572)

With these considerations regarding distribution, Hauff was the most modern of the fairy tale authors of his time, Heinz Rölleke (1990, 572 f.) emphasizes. Providing texts for girls and boys alike, making them interesting – i.e. also entertaining and exciting – and dispensing with the clear formulation of a utilitarian application was highly unusual at the time. Implicitly, an address to adults is also formulated here, for the remark that "perhaps not unwelcome, especially in the higher classes" probably refers to the parents who were supposed to enjoy the reading of their children.

Hans-Heino Ewers describes Hauff as a writer who was familiar with the finesses of market-oriented literary production:

> The young author, extremely well-read and literary versed, knows and masters the common narrative styles that his present day offers him. He knows how to strike the moral, the humorous-witty, the eerie-fantastic or Tieck-Hoffmannian, but also the pious-romantic tone in his collection of fairy tales. None of the traditional settings is left out, neither the Oriental nor the fairy tale, the gruesome-literary, the (sea-)adventurous, the socially critical or the romantic-homely in the shape of the Spessart or the Black Forest. [...] With their highly effective mixture of bourgeoisie and colourful adventurousness, Hauff's fairy tales form a pleasant contrast to the maudlin children's fairy tales of the Biedermeier period.[3] (Ewers 1990, 132 f.)

---

[3] The combination of adventurousness (in its various genre varieties) and bourgeoisie also proved successful for other, later nineteenth century *Stoffe*, if one thinks, for example, of the media reception history of various novels by Alexandre Dumas, Jules Verne or Robert Louis Stevenson.

In the reception of the texts, however, Hauff's innovation was long ignored. Critics equated popularity with triviality, railed against entertainment, suspense, show effects and specific youth literature. On the other hand, Hauff's fairy tales were canonised as children's literature. They became school *Stoff*, then educational film, the so-called Kulturfilm (cf. Riebe 1975; on the relationship between fairy tale film and children's film, cf. Liptay 2004, 13–15). The focus was on *Die Geschichte von Kalif Storch* (1826), *Die Geschichte von dem kleinen Muck* (1826), *Das Märchen vom falschen Prinzen* (1826), *Der Zwerg Nase* (1827), and *Das kalte Herz* (1828).

It was only later research that tried to portray a different view on Hauff. The anthology *Wilhelm Hauff oder die Virtuosität der Einbildungskraft*, edited by Ernst Osterkamp, Andrea Polaschegg and Erhard Schütz (2005), illuminates the work in its aesthetic-historical context and at the same time devotes itself to its medial reception history. Thus it says in the summary on the cover:

> Wilhelm Hauff's (1802-1827) appearance on the literary stage of the Biedermeier era was brief, scandalous, and crowd-pleasing. This young author was a master at playing the keyboard of taste and the literary market. Nevertheless, his texts continue to have an effect today: Hauff's fairy tales have made their way through books and films into the fantasy worlds of our day [...]. Of course, this success has always been suspicious to researchers. [...] The supposed lightness of Hauff's prose turns out [...] to be the effect of a virtuoso play on the keys of imagination and narrative forms. (Osterkamp/Polaschegg/Schütz 2005)

Stefan Neuhaus characterises Hauff as an early realist and ironist who plays games with the reader on various levels:

> [...] in today's terminology, one can speak of multiple coding. Hauff's essays, novellas, fairy tale novellas and novels are an offer to the reader to play along on various levels of the work, to open up spaces of association via pre-texts, to trace the role changes, to make the constructions of the plot(s) transparent. Such a strategy of play aiming at reflection anticipates literary concepts of the 20th century. Concrete behavioural patterns are portrayed, defictionalized, ironized, and juxtaposed. This makes Hauff an eminently (post-?)modern author. (Neuhaus 2002, blurb)

Joachim Giera raises the question "Wilhelm Hauff – a screenwriter who came too soon?" (2002b) and cites assessments that put Hauff in this field of literature, including that he was able to "create (clear) situations, (to) convey vivid optical and acoustic impressions" (Groeger 1965). Citing Hilde Schulhof (1928, 130), Fritz Martini judges that "Hauff narrates, with a technique typical of him and the rest of the period, in pictures, with strongly mimic-accentuated purposeful movement, which rightly recalled cinematic arrangements" (1971, 461). Christoph Schmitt notes that Hauff's precision (depictions of milieus, characterisations of people through objects, clothing, and foibles) corresponded "in part to concrete stage directions, so that one must describe his style as cinematic in Kracauer's sense" (Schmitt 1993, 47, cf. 277).

The following focuses on some early film adaptations of Hauff's fairy tales.

Early Films of Hauff's Fairy Tales

"The future of cinematography undoubtedly lies in the field of fantastic composition, the magic play and especially fairy tale poetry, and once it has been steered in this direction, it will certainly be able to achieve even more outstanding things," wrote Ludwig Brauner in the journal *Der Kinematograph* (1908, 2). However, fairy tale films were not quite as fortunate; in many cases, the image of fairy tales as children's literature stood in the way of their production and reception (cf. Höfig 2008). It took over ten more years before a fairy tale by Hauff was adapted for the cinema.

On November 21, 1926, *Der Kinematograph* published an illustrated advertisement by Universum Film-Verleih for various fairy tale films: "All theater owners are playing the popular fairy tale films of UNIVERSUM-FILM-VERLEIH GMBH during the months of November – December." Listed were *Der falsche Prinz* and *Das kalte Herz*, among others. The illustration shows the Schatzhauser character from *Das kalte Herz* and a dark-skinned boy with the inscription, "D. KLEINE MUCK".[4] The details probably refer to the films: *Der kleine Muck. Ein Märchen aus dem Morgenlande* (1920/21; directed by Wilhelm Prager); *Der falsche Prinz. Ein deutsches Märchen im orientalischen Gewande* (1922; directed by Erwin Báron) and *Das kalte Herz: Der Pakt mit dem Satan* (1923; directed by Fred Sauer). I will now discuss in more detail these and other early film adaptations of the fairy tales *Der kleine Muck* and *Das kalte Herz*, as well as those of *Kalif Storch*.

Der kleine Muck

As Cornelia A. Endler (2006, 358) notes, Ernst Lubitsch's feature-length film *Sumurun* (1920), a *1001 Nights fantasy*, characterised on the poster by Mihály Bíró (1921) as "Der Wunder Film", was an early attempt by German film production to cinematically adapt the overall plot of a fairy tale while also catering to the needs of children. After the end of production on the film, Ufa no longer had any use for the fairy tale-fantastic ambience and the expensive buildings that had been specially made for *Sumurun*, so Ernst Waschneck, an employee of the Ufa feature film department and on the production staff of *Sumurun*, acquired them and produced the film *Der kleine Muck* (1920/21, 5 acts) with director Wilhelm Prager on the same sets. Compared with *Sumurun* the film was a low budget production, yet it was met with immense success. The fact that it was shown as a family film in the regular evening programme of the cinema played a decisive role: "Equally entertaining for adults and young people" was written on the poster (Waschneck 1920). On February 8, 1921, the film passed the censors and was declared *Jugendfrei*; after the premiere on February 11, the *Vossische Zeitung* wrote:

---
[4] See: https://bit.ly/2UWkuuE (22.03.2019).

> Rarely has a program found a more appreciative audience than this week's at "Tauentzien-Palast". The fairy tale film shown there is also open to young people, and the young crowd made extensive use of this rare opportunity to attend a real cinema performance. (13.02.1921, quoted after Endler, 358)

The film was very well received by the child audience. Against the background of the cinema ban on children at the time, the magazine *Der Film* praised the attempt to circumvent this with family screenings:

> It was a joyous moment when the little tots were allowed to see the adventures of their little friend in the Tauentzienpalast. First of all, the uplifting feeling of being allowed to go to a "real" cinema for the "real" evening show! [...] But little Muck (Willy Allen) was also too droll with his huge fuzzy head and monstrous turban. And then the cute kittens and dogs. And the way he dashes away on his slippers! But the funniest thing of all was the long noses which the miracle figs created. That was something, to see such a fairy-tale wonder with one's own eyes! [...] Wilhelm Prager's direction knows how to get something almost like real suspense out of this harmless plot, bubbles over with delightful ideas and has chosen a cast that many a film for the "grown-ups" cannot boast of. [...] The idea of the family film, which the Kulturabteilung of the Ufa has created with "Der kleine Muck", must be called an extremely lucky shot. It is precisely the serious damage that the rigorous ban on young people is inflicting on cinema owners that makes the attempt to draw parents and children together in this way to family screenings seem worthwhile. (No. 8, 1921, 47 f.)[5]

What is also interesting about this review is the clear acceptance of what the child audience particularly appreciated about this film – "droll", "cute", "funny", "delightful" are the key adjectives here. Emphasized, moreover, is the opportunity "to see such a fairy-tale wonder with one's own eyes!" Similarly to the cinema release photos of the 1921 premiere show, the film images[6] correspond in appearance to early Oriental photography, which with its exoticizing and culturally staging images from the *Morgenland* already had a major presence in science and popular culture from the mid-nineteenth century onwards (cf. Luchterhandt/Roemer/Suchy 2017, e.g. 222 f.).[7] On August 19, 1926, Prager's film received the rating *Volksbildend*.[8] Only three years later, in the journal *Der Film*, a writer with the initials rk criticized this type of film as no longer in keeping up with the times:

> Well, [...] there are fairy tale films [...] that the child of our present day looks at with most astonished eyes, as little magic tricks, as fun entertainment, but which do not penetrate its heart. Poetic raptures from the stork to Hauff's fairy-tale Orient no longer fit into the age of the machine. To the children of today a car or a zeppelin is closer to its imagination than a rose carriage or a Faustian magic carpet. (No. 52, 28.12.1929, quoted after Höfig 2008, 100)

As Manfred Hobsch (citing Drewniak 1987, 601 f.) explains, the fairy tale film was also a problem for the National Socialists, especially in view of American animated film productions (cf. Hobsch 2009, 48). According to Boguslaw Drewniak (1987,

---

[5] Quoted by http://www.kinotv.com/mobil/film.php?filmcode=46659&q=88&l=de (18.03.2019).
[6] Accessed at https://bit.ly/2WcaTjJ (21.03.2019); Source: Ebay (20.07.2017).
[7] Accessed at https://www.imhof-verlag.de/media/catalog/product/pdfs/853397aeb12712b123c4ccc0f4e99b4c_Orientbilder%20Blick%20ins%20Buch.pdf (21.03.2019).
[8] http://www.difarchiv.deutsches-filminstitut.de/filme/dt2tb01089.htm (21.03.2019).

602), the Americans, of all people, were the first to fall for the idea of bringing the German fairy tale world to cinematic life in funny animated films. Even at the beginning of the war, the *Film-Kurier* had complained: "It shames us, because it is we Germans of all people who have the obligation to lead the way in this field. We have obligations to the fairy tale, especially to the treasure of German fairy tales, which are valuable cultural assets" (quoted in Hobsch, 48).

The film *Der kleine Muck. Ein Märchen für grosse und kleine Leute* by Franz Fiedler from 1944, released by the censors as *Jugendfrei*[9] on 4 December 1944, but performed exclusively in matinees and special events (cf. Klaus 2002, 122), must be judged regarding the background of the National Socialist understanding of culture. The fairy tale was relocated to Germany, on the one hand into a courtly baroque milieu of the seventeenth and eighteenth centuries, and on the other hand – matching Hauff's origin – into a Biedermeier environment of the nineteenth century.[10] The film's only reminiscence of Hauff's fairy tale's setting in the Orient comes in the form of two *Moors in* the king's court, clearly made up in black makeup (today one would speak of *blackfacing*), whose face Muck touches, exclaiming, "Donnerwetter, die sind ja echt!"

There is something very sedate about the film's worn and pathetical style of acting and speaking; even the slapstick elements adopted from silent cinema do nothing to change this. The Man in the Moon acts as a benevolent narrator figure who keeps the birth register, guards the fate of the child protagonists and repeatedly intervenes in a directing manner. At the beginning of the film he says, referring to Earth: "Ja, ja, die bedrängten Herzen, davon kann man ein Lied singen, wenn man ein so alter Mondmann geworden ist wie ich. Viel Leid gibt's da unten. Aber auch viel Freud [...], denn Kinder sind Freuden."

One of these children is little Muck (the son of big Muck); here – and this most certainly has to do with the fact that this is a Nazi film – he is not a small sixteen-year-old with a head that is too big, but a handsome twelve-year-old orphan boy who has to get by on his own without possessions after his parents have died. One of the three creditors who want to collect the father's debts from the orphan matches stereotypes associated with Jews in his outward appearance and in his social function as a usurer (cf. Schlesinger 2017, 171).

The message that runs through the entire film, "Sei froh und tapfer!", which Muck receives as a guiding principle from the Man in the Moon and which he autosuggestively repeats to himself again and again, corresponds to contemporary National Socialist perseverance and film policy at a time where the downfall of the

---

[9] According to Schlesinger (2017, 155), the film is based on the stage play by Waldfried Burggraf, *Der kleine Muck. Ein Märchen für Kinder in fünf Bildern* (1930). In contrast, the film's opening credits state, "a fairy tale for old and young people by Ruth Hoffmann based on a stage play by Friedrich Forster." Film stills, poster and cover of the issue of *Film Bühne* on http://www.maerchenfilm.info/filme-derkleinemuck1944.html (21.03.2019).

[10] This multi-temporality corresponds to a now common historicizing approach, as practiced, for example, by ARD and ZDF in their fairy tale series. Ludger Scherer (2019) deals with this under the concept of *fairy tale time*, which is based on Mikhail Bakhtin's concept of the chronotopos.

so-called Third Reich was already foreseeable. At the end of the film, the message of the divinely acting Man in the Moon – this time to the audience – is once again insistently given on the way: "Und vergesst nicht: froh und tapfer! Das gilt auch für euch, Kinderchen!" This is NS propaganda suitable for children in a fairy tale film that is only supposedly free of ideology, Schlesinger (2010) also argues.

Kalif Storch

On June 2, 1927, *Der Kinematograph* carries an advertisement from Gloria-Film:

> The GLORIA's new big OUTFITTING FILM. KALIF STORCH. A fairy tale play in 5 acts based on Wilhelm Hauff. The film of breathtaking suspense. The film of fairy tale effects. The film of the wonders of the Orient. The film of modern mass direction. The film of enchanting costumes. The film of the most marvellous buildings – is ready to be shown. (Advertisement 1927)

What is probably meant here is the Austrian silent film *Kalif Storch*, directed by Hans Berger and Ladislaus Tuszinsky in 1921, a live-action film with trick technology that premiered in Vienna in August 1924 but did not receive *Jugendfrei* clearance in Germany during the Weimar Republic until May 24, 1927 (cf. Winkelmayer 2004, 134–136).[11]

Shortly after this film, in 1923, the first animated film of Hauff's *Das Märchen vom Kalif Storch* was produced, a silhouette film shot with incident light (cf. Cürlis 2005, 20). For a long time, this film, entitled *Kalif Storch*, was considered to be a work by Lotte Reiniger (cf. e.g. still Endler 2006, 370 f.)[12]; since the 1950s, it has been archived as such at the Danish Film Institute. In 2005, Jean-Paul Goergen provided the decisive clue for the identification of the complete copy in the Danish Film Institute with an illustrated article on the fragment of the filigree silhouette film *Kalif Storch* by Ewald Mathias Schumacher, which is in the Bundesarchiv-Filmarchiv Berlin (cf. Goergen 2005, 10–12, 15; ibid. 2008, 40 f.). Noteworthy, among other things, is the Arabic-like banner[13] unfolding in the film, with the instruction to transform and re-transform what has been reproduced, however, in Latin characters is written, whilst using the magic spell from Hauff's fairy tale "Mutabor!" (Hauff 2003, 19), which was also used for the title of this article – and here refers to the transformation of Hauff's fairy tales, which takes place again and again through changes of medium and adaptation.

Silhouette films were an innovation at the time; the first one was made in 1916. Three years later, in 1919, Hans Cürlis founded the Institut für Kulturforschung in

---

[11] https://www.filmportal.de/film/kalif-storch_352f0193a2e841d8a508b921b12569d1 (25.03.2019).

[12] Here Endler is probably referring to Lotte Reiniger's famous film *Die Abenteuer des Prinzen Achmed* (1926).

[13] Film still: https://bit.ly/2UVmMdy (25.03.2019).

Berlin, set up a "Tricktisch" there, and from then on a circle of female animators produced silhouette films, including Lotte Reiniger, a silhouette artist who was already prominent at the time (cf. Cürlis 2005, 20), and who was publicly attested to have high artistic potential as early as 1921. Since she too later created a *Kalif Storch* silhouette film, this interesting passage – also in relation to the perception of a female artist – from the article *Werdende Filme. Das Geheimnis der Silhouetten-Filme* in the *Film-Echo,* the supplement to the *Berliner Lokal-Anzeiger* of November 28, 1921, is cited here. The description also fits her *Kalif Storch* (1935/54), which will be discussed in more detail below:

> Somewhere there is what you can call the artistic film. [...] In the Institut für Kulturforschung, which has a department for scientific films, a very cultivated and also very pretty young lady wearing 'Schneckerln' works as a sub-department, so to speak, and cuts large and small figures, little temples and houses, bridges, lakes, mythical creatures, ornaments out of black plates, lost in the world and lost in the film, connects everything that is supposed to be movable with dainty eyelets, makes the frail limbs of their shadows firm and then breathes life into her creatures (quoted from Goergen 2005, 7).

Reiniger's films revealed "truly pure artistic possibilities", the *Film Echo* continues (quoted from ibid.).

The next animated film of *Kalif Storch,* a mixture of silhouettes and drawn and painted background scenarios, was created by the Diehl brothers:

> In a suburb of Munich, between meadows and forests, three idealists of film have set up a film studio equipped with very peculiar technical finesse. They are three brothers: a painter, a film technician and a scholar, who work here, literally to the exclusion of the public, on the creation of fairy tale films. [...] these idealists named Diehl want to supply German film exclusively with fairy tales. A great animated film, *Kalif Storch,* has a whole new effect within this film genre. Its buildings seem three-dimensional and not flat, as is usually the case with fairy tale films,

emphasised the *Film-Kurier* No. 186 on August 11, 1931 (quoted from Goergen 2017). And it is precisely this plasticity, as opposed to the flatness (with its emphasis on contours), that characterises the Diehl brothers' film. Unlike Schumacher, they used background scenarios drawn and painted in central perspective on non-transparent celluloids (200 in total) and then shot – as he did – with incident light (cf. here and in the following Basgier 1994, 24–32). The human and animal figures acting in front of them are worked out as silhouettes; the spatial effect is created by reducing or enlarging the silhouetted figures, each of which is then assigned to a particular spatial plane – foreground, middle ground, background – to suggest depth. It is the first film made by the Gebrüder Diehl Film-Produktion and their only film using this technique; in later years, the Diehls became known for animated puppet films. The film was made between 1928 and 1930; it was approved for screening in 1931, music was added in 1937, and re-scored in 1942 (see Silberman 2005, 260). In the Nazi state, it was considered youth-friendly and educational to the "Volk" and belonged to the category *Kulturfilm,* which also made it suitable for school screenings. In addition to the backgrounds, which strive for a plastic realism, the lettering MUTABOR[14], reminiscent of the typography of expressionist silent films, is striking. Narratively, the film corresponds to what the Diehl brothers practiced even later: the film is stringently narrated, reduced to relevant plot elements, and there is no development or differentiated portrayal of characters, according to Thomas Basgier's characterisation (ibid., 26). He continues:

> All instruments that could contribute to the dramatization of the story were avoided: de-individualization of the cinematic personage and de-dramatization of a plot that is already low on climaxes, whose individual sections are strung together like pearls on a string and thus almost take on the character of episodes – two constants of Diehl's process of fairy tale editing. (Ibid., 26)

Ferdinand Diehl later wrote that *Kalif Storch* had caused a sensation, especially in teaching circles, and that overall "the idealistic success of the film was considerable", which was, however, read as an admission of financial failure. The film's theatrical release was also massively hampered by the introduction of sound film. At the time, the Diehl brothers lacked the necessary finances to dub the production, which still had intertitles (cf. ibid., 32).

Ambivalent views were also expressed in 1934 in a review of the silent film in *Der Bildwart* in June 1934:

> The film has been shown to children and adults and has been judged quite differently. Many children claimed that it was an excellent reproduction of Hauff's fairy tale, while others said that it deviated so much that one could hardly recognize the fairy tale in it [...]. In the overall judgment, however, one agreed, admired the great effort, even if one could not refrain from pointing out that there are many persons who could not yet walk properly and therefore adopted the locomotion form of creeping. (Quoted from Endler 2006, 372 f.)

In 1935, when Lotte Reiniger had already made many films and was intensely involved in critical film discourse, her version of *Kalif Storch* was first released in Germany; it was the year she emigrated to England. As *Caliph Stork,* the film was released in Britain in 1954 with an English soundtrack, and was later re-released with a German soundtrack. This film is not about tangible plastic effects and realism. Lotte Reiniger, a filmmaker who belonged to the artistic avant-garde of the time and had been schooled by Paul Wegener and Walter Ruttmann, emphasized the possibilities of realizing the fantastic with animated film as early as 1921:

> This way of working has the advantage that the designing artist does not need to take into account the laws of gravity, of the coherence of matter, in short, the laws of nature that govern every natural movement. He can do as he pleases with his forms and shapes. [...] There are no limits to the most extravagant imagination. (Reiniger 2005, 19)

These possibilities are also important for the realization of the fairy tale of *Kalif Storch,* where fantastic elements have a plot-bearing function.

---

[14] Film still: https://bit.ly/2TtSUDO (25.03.2019).

Reiniger usually worked with transparent sheets of paper layered on top of each other, which she illuminated from behind or below, and in which each sheet represents a kind of separate pictorial spatial plane. All pictorial objects and backgrounds consist of scissors cuts. The consequences of cutting with scissors and the material for the recording technique were already presented by Reiniger in 1924:

> [...] the crucial thing is that in the films I make, everything and anything is *cut with scissors*. This naturally results in a sharply defined outline in the background and framing as well as in the figure and other shaping. The shooting technique is also dictated. The figures must be on a surface lit from below, and the apparatus must be upside down above the surface and looking down on it. The figures must be made out of cardboard and lead, for bare cardboard figures would become warm and ripple from the strong light. And finally, the backgrounds must consist of transparent paper. [...] The figures must be infinitely mobile and very carefully guided in order to make an artistic virtue out of the lack of all other means of expression – such as inner contour, softly painted backgrounds – and to say the same thing with a simple movement of the outline that is otherwise achieved by many single moments. (Reiniger-Koch 1924, 205, emphasis in original: spaced)

For the characterisation of the figures, only the outer outline of the silhouette remains, combined with strategic use of ornamental elements and imagery. This results in harsh contrasts of light and dark, faces and figures become almost abstractions (cf. Knop 2015, 30 f.). In 1926, she emphasized that her "shadow figures move with the greatest truth to life, so that one completely loses the feeling that they are not real actors." (Reiniger 2005, 19) This view corresponds to contemporary experiences with silhouette films in school lessons, as Cürlis described in 1942, partly in retrospect:

> In most cases, special reference was made to the fact that the transfer of the material into black silhouette would not have been an obstacle for the children, indeed, that when questioned, the children would not only not have taken offence at the black figures, but would have accepted them as self-evident and natural. Thus, children only very rarely mentioned this fact at all in oral or written reports of what they had seen, and described the figures as normal figures; for example, there had never been any mention of the actually black faces. On the other hand, the figures were occasionally embellished with all kinds of things that did not exist at all. [...] But the fact that the silhouette stimulates this is significant and important for the usefulness in school. For the adult, on the basis of his intellectual grasp of what is seen, tends easily to attach far too much importance to the fact that the silhouette is a completely black picture, in which the black face has no expression except in its outline, with regard to interpretability; indeed, he fears that the child's grasp may be impeded by the absence of colour and internal drawing. (Cürlis 2005, 21 f.)

Yet Lotte Reiniger's films never denied the material from which they were made, Goergen (2008, 12) points out; Reiniger wrote regarding her material in 1935:

> There has been a lot of debate lately about the artistic issues of this type of film. For me, the solution lies in the fact that I only work with scissors. I have thus arrived at a strictly two-dimensional style, which I have never felt to be an inhibition, but have only welcomed as a form of expression highly appropriate to the film screen and the material of paper. (Reiniger 1935, 117 f.)

Das kalte Herz

Hauff's fairy tale *Das kalte Herz* is probably his most frequently adapted fairy tale – certainly because of the *Stoff*, which is also of interest to adults and deals with social and psychological conflicts, and because of its plot, which touches on various genres. New and, in several respects, very different film adaptations continue to appear right up to present day, such as, in addition to the DEFA film by Paul Verhoeven (1950) already mentioned, adaptations by Werner Reinhold (1978), Irma Rausch (1981),[15] Hannes Rall (2013, an animated film), Marc-Andreas Bochert (2014) and Johannes Naber (2016), which, however, cannot be discussed here (cf. Schlesinger 2015; Tomkowiak 2021).

In 1923, Adolf Wenter's film *Das Wirtshaus im Spessart* also appeared as an early cinematic version of *Das kalte Herz,* analogous to Hauff's embedding of the fairy tale within the frame narrative about two journeymen craftsmen who, together with the guests of the inn in the forest, drive away their fear of being attacked by telling stories. The feature-length silent film of seven acts was released by censors on April 14, 1923 with the verdict "Jugendfrei" and premiered on May 25, 1923 in Berlin at the Alhambra am Kurfürstendamm.

Fred Sauer's silent film *Das kalte Herz. Der Pakt mit dem Satan*, which was made around the same time and lasts about an hour, spans six acts, deals exclusively with this fairy tale. Although it was censored shortly before Christmas 1923, it probably had its premiere in August 1924, at the Ufa Theater on Nollendorfplatz in Berlin. The film was shot in Berlin-Wannsee and in the Black Forest in order to give the fairy tale film "its characteristic character," as the *Film-Kurier* of June 4, 1923 put it (quoted from Schlesinger 2015). Peter's desire for wealth is justified in this film, which is very loosely based on the literary model, not only by the urge for social advancement, as Hauff had depicted it, but also by the desire to be able to marry Maria – as Hauff's Lisbeth is called here. This dramaturgically justified motif, which corresponds with the *love interest* central to popular culture products, was taken up again and again in later film adaptations of the fairy tale. And it also plays a role in the design of the ending, for Peter does not get his heart back by outwitting Holländer-Michel, but because, having stolen it from Holländer-Michel, he calls out "Maria" – depicted in Gothic letters – at the moment of greatest peril. The warm heart in his hand exchanges places with a cold stone in his chest.

According to a review in *Bilddokumente zur Geschichte des Films*, the tinted film (night: blue, forest: green, room: yellow, morning: pink, particularly exciting scenes:

---

[15] This is a Soviet film, which appeared in German under the title *Märchen in der Nacht erzählt* or *Die Märchen der Nacht* and embeds the fairy tale of the cold heart, as in Hauff, in a frame story about wandering journeymen craftsmen, thus also using motifs from *Das Wirtshaus im Spessart,* cf. https://de.wikipedia.org/wiki/Märchen_in_der_Nacht_erzählt (29.03.2019).

red) presents the course of action through imagery alone and does so without explanatory titles except for the directly spoken sentences – often in the form of dialogue inserts directly in the image. Despite numerous camera angles and short cuts, the presentation is still theatrical, according to the assessment, but is already symbolically condensed and nuanced in the direction of silent pantomime. Although an attempt was made to show fairy tale landscapes and backdrops through skilful lighting, a touch of fairy tale atmosphere rarely emerged (Institut für Film und Bild 1967, 56 f.).[16] Schlesinger, on the other hand, judged in 2015: "[...] it is not so much the nature shots, but the décor, costume and the actors' acting that bring the film close to a fairy tale-like film expressionism."

An interesting detail should be mentioned: In this film, Peter brings back a coloured man from his trip around the world, who is put on display in Peter's home country for amusement – a racist scene from today's perspective, reminiscent of the ethnological shows still practised at the time, or of the exploration and travel films of the 1930s to 1950s.[17]

The reference in Silberman (2005, 260) to a film *Das kalte Herz* (director unknown) produced by Mercedes Film München in 1929 could not be verified. In 1933, *Mein Film* (No. 372, 2) makes a brief reference to a film manuscript by Carl Zuckmayer based on *Das kalte Herz* by Hauff; however, a corresponding film could not be verified either.[18]

Finally, the film *Das kalte Herz,* made between 1931 and 1933 by the still young (born 1909) but at that time already internationally successful pianist Karl Ulrich Schnabel (director, screenplay, production, camera), should now be discussed in some detail (cf. here and for the following account Fluri 2017 and 2019).[19] This was a privately initiated and self-financed experimental film shot with friends and family, neighbours and acquaintances of the director mainly around Berlin. Peter Munk was played by Franz Schnyder, later one of the most prominent Swiss film directors, known for a series of Gotthelf adaptations and the color film *Heidi und Peter* (1955). Holländer-Michel was embodied by Stefan Schnabel, the director's brother, who later became a successful actor in the USA featuring in numerous films.

---

[16] The text incorrectly dates the film to 1918 in the heading to the quoted section – a statement that is then found repeatedly in the literature when Sauer's film is mentioned.

[17] Minutes of Raff Fluri, Burgdorf (CH), on his viewing of the film at the Bundesarchiv-Filmarchiv, Berlin, on April 6, 2018; he kindly provided them to me on 24 April 2018. Excerpts of Sauer's film are part of the documentary *Bilddokumente zur Geschichte des Films*, part four: *Deutsche Spielfilme 1914–1924*. Federal Republic of Germany: Institut für Bild und Film in Wissenschaft und Unterricht (FWU) 1967.

[18] Kind notification from Raff Fluri. There can be no confusion with Zuckmayer's play *Das kalte Licht* (1955), since the latter refers to events in 1950 (atomic espionage).

[19] I would like to thank Raff Fluri for generously providing further information and access to the film.

Karl Ulrich Schnabel's diaries from 1931 and up to July 18, 1932 provide a surprisingly detailed insight into the making of the film. It also becomes clear here how persistently Schnabel stuck to his project despite adverse circumstances. In the summer of 1931 in particular, he took advantage of every opportunity to film, including the time during his concert tours through Europe. Schnabel found further filming locations in the area around Potsdam, Babelsberg and Wannsee. On May 14, 1932, the first test shots with actors and actresses took place; filming was often spontaneous and without permission, sometimes with the help of passers-by. Only simple technical means were available, which also affected the trick shots, that turned out to be all the more effective for it. Fast camera movements were shot from a moving car.

On May 7, 1933, Therese Behr-Schnabel, the director's mother, wrote to her husband Artur Schnabel:

> Nothing works out with Ruli's [meaning Karl Ulrich Schnabel, I. T.] film, at first the copying will take time and it won't get through the censors either, too many foreigners are involved and the Aryan plays the main role in it too [...] there is little hope ... (Matterne/Schnabel-Mottier 2016, 1001)[20]

As so-called *Halbjuden* the brothers Karl Ulrich and Stefan Schnabel were racially persecuted, and other people involved in this project were also subject to National Socialist persecution or discrimination. On May 12, 1933, the film was screened internally before experts in a heavily abridged version. Therese Behr-Schnabel described the event to her husband the following day:

> So today the film was screened again in front of a film expert who might acquire Ruli's concoction [...]. Yes, they were all very moved by it and this gentleman, if only I had kept his name, wants to buy the film! Ruli won't give it away, hold on tight, under 80,000 marks, it is unbearable, Stefan is fuming. (Matterne/Schnabel Mottier 2016, 1001)

But nothing came of it. In the early Nazi state, the film could not be completed for political reasons. The very next day the family left Berlin for Italy – without the film strips – initially for the summer holidays, but they never returned. Only Karl Ulrich Schnabel returned to Berlin several times, where he continued to try to make progress as a pianist. However, the situation in Nazi Germany forced him to leave Berlin once and for all in the spring of 1934; in 1939 he finally emigrated to the USA. His brother Stefan went into exile as early as 1933, first to Great Britain, then to the USA in 1937 (cf. Matterne 2012; Fluri 2017, 61).

The film was lost for decades until it was picked up at the end of 1990 from the widow of the pianist Hans-Erich Riebensahm on behalf of Karl Ulrich Schnabel. Schnabel had searched for a long time for the film reels with the almost finished but heavily shortened film, but kept coming across the film reels with the negatives and

---

[20] According to Fluri (2017, 61), there is so far no evidence that Schnabel actually submitted the film for censorship. There is no *Zensurkarte*, as it is a cine film (which at the time, as *Kulturfilme*, were handled by the Zentralinstitut für Erziehung). However, there are hints that he did present the film: a small note with directions to the *Reichsministerium* as well as the letter from Karl Ulrich's parents (written message from Raff Fluri dated April 17, 2019).

working materials. The restoration was only recently made possible by a lucky find made in 2009 by Swiss filmmaker Raff Fluri and by subsequent extensive research. Fluri also arranged for the film to be re-framed so that it could finally premiere at the Neuchâtel International Fantastic Film Festival (NIFFF) on July 3, 2016. Since the original definitive version cannot be precisely defined on the basis of the available material (preserved parts of the film, original script, typewritten transcript, changes requested by Schnabel and instructions on notes), the aim of the reconstruction was to create as faithful a version as possible on the basis of the shortened version of May 1933, which would correspond to Schnabel's ideas, but at the same time also to today's viewing habits. Finally, a musical soundtrack was added, apparently not envisaged by Schnabel: the American composer Robert Israel designed it, combining works by well-known composers with his own compositions to create a multi-layered orchestral accompaniment to the visual performance.

As I said, the film was mainly shot in and around Berlin. It is not set in an unclear fairy-tale time, but rather locates itself within the scenic setting of the late nineteenth and early twentieth centuries. Some settings resemble social studies in interior spaces, appearing like photographs from the context of the late nineteenth century social-hygienic debate (Fig. 1a). Others resemble folkloric field recordings. In addition, there is an expressive use of typographic elements in central scenes (Fig. 1b). Landscape is staged as an expressive emotional space. There are dissolves, double exposures, negative images and deliberate blurs (Fig. 2a). Fast cuts and image changes alternate with very slow shots, both procedures can function as psychological studies, in the first case for the illustration of mental turmoil and destruction, in the second for the maturing of decisions (Fig. 2b).

Narratively, the film works within a linear main narrative with flashbacks, foreshadowing, and dream sequences. The interplay of visual and narrative strategies gives rise to the film's modernity, which from today's perspective is striking and has not been matched by any other adaptation since.

The shots of Peter's trip around the world, which make up about one-sixth of the running time of the entire film, with images of famous places and buildings in many countries, of an opera performance and of festivals, were partly taken during Schnabel's concert and holiday trips and were now used for the film. They seem like a report and, from today's perspective, have a documentary feel to them. Schnyder, as Peter, was partly inserted into the film afterwards by Schnabel,

> so that the viewer gets the feeling of wandering aimlessly through the world together with the protagonist Peter Munk. Through clever montage, he succeeded in creating symbols that subtly refer to Peter Munk's emotional world. In addition to the multi-layered symbolism and intelligent cross-references, he also succeeded in creating shots that became contemporary witnesses and give the film an important documentary component, which is why we left the entire journey unchanged in its original state.[21]

---

[21] Written message from Raff Fluri dated May 6, 2017; regarding the aforementioned intelligent cross-references, Fluri explains a scene filmed in the Berlin State Opera: There, the opera *Zar und Zimmermann* by Albert Lortzing is being performed and Peter does not find any joy in it. The subtle thing is that the opera is subtitled *Die beiden Peter*.

Fig. 1 (**a**) Peter finds refuge with a family in the countryside. Karl Ulrich Schnabel/Raff Fluri, *Das kalte Herz* (1933/2016), screenshot (© 2016 Ann Mottier-Schnabel/Raff Fluri), (**b**) Peter dreams of Holländer-Michel. Karl Ulrich Schnabel/Raff Fluri, *The Cold Heart* (1933/2016), screenshot (© 2016 Ann Mottier-Schnabel/Raff Fluri)

Fig. 2 (**a**) Holländer-Michel pursues Peter in the forest. Karl Ulrich Schnabel/Raff Fluri, *Das kalte Herz* (1933/2016), screenshot (© 2016 Ann Mottier-Schnabel/Raff Fluri), (**b**) Lisbeth considers whether to help the old man. Karl Ulrich Schnabel/Raff Fluri, *Das kalte Herz* (1933/2016), screenshot (© 2016 Ann Mottier-Schnabel/Raff Fluri)

The flyer for the film accurately states:

> The film was far ahead of its time. Its completion 80 years later leads to an incomparable cinematic experience: a mixture of archaic-analogue, vivid special effects, visual compensation for missing language, novel narrative structures and unusual camera work. Since the film was not produced by a major studio, the director and writer were free to exercise their imagination and love of experimentation. The result was a film whose limits were set only by the technical and financial possibilities of the time, and K. U. Schnabel spared no effort in overcoming these limits.[22]

---

[22] The flyer is available through the very informative website for the film (https://daskalteherz.com): https://www.dropbox.com/sh/22117ja9pftajxi/AACGUUWqTCus3G4yPgzraH1ba?dl=0&preview=DKH_flyer_a4_d_web.pdf (30.03.2019). The website also features film stills and other footage, as well as a trailer for the film.

Finally, to sum up this extraordinary film with Kristina Köhler (2016):

> With its nod to magic tricks, *Das kalte Herz* seems inspired by early cinema; with its exterior shots and surrealist moments, the film is at the same time oriented towards the elements of an avant-garde visual language that characterised the cinema of the 1920s.

Final Thoughts

The cinematic reception history of Hauff's fairy tales is extensive, beginning in the early twentieth century and continuing to present day. One reason for the media success may be the polyphony emphasized by Ewers (1990, 132 f.), an observation that can be applied not only to the texts but also to the cinematic adaptations. A related additional reason is the cinematic quality of Hauff's texts, attested early on, as also briefly discussed above. As far as the innovativeness of the most recent film adaptations is concerned – also with regard to the modernity of Hauff's texts as models outlined above – more detailed analyses are required; they were not the focus here. However, it can be attested that both Hauff's fairy tales themselves and some of the early film adaptations were much bolder productions than the more recent ones are – on an aesthetic, technical or even content/society-related level. This may have to do with the fact that current TV productions, for example, tend to be more conservatively oriented anyway (cf. Lötscher 2017; Scherer 2019); but this may also be due to the fact that innovativeness and experimentation in film are not currently located in the crossover segment of family films, to which the film adaptations of Hauff's fairy tales still belong. Only the film *Das kalte Herz* by Johannes Naber (2016) breaks new ground, for example by linking the depiction of the Schatzhauser character with archaic natural mythological ideas and ecologically based theses.

In connection with the film adaptations of Hauff's fairy tales, it is not possible to speak of a media network in the sense of a planned media network system, but these *literarische Stoffe* from the early nineteenth century have led to a multi-layered corpus of manifold media products that are all intertextually related to Hauff's fairy tale originals. The research on the early film adaptations has brought to light very different material. In the case of some films, we were able to find out more about production contexts, in the case of others, more about contemporary reception. All of these films, which have only been discussed here in the sense of a rough overview, deserve a more in-depth analysis, both in terms of the products themselves and with regard to aspects of their production, distribution and reception, as well as their contemporary political, social and film-aesthetic context. The films adapt the originals in their own specific ways – historicizing, actualizing, ideologizing, aestheticizing, psychologizing, popularizing (cf. Gast 1993, 49–52) – and thus contribute to their transformation (cf. Kreuzer 1981, 36–41) or to the innovative continuation (cf. Bogner 2004, 438), differentiation and diversification of the source text and its levels of meaning through expansion, modification and transposition (cf. Doležel 1998, 206 f.).

References

Primary Literature

Hauff, Wilhelm: Märchen von Wilhelm Hauff. Mit 100 Bildern nach Aquarellen von Ruth Koser-Michaëls. Gesamtauflage 151 000. München [u. a.] 1965.
Hauff, Wilhelm: Sämtliche Märchen. Mit den Ill. der Erstdrucke. Hg. von Hans-Heino Ewers [1986]. Bibliogr. erg. Ausg. Stuttgart 2003.

Filmography

The filmography does not include the more recent films on Hauff's fairy tales, which are only mentioned but not discussed in the text.

Das kalte Herz (D 1933). Regie, Drehbuch, Produktion, Kamera: Karl Ulrich Schnabel. Ausführende Produzenten: Hermann Hochgesand, Hans-Erich Riebensahm. Rekonstruktion (Schweiz 2016). Projektleitung, Produktion, Schnitt: Raff Fluri, Verein Nachtlicht Media, Burgdorf (CH) (BluRay).
Das kalte Herz: Der Pakt mit dem Satan (D 1923). Regie: Fred Sauer. Hermes Film. Standort: Bundesarchiv, Abt. Filmarchiv, Berlin (analog).
Das Wirtshaus im Spessart (D 1923). Regie: Adolf Wenter, Orbis-Film GmbH, Deutsches Filminstitut (analog).
Der falsche Prinz. Ein deutsches Märchen im orientalischen Gewande (D 1922). Regie: Erwin Báron. Universum-Film AG (Ufa) – Kulturabteilung. Standort: Friedrich-Wilhelm-Murnau-Stiftung, Wiesbaden (analog).
Der kleine Muck. Ein Märchen aus dem Morgenlande (D 1920/21). Regie: Wilhelm Prager. Universum-Film AG (Ufa) – Kulturabteilung. Standort: Bundesarchiv, Abt. Filmarchiv, Berlin (analog).
Der kleine Muck. Ein Märchen für große und kleine Leute (D 1944). Regie: Franz Fiedler. Sonne-Film. Deutsches Filminstitut (analog). TV-Sendung des rbb: 04.07.2004 und 19.02.2006. Zugänglich unter https://www.youtube.com/watch?v=JN0plalQZYI (31.03.2019).
Kalif Storch (A 1921). Regie: Hans Berger und Ladislaus Tuszinsky. Film-Werke AG, Deutsches Filminstitut (analog, mit Virage).
Kalif Storch [Silhouetten-Animationsfilm] (D 1923). Regie: Ernst Mathias Schumacher. Colonna-Film GmbH. Dänisches Filminstitut (analog); Bundesarchiv, Abt. Filmarchiv (analog; Fragment). Zugänglich: Die Klassiker von Lotte Reiniger [Teil 4]. Lotte Reinigers Doktor Dolittle & Archivschätze, Absolut MEDIEN/ARTE Edition (DVD).
Kalif Storch [Silhouetten-Animationsfilm] (D 1930/31 [stumm]; 1937 [vertont]; 1942 [neu vertont]). Regie: Ferdinand Diehl. Gebrüder Diehl-Filmproduktion. Deutsches Filmmuseum. Zugänglich (Fassung von 1937): Märchen Zauber. Die schönsten Märchen. Gebrüder Diehl Puppentrick-Edition, Tacker Film/Deutsches Filmmuseum (DVD).
Kalif Storch [Silhouetten-Animationsfilm] (D 1935). Regie: Lotte Reiniger; The Caliph Stork [Silhouetten-Animationsfilm] (Großbritannien 1954). Regie: Lotte Reiniger. Deutsches Filmmuseum. British Film Institute. Zugänglich: Lotte Reinigers schönste Filme. Eine Auswahl aus der Gesamtedition, Absolut MEDIEN / ARTE Edition, hg. in Zusammenarbeit mit dem Deutschen Filminstitut – DIF und Primrose Productions (DVD).
Sumurun (D 1920). Regie: Ernst Lubitsch. Projektions-AG Union (PAGU) für Universum-Film AG (Ufa), Transit Film (DVD).

Other Media

Bíró, Mihály: Sumurun [Plakat]. 1921, https://de.wikipedia.org/wiki/Sumurun_(1920)#/media/File:Sumurun_(1920)._Filmplakat_von_Mihály_B%C3%ADró.jpg (31.03.2019).

Secondary Literature Before 1945

Anzeige: Der neue große Ausstattungsfilm der GLORIA. In: Kinematograph 21 (1927) 1042 vom 02.06., 2.
Anzeige des Universum Film-Verleihs. In: Der Kinematograph 20 (1926) 1031 vom 21.11., 27.
Anzeige der Gloria-Film. In: Der Kinematograph 21 (1927) 1042 vom 02.06., 2.
Brauner, Ludwig: Spezialitäten-Kinos. In: Der Kinematograph 2 (1908) 89 vom 09.09., 1–2.
Reiniger-Koch, Lotte: Wie ich meine Silhouettenfilme mache. In: Edgar Beyfuss/Alex Kossowsky (Hg.): Das Kulturfilmbuch. Berlin 1924, 205–209.
Reiniger, Lotte: Das Papier als Filmdarsteller. In: Heinz Schnakenburg (Hg.): Zu den drei Fischen im Papier. Eine Chronik des Papierberufs. Berlin 1935, 117–118.
Schulhof, Hilde: Wilhelm Hauffs Märchen. In: Euphorion 29 (1928) 108–132.
Waschneck, Ernst: Der kleine Muck [Plakat]. 1920, http://www.filmposter-archiv.de/filmplakat.php?id=24181 (21.03.2019).

Secondary Literature After 1945

Basgier, Thomas: Die unentwegt Bewegenden. Die Gebrüder Diehl und ihre Filme. In: Adolf und Luisa Haeuser Stiftung für Kunst und Kulturpflege/Deutsches Filmmuseum (Hg.): Mecki. Märchen und Schnurren. Die Puppentrickfilme der Gebrüder Diehl. Ausstellungskatalog zur Retrospektive vom 19. November 1994 bis 15. Januar 1995. Frankfurt a. M. 1994, 6–69.
Bogner, Ralf Georg: Medienwechsel. In: Nünning, Ansgar (Hg.): Metzler Lexikon Literatur- und Kulturtheorie. Ansätze – Personen – Grundbegriffe. Akt. und erw. Aufl. Stuttgart [u. a.] ³2004, 437–438.
Cürlis, Hans: Der Silhouettenfilm [1942]. In: Filmblatt 10 (2005) 27, 20–23.
Doležel, Lubomír: Heterocosmica. Fiction and possible worlds. Baltimore, Md. 1998.
Drewniak, Bogusław: Der deutsche Film 1938–1945. Ein Gesamtüberblick. Düsseldorf 1987.
Endler, Cornelia A.: Es war einmal ... im Dritten Reich. Die Märchenfilmproduktion für den nationalsozialistischen Unterricht. Frankfurt a. M. 2006.
Ewers, Hans-Heino: Romantik. In: Reiner Wild (Hg.): Geschichte der deutschen Kinder- und Jugendliteratur. Stuttgart 1990, 99–138.
Fluri, Raff: Franz Schnyder und „Das Kalte Herz". In: Burgdorfer Jahrbuch 86 (2019) 93–118.
Fluri, Raff/unter Mitarb. von Frederik Lang und Philipp Stiasny: Ein verschollenes Herz. Die Auffindung und Rekonstruktion von Karl Ulrich Schnabels *Das kalte Herz* (1933). In: Filmblatt 22 (2017) 63, 50–63.
Gast, Wolfgang: Grundbuch Film und Literatur. Einführung in Begriffe und Methoden der Filmanalyse. Frankfurt a. M. 1993.
Giera, Joachim: Vom Kohlenmunk-Peter, dem kleinen Muck und seinen Leuten ... Märchenfilme aus den DEFA-Filmstudios. In: Gerndt, Helge/Wardetzky, Kristin (Hg.): Die Kunst des Erzählens. Festschrift für Walter Scherf. Potsdam 2002a (Schriftenreihe des Wilhelm-Fraenger-Instituts Potsdam; 3), 293–300.

Giera, Joachim: Wilhelm Hauff: „Das kurze Leben und der lange Ruhm". Ein Beitrag zum 200. Geburtstag. In: Kinder Jugend Film Korrespondenz 90–2 (2002b), http://www.kjk-muenchen.de/archiv/index.php?id=1289 (21.03.2019).

Goergen, Jeanpaul: Angewandt oder weltverloren … Erkundungen über den Silhouettenfilm. In: Filmblatt 10 (2005) 27, 5–16.

Goergen, Jeanpaul: Lotte Reiniger: „Ich glaube mehr an Märchen als an Zeitungen." In: Die Klassiker von Lotte Reiniger [Teil 4]. Lotte Reinigers Doktor Dolittle & Archivschätze. Booklet zur DVD. absolut MEDIEN 2008, 4–13.

Goergen, Jeanpaul: 1928/29. Ferdinand und Hermann Diehl eröffnen ihre Münchner Trickfilmproduktion. In: Deutsches Institut für Animationsfilm | Blog Detailseite, http://www.diaf.de/de/home/rubriken/Blog_Detailseite.html?b=343, 07.08.2017 (the website doesn't exist anymore).

Groeger, Alfred Carl: Märchendichter Wilhelm Hauff. In: Wilhelm Hauff, „Saids Schicksale" und andere Märchen. Husum [1965] (Hamburger Lesehefte; 101), 66.

Hahn, Ronald M./Jansen, Volker/Stresau, Norbert: Lexikon des Fantasy-Films. 650 Filme von 1900 bis 1986. München 1986.

Hobsch, Manfred: Ideologie für Kopf und Herz der Jugend. In: Schäfer, Horst/Wegener, Claudia (Hg.): Kindheit und Film. Geschichte, Themen und Perspektiven des Kinderfilms in Deutschland. Konstanz 2009, 39–55.

Höfig, Willi: Die stumme Märchenfrau. Märchen und Sage im Stummfilm. Beispiele und theoretische Überlegungen der Zeit. In: Schmitt, Christoph (Hg.): Erzählkulturen im Medienwandel. Münster [u. a.] 2008, 87–108.

Hurrelmann, Bettina: 1826–28. Wilhelm Hauff […]. In: Brunken, Otto/Hurrelmann, Bettina/Pech, Klaus-Ulrich: Handbuch zur Kinder- und Jugendliteratur. Von 1800 bis 1850. Stuttgart [u. a.] 1998, 890–904.

Institut für Film und Bild in Wissenschaft und Unterricht (Hg.): Bilddokumente zur Geschichte des Films. München 1967 [gemeinsames Beiheft zu den Filmen F 785 *Markt in Berlin*, F 1506 *Bilddokumente zur Geschichte des Films*, FT 1574 *Lumiere*].

Kittstein, Ulrich: Das literarische Werk Wilhelm Hauffs im Kontext seiner Epoche. In: Ders. (Hg.): Wilhelm Hauff. Aufsätze zu seinem poetischen Werk. Mannheim 2002 (Mannheimer Studien zur Literatur- und Kulturwissenschaft; 28), 9–44.

Klaus, Ulrich J.: Filmlexikon der abendfüllenden deutschen und deutschsprachigen Tonfilme nach ihren deutschen Uraufführungen, Bd. 13: Deutsche Tonfilme. Jahrgang 1944/45. Berlin/Berchtesgaden 2002.

Knop, Matthias: Zwischen Expressionismus und Avantgarde. Lotte Reiniger – die Filmdichterin der Schattenwelt. In: Blattner, Evamarie/Desinger, Bernd/Knop, Matthias/Ratzeburg, Wibke (Hg.): Animation und Avantgarde. Lotte Reiniger und der absolute Film. Animation and Avantgarde. Lotte Reiniger and Absolute Film. Tübingen 2015, 27–33.

Köhler, Kristina: Vorweihnachtlicher Semesterabschluss mit der Filmvorführung von „Das Kalte Herz" (1933), 29.11.2016, https://www.film.uzh.ch/de/newsarchive/Weihnachtsvorstellung-des-Fiwi-«Das-Kalte-Herz»-(1933).html (30.03.2019).

Kreuzer, Helmut: Medienwissenschaftliche Überlegungen zur Umsetzung fiktionaler Literatur. Motive und Arten der filmischen Adaption. In: Schaefer, Eduard (Hg.): Medien und Deutschunterricht. Vorträge des Germanistentags, Saarbrücken 1980. Tübingen 1981 (Medien in Forschung + Unterricht/Ser. B; 2), 23–46.

Liptay, Fabienne: WunderWelten. Märchen im Film. Remscheid 2004 (Schriftenreihe „Filmstudien"; 26). Zugl.: Mainz, Univ., Diss., 2002.

Lötscher, Christine: Teenagernöte im Freilichtmuseum. Die Märchenspielreihen „Sechs auf einen Streich" (ARD) und „Märchenperlen" (ZDF). In: Dettmar, Ute/Pecher, Claudia Maria/Schlesinger, Ron (Hg.): Märchen im Medienwechsel. Zur Geschichte und Gegenwart des Märchenfilms. Stuttgart 2017, 309–326.

Luchterhandt, Manfred/Roemer, Lisa Marie/Suchy, Verena (Hg.): Das *un*schuldige Auge. Orientbilder in der frühen Fotografie. Petersberg 2017.

Martini, Fritz: Wilhelm Hauff. In: Wiese, Benno von (Hg.): Deutsche Dichter der Romantik. Ihr Leben und Werk. Berlin 1971, 442–472.

Matterne, Britta: Karl Ulrich Schnabel. In: Maurer Zenck, Claudia/Petersen, Peter (Hg.): Lexikon verfolgter Musiker und Musikerinnen der NS-Zeit. Universität Hamburg 2012, https://www.lexm.uni-hamburg.de/object/lexm_lexmperson_00002655 (30.03.2019).

Matterne, Britta/Schnabel Mottier, Ann (Hg.): Ein halbes Jahrhundert Musik. Der Briefwechsel Artur Schnabel und Therese Behr-Schnabel 1900–1951, Bd. 2: Briefe 1925–1951. Hofheim 2016.

Neuhaus, Stefan: Das Spiel mit dem Leser. Wilhelm Hauff: Werk und Wirkung. Göttingen 2002

Osterkamp, Ernst/Polaschegg, Andrea/Schütz, Erhard (Hg.): Wilhelm Hauff oder die Virtuosität der Einbildungskraft. Göttingen 2005.

Polaschegg, Andrea: Biedermeierliche Grenz-Tänze: Hauffs Orient. In: Osterkamp, Ernst/Polaschegg, Andrea/Schütz, Erhard (Hg.): Wilhelm Hauff oder die Virtuosität der Einbildungskraft. Göttingen 2005, 134–159.

Pforte, Dietger: Koser-Michaels, Ruth. Koser, Martin. In: Doderer, Klaus (Hg.): Lexikon der Kinder- und Jugendliteratur, Bd. 2. Weinheim [u. a.] 1977, 248–249.

Reiniger, Lotte: Lebende Schatten. Kunst und Technik des Silhouettenfilms [1926]. In: Filmblatt 10 (2005) 27, 18–19.

Riebe, Harald: Hauff, Wilhelm. In: Doderer, Klaus (Hg.): Lexikon der Kinder- und Jugendliteratur, Bd. 1. Weinheim [u. a.] 1975, 524–525.

Rölleke, Heinz: Hauff, Wilhelm. In: Brednich, Rolf W. u. a. (Hg.): Enzyklopädie des Märchens, Bd. 6. Berlin [u. a.] 1990, 570–576.

Said, Edward: Orientalism. London 1978.

Scherer, Ludger: Märchenfilm und Populärkultur. Zur kinematographischen Inszenierung des Chronotopos ‚Märchenzeit'. In: Dettmar, Ute/Tomkowiak, Ingrid: Spielarten der Populärkultur. Kinder- und Jugendliteratur und -medien im Feld des Populären. Berlin [u. a.] 2019 (Kinder- und Jugendkultur, -literatur und -medien; 113), 151–170.

Schlesinger, Ron: „Heil dem gestiefelten Kater!" – NS-Propaganda in Märchenfilmen zwischen 1933 und 1945. In: Zukunft braucht Erinnerung. Das Online-Portal zu den historischen Themen unserer Zeit, 27.02.2010. https://www.zukunft-braucht-erinnerung.de/heil-dem-gestiefelten-kater-ns-propaganda-in-maerchenfilmen-zwischen-1933-und-1945/ (21.03.2019).

Schlesinger, Ron: Märchenhafte Drehorte: Wo das kalte Herz schlägt. In: Märchen im Film. Kritiken. Analysen. Interviews, 23.09.2015, http://maerchen-im-film.de/maerchenhafte-drehorte-wo-das-kalte-herz-schlaegt/#comment-3009 (29.03.2019).

Schlesinger, Ron: Märchenfilm im „Dritten Reich". In: Dettmar, Ute/Pecher, Claudia Maria/Schlesinger, Ron (Hg.): Märchen im Medienwechsel. Zur Geschichte und Gegenwart des Märchenfilms. Stuttgart 2017, 143–177.

Schmitt, Christoph: Adaptionen klassischer Märchen im Kinder-und Familienfernsehen. Eine volkskundlich-filmwissenschaftliche Dokumentation und genrespezifische Analyse der in den achtziger Jahren von den westdeutschen Fernsehanstalten gesendeten Märchenadaptionen mit einer Statistik aller Ausstrahlungen seit 1954. Frankfurt a. M. 1993 (Studien zur Kinder- und Jugendmedienforschung; 12). Zugl.: Marburg, Univ., Diss.

Shen, Qinna: The Politics of Magic. DEFA Fairy-Tale Films. Detroit 2015.

Silberman, Marc: Hauff-Verfilmungen der 50er Jahre. Märchen und postfaschistischer Medienwandel. In: Osterkamp, Ernst/Polaschegg, Andrea/Schütz, Erhard (Hg.): Wilhelm Hauff oder die Virtuosität der Einbildungskraft. Göttingen 2005, 238–262.

Tomkowiak, Ingrid: Vom Aufstiegswillen des bürgerlichen Subjekts. Wilhelm Hauffs *Das kalte Herz* und seine filmischen Variationen. In: Himstedt-Vaid, Petra/ Hose, Susanne(Meyer, Holger/Neumann, Siegfried (Hg.): Von Mund zu Ohr via Archiv in die Welt. Beiträge zum mündlichen, literarischen und medialen Erzählen. Münster [u. a.] 2021, 615–629.

Wiedemann, Dieter: Es war einmal … Märchenfilme in der Bundesrepublik Deutschland und in der DDR. In: Dettmar, Ute/Pecher, Claudia Maria/Schlesinger, Ron (Hg.): Märchen im Medienwechsel. Zur Geschichte und Gegenwart des Märchenfilms. Stuttgart 2017, 179–228.

Winkelmayer, Sylvia: Der österreichische Zeichentrickfilm in der Stummfilmzeit. Diplomarbeit. Universität Wien 2004

Classics in All Types of Media

Max und Moritz Across Media

And a Closer Look at the Early Comic Strip

Bernd Dolle-Weinkauff

Wilhelm Busch and the Genesis of the Bubenstreich-Erzählung[1]

In Wilhelm Busch's *Max und Moritz* (1865), not only do many individual references to previously known works, motifs, and characters converge as "precursors and parallels" (Ries 2002, 1278 ff.); rather, three genre-historical lines can be discerned that are almost prototypically united in *Max und Moritz* to constitute the new form of the Bubenstreich narrative (Fig. 1). The basic foil here is the moral tale, a genre of specifically children's literary provenance, which made it possible to successfully connect the work to the current trends of the children's literary market. Ever since the Enlightenment, the *evil child* has played a growing role in cultural history as an image of terror and pedagogical example, becoming the preferred subject of children's literature with a pertinent orientation (cf. Richter 1993, 199). The highly successful pedagogical cautionary tale since the late eighteenth century and the moral tale that developed from it in the nineteenth century substantiate the apparent intention and tone of Busch's verses, which at first glance seem to continue the genre tradition without interruption. This is preceded in the picture stories in Busch's early work by several examples of the reception and processing of typical features of the pedagogical cautionary tale. Examples include the verse story *Diogenes und die bösen Buben von Korinth* (*Diogenes and the Bad Boys of Corinth*), which first appeared in 1862 in *Fliegende Blätter* (issue 881) and one year later in a different

[1] Boy's prank narrative.

B. Dolle-Weinkauff (✉)
Frankfurt a. M, Germany
e-mail: dolle-weinkauff@rz.uni-frankfurt.de

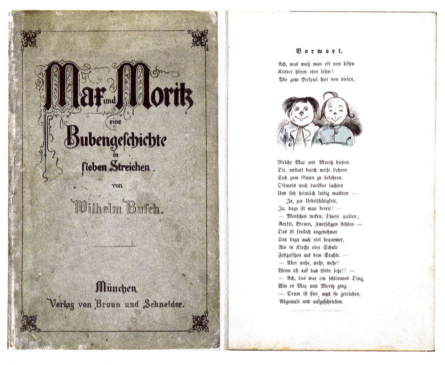

Fig. 1 First edition of *Max und Moritz*, cover and prologue (© Munich: Braun & Schneider, 1865)

layout as *Münchener Bilderbogen* (No. 350), and the *Münchener Bilderbogen* (No. 361) *Der hinterlistige Heinrich (The Cunning Henry)* of 1864. Both stories depict childish misdeeds that are marked as violations of good manners or educational commandments and – accompanied by pedagogical commentary – punished more or less drastically. The fact that in this phase Busch often operated with characters and plot elements that later recur in *Max und Moritz* is vividly demonstrated by the sketch of a complete picture story entitled *Der Kuchenteig (The Cake Dough)*, written in 1863 and rediscovered in 2008, which has not yet been provided with a written text (Platthaus 2010). The motif of the plot and its visual execution, as well as the appearance of the protagonist, a child with a sweet tooth who fell into the dough, seem like modules that are used again a little later in the 6th prank of *Max und Moritz*.

The line of tradition of the moral tale, which is carried entirely by didactic objectives, is amalgamated by Busch with borrowings from an entertaining folkloristic "art form of the fairground" (Braungart 1985, 9), the Bänkelsang,[2] whose origins go back to the sixteenth century. Also prefigured in the practice of Bänkelsang is precisely that inseparable linking of language and image that characterizes the narrative mode of the pictorial story. For *Max und Moritz*, the Bänkelsang – or murder ballad – was the godfather of the catchy rhythm of the verse narrative as well as of its content, the report of misdeeds and frivolous violations of the applicable law. Incidentally, it is the

---

[2] Street ballad usually narrating a dramatic event.

typical gesture of the balladeer who opens the narrative with a loud wail demanding attention ("Ach, was muss man oft von bösen/ Kindern hören oder lesen"), in order to immediately point with the pointer to the portraits of the heroes ("Wie zum Beispiel hier von diesen,/ welche Max und Moritz hießen"), whose misdeeds he then paints with pleasure: The panel sequence of the murder ballad storyboard is replaced by the picture sequence in the book, which bears some kinship to the picture sheets and accompanying booklets sold by nineteenth-century balladeers, but has the merit of being able to narrate in much greater detail. Here, too, it should not be overlooked that the link to the Bänkelsang is already very clearly evident in earlier works and forms "both typologically and developmentally basic patterns for works to come" (Pape 1981, 321). An example of this is Busch's contribution to *Fliegende Blätter* No. 796 of 1860, entitled *Trauriges Resultat einer vernachlässigten Erziehung* (*Sad Result of a Neglected Education*), which in some parts also refers to inspiration from Heinrich Hoffmann's *Struwwelpeter* (1845) (cf. Pape 1981, 322 ff.).

A third line of genre recognisable here is also already indicated in the text of the prologue of *Max und Moritz,* when it states about the heroes: "Die, anstatt durch weise Lehren/ Sich zum Guten zu bekehren/ Oftmals noch darüber lachten/ Und sich heimlich lustig machten." Neither the childish malefactors of the moral tales nor the tragic or sinister-murderous protagonists of the moritations exhibit such a tendency to the comic as is the case with Max and Moritz. Far more than the written text, the pictorial staging of the heroes bears witness to this, with the pleasure in the matter literally written on their faces at every prank. From the expectant joy in the preparation to the jubilation at the success of the attack; and even "Fein geschroten und in Stücken" their physiognomies still display that mischievous broad grin with which they were introduced in the first illustration in the prologue.

The type of hero that comes to light here can be traced back to the early modern mischievous jesters in the manner of Till Eulenspiegel and gained newfound popularity in the nineteenth century in the picaresque tales from Johann Peter Hebel's calendar stories, which bear witness to his special "inclination to literarize subcultural phenomena" (Franz 1995, 251). In Dieter Arendt's view, the tales collected in *Schatzkästlein des rheinischen Hausfreundes* (1811) are far less "moral and edifying [...] than we think we know from our textbooks" (Arendt 1985, 410 and 417), so that he defines the term "Schelmenerzählung" (picaresque story) for them – following Ernst Bloch. For him, therefore, the core pieces are the thieves' tales of Zundelheiner, Zundelfrieder and the Red Dieter, which deal with all kinds of trickery as well as high-spirited pranks. In contrast to many moritations, these tales do not deal with particularly brutal crimes – instead of the pleasure of horror, the audience is served amusing entertainment through more or less ingenious pranks. The prankster is not so much a criminal and certainly not a figure of terror, but shows himself either as a ridiculous clumsy fellow or as a cunning, sometimes quite sympathetic figure, although he too – for the sake of order and recognisably tongue-in-cheek – has to be reprimanded.

Thanks to these precursors, the moralising gesture of the verses in *Max und Moritz* takes on a naively draped, ironic hue; they are, as Friedrich Theodor Vischer judged, "funny even in themselves", taking on "quite a naïve appearance" (Vischer 1881, 121). The caricaturistic drawings and a corresponding picture direction often point beyond this "naïve appearance" (ibid.) by revealing the grotesque and the ridiculous undisguised. Even more so than in Heinrich Hoffmann's *Struwwelpeter* (1845), which is one of the immediate predecessors, in Busch's work the didactic message of the moral tale becomes a façade without disappearing entirely. Undermined by caricature and irony, the alibi of a moral lesson is preserved in the verses of the preface and epilogue and yet, especially on the pictorial level, gives room to the satirical and the clandestine joy in the effectively staged misdeeds. Busch thus decisively forces the break with the condemnation of the caricaturistic in children's literature, which Heinrich Hoffmann's *Struwwelpeter* had provocatively initiated – and thus the refunctioning of the moral into a boy's prank narrative – by recourse in particular to the picaresque story and the folkloristic tradition of the Bänkelsang.

Max und Moritz as a Media Phenomenon (1865–1930)

Wilhelm Busch's picture book from 1865, which appears to have been so successful in historical retrospect, was by no means an instant bestseller. When the author finally succeeded in having the work, which had already been completed in essential parts at the end of 1863, published by Braun & Schneider in Munich, he was faced with an unexpected rejection by the Dresden based publisher J. Heinrich Richter, who had published his *Bilderpossen* (picture farces) shortly before. However, the demand for the volume at Braun & Schneider was also initially disappointing (cf. Weissweiler 2007, 127). Although there are no statements from the time immediately after publication, the publisher later stated that the picture book had been met with massive rejection on the part of educators and that booksellers had therefore not believed that a further edition would be produced at all (cf. Ries 2002, 1339). Thus the sale of the four thousand copies of the first edition dragged on until 1868. However, this year saw a turnaround; the second edition was followed by a third in the same year, and after that hardly a year went by until the 1930s without at least one, or more often two or even several new editions appearing, so that in 1925 the hundredth edition was published in German by Braun & Schneider (cf. Liebert 1990, 141 ff.).

Translations were also soon distributed abroad, beginning with an edition in Danish in 1866. By 1930, *Max und Moritz* had appeared in 20 languages, with Eastern Europe forming the main focus (cf. Görlach 1982; Görlach 1997, 84 ff.). Particularly in the Anglophone world, Busch's picture books and picture stories in general were already widely read before the turn of the century, even though many of them were unauthorized translations and plagiarisms. Facilitated by "the failure of new efforts to legislate and enforce copyright vis-á-vis small fry like cheap magazine illustrations" (Kunzle 1992, 99), authors and publishers of picture stories in Great Britain and the USA in particular seem to have taken considerable advantage of Busch's works (ibid., 100 ff.). This finding is confirmed by Kevin Carpenter's research on the mass press regarding comedy in England from the last third of the nineteenth century to the beginning of the First World War. Particularly with regard to stories featuring "bad boys" and their misdeeds, he sees Wilhelm Busch's Bilderbogen and Bildgeschichten as key instigators for the emergence of numerous "homegrown young scamps" who wreaked havoc in London's funny papers in the 1890s, often as pairs of twins (Carpenter 2018). Even in the USA, where the first plagiarism appeared as early as 1862 (cf. Jones/Brown 2007, 197), Wilhelm Busch's work was not unknown towards the end of the century and enjoyed considerable popularity. Kunzle even goes so far as to claim that "Busch's style and subject-matter (if not his name) were disseminated […] especially in Britain and the United States, to literally millions of readers" (Kunzle 1992, 99).

The first English-language translation of *Max und Moritz* was published in 1871 under the title *Max and Maurice* in the translation by Charles Brooks in a Boston publishing house – even before the first British translation in 1873. Until 1914, ten US-American editions or reprints are attested (cf. Jones/Brown 2007, 180 and 193). Individual authors have also published more or less fragmentary adaptations. Rühle (1999, 508) lists *The Adventures of Teasing Tom and Naughty Ned* by Clark's Spool Cotton from 1879, which was apparently published in a large number of copies, with H. Bashfield as the author. The picture story, which closely follows the two widow Bolte pranks, demonstrates how Bolte's chickens are hunted down with ONT sewing thread. Furthermore, the picture story *The Revenge of the Persecuted Baker*, for example, published by Franklin Morris Howarth in the satirical magazine *Judge* in 1891,[3] arguably suggests the model of *Max und Moritz*'s sixth boy prank in the bakery (cf. Galway 2001, 189; Gravett 2005, 167). Harry Greening, on the other hand, created easily recognisable recreations of the Max and Moritz characters with the protagonists of the short-lived series *The Tinkle Brothers,* published in the *New York Journal* in 1897 and discontinued after only a few episodes (cf. Gordon 1998, 33), which even made the front page of the magazine insert *American Humorist* on October 3.[4]

The "Buschiade" as a Follow-Up: Imitation – Adaptation – Parody

These latter examples belong to a complex of literature, which occupies a prominent position in the history of *Max und Moritz*'s impact. Just as Hoffmann's picture book inspired numerous imitations and more or less creative adaptations in the form of so-called *Struwwelpetriaden*, *Max und Moritz* found its expression in a multitude of subsequent publications that are referred to as *Max-und-Moritziaden* or *Buschiaden*. The latter designation goes back to one of the longest relevant adaptations in the German-speaking world, which even up to the present day has appeared in ever new variants adapted to contemporary tastes and may be regarded as the

---

[3] For an illustration, see Kunzle 1998, 167.
[4] The resemblance to Max and Moritz goes so far that they were not recognized as the *Tinkle Brothers* by the editors of an anthology of contributions to the forerunners of the comic strip in the nineteenth century, whose cover they adorn, but were referred to as "Max and Moritz […] by the German Wilhelm Busch". Cf. Lefèvre/Dierick 1998, 4 [comment in the picture credits on the imprint page].

gender-specific counterpart to Wilhelm Busch's boy's prank stories: *Lies und Lene, die Schwestern von Max und Moritz (Lies and Lene, the sisters of Max and Moritz)*, probably first published in 1896 and already reaching its 10th edition in 1897. Written by Hulda von Levetzow and drawn by Franz Maddalena, it is called in the subtitle *Eine Buschiade für Groß und Klein in 7 Streichen*.[5]

Works of this kind, which I have called follow-ups, are characterized by a recurring, close connection to Busch's *Max und Moritz,* which not infrequently – as in *Lies und Lene* – culminates in an explicit reference to the model. Among the early examples are titles such as *Eduard und Ferdinand, mit Max und Moritz nah verwandt* (c. 1900) by Robert Hertwig or those without an author being named such as *Max und Moritz. Bubengeschichten in Streichen für Groß & Klein* (c. 1890) and *Neuer Max und Moritz. Eine Bubengeschichte in 5 Streichen* (c. 1893), in which some of Busch's pictures were accompanied by new written texts. This continued after the turn of the century in more and more new publications, such as *Max und Moritz im Luftballon. Allerhand lustige Fahrten zweier Lausbuben* (around 1905) by Joseph Kohn, *Fritz und Franz ein Brüderpaar, wie es Max und Moritz war* (around 1915). That well-known authors and illustrators also liked to fall back on the *Buschiaden* pattern and understood this as a tribute to Busch is shown, for example, by the little volume *Die bösen Buben* by Ludwig Thoma and Thomas Theodor Heine, published in 1903 for Busch's 70th birthday. For the period from 1911 to the end of the 1920s, Rühle records a peak in production with 40 titles alone (Rühle 1999, 527 ff.), whereby only the picture books are recorded, but not the equally numerous small forms that were published as adaptations and parodies in magazines and newspapers.

The Buschiade remains recognisably attached to its model and remains largely fixed in its inventory of forms and characters as well as in the conflict schemes of the plot. It is therefore not identical with the boy's prank story as such. Thematically and concerning the subjects, however, the Buschiaden often open up new terrain or can be applied to very different areas of application and can certainly be subjected to contradictory intentions. Thus, as in the aforementioned example of Heine and Thoma, the *Bösen Buben* can appear in 1903 as vehement critics of the Wilhelmine order, just as in *Die Luftbuben* (1915) by Curt von Frankenberg, as well as drawings

---

[5] In contrast, Reiner Rühle, bibliographer and commentator on a comprehensive list of adaptations of the *wicked children*, both Hoffmann's and Busch's prefers the term *Max-und-Moritziaden* in his 1999 publication. The titles listed there include not only the "pictorially or textually altered editions of *Max und Moritz*" but also all titles considered by Rühle to be "imitations, parodies, and adaptations" (Rühle 1999, 15); these terms are, however, overly broad in various respects: Thus, as *Tier-Max-und-Moritziaden* with *Fipps der Affe* (1879) and *Plisch und Plum* (1882), not only later works of their own are subsumed under them, but also those that, like *Diogenes und die bösen Buben von Korinth,* were written before *Max und Moritz.* In addition, quite a few stories are listed that have nothing more in common with Busch's *Max und Moritz* than belonging to the genre of boy's prank narrative in the form of a picture story. The term *Max und-Moritziade* thus nominally provides a specification that is to be missed elsewhere. I therefore prefer the term *Buschiade* and use it for those among the large number of boy's prank narratives in the succession of *Max und Moritz* that reveal manifest references to the pre-text in word, image, and narrative style.

by Robert L. Leonhard and – not identified in the title: by Walter Trier (cf. Rühle 1999, 532) – they are made serviceable for patriotic purposes with their pranks. The treatment of technical innovations, in this case aviation, which is also prominent here, is another common feature of not a few Buschiaden. What becomes clear here is a function reminiscent of the medial forefathers, Bilderbogen and Moritat. The fairground art of the Bänkelsang and the broadsheets were also, as it were, flexible media that served their audience with familiar forms on the one hand and unheard-of news on the other. Thus, the Buschiaden are obviously also about serving contemporary phenomena to the audience as fascinating curiosities, whereby the recourse to Busch's figures and topoi exploits and perpetuates their popularity in equal measure. In the history of the Buschiaden, this trait can be very vividly traced back as a unity of formal stereotypes and actualisation of themes and subjects up to present day (cf. Rühle 1999, 498 ff.).

In the 1920s in particular, they are often used for advertising purposes (ibid., 547 ff.) and, on the other hand, in three episodes drawn by Harry Rotziegel, they become contributors to the communist children's newspaper *Die Trommel* (1926). Most of the Buschiaden, however, remain rather apolitical and spend their creativity on inventing everyday pranks, attacks on supposed or actual authorities and more or less peaceful contemporaries. They orient themselves more closely or more widely to striking motifs and details from Busch's work, to the appearance of the heroes, to certain formal features such as the format of a series of several pranks with two protagonists, to the linguistic setting as verse text, and strictly follow the principle of the narrative sequence of images. The final punishment, not seldomly – as in Busch – death – is not obligatory. It is omitted to the extent that the protagonists are openly and undisguisedly created as sympathetic figures whose deeds serve a higher purpose, whatever it may be. The modifications of the retellings mostly consist of general modernisations of the milieu and the props, of gender-varied protagonists and plots, and of adaptations to contemporary, historical circumstances and events which, for instance, led to a boom of the Buschiade as parody in the era of the First World War (cf. Dolle-Weinkauff 2015, 46 f.; Sackmann 2016), for which here as one of many examples *Max und Moritz im Felde. Eine lustige Soldatengeschichte* may be mentioned as one of many examples (Fig. 2). It makes clear how Wilhelm Busch's model is continued in the portrayal of the protagonists and in the language of the written text, while the story treads its own paths.

Max und Moritz on Stage ...

Almost all dramatisations known so far in the period up to 1930 can also be characterized as Buschiaden, beginning with the first one of 1877, which – as Ries (2002, 1346) rightly proves – describes itself as a stage adaptation approved by Busch. *Max und Moritz. Ein Bubenstück in 7 Streichen (2 Abtheilungen)* by Leopold Günther, with music by Fritz Becker, was published by the Berlin publishing house of the theatre bookshop Kühling & Güttner in 1877. The first performance took

Fig. 2 The Buschiade as war satire: *Max und Moritz im Felde* (© Berlin: Schneider, [1915])

place on March 3 of the following year at the Grand Ducal Court and National Theatre in Mannheim (Görlach 1990, 130). According to the *Handbücher des ehemaligen Württembergischen Hoftheaters* in Stuttgart, after the first performance there in 1882, a total of 14 annual revivals can be documented for the years 1883 to 1902 (cf. Krekler 1979, 247). Further performances are documented for the Grand Ducal Theatre in Oldenburg in 1894 and 1907, in the Vienna Prater in 1900 and in the Bonn City Theatre in 1914.

It speaks for the certainly not insignificant importance of this dramatisation throughout the Wilhelmine era when Astrid Lange-Kirchheim demonstrates in her work on the reception of *Max und Moritz* in Franz Kafka's work that Günther's adaptation was still being performed extremely successfully 40 years after its premiere in the 1916/1917 season at the New German Theater in Prague. As the daily newspaper *Bohemia* reports, there was an extraordinarily brisk demand for tickets for the "Kinderschwank" (Lange-Kirchheim 2004, 164 f.). When Torsten Körner states in his Heinz Rühmann biography that the latter also took on the role of Max in a production of Leopold Günther's adaptation at the Munich Kammerspiele in 1925, it becomes clear that this story continued into the years of the Weimar Republic (cf. Körner 2001, 413). Under these circumstances, it is at least not improbable that a report in the *Film-Kurier* about a 1913 *Max und Moritz* performance at the Luisentheater in Berlin-Kreuzberg, in which Veit Harlan, later an actor and director loyal to the Nazi rulers, is said to have participated in his younger years, also refers to a production of Günther's play (cf. Kienzl 1942, 3 f.).

By 1930, a good dozen further dramatisations of the *Max und Moritz* material by various authors can be identified, the vast majority of them as printed stage texts from various publishers, a few also through press releases and archived playbills (cf. Rühle 1999, 605 ff.). Like Leopold Günther's play, some of them, if not most, were designed as Christmas plays, such as *Max' und Moritz' Weihnachtsfahrt. Ein Kinderspiel zum Weihnachtsabend* by Regina Angres and *Max und Moritz in der Himmelswerkstatt. Ein Weihnachtsspiel für Kinder mit Gesang und Tanz in drei Aufzügen* by Rudolf Göthner (1925). Throughout, these are farces and comedies with musical accompaniment; some, such as *Max und Moritz als Schulschwänzer* (1906), are identified as pantomimes. The latter – along with *Max und Moritz auf dem Ferkelmarkt* by Emmeran Gleißner (1927) – is among the minority of those plays in which the mischievousness of the heroes is celebrated in an almost unsanctioned manner. Rühle notes that the protagonists here "instead of going to school, steal sausages from the butcher and rolls from the baker" and considers it the "climax of this victorious and unpunished anarchy [...] that they also ring the school bell, and therefore all the schoolchildren can go home early" (Rühle 1999, 607). The majority, on the other hand, takes a decidedly moralising approach and thus moves the Buschiade much closer to the tradition of moral narrative. Not infrequently, the motif of conversion and purification, which is rather alien to the rascal story, appears here, as for example in the patriotic "Jungmannen-Spiel" by Margarete Reichert *Max und Moritz im Schützengraben (Max and Moritz in the Trench)* from the war year of 1916, which is about the healing of a notorious boaster.

The printed texts are not always intended for public performance on stages or for amateur play practice. Another medium that comes into play here is the paper theatre intended for implementation in nurseries, of which Ernst Siewert's booklet *Max und Moritz oder Wer andern eine Grube gräbt, fällt selbst hinein (Max and Moritz or Whoever digs a pit for others falls into it)*, first published in 1887 by Schreiber in Eßlingen, bears witness (Fig. 3). Here, the printed version offers not only the text, but also, in the appendix, coloured figures to be cut out for performance on a paper stage.

A photograph from the early twentieth century[6] that is informative in some respects for the dissemination of *Max und Moritz* plays and performance practice can be found in the volume *125 Jahre Max und Moritz* (Görlach 1990, 136). The photograph shows an impromptu street stage surrounded by festively dressed audiences in an inner-city square, accessed by a wide flight of steps and topped by a curved large-scale sign with the Cyrillic inscription Макс и Мориц, below which is 'Max und Moritz' in smaller Latin letters. In the central background of the picture is a stage set covering the entire front of the house, with numerous drawings that can be identified as quite faithful enlargements of individual figures and scenes from Wilhelm Busch's picture story. In front of it, the actors of the performance – the widow Bolte as well as the protagonists are clearly visible – have settled down on

---

[6] The location of the photograph is given as St. Petersburg. The caption dates the photograph "before 1918". However, it can be assumed that it was taken before the war, more precisely before 1914, because the city was renamed Petrograd in 1914.

Fig. 3 *Max und Moritz* in the paper theatre. Play by Ernst Siewert (© Eßlingen: Schreiber, 1887)

chairs, together with further female and male people, mostly costumed in historical uniforms. It is rather unlikely that this is a performance by a professional ensemble. The surroundings, the design of the stage set and the presentation of the participants suggest that an amateur acting group is performing here. In the background to the left of the stage a group of men can be seen, dressed as historical heralds. The scene is framed by flags and garland decorations on the houses and across the street. This suggests that it is a performance in the context of public celebrations, possibly a city anniversary or the like. If the name of the location St. Petersburg is correct, it could be a scene from a 1903 celebration of the 200th anniversary of the founding of the city by Peter I (1672–1725) in 1703. The performance might then have been a contribution from the ranks of the German community, which constituted the numerically largest minority in the city, or from one of the numerous nearby German colonies (cf. Busch 1995).

… and on the Screen

The new medium of film also apparently took on Wilhelm Busch's prank story on a larger scale. There is evidence of about 20 film adaptations of varying kinds up to 1930, of which, however, very few have survived or can be found. The references in the literature regarding these are far less precise and detailed than in the case of the print media and can hardly be checked in detail.[7] The first *Max und Moritz* productions mentioned here date from the years 1906 to 1908 and are all attributed to the

---

[7] The evidence comes from reports and advertisements in the contemporary issues of *Film-Kurier* and *Der Kinematograph* as well as the *German Early Cinema Database* of the Universität Köln. Cf. https://filmwissenschaftumsonst.wordpress.com/2014/10/17/the-german-early-cinema-database (19.10.2019).

Berlin Kinematografen- und Lichtbildgesellschaft (sometimes also Lichteffekt-Gesellschaft); these seem to be predominantly purely cinematic recreations of episodes from the printed picture stories.

In the following period, a number of different studios were active, so that the production was probably relatively broadly spread in terms of producers. Titles such as *Max und Moritz als Butterhändler* (1906), *Max und Moritz in der Arche Noah* (1910) or the film *Max und Moritz in der Großstadt* (1912), interestingly produced by Siegmund Lubin in Philadelphia/USA, signal an extensive detachment from the original plot while retaining the main characters. Others, such as *Max und Moritz im Himmel* (1921/22), could indicate cross-references to plays with similar themes, such as Regina Angre's *Max' und Moritz' Weihnachtsfahrt* (1911) or *Max und Moritz in der Himmelswerkstatt* (1925) by Rudolf Göthner. In contrast, adaptations of plots from the numerous Buschiaden in the print media are not to be found. Mostly the titles are described as comedies or feature fictional narratives. Exceptions here are the films *Max und Moritz* and *Max und Moritz lernen schwimmen* as well as *Eine fidele Schwimmstunde* presented by Ufa in 1921 and 1922, directed by Walther Zürn, which are both classified as short documentaries.

As far as the respective production techniques are concerned, these are rarely identified in the relevant directories. Among the exceptions is the 1908 flick *Max und Moritz,* produced by the Berlin Kinematografen – und Lichtbildgesellschaft, which is listed as a "Ton-Bild-Produktion".[8] Although only some, such as *Max und Moritz. Eine Bubengeschichte in sieben Streichen* (1907) or the film of the same name, in this case released by Hamburg's Vera-Film, are explicitly designated as animated films, it can be assumed that the majority were animated films (Fig. 4). With *Max und Moritz* by Messter-Film GmbH and *Max und Moritz von heute: Der Haupttreffer* by Willy Heß Filmgesellschaft – one of the few films banned by censors for young people – pieces in this genre first appeared in 1917 that were described as feature films. In accordance with the contemporary use of the term, these were probably not only films with fictional content, but in contrast to animated films, films with human actors. This assumption is also supported by the fact that in the latter case Edmund Edel, who was also known as an illustrator and commercial artist, was a veritable scriptwriter and director, and the actors were the brother and sister Ilse and Curt Bois.

The only relevant film in the period examined in this paper that was accessible to the author is available at the Bundesarchiv Berlin and can be viewed there. It is a 1921 35 mm silent film production by the Hamburg-based Vera-Filmwerke AG entitled *Max und Moritz. Eine Bubengeschichte in 7 Streichen,* which has a length of 228 metres. Vera-Filmwerke AG lists another film with the same title, but without subtitles, for 1923, which is possibly identical in whole or in part to the one from 1921; here Curt Wolfram Kießlich is named as the director, who was active as a

---

[8] A technical format in which picture and sound are recorded synchronously but separately and a picture projection device synchronised with a gramophone is used for the screening (cf. Müller 1994, 79 ff.).

Fig. 4 Advertisement of a *Max und Moritz* film produced by the International Cinematograph and Light Effects Society, Berlin (© *Der Kinematograph* (1907), issue 17)

screenwriter as well as an actor during the silent film era and had emerged as a poster painter with patriotic motifs during the World War.

The animated film of 1921 is divided into two parts, which correspond to the first two boy pranks in Busch's *Max und Moritz*, whose victims, as is well known, are widow Bolte and her chickens. The film closely follows the original and uses the almost unchanged verse text of the original, shortened only in longer passages such as the prologue, which is inserted in its own block proportions in the manner customary in silent films. The image setting is usually a rectangle, but not infrequently also a circle. The effort to create as few deviations as possible in the animated film drawings from those of the original picture Ton-Bild-Produktion[9] and its sequence of images is recognisable. Nevertheless, the deviations from Busch's graphic handwriting are clearly identifiable, as are modifications in pictorial detail: for example, the widow scoops her sauerkraut from the left instead of from the right as in Busch's work.

More interesting are the medial- or format-related changes. These include the reproduction of vertical-format images, such as the view of Bolte's house with the evildoers fishing for chickens on the roof, either in a sequence of cut-outs or in tracking shots. Furthermore, it is not uncommon for short, additional scenes to be inserted, such as Max and Moritz with the ladder on their way to widow Bolte's house. In a few places, there are even brief insertions of individual motifs from other pranks, such as uncle Fritz (5th prank) in bed, or illustrations taken from completely

---

[9] A technical format in which picture and sound are recorded synchronously but separately and a picture projection device synchronised with a gramophone is used for the screening (cf. Müller 1994, 79 ff.).

different picture stories by Busch, such as the greedy Tobias Knopp at the table (from *Herr und Frau Knopp*, 1876); both are inserted into the introduction of the widow Bolte. In this way, the filmmakers manage to avoid having the verse text insertions span more than four lines.

Given the intensive efforts to remake Busch's imagery, it is not surprising that the transitions from non-moving images to cinematic movement are dominated by relatively simple partial animation techniques. These are limited to mimic elements such as rolling the eyes and sticking out the tongue, turning the heads sideways, the gestures of individual limbs, as well as animal movements such as wagging the tails. Particular comedy unfolds whenever movements are involved that do not necessarily follow natural processes, but aim at grotesque-comical effects: For example, the animation of Moritz's hair curl, widow Bolte's bosom heaving up and down with excessive grief, and Max and Moritz's fantastically inflating bellies after eating the chickens. Further comical effects are created by borrowing from the graphic conventions of comics and their metafictional games. Thus the tears from the eyes of the widow Bolte not only flow profusely, but through closed doors; when Spitz the dog is beaten up, it hails asterisks of pain and the widow's fantasy of a juicy roast chicken is set in the pictorial space by a corresponding vignette – a thought bubble without a bubble, as it were.

Max und Moritz as the Initial Spark of the Comic Strip

The Beginnings of the "Katzenjammer Kids" by Rudolph Dirks

A completely new chapter in the history of the impact of *Max und Moritz* opened up in the press in the USA with the project of a young, German-born cartoonist named Rudolph Dirks, who at the end of 1897 began to draw a boy's prank picture story for *The American Humorist,* the weekly entertainment supplement of the *New York Journal.* Published by William Randolph Hearst, the paper was in fierce competition with Joseph Pulitzer's press empire, which included the *New York World,* and was eager to take the market lead by poaching particularly appealing cartoonists from the competition and developing promising new series. A number of anecdotes and more or less precisely provable statements by contemporaries suggest that Dirks was urged to draw inspiration from the children in Wilhelm Busch's illustrated stories, especially the *Max und Moritz* pranks – role models whose knowledge Dirks confirms in 1926 in a review of his beginnings quoted in Eckart Sackmann (2018, 92). As Jörg Thunecke documents, citing contemporary witnesses, Rudolph Block, also of German descent and employed the year before as art director of the Hearst paper, had even explicitly demanded picture stories from Dirks in the manner of Wilhelm Busch's *Max und Moritz* (cf. Thunecke 1987, 47; Goulart 1990, 212). That Hearst himself was involved in this idea is not proven beyond doubt, but it is certain that he stocked up on a large number of picture books during a stay in Germany in 1873. It is also reported by a biographer that Hearst showed his picture book collection to the young Dirks, not so much out of artistic as of commercial interest, and that Dirks then set to work on the new series (cf. Thunecke 1987, 62, notes 48 and 49).

The first installment of what Rudolph Block (Goulart 1990, 212) calls *The Katzenjammer Kids,* published in December 1897, offers a numbered sequence of six images without habitus, which – with the exception of the title "Ach! Those Katzenjammer Kids!" – operates entirely without written text. In the plot, three boys playing with marbles, one of whom bears a striking resemblance to Outcault's Mickey Dugan alias *The Yellow Kid* (cf. Blackbeard 1995) in his physiognomy as well as his conspicuously protruding ears, are driven apart by a neighbour with a garden hose. The three boys, however, know how to retaliate very effectively for the disruption of their harmless game by locking the elderly gentleman in his garden shed and then vigorously submerging him themselves.

The strip, which was subsequently printed – by no means regularly every week – in the Sunday supplements, went through a development phase of several years with regard to the pictorial narrative form and the inventory of characters, in which Dirks seems to experiment with different components, although the principle of the multi-part sequence of images and the plot pattern of the boy's prank are always retained. In addition, the recognisable motivic borrowings from Wilhelm Busch appear again and again, and the standardisation of the main characters makes progress. Thus, already in the second episode of December 19, 1897, the third Bengel – resembling the *Yellow Kid* – is omitted; in some episodes even only one protagonist acts against changing adversaries. In the second episode of December 19, 1897, "Mamma," whose appearance is at first somewhat reminiscent of widow Bolte's and who later becomes increasingly voluptuous, appears as the first standing figure, both as a victim and as a authority of punishment; the figure of "Papa" or "Grandpa," on the other hand, is limited to a guest appearance of several years. "Grandpa", whose role as a permanent male counterpart to the matron is taken over after the turn of the century by "the Captain", who after a while is joined by "the Inspector", a representative of an ominous school authority.[10] The classic arsenal of characters of the *Katzies* is thus complete.

Transdiegetic Narrative and Characteristic Figure Speech

Up to the turn of the century, Dirks predominantly retained the pantomimic picture sequences, only very occasionally using captions in verse or in prose; speech bubbles are encountered rather rarely, although these were also not unfamiliar to Dirks and already appear in the beginnings in an episode from January 30, 1898 (cf. Thunecke 1987, 63). From the spring of 1900, however, the wordless sequences occur only rarely and the use of speech bubbles, as well as bordered panels, motion

---

[10] According to Ron Goulart, "the Captain" first appears in the episode of August 31, 1902 and "the Inspector" on January 15, 1905 (cf. Goulart 1990, 212). On the development of the character ensemble and the settings of the series, see Brebeck 2018, 98 ff.

lines, sound words, pictorial symbols and pictogrammatic signs becomes the rule.[11] Although these elements can be found in isolated instances much earlier, as an ensemble in the comic they gain a completely new quality. The simultaneous use of these elements, which has now become a convention, is therefore not simply a summation of means of representation that are generally considered to be specific to comics. Rather, it is the first comprehensive establishment of a system of signs that Thierry Smolderen regards as constitutive for the narrative form of the comic and has used the term "l'audiovisuel sur papier" (Smolderen 2009, 118 ff.). What is meant by this is that in the course of the further development of the picture story, the comic develops a form of translation of linguistic, acoustic, and movement-simulating signs that corresponds to the print media and uses them in a systematically coordinated manner in the narrative plot. The separation between pictorial narration through the image and the verbal narrative text, which is spatially separated from it, that predominates in the picture story is abolished in a new organic unity.

Even more precisely than Smolderen, Eike Exner emphasizes the transdiegetic character of such signs as a unique selling point of comics compared to other narrative forms and media, such as the picture story in the manner of Busch and Toepffer and film (cf. Exner 2018/19). This designation aims at the fact that these elements of representation are in part to be understood as components of the narrated world, but in other parts they are not. Looking at the speech bubble as one of the most prominent among them, it can be stated that its communicative contents are part of the fiction, for instance in the form of a conversation between the characters in the plot. The characters perceive these contents, they exchange and react to each other. The speech bubble itself, on the other hand, the area left out of the pictorial space, its border, the shape of the thorn, and the like, elude the perception of the fictional characters, but not that of the reader, who understands the linguistic content and the graphic staging as "l'audiovisuel sur papier". As Exner (2018/19, 52 ff.)[12] points out, it was Rudolph Dirks who was the first among the press illustrators at the end of the nineteenth century to know how to use this transdiegetic instrumentarium in his work and who further perfected it in the first years of the twentieth century in association with Francis Burr Opper, who created the *Happy Hooligan* series in 1900.

The *Katzenjammer Kids* have now reached a form that makes Dirks's series the "first true comic strip" (Goulart 1990, 212). The two fiends now bear the German names Hans and Fritz and are also unmistakably marked in their appearance with certain stable features as descendants of Max and Moritz, although not identical to Busch's figures (cf. Eckhorst 2012, 85 ff.). Quite differently from the starting episode of 1897, where they as a trio actually only react to the assault of an arrogant adult, they have developed into notorious pests who never miss an opportunity for the most malicious pranks possible. However, every episode now also ends with an obligatory spanking, most of which is administered to them by the Mamma or the

---

[11] Jörg Thunecke (1987, 63) has presented an informative overview of the episodes from 1897 to the end of 1900.

[12] The article by Eike Exner is an internet publication with numbered sections; therefore, not the page but the section number is given in the citation.

Fig. 5 Rudolph Dirks' Wilhelm Busch-inspired series *The Katzenjammer Kids* was the first to develop the complete semiotic inventory of comics. – Episode from December 29, 1901 (© *New York Journal*)

Captain. An example of this stage of development can be seen in an episode of six pictures from April 14, 1901, which, with the bridge assassination of Mamma Katzenjammer, moreover very clearly takes up one of the best-known plot motifs from *Max und Moritz,* which the latter had at the time exemplified on Schneider Böck.[13] Indicative of Dirk's inexhaustible ideas in adapting Busch motifs in various stages, as well as of the increasingly blurred relationship to the original, is the episode *Mamma Katzenjammer Makes a New Year's Resolution and Promptly Breaks It* from December 29, 1901, in which the bridge assassination is repeated in the bedchamber (Fig. 5).

This example also makes it very clear why Dirks' strip concept primarily relied on the sequential sequence of images for a relatively long time and why the linguistic component remained rather marginal. The plot as such, i.e. the prank and the punch line, are initially hardly dependent on any additional written exposition – quite in contrast to Busch's picture stories, for example, which develop a complex network of verbal and pictorial elements (cf. Ries 2009). In the episodes with little written text from the first period, however, the *Katzenjammer Kids* have not yet found their own distinctive form, as it were; they lack a very specific tone. With the

---

[13] Retrieved from http://germanic.ku.edu/origins-comics-united-states-1897-1902-under-influence-wilhelm-busch-comics-rudolph-dirks (19.10.2019). – Thunecke 1987 also presents a whole series of images that refer to Busch's model. However, neither the specific episodes of the series are mentioned, nor the titles and issues of the newspapers from which they were taken.

direct character speech, however, Dirks then introduces a level of meaning that is completely independent of the picture narrative, which has a profiling effect as an essential element of character design and increasingly constitutes the specific humor of the *Katzies*.[14] The attempts with fragments of this pidgin German in title lines and subtexts, which Dirks already makes in the beginning, still seemed somewhat awkward: the place of this language is the bubble directly assigned to the speaker and only achieves its full effect here in the dialogue: "Poor Ma", "She Iss Caming" (Panel 4) – "Ach! Der Darlings Is Sleeping. Such Angel Boys" (Panel 5) – "I'll Make A Swear Nefer Will I Whip Der Darlings Again" (Panel 6) (*Katzenjammer Kids,* December 29, 1901; Fig. 5). Unfortunately, the phrase "Mit dose Kids, society iss nix", so typically attributed to the Inspector by Coulton Waugh (1947, 45), has not yet been verified; it has been repeated time and again since then, but cannot be substantiated in any episode of the Katzies.[15] Nonetheless, the American English of the protagonists, which is generally deformed with unorthodoxly twisted German chunks, abstinence in punctuation, tense and pronunciation errors, gives the simple plot its polish and soon becomes indispensable to the series.

The Establishment of the "Kid Strip" and Its Transformations

The further development of the series sometimes shows complicated production sequences with unbroken or still increasing popularity – this is true even for the period of the First World War, when the growing political dislike of the German Empire made it advisable to temporarily change the names of the protagonists and the series title. Prior to that, however, during the first decade after the turn of the century, the *Katzies* were presented in their own German-language versions in other Hearst papers aimed at German immigrants, such as the *Morgen-Journal,* in addition to the English-language one in the *New York Journal* – significantly, without shying away from their models, using the names Max and Moritz.[16] In addition, the pattern of success created by Dirks remained available to the public in literally twin forms for over 65 years: When Dirks left the *New York Journal in* 1913, the *Katzenjammer Kids* was continued by Harold Knerr, while Dirks won the right to continue running his own series in Pulitzer's rival paper, the *New York World,* begin-

---

[14] It should only be noted here that while this linguistic form is unmistakably related to the author's origins, it is by no means an attempt to make the strip commensurable for (German) immigrants who do not know English. Rather, a command of correct English is an indispensable prerequisite for understanding these language gags: "One had to know correct English to understand the broken English spoken by Hans and Fritz" (Inge 2016, 12).

[15] Unfortunately, this also applies to the extensive volume with a collection of early comic strips, which even carries this sentence in its title (Maresca 2013, 5).

[16] For example, in the issue of April 16, 1905, with the episode *Max und Moritz versuchen zu angeln,* http://www2.ku.edu/~germanic/eutin/images/14.jpg (19.10.2019). Others are printed in Neyer 2007, 19 ff.

ning in 1914, first under the title *Hans and Fritz*, and from 1918 as *The Captain and the Kids*. Later drawn by son John Dirks, this too lasted until 1979.[17]

Although a look at the *Katzenjammer Kids* in their different variants clearly shows Busch's influence on the genesis of the comic strip, it goes far beyond the influence of just this one series. As Bill Blackbeard postulates, an overview of the entire range of comic strips in the period from 1896 to 1916 shows the clear dominance of a specific character concept: "Three comic figures of popular fiction dominated virtually to the exclusion of all others: the demon child, the clownish innocent and the humanized animal. And the demon child led all the rest" (Blackbeard 1977, 19). It should be emphasized here that it were the strips with child protagonists that helped the comic strip to break through in the first place. As the examples cited by Blackbeard show, it is the pranksters and the unruly child characters who have outgrown the moral tale that predominantly make up the protagonists of the early strips. It is noticeable that it were not the consistently well-known naughty children of native Anglophone literature such as Mark Twain's *Tom Sawyer* (1876) and *Huckleberry Finn* (1885) or George W. Peck *Peck's Bad Boy* (1883) that were adopted as leading examples. However, it may have played a role that the models from Germany already existed in the form of picture books and picture stories, whose pictorial narrative and design could be directly linked to. Although related in some respects, Richard F. Outcault's character *Yellow Kid* (1895), who appeared in the cartoon series *Hogan's Alley* from 1895 onwards and is erroneously associated with Busch by Ries (2002, 1344), does not quite fit into the tradition of the boy's prank picture *story* and the comic strips that developed from it. Outcault's Mickey Dugan, alias the *Yellow Kid,* seems rather atypical in this context: the slum brat character might have had the makings of a knavery hero, but is persistently kept by in the role of a commentator on his surroundings; his impudence is always a verbal one, and the execution of misdeeds, not uncommon even in *Hogan's Alley* and *The Yellow Kid*, is always left to other characters. It is therefore the *Katzenjammer Kids* with the protagonists Hans and Fritz and their increasingly aggressive pranks that find numerous imitators in other strips, while *The Yellow Kid* was discontinued in 1899.

With the series *Buster Brown*, beginning in 1902, Outcault then rejoins the contemporary dominant trend of the kid strip as well as the formal standards shaped by Dirks and Opper with a completely independent contribution. The hero of the new series and his milieu are conspicuously reminiscent of Frances Hodgson Burnett's *Little Lord Fauntleroy* (1886), as it is visualized in Reginald Birch's illustrations, and to a certain extent represent the emblem of a culture oriented towards aristocratic models, which the bourgeois upper class also emulates in the USA. This is a stark antithesis to the modest world of lower-class immigrants as it appears in *Katzenjammer Kids* and even more so to that of *Hogan's Alley* and its successor series *McFadden's Row* – a greater contrast than that between the slum brat Mickey

---

[17] On the further development of the *Katzenjammer Kids,* see the catalogue rich in material of the Dirks exhibition at Museum Heide/Museumsinsel Lüttenheid, especially the contributions by Alexander Braun (23–60) and Tim Eckhorst (61–86) (Brebeck 2018).

Dugan and the fine toff Buster, who, like his literary predecessor Cedric, even shapes contemporary children's fashion in the relevant circles, is hardly conceivable. However, Buster – here in contrast to Cedric – has it all wrong with his slyness and a mixture of hypocrisy and malice. As is evident here, Outcault does not simply imitate the boy prank pattern that was so successful in its day, but restages it in its own way in a new social setting. The outwardly turned gentility conceals a pronounced tendency to misdeeds, which are all too readily directed against socially inferior individuals or the family. Only very seldom is the devil's brat, who is posing as a gentleman, put over his mother's knee for this. Instead, the end of each episode consists of a sermon of chivalry delivered by himself, which contains pure apology, since it is a notoriously hypocritical expression of remorse, combined with a list of sayings and commandments tailored to his own justification, as for example at the end of the episode about a treacherous snowball assassination, which was printed in an anthology in 1914, with the title *It probably was good for the lad:* "I didn't do this to get revenge. I did it to get a laugh. I would do a lot to get a laugh. Because it is sane & healthy too. 'Laugh and grow fat' says the proverb." (Outcault 1914, n.d.)

However, the new generation of comic strip rascals after the turn of the century gradually showed more harmless tendencies than the *Katzenjammer Kids* and their immediate adepts. The gradual disappearance of the doubling of the heroes as twins or pairs of siblings, which ultimately always refers to *Max und Moritz,* is already striking. Nor does it remain with the social nobilisation of the protagonists and their milieus and their embedding in decidedly bourgeois conditions of existence that can already be observed in *Buster Brown.* One example of this is James Swinnerton's *Little Jimmy,* which, with a running time of over 50 years, is also one of the most enduring of its kind to be printed. The kid strip, again published in the *New York Journal,* presents a little hero in a well-equipped home, the parents and their company portrayed as rather well-off contemporaries in their manner and dress. Jimmy's pranks are characteristically accidents, caused by his childish play instinct, lack of zeal in carrying out parental orders or attacks by strangers through no fault of his own: Sometimes – as in the starting episode of February 14, 1904 – the milk jug breaks on the way home from the store, or on the way to the doctor, seduction lurks in the form of friends who provide distraction. The obligatory beating, however, is also mercilessly carried out here on the better-off people for the slightest offence.

In this way, new variants emerge within the framework of the kid strip. Alongside the surviving rascals, who also appeared in ever new series variants – such as Perry from Martin Branner's *Winnie Winkle the Breadwinner* (1920–1996), which was also distributed in the 1930s in a German-language edition under the title *Kalle, der Lausbubenkönig (Kalle, the Rascal King)*, or Hank Ketcham's *Dennis the Menace* (since 1951) – child protagonists increasingly appeared without the previously indispensable gesture provocatively directed against the adult world. While the *Naughty Pete* strips by Charles Forbell, for example, published in 18 episodes in the *New York Herald in* 1913, still show remnants of the prank scheme in the outer plot of the establishment of a commandment, its transgression and the final catastrophe, these are also abandoned in other kid strips. Even further removed from its origins, as Ulrich Luckhardt notes, is the short-lived strip *The Kin-der-Kids*, drawn by

Lyonel Feininger and published in the *Chicago Sunday Tribune in* 1906 (Luckhardt 1990, 91). Here, the whimsical child characters Daniel Webster, Strenuous Teddy, and Piemouth were no longer at all out to cause confusion in the adult world. Rather, this trio of heroes has given up all initiative and, fleeing from the strict Aunt Jim-Jam, is forced to embark on a journey around the world, the disciplinarian with her cod liver oil as a miracle cure for the resocialisation of the disobedient always on their heels.

Above all, some of Winsor McCay's strips must be cited as early prominent examples. For example *Little Sammy Sneeze* (1904), whose child protagonist is only reminiscent of his antecedents through his catastrophic sneezing fits, without sharing their destructive tendencies: here the prank is turned into a not culpably caused spectacle. Not to forget *Little Nemo in Slumberland* (1905–1913, 1924–1927), who dreams himself away to Slumberland every night in his sleep to have fantastic adventures of all kinds. It seems that the protagonist, who was not particularly popular at the time and was conceived as more sensitive than terrible, no longer has anything in common with Hans and Fritz or their kind. Nevertheless, it can be assumed that children's heroes like *Little Nemo* would hardly have entered the stage of comic strips for adults without the brute door openers in the shape of Max and Moritz, Hans and Fritz and their adepts.

Max und Moritz: A Media Network?

Without a doubt, it can be stated that already at the beginning of the twentieth century almost all contemporary media, including the new medium of film, appropriated the material and the characters of Wilhelm Busch's picture stories and developed continuations of very different kinds. Busch's picture story is thus an artefact in the sense of Kurwinkel (2013) and the vast majority of recent media theories, which could form the starting point or the centre of a media network, understood as the "cross-media dissemination of popular cultural plots and forms" (Weinkauff 2014, 131). In my account, the diverse print media from picture books to magazines to the weekly press were considered in more detail, and some attention was also paid to theatre and film. Rühle (1999, 611 ff.) also lists a number of musical settings of *Max und Moritz*, some of which are independent of plays. Furthermore, light picture series are documented[18] in the period shortly after the turn of the century and, with the beginning of radio history in the 1920s, a considerable number of radio plays. Here, too, there is obviously a certain variety in adaptation and production, as some of the titles might suggest: for example, in 1927 SWR Frankfurt produced a reading of *Max und Moritz, vorgetragen von der Märchentante (recited by the fairy tale aunt)*,[19]

---

[18] The trade journal *Der Kinematograph*, for example, published a series of *Wilhelm Busch in Lichtbildern* in two issues in 1908 (cf. Borger 1908 and Wilhelm Busch in Lichtbildern).

[19] Cf. Der deutsche Rundfunk 5 (1927) 3, 184.

and in 1929 by the Ostmarken Rundfunk AG (ORAG) in Königsberg Otto Wollmann's *Max und Moritz. Hörspiel für den Kinderfunk (freely adapted from Wilhelm Busch)* was broadcast.[20] At a relatively early stage, games and toy manufacturers also offered corresponding products (cf. Rühle 1999, 614 ff.). According to Ries (2002, 1348), plastic replicas of characters from *Max und Moritz* and toy dolls were offered as early as 1887. With the exception of the print media, however, all of these medial productions have so far been recorded only rudimentarily, and even less has been researched in depth. If one takes into account that there are still numerous desiderata even in the field of the print media, it becomes clear that literary and media historiography still has great tasks ahead of it in this subject, the accomplishment of which will only make it possible to provide comprehensive information about the nature and essence of a *Max und Moritz* media network. The conclusions I have attempted to draw here can therefore only be of a provisional nature.

An important feature of this complex is the extraordinary vitality of the original work over the many decades. This is ensured by high numbers of printed copies of the legitimate original edition of the picture book into the 1930s as well as by repeatedly published unauthorized reprints, which, however, do not change the artefact at all or only insignificantly. By the beginning of the twentieth century at the latest, the characters Max and Moritz and the picture book narrative about them had become so deeply engrained in the cultural memory of Germany in particular that they did not even need to be promoted by other media variants, but on the other hand, new attempts were constantly being made to profit from their success. This embedding in the contemporary collective memory of the Germans also constitutes the prerequisite for *Max und Moritz* – as the photo of the St. Petersburg performance of 1903 vividly demonstrates – to function abroad as a representative of German (popular) culture.

Nevertheless, all these reformulations in theatre, film, radio, etc., as well as the merchandising products, contribute to an additional increase in the popularity of the original work. Henry Jenkin's statement, applied to modern media networks, that a transmedial narrative "unfolds across multiple media platforms, with each new text making a distinctive and valuable contribution to the whole" (2006, 95 f.) is therefore inaccurate in the given context. The relationship to Busch's model is exceedingly one-sided, regardless of whether it is a matter of re-creations, imitations, parodies or only distant borrowings. The respective new media creations permanently refer back to the model; insofar as they undertake new or further narratives, as a number of plays and films have evidently attempted, these are in turn not passed on. In this context, it is also striking that apparently only one *Max und Moritz* stage play has been performed over several decades. Significantly, it is the very first one, written in 1877 by Leopold Günther, which partly uses original text and is limited to the original arsenal of characters except for the addition of an Eulenspiegel as moderator.

---

[20] Cf. Der deutsche Rundfunk 7 (1929) 22, 2.

As becomes quite clear here, the theoretical models of media networks, media convergence, media mix and multimediality, which are oriented towards the media society of the late twentieth century, must themselves be historicised in some parts if they are to be used retrospectively to analyse and explain possibly similar phenomena in the past. In the present case, this means that both the theatre, which is listed as a primary medium in Harry Pross's (1972) media classification, and the tertiary media of broadcasting and film are of secondary importance in terms of the number of titles and production figures compared to the print media, which Pross lists as secondary. When Heinz Hengst (1994, 240) states for the modern media networks of the late twentieth century that their scripts were usually characterized by an electronic audiovisual lead medium, this cannot be applied to the *Max und Moritz* complex. This is not only due to the continuing, stable transmission of the original work, but also to the fact that it is the field of print media as such that exhibits a decisive dynamic for the further development of the artefact in terms of approaches to media network structures: the transition from the reproduction or imitation of the work to a fragmentary transmission of certain motifs and parts of the plot, combined with the transformation of the characters into serially reproducible creations, consequently into characters. The print media involved – picture book, humorous-satirical magazine, weekly and finally daily press – do not form a network in the sense of coordinated media geared to the purpose of commercial exploitation, but it is the – certainly modest from the point of view of the present – mere multimediality generated from different types of printed matter that ensures the dynamics of development.

In this way, the Buschiaden create numerous readings of a species of boys' and – mutatis mutandis – girls' prank stories, which, in their adherence to the model, form their own lineage of this genre. The seriality of the Buschiaden, which are published quite predominantly as singular book publications or as one shots in humorous journals, remains an incomplete one, insofar as it is limited for long stretches to the iteration of certain character types as well as plot and conflict schemes: it is not about the continuation of the adventures begun by Max and Moritz, but about their variations in ever new and different milieus. The fact that the protagonists, such as Lies and Lene, Fritz and Franz, Michel and Sepp, Maus and Molli, etc., always go by new names is just as much a sign of the independence they claim as the fact that new fictional spaces of action are always being created, so that there can be no talk of a uniform serial "cosmos" (Dolle-Weinkauff 2014, 157). This step only takes place with the successive implementation of the Buschiaden and the establishment of the kid strip by Rudolph Dirks' *Katzenjammer Kids* at the turn of the nineteenth and twentieth centuries.

The decisive basis for further development was the expansion of the ensemble of media involved until then to include another print medium, whose production conditions and format specifications set entirely new parameters for the authors. Compared to the book, the restriction to one or half a newspaper page, as envisaged by the entertainment sections of the contemporary US weekly press, represented a significant break. As periodicals that strove to continue successful offers with new episodes every week, however, they opened up entirely new possibilities for longer-term publications. Busch's *Max und Moritz* not only presented attractive starting points in terms of characters, plot and motifs, but with its form of episodic storytelling in a loose form of pranks it provided a conceivably favorable template for the establishment of a series such as Dirks then created with *Katzenjammer Kids* beginning in 1897. Dirks basically succeeded by picking up with his stories where the conventional Buschiaden left off. The transition from episodic to serial storytelling was not only the key to a prank universe ad infinitum, as the *Katzenjammer Kids* and their imitations successfully presented it for decades. Far more consequential, however, proved to be the innovations in narrative form that Dirks and other cartoonists involved pushed as they perfected their series: The development of a transdiegetic drawing inventory that represented the evolution of the traditional nineteenth-century pictorial story into the comic strip and the comic book in the twentieth century. This, however, is no longer the history of the *Max und Moritz* media network, but a completely new one.

References

Primary Literature

[Bashfield, H.]: The Adventures of Teasing Tom and Naughty Ned with a Spool of Clark's Cotton. New York: F. B. Patterson, 1879.
[Branner, Martin]: Kalle, der Lausbubenkönig. 60 lustige Streiche. Berlin: Zeitschriften-Verl. A. G., 1935.
Brantl, Ign./Roth, Hermann/Ringler, Ludwig: Fritz und Franz im Schützengraben. Lustige Streiche zweier Knaben. München: Alfred Schmidt Nachf., 1915.
Burnett, Frances Hodgson: Little Lord Fauntleroy. New York: Charles Scribner's Sons, 1886.
Busch, Wilhelm: Trauriges Resultat einer vernachlässigten Erziehung. In: Fliegende Blätter 16 (1860) 796, 108–110.
Busch, Wilhelm: Diogenes und die bösen Buben von Korinth. In: Fliegende Blätter 17 (1862) 881, 164–166.
Busch, Wilhelm: Diogenes und die bösen Buben von Korinth. Münchener Bilderbogen 13 (1863) 350.
Busch, Wilhelm: Der Kuchenteig [1863, unveröff. Skizze]. Repr. Hg. von Platthaus, Andreas. Berlin: Insel, 2010.
Busch, Wilhelm: Der hinterlistige Heinrich Münchener Bilderbogen 14 (1864) 361.
Busch, Wilhelm: Bilderpossen. Dresden: J. Heinrich Richter, 1864.
Busch, Wilhelm: Max und Moritz. Eine Bubengeschichte in sieben Streichen. München: Braun & Schneider, 1865.
[Busch, Wilhelm]: Max and Maurice. A Juvenile History in Seven Tricks by William Busch. From the German by Charles T. Brooks. Boston: Roberts Brothers, 1871.
Busch, Wilhelm: Herr und Frau Knopp. Heidelberg: Bassermann, 1876.
Busch, Wilhelm: Plisch und Plum. München: Bassermann, 1882.
[o. V./Busch, Wilhelm]: Neuer Max und Moritz. Eine Bubengeschichte in 5 Streichen. München [o. Verl.] [ca. 1893].
Dirks, Rudolph: Ach, those Katzenjammer Kids! In: New York Journal 16 (1897) vom 12.12., Beil. *The American Humorist*, 8.

Dirks, Rudolph: Ach, Those Katzenjammer Kids Once More! Already Again They Make Troo o o oble! In: New York Journal 16 (1897) vom 19.12. Beil. *The American Humorist*, o. S.

Dirks, Rudolph: [The Katzenjammer Kids] In: New York Journal 20 (1901) vom 14.4., Beil. *The American Humorist*, o. P.

Dirks, Rudolph: Mamma Katzenjammer Makes a New Year's Resolution and Promptly Breaks It. In: New York Journal 20 (1901) vom 29.12., Beil. *The American Humorist*, o. S.

Dirks, Rudolph: Max und Moritz versuchen zu angeln. In: Morgen-Journal (1905) vom 16.4., Beil. *Lustige Blätter*, o. S.

Feininger, Lyonel: The Kin-der-Kids. Darmstadt: Melzer, 1985 [Repr. dt.].

Forbell, Charles: Naughty Pete. In: New York Herald 77 (1913) vom 31.08.

Frankenberg, Curt von/Leonhard, Robert L.: Die Luftbuben. Berlin-Charlottenburg: Verlag „Luftfahrerdank", 1915.

[o. V.]: Fritz und Franz ein Brüderpaar, wie es Max und Moritz war [ca. 1915].

Greening, Harry: How the Tinkle Brothers Got in the Neck. In: New York Journal 16 (1897) vom 03.10., Beil. *The American Humorist*, 4.

Hebel, Johann Peter: Schatzkästlein des rheinischen Hausfreundes. Tübingen: Cotta, 1811.

Herbert, Wilhelm/Storch, Carl: Maus und Molli. Eine Mädelgeschichte nach Wilhelm Busch in sieben Streichen. München: Braun & Schneider, [1920].

Hertwig, Robert: Eduard und Ferdinand, mit Max und Moritz nah verwandt. Neueste Bubenstreiche. [o. O.] [o. Verl.] [ca. 1900].

Hoffmann, Heinrich: Lustige Geschichten und drollige Bilder für Kinder von 3–6 Jahren. [Ab 4. Aufl. 1847 u. d. T. Der Struwwelpeter]. Frankfurt a. M.: Literarische Anstalt, 1845.

Howarth, Franklin Morris: The Revenge of the Persecuted Baker. In: Judge 11 (1891) vom 11.7.

Ketcham, Hank: Hank Ketcham's Complete Dennis the Menace 1951–1952. Seattle: Fantagraphics Books, 2005 [Repr.].

Kohn, Joseph: Max und Moritz im Luftballon. Allerhand lustige Fahrten zweier Lausbuben [ca. 1905].

Levetzow, Hulda von/Maddalena, F. [Franz] (Ill.): Lies und Lene, die Schwestern von Max und Moritz. Eine Buschiade für Groß und Klein in 7 Streichen. Hamburg: Fritzsche, 1896.

McCay, Winsor: Little Sammy Sneeze. Er wußte nie wann's passiert. Das Beste aus den Jahren 1904–1907. Übers. von Jonas und Uwe Baumann. Bonn: Bocola 2010 [Repr.]

McCay, Winsor: The Complete Little Nemo. 1905–1927. 2 Bde. Köln: Taschen, 2017/2019 [Repr.].

[N. N.]: Max & Moritz. Buben-Geschichten in Streichen für Groß & Klein. [ca. 1890].

Outcault, Richard F.: At the Circus in Hogan's Alley. In: New York World 35 (1895) vom 05.05.

Outcault, Richard F.: McFadden's Row of Flats. In: New York Journal 15 (1896) vom 18.10., Beil. The American Humorist.

Outcault, Richard F.: The Yellow Kid and His New Phonograph. In: New York Journal 15 (1896) vom 25.10. Beil. *The American Humorist*.

Outcault, Richard F.: Buster Brown Has a Birthday Party. In: New York Herald 62 (1902) vom 19.10.

Outcault, Richard F.: It Probably Was Good for the Lad. In: Ders.: Buster Brown and Tige Here Again. New York: Frederick A. Stokes Company, [1914] [no page number].

Peck, George W.: Peck's Bad Boy And His PA. Chicago: Belford, Clarke & Co., 1883.

Rotziegel, Harry: Max und Moritz. 1. und 3. Streich. In: Die Trommel. Zeitschrift für Arbeiter- und Bauernkinder 6 (1926). 1. Streich [o. Titel] Heft 6, 16; 2. Streich Max und Moritz reisen nach Moskau, Heft 7, 16; Dritter Streich Max und Moritz im Ferienlager, Heft 8, 16.

Schneider, A.: Max und Moritz im Felde. Eine lustige Soldatengeschichte. Berlin: Otto Schloß [1915].

Swinnerton, James: Jimmy. He Goes for the Milk. In: New York Journal 23 (1904) vom 14.02.

Thoma, Ludwig/Heine, Thomas Theodor: Die bösen Buben. München: Albert Langen, 1903.

Twain, Mark: The Adventures of Tom Sawyer. Hartford: American Publishing Company, 1876.

Twain, Mark: The Adventures of Huckleberry Finn. New York: Charles L. Webster 1885

Widmann, Wilhelm/Jaeger-Mewe, H.: Michel und Sepp. Die tapferen Zwei dreschen die Lug- und Trug-Kumpanei. Stuttgart und Wien: Loewes, [1915].

Filmography

Max und Moritz als Butterhändler [Spielfilm] (D 1906), Internationale Kinematograph- und Lichtbild-Ges. Berlin.
Max und Moritz. Eine Bubengeschichte in sieben Streichen [Zeichentrickfilm] (D 1907). Nach dem gleichnamigen Buch von Busch, Internationale Kinematographen- und Licht-Effekt-Gesellschaft mbH, Berlin.
Max und Moritz [Tonbild] (D 1908), Kinematographen – und Lichtbildgesellschaft, Berlin
Max und Moritz. Eine Bubengeschichte in sieben Streichen (D 1908), Vera-Film, Hamburg.
Max und Moritz in der Arche Noah [Lustspiel] (D 1910).
Max und Moritz in der Großstadt (USA 1912), Siegmund Lubin, Philadelphia/USA.
Max und Moritz [Spielfilm] (D 1917), Messter-Film GmbH 1917 [Jugendverbot. – Zensur: 01.1917.BZ40225].
Max und Moritz von heute: Der Haupttreffer. [Spielfilm] (D 1917). Drehbuch und Regie: Edmund Edel. Mit Ilse Bois und Curt Bois, Willy Heß Filmgesellschaft und Filmfabrik, Berlin.
Max und Moritz. Eine Bubengeschichte in 7 Streichen [Animationsfilm] (D 1921), Vera-Filmwerke AG, Hamburg.
Max und Moritz [Kurz-Dokumentarfilm] (D 1921), Ufa.
Max und Moritz lernen schwimmen. Eine fidele Schwimmstunde [Kurz-Dokumentarfilm] (D 1922). Drehbuch und Regie: Walther Zürn, Ufa.
Max und Moritz im Himmel [Kurz-Spielfilm] (D 1921/22). Contag-Film AG, Berlin.
Max und Moritz [Animationsfilm] (D 1923). 2 Akte. Regie: Curt Wolfram Kießlich, Vera-Filmwerke AG, Hamburg.

Audiography

Max und Moritz, vorgetragen von der Märchentante (D 1927). SWR Frankfurt.
Max und Moritz. Hörspiel für den Kinderfunk (D 1929). Otto Wollmann (Frei nach Wilhelm Busch). Ostmarken Rundfunk AG (ORAG), Königsberg.

Theatrography

Angres, Regina: Max' und Moritz' Weihnachtsfahrt. Ein Kinderspiel zum Weihnachtsabend. Berlin: Bloch-Theaterverlag, 1911.
Gleißner, Emmeran: Max und Moritz auf dem Ferkelmarkt. Posse mit Gesang in einem Aufzug. Metten: Druck und Verlag der Abtei Metten, 1927.
Göthner, Rudolf: Max und Moritz in der Himmelswerkstatt. Ein Weihnachtsspiel für Kinder mit Gesang und Tanz in drei Aufzügen. Musik von Max Petzold 1925. Leipzig: Glaser, Musikalien- und Theaterverlag, [1925].
Günther, Leopold: Max und Moritz. Ein Bubenstück in 7 Streichen (2 Abtheilungen). Musikalisch unterlegt von Fritz Becker. Berlin: Verlag der Theaterbuchhandlung Kühling & Güttner, 1877.
Reichert, Margarete: Max und Moritz im Schützengraben. Jungmannen-Spiel. Berlin: Bloch, 1916 (Jungdeutschland-Bühne; 5).
Sack, F.: Max und Moritz als Schulschwänzer. Bonn: Heidelmann, 1906 (A. Heidelmann's Pantomimen; 7).
Siewert, Ernst: Max und Moritz oder Wer andern eine Grube gräbt, fällt selbst hinein. Ein lustiges Bubenstück in fünf Streichen, nebst Vorstreich, Nachstreich und Prolog. Eßlingen: Schreiber, 1887 (Schreibers Kindertheater; 27).

Secondary Literature Before 1945

Borger, C.: Frankfurt a. M. In: Kinematograph (1908) 62 vom 04.03., 8.
Kienzl, Florian: Veit Harlans Werdegang. Der Gestalter des Ufa-Farbfilms *Die goldenen Stadt*. In: Film-Kurier 24 (1942) 79 vom 04.04., 3–4.
Max- und Moritz. Eine Bubengeschichte in 7 Streichen. [Anzeige]. In: Der Kinematograph 1 (1907) 17, [o. S.].
Vischer; Friedrich Theodor: Satyrische Zeichnung. Gavarni und Töpffer. Mit einem Zusatz über neuere deutsche Karikatur. In: Ders. (Hg.): Altes und Neues. Heft 1, Stuttgart 1881, 61–151.
Wilhelm Busch in Lichtbildern [Anzeige]. In: Kinematograph (1908) 57 vom 29.01., 15.

Secondary Literature After 1945

Arendt, Dieter: Der Hausfreund als Bürgerschreck oder Die Sippschaft der Zundelschelme. Zum 225. Geburtstag von Johann Peter Hebel. In: Schweizer Monatshefte 65 (1985) 5, 409–424.
Blackbeard, Bill: Struwwelpeter, Pagliacci and Puss in Boots. Folklore Figures in the Early Sunday Comic Strip 1896–1916. In: Ders./Williams, Martin (Hg.): The Smithsonian Collection of Newspaper Comics. Washington, D.C. 1977, 19–21.
Blackbeard, Bill: R. F. Outcault's *The Yellow Kid*. A Centennial Celebration of the Kid, who Started the Comics. Northampton 1995.
Braungart, Wolfgang (Hg.): Bänkelsang. Texte – Bilder – Kommentare. Stuttgart 1985.
Brebeck, Benedikt: Durch Streiche zum Ruhm. Zwei Lausbuben wüten durch die Comic-Geschichte. In: Ders./Museumsinsel Lüttenheid (Hg.): Rudolph Dirks – Zwei Lausbuben und die Erfindung des modernen Comics. Berlin 2018, 95–120.
Busch, Margarete: Deutsche in St. Petersburg 1865–1914. Identität und Integration. Essen 1995.
Carpenter, Kevin: „wonderfully vulgar". British Comics 1879–1939 [Online Exhibition]. Bibliotheks- und Informationssystem der Carl von Ossietzky Universität Oldenburg 2018, http://www.wonderfullyvulgar.de (01.04.2019).
Dolle-Weinkauff, Bernd: Deutschsprachige Kriegsbilderbücher 1914–1918. Ein Abriss der Themen, Typen und Tendenzen. In: Kinder- und Jugendliteraturforschung 2014/2015. (2015), 27–47.
Dolle-Weinkauff, Bernd: Comic, Graphic Novel und Serialität. In: Hochreiter, Susanne/ Klingenböck, Ursula (Hg.): Bild ist Text ist Bild. Narration und Ästhetik in der Graphic Novel. Bielefeld 2014, 151–168.
Eckhorst, Tim: Katzenjammer, Kids und Kauderwelsch. Monografie zu Leben und Werk von Rudolph Dirks. [Wewelsfleth] 2012.
Exner, Eike: The Creation of the Comic Strip as an Audiovisual Stage in the *New York Journal* 1896–1900. In: Imagetext. Interdisciplinary Comics Studies 10 (2018/19) 1, http://imagetext.english.ufl.edu/archives/v10_1/exner (23.03.2019).
Franz, Kurt: Kalendermoral und Deutschunterricht. Johann Peter Hebel als Klassiker der elementaren Schulbildung im 19. Jh. [Tübingen 1995] Repr. Berlin [u. a.] 2016.
Galway, Carol: Wilhelm Busch: Cryptic Enigma. Diss., University of Waterloo (Ontario/ Canada), 2001.
Gordon, Ian: Comic Strips and Consumer Culture 1890–1945. Washington, D.C. [u. a.] 1998.
Görlach, Manfred: Bibliographie der Übersetzungen. Stand 1990. In: Wilhelm Busch Gesellschaft (Hg.): 125 Jahre *Max und Moritz*. Entstehung und Wirkung des berühmten Buches. Stuttgart 1990, 149–164.
Görlach, Manfred: Max und Moritz in aller Munde. Wandlungen eines Kinderbuches. Eine Ausstellung in der Universitäts- und Stadtbibliothek Köln 27. Juni – 30. September 1997 (Kleine Schriften der Universitäts- und Stadtbibliothek Köln; 3).

Görlach, Manfred: Max und Moritz polyglott. München 1982.
Goulart, Ron: The Encyclopedia of American Comics. From 1897 to the Present. New York [u. a.] 1990.
Gravett, Paul: Graphic Novels. Stories to change your life. London 2005.
Hengst, Heinz: Der Medienverbund in der Kinderkultur. Ensembles, Erfahrungen und Resistenzen im Mediengebrauch. In: Hiegemann, Susanne/Swoboda, Wolfgang H. (Hg.): Handbuch der Medienpädagogik. Opladen 1994, 239–254.
Inge, M. Thomas: Origins of early Comics and Proto-Comics. In: Bramlett, Frank/Cook, Roy T./Meskin, Aaron (Hg.): The Routledge Companion to Comics. London [u. a.] 2016, 9–15.
Jenkins, Henry: Convergence culture. Where old and new media collide. New York [u. a.] 2006.
Jones, Gregory/Brown, Jane: Wilhelm Busch's Merry Thoughts. His Early Books in Britain and America. In: The Papers of the Bibliographical Society of America 101 (2007) 2, 167–204.
Josting, Petra: Kinder- und Jugendliteratur im Medienverbund. In: Lange, Günter (Hg.): Kinder- und Jugendliteratur der Gegenwart. Ein Handbuch. Baltmannsweiler 2011, 391–420.
Körner, Torsten: Ein guter Freund: Heinz Rühmann. Biographie. Berlin 2001.
Krekler, Ingeborg: Katalog der handschriftlichen Theaterbücher des ehemaligen Württembergischen Hoftheaters. Wiesbaden 1979.
Kunzle, David: Busch Abroad: How a German Caricaturist Willy Nilly Helped Launch the New Cheap Comic Magazines in Britain and the United States. *Victorian Periodicals Review* 25 (1992) 3, 99–108.
Kunzle, David: Precursors in American Weeklies to the American Newspaper Comic Strip. A Long Gestation and a Transoceanic Cross-Breeding. In: Lefèvre, Pascal/Dierick, Charles (Hg.): Forging a New Medium. The Comic Strip in the Nineteenth Century. Bruxelles 1998, 157–186.
Kurwinkel, Tobias: Medienverbund. In: Schäfer, Horst (Hg.): Lexikon des Kinder- und Jugendfilms im Kino, im Fernsehen und auf Video. Teil 6: Genres, Themen und Aspekte. 42. Erg.-Lfg. Meitingen 2013, 1–5.
Lange-Kirchheim, Astrid: Zur Präsenz von Wilhelm Buschs Werken in Franz Kafkas Texten. In: Liebrand, Claudia/Schößler, Franziska (Hg.): Textverkehr. Kafka und die Tradition. Würzburg 2004, 161–204.
Lefèvre, Pascal/Dierick, Charles (Hg.): Forging a new medium. The comic strip in the nineteenth century. Bruxelles 1998.
Liebert, Ute: Bibliographie der Originalauflagen von 1865–1958. In: Wilhelm Busch Gesellschaft (Hg.): 125 Jahre *Max und Moritz*. Entstehung und Wirkung des berühmten Buches. Stuttgart 1990, 140–148.
Luckhardt, Ulrich: *Max und Moritz* in Amerika. In: Wilhelm Busch-Gesellschaft (Hg.): 125 Jahre Max und Moritz. Entstehung und Wirkung des berühmten Buches. Stuttgart 1990, 92–102.
Maresca, Peter: Society is nix. Gleeful Anarchy and the Dawn of the American Comic Strip 1895–1915. Palo Alto/CA 2013.
Müller, Corinna: Frühe deutsche Kinematographie. Formale, wirtschaftliche und kulturelle Entwicklungen. Stuttgart 1994.
Neyer, Hans Joachim: Wilhelm Busch, seine Bildgeschichten und der amerikanische Comic. In Comixene 35 (2007) 101, 8–19.
Pape, Walter: Das literarische Kinderbuch. Studien zur Entstehung und Typologie. Berlin [u. a.] 1981.
Platthaus, Andreas (Hg.): *Der Kuchenteig* von Wilhelm Busch. Mit einem Essay von Andreas Platthaus. Berlin 2010.
Pross, Harry: Medienforschung. Film, Funk, Presse Fernsehen. Darmstadt 1972.
Richter, Dieter: Hexen, kleine Teufel, Schwererziehbare. Zur Kulturgeschichte des bösen Kindes. In: Deutsches Jugendinstitut (Hg.): Was für Kinder. Aufwachsen in Deutschland. München 1993, 196–202.
Ries, Hans: Das Verhältnis von Bild und Wort in Wilhelm Buschs Bildergeschichten. In: Kinder- und Jugendliteraturforschung 2007/2008 (2009), 23–35.

Ries, Hans (Bearb.): Busch, Wilhelm: Die Bildergeschichten. Historisch-kritische Gesamtausgabe in drei Bänden. Im Auftr. der Wilhelm-Busch-Gesellschaft hg. von Herwig Guratzsch und Hans Joachim Neyer. Bearb. von Hans Ries. Unter Mitw. von Ingrid Haberland. Hannover 2002 (Bd. 1 Frühwerk).

Rühle, Reiner: „Böse Kinder". Kommentierte Bibliographie von Struwwelpetriaden und Max- und-Moritziaden mit biographischen Daten zu Verfassern und Illustratoren. Osnabrück 1999. (Bibliographien des Antiquariats H. Th. Wenner; 4).

Sackmann, Eckart: Big and Little Willie – und Max und Moritz noch dazu. In: Ders. (Hg.): Deutsche Comicforschung 12 (2016), 56–63.

Sackmann, Eckart: Wilhelm Busch – die falsche Traditionslinie. In: Matthias Winzen (Hg.): Wilhelm Busch. Bilder und Geschichten. Baden-Baden 2018, 65–110.

Smolderen, Thierry: Naissances de la bande dessinée. De William Hogarth à Winsor McCay. Bruxelles 2009.

Thunecke, Jörg: Wilhelm Busch's *Max und Moritz* and Rudolph Dirks' *Katzenjammer Kids*. Aspects of a cultural exchange. In: Ders. (Hg.): Wilhelm auf den Busch geklopft. Essays and translations in honour of Dieter Paul Lotze. Nottingham (UK) 1987, 42–66.

Waugh, Coulton: The Comics. New York 1947.

Weinkauff, Gina: Das Sams. Betrachtung eines prominenten kinderliterarischen Medienverbunds und seiner Rezeption in der Fachöffentlichkeit. In: Weinkauff, Gina/Dettmar, Ute/Möbius, Thomas/Tomkowiak, Ingrid (Hg.): Kinder- und Jugendliteratur in Medienkontexten. Adaption – Hybridisierung – Intermedialität – Konvergenz. Frankfurt a. M. [u. a.] 2014 (Kinder- und Jugendkultur, -literatur und -medien; 89), 127–146.

Weissweiler, Eva: Wilhelm Busch: Der lachende Pessimist. Köln 2007.

Robinsonades between 1900 and 1945

From Silent Film Classic to *Radio-Robinson*

Sebastian Schmideler

Theoretical Framework: On the Significance of Children's and Youth Media

Under the heading *Blickpunkte, Tagesschau online* ran the headline on April 25, 2019 with the *pictures of the day*, which showed a photograph in first place of the title page of the first edition of *Robinson Crusoe:* "300 years ago today, *The life and strange surprising adventures of Robinson Crusoe* was published. Daniel Defoe's novel is considered the first bestseller in world literature. No other novel has been printed, translated and adapted so often to this day."[1] German-language research on children's and young people's literature has also made a similar observation with regard to the novel's long-term success: "Statistics prove that *Robinson Crusoe* is the most widely read book in the entire world after the Bible" (Franz 2012a, 1). It is astonishing that in the context of the rapid, accelerated change of the literary market and the scarce, predominantly present-fixated media attention to the past, a book from 1719 still has such a high-profile scope and significance three hundred years after its first publication that it can be considered part of literary general education and even serve as the headline of a serious news magazine of the public broadcaster. This is not only evidence of the unbroken high significance of this book's impact, but also proof of a particularly vibrant aesthetic surplus. This specific work has developed a specific literary momentum of its own. It is not only thanks to its media mutability that it has been able to be preserved in cultural memory for so long.

---

[1] https://www.tagesschau.de/multimedia/bilder/blickpunkte-4667.html (05.09.2019).

S. Schmideler (✉)
Faculty of Education, Elementary School German Didactics, University of Leipzig, Leipzig, Germany
e-mail: sebastian.schmideler@uni-leipzig.de

The anthropological dimension of the *Stoff* contributes to this. In the model of the insular exile situation of man thrown back on himself and his original existence, fundamental questions about the relationship between nature and culture in the process of civilisation are negotiated in an exemplary manner that always remains topical. The causes and consequences of human progress are discussed. Based on Robinson's story and on the *literarische* and medial Stoffe circulating around him, complex and demanding, ambiguous ambivalences of the achievements of human civilisation of Central European influence and Christian tradition are shown in plain images and simple but fascinating scenes.

However, it is precisely because of its unmistakable civilisational tendency towards colonisation in this context that the work is increasingly being put under pressure to legitimize itself in a globally networked and connected world. The reason for this is the literary depiction of the subjugation of the foreigner, the more or less ruthless exploitation of nature in disregard of its naturally developed and evolved needs, the sometimes excessively propagated gesture of superiority, and the fantasies of omnipotence of the *white master race*. Problematic, moreover, are the predominantly frivolously optimistic beliefs in technology and the tendency towards the resulting Eurocentrism, which tends towards racist ideology, especially in the *Friday* episode. Under these circumstances, Robinson can only serve as a model to a limited extent. It is obvious that the world view represented in this novel has already shown itself to be too corruptible and contaminated by unilateral claims to power, especially from the experience of the global political, but also climatic and technical development of the twentieth and early twenty-first century. In the end this attitude has done more harm than good to mankind and nature. A postmodern worldview that is open to interpretation, on the other hand, is absolutely dependent on the acceptance of heterogeneity, diversification of lifestyles, multi-perspectivity and ideas of reality that are perceived as constructive. It sees in this the basis for a common coexistence capable of compromise on an earth often endangered by the incalculable consequences of civilisation. The postmodern worldview therefore consciously renounces the binding force of ideological systems and religious patterns of world interpretation. It can and may therefore no longer unquestioningly accept the dominance of the world view prevailing in *Robinson Crusoe* as an all-time valid model. This is particularly evident in the interpretations of this novel from the field of *postcolonial studies* that are prevalent in English and American studies.

In German-language research on children's and young people's literature, the work continues to be legitimized as an important novel in the children's and young people's literary tradition through the discussion of classics, the canon, and valuation (cf. Ewers 2013, among others). There, it is even valorized as a particularly significant reference object of literary studies discussion: Robinson "continues to survive as a literary classic, perhaps even as the prototype of the classic par excellence" (Franz 2012a, 1; cf. also Franz 2012b). Contributing to this is the "ubiquity of *Stoff* and motif" (Franz 2012a, 22 ff.) in the various genres of children's and young adult literature and media that persists to this day. Moreover, international cultural studies research on children's literature has attempted to establish *Robinson* as part of a seemingly timelessly binding world literature for children. This was intended to secure the novel's long-term status as a classic. The reflections of the French cultural and literary historian Paul Hazard (cf. Hazard 1952, 76–85), which are not free of one-sided, child-idealising considerations, but which are full of consequences and almost believing in predestination, are revealing here. *Robinson Crusoe* had been "chosen by the race of children, a very numerous and very affectionate people, who do not easily forget their gods. Defoe had not written it for children? Well, the children appropriated it without much trouble" (ibid., 78).

This reception did not remain concentrated on children's and youth literature specific to books and print media, but was modernized between 1900 and 1945 with new media such as radio and film. The media network discussion interwoven with this takes on a special appeal in the media history conception of the Lüneburg media historian Werner Faulstich. In this theory, the social and communication science as well as the system theory media character of individual media is particularly accentuated in their specific capacity. Media is viewed as an organized communication channel in its system context, its social dominance, its institutionalisation historically differentiated under the aspect of media change. This can show the process of modernisation particularly clearly (cf. Faulstich 2006). The phase from 1900 to 1945 is characterized by the transition from the "industrial and mass age" (ibid., 59–107), which was dominated by print media such as magazines, booklets or postcards, and the first electronic media such as telegraphy etc., to the historical phase of the "new electronic world" (cf. ibid., 116–120), which gave rise to new electronic mass media such as radio, but also film. For the context relevant here, it is particularly decisive how this transition from the "industrial and mass age" to the "new electronic world" manifests itself in concrete Robinsonades and Robinson adaptations for children and adolescents. The question is which particular conditions regarding reception influence the exploitation in the media network and in the new electronic as well as in the traditional print media. It is also of particular interest to concretely confront the medial transition phenomena with the observed, reconstructed and contextualized results of the Robinsonades and Robinson adaptations studied, so that they can form an informative media-historical case study.

On the Systematics of Robinson Adaptations and Robinsonades for Children and Adolescents

Daniel Defoe's genre-constituting prototype, the novel *Robinson Crusoe* (Defoe 1719), published in 1719, takes up a specific kind of motif combination that is "characterised by partial seclusion of an individual or a group of people" (Stach 1999, 1). This motif combination "belongs, even before Defoe, to world literature" (Rehm 1929, 59; cf. also Stach 1999, 1 f.). In terms of content, the development of the Robinsonade into a literary genre feeds on this motivic *Stoff*. Defoe "creates the actual work that gives the genre its name" (Rehm 1929, 60). Thus it is the "insular seclusion, exploited either as the main motif or yet as an episode", as well as the "exilic character of the sojourn, i.e. involuntary imprisonment with the lively longing to be set free again", which, in terms of motif history, form the two main characteristics of the genre of the Robinsonades. In addition, and specifically in the literary context, there are formal narratological characteristics as signals of fictionality, such as the taking up of elements of the "adventurous *description of life and travel*" as "a literary narrative pattern in which travel and biography are intermediated in typical form, [...] the ensemble of these moments can be called a Robinsonade" (Fohrmann 1981, 49).

Robinsonades (cf. also Schlaeger 2003) are therefore either literary or media adaptations of the genre-constituting prototype of *Robinson* (such as addressee-specific retellings of the plot, picture book versions, etc.). At the same time, they include more or less independent, productive testimonies of reception, such as extensions, reworkings, new designs of the original or innovative representations through creative combinations of motifs. This also includes the conventional or novel take-up of genre patterns including satirical-parodic perspectives etc. as literary or media works. Motifs from the original are used implicitly or explicitly in a targeted aesthetic manner.

In this context, the reception within the children's and young people's literary system of action and symbols occupies a special position (cf. Ewers 2012). On the one hand, Robinson adaptations for children and adolescents become part of intentional children's and youth literature through the addressee-specific adaptation (so-called accommodation) of the originally adult *literarischer Stoff* (cf. ibid., 171). On the other hand, the genre becomes distributively and qualitatively more significant through its independent production in the history of reception; it becomes specific or original children's and youth literature. In this respect, the Robinsonades of children's and youth literature "are to be regarded as a sub-genre of the genre [of Robinsonades; the author.]. The spectrum is broad, and the transitions to adult literature are fluid" (Stach 1999, 30).

A distinction must therefore be made between the direct, addressee-specific adaptations of Defoe's *Robinson* for children and adolescents and the Robinsonades actually created for this group of addressees. Among these, in turn, the adaptations of adult literary Robinsonades for children and adolescents are to be differentiated. This includes, for example, the special case of the *Felsenburgiades* (versions of the novel "Insel Felsenburg") Of particular interest here are the children's and youth literary adaptations of Johann Gottfried Schnabel's tetralogy *Wunderliche FATA einiger SEE-Fahrer/Insel Felsenburg* (1731–1743) (Schnabel 1731–1743; on the history of reception, cf. Schmideler 2012) such as Christian Carl André's philanthropic, youth literary Felsenburgiade *Felsenburg, ein sittlichunterhaltendes Lesebuch* (cf. André 1788/89; Schmideler 2008). By far the most impactful and significant part of the genre tradition is formed by the Robinsonades as part of children's and youth literature, written specifically for children and young people. Outstandingly successful examples include Campe's *Robinson der Jüngere* (Campe [1779/80] 2000), *Der Schweizerische Robinson* by Wyss (Wyss 1821–1827), and the German translation *Sigismund Rüstig* based on Marryat's *Masterman Ready*

(Marryat 1843a, b).[2] The same applies to aesthetic exploitation in individual types of media such as radio adaptations (e.g. radio plays), film adaptations or television versions, or in the ensemble of a media network. The Robinsonades published in German-language literature up to 1990 are bibliographically recorded, albeit not completely, including films, radio plays and musical pieces (cf. Stach 1991).

In summary, the figure of Robinson is an ideal-typical character. The genre of the Robinsonades represents a model staging of a narrative pattern that aims to illustrate the tense relationship between civilisation and culture:

> Robinson is an ideal-typical figure and every Robinsonade an ideal-typical design of human life. It is created under the religious, ethical, social, philosophical and pedagogical conditions of its time in order to hold up a mirror to the changing society and to initiate the design for a more humane development of the world. (Stach 1984, 190)

This tradition-conscious, progress-optimistic, utilitarian approach to interpretation, which lays claim to a progressive view of history, is increasingly being overshadowed by criticism in the context of the currently dominant poststructuralist, postcolonial and deconstructivist patterns of interpretation. The cause is the aforementioned colonialist and Eurocentric perspective of the Robinsonades. This critique culminates – following Friedrich Forster's media network *Robinson soll nicht sterben* – in the demand "Robinson must die" as a postcolonial cultural studies response to the possible contamination of the entire Stoff circle with colonialist ideals of thought and behaviour, which are to be uncovered and overcome in an ideology-critical manner (cf. Bauer 2009).

Historical Contextualisation I: On the Impact History of the Successful Model of the Robinsonades

In order to assess the medial reception of the *Stoff* in the first half of the twentieth century, it is imperative to reconstruct and contextualize the historical development in the preceding phase because of the intensity and density of the reception documents. If one concentrates solely on the productive literary reception of Defoe's *Robinson Crusoe* of the German-speaking world in the eighteenth and early nineteenth centuries, the proportion of Robinsonades published here is enormous, and they are to be counted predominantly among adult literature. In the words of a contemporary anthologist of these Robinsonades, Johann Christian Ludwig Haken, from 1805, it can be stated: "Set in motion by the model of Defoe's *Robinson Crusoe*, it rained Robinsonades [...] for several decades of the past century" (Haken 1805, II; cf. also Stach 1984, 188). The *Robinson* story and its numerous

---

[2] Stach further differentiates between "apocryphal Robinsonades", which do not explicitly refer to Robinson in their title, and "pseudo-Robinsonades", in which apart from "the main criteria, insular existence and civilisational isolation, other criteria such as initial situation, living conditions and social order only play a subordinate role" (Stach 1991, I–III).

adaptations or Robinsonades in the true sense were thus already very successful popular reading *Stoff* for adults in the eighteenth century, before children's and youth literature made use of this genre (cf. Zupancic 1976; Liebs 1977 et al.).

Although Johann Karl Wezel's *Robinson Krusoe* (1779/1780), which is critical of civilisation, excitingly narrated, and activates independent reflection (Wezel 2016; on the significance of this work, cf. Ilbrig 2008) was not successful in terms of publishing and children's literature, but the knowledge-providing and strictly philanthropic Robinsonade *Robinson der Jüngere* by Joachim Heinrich Campe (2000), which is formally structured in educational dialogues within narrative evenings, was all the more successful (cf. also Wild 1986; Schlaeger 2003, 310). Campe's adaptation of Robinson, which followed a suggestion by Jean-Jacques Rousseau (see, among others, Stach 1999, 4–5; Franz 2012a, 10–11), virtually outstripped Defoe's original in the eighteenth and nineteenth centuries. Campe's children's book appeared in "120 editions, translated into 25 languages" (Rehm 1929, 61), was read "from Kadix to Constantinople" (Stach 1984, 189), and was considered "the new Bible of all children of educated classes" in the eighteenth and nineteenth centuries (Wolfgang Menzel; quoted in Ewers 1982, 232 f., quotation, 232). Through Ludwig Richter's widely distributed illustrations of 1848, the book also fully became popular reading *Stoff* for the education-loving and progress-optimistic bourgeoisie of the nineteenth century (cf. Stach 1999, 6; Franz 2012a, 11). As a projection of striving for perfection, progress optimism, utilitarianism, criticism of civilisation, of the bourgeois and Christian performance ethos, of moral teachings and virtues, as well as for the purpose of conveying the mastery of affect, the philanthropist-inspired children's book was ideally suited for the popularisation of an Enlightenment worldview guided by reason. Robinson advanced to the genre character of a busy and industrial man. He traverses the history of human development *in nuce*: from hunter-gatherer, farmer and stockbreeder to specialized craftsman, in God-fearing faith, with a civilising drive and, in the episode with the figure of Friday, also with colonialist pretensions. As a children's literary goal and aesthetic purpose, the character was intended to propagate the binding exemplary function of the Enlightenment, bourgeois, philanthropic worldview. Robinson thus became "a leading pedagogical figure" (Stach 1999, 6). Through its strong presence, especially on the book market, it continued to be transmitted uninterruptedly and powerfully in its ideological and moral-moral role model function in schools and homes until the 1930s and 40s.

But already during the period under study, for example in a fundamental literary encyclopedia article of 1929, people distanced themselves from Campe's pedagogical use of Robinson for aesthetic and ideological reasons: "The crass utilitarian viewpoint of the eighteenth century was the only thing that could lead to this boring transformation of the original, which had thus been completely pushed aside" (Rehm 1929, 61). This increasingly strong criticism was also supported by literary pedagogy from the late nineteenth century onwards from the environment of the youth writing movement around Heinrich Wolgast (cf. Stach 1999, 7; Franz 2012a, 14, 16). Therefore, not only was Campe's original itself further transmitted in the Kaiserreich, but special adaptations intended for school and private reading were also produced. These adaptations picked up on these aspects of criticism and were, in turn, wildly successful because of these updates. "Next to Campe's *Robinson der Jüngere,* Gustav A. Gräbner's reworking of Campe's original was the most widespread version into the 1930s" (Stach 1984, 189; Franz 2012a, 15; on the editions, cf. in detail Stach 1991, 93 f.); a 45th edition of this adaptation appeared as late as 1945 (cf. ibid., 94).

It is therefore also Robinsonades, which, in contrast to Campe's children's book, correspond more closely to the entertaining, tension-demanding, adolescent reading needs of the adventure genre, that gained importance in the nineteenth and twentieth centuries. They document the process of literarisation of children's and young adult literature. Here, suspense, actionism (Aktionimus in German), the play on the young reader's fearfulness, as well as fantasies of grandiosity, are evidence of anchoring in the adventure genre, which at that time was becoming more popular. Even in the first half of the twentieth century, these adventure books were still extremely present as Robinsonades, especially on the book market, so that extensive continuities could emerge and grow here. Marryat's *Masterman Ready* of 1841 – known through a transmission by the children's and youth author Franz Hoffmann of 1843 (Marryat 1843a), becoming popular in German-speaking countries as *Sigismund Rüstig* in Heinrich Laube's translation (Marryat 1843b) and distributed in numerous adaptations and editions – stands for this tendency (cf. Stach 1991, 99–112). *Sigismund Rüstig* became "the most popular German-language Robinsonade in the second half of the 19th century" (Franz 2012a, 6 f.). This strand of reception of the Robinsonades, which is particularly enduring in the adventure genre, also documents "an enduring popularity and an unbroken interest in reading" (Stach 1999, 11). Both still had a strong impact in the first half of the twentieth century, as the presence of the Robinsonade on the book market for children and young people can attest.

This is no less true for the four-volume *Der Schweizerische Robinson* by Johann David and Johann Rudolf Wyss (Wyss 1821–1827), one of the most internationally successful children's and youth books ever from Switzerland (cf. Kortenbruck-Hoeijmans 1999; Rutschmann 2002, 159). Between 1811/1812 and 1980, "671 different editions in German, French and English" (Rutschmann 2002, 159) as well as numerous media adaptations can be traced – from picture book versions to film classics (cf. Kortenbruck-Hoeijmans 1999, 190–202). *Der Schweizerische Robinson* is first and foremost an educational book and a family Robinsonade, since here an entire Swiss preacher's family finds itself on a desert island. The tradition, particularly philanthropic, of instructive, morally entertaining educational dialogues is continued here (cf. ibid., 119–121), although the action of the adventurous narrative is part of what happens on the desert island and does not require mediation by the father speaking in dialogues, as in Campe's Robinsonade. Moreover, it is a "narrated encyclopedia" (Rutschmann 2002, 171 f.). With a view to educating the young readership in the field of natural history alone, instructive information about more than "140 different animal species and 92 plant varieties" can be traced in the tetralogy, in part with exact and very specific details about their occurrence and way of life (cf. Kortenbruck-Hoeijmans 1999, 130). Since among them the Virginian ruffed grouse is represented together with giraffes, kangaroos and elephant seals on an island, the animals appear here less as part of a realistic environmental history than as living models in an encyclopedia for children that has become a narrated plot and primarily serves to impart knowledge.

In addition, children's and youth Robinsonades, which belong to the genre of the girls' book, were also successful (cf. Stach 1999, 17–21). Robinsonades have also been widely distributed on the level of visual storytelling in genres such as picture books and in special forms of broadsheet printing such as the Bilderbogen (cf. ibid., 21–25; Stach 1991, 215–222). Likewise, dramatic as well as lyric adaptations can be traced (cf. Stach 1999, 25–28; Franz 2012a, 26–29; Stach 1991, 226–229). This great breadth of genres and this diversity of forms once again demonstrate the astonishing momentum of reception in this literary field. It continued unbroken into the first half of the twentieth century. Just how firmly and deeply rooted these Robinsonades were, especially in the nineteenth century, as the foundation of reading socialisation on the basis of a bourgeois worldview, is demonstrated, for example, by an anonymously published Nuremberg picture and reading book from 1858. Here, the core of the plot patterns of the most famous Robinsonades, such as *Sigismund Rüstig* or the *Insel Felsenburg,* are described in pictures and words in an instructive and entertaining manner to three- to five-year-olds, who were then to become acquainted with the original versions in school and at home in the further course of their literary and aesthetic education (cf. Robinsonades 1858). The appreciation of the *Stoff* for bourgeois reading culture in the nineteenth century is also clear from an effusive characterisation by Bogumil von Goltz: "O Robinson, you wonder-man, you hero of childhood! […] O Robinson, thou book of books, thou holy scripture written in children's hearts, thou true children's Bible of all times" (quoted in Franz 2012a, 10). With this in mind, the enormous success of the Robinsonades can still be explained on the book market of the first half of the twentieth century. For example, of Fritz Gansberg's *Die Geschichte von Robinson für unsere Kleinen* (1930), "an edition was published as a complete work for literature classes in its 20th edition as late as 1941" (Stach 1999, 8; Gansberg 1941; cf. also Stach 1991, 92).

If one attempts to add together the formal-structural specificities of the Robinsonades in children's and youth literature since the eighteenth century, the following becomes apparent: A first genre pattern – such as the adaptations by *Sigismund Rüstig* – emphasizes in particular the anchoring of the Robinsonades as part of narrative adventure literature as a result of a process of increasing literarisation of children's and youth literature as a model of fictionality. A second genre pattern accentuates – such as Campe's *Robinson der Jüngere* – Robinsonades as factual *Stoff* imparting knowledge and thus as part of a reality or factuality model of worldview formation for children and adolescents. This also includes the pedagogical instrumentalisation of the Robinson *Stoff* for the context of school use with explicit educational, instructional, and pedagogical intentions:

> All subjects have a share, namely drawing, singing, German (reading and writing), arithmetic and natural history, which also includes geography, technology and cultural history (with the introduction to historical thinking). (Franz 2012a, 16)

Both models have a common hybrid interface with regard to the implicitly or explicitly conveyed moral-educational function as a specificity of the addressee orientation in the process of accommodation of the adaptation of the *Robinson-Stoff* for children and adolescents. These addressee-specific Robinsonades are therefore, in varying degrees, always also morally instructive educational writings. This interface with moral education is an expression of the tensions in eighteenth and nineteenth century children's and youth literature between the demand for instruction and the intention to entertain, in which the Robinsonades still oscillate and vary in the first half of the twentieth century. In the widely received Robinsonades by Campe and Wyss, these instructional components are still particularly pronounced in the educational dialogues and the philanthropic-pedagogical educational program of moral-educational values and norms. This proportion gradually declines in favour of the intention to entertain and the accentuation of literariness.

Historical Contextualisation II: On the History of Reception between 1900 and 1945

However, in what context was the Robinson *Stoff* specifically received between 1900 and 1945? Due to the presence of the *literarischer Stoff* of *Robinson Crusoe* in adult literature and the broad reception of the Robinsonades in the field of children's and youth literature, the work was already extremely popular in the nineteenth century, both as private and family reading and as a subject for teaching and school reading. Robinson therefore brought considerable credit from the two-hundred-year tradition of its reception, which had remained unbroken until then. In the school curriculum of the nineteenth century, *Robinson Crusoe* was a so-called concentration *Stoff* within Johann Friedrich Herbart's pedagogical theory. The *Stoff* was especially received pedagogically in the context of the cultural stage model of Tuiskon Ziller's pedagogical theory of education (see, among others, Fuchs 1893). The basic idea was that the "objects of instruction" were concentrated in the subjects in the proper sense, in that they "relate to the development, expression and expansion" of a "thought" (Franz 2012a, 15). This occurred in a developmental context of cultural stages, in that "the child in its development – in fast motion – once again passes through the same stages as in their overall development, that is, ontogenesis and phylogenesis are seen as analogous to each other" (Ibid.). *Robinson Crusoe* was intended for the second school year as so-called Gesinnungsstoff (*literarischer Stoff* for the acquisition of established ethical views or attitudes.). Understandably, it had obligatory reference status because of its special anthropological suitability for illustrating the aims of the concentration *Stoff* in the context of the culture level theory. Separate school versions were conceptualized for this compulsory reading. *Robinson Crusoe* was a compulsory subject of instruction and once again gained importance for the school of the Kaiserreich after 1900 (cf. in detail ibid., 14–16).

The *Stoff* was therefore already sufficiently established at the turn of the century to be considered a central point of reference for the aesthetic and moral education of children and young people, both from the perspective of children's and young people's literature and from an educational perspective. Reform pedagogical currents such as the work-school movement further developed this already strong potential. Robinson was declared to be the "prototype of independence", and his story was used to test practical activities based on his model, which constituted updates and innovations of the traditional reception of the nineteenth century: "At school, pupils are now taught to do handicrafts, pottery, sawing, planing and hammering, in fact to carry out many activities such as those specified in *Robinson Crusoe*" (Franz 2012a, 17).

Such a successfully cultivated field did not remain uninfluenced by the burgeoning psychological research on young readers and reading socialisation theory. It was the psychologist and reading socialisation researcher Charlotte Bühler, wife of the author of the *Organon* model of language, Karl Bühler, who is still well-known today, who attached a special conceptual significance to Robinson's figure in her theory of the different *Lesealter/reading ages*. She thus perpetuated the already strengthened reference status of the work for reception in school and private reading continuously for the needs of the twentieth century. Bühler resorted to both qualitative and quantitative scientific arguments in order to legitimize the specific meaning of the *Robinson Stoff* for her purposes. Her "extensive empirical research," which "surveyed, among others, 8000 children and adolescents in Vienna about their reading interests," showed a striking concentration "between 10 and 18% each" among "8–14 year-old boys" (Franz 2012a, 19) – and even among 10–13 year-old girls still between 10 and 12% – in relation to *Robinson.* This preference for the adventurous on the basis of *Robinson Crusoe* as reading *Stoff* also determined Bühler's definition of the age-group specificity of her theory:

> I believed I could recognise three stages in the child's need for literature: the *Struwwelpeter age,* the *fairy-tale age* and the *Robinson age.* In the first stage, the child loves small, simple stories [...]; in the fairy-tale age, the child allows himself to be led far away into the world of wonder; in the Robinson age, he returns to the real world. (Charlotte Bühler; quoted from Franz 2012a, 20)

Even if the term "Robinson age (also: adventure age)" was "disputed and questioned" after 1945, since "reading preferences depend on the respective range of books and the reading interests of a developmental phase cannot be captured and characterized by one type of book and certainly not by a single work" (Dahrendorf 1984, 191), Bühler's reading age classification was innovative and formative for the reception period between 1900 and 1945. Here, reception traditions were taken up, expanded in terms of reader psychology, and thus already existing lines of tradition could be consolidated.

However, one should also place other empirical results of contemporary young readers' research alongside the figures collected by Bühler as a corrective. They provide a far more differentiated picture of the reception of *Robinson Crusoe in* terms of the reading interests of children and young people. For example, a study

Fig. 1 Cover of the brochure *Was liest unsere Jugend?* (Siemering/Barschak/Gensch © Berlin: R. von Decker, 1930)

(Fig. 1) with statistical surveys on the reading of boys and girls in the Weimar Republic in the survey period 1929/1930 shows astonishing details with regard to *Robinson Crusoe* (cf. Siemering/Barschak/Gensch 1930).

The method of direct questioning was chosen; 25,000 pieces of paper were evaluated throughout Germany, with male and female youth, large cities and small towns as well as different types of schools being recorded in a differentiated manner. An evaluation at a boys' high school in a large city in a proletarian quarter of a student body aged 13 to 16 shows that *Robinson* was mentioned only 13 times as a reading preference, while Remarque's *Im Westen nichts Neues* was mentioned 49 times (cf. ibid., 84). This not only impressively demonstrates the class-specificity of the phenomenon of reading *Robinson Crusoe*. The fact that, with regard to the popular cultural development of the mass reading of booklet and serial literature, quite different reading preferences set the tone among reading youth than *Robinson Crusoe is* impressively illustrated by statistics of the overall results of a small Prussian town with less than 30,000 inhabitants with regard to boys' reading at the age of 14: The booklet series *Frank Allan – Der Rächer der Enterbten* (cf. also Galle 1988, 100–112), published between 1920 and 1932, was mentioned by 14-year-old boys no less than 1684 times in total, while *Robinson Crusoe* was mentioned only a whole 5 times (cf. Siemering/Barschak/Gensch 1930, 56 f.).[3] Frank Allan was considered the "epitome of the serial hero in the Weimar Republic", the series was committed to the "detective adventure in the genre of the staple novel", whose popular spread was also due to the emergence of the film detective in the silent film era; the success was "resounding", the hero's name became "a fixed term" (Galle 1988, 110 f.). As a result, this striking value alone puts Bühler's investigations into considerable perspective. The statistical value puts the classic status of the reading *Stoff* in proportion to the contemporary typical reading of fashionable booklet and serial literature as part of a "transmedial expansion" (Faulstich 2006, 95–100), which was obviously actually preferred by the masses.

Where the school system, especially of the Kaiserreich, the Weimar Republic, but also of National Socialism, placed great value on high-quality readings of the classics in the school context (here, too, there were astonishing continuities; cf. Gansberg 1941), nevertheless, the old pattern of reading *Robinson,* inherited from the nineteenth century, apparently still functioned. In a survey of the reading of a first class in secondary school (14 years old), *Robinson Crusoe* is mentioned in the category "Good juvenile writings" as many as 7 times; Wilhelm Speyer's *Kampf der Tertia,* in comparison, 5 times (cf. Siemering/Barschak/Gensch 1930, 42).

Overall, it becomes apparent that the reception of the *Stoff* varied in different ways during the period under investigation. The field of tension moves between the socialisation of reading inherited from the nineteenth century as a reading of the spirit and concentration *Stoff* in the school of the empire, work-school-specific updates, the learning-psychological revaluation of the book through the establishment of the *Robinson age* in Charlotte Bühler's reading age theory and the statistically verifiable displacement by modern reading *Stoffe* such as booklets and serial literature.

Robinsonades in the Media Network

As should have become clear from the previous remarks, *Robinson Crusoe* was extremely present from a multifaceted literary tradition in its reception as compulsory school reading *Stoff* and in private reading from the eighteenth century and throughout the entire nineteenth century until the end of the period under investigation. A media network use therefore did not need to be inaugurated and aesthetically justified in terms of children's and young people's media. Nevertheless, despite

---

[3] Cf. ibid., 60: "The overwhelming share that Frank Allan has here is not noticed everywhere, but he appears almost without exception even in every village. Individual inquiries at schools [...] revealed that he was also present there. One can also be sure of finding him in every youth community."

these very favourable initial conditions, the proportion of media networks in the true sense, i.e. a conscious intermedial interplay of a concrete *literarischer Stoff* of a Robinsonade in reception-specific media for listening, seeing and reading in the first half of the twentieth century, is evidently far less pronounced than one might initially assume. This is obviously essentially related to the fact that the reception of *Robinson Crusoe* and the addressee-oriented Robinsonades was still traditionally strongly tied to the genres and genres of book- and print media-centered children's and youth literature in schools and at home during this period as a late consequence of the nineteenth century.

Individual media networks nevertheless stand out from this observation. One conspicuous media network with an intense reception was Friedrich Forster's (i.e. Waldfried Burggraf) children's *literarischer Stoff Robinson soll nicht sterben*, which was present in individual media over the decades from the 1930s to the 1950s. Primarily as a play (Forster 1932 et al.), but also as a story (Forster 1948 et al.), as a radio play adaptation (Forster 1950; cf. Stach 1991, 252) and as a film adaptation (Forster 1956), it formed an overall, time-dispersed, media-network-specific unit. The play was "written in 1931 and premiered on September 19, 1932 at the Altes Theater in Leipzig by Detlef Sierock. Forster dramatizes the life of Daniel Defoe" (Stach 1991, 209; Reinhard 1994); the *Stoff* is "a tribute to Daniel Defoe" (Franz 2012a, 1). Thematically, *Robinson soll nicht sterben* stands strongly in the educational tradition of addressee-specific Robinsonades for children and adolescents. The impoverished, elderly Defoe and his morally deficient, lazy, spoiled son Tom open up a dichotomous constellation of characters that culminates in the contrastingly conceptualized child heroes. Tom is joined by the hard-working, morally virtuous Maud. She is supposed to produce the educational role model effect. Defoe, on the other hand, represents modern eighteenth century Rousseauist and philanthropic views. He sees childhood as an independent phase of life with the right to play and education, rather than an obligation to early child labor. The insular situation of Robinsonade is here enacted in the isolation and helplessness of Defoe and the group of children with these Enlightenment views of childhood. The protagonist Maud overcomes this isolation by mustering up the courage to go to the king to demand her rights. In turn, this virtuousness also produces a purification process in Tom. It eventually transfers to the king's son, who takes up Robinson's play in a way that is critical of civilisation and embraces the new childhood ideal as a beacon of hope for a new, enlightened social order. In this context, Robinson is staged as an Enlightenment model of the will to self-activity, which children of all classes should follow. The advocacy of children's rights, the critique of child labor, the effort to create the social conditions for a happy childhood in peace and freedom give the children's *literarische Stoff* a topical tendency in the sign of modernisation. Beyond Defoe's death, these ideas live on in the figure of Robinson and his fate in the book: *Robinson soll nicht sterben*. In the film version, the problem of enforcing international children's rights, which became virulent after 1949 and was juridically passed in 1989 at the UN Convention on the Rights of the Child, is characterized even more strongly by the three boys Ben, Charly and Jim: they are younger than the heroes of Forster's play. In this way, the aspect of child labour is more clearly illustrated, which also plays a greater role in the film version. Within the media network of Forster's children's *literarischer Stoff*, the moral and ethical programme of the Robinsonades as a whole is subjected to updating and internationalisation. Both are intended to make the Robinson *Stoff* adaptable to the present. Beyond the colonialising tendency, an optimistic, enlightened dimension should be attempted to be inaugurated in Robinson for Children with a view to children's rights.

If we are dealing here with a specifically children's literary media network, the media network of the *Swiss Family Robinson/Dschungel der tausend Gefahren* (cf. also Stach 1991, 237–250), which is based on the *Der Schweizerische Robinson* (Wyss 1821–1827) and extends from the 1940s to the 1960s, is a typical example of a family-addressed reception of a Robinsonade. It is addressed to several generations at once. However, it only became popular after 1949 and was distributed in a media network, including merchandising products such as comic books for the film or cine film versions for home cinema – for example with a version for US television. This media network therefore extends beyond the period under investigation. The media network system appears to be more typical of serially marketed US media network systems after 1945.

Film, Radio, Book: Robinson and Robinsonades in Individual Specific Types of Media

Movie Versions

The theatrical versions of the Robinsonades, of which Forster's play was the best known from the German-speaking world in the first half of the twentieth century (cf. Forster 1932), were – like Paul Mochmann's *Robinsons Abenteuer*, for example – predominantly still strongly inspired by educational intentions of moral formation of the addressed target group (Mochmann [1932]). Thus, it can be summarised from this play of Mochmann's: "Robinson changes from a haughty merchant's son to a man capable of living" (Stach 1991, 212). Compared to the massively distributed, book-centered versions, the manageable film versions produced between 1900 and 1945 have not all been preserved (cf. also the indexed films in Stach 1999, 237–250). For this reason, it is sometimes difficult to make characterising statements about the reception specificity, for example, of the intended addressees, retrospectively.

The film plot of the two-part 1920, ten-minute animated silent film by Louis Seel, *Robinson,* reproduces Robinson's fate according to Defoe in a condensed form in short individual scenes with inserted intertitles with text panels. Children already had to be able to read if they wanted to understand the film not just by watching it, but by actively receiving it. After all, this silent film version is early, preserved proof that the genre of animated films already used this *Stoff* in its first phase of development. For obvious reasons, it is the familiarity of the *Stoff* that may have provided the incentive for this cinematic adaptation. In terms of form, the film is particularly influenced by the expressionist aesthetics of the Wiesbaden painter and internationally active film producer and director Louis (also Luis/Ludwig) Seel (on his biography, see, among others, Giesen/Storm 2012, 166). For example, the heath landscape of Robinson's childhood home (Seel 1920, Part 1, 00:00:38), characterised by birch trees and a half-timbered farmhouse, is unmistakably influenced by Seel's expressionist landscape painting; the image is ready for exhibition. Seel's landscape style is incorporated into the animated silent film as a hallmark of his expressionist visual language, which was influenced by fine art. The scene seems almost like a painting, i.e. an expressionist landscape painting by Seel, who is also highlighted in the opening credits of the first part as being responsible for the design of the animated film (ibid., 00:00:13). This conspicuous incorporation of expressionist landscape painting, however, is likely to have been directed more at adult audiences.

The 1924 Robinsonade *Little Robinson Crusoe/Jackie, der kleine Robinson*, on the other hand, already indicates in the German-language version of the film title that this children's film was tailored to the popularity of the child star Jackie Coogan. Coogan went down in international film history as the hero of the Charlie Chaplin film *The Kid* (1921). The child star, whose childlike grace the film's plot deliberately stages, was also a cult figure for children in the world of the Weimar Republic. This shows the internationality of the film industry's marketing. Jackie Coogan plays Mickey Hogan, a ship's boy rhyming with his name, who is shipwrecked, marooned on a desert island, and pursued by cannibals, who are portrayed in the stereotyping typical of the time.

Already at the age of four, Jackie Coogan was discovered by a film actress and used for public dance performances in the USA: "Under the loud cheers of the audience, the little artist had to repeat his dances, which he mastered, over and over again" (Der kleine Jackie Coogan 1926, [10]). On a train ride, as a five-year-old, he happened to meet Charlie Chaplin, who, thrilled by his comic talent, cast him in the lead role in *The Kid*; at least that is how the story is told to the child audience of the Weimar Republic in a 1926 radio magazine: Jackie "brazenly sat down on his [Chaplin's; S. Sch.] knees and plucked him by the ears, the nose, the hair, the watch chain, and everything he could obtain with his ten naughty little fingers with such funny gestures that Chaplin bent over with laughter" (Ibid.). A new child star in film history had been inaugurated, who could also celebrate his commercially lucrative success with a Robinsonade.

The US *South Seas* film parody of 1932, *Mr. Robinson Crusoe,* is once again dominated by elements of film comedy that humorously take aim at *Robinson's Stoff.* Robinson alias Steve Drexel, played by Douglas Fairbanks in the leading role, has a mistress belonging to the indigenous population of the island, whom he calls Saturday. This results in some erotic passages that make the film not necessarily suitable as a children's film; consequently, the DVD has an age restriction (FSK 12). Interesting for the media change in the first half of the twentieth century is the media-integrative staging of technical innovations. The new mass medium radio becomes a decisive part of the film plot. The staging of radio is deliberately used to create specifically comic film effects arranged in a way that is critical of civilisation. Drexel and Saturday enjoy listening to the disaster news from civilisation on the radio. Thus they can enjoy the island paradise in the *South Seas* all the more relaxed. However, the radio, of all things, as an expression of modern civilisation, also saves the lives of the two film heroes in the wilderness. Cannibals from a neighboring island want to kidnap and barbecue the two protagonists, when the trained monkey Drexels manages to turn on the radio. The cannibals are so startled by the sounds of the radio broadcast that they flee in horror. Saturday is able to free Drexel, who in turn succeeds in catching the cannibals in a net trap. In a parodic way, the film plot thus takes an unusually comic aspect out of the achievements of technology, showing the ambivalence of technical progress as a punch line. But the inevitable consequence of modernisation is also already visible. Even on a seemingly deserted island, one can no longer escape the global mass media.

The Robinsonade designed as a nature film *Ein Robinson. Das Tagebuch eines Matrosen* from 1940 is the last feature film by mountain filmmaker Arnold Fanck, who made film history in this genre with films such as *Die weiße Hölle vom Piz Palü* (1928). The film was shot in South America on the "Robinson Island" of Juan Fernández. Since the film was and is released for young people, it can be considered here as a reception document. It tells the story of Carl Ohlsen, a chief sailor, who escapes to this deserted island during the First World War, voluntarily as an outcast. The island is shown in the visual staging of an authenticity fiction as a setting with the aesthetic play of an *original* Robinson plot in *authentic* nature shots. The grandson of the director recalls:

> It was the story of the German sailor Hugo Weber that inspired my grandfather. Weber lived on the legendary island of Juan Fernández: the island in the South Pacific where, around 1700, the privateer Alexander Selkirk, who would later become world famous as *Robinson Crusoe*, had already held out. Fascinated by Weber's biography, my grandfather learned how the signal mate of the German Imperial Navy first reached the island by swimming in 1915 because the British had boarded his ship, the *SMS Dresden*. Years later, Weber returned to the distant island to live a Robinson life. (Fanck 2015)

It is revealing that genuine National Socialist contemporary color became the subject of this nature genre film, which is remarkable for its impressive nature shots of the island paradise:

> In the film, the new *Dresden* of the Nazi fleet calls at the island briefly, but Weber notices this too late and then pursues her, first in his small sailboat and later on foot through Tierra del Fuego and Patagonia. There *Carl Ohlsen*, as the historical Weber is called in the film, finally reaches the *Dresden* – and returns home to the Reich with her. (Ibid.)

In summary, it remains to be stated: In comparison to the book-medium tradition of the genre, the film-medium reception of Robinsonades for children and adolescents in the period under study is rather atypical and specific to the target audience. Insofar as it is still possible to make concrete statements about their characteristics in order to interpret their meaning due to the difficult source situation, they take up specific film genres (especially Fanck: nature film, Fairbanks: film parody or film comedy). However, apart from *Little Robinson Crusoe/Jackie, der kleine Robinson*, they are not primarily committed to the intentional tradition of addressed Robinsonades for children and young people of the eighteenth and nineteenth centuries. In comparison to other addressee-specific media network adaptations of

Robinsonades (with the exception of the diachronically developed media network of Forster's *Robinson soll nicht sterben*), there is predominantly no evidence of typical media network adaptations. What is more typical is a reception in individual types of media such as film, which reveals a continued strong dominance of the book-oriented strand of reception. This is also proven by the reception of Robinsonades in the new mass medium of radio.

"Robinson" on the Radio

Radio as a new mass medium of the Weimar Republic and National Socialism experienced its heyday in the first half of the twentieth century. In the sense of Werner Faulstich's definition of the media, it had special significance of a leading medium in this historical phase. It marks the media-historical transition in the media order of Harald Pross and Werner Faulstich from the print medium (secondary medium) with the use of technology on the production side to the electronic, auditory medium (tertiary medium) with the use of technology on the production and reception side. It belongs to the historical phase of the "new electronic world" and creates a "new radio public" (cf. Faulstich 2006, 116–120). It is also addressed specifically to children and young people.

However, the source situation of audio documents from this period is also complicated with regard to the verifiable reception of radio-specific Robinsonades. Often, broadcast programs handed down in radio journals are the only evidence of the existence of these broadcasts. After evaluating these sources, it is first noticeable that traditional Robinsonades known from book-centered reception were part of the addressee-oriented adaptation for children's and youth radio of the Weimar Republic. The radio adaptation *Philipp Ashton, ein neuer Robinson* (*Philipp Ashton, a new Robinson*, cf. Schubert 1928a, b, c), broadcast by the Kölner Werag on October 19, November 2 and November 23, 1928, is based, for example, on a Robinsonade by Gottlieb Heinrich von Schubert (1849), a very well-known natural scientist and writer in the nineteenth century, based on eighteenth-century memoir literature. It was still successfully distributed in various editions on the youth book market in the early twentieth century (cf. Stach 1991, 117 f.). It tells the story of Philip Ashton, who "is captured by pirates" and flees to the West Indian island of Ruatan, "where he lives (as Robinson) for twenty-five months" (ibid., 118). Schubert's original is in the tradition of the moral-educational perspectivisation of the Robinsonades of youth literature. In Schubert's own words, the aim is to see in Ashton's fate "the serious, faithful adherence to God's word and commandment", the "heroic courage of faith, even in the face of the dangers of death", and to show his "actions and nature" as a lonely man on the island "as a model of what church, school and parental home [...] can make of the youthful, pictorial nature of man" (Schubert 1849, Preface to the first edition, VII f.). In addition, there are knowledge-conveying aspects from natural history that are committed to the reality and factuality model. It can be assumed that the radio version followed this tradition. Even if concrete evidence of this cannot be found at present, the popularity and dissemination of the book version of this Robinsonade is very likely the reason for this radio version.

A reading by Fr. Staude *Von Robinson Crusoes Schicksalen (2. Abend)* broadcast in the afternoon program of the Vienna radio station on June 2, 1925, also suggests a radio series in the family program, for which children and young people could also have been intended as listeners (cf. Der deutsche Rundfunk 3 (1925), 1426).

Decidedly addressed to children was the children's revue *Funkheinzelmanns Bilderbuch,* broadcast on December 20, 1927 by the Hamburg radio station from the Carl-Schultze-Theater in Langenreihe, announcing it as the 15th picture of the revue *Der neue Robinson* (cf. Der deutsche Rundfunk 5 (1927), 3516). In the period under investigation, this designation could refer to both a radio adaptation after Marryat (cf. Marryat 1843a, b) and after Gotthilf Heinrich von Schubert (cf. Schubert 1849). Both had the term *neuer Robinson* in the title. It is also conceivable, however, that this was a radio adaptation of its own, following a reception specific to the *Funkheinzelmann.* In this context, the transmedial tendency of the children's revue is nevertheless conspicuous, which intends to bring the forms of the picture book synaesthetically as sound and audio image in a kind of audio collage to the children as listeners as an opportunity for aesthetic and literary education. The broadcast date of this children's revue shortly before Christmas as well as its transmission from the Carl-Schultze-Theater in Hamburg are moreover in the typical tradition of the popular Christmas fairy tale in the city theaters, which had been established since the Kaiserreich (cf. Reiß 2008).

Another conspicuous feature of radiomedial reception is that celebrities and stars of the Weimar Republic, who were very present in the media, tried to make themselves popular in connection with children's and youth literature Robinsonades and addressee-specific Robinson adaptations. For example, the child star Jackie Coogan, who was known not only for the Charlie Chaplin film *The Kid* but also for the aforementioned film *Little Robinson Crusoe/Jackie, der kleine Robinson*, appeared on German children's radio (cf. Coogan 1930). And radio magazines also tried to arouse children's interest in the prominent child star. In 1926, for example, the radio magazine *Funkheinzelmann* stated, "Who among the children has not heard of little Jackie Coogan or perhaps even seen him wriggling on the flicker screen in a movie theater?" (*Der kleine Robinson* Jackie Coogan 1926). Conversely, radio pioneers and, in the Weimar Republic, specifically radio celebrities such as Hans Bodenstedt also productively dealt with the *Robinson-Stoff* in their media careers. Of all people, a literary adaptation of *Robinson Crusoe* in the context of book-centered reception can be traced from the radio-savvy Bodenstedt[4] (cf. Defoe/Bodenstedt [1912]). This once again demonstrates the importance of book-media reception for the period under investigation.

---

[4] Bodenstedt "helped build the Hamburg radio program in 1924, later director of NORAG. Dismissed by the Nazis in 1933, after 1945 employee at the children's radio of the NWDR in Hamburg". https://www.robinsone.de/auth/defoe-alles.htm (17.09.2019). Cf. also the contribution by Annemarie Weber in this volume.

Tendencies of Modernisation in the Book Reception of the Robinsonades

The first half of the twentieth century is characterized in the German-speaking world by a conspicuous surge in modernisation. It is therefore not surprising that in the literary, book-centered reception of the Robinsonades in particular, the incorporation of technical innovations becomes typical as a striking feature. Media and technical achievements become part of these adaptations of children's and young people's literature. The proportion of book-centered Robinsonades is so dominant in comparison to the demonstrable single-media adaptations in film and radio that this aspect can be seen as the comparatively most significant innovative push in reception. The modernised continuation of their traditional affinity to the model of the factual *Stoff* imparting knowledge is particularly evident in the open-mindedness towards the thematisation of new technology in the Robinsonades. Telegraphy, radio, airplanes, and war technology become the preferred subject of Robinsonades, which update this tradition in the first half of the twentieth century.

In this context, the unbroken continuation of the typical colonialising tendencies of such Robinsonades is also conspicuous, for example, in the scientific instructional youth book *Professor Robinson* (Felsing 1906), "a natural history study with colonialist ideas" (Stach 1999, 15). The phenomenon of urban-rural dichotomisations, crucial to the modernisation process, also has an innovative tendency in the children's and youth media expression of metropolitan Robinsonades in the metropolitan theme. An example of a Robinsonade in contrast to the metropolitan tendency (New York, Berlin) is Lisa Tetzner's fifth volume of the so-called *Kinderodyssee* (Tetzner [1944/45] 1989; cf. also Weinkauff 1995), written in exile, and is at the same time an outstanding example of Robinsonades produced in children's and youth literature in exile (cf. Mikota 2009). Characteristic of the glorification of the country is the three-volume so-called Alpine Robinsonade *Die Höhlenkinder* by Alois Theodor Sonnleitner (i.e. Alois Tlučhoř) (Sonnleitner 1918–20; cf. also Franz 2012a, 7), which was still actively read by young people after 1945. The *Stoff* was used for television several times: in 1962, a twelve-part television series was produced for WDR (Die Höhlenkinder 1962); this was followed in 1982 by a ten-part Italian television series (Die Höhlenkinder 1982), which was also broadcast on ZDF in 1985.

The affinity for technology and the genre's inclination towards innovations of modernisation for the masses ensured the Robinsonades the necessary attention among the reading youth. Such Robinsonades therefore already bear their conspicuous claim to modernity in their title, for example Wilhelm Ziegler's *Radio-Robinson. Eine moderne Robinsonade für die Jugend* (1924, Figs. 2 and 3).

This Robinsonade is also in the tradition of the model of knowledge representing *subject-Stoff*. It uses the topic of ship radio, embedded in an exciting and adventurous plot about a ship radio operator, to teach the physical basics of acoustics in an appendix, which are shown using the examples of telegraphy, telephony and radio:

Fig. 2 Front cover of *Radio-Robinson. A modern Robinsonade for the young* (Ziegler © Reutlingen: Bardtenschlager, 1924)

> Two shipwrecked men salvage the technical equipment of a ship on a deserted island. They build a power station with a waterfall and can protect themselves from the natives with the help of energised barriers. By radio they reach a rescuing ship. (Stach 1991, 129)

It is no longer the traditional ethos of productivity and the progress optimism of the eighteenth century that determine the basic ideas of this knowledge-providing Robinsonade, but rather the special knowledge of the electrical and electronic age that alone makes survival on the desert island possible here. The heroes are saved by wireless telegraphy as a mark of the process of modernisation in the conflict of nature and culture. The message of these Robinsonades is: survival is possible for those who can arm themselves against the challenges of nature through thorough knowledge of the modern scientific and technical achievements of twentieth century civilisation.

This is also evident in relation to the war-relevant technology of aircraft construction. The technology-believing confidence in the future viability of German aeronautics is expressed in Paul Georg Ehrhardt's 1934 Robinsonade *Der Flieger-Robinson* (Ehrhardt 1934). The book was distributed in its fifth edition in 1937. The

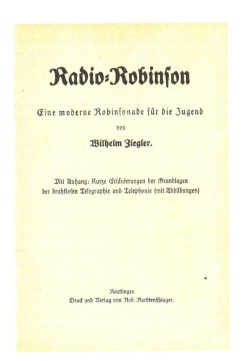

Fig. 3 Title page and frontispiece of *Radio-Robinson. A modern Robinsonade for the young* (Ziegler © Reutlingen: Bardtenschlager, 1924)

modern young hero of this Robinsonade is a hero of technology. It tells the "story of a young aviator who is forced to land in the Pacific Ocean. On an uncharted island he experiences a seven-year Robinsonade until, with the help of a homemade airplane, he manages to be rescued" (Stach 1991, 90). The novel's fiction of authenticity, significant to the reading youth, is evident in the dedication: "Dedicated to the ocean aviator Hermann Köhl, once my observer in the *Albatros B3* airplane" (Ehrhardt 1934). Köhl crossed the Atlantic in 1928 in a Junkers aircraft. This was the first crossing of the ocean on a flight from Europe to America by a powered aircraft. The superiority of German technology and the Dessau aircraft manufacturing company Junkers here with the heroic achievement of the *Flieger-Robinson* form the fascinating modernisation phenomenon, which was supposed to captivate the youthful readership.

Conclusion: Reflections and Theses on the Media Network Discussion

As a result of the Robinson and Robinsonades reception between 1900 and 1945 it can be stated: The modernisation process is evident in the affinity to the thematisation of innovative technology such as telegraphy, radio, aircraft construction, war technology in literary book-centered Robinsonades such as *Radio-Robinson* and *Flieger-Robinson,* but also in US film parodies such as *Mr. Robinson Crusoe.* The continuation of traditional book-medial Robinsonades (adventure type, non-fiction type) is quantitatively and qualitatively greater than their qualitative innovation value in use in the media network, despite the radio and film adaptations that are open to new mass media. Media networks such as Forster's *Robinson soll nicht sterben* are conspicuous exceptions. What is more typical is a system of addressee-specific reception of the *Robinson-Stoff* in the individual media of book, film and radio. Market-relevant, addressee-specific media networks only emerged after 1945 in an international context *(Swiss Family Robinson).* The reason for this in the German-speaking world is above all the firmly anchored reception of the *Robinson* story in schools. Typical media-historical developments in the sense of Werner Faulstich's media-historical development model for mass-media markings are more evident in phenomena on the margins: The dominance of booklet reading as one of the leading literary media of the era is nowhere more evident than in the data on the booklet series *Frank Allen – Der Rächer der Enterbten,* which, as mentioned, was mentioned as boy's reading in a contemporary statistical survey no less than 1684 times in total, while *Robinson Crusoe* was mentioned a mere 5 times (cf. Siemering/Barschak/Gensch 1930, 56 f.). This shows *in nuce,* and to a certain extent as the tip of an iceberg, how pronounced the ambivalence was between the perpetuation and transmission of the educational-historical value of Robinson and Robinsonades reception in the lingering bourgeois claim to education and the associated reading and media socialisation with the actual reading, entertainment and media use needs of children and adolescents in the period under study, which was no longer dominated by exciting Robinsonades alone.

Whether and how it will be possible to successfully keep Robinson's reception in children's and young people's literature and media permanently alive in the future in the face of increasing postcolonial criticism remains an open question. The Regensburg-based scholar of children's and youth literature Kurt Franz was optimistic in 2012:

> Even today […] *Robinson* has not died, neither in terms of the history of mentality nor the history of reception, although it no longer stands out as a title for children and young people, even in the school reading canon, but it continues to survive as a literary classic, perhaps even as the prototype of the classic par excellence. (Franz 2012a, 1)

Literature

Primary Literature

André, Christian Carl: Felsenburg. Ein sittlichunterhaltendes Lesebuch. 3 Bde. Gotha: Ettinger, 1788–1789.
Campe, Joachim Heinrich: Robinson der Jüngere, zur angenehmen und nützlichen Unterhaltung für Kinder. [1779/80] Nach dem Erstdr. hg. von Alwin Binder und Heinrich Richartz. Bibliographisch erg. Ausg. Stuttgart: Reclam, 2000.

Defoe, Daniel: The Life and Strange Surprizing Adventures of Robinson Crusoe of York [...]. London: Taylor, 1719.
Defoe, Daniel/Bodenstedt, Hans: Robinson Crusoe. Für die Jugend neu bearbeitet von Hans Bodenstedt. Mit einem Begleitwort von August Scholz. Ill. von Hans Bruch und Karl Simunek. Unter Mitarbeit von August Scholz, Hans Bruch und Karl Simunek. Berlin: Oestergaard, [1912] (Oestergaards Jugendbücher).
Ehrhardt, Paul Georg: Der Flieger-Robinson. Stuttgart: Herold, [1934].
Felsing, Otto: Professor Robinson. See- und Inselabenteuer. Elberfeld: Lucas, 1906.
Forster, Friedrich [d. i. Waldfried Burggraf]: Robinson soll nicht sterben. Mit Bildern von Hans Meid. München: Desch, [1948].
Gansberg, Fritz: Die Geschichte von Robinson für unsere Kleinen. Langensalza: Beltz, 1930, [²1941].
Marryat, Frederick: Der neue Robinson oder Schiffbruch des Pacific. Eine Erzählung für die Jugend. Nach dem Engl. bearb. von Franz Hoffmann. Stuttgart: Schmidt und Spring, 1843a.
Marryat, Frederick: Sigismund Rüstig der Bremer Steuermann. Ein neuer Robinson nach Capitain Marryat. Frei für die deutsche Jugend bearb. [von Heinrich Laube]. 2 Bde. Leipzig: Teubner, 1843b.
Robinsonaden. Neues Bilder- und Lesebuch für die Jugend. Mit 8 colorirten Lithographien im Tondruck. Nürnberg: Lotzbeck, 1858.
Schnabel, Johann Gottfried: Wunderlich FATA einiger SEE-Fahrer [...]. 4 Bde. Nordhausen: Groß, 1731–1743.
Schubert, Gotthilf Heinrich von: Der neue Robinson oder die Schicksale des Philipp Ashton, während seines erzwungenen Aufenthalts unter den Seeräubern und auf der unbewohnten Insel Roatan. Eine wahre Geschichte. Für die deutsche Jugend bearb. Calw [u. a.]: Vereinsbuchhandlung/Steinkopf, 1849.
Sonnleitner, Alois Theodor [d. i. Alois Tlučhoř]: Die Höhlenkinder. 3 Bde. Stuttgart: Franckh, 1918–1920.
Tetzner, Lisa: Die Kinder aus Nr. 67, Bd. 5/6: Die Kinder auf der Insel/Mirjam in Amerika. [1944–1945] Aarau [u. a.]: Sauerländer, ³1989.
Wezel, Johann Carl: Robinson Krusoe. Hg. von Wolfgang Hörner und Jutta Heinz. Heidelberg: Mattes, 2016 (Gesamtausg.; 2,2).
Wyss, Johann David: Der Schweizerische Robinson oder der schiffbrüchige Schweizer-Prediger und seine Familie. Ein lehrreiches Buch für Kinder und Kinder-Freunde zu Stadt und Land. Hg. von Joh. Rudolf Wyß. 4 Bde. Zürich: Orell, Füßli 1821–1827.
Ziegler, Wilhelm: Radio-Robinson. Eine moderne Robinsonade für die Jugend. Reutlingen: Bardtenschlager, 1924.

Filmography

Die Höhlenkinder [zwölfteilige Fernsehserie für den WDR] (D 1962). Regie: Peter Podehl.
Die Höhlenkinder/I Ragazzi della valle miseriosa (I 1982). Regie: Marcello Aliprandi.
Die weiße Hölle vom Piz Palü [Naturfilm] (D 1928). Regie: Arnold Fanck.
Robinson soll nicht sterben (D Forster 1956). Regie: Josef von Báky. N. d. Theaterstück *Robinson soll nicht sterben* von Friedrich Forster [d. i. Waldfried Burggraf] [EA 1932].
Robinson Crusoe [zweiteiliger Animationsstummfilm] (D 1920). Gestaltung: Louis Seel.
Little Robinson Crusoe/Jackie, der kleine Robinson [(Kinder-)Film mit Kinderstar Jackie Coogan] (USA 1924). Regie: Edward F. Cline.
Mr. Robinson Crusoe [Abenteuerfilm- und Robinsonadenparodie] (USA 1932). Regie: A. Edward Sutherland [DVD].
Ein Robinson. Das Tagebuch eines Matrosen [Naturfilm] (D 1940). Regie: Arnold Fanck.
The Kid/Der Vagabund und das Kind [Stummfilm-Tragikkomödie] (USA 1921). Regie: Charlie Chaplin.

Audiography

Funkheinzelmanns Bilderbuch. Eine Kinderrevue [Übertragung aus dem Carl-Schultze-Theater Hamburg] (1927). Norag Hamburg, 20.12.1927. Quelle: Der deutsche Rundfunk 5 (1927) 51, 3456.
Jackie Coogan stellt seinen Vater vor. Unter Mitarbeit von Jackie Coogan (Von Kindern für Kinder) [Radiosendung] (1930). Funk-Stunde Berlin, 13.02.1930. Quelle: Der Deutsche Rundfunk 6 (1928), 46.
Von Robinson Crusoes Schicksalen (2. Abend) [Radiolesung] (1925). Gesprochen von Fr. Staude. Rundfunksender Wien, 02.06.1925. Quelle: Der deutsche Rundfunk 3 (1925) 22, 1426.
Schubert, Gotthilf Heinrich von: Philipp Ashton, ein neuer Robinson. (1) Unter Räubern. Die Flucht. Unter Mitarbeit von Rudolf Simon (Jugendfunk). (1928a) Werag Köln, 19.10.1928. Quelle: In: Die Sendung 5 (1928) 42, XXV.
Schubert, Gotthilf Heinrich von: Philipp Ashton, ein neuer Robinson. (2) Traurige Tage und große Not – Die Rettung. Unter Mitarbeit von Rudolf Simon (Jugendfunk). (1928b) Werag Köln, 02.11.1928. Quelle: Die Sendung 5 (1928) 44, XXV.
Schubert, Gotthilf Heinrich von: (1928c): Philipp Ashton, ein neuer Robinson. Traurige Tage; Die Rettung. Unter Mitarbeit von Rudolf Simon (Jugendfunk). Werag Köln, 23.11.1928. Quelle: Der Deutsche Rundfunk 6 (1928) 47, 3232.
Robinson soll nicht sterben [Hörspiel nach Friedrich Forster]. Bayrischer Rundfunk/Südwestfunk Baden-Baden/Rundfunk Bremen/Wiener Hörfunk Forster 1950/1955/1957/1964 (erschlossen; vgl. Stach 1991, 252.

Theatrography

Friedrich Forster [d. i. Waldfried Burggraf]: Robinson soll nicht sterben. Ein Stück in drei Akten. Leipzig: Kurt Scholze Nachf., 1932 (UA Leipzig 1932).
Mochmann, Paul: Robinsons Abenteuer. Ein Kinderstück. Berlin: Henschel, 1932 (UA unbekannt).

Secondary Literature Before 1945

Der kleine Jackie Coogan. In: Funkheinzelmann 1 (1926) 1, 9–10.
Fuchs, Arno: Robinson als Stoff eines erziehenden Unterrichts in Präparationen und Konzentrationsplänen. Nach Herbart-Zillerschen Grundsätzen bearb. Jena 1893.
Haken, Christian August Ludwig: Bibliothek der Robinsone, Bd. 1. Berlin 1805.
Rehm, W.: Robinsonade. In: Paul Merker/Stammler, Wolfgang (Hg.): Reallexikon der deutschen Literaturgeschichte, Bd. 3. Berlin 1928/1929, 59–62.
Siemering, Hertha/Barschak, Erna/Gensch, Willy: Was liest unsere Jugend? Ergebnisse von Feststellungen an Schulen aller Gattungen und Erziehungsanstalten sowie bei Jugendorganisationen und Jugendlichen. Berlin 1930.

Secondary Literature After 1945

Bauer, Matthias: Robinson muss sterben. Jack Golds *Man Friday* (1975) als Ideologiekritik kolonialistischer Denk- und Verhaltensmuster. In: Bieber, Ada/Greif, Stefan/Helmes, Günter (Hg.): Angeschwemmt – Fortgeschrieben. Robinsonaden im 20. und beginnenden 21. Jahrhunderts. Würzburg 2009, 139–154.

Dahrendorf, Malte: Robinsonalter. In: Doderer, Klaus (Hg.): Lexikon der Kinder- und Jugendliteratur. Sonderausg., Bd. 3. Weinheim [u. a.] 1984, 191.

Ewers, Hans-Heino: Art. Joachim Heinrich Campe: Robinson der Jüngere. In: Brüggemann, Theodor/Ders. (Hg.): Handbuch zur Kinder- und Jugendliteratur. Von 1750 bis 1800. Stuttgart 1982, Sp. 215–233.

Ewers, Hans-Heino: Literatur für Kinder und Jugendliche. Eine Einführung. Paderborn ²2012.

Ewers, Hans-Heino: Kinder- und Jugendliteratur. In: Rippl, Gabriele/Winko, Simone (Hg.): Handbuch Kanon und Wertung. Theorien, Instanzen, Geschichte. Stuttgart [u. a.] 2013, 350–356.

Fanck, Matthias: Bergfilmpionier Arnold Fanck. Vergessener Star. In: Spiegel online (2015) vom 11.10. https://www.spiegel.de/geschichte/ein-robinson-von-arnold-fanck-erinnerung-an-den-bergfilmpionier-a-1051946.html (01.03.2020).

Faulstich, Werner: Mediengeschichte. Von 1700 bis ins 3. Jahrtausend. Göttingen 2006.

Franz, Kurt: Robinson Crusoe als Schullektüre. In: Kurt Franz (Hg.): Kinder- und Jugendliteratur. Ein Lexikon. 47. Erg.-Lfg. Meitingen 2012a, 1–34.

Franz, Kurt: Robinson und Robinsonaden. Vom Abenteuerroman zum Schulklassiker. In: Schilcher, Anita/Pecher, Claudia Maria (Hg.): „Klassiker" der internationalen Jugendliteratur, Bd. 1: Kulturelle und epochenspezifische Diskurse aus Sicht der Fachdisziplinen. Baltmannsweiler 2012b, 55–82.

Fohrmann, Jürgen: Abenteuer und Bürgertum. Zur Geschichte der deutschen Robinsonaden im 18. Jahrhundert. Stuttgart 1981.

Galle, Heinz J.: Groschenhefte. Die Geschichte der deutschen Trivialliteratur. Frankfurt a. M. [u. a.] 1988.

Giesen, Rolf/Storm, J. P.: Animation Under the Swastika. A History of Trickfilm in Nazi Germany, 1933–1945. Jefferson [u. a.] 2012.

Hazard, Paul: Kinder, Bücher und große Leute. Vorwort von Erich Kästner. Hamburg 1952.

Ilbrig, Cornelia: „Sic transit gloria mundi". Aufbau und Zerstörung einer Inselwelt in Wezels *Robinson Krusoe*. In: Schnabeliana 9 (2008), 73–89.

Kortenbruck-Hoeijmans, Hannelore: Johann David Wyß' *Schweizerischer Robinson*. Dokument pädagogisch-literarischen Zeitgeistes an der Schwelle zum 19. Jahrhundert. Baltmannsweiler 1999.

Liebs, Elke: Die pädagogische Insel. Studien zur Rezeption des *Robinson Crusoe* in deutschen Jugendbearbeitungen. Stuttgart 1977.

Mikota, Jana: Die Kinder auf der Insel – Insu Pu – Das Eismeer ruft. Die Robinsonade in der Kinder- und Jugendliteratur des Exils. In: Bieber, Ada/Greif, Stefan/Helmes, Günter (Hg.): Angeschwemmt – Fortgeschrieben. Robinsonaden im 20. und beginnenden 21. Jahrhunderts. Würzburg 2009, 36–54.

Reinhard, Angelika: Die Karriere des *Robinson Crusoe* vom literarischen zum pädagogischen Helden. Eine literaturwissenschaftliche Untersuchung des Robinson Defoes und der Robinson-Adaptationen von Campe und Forster. Frankfurt a. M. [u. a.] 1994.

Reiß, Gunter (Hg.): Kindertheater und populäre bürgerliche Musikkultur um 1900. Studien zum Weihnachtsmärchen (C. A. Görner, G. von Bassewitz), zum patriotischen Festspiel, zur Märchenoper, zur Hausmusik (C. Reinecke, E. Fischer) und zur frühen massenmedialen Kinderkultur. Frankfurt a. M. [u. a.] 2008 (Kinder- und Jugendkultur, -literatur und -medien; 55).

Rutschmann, Verena: "Der Schweizerische Robinson" – eine erzählte Enzyklopädie. In: Tomkowiak, Ingrid (Hg.): Populäre Enzyklopädien. Von der Auswahl, Ordnung und Vermittlung des Wissens. Zürich 2002, 159–173.

Schlaeger, Jürgen: Robinsonade. In: Müller, Jan Dirk (Hg.): Reallexikon der deutschen Literaturwissenschaft, Bd. III. Berlin [u. a.] 2003, 309–310.

Schmideler, Sebastian: Die Insel Felsenburg als philanthropische Mädchenschule – Die Jugendbearbeitungen der *Wunderlichen FATA* von Christian Carl André (1763–1831). In: Schnabeliana 9 (2006–2008). St. Ingbert 2008, 91–181.

Schmideler, Sebastian: Metamorphosen. Wie die Insel Felsenburg in den literaturwissenschaftlichen Kanon aufgenommen wurde. Eine Spurensuche. In: Schnabeliana 10 (2012), 137–170.

Stach, Reinhard: Robinsonade. In: Doderer, Klaus (Hg.): Lexikon der Kinder- und Jugendliteratur. Sonderausg., Bd. 3. Weinheim [u. a.] 1984, 188–191.

Stach, Reinhard: Robinson und Robinsonaden in der deutschsprachigen Literatur. Eine Bibliographie. Würzburg 1991.

Stach, Reinhard: Robinsonaden in der Jugendliteratur. In: Franz, Kurt (Hg.): Kinder- und Jugendliteratur. Ein Lexikon. 7. Erg.-Lfg. Meitingen 1999, 1–34.

Weinkauff, Gina: Natur und Stadt in Lisa Tetzners Kinderodyssee. In: Nassen, Ulrich (Hg.): Naturkind, Landkind, Stadtkind. Literarische Bilderwelten kindlicher Umwelt. München 1995, 107–121.

Wild, Reiner: Die aufgeklärte Kinderliteratur in der Literaturgeschichte des 18. Jahrhunderts. Zur Kontroverse um die Robinson-Bearbeitung zwischen Joachim Heinrich Campe und Johann Carl Wezel. In: Grenz, Dagmar (Hg.): Aufklärung und Kinderbuch. Pinneberg 1986, 47–78.

Zupancic, Peter: Die Robinsonade in der Jugendliteratur. Bochum 1976. Zugl.: Bochum, Univ., Diss., 1976.

School Stories in the Theatre, Book and on the Screen

Beyond Romy and Lilli

Christa Winsloe's Boarding School Story and Its Forms of Presentation in the Media

Gabriele von Glasenapp

Preliminary Considerations

If one considers a media network in terms of the multitude of its medial and interrelated manifestations, its temporal dimensions, its geographical extent, the extent of its reception history, as well as its intermedial references – also with regard to other media networks – Christa Winsloe's story about the girl Manuela and her failing socialisation at a girls' boarding school, written at the beginning of the 1930s, certainly occupies a prominent place within the numerous and quite diverse media networks whose emergence falls within the Weimar Republic. Based on recent research, according to which a media network media network is to be understood as "the fact that a *Stoff* is present in various media, that is, that there is cross-media marketing and, in addition, in many cases a large number of fan articles" (Josting 2012, 391) and based on the parameters listed at the beginning, the *Stoff*, which was treated a total of four times in different media by the author during her life (1888–1944) and under different titles represents a media networkmedia network which is as dynamic as it is branched. In addition to the criteria mentioned above, the specifics of this network include the very different perceptions of the individual media relevant here – stage manuscripts, film scripts, film, novel – the consistently very explicit reference character of the individual type of media to others, the popularity factor (especially concerning the film and novel versions), as well as a very complex reception history that is subject to several extensions and caesurae: In terms of time, it can be divided into processes that took place during the author's lifetime and were partially initiated or controlled by her, and those that began after 1945, i.e. after Christa Winsloe's death, and show a spectrum whose medial

G. von Glasenapp (✉)
ALEKI, University of Cologne, Cologne, Germany
e-mail: g.glasenapp@uni-koeln.de

© Springer-Verlag GmbH Germany, part of Springer Nature 2024
P. Josting et al. (eds.), *German-Language Children's and Youth Literature In The Media Network 1900–1945*, https://doi.org/10.1007/978-3-476-05892-8_16

bandwidth extends from new productions, editions, and film adaptations to radio plays, translations, and adaptations of her *Stoff* in very different types of media.

In the following article, the narratives surrounding Christa Winsloe's protagonist Manuela will be more closely examined with regard to their media network characteristics – taking into account the indicators listed here – in two separate but nevertheless interrelated steps: first, the network characteristics will be examined in a narrower sense from a diachronic perspective, i.e. in which media is the story *conveyed*, how are these types of media related to each other, or can reciprocal references be identified. Approaches regarding the history of reception are linked to this – in particular with regard to the contemporary popularity of the *Stoff* as well as the translations that appeared at the time. In the second part, which will be synchronous, the focus will be put on aspects of a broader concept of media networksmedia network, i.e. where can references to similar structures of *Stoff* and other media networksmedia networks be identified, how are these references established, and by whom are they initiated. This approach, however, is based on the premise that the individual aspects of a narrow and a broader concept of media networksmedia network cannot always be as strictly separated from one another as the approach outlined here would suggest.[1]

History and Genre Traditions

The story about the girl Manuela von Meinhardis is conveyed – to use a term appropriate to the media with regard to the different forms of manifestation – when, after the death of her mother, she against her will is sent to the Potsdam Princess Helene Convent, a boarding school for young girls. There, Prussian soldierly drill, and discipline – represented by the figures of the matron as well as the governesses, i.e. age (and the principles it represents) rule over the youth of the pupils. There the girls are prepared for their future role as wives and mothers of officers, just as the majority of them are themselves daughters and granddaughters of officers, i.e. they are seen as part of a community shaped by soldierly Prussian principles and thus at the same time as part of a succession of tradition constituting the state. The boarding school thus appears as a place where the girls are not so much educated as barracked and drilled – like male soldiers, they wear a kind of uniform, which is also explicitly called such. In this environment, however, which postulates affect control as the highest good, the girls nevertheless have forbidden crushes both on each other and on the young governess, Fräulein von Bernburg, whose upbringing emphasises affection in the girls instead of drill. The motherless Manuela in particular is attracted to the governess, and after the performance of a play in which the girl plays

---

[1] For reasons regarding the extent of this paper, the numerous productions of the play as well as the translations of the stage version, the novel and the cinematic subtitles can only be dealt with in rudimentary form.

the male lead, she, intoxicated by alcohol and her acting success, made bold by the men's clothes she wears, openly expresses her affection, a fundamental breach of the rules that is met with draconian punishment: For the purpose of better supervision, Manuela is isolated from all her classmates in the future, and Fräulein von Bernburg is to leave the convent. In deepest despair, the girl sees only one way out for herself: suicide.

Although the protagonist Manuela is barely 15, Winsloe did not address any of the four versions of her story to adolescents. The plot outlined here, however, clearly reveals the structural features of both the Backfisch or boarding school narrative and the schoolboy novel, which were evidently drawn upon here. The texts attributed to this corpus are analogous to the genre of the Bildungsroman, the coming-of-age novel, or the adolescent novel, to which the boarding school narratives and school novels can also be counted in the broadest sense, and are located, regardless of their address, in a *borderline area* between adult and juvenile literature, since they all deal with the identity-finding processes of adolescents, the majority of which are portrayed as a profoundly crisis-ridden stage of development – which researchers have meanwhile subsumed under the term "disturbance" i.e., as an antithesis to order, norm, and undisturbedness (Gansel 2011, 42).

In this text corpus, which has experienced a heyday in German-language adult and youth literature since the last third of the nineteenth century, two basic variants can be identified. What both variants have in common is that the plot centres on the crisis-ridden enculturation processes of adolescence. The socialisation processes associated with this, however, do not usually take place in the parental home, but rather in schools, boarding schools, or so-called convents located at a considerable distance from it, whereby – due to the times – the majority of these are single-sex universes. The education received there was intended to enable the individual to participate in bourgeois society – a claim, however, that the narrations put into practice in very different ways.

Two antagonistic narratives can be distinguished. The first, largely affirmative, is found in the Backfisch or boarding school narratives explicitly addressed to adolescent female readers. As Gisela Wilkending has shown in her research, they almost universally follow an analogous pattern: a girl who is conspicuous for her wildness or other atypical female behaviour is sent by her parents to a boarding school, often against her will. There she learns to internalise and accept the given and never questioned social values in the form of educational maxims, in dealing with her peers, through warning stories as well as interactions with the governesses, for which in the end she receives the deserved gratification in the form of a bridegroom or at least a serious suitor. The prototype of the genre is Emmy von Rhoden's 1885 novel *Der Trotzkopf. Eine Pensionsgeschichte für erwachsene Mädchen* (cf. inter alia Wilkending 1999, 104–116).

The second – the critical school narrative – is different. It is best known from today's classics of the school novel, such as *Unterm Rad* (1906) by Hermann Hesse or *Der Zögling Törless* (1906) by Robert Musil. In these narratives, which are not addressed to adolescent readers, the adolescent is unable or unwilling to internalise society's values, to chalk up adaptation as an individual gain; the conflict between the individual and society seems insurmountable, or to put it another way: In the end, the principles of disciplinary society triumph over life, drive suppression over sexuality, age (in the form of teachers) over youth, societal maxims over the inner nature of the adolescent, conformity over individualism, and not infrequently death or at least regression over empathetic life (cf. Hamann 2016, 20–22). In these narratives, school appears as a heterotopia turned negative, i.e. as the incarnation of a disciplinary and surveillance society that not only prevents the adolescent individual from developing, but literally deprives him or her of the air to breathe.

Analogous to the address of the texts – Backfisch and boarding school narratives were explicitly addressed to adolescents, the other texts to a general audience – is the gender assignment. The majority of female socialisation processes does not involve many crises and are successful – their literary representation is reserved for the Backfisch narratives and thus for specific youth literature. The literary representation of male socialisation, however, often ends in disaster. The adolescent fails because of the antagonisms between life and school that are insurmountable for him.

Research has only in exceptional cases – in connection with the story of Winsloe – taken a look at these genre-typological contexts, and even then only to some extent (cf., among others, Koch 1987, 81–89; Luserke 1999, 100–108; Johann 2003, 492–495; Birkner 2009, 95–99), instead preferring to focus on the implications of the love relationship between Manuela and Fräulein von Bernburg. Such a focus is justified, considering that homoerotic and also homosexual relationships (as part of a complex and by no means straightforward process of finding one's identity) do play a role in most of the school novels (*not* the Backfisch stories!) – albeit always among peers and not between members of different generations. However, this fixation of perception is certainly also due to the fact that the author Christa Winsloe and her work were only rediscovered at the beginning of the 1980s by the second German women's movement (cf., among others, Gramann/Schlüpmann 1981, 28–41; Reinig 1983, 239–248), which, like the so-called women's or feminist research that emerged from it, yet, attracted considerably more interest. Feminist research, however, was clearly more interested in the positively connoted portrayal of a love affair between two women, which had been absent from media representations, than in the genre characteristics of Backfisch or school novels at the turn of the century. Since the first biography of Winsloe did not appear until the early 2010s (Hermanns 2012a), the examination of the author and her oeuvre has been reserved for different, partially overlapping fields of scholarship, including queer studies (see, among others, Fest 2012, where further references can be found), exile studies (see, among others, Hermanns 2013, 62–71), theatre studies (cf. among others, Stürzer 1993, 96–111), but above all film studies, which dealt with the cinema of the Weimar Republic (cf. among others, McCormick 2009, 271–289) or the history of queer cinema (cf. among others, Boxhammer 2007; Dyer 2003, 23–62), and more recently also the didactics of literature (Birkner 2009, 95–99). Established German studies, literature, and cultural studies,[2] but also research on children's and young people's literature, however, have so far shown little interest in the *Stoff*; nor has it been examined with regard to its media-specific or transmedial manifestations, despite the fact that the various medial manifestations are nearly universally mentioned in the research literature.[3]

Christa Winsloe's Boarding School Story in the Media Network (1930–1936)

Christa Winsloe herself initially played a major role in the various media versions of the story – stage manuscripts or plays, film script, novel – and in all cases as author; only in the case of the screenplay did F. D. Andam (i.e. Friedrich Andamm, 1901–1969) assist her as scriptwriter. Characteristic of this first media network, consisting of two plays, a feature film and a novel, is its very short creation time of less than a year, the different titles of the individual media products, some of which were accompanied by significant shifts in emphasis, the openly stressed intermedial references, on the one hand to already existing media versions of the story, on the other hand – and this rather implicitly – to further media networks, and last but not least the immense response of the audience, which contributed decisively to the rapid expansion of the media network.

The beginning of the network was marked by the premiere of the play *Der Ritter Nérestan (The Knight Nérestan)* by the then completely unknown author Christa Winsloe at the end of November 1930 at the Leipzig Schauspielhaus (cf. Stürzer 1993, 102–107). Although this first version of the story clearly emphasises the two central plot moments – the sharp criticism of the educational maxims that are singled out as hostile to humanity and the emotional relationship between pupil and educator that ends with the protagonist's suicide – the scandal fails to materialise; the response from audiences and critics is friendly but restrained.

Christa Winsloe reacts by rewriting the play; in doing so, above all she "defuses" (ibid., 103) the figure of the governess by removing scenes that explicitly refer to homosexual connotations (cf. ibid., 104 f.). Fräulein von Bernburg's feelings are relegated to the secondary text, i.e. to non-linguistic gestures, and thus ultimately left to the interpretation of the audience. Her linguistic utterances to Manuela are

---

[2] This can be seen not least in the fact that Winsloe's history is still not mentioned in German-language literary histories (on the era of the Weimar Republic); cf. as a prominent example Kiesel 2017. Even the historiography of women's literature that emerged in the 1980s mentioned Winsloe at best passim (cf. Fischer-Lichte 1988, 379) or not at all (cf. Gnüg/Möhrmann 1999; Fähnders/Karrenbrock 2003). Analogously, the author and her story are not mentioned in the numerous studies on the literary representation of school, apart from a few exceptions.

[3] Even in the publications whose titles suggest a preoccupation with the media manifestations of the *Stoff*, an examination of it in the final analysis takes place at most in rudimentary form (see, among others, Puhlfürst 2000; Iurascu 2019).

kept more general, her proleptic utterance to the matron to leave the convent together with Manuela softened to the effect that only she wants to leave the asylum (Winsloe 1930, 121). Although Winsloe retains the central plot elements of the first version, the new version bears a distinctly more polyvalent character, at least with regard to the relational nature of the two main protagonists. The new version also receives an altered title, from which the shifts in emphasis can be read, at least implicitly: Whereas the first title, *Der Ritter Nérestan*, had focused on the protagonist Manuela (in a theatrical performance of Voltaire's drama *Zaire* on the occasion of the matron's birthday, she takes on the role of the knight Nérestan), the renaming as *Gestern und Heute (Yesterday and Today)* shifts it to the socio-political aspect of the drama, i.e. the critique of the boarding school's repressive educational maxims. The thrust of this criticism was not least the fact that, as is pointed out in the very first scene, although the plot is set in the author's present, i.e. the Weimar Republic, the traditional principles of the imperial era remain unchanged (cf. Winsloe 1930, 8 f.) and thus at the same time bear a profoundly anti-republican character (cf. Fest 2012, 461–464).[4] The premiere of *Gestern und Heute* took place at the beginning of April 1931 in Berlin's Theater an der Stresemannallee; its resounding success with audiences and critics provided the occasion for a renewed expansion of the media network, which at this point was still very manageable – as early as the summer of 1931, the film producer Carl Froelich (1875–1953) initiated the film adaptation of the play. The theatre director Leontine Sagan (1889–1974), who had already directed the stage version of *Gestern und Heute*, was engaged as director (cf. Sagan 2010, 174–181). The media network thus exhibits another specific feature that can be attributed in part to the author, but was to become increasingly independent, the appearance of certain actors across media boundaries – in this case the director Leontine Sagan, but above all the actress Hertha Thiele, who played the protagonist Manuela in both versions of the drama as well as in the film version (Stürzer 1993, 287), something Winsloe had explicitly insisted on (cf. Sagan/Eckardt 2010, 179). Sagan's commitment, on the other hand, was due to Carl Froelich himself (ibid., 177–179). In both cases, however, such a selection, whether explicit or implicit, helped to highlight the composite nature of the individual media. This aspect was also emphasised in the titles of the individual types of media: when the two drama manuscripts were published, the title of the first drama version, *Der Ritter Nérestan* (Winsloe 1930, 1973), was written in brackets on the cover of both the first and new editions of *Gestern und Heute*; analogously, in the film credits, reference was made to the "stage play *Gestern und Heute*" under the heading *Original*.

---

[4] The fact that Winsloe had conceived the new version of her drama as a period piece can also be seen in the stage manuscript, where the time of the action is explicitly stated as "Today" (Winsloe 1930, 4). In the new edition of the stage play, the time was changed to "end of the twenties" (Winsloe 1973, 4), which – probably unintentionally – emphasises the temporal distance to the events. Research has so far only marginally addressed the socio-political aspects of the drama (cf. in part Fest 2012, 462–464).

The film premiered in Berlin at the end of November 1931, and its resounding success[5] – it is considered one of the most successful films of the year, both at home and abroad (cf. Stürzer 1993, 100; Prinzler 1995, 98)[6] – is due not only to Sagan's directing, cinematography and the performances of the actresses, but also to the film title *Mädchen in Uniform*, which presumably goes back to Carl Froelich – who acted as the film's "artistic director" (according to contemporary film posters).[7] With the film version, however, the *Stoff* was not only adapted for a new medium, but a new story was also told: almost all concrete references to time that the stage plays still had (cf. above)[8] were erased in favour of temporal ambiguity (cf. Fest 2012, 465); the originally performed stage play *Der Ritter Nérestan* becomes Schiller's *Don Carlos*, but the most important thing is the changed ending: unlike in the stage versions, the schoolmates are able to prevent the protagonist's suicide at the last moment.

This softened ending was quite obviously also due to one of Froelich's numerous interventions; Winsloe herself, who had collaborated on the screenplay, was highly dissatisfied with it, which can be seen from the fact that she only permitted productions of the play if the tragic ending she had envisaged was also performed in them (cf. Stürzer 1993, 100 f.). With regard to the successively expanding media network, one can speak here of medial penetration processes: Not only was a successful play adapted for film by its author, the great success of the film in turn prompted dramaturges to integrate elements of the film into their own productions, which Winsloe, however, obviously tried to prevent. It becomes clear that within a short period of time it was no longer the play but the film adaptation that was seen as the dominant medium to which the other media that took up the *Stoff* wanted to refer.[9]

---

[5] Contrary to what can be read in older publications, the film did not cause any form of scandal, neither at its premiere nor after the transfer of power (cf. Nowak 2015, 131 f.).

[6] It competed with such successful films as *Die Drei-Groschen-Oper* (director: G. W. Pabst), *M* (director: Fritz Lang), *Der Kongress tanzt* (director: Eric Charell), *Berlin Alexanderplatz* (director: Phil Jutzi), *Emil und die Detektive* (director: Gerhard Lamprecht), *Der Hauptmann von Köpenick* (director: Richard Oswald); *Im Westen nichts Neues* (director: Lewis Milestone), as can be read in Prinzler (1995, 97 f.).

[7] The oxymoron *Mädchen in Uniform*, deliberately placed here, may owe something to the title of the extremely successful anti-war novel *Die Katrin wird Soldat* (1930) by Adrienne Thomas (1897–1980), which was published at almost the same time and is based on the same rhetorical figure. Herta Thiele, on the other hand, suspected that Froelich chose this title in order to tie in with the popular soldier's tales of the early 1930s (cf. Gramann/Schlüpmann 1981, 41).

[8] The references to time were only retained (or even intensified) when Froelich thought it opportune: in the drama, for example, the character Ilse *outed* herself as a fan of Hans Albers and Greta Garbo (cf. Winsloe 1930, 20); in the film version, however, the actress Henny Porten is named instead of Garbo, with whose production company Froelich had merged shortly before.

[9] This manifests itself particularly clearly in the contemporary translations of the play *Gestern und Heute*, for example in the English translation by Barbara Burnham, who chose *Children in Uniform* as the title and added "Adapted from the same play as *Mädchen in Uniform*" as a subtitle (Winsloe 1933b). The French translation proceeded quite similarly; there the title of the translated play was *Demoiselles en Uniforme*, which was subtitled "Traduction fidèle de la pièce Allemande *Gestern und Heute* d'où a été tiré le film sensationnel *Mädchen in Uniform* sous le titre *Jeunes Filles en Uniforme*" (Winsloe 1932). A slightly *softened* version can be found in the Danish translation of the play, which adopted the original title with *Igår og idag (Gestern und Heute)*, but placed the film title in brackets *(Piger i uniform)* after it in Danish.

Winsloe took both factors into account – the great popularity of the film as well as her dissatisfaction with what she saw as an unacceptable ending – a decision that resulted in a renewed expansion of the existing media network within two years: Winsloe tells the boarding school story a fourth time, but now in the form of a novel. Again, it is partially a new narrative: the prequel is now also told, i.e. the protagonist's childhood, the death of her mother, her stay with a family friend, where the girl feels attracted to her friend's mother, and her transfer to the boarding school. Much more emphasis (than in the previous versions) is placed on the emotional relationship between the pupil and the governess, which is further reinforced by the alternation between internal and zero focalisation (which also allows a glimpse into the emotional world of the governess). These narrators' accounts are contrasted, as it were, with longer dialogue passages, some of which are taken verbatim from the drama versions and at the same time recall the origin of the text as a drama text (cf. Luserke 1999, 101).

Analogous to the drama versions, Manuela is also *allowed to* die at the end in the novel version; she throws herself out of the window. For this new story, Winsloe also chooses a new title, *Das Mädchen Manuela* (Winsloe 1933a), as well as a subtitle: "Der Roman von *Mädchen in Uniform*."[10] As awkwardly formulated as this subtitle is, it is nevertheless of central importance with regard to the intermedial reference that appears – is supposed to appear – here. Even if Winsloe had been extremely critical of Froelich's changes, the great success of the film had not left her unimpressed, and so she insinuated with the title and subtitle that the actual story was being (re)told here – certainly in imitation of the successful film.[11]

However, the effectiveness of media networks is not only subject to the content negotiated in them, it is also always highly context-dependent. These contexts, however, had fundamentally changed in Germany at the end of January 1933 with the handover of power to the National Socialists. This did not affect the film version of Winsloe's play; although she had not lived in Germany since 1932 and Leontine Sagan had emigrated to England in the same year, this did not dampen the success of the film. The film's great success can be seen in the relevant contemporary periodicals such as the film journal *Der Kinematograph* or the daily *Film-Kurier*, which was shown not only in Germany but also in European and non-European countries, including Algeria and Palestine. Even after the start of the war in Germany, the film

---

[10] The publisher also advertised the novel with a corresponding banderole: "Sensational new release. The novel of the famous film *Mädchen in Uniform*" (Hermanns 2012a, 154).

[11] The majority of translations published between 1933 and 1943 proceeded in a similar manner; of the ten translations in total, there are only three that make no reference to the film title: the editions in Catalan (1934) and in Czech (1935), both of which are limited to the name *Manuela*, as well as the Dutch edition *Het meisje Manuela* (1935). The Italian (1934), Portuguese (1934), Spanish (1934), Polish (1936), and Hungarian (1943) translations each mentioned only the film title, and only the English (1933) and French (1934) editions followed the German supertitle and subtitle verbatim. Some of the translations also featured film stills on their covers.

was shown again and again in various cities, and at the same time was repeatedly cited as a reference for other films until the 1940s. The fact that the film, despite its author and director, was not subject to any restrictions from the side of those in power during the Nazi era (cf. Weinstein 2019, 144–165) was obviously paradoxically due to the former "artistic director-in-chief" Carl Froelich, who had not only joined the party as early as 1933, but also served as president of the Reichsfilmkammer since 1939 (cf. Schrader 2008, 100–102). *Mädchen in Uniform* could thus be perceived as a film by Froelich and the participation of other politically disliked or persecuted actors (the leading actress, Hertha Thiele, had also been banned from working since 1936 and had emigrated to Switzerland in 1937) could be ignored.

Unlike the film, Winsloe's novel was not initially published in Germany in 1933, but by the Amsterdam publishing house of Allert de Lange,[12] which in turn had reached an agreement with the Viennese publishing house of Ernst Peter Tal to distribute selected works of the publisher in Germany, including the novel *Das Mädchen Manuela* (cf. Hermanns 2012a, 152–155). Since Winsloe herself was neither banned from her profession nor persecuted, her works were initially not subject to censorship either; they were also not affected by the burning of books in 1933, nor did she apparently belong to the circle of emigrated authors (cf. Schoor 1992, 135). The decision to publish her works with Allert de Lange was (at first) to prove extremely sales-promoting, thanks to the publisher's international contacts in conjunction with the film version, which was also shown in other countries. It was not until the mid-1930s, when the German authorities discovered that Winsloe's works were published by a publishing house (Tal) that also published the works of émigrés or authors whose writings were on the *Liste des unerwünschten Schrifttums* or deemed harmful, that her works were also banned in Germany (cf. Hermanns 2012a, 156); by 1936 Tal was no longer able to sell any works in Germany (cf. Schoor 1992, 145). Although the film *Mädchen in Uniform* could continue to be shown in Germany even after the novel was banned, the measures nevertheless marked the end, or at least an interruption, of the first media network, namely the one that Christa Winsloe had initiated and to whose continuous expansion she herself had contributed in a decisive way. Winsloe was murdered in France in June 1944; with her death, however, a new chapter in the history of the media network based on her texts begins, albeit with a time delay, but now with other actors.

---

[12] In April 1933, the publishing house was approached to establish a separate department for authors who had emigrated from Germany (cf. Schoor 1992, 14). In order to ensure the economic stability of the company, they tried to publish novels that had either already been successful in Germany or works that were promising due to their resonance (in other media, among others), including – after the film adaptation – Winsloe's novel (ibid., 31). *Das Mädchen Manuela* was among the first novels published by Allert de Lange; in 1933 and 1934, a total of two editions with a total of 7000 copies were published (ibid., 94; cf. also Hermanns 2012a, 151–153).

Transmedial Narrative Worlds Since the 1950s

In an examination of the media network that began after Winsloe's death, a distinction should be made between a media network in the narrower and in the broader sense, as explained above. A media network in the narrower sense is understood/ subsumed to include all media products that refer in an explicit, unambiguous way to the media products that already existed before 1944 (plays, film, novel). In contrast, the so-called broad media network, which will be more closely examined in the last section of this text, is characterised – in the present case – primarily by its implicit references and thus by its rhizomatic character, i.e. by its contact with other media networks, by structures that reveal references to other types of texts, by intertextual references on the level of content.

The media network in the narrower sense initially comprises the same range of media production as before: new editions of the novel (including new editions of translations), a new edition of the play, new film adaptations, new productions of the play *Gestern und Heute*. Extensions of the media spectrum include a radio play, the television broadcast of a previously recorded theatrical production, a continuation of the story (in two versions), and fan fiction that has been circulating on the web since the 2010s. The temporal dimension stretches from the beginning of the 1950s to the immediate present, although a striking caesura after the end of the 1950s stands out: it takes a good two decades before Winsloe's story (and its media realisations) is rediscovered by the German women's movement in the early 1980s.

Characteristic of this second phase of the media network in its entirety is once again its open, i.e. intended, reference to other products of the same network, which manifests itself on a textual, paratextual, and medial level, but also with regard to the actors. In this context, another central feature is the dominance of the film title *Mädchen in Uniform (Girls in Uniform)*, which, with the beginning of this second phase of the media network, is definitively used for almost all forms of media representation, often without mentioning the titles of the preceding media products. This continues and reinforces a practice that, as shown above, had already begun immediately since the film's first showing and that Winsloe himself had also adopted. Since the 1950s at the latest, one can therefore speak of a media network of *Mädchen in Uniform* that encompasses a multitude of media manifestations whose membership in the same media network manifests itself not least in the use of one and the same title.

From a diachronic perspective, a new medium stands at the beginning of the new phase of this media network: the radio play. On May 18, 1949, Bayerischer Rundfunk broadcast the radio play *Mädchen in Uniform* – with a prominent cast including Lina Carstens, Maria Wimmer, Pamela Wedekind – and Ellen Schwanneke as Manuela. Schwanneke (1906–1972) had already appeared in the 1931 film version (Kühn 2007) – but there in the role of Manuela's classmate Ilse von Westhagen. Since the radio play was obviously not archived (cf. Winsloe 1949), it is also no longer possible to trace which model the editor, the well-known theatre director Heinz Coubier (1905–1993), referred to.

Even the new editions of the novel that appeared simultaneously in the early 1950s in the publishing houses of Allert de Lange, Kiepenheuer, Verkauf, and a publishing house in St. Gallen (cf. Winsloe 1951)[13] were only distributed and advertised under the title *Mädchen in Uniform*, and thus at the same time placed in an explicit connection to the film;[14] the title *Das Mädchen Manuela* chosen by Winsloe at the time is also no longer found in the paratextual field. The comparatively high sales figures were possibly also due to the fact that a first remake of the *Stoff* had been released in German cinemas in March 1952: *Muchachas de Uniforme* (1951), directed by Alfredo B. Crevenna (1914–1996). Despite the fact that it was formally a Mexican film with a plot set in Mexico, the film version can nevertheless be described as a genuinely German project for long stretches: The director came from Germany and had worked for Ufa until his emigration in 1938;[15] the producer was Rodolfo (actually Rudolf) Loewenthal (1908–1982), who had been employed by the Terra Film production company in Berlin before his emigration (see Weniger 2011, 592). Egon Eis (1910–1994), a native of Vienna, is named as co-author of the screenplay (cf. ibid., 152 f.). In terms of content, it was closely based on the 1931 film version, but the criticism of the Prussian-soldierly educational drill was transformed into a critique of the harshness of religious principles that break the girls.

While the Mexican version had adopted the original German title verbatim, a new title – *Mädchen ohne Liebe* – had to be chosen for the German version, which did not immediately indicate that it belonged to the existing media network. Nevertheless, the film possibly provided the occasion for the German side to take up the *Stoff* once again.

A second remake of the film was released in the summer of 1958 as a German-French co-production directed by Géza von Radványi, now again under the title *Mädchen in Uniform*. Winsloe's play *Gestern und Heute* is again cited as the source in the credits, rather than the 1931 film, although F. D. Andam was involved in the screenplay as in the first version, i.e. a phenomenon typical of many remakes of the

---

[13] Allert de Lange had sold the rights to Kiepenheuer, which resulted not least from the history of both publishing houses; Hermann Kesten, publishing director at Kiepenheuer before 1933, had moved to Allert de Lange in Amsterdam after his emigration and helped him there to build up the German department of the publishing house. Many authors who had been forced into emigration and had previously published their works with Kiepenheuer also moved to Allert de Lange after 1933. After 1946, it was Fritz Helmut Landshoff, managing partner of Kiepenheuer Verlag before 1933 and head of the German department of the Amsterdam-based Querido Verlag after his emigration, who brokered a collaboration between Allert de Lange and Kiepenheuer that also included the acquisition of rights for individual authors (cf. Boge 2011, 226 f.). Among other things, Kiepenheuer took over the rights to Winsloe's novel, which was included in 1951 in the series of *Kiepenbücher* that he had newly founded (cf. ibid., 229), and granted licenses to W. Verkauf's Austrian publishing house and the St. Gallen publishing house. The comparatively high sales figures illustrate how present Winsloe's novel still was in the minds of readers; in November 1951, 6500 copies of the novel had already been sold (cf. ibid., 239).

[14] "Mädchen in Uniform. Who does not remember at this title the internationally known film, one of the greatest [sic!] successes of German cinemas? To it we owe this novel, which tells the story of the girl Manuela." (Winsloe 1951, blurb).

[15] Cf. https://it.wikipedia.org/wiki/Alfredo_B._Crevenna (15.07.2019).

1950s, namely personnel continuity, played a not insignificant role here (cf. Frank 2017, 19). Unlike the first version, in which the majority of actresses had either already appeared in the play or were known as theatre actresses, popular film actresses were now primarily used, first and foremost Lilly Palmer as Fräulein von Bernburg and Romy Schneider (as Manuela), who was already one of Germany's most popular actresses in the 1950s due to her leading role in the three *Sissi* films (1955–1957). In terms of content, the film was largely based on the original 1931 film (i.e. not the play), with the central difference that instead of the temporal ambiguity of the first film version, a map of Prussia and the year 1910 were inserted at the beginning. At the same time, this took into account the German public's obvious penchant for historical films; in the years before, in addition to the *Sissi* films, films about *Ludwig II* (1955) and the *Hauptmann von Köpenick* (1956) – both directed by Helmut Käutner – had already been released, all of which perfectly met the obvious longing for a largely transfiguring view of the past.[16] The remake of *Mädchen in Uniform* was also the expected big hit with audiences, although it failed to convince critics: Unanimous criticism was levelled at the watering down and over-reconciliatory tendencies of the *Stoff*, which in this way had lost all critical potential.

The film event was accompanied by a reissue of the novel in the Bertelsmann Lesering (cf. Winsloe 1959), which in turn not only bore the same title as the film, but whose cover also featured a central film scene between Palmer and Schneider, so that it was once again insinuated that this was indeed 'the book to the film'. Radványi's film was also shown abroad, including in France, the Netherlands and England – where new editions of the 1930s translations also appeared almost simultaneously.

The examples cited here prove that the media network also functioned according to the same laws in the 1950s as it did in the decade of its creation – marketing strategies and the obvious continuing popularity of the *Stoff* were mutually dependent. In addition to cinematic remakes and new editions of the novel, there have also been numerous theatrical productions of the *Stoff* since the 1970s, including one by Hartmut Gehrke in 1973 at the Bochum Schauspielhaus under the direction of Peter Zadek, which was recorded and broadcast by ZDF[17] in 1974 due to the positive response. This as well as the following productions – among others In 1976 again by Hartmut Gehrke at the Berlin Volksbühne, and after the turn of the millennium at the Landestheater in Wiesbaden – emphasised their affiliation with the expanding media network through the consistently used film title *Mädchen in Uniform (Girl in Uniform)*, the 1976 production also by casting Dorothea Wieck in the role of the Headmistress, who had embodied the governess Fräulein von Bernburg in the 1931 film version, which was also explicitly referred to in the program.

---

[16] Remakes can be described as "a diverse production practice in the popular cinema of the young Federal Republic […]. [Through] the revivals of previously filmed material [it was possible] to create a line of continuity to (positively occupied) film memories from a culturally formative phase" (Frank 2017, 22 f.). On the remake of *Mädchen in Uniform in* the context of productions of past monarchies, cf. ibid., 305.

[17] "Zweites Deutsches Fernsehen" German TV Broadcasting channel.

Fig. 1 Cover *Das Mädchen Manuela. The novel to the film "Mädchen in Uniform"* (Winsloe © Berlin: Krug & Schadenberg, 2012)

As already mentioned, the interest of the German women's movement in the *Stoff*, but also of film studies in the history of film during the Weimar Republic since the end of the 1970s,[18] again marks a clear caesura in the history of the media network. Although this does not manifest itself in a fundamental change of media – on the contrary, the focus continues to be on the traditional medium of the book, with a clear reference to the two film versions (Fig. 1), while retaining the media network title *Mädchen in Uniform (Girl in Uniform)* – the focus is now increasingly on the author herself, her life story and thus at the same time the history of her work, i.e. the continuously expanding media network is accompanied by a presentation of or reflection on the history of its creation. In view of these changed interests, the marketing aspects are increasingly taking a back seat, although they continue to be

---

[18] In 1977, the 1931 version of the film was shown in public again for the first time; it was broadcast in several third programs, including NDR in May 1978, on the 70th birthday of the actress Hertha Thiele, who also commented on the film there (cf. Gramann/Schlüpmann 1981, 28). The storage medium of the video cassette, which also emerged in Germany at the end of the 1970s, contributed additionally to the dissemination or rediscovery of this version.

served by the still open dwelling character of the individual media and at the latest since the emergence of new storage media (video cassette, DVD, streaming platforms), which at least make book and film versions accessible to everyone.

Characteristic for this caesura is furthermore the fact that it takes place in a fictional approach as well as on a scientific level. In 1981, Christa Reinig publishes the narrative *Mädchen ohne Uniform*, which she situates on several time levels (cf. Luserke 1999, 126; Pfleger/Steward 2019, 166–185). It is about the historical person Christa Winsloe, who once again returns to her school and reviews some disjointed scenes in her mind's eye that she herself experienced there, scenes that merge seamlessly into analogous cinematic as well as novel scenes – thus clear as well as character names are mentioned and in this way the plot of the story is identified as genuinely autobiographical. The third temporal level is set in the author's present and again in a school, in which a close relationship develops between the pupil Manuela and her mathematics teacher Bern, which in the end does not lead to catastrophe, but to a utopian-open conclusion, which at least makes a common future seem possible (cf. Ewering 1992, 107–109). Reinig's rewriting and continuation proceeds in a fundamentally different way from the previous versions with regard to its referential character; her narrative presupposes knowledge of the pretexts and films, and only in this case do the three levels and their interrelationships become accessible. While in the first edition of 1981 these contexts are at least still implicitly referred to by the counterfactual title *Mädchen ohne Uniform* (*Girls without Uniform*), in the following editions it recedes further by the new title *Die ewige Schule* (Reinig 1981, 1986), which were also published by new publishers.[19]

At the same time, scholarly discussion of Winsloe's work began (which will be discussed here only insofar as it is of importance for the Medienverbund), or of the still-living actors from the early days of the Medienverbund. In June 1981, Karola Gramann and Heide Schlüpmann published an article in the magazine *Frauen und Film* about the films *Mädchen in Uniform* and *Anna und Elisabeth* (1933), in which Hertha Thiele and Dorothea Wieck once again appeared together in front of the camera (cf. on this below), as well as a longer interview with the actress Hertha Thiele, in which she provided information about the production conditions of the film, the relationship between Carl Froelich and Leontine Sagan, the involvement of the author Winsloe, and the visualisation of lesbian desire in both the stage and film versions (cf. Gramann/Schlüpmann 1981, 32–42). What had previously been outsourced to a few signals in the paratexts was thus made explicit for the first time and exhibited as if under a burning glass, to which the focus on the actors who actually existed (in the form of a contemporary witness interview) played a decisive role.

---

[19] The first edition was published in 1981 by the Eremiten-Presse, with graphics by Klaus Endrikat. However, Reinig took offence at these graphics because of what she saw as their pornographic character (Ewering 1992, 101 f.) and published the new edition of her story in a slightly different form a year later under the title *Die ewige Schule* (*The Eternal School*) in an anthology with the same title published by Frauenoffensive (cf. Reinig 1982, 65–93). The story was reprinted in the volume *Gesammelte Erzählungen* (cf. Reinig 1986, 264–288).

Gramann and Schlüpmann's contribution, however, not only marks the beginning of a scholarly preoccupation above all with the beginnings of the media network from a new (feminist-film studies) perspective; the approach taken here for the first time, namely to consider the individual media in the network and in their historical context, is also reflected in the new editions of the novel. All three editions of the novel published between the 1980s and the 2010s (cf. Winsloe 1983, 1999, 2012) are not limited to a mere reprint of the text, but must be regarded as editions, for each of the editions is accompanied by a lengthy afterword by the respective editor (cf. Reinig 1983, 239–248; Amrain 1999, 275–281; Hermanns 2012b, 273–293), in which the history of the novel and the film as well as the author's biography are discussed in detail, thus also making them recognisable as parts of a media network that now spans a long history. What all three editions have in common is that the relationship between novel and film is accentuated, not least by the fact that the covers are again provided with film stills – the majority from the 1931 film version.[20]

Seventy years after Christa Winsloe's death, the copyright to her works expired at the end of 2014; the now existing public domain of her oeuvre was reflected in a large number of e-publications of her novel (a total of eight in the years between 2015 and 2019; in addition, the text was posted in the *Projekt Gutenberg – Klassische Literatur online*). In contrast to the print editions, the e-publications resume the traditions of earlier editions in that references to the existence of the media network are once again reserved exclusively for the title and/or the content text.

Intertextual and -medial References Within the Drama, Film, and Novel Version(s)

The special features of the media network examined here also include the references to other texts and media that manifest themselves in very different ways in the individual types of media, the majority of which also belong to media networks. A distinction must be made between explicit references, most of which are made by naming the titles of works, and implicit references, which can be seen either in the invocation of genre conventions[21] or in the context of marketing, especially of the

---

[20] In the edition edited by Christa Reinig (1983), her biographical essay is followed by several unpaginated pages with a total of 16 film stills.

[21] Among these more implicit references are the numerous novels about pupils, in which either emotional relationships between pupils and teachers also occur, including *Claudine à l'école* (1900) by Colette as well as *Regiment of Women* (1917) by Clemence Dane, or stories in which pupils are driven to their deaths by the behavior of teachers; the most prominent example is the novel *Der Schüler Gerber hat absolviert* (1930) by Friedrich Torberg, in which the protagonist, worn down by the ongoing power struggle with the teacher Kupfer, throws himself out of the window. In order to narrow down this field of references, only texts have been cited here that either appeared close in time to Winsloe's works or in which clear analogies appear at the plot or character level. Cf. on Colette's novel the remarks in the following chapter. The references between Winsloe's film and Clemence Dane's novel seemed so obvious, at least to contemporaries, that in the mid-1930s Winsloe and Carl Froelich were accused of plagiarism by a French newspaper, which Winsloe had to counter with an affidavit (cf. Hermanns 2012a, 212).

film *Mädchen in Uniform (Girls in Uniform)*, and thereby attempt to identify Winsloe's film itself as part of a large, arbitrarily expandable media network.

A characteristic of explicit references, as already mentioned, is that they are often reserved for the individual media, i.e. they are not retained within the network but change, and further that they are consistently subject to a comparatively unambiguous semantisation, which, however, only unfolds through a reference to the actual plot.

The play with intertextual references is already inherent in the stage versions of Winsloe's story, and here especially in the first version, as can already be seen from its title *Der Ritter Nérestan*. Nérestan is one of the protagonists in Voltaire's drama *Zaïre* (1732), the play performed by the schoolgirls at the convent to celebrate the matron's birthday, thus representing both the climax and the catastrophe of the plot. The title character, Zaïre, is a slave and mistress in the harem of Sultan Orosmane. She is actually of Christian origin, but not baptised. Disaster strikes when her brother Nérestan, whose role is played by Manuela, secretly wants to have her baptised, but the Sultan mistakes him for Zaïre's lover. Furious with jealousy, he kills her and then takes his own life. The dwelling character of the plot is unmistakable: The topoi of liberation, love, as well as the devastating effect of any dogmatism (here symbolised in religious constraints) also play a decisive role in Winsloe's drama; the Sultan's suicide proves in retrospect to be an implicit prolepsis to the protagonist's suicide. The play is also inscribed with the character of a reference in terms of its media network: Through title, plot, and the character of Nérestan, references are made to a prominent media network that had its beginnings in the 1730s. *Zaïre*, translated into numerous languages, including German, was Voltaire's most successful play: for two hundred years it was on the repertoire of the Comédie Française, during which time it was set to music for a total of thirteen operas, and there is at least one other libretto – that for Mozart's unfinished opera *Zaide*.

Manuela also plays the knight Nérestan in the second theatrical version; only with the change of media (from stage play to film) is Voltaire's tragedy replaced by Schiller's drama *Don Carlos* (1787), possibly because it was assumed that Schiller's drama was more familiar to the audience than Voltaire's tragedy. The implications that also constitute the plot of Winsloe's story are even clearer in Schiller's work: the topoi of freedom, generational conflict, rebellion – but also, as in Voltaire's work, a love affair against the rules (here between the protagonist and his stepmother Elisabeth of Valois, who has much more in common with the figure of Elisabeth von Bernburg than just the first name). The fact that Schiller's drama was also part of a media network begun in the eighteenth century (whose central components consist of historical treatises, Schiller's drama, and Verdi's opera of the same name – to name only the most important individual media here) should only be mentioned here in passing, as should the easily decipherable reference to the plot of the film.

While Winsloe returned to Voltaire's drama *Zaïre* for the novel version, a third play was chosen for the 1958 remake: Shakespeare's tragedy *Romeo and Juliet* (1597), the epitome of all unhappy love stories, so to speak – at the same time the play that belongs to a media network that is characterised both by an almost unmanageable number of individual types of media (including operas, musicals, paintings, film adaptations) and by the greatest temporal extension (of more than 400 years).

As different as the references may be, what they all have in common, apart from the dwelling character, is the story of two lovers who (for different reasons) cannot or are not allowed to visit each other, because their love violates existing conventions. Furthermore, the dramas all have in common that they open up a metadiegetic level on which the intradiegetic protagonist acts as a male character in a way that forms a decisive prerequisite for openly articulating her feelings later, now again on an intradiegetic level, with which the catastrophe takes its course: For the moment, she is no longer able to distinguish between the level of the play and the *narrated* reality.

Analogous to the media network around Christa Winsloe's boarding school story, the cited plays are also characterised, in addition to their specific plot constellation, by their high degree of familiarity (which still applies to Voltaire's tragedy in the 1930s); only for this reason can they be called upon as reference texts, a popularity that is to be seen in obvious connection with those media networks of which they are a part.

A similar dramaturgy – but altogether much more concise – is followed by two further reference texts, which are, however, only mentioned in the stage versions: Upon entering the convent, the protagonist is required to hand over her personal belongings, including money, sweets and – books. Of these books, two novels are mentioned by name and specified by the protagonist as follows: "One is *Maya the Bee*, that's my favorite book, the other one I haven't read yet, my dad gave it to me for the trip. It's called *Alraune*." (Winsloe 1930, 17).[22] Both novels, written in the early 1910s, were already part of a rapidly expanding media network in the Weimar Republic, i.e. in the author's present, above all through film adaptations,[23] some of them several times; at the same time, they were extremely popular works with high

---

[22] Waldemar Bonsels: *Die Biene Maja und ihre Abenteuer* (1912); Hanns Heinz Ewers: *Alraune. Die Geschichte eines lebenden Wesens* (1911). In the two film versions, the mention of books is missing entirely in the corresponding scene; in the novel version, it is Émile Zola's novel *Der Bauch von Paris* (1873), which Manuela has independently pulled out of her father's bookcase (cf. Winsloe 1933a, 147).

[23] The novel *Alraune* became an international bestseller immediately after its publication; in 1928 it had a circulation of more than 400,000 copies and had been translated into more than twenty languages. Between 1919 and 1928, the novel was filmed a total of four times, including in 1928, i.e. in the immediate temporal context of the creation of Winsloe's dramatic versions, by Richard Oswald (cf. Knobloch 2002, 26).

circulations.[24] The mention of these two texts in particular can therefore also be interpreted as a further sign of the topicality of the play in its entirety.[25]

The contextual references to Winsloe's drama are more implicit, but can certainly be established, in *Alraune,* for example, through the apostrophised "abnormality" of the protagonist, who owes her creation to a fertilisation without sexual intercourse – her mother is a prostitute, the sperm was taken from a lust murderer who had just been executed, i.e., the novel "can easily be read as an allegorical treatise on the fatal consequences of sexual desire" (Delabar 2014, 132). After Alraune has driven people to their deaths through her libidinous behavior, among other things, she plunges herself to her own death – also an implicit prolepsis with regard to Manuela's own fate.

In the case of Bonsels' novel, the references are more complex and at the same time more polyvalent: In a first reading, both narratives marked, as it were metaphorically, the cornerstones of Manuela's stage of development: as an almost 15-year-old, Manuela has already outgrown the universe of Maya the Bee's ordered insect state, which is sketched out in the *Roman für Kinder* (thus the subtitle), but she has not yet reached the (also sexually) disordered, unhinged world of Alraune; the girl is in a kind of moratorium of no longer being a child, but also not yet an adult. However, Bonsels' novel was by no means received exclusively as a children's novel, and the corresponding subtitle was therefore no longer used after 1918 (cf. Weiss 2014, 12); rather, it is typical crossover literature, that is, a text that was (initially) explicitly addressed to children, but implicitly always to adult readers as well; during the First World War, the novel was among the favourite literature read by German soldiers (cf. Kümmerling-Meibauer 2014, 46). The novel, and here especially the depiction of the beehive, could also be read as a political allegory, as a "conception of order that on the one hand reflects power relations and on the other the relationship between the individual and the community" (ibid., 55), meaning of course one's own, the German community. It is precisely this reading that becomes a proleptic counterfactual in Winsloe's dramas – the community between girls and governesses depicted here is dominated by anachronistic power relations in which the relationship between the individual and society has long been out of joint to the detriment of the individual.

Last but not least, Bonsels' narrative can also be read as a representation of a female universe – the bee-state is ruled by a queen, Maja is instructed by a governess, a utopian world if one relates it to the world depicted in Winsloe's dramas. At the same time, Bonsels' novel invokes genre conventions that are also constitutive for Winsloe's story – the patterns of popular Backfisch and girls' literature (cf. ibid.,

---

[24] By 1932, shortly after the performances of Winsloe's plays, 745,000 copies of Bonsels's novel had been sold; it is thus considered one of the most successful works of the 1920s/30s (cf. Weiss 2012, 141–147).

[25] Against this background, Ilse's reaction, especially to the mention of the second novel, becomes understandable: "Haach great. That's exciting. Give me that, it's by Hanns Heinz Ewers. […] I wasn't even allowed to read that at home." (Winsloe 1930, 17).

49), the schema of which is both cited and modified by both authors: in Bonsels' case, by coupling the pattern with elements of the adventure narrative; in Winsloe's, by depicting a failure of female socialisation, a course that, as already mentioned, had yet been without precedent within girls' literature.[26]

The Film *Mädchen in Uniform* as a *Brand* and Reference Text

The rhizomatic traits evoked in this way, through which ever new narrative universes are opened up, do not, however, only concern the intertextual or -medial references that are called up within the media network by Winsloe's texts themselves; after the great success of the film, it in turn served, initially above all in connection with marketing strategies, as a point of reference and reference narrative for further films. For reasons of space, only the films in which these references are explicitly made, mostly in the epitextual environment, are listed in this context.

What is particularly striking in this context is the broad temporal and geographic spectrum that opens up upon closer examination. The period stretches from 1932, i.e. approximately one year after the premiere of *Mädchen in Uniform*, to after the turn of the millennium and includes films from Germany, France, England, Japan, Canada, and the USA. These are exclusively films in which predominantly female universes are portrayed, for example an all-female rowing team (*8 Mädels im Boot*, Germany 1932), whose great success is explicitly compared to that of *Mädchen in Uniform* (cf. Pariser Filmbrief 1933). The references are clearer in the film *Anna und Elisabeth* (D 1933) by Frank Wysbar about the close, religiously based relationship between a landowner and a peasant girl. The two characters were embodied by Hertha Thiele in the role of Anna and Dorothea Wieck as the landowner; this cast alone constantly referred to the previous film,[27] both in the announcements and in the few reviews that the film, which was released in April 1933, still received; only 14 days after its premiere, it was banned by the National Socialists, on the one hand because of its religious underpinnings (cf. Gramann/Schlüpmann 1981, 43), and on the other hand because of its Jewish production background (the music was by Paul Dessau).

In December 1937, the film version of Colette's novel *Claudine à l'école* was released in Paris, and before the film was even shown in Germany, it was advertised

---

[26] The fact that Winsloe's pre-texts also included Emmy von Rhoden's novel *Der Trotzkopf*, which is still regarded as a prototype of the genre, becomes clear not only in the constellation of characters, i.e. in the emotional interplay and counter-play between matron, governess and pupil, but also in the ironic reference to the character Ilse Macket, the protagonist of von Rhoden's novel. When introducing her fellow pupils, Manuela is asked by them to address some of them only by their surnames, saying that there are so many Ilses here, one would otherwise not be able to tell them apart (cf. Winsloe 1930, 15). This scene also exists exclusively in the dramatic version.

[27] There are also continuities in the director and cameraman: Frank Wysbar worked as an assistant and Frank Weimayr as a cameraman on *Mädchen in Uniform*.

as the "French counterpart to *Mädchen in Uniform*" (*Girls in Uniform*);[28] in the perception of the film, both the content and the media references obviously played an equally important role:

> It is not saying too much to call this film a French "girl" in uniform, if one wants to disregard the novelty and the unique quality of this German film. [...] The famous French writer Colette, who, by the way, significantly contributed to the film's triumphant run-up at the time by her French subtitles for the German film, had her juvenile novel *Claudine à l'école* filmed here, with which she became famous before the war, and which is still one of the most widely read books today. It deals with the same subject of *Mädchen in Uniform*. (A French counterpart to "Mädchen in Uniform" 1937)

It is only hinted at what "the same theme" consists of – the "love of an adolescent [...] girl for her teacher". Significantly, in this case, too, reference is made exclusively to the film – quite obviously, it was assumed that it was still completely present in the public's consciousness six years after its premiere; added to this was the fact that Winsloe's novel had already been banned at that time and Colette's novel had not yet even been translated into German.[29] Four years later, in the summer of 1941, the film *Aufruhr im Damenstift*, an adaptation of the stage play *Frøkenklostret*[30] by the Danish playwright and screenwriter Axel Breidahl (1876–1948), premiered in Berlin. F. D. Andam was the director and responsible for the screenplay. He had also written the screenplay for the two film versions of *Mädchen in Uniform*, a fact that was referred to several times in the course of the extensive advertising campaign for the film (cf. Ein männerloser Film 1941; Aufruhr im Damenstift 1941; Von der Begegnung zweier Welten 1941, 3). The film version, which received a great deal of attention in the form of announcements, repeated reviews, articles, and a one-page "Bilderbogen" (1941) with numerous film stills in the relevant periodicals, is not only characterised by a continuity of personnel with regard to *Mädchen in Uniform*, however; the subject, setting, and constellation of characters are also cited. Although *Aufruhr im Damenstift* is a so-called "serious comedy" (Von der Begegnung zweier Welten 1941, 3), it is also a "manless" or "women's film" (Frauen-Filme in männlicher Zeit 1941, 2; Ein männerloser Film 1941), as is explicitly emphasised several times. The girls' boarding school is now replaced by a so-called ladies' convent, which also adheres completely to the principles of a time long past, until the closed-off world is upset and broken up by a young girl. In this case, however, the confrontation between "yesterday and today" does not end in tragedy, but with a victory of youth over age; true to the conventions of comedy, it comes to a good end, the generations develop understanding for each other, the

---

[28] In the early 1930s, Colette had already been responsible for the subtitles in the French version of *Mädchen in Uniform* (cf. Virmaux 2004, 243–246); a fact that was repeatedly referred to in the later advertising campaign.

[29] The first German translation of *Claudine à l'école* was not published until 1958 by Paul Zsolnay Verlag, under the title *Claudine erwacht*.

[30] The original Danish version *Frøkenklostret. Komedie i 10 Billeder* was written in the late 1930s. A German-language version was first performed in Zurich in 1940.

ladies of the convent open themselves and their cosmos to the demands that the contemporary world places on them.

The film stills show that Andam attempted to adapt the visual language of Sagan's film, but the quotations in the constellation of characters are even more obvious: In Andam's film version, too, the plot is driven forward by a constellation of three characters in the shape of the old, unyielding abbess, the young, understanding Stiftsdame Fräulein von Benzon, and the teenage protagonist; the description of the abbess refers to her model in Sagan's film version: "With a respectful cane in black and silver, gravely measured, long since beyond all longings of life, so this abbess strides through the spaces that are the world to which she has committed herself." (Von der Begegnung zweier Welten 1941, 4).

"We all remember the film *Mädchen in Uniform (Girls in Uniform)*, which appeared almost a decade ago" (Ein männerloser Film 1941), was the first sentence of a report on *Aufruhr im Damenstift*, which appeared almost half a year before the premiere of the film and in this way from the outset determined the cinematic tradition in which the announced film stood and was to be received.

However, this procedure of bringing attention (and thus success) to the respective film by pointing out intertextual references, while at the same time steering its reception, was not successful in all cases – and obviously not desired in all cases either, notwithstanding the enduring appreciation of the cinematic pre-text. While, as noted above, despite the fact that both director Leontine Sagan and Christa Winsloe herself (who was always credited as a screenwriter in the credits of *Mädchen in Uniform*) had long since left Germany and Winsloe's works had been on the *Liste des unerwünschten Schrifttums* since 1935, *Mädchen in Uniform* was not only able to be screened in Germany after 1933, but was also evidently held in high esteem by filmmakers throughout (which was undoubtedly due to the political position of the former artistic director), films were rigorously banned in other cases if it turned out that their drafts came from authors of Jewish origin.

In February 1938, the *Film-Kurier* announced the screening of two successful French films, including *Gefängnis ohne Gitter*, "a film similar to *Mädchen in Uniform* set in a girls' educational institute" (Drei Auslandsfilme im Cando-Verleih 1938). However, the film was not actually shown in Germany; most likely the censorship authorities had in the credits discovered the names of Gina Kaus (1893–1985) and the brothers Egon and Otto Eis, on whose play of the same name the film was based (cf. Kaus/Eis 1936).[31] Kaus' literary works had previously already become victim of book burning in 1933 (cf. Treß 2009, 510 f.); in March 1938, one day after the so-called Anschluss of Austria, she fled with her family via Zurich to Paris, while the Gestapo had already confiscated her Vienna apartment (cf. Hofeneder 2013, 33–35).

---

[31] While the play "modelled on Christa Winsloe's *Mädchen in Uniform*" (Hofeneder 2013, 33), which only had four performances in Zurich in 1936, did not receive a great response, the French film version *Prison sans barreaux* (1938) was so successful that an English remake *(Prison Without Bars)* was made the same year – with the participation of the French actress who had also played the leading role in the first film version (cf. ibid., 301).

Whether and to what extent the play and film were actually oriented towards Winsloe's dramatic, or cinematic pre-text remains open; at the centre of the plot is not a boarding school, but a closed home for female adolescents with educational difficulties or socially conspicuous, as well as the educational measures practised there. However, in Kaus's play and film, too, the plot is constituted by the debate about traditional and reform-oriented educational measures – positions that are personified by corresponding (female) actors, who at the same time struggle for the fate of the young protagonist.[32]

Prison sans Barreaux was the last film to be advertised with an explicit reference to *Mädchen in Uniform* as a cinematic pre-text. Since the 1950s, i.e. after the remakes, but especially after the rediscovery of the first film version in the late 1970s, the intertextual references took place in a different context: they no longer served to promote a film with similar subject matter or analogous character constellations but were primarily indebted to a media-historical context, in this case the reception history of *Mädchen in Uniform*. In addition to the two new film adaptations, the Japanese film *Onna no Sono* (女の園*;* English.: The Women's Garden, 1954) by Keisuke Kinoshita is still mentioned today (cf., among others, Anderson/Richie 1982, 293; Boxhammer 2007, 149), which centers on four young women who attend a private high school where they come into serious conflict with the outdated, authoritarian educational system. Thus, *Onna no Sono*, like *Lost and Delirious* by Léa Pool (Canada 2001), is one of those films *in* which motifs of *Mädchen in Uniform are* recognisable yet based on a different textual template.[33] Pool's film is also set in a girls' boarding school, but the focus here is not on an examination of outdated educational ideas, but on a love story between two schoolgirls that ends tragically, i.e. by suicide. The references appear more clearly in Katherine Brooks' film *Loving Annabelle* (USA 2006), which tells the story of a rebellious senator's daughter who is sent to a strict Catholic boarding school for girls and falls in love with her teacher there. The reference to Winsloe's pre-text is hardly missing in any of the numerous American and German reviews; even the American Wikipedia article mentions it prominently in its first sentence.[34]

In contrast to these numerous films, in which references to *Mädchen in Uniform* can be found explicitly or covertly, there is so far only one narrative that, if we take

---

[32] In her memoirs, Gina Kaus herself commented on the creation of the drama, its success in the course of film adaptations, and especially on the role of her co-authors, the Eis brothers, but not on possible models (cf. Kaus 1979, 196, 199, 212); however, it hardly seems conceivable that Kaus had no knowledge of Winsloe's drama or its film adaptation. Moreover, it can be considered certain that the Eis brothers knew either the drama or the film version; in 1951, Egon Eis was co-author of the screenplay for the Mexican remake *Muchachas de Uniforme* (see above).

[33] The film is based on the novel *Jinkō Teien* (人工庭園*;* dt.: Ein falscher Garten) by Japanese author Tomoji Abe (1903–1973). Pool's film was based on the novel *The Wives of Bath* (1993) by Canadian author Susan Swan. The film was also released in Germany under the title *Lost and Delirious – Verrückt nach Liebe* or *Lost and Delirious – Bezaubernde Biester.*

[34] "*Loving Annabelle* is a 2006 American romantic drama film directed by Katherine Brooks. In the tradition of *Mädchen in Uniform,* it tells the story of a boarding school student who falls in love with her teacher.", https://en.wikipedia.org/wiki/Loving_Annabelle (21.06.2019).

a narrower concept of intertextuality as a basis, shows traces of the film, but also of Winsloe's novel, on various levels – Judith Schalansky's novel *Der Hals der Giraffe* (The Neck of the Giraffe), which was first published in 2011, has won many awards and has since been translated into numerous languages. However unlike the case of the films cited, these references only reveal themselves to recipients who actually have a precise knowledge of the pre-texts, since they are not even hinted at in the peri- or epitexual field of Schalansky's novel. The references themselves manifest themselves on very different levels of the novel – first in the context of a surface structure that is not of central importance to the course of the plot: among the colleagues of the protagonist Ingrid Lohmark there are several whose names are taken from both the film and the novel: There are teachers named Bernburg and Schwanneke, and two teachers named Thiele and Meinhard (cf. Hermanns 2012b, 290).[35]

Even if these protagonists play a rather subordinate role in the progression of the plot, they are certainly subject to a semanticisation through their naming in such a way that they explicitly refer to the cinematic pre-text, the traces of which can then also be recognised at the level of genre as well as in the deep structures of the novel. Schalansky chose the subtitle *Bildungsroman* for her novel, and in doing so she simultaneously calls up the manifold forms of this genre, including the counteracting patterns, that is, those that tell precisely not of a successful process of self-discovery, but of its failure (cf. Mielke 2016, 357). It is precisely in this failure that Winsloe's and Schalansky's texts meet – both protagonists ultimately fail to find a place in society or lose it. The traces are even clearer (in a modified way) in the context of central plot elements: The protagonist Lohmark also develops special feelings for one of her students, but without being able to account for them herself. While in Winsloe's film and novel the relationship between Manuela and Fräulein von Bernburg oscillates between homoerotic and mother-daughter feelings until the governess finally retreats to the role of teacher and thus brings about the catastrophe, Lohmark compensates for the failed relationship with her own daughter Claudia in her feelings for the pupil, which are also "sensually charged" (ibid., 374). Analogous to the pre-text, there is also a central scene in Schalansky's novel in which the daughter asks for her mother's assistance but is denied it: "Natürlich war sie ihre Mutter. Aber zu allererst ihre Lehrerin. […] Niemand ging zu ihr. Niemand tröstete sie. Auch sie nicht. Es ging nicht. Vor der ganzen Klasse. Nicht möglich. Sie waren in der Schule. Es war Unterricht. Sie war Frau Lohmark" (Schalansky 2011, 218 f.).[36]

---

[35] Strictly symmetrically, the names refer both to the two central film or novel characters (Fräulein von Bernburg and Manuela von Meinhardis) and to two actresses: Hertha Thiele, who embodied the character of Manuela, and Ellen Schwanneke, who also embodied the character of Ilse von Westhagen in the film.

[36] "Of course she was her mother. But first and foremost her teacher. […] No one went to her. No one comforted her. Not even her. It didn't work. In front of the whole class. Not possible. They were in school. It was class. She was Frau Lohmark".

Conclusion

Schalansky's novel – published exactly eighty years after the cinematic pretext *Mädchen in Uniform* – marks – together with the new edition of the novel by Doris Hermanns, further recent fan-fiction narratives[37] and numerous film stills on the Internet – the current state of this media network, which began in the Weimar Republic, extended from Germany across European borders to the USA, Palestine and North Africa within a few years and, regardless of the political changes in the following decades, presented itself again and again in different manifestations and emphases.

Characteristic of this media network, apart from its complexity, is also its heterogeneity, which manifests itself in the ongoing publication and translation history of the novel as well as in the new film adaptations. The media references are also of central importance to other media networks, which can be found above all in the drama as well as the novel version, the great popularity of the *Stoff*, to which the producers (first and foremost Christa Winsloe herself) immediately react by referring above all to the filmic pre-text by means of intertextual procedures or the identification of analogous motifs, character constellations and settings. A dominant position within the media network, especially in recent years, is occupied by processes of reception and, at the same time, processes of updating, which are reflected primarily in films, but also in part in narratives.

As a cross-temporal characteristic of this media network around Christa Winsloe's boarding school history, which has steadily been growing until today and is ultimately unfinished, one can therefore cite its inherent referential character for over eight decades – not as a genuine unique selling point, but as a specific feature that is also inherent in a referential character, namely to the *Stoff* itself, which enables very different reception and marketing processes in different generations and contexts – and will certainly also enable them in the future.

References

Primary Literature

Kaus, Gina: Und was für ein Leben … mit Liebe und Literatur, Theater und Film. Hamburg: Knaus, 1979.
Kaus, Gina/Egon und Otto Eis: Gefängnis ohne Gitter. Stück in acht Bildern. Wien: Marton, 1936.
Reinig, Christa: Mädchen ohne Uniform. Erzählung. Offsetlithographien von Klaus Endrikat. Düsseldorf: Eremiten-Presse, 1981.

---

[37] These are exclusively narratives with alternative conclusions: After Manuela's suicide, which is thwarted at the last moment, the two protagonists find each other and leave the boarding school together.

Reinig, Christa: Die ewige Schule. In: Dies.: Die ewige Schule. Erzählungen. München Frauenoffensive, 1982, 65–92.
Reinig, Christa: Die ewige Schule. In: Dies.: Gesammelte Erzählungen. Darmstadt [u. a.]: Luchterhand, 1986, 264–288 (Sammlung Luchterhand; 656).
Schalansky, Judith: Der Hals der Giraffe. Bildungsroman. Berlin: Suhrkamp, 2011.
Winsloe, Christa: Das Mädchen Manuela. Der Roman von Mädchen in Uniform. Amsterdam: de Lange; Leipzig: Tal & Co., 1933a.
Winsloe, Christa: Mädchen in Uniform. Roman. Amsterdam: de Lange; Köln: Kiepenheuer; Wien: W. Verkauf; St. Gallen: Allgemeiner-Verlag, 1951.
Winsloe, Christa: Mädchen in Uniform. Gütersloh: Bertelsmann Lesering, 1959.
Winsloe, Christa: Mädchen in Uniform. Roman. München: Frauenoffensive, 1983.
Winsloe, Christa: Mädchen in Uniform. Mit einem Nachwort von Susanne Amrain. Göttingen: Daphne, 1999.
Winsloe, Christa: Das Mädchen Manuela. Der Roman zum Film *Mädchen in Uniform*. Hg. und mit einem Nachwort versehen von Doris Hermanns. Berlin: Krug & Schadenberg, 2012.

Filmography

8 Mädels im Boot (D 1932). Regie: Erich Waschneck, Fanal-Filmproduktion GmbH, Berlin.
Anna und Elisabeth (D 1933). Regie: Frank Wysbar, Kollektiv-Film GmbH, Berlin.
Aufruhr im Damenstift (D 1941). Regie: F. D. Andam (d. i. Friedrich Andamm). Nach der Komödie *Frøkenklostret* von Axel Breydahl [EA 1940], Algefa-Film GmbH, Berlin.
Claudine à l'école (F 1937). Regie: Serge de Poligny. N. d. Roman *Claudine à l'école* von Colette [EA 1900].
Lost and Delirious (Can 1991). Regie: Lea Pool. N. d. Roman *The Wives of Bath* von Susan Swan [EA 1993].
Loving Annabelle (USA 2006). Regie: Katherine Brooks.
Mädchen in Uniform (D 1931). Regie: Leontine Sagan. N. d. Drama *Gestern und Heute* von Christa Winsloe [EA 1930], Deutsche Film-Gemeinschaft GmbH, Berlin.
Mädchen in Uniform (D 1958). Regie: Géza von Radvanyi. N. d. Drama *Gestern und Heute* von Christa Winsloe [EA 1930], CCC-Film GmbH, Berlin.
Muchachas de Uniforme (Mex 1951). Regie: Alfredo B. Crevenna.
Onna no Sono [Garten der Frauen] (JPN 1954) Regie: Keisuke Kinoshita. N. d. Roman *Jinkō Teien* [Ein falscher Garten] von Tomoji Abe [EA 1953].
Prison sans barreaux (F 1938). Regie: Léonide Moguy. N. d. Drama *Gefängnis ohne Gitter* von Gina Kaus [EA 1936].

Audiography

Winsloe, Christa: Mädchen in Uniform. Hörspiel. Bayerischer Rundfunk. Erstsendung: 18.05.1949 In: ARD-Hörspieldatenbank http://hoerspiele.dra.de/vollinfo.php?dukey=1542562&vi=1&SID (21.06.2019).

Theatrography

Winsloe, Christa: Gestern und Heute (Ritter Nérestan). Schauspiel in 3 Akten und 12 Bildern. [Unverkäufl. Bühnen-Ms.] Wien: Marton, 1930.
Winsloe, Christa: Demoiselles en Uniforme. Pièce en trois actes et douze tableaux. Traduction fidèle de la pièce Allemande *Gestern und Heute* d'où a été tiré le film sensationnel *Mädchen in Uniform* sous le titre *Jeunes Filles en Uniforme*. Paris: Fasquelle Editeurs, 1932.
Winsloe, Christa: Girls in uniform. A Play in Three Acts. Adapted from the German play *Gestern und Heute* upon which the film *Mädchen in Uniform* is based. Übers. von Barbara Burnham. London: Victor Gollancz 1933b; Boston: Little, Brown, and Co., 1936.
Winsloe, Christa: Mädchen in Uniform („Ritter Nerestan"). Schauspiel in 3 Akten und 12 Bildern. Wien [u. a.]: Sessler Neue Edition, 1973.

Secondary Literature Before 1945

Aufruhr im Damenstift. In: Film-Kurier 23 (1941) 185 vom 09.08., 2.
Bilderbogen. „Aufruhr im Damenstift". In: Film-Kurier 23 (1941) 57 vom 07.03., o. S.
Drei Auslandsfilme im Cando-Verleih. In: Film-Kurier 20 (1938) 36 vom 12.02, 1.
Ein französisches Gegenstück zu „Mädchen in Uniform". In: Film-Kurier 19 (1937) 302 vom 29.12, 3.
Frauen-Filme in männlicher Zeit. Keine thematische Einseitigkeit im deutschen Filmschaffen. In: Film-Kurier 23 (1941) 75 vom 29.03., 1–2.
Ein männerloser Film. Ein Kind verwandelt ein Damenstift. In: Film-Kurier 23 (1941) 76 vom 31.03., 2.
Pariser Filmbrief. In: Kinematograph 27 (1933) 22 vom 01.02., 4.
Von der Begegnung zweier Welten. Ein ungewöhnliches Thema und seine Gestaltung. In: Film-Kurier 23 (1941) 43 vom 20.02., 3–4.

Secondary Literature After 1945

Amrain, Susanne: Christa Winsloe – die berühmte Unbekannte. Ein Nachwort. In: Winsloe, Christa: Mädchen in Uniform. Göttingen 1999, 275–281.
Anderson, Joseph I./Richie, Donald: The Japanese Film. Art and Industry. Princeton 1982.
Birkner, Nina: „Ich mag keine Frau werden – ich möchte ein Mann sein". Weibliche Adoleszenz und Bildungskritik in Schulgeschichten des 20. Jahrhunderts. In: Der Deutschunterricht 61 (2009) 4, 95–99.
Boge, Birgit: Fritz H. Landshoff – Ein nützlicher Mann. Die Zusammenarbeit von Joseph Caspar Witsch und Fritz H. Landshoff 1949–1952. In: Lokatis, Siegfried/Sonntag, Ingrid (Hg.): 100 Jahre Kiepenheuer Verlage. Berlin 2011, 224–243.
Boxhammer, Ingeborg: Das Begehren im Blick. Streifzüge durch 100 Jahre Lesbenfilmgeschichte. Bonn 2007.
Delabar, Walter: Unschlüssigkeit? Einige Überlegungen über die Begründung des Phantastischen aus der Moderne am Beispiel von Hanns Heinz Ewers' *Alraune* (1911). In: Murnane, Barry/Godel, Rainer (Hg.): Zwischen Popularisierung und Ästhetisierung. Hanns Heinz Ewers und die Moderne. Bielefeld 2014, 115–134 (Moderne-Studien; 16).
Dyer, Richard: Now you see it. Studies in Lesbian and Gay Film. London [u. a.] 2003.
Ewering, Cäcilia: Frauenliebe und -literatur. (Un)gelebte (Vor)Bilder bei Ingeborg Bachmann, Johanna Moosdorf und Christa Reinig. Essen 1992 (Literatur: Männlichkeit/Weiblichkeit; 4).

Fähnders, Walter/Karrenbrock, Helga (Hg.): Autorinnen der Weimarer Republik. Bielefeld 2003 (Aisthesis Studienbuch; 5).

Fest, Kerstin: Yesterday and/or Today. Time, History and Desire in Christa Winsloe's *Mädchen in Uniform*. In: German Life and Letters 64 (2012) 4, 457–471.

Fischer-Lichte, Erika: Frauen erobern die Bühne. Dramatikerinnen im 20. Jahrhundert. In: Brinker-Gabler, Gisela (Hg.): Deutsche Literatur von Frauen. Zweiter Band. 19. und 20. Jahrhundert. München 1988, 379–392.

Frank, Stefanie Mathilde: Wiedersehen im Wirtschaftswunder. Remakes von Filmen aus der Zeit des Nationalsozialismus in der Bundesrepublik 1949–1963. Göttingen 2017 (Cadrage. Beiträge zur Film- und Fernsehwissenschaft; 4). Zugl.: Berlin, Humboldt-Univ., Diss., 2015.

Gansel, Carsten: Zwischenzeit, Grenzüberschreitung, Störung – Adoleszenz und Literatur. In: Ders./Zimniak, Pawel (Hg.): Zwischenzeit, Grenzüberschreitung, Aufstörung. Bilder von Adoleszenz in der deutschsprachigen Literatur. Heidelberg 2011, 15–48.

Gnüg, Hiltrud/Möhrmann, Renate (Hg.): Frauen Literatur Geschichte. Schreibende Frauen vom Mittelalter bis zur Gegenwart. Stuttgart [u. a.] 1999.

Gramann, Karola/Schlüpmann, Heide: Momente erotischer Utopie – ästhetisierte Verdrängung – Zerrbilder des Begehrens. In: Frauen und Film (1981) 28, 28–47.

Hamann, Christof: Institutionen der Pädagogik in Literatur und Film. Einleitung. In: Metin Genç/ Christof Hamann (Hg.): Institutionen der Pädagogik. Studien zur Kultur- und Mediengeschichte ihrer ästhetischen Formierungen. Würzburg 2016, 9–39.

Hermanns, Doris: Meerkatzen, Meißel und das Mädchen Manuela. Die Schriftstellerin und Tierbildhauerin Christa Winsloe. Berlin 2012a.

Hermanns, Doris: „Der große Geist der Liebe, der tausend Formen hat". Nachwort. In: Dies. (Hg.): Christa Winsloe: Das Mädchen Manuela. Der Roman zum Film *Mädchen in Uniform*. Berlin 2012b, 273–293.

Hermanns, Doris: „Ich lebe vom Heimweh". Die Schriftstellerin und Bildhauerin Christa Winsloe. In: Exil 33 (2013), 62–71.

Hofeneder, Veronika: Der produktive Kosmos der Gina Kaus. Schriftstellerin – Pädagogin – Revolutionärin. Hildesheim, Zürich, New York 2013 (Germanistische Texte und Studien; 92).

Iurascu, Ilinca (Hg.): The Media Histories of *Mädchen in Uniform*. In: seminar. A Journal of Germanic Studies 55 (2019) 2, 89–93.

Johann, Klaus: Grenze und Halt. Der Einzelne im „Haus der Regeln". Zur deutschsprachigen Internatsliteratur. Heidelberg 2003.

Josting, Petra: Kinder- und Jugendliteratur im Medienverbund. In: Lange, Günter (Hg.): Kinder- und Jugendliteratur der Gegenwart. Ein Handbuch. Korr. und erg. Aufl. Baltmannsweiler ²2012, 391–420.

Kiesel, Helmuth: Geschichte der deutschsprachigen Literatur 1918 bis 1933. München 2017 (Geschichte der deutschsprachigen Literatur von den Anfängen bis zur Gegenwart; X).

Knobloch, Marion: Hanns Heinz Ewers. Bestseller-Autor in Kaiserreich und Weimarer Republik. Marburg 2002. Zugl.: Marburg, Univ., Diss., 2001.

Koch, Friedrich: Schule im Kino. Autorität und Erziehung. Vom *Blauen Engel* bis zur *Feuerzangenbowle*. Weinheim [u. a.] 1987.

Kühn, Volker: Schwanneke, Ellen. In: Neue Deutsche Biographie 23 (2007), 789–790 [Online-Version], https://www.deutsche-biographie.de/pnd117351407.html#ndbcontent (21.06.2019).

Kümmerling-Meibauer, Bettina: Nicht nur „ein Märchen für Kinder". *Die Biene Maja* als Crossover Literatur. In: Weiss, Harald (Hg.): Hundert Jahre Biene Maja. Vom Kinderbuch zum Kassenschlager. Heidelberg 2014 (Studien zur europäischen Kinder- und Jugendliteratur; 1), 45–63.

Luserke, Matthias: Schule erzählt. Literarische Spiegelbilder im 19. und 20. Jahrhundert. Göttingen 1999 (Kleine Reihe V&R; 4016).

McCormick, Richard W.: Coming Out of the Uniform. Political and Sexual Emancipation in Leontine Sagan's *Mädchen in Uniform* (1931). In: Isenberg, Noah (Hg.): Weimar Cinema. An Essential Guide to Classic Films of the Era. New York 2009, 271–289.

Mielke, Angela: „Philosophie hätte ich auch unterrichten können". Judith Schalanskys *Der Hals der Giraffe* als vielschichtige Spielart eines Bildungsromans. In: Genç, Metin/Hamann, Christof(Hg.): Institutionen der Pädagogik. Studien zur Kultur- und Mediengeschichte ihrer ästhetischen Formierungen. Würzburg 2016, 357–391.

Nowak, Kai: Projektionen der Moral. Filmskandale in der Weimarer Republik. Göttingen 2015 (Medien und Gesellschaftswandel im 20. Jahrhundert; 5). Zugl.: Gießen, Univ., Diss., 2015.

Pfleger, Simone/Steward, Faye: In and Out of Uniform. Imagining and illustrating Queer Subjects, Institutional Spaces, and Counterpublics in Christa Reinig's *Mädchen ohne Uniform* and *Die ewige Schule*. In: seminar. A Journal of Germanic Studies 55 (2019) 2, 166–185.

Prinzler, Hans Helmut: Chronik des deutschen Films 1895–1994. Stuttgart [u. a.] 1995.

Puhlfürst, Sabine: Christa Winsloes *Mädchen in Uniform*. Theaterstück – Verfilmung – Romanfassung. In: Hergemöller, Bernd Ulrich (Hg.): Homosexualität in der Weimarer Republik (1919–1933). Hamburg 2000 (Inventio. Jahrbuch für die Geschichte der Homosexualitäten), 34–57.

Reinig, Christa: Über Christa Winsloe. In: Christa Winsloe: Mädchen in Uniform. Roman. München 1983, 239–248.

Sagan, Leontine/Eckardt, Michael (Hg.): Licht und Schatten. Schauspielerin und Regisseurin auf vier Kontinenten. Berlin 2010 (Jüdische Memoiren; 16).

Schoor, Kerstin: Verlagsarbeit im Exil. Untersuchungen zur Geschichte der deutschen Abteilung des Amsterdamer Allert de Lange Verlages 1933–1940. Amsterdam, Atlanta, GA 1992 (Amsterdamer Publikationen zur Sprache und Literatur; 101).

Schrader, Bärbel: „Jederzeit widerruflich". Die Reichskulturkammer und die Sondergenehmigungen in Theater und Film des NS-Staates. Berlin 2008.

Stürzer, Anne: Dramatikerinnen und Zeitstücke. Ein vergessenes Kapitel der Theatergeschichte von der Weimarer Republik bis zur Nachkriegszeit. Stuttgart [u. a.] 1993.

Treß, Werner (Hg.): Verbrannte Bücher 1933. Mit Feuer gegen die Freiheit des Geistes. Bonn 2009.

Virmaux, Alain und Odette: Colette et le cinéma. Paris 2004.

Weinstein, Valerie: The Uniform in the Closet. *Mädchen in Uniform* in Nazi Germany. In: seminar. A Journal of Germanic Studies 55 (2019) 2, 144–165.

Weiss, Harald. Einleitung: Hundert Jahre Biene Maja. In: Ders. (Hg.): Hundert Jahre Biene Maja. Vom Kinderbuch zum Kassenschlager. Heidelberg 2014, 7–19 (Studien zur europäischen Kinder- und Jugendliteratur; 1).

Weniger, Kay: „Es wird im Leben dir mehr genommen als gegeben …". Lexikon der aus Deutschland und Österreich emigrierten Filmschaffenden 1933 bis 1945. Eine Gesamtübersicht. Hamburg 2011.

Wilkending, Gisela: Die Pensionsgeschichte als Paradigma der traditionellen Mädchenliteratur. In: Gnüg, Hiltrud/Möhrmann, Renate (Hg.): Frauen Literatur Geschichte. Schreibende Frauen vom Mittelalter bis zur Gegenwart. Stuttgart [u. a.] 1999, 104–116.

Traumulus

From Naturalistic Drama to National Socialist Film Adaptation

Petra Josting

Introduction

The naturalistic drama *Traumulus* (1905) by Arno Holz (1861–1928) and Oskar Jerschke (1861–1928) was a great success with audiences on German-language stages at the time of its publication and even up to four decades later. It can be assumed that young people from middle-class circles with an affinity with theatre also saw performances, but it was primarily *Stoff* addressed to adults. This only changed with the film adaptation carrying the same name in 1935, because the state-awarded film was not only shown in public cinemas but was also recommended for young people by both the Nazi Teachers' Association and the Hitler Youth (HJ) and shown nationwide in the HJ[1]'s so-called youth film lessons.

In the following, we will first focus on the drama, its authors and reception, with particular emphasis on clarifying the origins of its success in the first decades of the twentieth century. Related to this is the question of what else was so appealing about the *Stoff* under National Socialism that it was made into a film and awarded the rating of *staatspolitisch besonders wertvoll*. To answer these questions, it is not sufficient to focus on the film alone and comparing it to the literary original, that is, to concentrate on semiotic analyses. Rather, following S. J. Schmidt's media compact concept, it is necessary to look at the systematic interrelationship of communication instruments, technical resources, social institutionalisations, and media availability

---

[1] Cf. Hoffmann 1991, chap. IV, 4 and Belling/Schütze 1937, chap. V.

P. Josting (✉)
Faculty of Linguistics and Literary Studies, German Studies, Bielefeld University, Bielefeld, Germany
e-mail: petra.josting@uni-bielefeld.de

or supply, that is, to pursue process systems and process interrelationships as media supplies are always "highly dependent results of the interaction of highly complex social processes." (Schmidt 2013, 41).

The "Production Community"[2] Between Arno Holz and Oskar Jerschke

While Oskar Jerschke worked full-time as a lawyer, wrote poems and dramas only on the side, and plays a rather insignificant role in literary history, Arno Holz, who came from the East Prussian town of Rautenberg (today Kętrzyn), consistently began his path as a writer at the age of 18, after he had failed to transfer to the Obersekunda and had dropped out of school (cf. Fricke 2010, 17).[3] He was one of the leading figures of naturalism, first trying his hand as a lyricist, later as a dramatist, and is also considered an important art theorist of his time (cf. Hechler 1981). Holz and Jerschke met in Berlin in the setting of the *Kyffhäuser-Zeitung*, the *Wochenschrift für alle Universitäts-Angehörige deutschen Stammes und deutscher Zunge; Organ der deutschen Studenten*, so the subtitle. Until Jerschke's death they were united by "a friendship that was not always free of tension, but extremely close" (ibid., 29); their first jointly published work is the poetry collection *Deutsche Weisen* (1884). The two friends intensified their joint drama[4] work in the late 1890s. A central reason for this

> was a deep-seated problem of creativity on Holz's part: as precisely as Holz knew how to use language and as easy as it was for him to work on and refine what he had begun, he found it difficult to come up with a viable literary subject. [...] When Jerschke learned of Holz's renewed difficulties [...] in March 1897, he offered himself from Strasbourg as a supplier of ideas and collaborator. (Ibid., 384; cf. also Sprengel 1993, 93)

Another reason for Holz's writing was the need to earn money, which is why success was at times more important to him than the art itself (cf. Stüben 2001, 201). Thus, starting in the summer of 1900, the two friends met and isolated themselves for a few weeks each year to write together, relying on entertaining stories and popular themes, foregoing tragic conflicts in most cases. Between 1900 and 1911 they produced, among other things, five dramas, the *Deutsche Bühnenspiele*: the so-called men's comedy *Frei!* (1907), the play *Gaudeamus!* (1908), the comedy *Heimkehr* (1909), the tragic comedy *Traumulus* (1905) and the comedy *Büxl*

---

[2]This is the term used by Stüben (2001) in the subtitle of his article.

[3]Fricke offers a comprehensive insight into the biography and work history of Arno Holz in his book *Arno Holz und das Theater* (2010), in which the play *Traumulus*, however, only plays a marginal role.

[4]On the collaboration between Holz and Jerschke, see also Stüben 2001. On the joint work of Holz and Johannes Schlaf, see Sprengel 1994.

(1911).[5] The first three plays were initially written under the pseudonym Hans Volkmar, because Holz did not want to give his name for these works. In fact, most of the theatres that asked for the plays rejected them; only *Heimkehr* found both a publisher and acceptance with the then director of the Berlin theatre, Paul Lindau, where it premiered on 17.01.1903, but was taken off the programme again after only two weeks due to poor reviews. Even at that time, all of the *Bühnenspiele* were considered "merely unspectacular utility pieces that exhaust themselves primarily in the demonstration of fully naturalistic craftsmanship" (Fricke 2010, 392). To this day, they play a marginal role in specialist literature. Holz even refrained from including them in the ten-volume Gesamtausgabe of his works published in 1924/1925, and the post-war edition does not contain the *stage plays* either (cf. Pertsch 2013, 119 f.).

However, immediately after its completion in 1904 the play *Traumulus* was met with great acclaim, and the newly founded publishing house Piper included it in its programme in 1905. Otto Brahm, who was the director of the Lessing Theater in Berlin at the time, premiered the play on September 24, 1904, and it ran for more than 150 performances, starring the then famous actor Albert Bassermann. With almost 800 performances in the 1904/1905[6] season, it advanced to become one of the biggest stage successes of that season in Germany and finally brought Holz notable royalties (cf. Fricke 2010, 386 ff.). Due to the sensational success of the *Traumulus*, the last remnants of self-doubt disappeared within in the mind of the author, who had Robert Reß write the "(in parts also pre-written) book of homage to *Arno Holz und seine künstlerische, weltkulturelle Bedeutung*" (Reß 1913, 393) for his 50th birthday.

Traumulus: Pupil Drama and Pupil Suicide in the Wilhelminian Era

With *Traumulus,* Holz and Jerschke took up the motif of pupil suicide, which had already successfully established itself around 1900 as a new literary genre in both epic poetry and drama (cf. Barnstorff 1917). Suitable examples are Frank Wedekind's *Frühlings Erwachen* (1891) or Emil Strauß's *Freund Hein* (1902). School criticism expressed itself in literature as cultural criticism and cultural struggle. Already with the beginning of the Kaiserreich, critical voices against the military orientation of schools had increased, which gradually led to a change in the elementary schools, but left grammar schools largely untouched (cf. Weber 1999, 64). The foundation of this was constituted by the structures of Wilhelmine society in general, or rather of

---

[5] The dates refer to the year of creation (cf. Fricke 2010, 388 ff.); some of the plays were published later. Cf. the theatrography in the bibliography.
[6] According to Correns (1956, 174), the play spread from Berlin throughout Germany and was performed in 137 cities in the 1904/1905 season. There were 42 performances in Leipzig, 40 in Hanover, 37 in Munich, 21 in Stettin, 20 in Hamburg and 19 in Breslau.

the school system, which were geared towards authoritarianism and taught passivity and blind obedience to authority (cf. Noob 1997, 102). Young men suffered so much under authoritarian fathers and teachers that they sometimes saw suicide as the only way out.[7]

In the tragicomedy *Traumulus* (Fig. 1), which combines the tragic and the comical, the central teacher figure is headmaster Dr. Gotthold Niemeyer at the Königliches Gymnasium. He is not one of the usual tyrants, but always anxious to "guide the youth by kindness and to look into and understand their faults" (Holz/Jerschke 1905, 153), as he says himself. In accordance with his humanistic ideals, he believes in the good in people and especially in youth, thus standing in stark contrast to, for example, Heinrich Mann's insidious and malicious Professor Unrat (1905). His

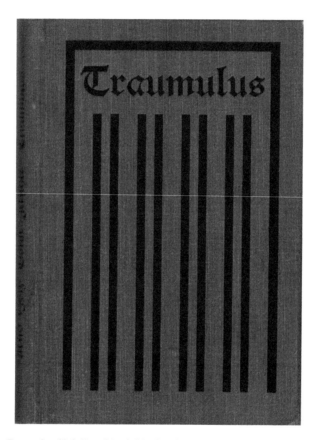

Fig. 1 Cover *Traumulus* (Holz/Jerschke © Munich: Piper, 1905)

---

[7] In 1903, the physician Alfred Eulenburg analysed the figures registered and partially documented by the Preußisches Kultusministerium from 1883 onwards, according to which 1017 cases were involved (cf. Neumann/Neumann 2011, 13).

students nicknamed him Traumulus because of his unworldliness. The unworldliness that gives him comical traits manifests itself, for example, in the fact that in his German lessons he deals exclusively with classical texts, since contemporary literature, in his opinion, comprises only "immoral books" (Holz/Jerschke 1905, 127). Or, another example: even the almost adult pupils are only allowed to visit a single inn in the village to drink a glass of beer, and even that only on Thursdays between 6 and 7 pm. He has this arrangement, as his favourite pupil von Zedlitz explains,

> nicht getroffen, um Sie in Ihrer Freiheit zu beschränken ... o nein, die Jugend soll Freiheit haben ..., sondern um Sie vor gefahren zu behüten, von deren Vorhandensein sie noch gar keine Ahnung haben! (Ibid., 60)[8]

Niemeyer fails to recognise that youth must gain experience on their own and has no idea of their doings, even though some of the students lodge with him. Thus, he is at the same time a tragic figure who fails because of his "blind pedagogical idealism" and ultimately because of his "tragic blindness" towards the pupil Kurt von Zedlitz as well as the other pupils (Weber 1999, 79 f.).

The five-act play is set in the Prussian provinces of the German Empire around 1900; there is no precise indication of time or place. The action takes place over a period of only twelve hours; the back story, into which the reader or audience is gradually introduced, goes back further and is of central importance to the course of the plot. Principal Niemeyer was transferred a little over a year ago because, in the opinion of his superiors, he did not teach his students discipline and order. This punitive transfer was accompanied by a pay cut, which prompted him to take in students as boarders in order to mitigate the financial cut in this way. In addition to this professional flaw, which only people in the know such as the district administrator von Kannewurf are aware of, his circumstances regarding family are also not in good shape in the opinion of the small-town, narrow-minded society. They view with great suspicion the activities of Niemeyer's second wife Jadwiga, who is said to be a spendthrift and an obsessive cleaner, as well as his son Fritz from his first marriage, who is considered to be reckless. Adding to the debacle is the supposed miscasting of a single role in the play Niemeyer has written especially for the festive monument unveiling in honour of the German Kaiser, which is to be performed in a few days. He wants to stage the play with his students, who have been rehearsing every day, but he has cast a young actress from the local theatre in a female role, who does not enjoy a good reputation and with whom his favourite student von Zedlitz has begun an affair, i.e. spent the last night. Consequently, for a small town at that time these are untenable conditions.

The actual plot begins the following morning.[9] In the first act, the town's dignitaries meet in the casino on Sunday morning to discuss the upcoming festivities on the occasion of the Kaiser's visit. Some gentlemen speak Berlin dialect. Landrat von Kannewurf, who unapologetically shows himself to be Niemeyer's opponent,

---

[8] not to restrict your freedom ... no, the youth should have freedom ... but to protect you from dangers of whose existence they have no idea!
[9] For the following summary, see also Correns 1956, 144 ff. and Neumann/Neumann 2011, 73 ff.

reports that von Zedlitz, the best of the Prima (best of the class), had spent the evening first in the dubious *Goldener Pfau* pub with the disreputable actress Lydia Link and then at her home. He knew this because he had had Niemeyer's pupils under police surveillance since he had taken up his post without his knowledge, in order to expose him to a scandal and as a result to obtain his dismissal. Niemeyer, who arrives some time later, is confronted with the accusations against von Zedlitz, but vehemently rejects them, taking his pupil's side. In the second act, when Niemeyer interrogates von Zedlitz in his living room at home, the latter, on the advice of Niemeyer's son Fritz, who sees his father's position endangered, confesses only to the visit to the pub and is grounded for it. This reassures Niemeyer, especially since Lydia Link confirms this statement. The third act shows the cellar rooms of the baker Schladebach, where the secret student fraternity of the grammar school, the *Antityrannia*, meets in the afternoon for the second foundation party; the baker himself also takes part. The boys are boisterous, like students of the corps they make use of turgid phrases, they make fun of the headmaster and his wife, but it is also clear that they like him. When von Zedlitz appears in spite of his confinement to his room and asks his fellow students to dissolve the secret society so as not to endanger Niemeyer any further – he himself is no longer a member from now on – the police suddenly appear and remove all those present. The fourth act takes place at the police station. Von Zedlitz is confronted by Lydia Link, who stands by her statement. He refuses to testify because he wants to spare his teacher. Disappointed, the rushing Niemeyer has to realize that his favourite student also belongs to the secret society. In addition, the affidavit of a police officer shows him that von Zedlitz did spend the night with Lydia Link. Zedlitz implores his teacher to forgive him, wants to explain, but Niemeyer sends him away, calls him a criminal, never wants to see him again. After he learns that von Zedlitz declared upon his arrest that he had left the secret society, he suspects the danger his pupil is in. The fifth act takes place in Niemeyer's study. His wife appears, tells of the gambling debts and forged bills of his son, who has blackmailed her for infidelity; she wants to divorce him. Niemeyer still hopes to see von Zedlitz again, but late in the evening comes the news that his student has shot himself. With this, Niemeyer considers himself the murderer; he announces his resignation and collapses. Von Kannewurf is also shocked by the suicide and asks Niemeyer for reconciliation.

Traumulus' Reception on Stage

As noted above, the nearly 800 performances of *Traumulus* in numerous German cities during the 1904/05 season demonstrate its immense success. Correns, who analysed the play with regard to its success, comes to the conclusion that the great effect on the audience has three causes. Firstly, the plot was built up in an extremely exciting way, because the audience was "smarter than the bearer of the plot from the beginning"; at the same time, however, they did not learn everything that had happened in the past, "but always just as much as was necessary" to keep Niemeyer one step ahead (Correns 1956, 168). Secondly, the choice of conflict struck a chord. With the teacher figure Niemeyer, the audience was reminded of their own school days, of the personally experienced "teacher-pupil conflict" (ibid., 171), of unworldly teachers. The fact that Niemeyer was "blind" not only to his students, "but also at home, that was taken as confirmation of how right one had already been at school to betray him." (Ibid.) Thirdly, the audience was very receptive to the portrayal of the "German Spießbürger" (ibid.) because they sympathised with them: the Sunday morning pint "in a circle of equals corresponded to their ideas of the well-situated bourgeoisie" (ibid.); the men gathered there, such as the district administrator, sanitary councillor, lawyer, assessor, and Jewish factory owner, belonged to the circles in which they themselves frequented. The behaviour of the *Antityrannia* in the cellar, which was reminiscent of their own time in the Burschenschaft, was also met with the approval of the male spectators. With the change from the cellar party to the police station, there was then a change of scene that "frightened and outraged the German Spießbürger" (ibid., 172), i.e. appealed to the emotions once again. And finally, he is receptive to the sentimental when, at the end, Niemeyer is asked by Landrat von Kannewurf for reconciliation (cf. ibid., 173).

The enthusiasm of the audience becomes clear from the many performances, as can be read in the theatre reviews of the premiere (cf. ibid., 176 ff.). The critics praise the great acting performance, the majority likewise the play, but there are also negative voices, such as that of Gustav Zieler in the *Literarisches Echo*: "What deep shock could this *Stoff* cause", but Traumulus "does not make us shudder before the sublime fate." (Ibid., 176) The review of the famous theatre critic Alfred Kerr in the journal *Der Tag* published on 27th of September 1904 also aims in this direction, attesting to the brilliant performance of the leading actor Bassermann and to the "striking excellence" of the performance (Kerr 1998, 203), but he scorns Holz as a poet. The figure of Niemeyer

> is only an oaf with tolerably kindly features. However, in order to impress the viewer, he should have been an oaf with shining features. In other words, his good sides should have been made more luminous by the poet. [...] The Holzian average of life does not suffice here. [...] Holz's mistake is not that he wants to shape the average out of life, but that his shaping is average. [...] Holz gives the sufficient, not the ultimate. Here he separates himself from a poet who gives the ultimate, not only the sufficient. Most of what this schoolman says is true; [...] but that, my dear fellow, is far too little. Truth is the least; it remains a prerequisite. It is only on this basis that things are supposed to start. It does not start with Holz. Here lies the original fault of the piece. [...]
>
> With all this the craftsmanship of Holz' work is quite worthy of respect. As then Holz represents a tight talent on the side of the energetic-proficient. He accomplishes what one can accomplish, without being a genius, to the serious applause of even opposing contemporaries. Without being a genius; without having the spark, without the distant glimmer of a spark in him. The man has no music. He is a literary carpenter of great precision, in the least no created poet. He is one who treats art by stiffening and mocking himself to be right. In this way he gains a mastery that is bruised; such a noisy, unsympathetic, cuddly, beam-steady certainty. (Ibid., 200 ff.)

The scathing criticism by Alfred Kerr, who like many other intellectuals went into exile in 1933, is unlikely to have interested the Nazi rulers and their henchmen.

Directors, dramaturges, and audiences continued to be enthusiastic about the play well into the 1940s, as evidenced by performances in Berlin,[10] Weimar[11] and Vienna,[12] for example. In the program booklet of the Berlin Staatstheater, where the *Traumulus* was performed in a new production in 1940, there is an excerpt from Karl Turley's dissertation *Arno Holz. Der Weg eines Künstlers* (1935), which praises, among other things, Holz's "contrary position" in relation to his time as well as his "sharp criticism of everything entrenched" (Turley 1940, n.d.). In Hamburg, to give another example, the first performance took place in 1917 at the Altonaer Stadttheater. On Holz's 60th birthday in 1923, the first performance took place at the Thalia Theater; further new productions followed here in 1935, 1952, and 1980 (cf. Thalia Theater 1980, n.d.). The performance at the Thalia Theater in 1980 was a guest production by the GDR director Klaus Dieter Kirst. The excerpts on questions of education from works by Immanuel Kant, Arthur Schopenhauer and Theodor W. Adorno printed in the programme booklet provide clues to the interpretation of the play (cf. ibid.), or rather Adorno's dictum of education for maturity.

In contrast, the Nazi system also criticized the Prussian authoritarian state and its educational system but relied on a new understanding of education that aimed at "alignment," "Gleichschaltung," and "manipulation" (Flessau 1987, 81). In the National Socialist concepts of education, the terms *Bildung* (*education*) and the *individual* are therefore no longer found; the transfer of knowledge through *Bildung* was replaced by the training of character, and the place of the individual was taken by the *Volk* (*the people*) and *community* (cf. Hopster/Nassen 1983, 32). Parallel to this, a Nazi media culture was established, which in this sense attempted to establish a *Volkserziehung* (*societal education*) that served to control and regiment all cultural spheres. With regard to the characteristics of the culture of the Nazi period, Faulstich is to be agreed with, according to whom "descriptively one can only speak of a 'culture of annihilation'", "normatively of the rejection of culture altogether" (Faulstich 2009, 24), because, as in the Soviet Union under Stalin, the entire cultural sphere was placed under the so-called primacy of politics, with the aim of exerting influence accordingly via competing, different party official and state institutions. To this end, the Reichskulturkammer was established in 1933, which was divided into the following chambers, which were like professional associations with compulsory membership and generally refused admission to politically and religiously *undesirable persons,* which basically was a professional ban: Reichsmusikkammer,

---

[10] According to the programme of the Staatstheater Berlin Kleines Haus at Nürnberger Straße 70–71 (today Budapester Straße 35), the play was performed for the 18th time on March 16, 1940. The acclaimed new production took place here on 16.02.1940 under the direction of Wolfgang Liebeneiner and Werner Krauß in the role of the teacher Niemeyer (cf. Herzberg 1940). The theatre was originally the privately run Deutsche Künstlertheater. Max Epstein, who ran it from 1913, was expropriated by the Nazi rulers in 1935, and Gustaf Gründgens was general director from 1935 to 1943, until the house was destroyed in a bombing raid (see https://de.wikipedia.org/wiki/Deutsches_K%C3%BCnstlertheater (08.05.2019).

[11] Cf. Weimar playbills posted online: http://www.theaterzettel-weimar.de; keyword "traumulus" (28.11.2019).

[12] The first performance took place at the Burgtheater in Vienna on 11 February 1905 (cf. Graf 1905).

Reichskammer der bildenden Künste, Reichstheaterkammer, Reichsschrifttumskammer, Reichspressekammer, Reichsrundfunkkammer and Reichsfilmkammer (cf. Hinkel 1937).

The Film Sector of the National Socialist Era

What attracted the *cultural creators* – the common term in the *Third Reich* – not only to stage the *Traumulus* on German-speaking stages, but also to film it? To recommend it to a broad public of adults and to show it in the *Jugendfilmstunden* of the HJ, which increased the number of viewers many times over? And what was so fascinating about this *Stoff* that it was adapted for the most powerful medium of those years? According to Fritz Hippler – who had been the Reich's film director since 1942 and, among other things, produced the anti-Semitic inflammatory film *Der ewige Jude* (*The Eternal Jew*, 1940) – people were aware that the medium of film was

> by its characteristic of primarily affecting the visual and emotional, i.e. the non-intellectual, it has a particularly penetrating and lasting psychological and propagandistic effect on the masses. [...] it grasps the broad masses. It thus achieves sociological effects which can often be more lasting than those of school and church, or even books, the press, and radio. (Hippler 1943, 14)

If we first look at the film industry in general as one of several major cultural sectors, then, like the book market for example, it is associated in the collective memory with *Gleichschaltung,* censorship and propaganda with regard to the Nazi era – which is associated with the idea that a specific film culture was decreed by the state in 1933, which came to an end when the tyranny was overthrown. This is not the case, however, because on the one hand most of the so-called filmmakers were active in the Federal Republic until well into the 1960s, and on the other hand the basic structures of the film industry were already laid out in the final phase of the Weimar Republic due to various crises: Firstly, foreign competition, especially American film, led to stagnation in domestic sales; secondly, the introduction of sound film required high investment costs from producers and cinemas, which led many companies into insolvency; and thirdly, the world economic crisis did not spare the film industry insofar as the number of visitors declined rapidly. As a result of these circumstances, by 1933 only the four major companies Ufa, Tobis, Terra and Bavaria controlled 40% of German film production (cf. Strobel 2009, 129). Ufa, in which all film industries (production and distribution companies, copying plants and most cinema theatres) were only merged in 1942 and which was thus nationalised relatively late, had already been majority-owned by Alfred Hugenberg, the chairman of the German National People's Party and one of many pioneers of National Socialism, since 1927. For the restructuring of Europe's biggest film company Ufa he appointed Ludwig Klitzsch who was also president of the top organisation of the German film industry (SPIO). As early as 1932, this organisation developed the plan to transform Ufa into a state film authority, including its own credit bank, so that by mid-March 1933 the Nazi system was able to draw on precisely these new plans and only had to implement them. The implementation and expansion of the plans included, among other things: the establishment of a Reich Film Chamber and a film credit bank, a *film* department within the Reichsministerium für Volksaufklärung und Propaganda under Joseph Goebbels, the appointment of a Reich film dramaturge to whom every screenplay had to be submitted for approval, a film censor with the highest predicates of *Film der Nation* and *staatspolitisch und künstlerisch besonders wertvoll film,* the regulation of *film lessons* for *young people,* the introduction of *Filmbetrachtung (film viewing)* instead of film criticism, the establishment of a star cult and, last but not least, the founding of the Deutsche Akademie für Filmkunst in Babelsberg in 1938, which was intended to secure influence on education in the film sector (cf. ibid., 130 ff.).

With regard to the number of films produced and screened in Germany during the Nazi regime, the figures vary only slightly. While Strobel assumes 1094 feature films plus 24 co-productions with foreign companies (cf. ibid., 136), Hobsch puts the figure at around 1200 feature films, the majority of which were "melodramas, love stories, comedies, adventure, revue, hit, costume and Heimat films, folk plays and harmless crime films"; plus "many times that number of short non-fiction and documentary films" that were of propagandistic importance because they addressed "racial doctrine, blood-and-soil ideology and military themes" (Hobsch 2009, 39). In view of the fact that many actors in the film industry had gone into exile after 1933 or were banned from their professions, i.e. there was a shortage of personnel at all levels, the number of productions is not low.

As far as the number of films produced specifically for children and young people is concerned, according to Hobsch, it is only four percent of the total spectrum of the time (cf. ibid.).[13] The publication on youth film in the *Third Reich,* which dates from the Nazi period and was commissioned by the NSDAP and published by Anneliese Sander and contains the results of a large, but not representative, survey on film[14] among leaders of the HJ, lists only ten films (cf. Sander 1944, 30).[15] As a rule, however, 20–25% of German film production received the rating *jugendfrei*;[16]

---

[13] The number is considerably higher. Cf. the contribution by Marlene Antonia Illies on *children's and youth film from 1900 to 1945 in* this volume.

[14] Funk (1934) conducted another survey of the psychological after-effects of film in the lives of vocational school youth as part of a dissertation.

[15] One of the interesting things about this study, which was published by the ranks of the party, is that in the case of youth films, firstly, the low number is criticised as follows: "In 15 years, Germany has thus released 12 youth films" (Sander 1944, 30) and secondly, that at the beginning of this list there are still two films from the Weimar Republic, *Emil und die Detektive* and *Der Kampf der Tertia* (cf. ibid.).

[16] Stelzner-Large (1996, 295–307) compiled a chronologically structured list of feature films that carried the notation *jugendfrei* and *jugendfrei ab 14 Jahren* for the period 1933–1945 in her dissertation. More informative, however, are those of Sander (1944, 145–154), even if they do not cover the entire period. Here one finds the *Liste der von der RPL. für Jugendfilmstunden zugelassenen Filme für Kino und kinolose Orte* (differentiated according to *youth-free* and *youth-free from*

whether they were also *jugendgeeignet* and should be shown was a matter of controversial debate. Only the predicate *jugendwert,* introduced in 1938, meant that young people should be able to view the film (cf. Hobsch 2009, 40). Sander laments the small number of specific feature films for the youth, who had to make do predominantly with films addressed to adults, and attributes this to the film industry, which was of the opinion that the low admission prices in the context of the *Jugendfilmstunden* of the HJ attended by boys and girls were not economically lucrative enough. It attempts to refute this assumption with statistics according to which in 1942/1943 over 45,290 *Jugendfilmstunden* were held with 11,215,000 visitors (cf. Sander 1944, 72). It remains to be asked whether the film industry, which had long since been nationalized by this time and saw youth as the guarantor of the future, was really not prepared to invest more money (cf. also Sander/Reese 1984, V), or whether there was not a lack of suitable people who could have met the ideological and at the same time qualitative demands of the Nazi rulers in the film sector, as is known from the field of children's and youth literature. The conclusion at the end of Sander's study is instructive for assessing which youth films the HJ had in mind, stating:

> The youth feature film in its early stages. "Hitlerjunge Quex", "Kadetten", "Hände hoch!" are milestones in the development of German youth feature filmmaking. The film in progress, "Junge Adler", promises to bring further progress. Quantitative and qualitative further work is necessary here. (Sander 1944, 135)

In accordance with the new understanding of art, film is supposed to be "Volkskunst" (*people's art*); this is called upon to "set up ideals itself, to demonstrate them; to align 'attitude, world view and taste', to help shape them (ibid., 12). And this Volkskunst" steps "out of the realm of the merely aesthetic into that of the also-political" and thus becomes "[...] – a means of leadership." (Ibid.).

Traumulus (1935): Rated as *State-Political and as an Artistically Especially Valuable Film*

At the time of the black-and-white film *Traumulus*' production in 1935, the Nazi system is at the end of its consolidation phase, i.e., *Gleichschaltung* is largely complete, party official and state institutions have been expanded to function. It is speculative to answer the question of why the actors from the most diverse areas of the film sector decided to film Holz and Jerschke's *Traumulus* drama. It can be assumed that at this point in time, people were still very keen to distance themselves from the old system and thus to criticise the old conditions. In order to reach the broad masses

---

14 years of age) as well as a list of long feature films of domestic and foreign production from 1935 to 1943 (differentiated according to *jugendfrei* and *für Jugendliche ab 14 Jahren*), whereby it is also indicated which films were removed from the list in the course of the war.

as far as possible, a *Stoff* was chosen that is set in a school and almost caricatures the classic grammar school teacher.

People of rank and name or will still attain these attributes, are involved in this production. Director and producer is Carl Froelich (1875–1953), who was successful in the film business since the beginning of the nineteenth century. Froelich joined the NSDAP before 1933, continued to make many successful films during the Nazi era and was appointed president of the Reichsfilmkammer in 1939.[17] The screenplay was penned by Robert A. Stemmle (1903–1974) and Erich Ebermayer (1900–1970), both of whom conformed to the Nazi regime. Stemmle was a dramaturge at Tobis, later also a director and producer;[18] he was responsible for directing and writing the screenplay, for example, for the first filming of *Feuerzangenbowle* under the title *So ein Flegel*.[19] Ebermayer, who studied law, wrote several novels and light fiction in addition to screenplays, even into the Adenauer era.[20] Experienced cinematographer is Reimar Kuntze.[21] The leading role of headmaster Niemeyer is played by Emil Jannings (1884–1950), who had played the district administrator[22] in this play 20 years earlier (Fig. 2). He began his career as a stage actor in the provinces, received engagements in Berlin from 1914, where he worked with Max Reinhardt,

Fig. 2 Emil Jannings in *Traumulus* (1935) (© Beta Film GmbH, DFF – Deutsches Filminstitut & Filmmuseum/KINEOS Collection)

---

[17] Cf.   https://www.filmportal.de/person/carl-froelich_af360ddb231c48168439117c467bb5dd (31.12.2019).

[18] https://www.filmportal.de/person/robert-a-stemmle_7b58be5cf9db48709a0c88022b13f0a7 (31.12.2019).

[19] Cf. the contribution by Heidi Nenoff in this volume.

[20] https://de.wikipedia.org/wiki/Erich_Ebermayer (31.12.2019).

[21] Cf.   https://www.filmportal.de/person/reimar-kuntze_6016a45066514747bf0af79392419219 (31.12.2019).

[22] Cf. Arno Holz: "Jannings-Ia!" (1935), which refers to a letter in the Arno Holz archive from Max Wagner.

among others, and got his first (silent) film role in 1915. His success was so great that he took part in American movies at the end of the 1920s and was the first actor to receive an Oscar there. After his return Jannings was also a great star in Nazi Germany who remained unforgettable for a wide audience among others due to his portrayal of Professor Rath at Marlene Dietrich's side in *Der blaue Engel* (1929). Because of his Nazi past he received a lifelong professional ban, therefore he took the Austrian citizenship and left Germany.[23]

Before dealing with questions of reception and distribution, the focus will first be on the analysis of the film and thus, in the context of *post processing* (cf. Schmidt 2008), on the aspect of media change. Two studies are available for this, but they are largely classic ideology-critical, i.e. they concentrate on the content level (cf. Kanzog 1994; von der Osten 1998), but leave out film-aesthetic means (cf. Hickethier 2001) as well as questions of "audience gratification" (Welzel 1995, 212) and thus also emotions, which will therefore be considered in the following. Von der Osten and Kanzog, however, already included the screenplay for their investigation so that it becomes clear at which points the participants, probably the director, intervened.[24]

Both the plot of the film and the screenplay, as well as numerous character speeches and thus sequences of dialogue, are closely based on the printed original, and are even adopted verbatim in some cases. In contrast to the drama, however, the cinematic action does not begin in the casino, where the district administrator von Kannewitz confronts Prof. Niemeyer upon his arrival with the statement that his student von Zedlitz "has been cavorting tonight with a courtesan known in town in a public entertainment establishment of the most disreputable sort" (Holz/Jerschke 1905, 33). The film[25] begins with this backstory (04:45–16:22), embellishes it relatively broadly, and promises suspense; solely the images first tell the story: in bird's-eye view and accompanied by idyllic music, the camera captures a night watchman extinguishing the streetlights, including one in front of the bakery, in a small-town street where piles of snow can be seen in front of the houses. The camera pans up the wall of the house to a dark window, switching to a policeman standing freezing in the street, apparently watching this house (accompanied by music symbolising danger) and looking at his watch as light is seen behind the window. The next scene takes place in the stairwell of the baker's house; in bird's-eye view, a pair of lovers appears at the top of the stairs – at first only artfully visible as shadows – saying goodbye and apparently finding it difficult to part, which is underlined by the music radiating bliss. But at the same time a further danger looms, for the bakers are already at work and the young man does not want to be caught, which he succeeds in doing. Only the policeman continues to have him in his sights as he enters the street, and once again looks at his watch. For the viewers, who do not know the *Stoff*, it is only clear at this point that someone is being watched (whether because

---

[23] Cf. filmportal.de, https://www.filmportal.de/person/emil-jannings_3377e94609d3412cae1cc341360254ba (28.11.2019).

[24] Since the script was not available to me, I'll draw on von der Osten's passages for comparison.

[25] The version from the Federal Archives, which is not freely accessible, begins at 02:08 with the opening credits (film details), ends at 02:04:25, so covers about two hours.

of the tête-à-tête is still unclear) and that a pair of lovers has met, different emotions are thus addressed, presumably for all genders and ages. Temporally, they can locate the action in the Kaiserreich because of the woman's clothing and the civil servant's spiked Prussian helmet.

Only in the following scenes of the prequel does it become clear who the young man is: the boarding school student von Zedlitz, who with the help of his best friend Mettke (played by Hans Richter) gets into the common dormitory of the high school students via a rope ladder, but again not unnoticed, because his whistle, which wakes his friend, is heard by the caretaker, who looks at his alarm clock, which shows 05:55. When both are in bed, Mettke wants to know how it was, whereupon the following short dialogue (09:40–10:04) relaxes the viewer:

Zedlitz:	Du bist zwar mein bester Freund, aber das verstehst du nicht.
Mettke:	Wieso?
Zedlitz:	Ja, weil ich es selbst nicht verstehe.
aus dem Hintergrund:	Maul halten!
Mettke:	Was ist denn da groß zu verstehen?
Zedlitz:	Ach, ich hab' einen Menschen kennengelernt, Mettke, einen Menschen …[26]

Even though one can imagine how von Zedlitz spent the night, the verbal level emphasizes the woman as a person or as a human being and not as a sexual partner, while the script focuses on the experience, stating, "I experienced something tonight that I would never have believed could be experienced" (quoted from von der Osten 1998, 195). When he then tells Mettke that he wants to get engaged and that his beloved is the actress Lydia Link, the friend declares him crazy, that he should think about his family, but ends the conversation ironically with the remark, "you Zedlitz people already attracted unpleasant attention in the Middle Ages." Zedlitz himself is unimpressed by this, soulfully thinking back to the past hours, musically accompanied by the folk song *Du, du liegst mir im Herzen*.

Once again, the last part of the opening credits arouses completely different emotions, showing all the boys of very different ages in the dormitory after waking up, whispering, and putting their heads together and then making fun of the planned engagement of their classmate von Zedlitz, Mettke had told them about it. They congratulate their eldest with a bouquet of feather dusters, whereupon a funny-looking scuffle with water sprays unfolds, interrupted by the entering caretaker Schimke, who embodies a friendly figure. The camera is set to semi-close-up, foregrounding the situation: Schimke turns to Zedlitz, saying that as an old soldier he must report tonight's affair. He doesn't want to be dissuaded by the boys holding it together, and certainly doesn't want to be bribed with money. But to everyone's amusement, a way is found to use exactly this means, in that the boys pretend that a coin is lying on the floor, and Schimke claims that his wife has not sewn up the hole in his trouser pocket again.

---

[26] *Zedlitz:* You may be my best friend, but you don't understand / *Mettke:* Why? / *Zedlitz:* Yes, because I don't understand it myself. / *from the background:* Shut up! / *Mettke:* What is there to understand? / *Zedlitz:* Oh, I met a person, Mettke, a person …

Old and young alike are likely to have been captivated by these opening credits, which were newly created as part of the script. It arouses the curiosity of the viewers as to what the policeman is all about and what happens next with the love affair, and adults' memories of their own school days and their first time making love are evoked. The younger ones are confronted with their first sexual experiences, but Zedlitz's falling in love also creates insecurity among them due to their own inexperience, which ends in scuffles that spread comedy. At the same time, the boarding school students are thus introduced as likeable boys who stick together when it counts and are still full of mischief – quite unlike Holz's original, in which, as later in the film, they appear as high-strung members of a secret society who behave like fraternity members.

Even though the film, as mentioned above, is oriented towards the plot of the drama, it still makes use of its specific means by granting the simultaneity of events through the alternating view into different spaces of action. This becomes exemplarily clear after the prequel, when first (as at the beginning of the first act of the drama) four older men are shown chatting in the casino with a morning pint: Wollwein, Major, Sanitätsrat and Meyer.[27] Even before the Landrat, Falk and Niemeyer join the gentlemen, the plot shifts to Niemeyer's apartment after some of the gentlemen have made disparaging remarks about Niemeyer's much younger second wife. In the four-minute scene (19:28–23:28), Niemeyer's money problems are brought home to the viewers in a compact way, only leaving behind a negative impression. On the one hand, she seems to have a penchant for luxury and to be arrogant, for both the dressmaker's demands for money for her splendid dress and the baker's outstanding bills, which he repeatedly reminds her of, she rebuffs arrogantly and knows especially how to silence the baker with her charm. On the other hand, it becomes clear in the conversation with her stepson Fritz, who is making no progress with his studies and living large, that he regularly demands money from her and is now blackmailing her. He does so by saying that he has seen her with another man, of which Niemeyer must of course know nothing. This scene between stepmother and stepson, in which the camera repeatedly switches from one person to the other in close-up, shines through acting (on the one hand Fritz's sardonic smile and corresponding tone of voice, on the other the increasingly frightened wife in speech and facial expressions), but only gains authenticity through the camera angles and movements. Most of the characters are thus introduced within the first 21 minutes, in contrast to the drama also the boarding school students, who only enter the stage in the 3rd act and only as secret allies, thus offering young viewers little opportunity for identification.

As for the character of Niemeyer, who unlike most other teacher figures of his time does not appear as a tyrant but as an understanding person towards his pupils, the film also ultimately exposes his educational ideas, which are based on

---

[27] Meyer still bears the name Goldbaum in the original as well as in the screenplay. The reason for this change is the *Nürnberger Gesetze of* 15 September 1935, according to which Jewish names could only be used in films if they served to portray a negative character (cf. von der Osten 1998, 196).

humanistic educational ideals of the nineteenth century, as wrong, but in the end he goes one step further by professing his belief in the new educational ideas and the norms associated with them.[28] A teacher who defends his pupils because he believes in the good in them, as Niemeyer tries to do in the casino in his confrontation with the Landrat (38:40–43:29), can only have been met with enthusiasm of young and older viewers, for they would surely have wished for this themselves. In addition, there is Niemeyer's cordiality towards Zedlitz, whom he asks in the living room at the end of the conversation what was bothering him, whether he had been too harsh, and whom he embraces in a fatherly manner (01:08:29–01:09:44). The audience's sympathy with the good-natured teacher, however, is gradually coupled with a lack of understanding of his credulity and ultimately his blindness to reality, which he displays in his conversation with the flattering and lying Lydia Link, as well as the ensuing dialogue with von Zedlitz, whose distraction he misinterprets. However, he seems to suspect something, for in the film he subsequently goes to the *Goldener Pfau* pub, is shown the green salon in which von Zedlitz initially spent last night, and to his own horror realises that it is an establishment with barely dressed ladies (01:12:04–01:13:24). His faith in his own ideals begins to shatter when the lie is exposed, and he is told at the police station that von Zedlitz did indeed spend the night with Lydia Link. He is deeply hurt that his trust had been badly abused, that he has been so lied to. Upset, he berates his favourite student, yells at him that he is done with him, can't see him anymore, won't accept an apology (01:32:30–01:37:45). Nevertheless, as becomes apparent in the following conversation with the district administrator, Niemeyer does not want to abandon his principles because of this one sad case. After the context surrounding von Zedlitz's actions becomes clear to him, his suspicions that the Primus (best of the class) may have taken his own life are finally confirmed, making him feel guilty, seeing himself as von Zedlitz's murderer. While Niemeyer is in his study in the drama, the former pupil Falk at his side as well as the district administrator, and the final scene is kept relatively short, it is cinematically effective and fleshed out with a message.

In the film, after the stretcher with von Zedlitz's dead body has been carried into the school building, accompanied by his classmates, Niemeyer takes a seat on a chair next to the stretcher; the students stand together as a group, shaken, to the side of Niemeyer, who has his eyes fixed on the face of his dead classmate. Lovingly, Niemeyer looks at him, speaks softly and slowly, gradually leans deeper towards him:

> Also bist du doch zu mir zurückgekommen, Kurt von Zedlitz, hatte dich doch fortgeschickt, dir verboten, mir noch einmal unter die Augen zu treten. Welch sonderbarer Ungehorsam. [längere Pause] Wusstest du wirklich keine andere Entschuldigung als diese stumme

---

[28] Von der Osten (1998, 196) is mistaken when he also cites Niemeyer's statements to Zedlitz in this context, after the latter only admitted to being with the actress in the bar. The sentence "Moral purity is still the foundation of healthy development. For the individual, as well as for the community" (Holz/Jerschke 1905, 63) can already be found in the drama and proves once again that Nazi ideas usually do not originate in National Socialism, but that certain ideas had a long tradition, but were re-functionalized in the Nazi system.

Antwort, auf die kein Mensch eine Erwiderung hat? [längere Pause] So musst du nun Recht behalten. Ich bin Schuld an deinem Tod.²⁹ (02:01:22–02:02:28)

And addressing the students, he announces that he will resign from his office, that he will no longer be their teacher:

> Ihr nennt mich Traumulus. Ich weiß. Nur wir sind nicht da zu träumen, die Menschen blind zu lieben und dann in ihrer Not allein zu lassen. Ich habe euch nicht geführt, ich habe euch nicht gekannt, ich habe versagt. Ich trete ab. [Pause] Mein Gott, nun steht ihr da, ihr Kinder, und meint, der da war ein Held. Nein, er war kein Held. Denn wir sind nicht in dieses Leben geschickt worden, um ihm zu entfliehen, sondern um es zu bezwingen. Deshalb stählt und härtet euch, kämpft, siegt über euch selbst.³⁰ (02:02:56–02:02:18)

In the last sentence in particular, those virtues are addressed that the Nazi regime proclaimed from the beginning and to a certain extent included in its educational program. Apparently the idea for this Nazi related final passage goes back to the director, for it is reported of the shooting in the film studio that Carl Froelich "exchanges the verdict [...] after every rehearsal and every take" with Jannings, at the same time drawing ever new highlights into the dialogue until the scene is flawlessly expressed in play and language". (BeWo 1935). In any case, the ending does not come from the scriptwriters, because their script ends after "Ich trete ab. [Pause]" with the following words:

> Eines bewahrt euch von dieser Stunde, das letzte, was ich euch noch als Lehrer geben kann: Wir sind nicht in dieses Leben geschickt worden, um ihm zu entfliehen. Wenn es manchmal auch das Leichteste sein mag. Wir beide, mein Primus und ich, wir haben das leider getan.³¹
> (Quoted from von der Osten 1998, 197)

From a film aesthetic point of view, it should be emphasized that while Niemeyer is still at the police station, the Zapfenstreich begin outside, images of which are repeatedly faded in until the end, and its music can be heard again and again in the background while he speaks his words of farewell. His departure is thus heralded on a symbolic level before he himself has made this decision, and also acquires something honourable, even though he is a failure. Nonetheless, in this cinematic production he is not an "oaf with tolerably benevolent features" (Kerr 1998, 200), as the theatre critic at the premiere of Holz's drama in 1904 had sharply put it, but an "oaf with luminous features" who can "impress" (ibid.).

---

[29] So you came back to me after all, Kurt von Zedlitz, had sent you away, forbidden you to appear before my eyes again. What strange disobedience. Did you really know no other excuse than this silent answer, to which no man has a reply? So now you must be right. I am to blame for your death.

[30] You call me Traumulus. I know. Only we are not here to dream, to love people blindly and then leave them alone in their need. I have not led you, I have not known you, I have failed you. I resign. My God, now you stand there, you children, and think that this one was a hero. No, he was no hero. For we were not sent into this life to escape it, but to conquer it. Therefore, steel yourselves, toughen yourselves, fight, conquer yourselves.

[31] One thing keeps you from this hour, the last thing I have left to give you as a teacher: We were not sent into this life to escape it. Though sometimes it may be the easiest thing to do. You and I, my Primus and myself, we have unfortunately done that.

Reception and Distribution of the Film Version *Traumulus*

Already during its production in autumn 1935, as was usual in the past with other films, the *Film-Kurier* reported about the process. There it says among other things:

> This world, which constituted the inner attitude of the *schoolmaster* [emphasis added], had to fall in order to give the *educator* [emphasis added] of a new and yet always unchanging youth the possibility of rebuilding a new, more life-like one ... The work lives from this problem. (BeWo 1935).

A week later there is another report from the visit of the filming, where Emil Jannings was interviewed and told that he had been friends with Arno Holz. He had tried in vain to persuade the poet to work for the film a long time ago, but the poet refused because the film lacked sound at that time (cf. Vom Preußenkönig zum Gymnasial professor 1935).

The premiere took place on 23 January 1936 at the Ufa-Palast am Zoo in Berlin. In Berlin alone, the film was shown simultaneously in 53 premiere theatres, where 303,835 visitors are said to have been counted in the first six days (cf. Zahlen sprechen 1936). Two days after the premiere, a euphoric review appears in the *Völkischer Beobachter*, the party organ of the NSDAP, which gives a good indication of the new ideas of a successful film. The author begins by criticising the previous film producers, who had not understood that, in addition to the "what," the "how" was of the utmost importance (von Demandowski 1936). First and foremost, he praises the screenwriters who "skilfully revealed [...] the profound irony and the satire of the times", the "satire on Jugendstil (which is unmistakably announced on the opening title with a woodcut-like frame for connoisseurs)", and then the magnificent drawing of the dignitaries of Wilhelminism, "all the pettifoggers and guardians of virtue, the small-town moralists and gossip-mongers, on whom the only really valuable human being, [...], threatens to perish." (Ibid.) The director's ability to have "put the right actors in the right places with a sure view", to have "not let anyone play themselves into the foreground" and thus to have achieved a "seamless interplay" is particularly emphasized. (Ibid.) And also imagery, sound and construction were "like the actors, servants to the work as a whole." (Ibid.) Last but not least, he praises numerous actors, above all Emil Jannings, whom he sees "at the height of his character portrayal", he plays

> this Traumulus with infinite subtlety, each of his movements harmonizes with facial expression and speech, the development and heightening of this figure into the solely valid human, is staggering. His transitions from the humourless to the serious, from the comical to the tragic, his outbursts and his transformations are the best, the greatest art of representation par excellence. (Ibid.)

In a similar fashion, the *Berliner Lokal-Anzeiger* comments on the performance of the leading actor: "Jannings lets us experience fate: we smile with him, we fight with him, we suffer with him. (Fischer 1936) Like Demandowski in the *Völkischer Beobachter*, the managing director of the Reichskulturkammer, Hans Hinkel, praises the "excellent community spirit of all those involved in the work" and "the excellent characterisation of the milieu around 'Traumulus,'" a milieu for which he harbours only contempt because it lacks "any inner attitude" (Hinkel 1936). Today's youth "thankfully no longer know this empathy with this milieu, or only to a small degree. [...] For the most part, they have courageously escaped from this dull atmosphere of morality-producing bourgeoisie." (Ibid.) The film makes every German aware of "what the awakening of the new Germany in the National Socialist spirit means for all of us and for the future of our nation." (Ibid.) The leadership of the Nazi system, which received a copy in advance, was also enthusiastic, as can be seen from an entry by Goebbels in his diary. He sees the film in the evening at home on 11.01.1936, writes enthusiastically: "A very big hit. Pre-war Germany brilliantly caricatured. Wonderful!" (Goebbels 1987, 563) The next day he watches the film again with Hitler, who is apparently "enraptured," "Jannings excelling. And another set of the best acting performances." (Ibid.)

The statements quoted so far have in common the criticism of a certain time and its representatives, which one still personally experienced and suffered from. In the filmic realisation, it also fits that Niemeyer and the district administrator do not reconcile at the end as in the drama. The equally positive criticism of the Reichsjugend-Führung (RJF), which claimed to be the sole educator in contrast to the NS-Lehrerbund, focuses on a different issue, namely education. Apparently, the RJF also enjoyed the privilege of being able to show films before their first screening. Comsequently, *Traumulus* was screened one day before its official premiere to all Berlin leaders of the HJ and the Bund Deutscher Mädel (BDM). The reactions of the young people were "extraordinarily appreciative", they "praised its educational values and decided to use it in special youth film lessons" (Ein Film zur Erziehungsfrage 1936). In this context, the RJF's press service pointed out that there had been a lack of films devoted to the subject of "youth and youth education" since the Nazi takeover; in this respect, *Traumulus* represented "after a long time, a first and at once also outstandingly successful foray into an area that had not been taken into account." (Ibid.) Even the representatives of the NS-Lehrerbund were more than open-minded. Of course, one had to ask oneself whether such a film did not violate the "sense of professional ethics" and "professional honour". But this question had to be answered in the negative: "A little bit of *Traumulus*" was always carried by the "ideal-minded educator [...], in contrast to the flat utilitarian and realistic man". He must therefore "keep this side of his nature under constant control so that it does not become dangerous to him and the young people entrusted to his care" (Traumulus unter Kollegen 1936). And among students, too, the film was very well received or ranked first, as a survey conducted in 1937 revealed: important to them in films was the "portrayal of human fates" that immediately "seize" them, as well as "educational[...] values" (Studenten urteilen über Filme 1937).

With so much praise and recognition from different sides, it is not surprising that those significantly involved in the film, which was awarded the rating of being *staatspolitisch und künstlerisch besonders wertvoll* and was also given the endorsement of being *für Jugendliche ab 14 Jahren zugelassen* (Zensierte Filme 1936), received the highest awards. Already in May 1936 Goebbels presented the director

Carl Froelich with the National Film Award 1936[32] with the words that this film had been created "without an obtrusive tendency, but along clear, ideological lines" (Staatspreise überreicht 1936). Emil Jannings was appointed state actor by Göring in July 1936 (cf. Käthe Dorsch und Emil Jannings Staatsschauspieler 1936).

First performances outside Berlin followed relatively quickly. For example, from February 4, 1936 in southwestern Germany (cf. "Traumulus"-Start in Stuttgart 1936), because of the carnival in the Rhineland only from February 28, 1936 in the west (cf. Traumulus in Westdeutschland 1936) or in Königsberg (cf. "Traumulus" in Ostpreußen 1936). In addition, importance was attached to special screenings, such as for district leaders of the NSDAP in Kiel,[33] for participants of the Film Ball in Munich (cf. "Traumulus" in München 1936), the Winter Olympics ("Traumulus" in Garmisch 1936) and the Summer Olympics in Berlin (cf. "Traumulus" während der Olympiade 1936) —the latter in order to reach a foreign audience as well. Later in the war, so-called revivals of films were in vogue, to which *Traumulus* belonged like many other entertainment films, e.g. in 1942 (cf. w. st. 1942).

A particularly large number of viewers were reached through the *Jugendfilmstunden* of the HJ, especially after the introduction of compulsory membership in the youth organisation in 1939. However, *Jugendfilmstunden* at an admission price of 20 Pfennig were introduced as early as 1934, although they did not yet take place nationwide (cf. Hoffmann 1991, 104). They were intended to be a celebration for adolescents in contrast to the usual visits to movie theatres or cinemas, and it was also intended to exert an influence on the choice of films and, moreover, the leadership hoped that "communal discussions" (Belling/Schütze 1937, 46) would have an important educational effect. Shortly after its screening, *Traumulus* was included in the directory for *Jugendfilmstunden* (cf. Für die Jugendfilmstunden empfohlen 1936) and could was thus ensured wide distribution. In order to promote valuable films in the best possible way from the point of view of the state, one also thought about advertising measures on the radio, which was still very rarely used, whereby one thought less of conventional reviews, but rather of appearances of the actors, but possibly also of the other participants in front of the microphone (cf. Eckert 1936). And let's not forget television, which at the time still had a very limited distribution. However, the first television parlors worldwide were set up in Berlin as early as 1935; in the TV program, *Traumulus* can be found on April 5, 1937, at Paul Nipkow's television station in Berlin-Witzleben.[34]

Regarding distribution, it is interesting to note that the film was also seen outside of Germany, and quickly attracted great interest and recognition in several countries. The Christian *Kleine Volksblatt* in Vienna, for example, called it "the most interesting and mature film of the new Germany" (quoted in Das Neueste aus dem Ausland 1936, 1). The *Prager Tageblatt* spoke of "a peak film [...] of world film

---

[32] In 1935, Leni Riefenstahl received it for her film *Triumph des Willens*. Froelich received the State Prize a second time in 1939 for the film *Heimat*. In 1942 Froelich was honoured for four decades of film work (cf. G. H. 1942).

[33] Cf. the note in *Film-Kurier* 18 (1936) 42 of 03.02., 2.

[34] The reference is found in the journal Die Sendung 14 (1937) 14 of 05.04.

production" (quoted after "Traumulus" im Prager Urteil 1936). Further screening notices can be found for Zurich,[35] Copenhagen,[36] Hungary[37] and the USA,[38] among others.

Conclusion and *Traumulus* Today

As a playwright, Arno Holz is one of the most important representatives of naturalism, and his *Traumulus* was one of the most successful plays performed on German-language stages for over four decades. According to the available evidence, it was last performed in Hamburg forty years ago, with the present programme booklet revealing hints of a critical new production in the direction of education for maturity in Adorno's sense. The question of how exactly the play was interpreted in the individual productions must remain unanswered at this point. In addition to program notes and reviews in the press, this would require an examination of the respective dramaturgical interventions in the stage play.

The analysis of the film version shows that it is a media network in which the film adaptation closely follows the drama; many character speeches were adopted verbatim. The screenwriter, director, and actors, above all Emil Jannings, and others involved created an award-winning film that delighted its contemporaries in terms of content, technique, and aesthetics: young and old audiences, party, and national leaders, and not least the critics. It did not achieve this effect because, like typical propaganda films and propagandistic feature films of those years (on this question of genre, cf. Strobel 2009, 134 ff.), it focused on Nazi ideology. Apart from Niemeyer's closing words ("For we have not been sent into this life to escape from it, but to conquer it. Therefore steel yourselves, toughen yourselves, fight, conquer yourselves") and the dialogue of two boarding school students ("I'm definitely going to join the Schutztruppe one day, [...], riding through the steppe like this and driving the blacks before them"), the film is neither racist nor overtly propagandistic. But it is covertly propagandistic and political in the way it ridicules past times and their representatives, including their moral and educational ideas, so that the Nazi rulers could functionalize it for the new Germany.

It is therefore not surprising that the film was released after 1945 (Fig. 3) with only a few editing restrictions. According to Kanzog, the Tobis sign and the dialogue of the two students quoted above had to be removed in accordance with the 1950 and 1969 examinations (cf. Kanzog 1994, 112). In addition, other passages

---

[35] Cf. the note in *Film-Kurier* 18 (1936) 118 of 22.05., 3. On the uncritical reception in Switzerland, cf. Prodolliet (1999), 60 ff.

[36] Cf. the note in *Film-Kurier* 18 (1936) 81 of 04.04., 1.

[37] Cf. the note in *Film-Kurier* 18 (1936) 154 of 04.07., supplement, 2. Here we also find the note that the film was initially banned in Hungary.

[38] Cf. the note in *Film-Kurier* 18 (1936) 277 of 28.09., 3.

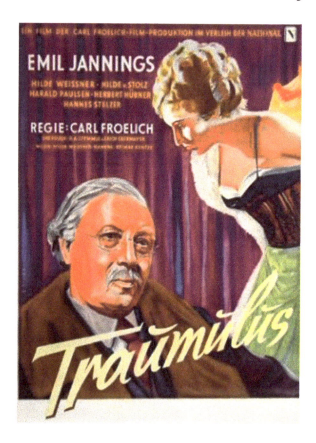

Fig. 3 Poster by B. Arndt for the re-release of *Traumulus* from 1949 (© DFF – Deutsches Filminstitut & Filmmuseum)

were removed, because the shortened and censored version only has a running time of 95 minutes, which is 25 minutes shorter than the original two-hour version. It was broadcast by ZDF in 1998, by ORF2 in 1999 and by sky several times in the summer of 2009.[39] The comparison of both versions showed that the cuts refer to the picture sequence in many scenes, no scene was cut completely, larger cuts refer only to the fade-ins of the Zapfenstreich. To my amazement, even Niemeyer's final line, in which he appeals to the often-praised Nazi virtues of steeling oneself, hardening oneself, fighting, winning, was not cut. While the original length of the film can only be obtained for scholarly purposes through the Bundesarchiv, the abridged version, identical in its message, is freely available, with no references to its original version, its context of origin, contexts of effect, etc. It would be worthwhile to investigate the reception of this version by young people and adults today.

---

[39] Cf. https://www.fernsehserien.de/filme/traumulus (05.01.2020).

References

Primary Literature

Holz, Arno/Oskar Jerschke: Deutsche Weisen. Berlin [u. a.]: Parrisius, 1884.
Mann, Heinrich: Professor Unrat oder das Ende eines Tyrannen. Roman. München: Langen, 1905.
Strauß, Emil: Freund Hein. Eine Lebensgeschichte. Berlin: Fischer, 1902.

Filmography

Der blaue Engel (D 1929/30) [Spielfilm]. Regie: Josef von Sternberg, Drehbuch: Robert Liebmann und Karl Vollmoeller, Musik: [u. a.] Friedrich Holländer, Ufa Berlin.
Traumulus (D 1935) [Spielfilm]. Regie: Carl Froelich, Drehbuch: Robert A. Stemmle und Erich Ebermayer, Musik: Hansom Milde-Meißner, Froelich-Film GmbH, Berlin (Bundesarchiv); gekürzte, frei zugängliche Fassung, TaurusVideo GmbH, München 1994.

Theatrography

Holz, Arno/Oskar Jerschke [Pseud. Hans Volkmar]: Frei! Eine Männerkomödie in vier Aufzügen. München: Piper, 1907.
Holz, Arno/Oskar Jerschke [Pseud. Hans Volkmar]: Gaudeamus! Festspiel zur 350-jährigen Jubelfeier der Universität Jena. Berlin: Sassenbach, 1908.
Holz, Arno/Oskar Jerschke [Pseud. Hans Volkmar]: Heimkehr. Berlin: Sassenbach, 1903 [später u. d. T.: Die Perle der Antillen. Komödie in vier Akten. Berlin: Bloch, 1909].
Holz, Arno/Oskar Jerschke: Traumulus. Tragische Komödie. München: Piper, 1905.
Holz, Arno/Oskar Jerschke: Büxl. Komödie in drei Akten. Dresden: Reißner, 1911.
Holz, Arno/Oskar Jerschke: Deutsche Bühnenspiele. Ausgabe in einem Bande. Inhalt: Frei, Traumulus, Büxl. Dresden: Reißner, 1922.
Wedekind, Frank: Frühlings Erwachen. Eine Kindertragödie. Zürich: Schmidt, 1891.

Secondary Literature Before 1945

Arno Holz: „Jannings-Ia!". In: Film-Kurier 17 (1935) 286 vom 07.12., 3.
Barnstorff, Hermann: Kind und Schule in der deutschen schönen Literatur unserer Zeit. In: Monatshefte für deutsche Sprache und Pädagogik 18 (1917) 2, 33–39.
Belling, Curt/Schütze, Alfred: Der Film in der Hitler-Jugend. Berlin 1937.
BeWo: Jannings – Traumulus. Carl Froelich dreht in Tempelhof. In: Film-Kurier 17 (1935) 257 vom 02.11, 3.
Demandowski, Ewald von: Emil Jannings in „Traumulus". In: Völkischer Beobachter (1936) 25 vom 25.01., o. S..
Eckert, Gerd: Filmwerbung des Rundfunks. In: Film-Kurier 18 (1936) 70 vom 23.03., 3.
Ein Film zur Erziehungsfrage. In: Film-Kurier 18 (1936) 21 vom 25.1., Beibl.

Fischer, Hans E.: Emil Jannings als Traumulus. Triumph der Schauspielkunst im Ufa-Palast am Zoo. In: Berliner Lokal-Anzeiger (1936) 21 vom 24.01.
Für die Jugendfilmstunden empfohlen. In: Film-Kurier 18 (1936) 55 vom 05.03., 3.
Funk, Alois: Film und Jugend. Eine Untersuchung über die psychischen Wirkungen des Films im Leben der Jugendlichen München 1934. Zugl.: München, Univ., Diss., 1934.
G. H.: Professor Carl Froelich 40 Jahre im Filmschaffen. In: Film-Kurier 24 (1942) 27 vom 02.02., 2.
Graf, Max: Traumulus. In: Neues Wiener Journal 13 (1905) 4062 vom 13.02., 1–2.
Herzberg, Georg: Im Rampenlicht. „Traumulus". In: Film-Kurier 22 (1940) 41 vom 17.02, 2.
Hinkel, Hans: „Traumulus" und sein Milieu. In: Film-Kurier 18 (1936) 91 vom 18.4., Beibl.
Hinkel, Hans (Hg.): Handbuch der Reichskulturkammer/bearb. von Günther Gentz. Berlin 1937
Hippler, Fritz: Betrachtungen zum Filmschaffen. Mit einem Vorwort von Carl Froelich und einem Geleitwort von Emil Jannings. Neu bearb. und erw. Aufl . Berlin ^{5}1943 (Schriftenreihe der Reichsfilmkammer; 8).
Käthe Dorsch und Emil Jannings Staatsschauspieler. In: Film-Kurier 18 (1936) 168 vom 21.07, 3.
Das Neueste aus dem Ausland. In: Film-Kurier 18 (1936) 29 vom 04.02., 1–2.
Reß, Robert: Arno Holz und seine künstlerische, weltkulturelle Bedeutung. Ein Mahn- und Weckruf an das deutsche Volk. Dresden 1913.
Sander, Anneliese U.: Jugend und Film. Berlin 1944 (Das Junge Deutschland: Sonderveröffentlichung; 6).
Staatspreise überreicht. An Froelich und Schumann. In: Film-Kurier 18 (1936) 122 vom 27.05., 1.
Staatstheater Berlin, Kleines Haus: Traumulus. Programmheft. Berlin 1940.
Studenten urteilen über Filme. Das Ergebnis aus 500 Fragebogen. In: Film-Kurier 19 (1937) 129 vom 07.06, 3–4.
„Traumulus" im Prager Urteil. In: Film-Kurier 18 (1936) 144 vom 23.06, 1.
„Traumulus" in Garmisch. In: Film-Kurier 18 (1936) 32 vom 07.02., 331.
„Traumulus" in München. In: Film-Kurier 18 (1936) 26 vom 31.01., 1.
„Traumulus" in Ostpreußen. In: Film-Kurier 18 (1936) 56 vom 06.03., 4.
Traumulus in Westdeutschland. In: Film-Kurier 18 (1936) 22 vom 27.01., 4.
„Traumulus" unter Kollegen. In: Film-Kurier 18 (1936) 46 vom 24.04., 3.
„Traumulus"- Start in Stuttgart. In: Film-Kurier 18 (1936) 31 vom 06.02, 3.
„Traumulus" während der Olympiade. In: Film-Kurier 18 (1936) 189 vom 14.08., 2.
Turley, Karl: Das Leben des Dichters. In: Programmheft des Staatstheaters Berlin, Kleines Haus, zur 18. Aufführung des *Traumulus* am 16.03.1940. Berlin 1940.
Vom Preußenkönig zum Gymnasialprofessor. „Traumulus" wird verfilmt – Gespräch mit Emil Jannings. In: Film-Kurier 17 (1935) 265 vom 09.11., 2.
w. st.: Leipzigs Spielpläne. Auch im August viele Wiederaufführungen. In: Film-Kurier 24 (1942) 224 vom 24.09., 2.
Zahlen sprechen. In: Film-Kurier 18 (1936) 60 vom 11.03., 2.
Zensierte Filme vom 13. bis 18. Januar 1936. In: Film-Kurier 18 (1936) 23 vom 28.01., 4.

Secondary Literature After 1945

Correns, Marie-Luise: Bühnenwerk und Publikum. Eine Untersuchung der Struktur von vier erfolgreichen Dramen um die letzte Jahrhundertwende in Berlin. (Sudermanns „Heimat", Halbes „Jugend", Hauptmanns „Fuhrmann Henschel" und Holz und Jerschkes „Traumulus"). Jena, Univ., Diss., 1956.
Faulstich, Werner: Einführung. Politik, Wirtschaft, Gesellschaft. In: Ders. (Hg.): Die Kultur der 30er und 40er Jahre. München [u. a.] 2009 (Kulturgeschichte des 20. Jahrhunderts; 2), 7–26.

Flessau, Kurt-Ingo: Schulen der Partei(lichkeit)? Notizen zum allgemeinbildenden Schulwesen des Dritten Reiches. In: Ders./Nyssen, Elke/Pätzold, Günter (Hg.): Erziehung im Nationalsozialismus: „… und sie werden nicht mehr frei ihr ganzes Leben!" Köln [u. a.] 1987, 65–82.

Fricke, Thorsten: Arno Holz und das Theater. Biografie – Werkgeschichte – Interpretation. Bielefeld: Aisthesis, 2010. Teilw. zugl.: Köln, Univ., Diss., 2000.

Goebbels, Joseph: Die Tagebücher. Hg. von Elke Fröhlich i. A. des Instituts für Zeitgeschichte und in Verbindung mit dem Bundesarchiv. Teil I, Bd. 2. München [u. a.] 1987.

Hechler, Manfred: Die soziologische Dimension der Kunsttheorie von Arno Holz. Frankfurt a. M. [u. a.]: Lang, 1981 (Europäische Hochschulschriften: Reihe 1, Dt. Sprache und Literatur; 461).

Hickethier, Knut: Film- und Fernsehanalyse. ³Stuttgart [u. a.] 2001.

Hobsch, Manfred: Ideologie für Kopf und Herz der Jugend. In: Schäfer, Horst/Wegener, Claudia (Hg.): Kindheit und Film. Geschichte, Themen und Perspektiven des Kinderfilms in Deutschland. Konstanz 2009 (Alltag, Medien und Kultur; 5), 39–55.

Hopster, Norbert/Nassen, Ulrich: Literatur und Erziehung im Nationalsozialismus. Deutschunterricht als Körperkultur. Paderborn [u. a.] 1983 (Informationen zur Sprach- und Literaturdidaktik; 39).

Hoffmann, Hilmar: „Und die Fahne führt uns in die Ewigkeit". Propaganda im NS-Film. 6.–7. Tsd. Frankfurt a. M. 1991.

Kanzog, Ulrich: „Staatspolitisch besonders wertvoll". Ein Handbuch zu 30 deutschen Spielfilmen der Jahre 1934 bis 1945. München 1994 (Diskurs Film; 6).

Kerr, Alfred: „Ich sage, was zu sagen ist". Theaterkritiken 1893–1919. Hg. von Günther Rühle. Frankfurt a. M. 1998.

Neumann, Helga/Neumann, Manfred: Vom Pauker zum Pädagogen. Ein literarischer Streifzug durch die Schule im „Jahrhundert des Kindes". Stuttgart 2011 (Kröners Taschenausgabe; 408).

Noob, Joachim: Der Schülerselbstmord in der deutschen Literatur um die Jahrhundertwende. Heidelberg 1998 (Beiträge zur neueren Literaturgeschichte; Folge 3; 158). Zugl.: Oregon/USA, Univ., Diss., 1997.

Osten, Ulrich von der: NS-Filme im Kontext sehen! „Staatspolitisch besonders wertvolle Filme" der Jahre 1934–1938. München 1998 (Diskurs Film: Bibliothek; 13). Zugl.: München, Univ., Diss., 1996.

Pertsch, Dietmar: Traumulus – Vom Theaterstück zum einzigen Spielfilm nach einem Werk von Arno Holz und Oskar Jerschke. In: Szatrawski, Krzysztof (Hg.): Arno Holz und sein Werk. Zum 150. Geburtstag des Dichters; Materialien zum historisch-literarischen Symposion Kętrzyn, 26.–27. April 2013. Kętrzyn 2013, 117–129.

Prodolliet, Ernest: Der NS-Film in der Schweiz im Urteil der Presse 1933–1945. Eine Dokumentation. Zürich 1999.

Sander, Anneliese U./Reese, Hartmut (Kommentar): Jugendfilm im Nationalsozialismus. Dokumentation und Kommentar. Nach der Sonderveröffentlichung Nr. 6 der Zeitschrift „Das junge Deutschland" (1944). Münster 1984 (Geschichte der Jugend; 7).

Schmidt, Siegfried J. (2008): Der Medienkompaktbegriff. In: Münker, Stefan/Roessler, Alexander (Hg.): Was ist ein Medium? Frankfurt a. M. 2008, 144–157.

Schmidt, Siegfried, J.: Medien – Materialitäten – Räume. Zur Analyse eines Wirkungszusammenhangs. In: Dander, Valentin/Gründhammer, Veronika/Ortner, Heike (Hg.): Medienräume. Materialität und Regionalität. Innsbruck 2013 (Medien – Wissen – Bildung) 37–49.

Sprengel, Peter: Holz & Co. Die Zusammenarbeit von Arno Holz mit Johannes Schlaf und Oskar Jerschke – oder: Die Grenzen der Freiheit. In: Text + Kritik (1994) 121, 20–32.

Sprengel, Peter: Literatur im Kaiserreich. Studien zur Moderne. Berlin 1993 (Philologische Studien und Quellen; 125).

Stelzner-Large, Barbara: „Der Jugend zur Freude"? Untersuchungen zum propagandistischen Jugendfilm im Dritten Reich. Weimar 1996. Zugl.: Bonn, Univ., Diss., 1996.

Strobel, Ricarda: Film- und Kinokultur der 30er und 40er Jahre. In: Faulstich, Werner (Hg.): Die Kultur der 30er und 40er Jahre. München [u. a.] 2009 (Kulturgeschichte des 20. Jahrhunderts; 2), 129–147.

Stüben, Jens: „Ich warte sehnsüchtig [...] auf den ‚Stoff', den Du mir schenken solltest". Arno Holz' Produktionsgemeinschaft mit Oskar Jerschke. In: Plachta, Bodo (Hg.): Literarische Zusammenarbeit. Tübingen 2001, 197–215.

Thalia Theater: Traumulus [Programmheft]. Hamburg 1980.

Weber, Albrecht: Literatur und Erziehung: Lehrerbilder und Schulmodelle in kulturhistorischer Perspektive, Bd. 3: Einem neuen Zeitalter entgegen? Frankfurt a. M. [u. a.] 1999.

Welzel, Birgitta: „Staatspolitisch besonders wertvoll". Neue Wege in der Forschung zum nationalsozialistischen Film. In: Internationales Archiv zur Sozialgeschichte der Literatur 20 (1995) 2, 209–214.

"Da stelle ma uns mal janz dumm"

Die Feuerzangenbowle: A Media Network Analysis

Heidi Nenoff

Introduction: Surveying the Current Situation

The multiple exploitation of a narrative *Stoff* in print media, as film, radio play and audio book in a media network is a cultural phenomenon of society in the age of the "culture industry" (Horkheimer/Adorno 2002, 128 ff.). This phenomenon must first be described, then analysed and evaluated regarding the production processes and actors involved, if one wants to understand current media development and make meaningful use of the potentials of such media networks.

The film adaptations and the radio play or audio book adaptations of the novel (Fig. 1) *Die Feuerzangenbowle* (1933) by Heinrich Spoerl[1] (1887–1955) form an impressive media network, which can be used as an example to show how the culture industry can function and how the *Stoff* changes in different media. The main thing that becomes visible is how it spreads exponentially through different media, so that in the end literally every child knows *Feuerzangenbowle*. In analysing the

---

[1] Spoerl wrote the novel in co-authorship with Hans Reimann (1889–1969). For strategic and political reasons ("In the summer of 1932, Reimann's name [...] was anything but a recommendation among publishers"; Ohmann 2010, 29), Spoerl offered the work to the publishers as sole author. However, both authors consistently shared royalties for *Feuerzangenbowle for the rest of* their lives. Currently, the descendants of the two authors are still fighting over its rightful authorship (cf. ibid., 20 ff.).

H. Nenoff (✉)
Faculty of Education, German Elementary School Didactics, University of Leipzig, Leipzig, Germany
e-mail: heidi.nenoff@uni-leipzig.de

© Springer-Verlag GmbH Germany, part of Springer Nature 2024
P. Josting et al. (eds.), *German-Language Children's and Youth Literature In The Media Network 1900–1945*, https://doi.org/10.1007/978-3-476-05892-8_18

Fig. 1 Cover *Die Feuerzangenbowle* (Spoerl © Reprint [1933], with an addendum by Joseph A. Kruse, 2008)

media network, by Schmidt[2]'s (2008) media compact concept will be referenced, which allows a systematic approach to this phenomenon and through which the structures of such a media network can be revealed in terms of levels of action and components of media. This is necessary in order to reconstruct who acts with whom and why in the creation of media products and how what works in which processes

---

[2]With the *media compact concept*, I also refer to the introductory lecture by Petra Josting and Annemarie Weber for the conference at Bielefeld University on 15 June 2018 for the project *Deutschsprachige Kinder- und Jugendliteratur im Medienverbund 1900–1945, in* which Siegfried J. Schmidt's /*media compact concept* is briefly introduced. Schmidt/Zurstiege (2000) and Schmidt (2008) serve as basic literature for the theoretical foundation.

and how this is reflected in the respective process results, which have an effect up to our present day.

It all began on April 19, 1933 with the publication of the first part of the novel *Die Feuerzangenbowle,* which was printed as a sequel until May 26, 1933 in the liberal daily newspaper *Der Mittag,* owned by the publisher Heinrich Droste. From this a media network arose over the past 86 years consisting of: (a) Spoerl's novel with about half a million copies printed (cf. Vitz 2004, 21) until 1945 and from 1945 until 1998 almost annually a new edition in several publishing houses with an immense number of printed copies, (b) the first film version with Heinz Rühmann (1902–1994) under the title *So ein Flegel* from 1934, (c) the film version with Heinz Rühmann *Die Feuerzangenbowle* from 1944 and (d) the film version with Helmut Käutner *Die Feuerzangenbowle* from 1970. The journalist and chief reporter of the *Berliner Tageszeitung (B. Z.),* Oliver Ohmann, writes in his 2010 published work *Heinz Rühmann und "Die Feuerzangenbowle":* "The *Feuerzangenbowle* is an integral part of culture. For decades, Heinz Rühmann as the 'Pfeiffer with three f's' has thrilled his audience." (Ohmann 2010, blurb).

In fact, the 1944 film comedy referred to here (Fig. 2) can be considered to be very popular in Germany, as proven, for example, by reports of the 2017 television ratings on the internet: "*Feuerzangenbowle* on ARD clearly dominated the primetime ratings on Christmas Eve." (Sallhoff 2017) Each year during the Christmas season, the 1944 film airs multiple times on television.[3] This continued success on television resulted from its regular screening in cinemas in both parts of Germany throughout Germany's postwar history. In the 1960s, the film had "mastered the leap from cinema to television" (Ohmann 2010, 149). It was said to have been "an all-German love at a time of seperation" (ibid., 153) and a "street sweeper" (ibid., 155). In addition, the novel was always present on the book market. The 1944 film adaptation and the book market benefited from each other for over 70 years, as evidenced by numerous cover designs featuring Rühmann (as if these editions were the "book to the film"). The amount of printed matter is so substantial that the number of books actually produced may well reach two million.

Long before Rühmann's death in 1994, the film (1944) also reached German universities with annual screenings at Christmas time. This gave rise to the so-called *Feuerzangenbowlen-Kult* accompanied by hot alcoholic drinks. Göttingen and Aachen are the strongholds of the *Rühmann-Kult*. In total, until today it has become a tradition at 30 universities, cultivated mainly by students (cf. ibid., 161 f.). Quotes such as: "Bah, wat habt ihr für ne fiese Charakter!", "Aber Herr Direktor, nor deesen wentzigen Schlock!", "Wat is ne Dampfmaschin? Da stelle ma uns mal janz dumm", with the speech characteristics of the figures of Professors Bömmel and Schnauz (Crey) quickly became catchphrases (cf. Brenner 2004, 15), especially among teachers.

However, the two other film versions, *So ein Flegel* (1933) and *Die Feuerzangenbowle* (1970), are only marginally received, always against the backdrop of the 1944 film version in comparison or for special Rühmann friends. The

---

[3] Cf. *Die Feuerzangenbowle.* In: Quotenmeter, http://www.quotenmeter.de/tag/Die+Feuerzangenbowle (24.08.2019).

Fig. 2 Cover of *Die Feuerzangenbowle* (© Kinowelt Home Edition GmbH, 2009)

1944 film was the trigger for further *self-releases* in other media contexts, which were particularly promising in terms of market strategy due to the collective memory of Rühmann as Pfeiffer, Erich Ponto as Schnauz (Professor Crey) and Paul Henckels as Professor Bömmel.

There is a 1970 radio play adaptation directed by Heinz Günter Stamm and Bernd Grasshoff.[4] This was followed in 2003 by an audio book version by entertainer Götz Alsmann.[5] The composer Thorsten Wszolek produced a musical in 2004, thus ushering in a veritable stage era for the *Stoff*. Especially in Düsseldorf, the birthplace of Heinrich Spoerl, the play became a tradition; e.g., in memory of Spoerl, as a son of this city. Currently, there is talk of a veritable *Feuerzangenbowlen-Boom* at German theatres, this being a particular "chapter of success" (Ohmann 2010, 166). From the 1980s onwards video distribution also benefited from the

---

[4] Cf. ARD Listening Database, http://hoerspiele.dra.de/vollinfo.php?dukey=1476455&vi=41&SID (24.08.2019).

[5] Cf. Alsmann's Web site, https://www.goetz-alsmann.de/?page_id=34 (24.08.2019).

enduring success of *Feuerzangenbowle*. DVD editions followed from 1999 and most recently Blu-ray discs in the *Zweitausendeins Edition* in 2009 (cf. ibid., 149 and 176).

The Media Compact Concept as an Instrument of Analysis for the Media Network System *Feuerzangenbowle*

With his theory of media as a compact concept Schmidt tries to capture the systemic nature of media and media networks. Various types of media are always integrated into a complex system consisting of different *spheres of action* with their *actors* (actants) and of different *components* that all constitute each other reciprocally. "Media systems are process systems, i.e. interdependencies of effects in the sense of general systems theory." (Schmidt 2008, 150).

Analysing and interpreting individual media offers is not sufficient, because they are not able to adequately grasp the complex set of conditions, the context, the historical dimension and the actors involved with their intentions as well as the effects of media. For media offers are always the results of complex processes, and as such they must be analysed, interpreted and evaluated (cf. ibid., 148).

At the level of the *spheres of action, production, distribution, reception* and *processing* are to be mentioned. By *processing* Schmidt understands such processes "in which media offers are made the object of the production of new media offers, such as the filming of the novel" (ibid., 148). On the level of the *components of* media, four components have to be considered in the analysis, interpretation and evaluation: 1) varying types of media are instruments of communication, 2) are produced by media techniques, and 3) require institutional bodies or organisations such as publishers or broadcasters in order to apply, administer, finance, politically and legally represent media techniques, and 4) it is the media offers themselves (cf. ibid., 144 f.) "which emerge from the interaction of all the factors mentioned" (ibid.). The "process results" carry with them the conditions of the respective media system as specific characteristics (cf. ibid.).

What does the first component "media are instruments of communication" (ibid., 144) mean for the analysis? If one focuses on the *instrument,* then one sees in the medium the essential form of conveying messages via the written word or the spoken word preserved on sound carriers, via music and images stored on film reels, which always has to be considered in the interpretation, whereby the temporal and spatial limitation is overcome (cf. Hickethier 2010, 41 f.), but is also ordered in a conspicuous way by a producer according to his intention, aesthetically designed and, above all, reproduced and disseminated. The peculiarity of always solely being a limited material means of transport/medium necessarily requires the selection and weighting of statements. In the analysis, it is important to consider that this material means of transport is *produced by someone*: "Media are produced by media techniques" (Schmidt 2008, 146). Behind a medium there is usually a whole armada of producers who, with their limited technical and financial possibilities, have to select and make a selection depending on their intentions. For Schmidt's definition: "forms of media are instruments of communication" includes the communication model (again, a systemic set of conditions) in which the actants (cf. Hickethier 2010, 38 f.), sender and receiver, are inscribed, who always change their roles and who mutually condition each other. For the interpretation of media, it is not irrelevant to closely look at who the actants are and what intentions (cf. ibid., 47) they pursue in the respective situations and what expectations are present on both sides. This simultaneously addresses Schmidt's third component: 'forms of media require institutional institutions or organisations'.[6] In the case of *Feuerzangenbowle*, the following sender-actants and institutions can be determined: the two authors Spoerl and Reimann, the publishers (especially Droste Verlag), the film industry (the film production company Ufa), and those involved during the Nazi dictatorship. Each actor in this field of action pursues intentions in the production of films and books; aesthetics is not necessarily involved.

Die Feuerzangenbowle was originally written as a screenplay for a cinematic film, rewritten by the authors as a novel and printed in the spring of 1933 in the daily newspaper *Der Mittag* as a serial novel, which was met with success. (cf. Ohmann 2010, 22 f.) In the same year this was followed up by the first edition and in December filming began on *So ein Flegel*. Thus, *Feuerzangenbowle* found its way into German cinemas after all and became a profitable business, because the "collective recipients" (Schmidt 2008, 148) in the cinemas were ideal multipliers. In 1943, 1116.5 million cinema-goers were counted in Germany; this means 14.4 cinema visits per inhabitant per year (cf. Lowry 1991, 4) – cinema was a cultural mass phenomenon. Within a very short time, the *Feuerzangenbowlen* story was thus probably known throughout Germany, especially since *So ein Flegel* was highly praised in the trade press.[7] With the cinema screenings, the book again sold very well, as evidenced by the print runs and the number of prints.[8] In 1943 the continuing success of the book then led the producers to assume that a new film version would also fill the cinema halls well.

The reception and distribution history of the *Feuerzangenbowlen Stoff* thus clearly shows that this is an industrial production of a commodity for which there is a market. The market value increases in particular due to the demand for cheerful films and books that manage to disperse the audience through humour. Producers

---

[6] With the exception of the medium of the *letter*. The letter does not require an institution (cf. Schmidt, 144).

[7] A detailed, very laudatory review can be found, for example, in *Der Kinematograph* (So ein Flegel 1934).

[8] With the help of the Karlsruhe Virtual Catalogue (KVK), the following number of printed copies in the editions of the Droste-Verlag Düsseldorf could be reconstructed: 20 thousand in 1933, 50 thousand by 1937, 80 thousand by 1938, 227 thousand by 1940, 350 thousand by 1941, no information on the number of printed copies in 1942 (Propaganda Ostland), 515 thousand by 1943 (*Feldpostausg.*), no information on the number of printed copies in 1944 (*Wehrmachtsausg.*). In total, it can be assumed that about half a million copies were printed from 1933 to 1945.

serve the needs of their customers, whose "ideology is the business" (Horkheimer/ Adorno 2002, 145). In this sense, the two authors are just as much "producers" rather than writers or artists. Already the plan to write a screenplay in pairs conveys the intention of the two (teamwork is typical for literary commodities; cf. Nusser 1991, 41): it is about a market concept and profit. Ernst Eckstein's school humoresque *Besuch im Karzer* (1875) served as the raw material from which entire passages of text were taken, along with the linguistic idiosyncrasies of the characters (cf. Ohmann 2010, 19).

For the "optimal mercantile exploitation" (Nusser 1991, 42) of the *Stoff*, the film was made a second time ten years after the premiere of *So ein Flegel*. It is possible that Spoerl was not satisfied with the version of the first production, which considerably deviated from the book, and now saw the opportunity to produce a better version, but he also struck a chord with the times, for light-hearted films were not only in demand in 1943/1944, but also politically desired. The German film production was under the leadership of the Reichspropaganda minister Goebbels and therefore in the service of the dictatorship. Goebbels imposed the Babelsberg film production facility to produce 110 films per year. "In the fiscal year 1943/1944, Ufa made a net profit of 175 million *Reichsmark*. A large sum of this went to armaments." (Ohmann 2010, 138) The Nazi state pursued mercantile interests as much as authors and film producers. The production of films was an important source of revenue for the state to finance armaments and war. Cheerful films were considered particularly suitable under the Nazi leadership.

However, the production of light-hearted flicks offered many more advantages than merely good revenues. In 1944, Horkheimer and Adorno, who lived through the Nazi era in exile, in a highly media-critical manner analysed the advantages of the special effect of light-hearted films, which went beyond mercantile interests. In laughter, the "echo of the escape from power" resounds – laughter "copes with fear," but only apparently, and thus becomes "the instrument of the deception of happiness," for "[i]n such harmony they offer the distortion of solidarity." (Horkheimer/Adorno 2002, 149). Especially under conditions of dictatorship and war, cheerful films have a dictatorship-friendly, quietising effect, for they would not give the consumer "a moment's inkling of the possibility of resistance" (ibid., 150) and they make "all needs [...] appear to be fulfillable." For the powerholder, this context is particularly favourable: "Pleasure means being in agreement. [...] Not having to think about it, forgetting suffering, [...] escape from thoughts of resistance" (ibid., 153). "Fascism [...] hopes to reorganise the gift-receivers trained by the culture industry into a regular forced following." (Ibid., 170) For this reason, more than half of all films made at this time were so-called *H-films*, cheerful films (cf. Curstädt 2018, 404). Research by Ben Urwand also shows Hitler's affinity with film. Hitler had believed in a "mysterious, almost magical power" (Urwand 2017, 21) of films; books, on the other hand, were worthless compared to film (ibid., 22). This is because film would bring far greater propaganda success with much less effort. Urwand supports this statement with a quote from Hitler: "The picture brings in a much shorter time, almost I would like to say at one stroke, to man an enlightenment which he receives from written material only through protracted reading."

(Hitler; quoted in Urwand, ibid., 22 f.) With the help of the new cinema technology, the "views of a large crowd could possibly change quickly and without a lot of fuss [...]" and have a "powerful effect" (ibid., 23).[9] In particular, people swore by the subtle effective power of *H-films*. Goebbels had advocated producing more *blameless* films, since "propaganda is most effective" "when it is not immediately seen through as such by the audience." (Hoffmann 2017, 89) Source research brought to light that film producers in Babelsberg completely submitted to these intentions and goals, as shown in an exchange of letters from 1933 between Ufa's head of business Wilhelm Meydam and manager Ernst Hugo Correll. Wilhelm Meydam (Ufa management/head of business) writes:

> So we have to be clear that the masses of viewers inside and outside the German borders are looking for relaxation, so that in our whole endeavor the cheerful film must play the first role. (Quoted from Rother 2017, 26)

Ernst Hugo Correll (manager of Ufa since 1928, director of Ufa) answers:

> Ufa also has a cultural task to fulfill, which for the near future can only consist of promoting the government's state-political views and world views. (Quoted from ibid., 27)

Ufa was demonstrably in the service of "the government" and even participated in the war crime of "forced labor".[10] These research findings ultimately result in fairly uniform assessments on the part of film scholars about Nazi cinematic entertainment: The "supposedly apolitical films have an eminently ideological function" (Lowry; quoted in Mailänder 2017, 117). These films provided a "whitewashed image of National Socialism" (ibid.). Curstädt sums up, "Nazi cinema is perhaps the most lingering and richest example of a forced appropriation of the seventh art by reasons of state." (Curstädt 2018, 404) *Feuerzangenbowle* was a "warm-hearted droll that in 1944 was no longer intended to win anyone over to the ideas and ideals of the National Socialists [...] but to serve as a humorous diversion and distraction from the dreary everyday life of bombing and war" (ibid., 407). With regard to the "National Socialist ideology, the film was neither necessarily good nor evil, but certainly not innocent" (ibid.).

---

[9] For this purpose, Hitler distinguished two divisions films: art and propaganda. For an important propaganda film, Hitler himself became a film producer. For example, he commissioned the director Leni Riefenstahl to record the Nuremberg Party Congress of 1934. The result was the film *Triumph des Willens* (ibid., 47) and other such films by Riefenstahl that followed.

[10] Forced labor was organized by Friedrich Sauckel, General Plenipotentiary for the Labor Deployment of Five Million People. Only 200,000 came to Germany voluntarily. Sauckel was sentenced to death by hanging at the main Nuremberg war crimes trial in 1946 (see Püschel 2017, 163). Babelsberg was Europe's largest film company in 1939, with 65 defense-related operations employing nearly 13,000 people. Ufa's workforce consisted of 4500 employees (ibid., 165). Forced labor in the Babelsberg film city "took place according to the same regularities as in all other operational areas" (ibid.). Forced laborers were housed in camps. There, those deported from all over Europe were separated according to nationalities with hierarchies. Those deported from Eastern Europe were considered racially inferior and were treated accordingly (cf. ibid.). Next to the Ufa site, an area was purchased by the company and a barracks camp for 600 inmates was built (ibid., 166).

The film *Die Feuerzangenbowle* was thus produced under conceivably unfavourable circumstances in the period between March 18, 1943, and January 28, 1944 and even had start-up difficulties despite the promotion of *H-films*. Goebbels wanted to ban this film because of its denigration of the teaching profession. Rühmann therefore personally travelled to the Wolfsschanze, the Führer's headquarters, with the film reel in his luggage to get the film's approval from Hitler. Hitler is said to have merely asked whether this film was funny, and in answering this question in the affirmative, released the film (cf. Ohmann 2010, 114 ff.).

This historical context must always be taken into account when analysing the "process results" that "the conditions of the respective media system entail as specific characteristics" (Schmidt 2008, 144 f.). The success of books and film after 1945 proves that a media system is constitutively a "self-organising" one (ibid., 145), albeit made by people and shaped by their (mercantile) interests in the supply-demand mechanism. Like the growth of a rhizome, the significance of *Feuerzangenbowle* grew over the past 85 years, as shown above, to the point where it became a part of popular culture itself, the Germans' favourite film. Heinz Rühmann, who was cynically called "Reichsgaudibursche" by Karl Valentin (cf. Winkler 1992), has played a significant role within this pupularity.

The Novel *Die Feuerzangenbowle* (1933)

Spoerl's books are said to have brought "laughter and joy" and to have been "clear and entertaining, unfussy and unobtrusive" (Ohmann 2010, 204). They are undoubtedly professionally crafted popular entertainment novels. The *Feuerzangenbowle* by Spoerl and Reimann is also clear and entertaining.[11] It can be shown here that this novel has typical characteristics of popular literature and can be named among the "reading *Stoffe* of the 'little people'" (Nusser 1991, 46), which can also explain its popularity.

The structure of the novel can be described as follows: Four wealthy, middle-class gentlemen sit in a tavern over a Feuerzangenbowle[12] and recall their past school pranks. This lively company forms the framework of the narrative. The episodes framed in it result from an (apparent) problem of the character of the writer Hans Pfeiffer, which is presented from the perspective of a superior narrative instance (auctorial narration). Pfeiffer's problem consists in having missed such pranks. With the decision to make up for what he has missed, the narrative gets underway. "A pipe dream becomes a deed" (ibid., 13): Pfeiffer slips into the A level

---

[11] Since Spoerl is noted as the sole author on the covers of the editions for the above-mentioned reasons, in the following I will also mark the quotations only with "Spoerl".

[12] Feuerzangenbowle is a traditional German alcoholic drink for which a rum-soaked sugarloaf is set on fire and drips into mulled wine.

pupil uniform and goes to the grammar school in the small town of Babenberg,[13] where farcical school pranks are strung together, rising in stages, culminating in a finale. A love story is also woven into this story. Hans falls in love with the headmaster's daughter, Eva. The novel ends in a "sad happy ending" that serves to expose the story as fiction. The narrator speaks to the reader, reporting with a pathos of a melancholy worldly wise man that, alas, it was all fiction: "True of the story is only the beginning: the Feuerzangenbowle." (Spoerl 1990, 171).

Spoerl set the plot in the Wilhelminian Age (around 1910), a time that many contemporaries (1933) saw as the *Golden Age*, where the world was still in order, which is what the implicit narrator and the fictional readers long for. Indeed, narrator and readers form a "we-community" and desire the same thing, as the narrator's final speech shows, "True are the longings that drive *us*." (Ibid., emphasis added).

Typical features of folk tales can already be identified in the structure of the novel. With Pfeiffer's role reversal from writer to high school student, the novel bears the traits of a comedy of errors, in which the fun of the role reversal is intensified again at the end, when the supposed grammar school pupil disguises himself as teacher Schnauz. The comedic traditionally belongs to the poetry of the people anyway. The antics it contains, here as school pranks and mistaken identities, bear a structural resemblance to the popular *Schwank* (cf. Nusser 1991, 93).[14]This *Schwank*-like plot, the stringing together of antics, follows the "strategy of actionism" (ibid., 129) for such reading *Stoffe*.

Characteristic of popular reading *Stoffe* is also the typecasting of the characters, who align themselves with "certain role clichés" (cf., ibid., 41), whereby the main character Pfeiffer, is supposed to depict a figure of identification for the readers according to their wishful thinking and longing for the 'ideal world' (cf., ibid., 126). This is because these texts are written in such a way that they anticipate the supposed expectations of real readers.

Pfeiffer's eloquence and shrewdness, for example, are supposed to correspond to the readers' wishes. Pfeiffer is, moreover, a bourgeois writer with success and wealth: "As a young writer, he already has a big name", whose books "are being fought over by publishers today", his writings are "world-famous" (Spoerl 1990, 11), but also conservative and folkish, since he "works at the Vereinigte Werkstätten für Vaterländische Heimkunst" (United Workshops for Patriotic Home Art) (ibid., 14). Spoerl obviously intended to appeal to the (petit) bourgeois circle of readers who could be considered as buyers, and who would approve of this nostalgic, *völkisch* attitude.

---

[13] In the original 1933 version, Pfeiffer travels to the small town of Odernitz (cf. Spoerl 1933, 23). This town is only renamed "Babenberg" after the first film successes, in order to establish the connection to Babelsberg, to the film factory.

[14] The *Schwank* is "kept in a popular style", similar to an "anecdote, related to the short story", "with coarse and drastic, not infrequently raunchy content" (Straßner 1978, 1). It served "to ridicule", offered "light humour, harmless merriment without problematics" and "light-hearted cheerfulness" (ibid., 3). The *Schwank* is basically not a moral tale, since it does not exhort "to virtue", but rather tells with "disillusioning impetus [...] well-done pranks", which sometimes slide into the obscene (ibid., 3 f.).

Pfeiffer, this "Benjamin of society" (ibid.), is highly respected by representatives of the scholarly class (such as "der Justizrat", ibid., 8; the "Bankier", the "Herr Geheimrat", ibid., 154). His status and prestige allow him to temporarily break out of bourgeois life at times and, within certain bounds – within the realm of the harmless – to defy the norms (in Wilhelmine school life). He is nevertheless worthy of freeing the headmaster's daughter: "Here is my final school report, here my doctoral diploma, here my publisher's accounts, and here [...] my statement of income." (Ibid., 170) In his dealings with Eva, he behaves demurely in accordance with bourgeois conventions, almost naively chaste, as a game of blind man's buff shows as a love match (cf. ibid., 89). He does not need to break his marriage vows with his fiancée Marion, for Marion does this for him. Thus, Pfeiffer's moral loyalty in fundamental matters of life is not doubted at any point. The character Pfeiffer, despite this gained experience in the experiment of school and despite the change of partner, is a static and simple character, without development of personality, conflict or inner conflict. At the end of the novel he is what he had been at the beginning: the successful writer. His *problem* of having missed school pranks is hard to beat for shallowness.[15] Therefore, a development of this character is not to be expected at all.

Likewise, the teacher charaters are set up as "mere husks of persons" (Nusser 1991, 127) as the central figures of the comedy. Professor Crey (Schnauz) embodies the type of the ambitious, bourgeois educated and already somewhat elderly, quirky bachelor with a caricature-like appearance (pointed belly, golden watch chain; cf. Spoerl 1990, 18). This ambitious teacher is open to new teaching methods (cf. the episode in the chemistry cabinet, which shows that the experiment serves to make the lesson more vivid), yet he is the *failure* who ultimately teaches nothing at all because he has trouble getting the students to see reason. In the novel, Schnauz and Pfeiffer rival for Eva's favor, with Schnauz coming off miserably. On the seesaw in the park, Schnauz is finally exposed to ridicule by Eva.

Spoerl endowed Crey and Professor Bömmel with the dialect joke, with that popular local farce with which the deviant can be made the object of ridicule. It is precisely this "entertainment effect" that is supposed to be particularly "ideologically effective" (Nusser 1991, 93). Professor Bömmel embodies the old, already somewhat plodding, anti-authoritarian type of teacher who, because of his age and his school experience, has given up any effort to want to make a difference with pupils. The youthful teacher with the speaking name of Dr. Brett "is one of those teachers who have no need to make the dry subject matter palatable through tortured jokes" (Spoerl 1990, 41). He is able to excite the students with the subject itself: "When he spoke, and in a restrained voice headed for the decisive effect, one could have heard the drop of a pin." (Ibid.) With gymnastics in a commanding tone, he has the gang of pupils under control, although they still get into mischief behind the teacher's back (cf., 21).

---

[15] Witte sees in this motivation for action, having missed school passes, the "baroque motif of becoming aware of 'I have not lived': ubi sunt, it was once said. [...] the realization of the missed life [is] recast as a substitute memory of the good old days." (Witte 1995, 241)

With Prof. Knauer, the headmaster, Spoerl associates the type of the supposedly aloof authority figure, who was therefore nicknamed Zeus (cf., ibid., 27). Nevertheless, his authority is also undermined by characterising him as conflict-averse and "quirky": "Er war das Gegenteil eines Schultyrannen; seine Größe bestand darin, alle überflüssigen Konflikte [. . .] zu vermeiden und die kleine Anstalt mit Wohlwollen und Sanftmut im Geleise zu halten." (Ibid.). His "Schrulle bestand in einer kleinen Mappe, die er stets und ständig unter dem Arm trug. [. . .] Wahrscheinlich nahm er sie auch mit ins Bett" (Ibid.). In the dialogue between Pfeiffer and Knauer, his authority is finally disavowed, in which he asks Pfeiffer not to think and then to think anyway (cf. ibid., 28).[16]

Like the typicality of the teachers, the pupils are provided with characteristics that have a high recognition effect on the readers, as they correspond to general experiences. Thus, there is the "cadaverous" (ibid., 20) nerd Luck, who is the target of constant taunts from his classmates. In the novel, Luck, hustling for recognition by posting "Due to structural alteration [...] school closed" (ibid., 91), will carry out this prank without getting the recognition he craves, although he displays himself and hopes for punishment and thus fame among the students.[17] A second important student type is the leader of the class Rosen, who, however, surprisingly quickly gives way to the witty, resourceful Pfeiffer. With this typecasting of characters, the novel conforms to the principle of seriality, which popular novels require to serve popular tastes. In line with expectations, the novel delivers clearly delineated character types taken from the genres of popular literature (cf. Horkheimer/Adorno 2002, 142 and 163 f.). As already mentioned, Spoerl and Reimann have taken part of the whimsical teacher types from other school novels, thus making use of the seriality of the characters. This is even mentioned in the novel: "Does the man [Prof. Crey; note H. N.] really imitate Professor Heinzerling from Eckstein's 'Besuch im Karzer'?" (Ibid., 19).

In the we-community, readers are offered by the authors what they already know and can confirm. The depiction of complex interrelationships of social structures is avoided by orienting both characters and plot "to certain role clichés" (Nusser 1991, 41) and by limiting oneself to a "narrowly limited section of reality" (ibid., 51). The narrowly limited section of reality is the depiction of a high school in a small town. The big city, where Pfeiffer comes from, is not addressed at all in the novel. Social contexts are only ostensibly pointed out, but – as will be seen later – they are one-sided, simple, downright knit-patterned, and depict what a lay philosopher who is content with simple answers to complex questions thinks. The words of wisdom that the narrator mostly puts into the mouth of Pfeiffer, a sympathetic character, are nevertheless revealing and worthy of attention, for they provide insight into the history of mentality from the time when the novel was written. In the dialogue between Pfeiffer and Luck, the following image of man is conveyed:

---

[16] On the typicality of teachers, cf. also the detailed characterization of teachers in *Feuerzangenbowle* in Grimm/Rieger 2011, 65.

[17] On this point, the film (1944), which was shot later, deviates from the novel. In the film, Rosen tries to denounce Pfeiffer.

> Man by nature is crude and without compassion. Just like nature itself. Even the children still are. They torture animals, pluck the legs off flies, slice earthworms and think no evil. Pity is a cultural product and is instilled. [...]
>
> [I]n every place where men are formed, where man becomes a crowd, deep instincts stir. Think of the popular assemblies, of lynch law [says Pfeiffer to Luck, H. N.]. Apart from this, however, every individual has the need to vent his malice somewhere, or at least his bad temper. [...] According to the law of least resistance, one takes someone as weak as possible for this purpose. [...]
>
> They cannot bear this [being clever; H. N] [...] they will always prove to the weak that his cleverness is of no use to him. (Ibid., 69 f.)

So man is raw by nature, it says at first. This refers to a conception of man that is interwoven with the tradition of the Protestant doctrine of original sin and with an optimism of progress (of the nineteenth century) and cannot remain unreflective, since it plays the arguments to the representatives of the pedagogy of breeding, confirms Social Darwinism, which in history has proved to be discriminatory, and finally does not contradict in contemporary history the racial ideology that is on the rise.[18] This conception of man shows only one side of a traditional discourse of natural law, which precisely also knows a counter-position, namely the idea that the child is good by nature, since the natural is per se the good and desirable.[19] According to the idea expressed here, the human being needs ennoblement through upbringing and education. The mention of "popular assemblies" as a place where wickedness can be "let loose" (irony signals are not evident here) shows a clear rejection by the author of mass marches (the mob). The brutality that can come out in popular gatherings is therefore not in the sympathetic Pfeiffer's (and the implied narrator's) mind. Rather, this utterance allows us to draw conclusions about Pfeiffer's elitist thinking. This is also supported by the novel's inherent appreciation of the German Gymnasium with its specifically national education. The opening line, "Dieser Roman ist ein Loblied auf die Schule, aber es ist möglich, daß die Schule es nicht merkt"[20] is meant seriously. Pfeiffer therefore defends the Gymnasium (German grammar school) at several points in the novel:

> Das Gymnasium hat natürlich mit Beruf und Brotarbeit nichts zu tun. In diese Tretmühle kommt man früh genug. Ein Gymnasium ist keine Fortbildungsschule. Wenn es darum geht, schnell ans Verdienen zu kommen, und wer den Menschen nur nach Brieftasche

---

[18] Cf. Dieter Richter, who writes: "The Christian idea of the natural depravity of childlike nature [...] remained one of the defining moments of Western anthropology and educational theory" (Richter 1993, 3) and formative for "Protestant educational concepts" (ibid.). "A passionate debate about evil children [...] began towards the end of the nineteenth century following the publications of the Italian criminal anthropologist Cesare Lombroso" (ibid., 10). He was "committed to social Darwinist lines of thought, endeavored to work out characteristics [race, skull shape, physique; H. N.] of so-called 'born criminals' in large-scale empirical studies [...]. Lombroso cites as common characteristics of children and criminals the tendency to 'rotting', pleasure in cruelty to animals [...]." His work [...] on "minor criminals [was] a kind of key theme" (ibid.) during this period.

[19] An important opponent of the position presented here is, for example, J. J. Rousseau, whose positive image of childhood is rooted in the Stoic tradition and the ideas of the *Golden Age* (cf. Assmann 1978, 101).

[20] Transl.: "This novel is a paean to the school, but it is possible that the school will not notice".

und Bankkonto bewertet, der braucht allerdings kein Gymnasium. Der wird auch nie begreifen, daß es noch andere Werte gibt, die sich nicht in Mark und Pfennig ausdrücken lassen, geistiges Besitztum, das man nicht kaufen, aber auch nie mehr verlieren kann. Das einen aus dem Dreck des Alltags heraushebt, Erholung für gute Tage und Trost und Zuflucht, wenn es einem mal dreckig geht. Sehen Sie, dafür gehen wir aufs Gymnasium. (Ibid., 57 f.)

[D]as Gymnasium ist eine bürgerliche Institution und dient einem bürgerlichen Ideal. (Ibid., 140).

Fitting the bourgeois ideal, the school reading that is mentioned in the novel is accordingly chosen. One reads in German grammar schools the works of the German classics Goethe (ibid., 129), Schiller (ibid., 45) and Hölderlin (ibid., 129). However, not just any works by these authors are mentioned, but those about great, glorious heroes: Goetz von Berlichingen, Wilhelm Tell, Wallenstein, Hyperion, and Faust. The philosopher of superhumanity is added to this trio of classics, Friedrich Nietzsche (ibid., 129), and to crown it all, the poet of the ivory tower, Stefan George, twice (ibid., 103 and 137). It is the cadaverous nerd Luck, of all people – since it is part and parcel of a certain elitist thinking – who occupies his spare time with poems by George. During a drinking session in an atmosphere of "youthful brotherhood" (ibid., 138), Luck recites George and Hölderlin.

The praise of the school and of bourgeois education, the high esteem for the great German poets and their works about German knights and other heroic fighters, the mention of Friedrich Nietzsche, Friedrich Hölderlin, and Stefan George reveal an attitude-like pride of bourgeois conservative circles inscribed in the text. The fact that Pfeiffer also "works at Vereinigte Werkstätten für Vaterländische Heimkunst" (United Workshops for Patriotic Home Art) connects this pride of place with the *völkisch*-nationalist sentiments of this character. Added to this is Luck's fondness for the poems of Stefan George. Spoerl thus alludes to the adherence of a "circa 1919 [...] historico-political idea [that] developed considerable fascination in both conservative and progressive circles in the decades that followed" (Kiesel 2018, 121). Youthful aesthetes, such as the cadaverous Luck is said to embody, were fascinated by George's *Geheimes Deutschland* (*Secret Germany*), in which the poet and his followers lead Germans out of "his mountain and cave into the light" and give them "the deep confidence for a future" (George; quoted in Kiesel, ibid.). George's followers dreamed of the "Second Reich" and the "rebirth of the old 'Holy Roman Empire of German Nations'" (cf. ibid., 131 f.). Hölderlin's poems, which Luck mixes with George's poems, were considered to be the art of a poetic great of divine dimension, who had been an "important model" for George. He was the "seer-poet" that George also considered himself to be (cf. ibid., 130), of which Luck is equally completely moved by: "also [...] spricht [Luck] mit Geisterstimme seine tief empfundenen Kreuzungen zwischen Hölderlin und Stefan George. Er wurde selbst ganz erschüttert davon." (Spoerl 1990, 137) His classmates and Pfeiffer, on the other hand, laugh at Luck for this: "sie lagen unter den Stühlen und wälzten sich. Selbst Hans Pfeiffer lachte mit" (ibid.).

Pfeiffer and Luck are thus characterised as conservative, bourgeois, nationalistic and folk-minded. This also fits in with the idea of the role of women in the novel, which already seems antiquated to contemporaries around 1933, and which is still entirely rooted in the nineteenth century world of thought. The schoolgirls from the neighbouring Lyceum are humorously called "Gänse" or "Hühner" by Pfeiffer. Prof. Knauer "besaß eine beachtliche Hühnerzucht" (ibid., 27), which may be meant here in an exceptional double sense. Eva embodies the naïve girl from the provinces in need of a man's guidance. Her role as wife and mother is already established. Her character seems pale, reduced merely to her appearance. In her dealings with Pfeiffer, she behaves in an artificially affected manner. She is immediately ready to slap Pfeiffer whenever he attempts to give her a kiss, although she actually wants to be kissed. Pfeiffer's uttered petty wisdom about gender behavior, which is meant to make readers smile, then fits in with this artificial posturing:

> Frauen sagen Nein, wenn sie Ja meinen, Frauen sagen Ja, wenn sie Nein meinen. Oder Frauen sagen Ja, wenn sie Ja meinen [...] Verteufelt schwer, sich auszukennen. [...]. Die Frau liebt aus Naturbestimmung. Aber der Mann ist Dilettant. (Spoerl 1990, 89)

Pfeiffer's landlady, Frau Windscheit, also embodies the role cliché of a petit bourgeois housewife. The plump lady in her late forties is a mother through and through, exaggeratedly clean to the point of ridiculousness, domestic and caring (cf. ibid., 33). Marion, Pfeiffer's fiancée, presents the contrasting image of such a small-town landlady; she portrays the fine salon lady from the big city. On the whole, not a single woman in the novel is credited with the achievement of emancipation of the women of the Weimar Republic; on the contrary, they play only the role of an amusing ingredient in this male-dominated world of the *Feuerzangenbowle*.

The comic, popular novel *Feuerzangenbowle* possesses – as has been shown – all the qualities for rapid marketing. It works very strongly with patterns from the arsenal of popular literature, it transmits role clichés and conservative, bourgeois, *völkisch* attitudes that are close to National Socialist ideology. It is from this backward-looking nature of the novel that the narrator's famous final sentence can then be understood: "Wahr sind auch die Erinnerungen, die wir mit uns tragen; die Träume, die wir spinnen, und die Sehnsüchte, die uns treiben." (Spoerl 1990, 171).

"[M]an darf davon berührt sein, ohne jemals zu wissen, was eigentlich berührt," Curstädt says of this final sentence, attributing to it a vacuous emptiness (Curstädt 2018, 408). However, this sentence need not be empty. The longing of which the narrator speaks is the longing for the lost Holy Roman Empire of the German Nation, which, from the perspective of the national conservative, had been the *true thing*, as it were. This yearning, with its optimistic promise of salvation, serves the need of readers of entertainment literature for the ideal world and for a "happy ending" (Nusser 1991, 54). To sum up: The novel *Die Feuerzangenbowle* was the beginning of Spoerl's era of success. His novels such as *Wenn wir alle Engel wären* (1936) and *Der Gasmann* (1940) were also filmed with Heinz Rühmann in the leading roles. By the end of the 1930s, Spoerl was the "most successful entertainment writer of the Third Reich" (Ohmann 2010, 46). His literary production was extensive, "Spoerl apparently had no fear of contact with the regime". He also published his texts in the "Nazi inflammatory paper *Der Angriff*" and since 1935 had been a "member of the Reichsschrifttumskammer" but not of the NSDAP (ibid., 45).

Regardless of the ideological context, however, it is certain that his literary works and his friendship with Heinz Rühmann were financially rewarding. Spoerl, a lawyer, became "wealthy as a writer within a few years," with a villa on Wannsee (near Heinz Rühmann's residence), with a "maid and private secretary." (Ohmann 2010, 45).

The Film Versions from the Years 1934, 1944 and 1970

What essentially defines the *Feuerzangenbowle* media network is the novel and its three fundamentally different film adaptations: *So ein Flegel* (1934), *Die Feuerzangenbowle* (1944) by Helmut Weiss and *Die Feuerzangenbowle* (1970) by Helmut Käutner. In my comparative examination of these film adaptations, I would like to focus on only four aspects: 1) the placement of the film in its historical (and artistic) context, 2) a comparative analysis of the content of the film adaptation with the book original, 3) the use of technical and artistic means on the visual level, 4) the use of artistic means on the sound level, and the interpretive conclusions resulting from the analyses.

After the success of the novel in the summer of 1933, Cicero-Film GmbH began production of the black-and-white sound film *So ein Flegel in* the same year. It was shot in the Jofa studio in Berlin-Johannisthal within only two months, from mid-December to mid-February. The director was R. A. Stemmle, the screenplay was written by Hans Reimann. This film counts to the beginnings of sound film recordings. The costs for such sound films were still very high in the early 1930s (cf. Dorn 2004, 225). Film production facilities were under considerable financial pressure.[21] This required an effective production of numerous films in as short a time as possible, which explains why the time spent shooting was so considerably short. The actor who was already a star at this time, Heinz Rühmann, took over the double role of Hans and Erich Pfeifer (in this specific adaptation only with one "f"). The screenwriter Reimann, however, only roughly stuck to the novel. He changed the script for the film so extensively that his partner Spoerl is said to have been outraged by it (cf. Ohmann 2010, 42).

The first noticeable difference to the novel is the missing frame story, from which the novel got its title and why the film could not be called *Feuerzangenbowle,* but had to be renamed *So ein Flegel.* From the lack of an aldermanic round in the frame story follows the lack of motivation for the main plot, namely Dr. Hans Pfeifer's lack of school experience, which he only becomes aware of during the Feuerzangenbowle in the narrative circle. Reimann instead offers a different plot with a different (more plausible) plot motivation. He doubles the character Pfeifer. The man of letters, Dr. Hans Pfeifer, is joined by his younger brother Erich (in the dual role of Rühmann), who looks completely like him, the bum who has nothing to

---

[21] Cf. Dangerous "Reform" Plans 1934, 1.

do with school and behaves like a lout there. When he arranges for the school to be closed because of alleged building work, Hans Pfeifer is supposed to come to the school for a talk with the headmaster, and thus begins the comedy of errors. Hans is mistaken at school for his brother Erich and punished; Erich, on the other hand, flees to Berlin, where, as the supposed Dr. Pfeifer, he causes all sorts of mischief both at work and in his private life. The pranks described in the book, the scene in the chemistry cabinet about alcoholic fermentation and the final reenactment of Professor Crey are missing in the film. It is also not so much the pranks that dominate the comedy of the film, but rather the mix-ups in two parallel storylines in two locations (in Berlin and in Mittelsbach), in which the protagonists also swap partners, which is why the theme of love determines the plot much more clearly than in the novel.

On the visual level, the sophisticated professionalism of the producers is already evident in this early black-and-white sound film. It starts to show with the hiring of the well-known actor-star Rühmann for the double role as it proves to be a successful choice. Rühmann, small in stature, might have been just the right identification figure for the targeted cinema audience, namely that of the *little man*. Professionally done, however, are purposefully used camera angles and the editing technique in interaction with the dialogues and inserted texts, which create coherence and consciously direct the viewer's attention. The most unmarked camera angle is the semi-close-up (people are shown in the frame from the waist up). It serves to draw the viewer's focus to the character constellations. In a comedy of errors, the constellation of characters is therefore the most important thing, which is why this shot size dominates in this film. Other shots are only used sparingly; the *close-up* (from the navel up in the frame) to show facial expressions and gestures, or close-ups (only faces or texts on paper) are inserted at very exposed points (cf. Hickethier 2007, 54 ff.). Such special places are mostly the love scenes with Hans and Eva. They look at each other through a keyhole or a peep-box cinema window. In this way, the camera achieves a change of perspective from the outside view to the inside, because the spectator is supposedly looking through the eyes of the characters and thus receives information that goes beyond the character's speech. In this way, the viewer learns the title of Hans Pfeifer's play (coded as silly because of drastic exaggerations), which, as a play within a play,[22] self-ironically parodies this film comedy without words. The close-up of a book by Hans Pfeifer, which Eva and her friend are holding in their hands, in fact tells us about Pfeifer's work. His *Wandlungen der Venus*[23] is a frowned-upon erotic booklet, but he makes a lot of money from it, as the glamorous décor of his villa shows.

The actors' line of sight is arranged in accordance with the cinematic conventions of the 1930s. In the film *So ein Flegel,* the characters never look directly at the

---

[22] The fictional title of the school play is *Between Secunda and Prima.*

[23] An allusion to a book with "morally captious content" or to so-called "dirty literature": Benedict Leijo: Die Wandlungen der Venus. Vienna 1924, 6 f. In this slim, aesthetically sophisticated volume, three young librarians are locked in the library overnight. They use this opportunity to read stories to each other from forbidden books.

camera, but rather past it at an angle, or they direct their gazes at each other (cf. Hickethier 2007, 63 f.). The effect of this predetermined direction of gaze is startling. It conveys the impression that the game is in a separate (fictional) space, which the viewer only looks at from the outside. This trick marks the strict separation between the film world and the real world.

The editing technique and the design of the scenic transitions are remarkable in that transitions, which are always connected with a change of location, are always accompanied verbally by the characters and announced with a keyword. For example, the cue "Flegel" is followed by the hard cut, the change of location and the fade-in of the character Erich. These supposedly seamless transitions through the announcements suggest the simultaneity of the two storylines, although the viewer is only shown the scenes one after the other.

The background music by Harald Böhmelt corresponds to what the film is supposed to be: a light comedy. A schlager-like[24] dance song ("Und rechts herum der Fuß und links herum der Fuß, die Liebe, die Liebe ...") is used as a leitmotif in various scenes. Sometimes as orchestral, sometimes as salon piano music, the same catchy tune is heard, which also accompanies the frequent dance scenes. The lightness of the film is thus always indirectly expressed and it really struck a chord with the audience. It was a "great success with the public", "all the critics were enthusiastic" (Ohmann 2010, 43), but this is said to have been "primarily thanks to Heinz Rühmann", "who can give free rein to all humours in a splendid double role" (Völkischer Beobachter, 02.15.1934; quoted from Ohmann, ibid.).[25]

Perhaps the only person who was not satisfied with the result was Heinrich Spoerl. For he could also have understood Reimann's ironic portrayal of the writer's character as a personal blow against himself. Spoerl is said to have pushed the next film version of *Feuerzangenbowle* after the disappointment of *Flegel* in 1943. The director was Helmut Weiss, Heinrich Spoerl wrote the script himself for Terra-Filmkunst GmbH in Berlin. Heinz Rühmann was the production manager for the black-and-white film. All scenes were shot in the Babelsberg studio or there in the open. Filming started on March 18, 1943, exactly one month to the day after the arrest of the Scholl siblings in Munich, almost two months after the surrender of the German 6th Army at Stalingrad, in the midst of the first Allied air raids on Berlin from January 16 to March 30, 1943, coinciding with the Holocaust. On January 28, 1944, the film from the "dream factory" (Dorn 2004, 225) premiered in Berlin.

Spoerl now adhered more closely to the novel than Reimann, although he too made some changes (adaptations to the time around 1943). Crucial deviations from the novel are the following: The frame story is much more elaborately constructed in the film than in the novel. The plot in the novel takes the form of a progressive

---

[24] Schlager is a popular German genre of music associated with dancing.

[25] "A major component of the studio system is the star system, which was introduced as early as 1910. Film companies initially hired stage stars for film productions. Actors who were particularly well received by audiences were tied to a studio with high fees and contracts [...]." The concept worked out with Rühmann as the ideal figure: "Stars embody social types [...], serve as a foil for identification for the cinema audience." (Dorn 2004, 225).

chronological sequence of events: Decision of the experiment in the old men's meeting, Pfeiffer's experiment school, renewed meeting of the old men to evaluate the experiment. In the film, however, the group around the Feuerzangenbowle forms the framework. In the end, the experiences at the grammar school are exposed as mere creations of Pfeiffer's imagination. This frame story is thus an ironising signal of fiction, to be understood as a fantasy in alcoholic ecstasy. This makes any referencing to reality impossible. In the novel, however, the narrator does admit to having merely invented everything. It is possible that Spoerl wanted to avoid the Nazi censorship by making this change. Any reference to contemporary reality was to be avoided, which is why the plot was to be set in 1910 for everyone to see.

The love story between Eva and Pfeiffer was shortened, thus omitting the denigration of Professor Crey (Schnauz) and shifting the emphasis from love lust to a grammar school pupil story. Dr. Brett is a history teacher instead of a math teacher in the film, in order to be able to sneak in a concession to Nazi censorship after all. The film needed a representative of the *modern,* young, Nazi teacher who dominates the students through discipline while all the other old teachers fail. Appropriately, the history lesson deals with the history of the Goths, who, in the ideology of National Socialism, were the original Aryans who founded the *Deutschtum.* The image of the teacher was not to be denigrated too much. However, it also seems important to change the actions of the character of the geek Luck. In the novel, Luck commits the school closing prank, but in the film Pfeiffer is the perpetrator. The pupil Rosen intends to snitch on Pfeiffer, but he is threatened with punishment because of it. Thus, surprisingly, accusation is not portrayed positively in the film.

In the novel, there are numerous intertextual references and statements of the character Pfeiffer with a *völkisch-*nationalist worldview packaged as life wisdom. This is dispensed with in the film. Only a brief statement by the teacher Dr. Brett, which again is not found in the novel, hints at Nazi sentiments. Dr. Brett says, "A new age must show new methods. Discipline must be the bond that binds pupils like young trees." Witte finds in this inserted phrase (which can originally be traced to a famous parable by Immanuel Kant[26]) a reference to the Nazi propaganda film *Ewiger Wald* (1936): " *Ewiger Wald* already pivoted from Friderician soldiers to nursery, dreaming the ideal of order from the perfectly aligned state as second nature." (Witte 1995, 244) In the film, Dr. Brett embodies the ideal of the Volksgemeinschaft, in which the individual should only serve the purpose of the whole. The task of the school, according to this view, is to enable people to become part of the Volksgemeinschaft through discipline.

---

[26] Immanuel Kant writes: "so wie Bäume in einem Walde eben dadurch daß ein jeder dem andern Luft und Sonne zu benehmen sucht, einander nötigen, beides über sich zu suchen, und dadurch einen schönen geraden Wuchs bekommen; statt daß die, welche in Freiheit und von einander abgesondert ihre Äste nach Wohlgefallen treiben, krüppelig, schief, und krumm wachsen". In: Idee zu einer allgemeinen Geschichte in weltbürgerlicher Absicht. Vierter Satz. (Kant, Immanuel.: Schriften zur Anthropologie, Geschichtsphilosophie, Politik und Pädagogik. Erster Teil. Kant Werke, Bd. 9, Darmstadt 1994, 40).

On the visual level of the black-and-white film, innovations can be observed in comparison to the film *So ein Flegel*. It is new that the narrator in the frame *story* addresses the audience directly while looking into the camera. This breaks up the closed nature of the film's plot. The scene transitions are also new, each of which is combined with a change of location as well as a change of camera angles. Instead of the hard cut, flowing transitions are created by slowly fading out one image and slowly fading in the other, which reinforce the coherence of the plot beyond the spoken word and contain unspoken messages. An example of this is the smooth transition of the following images: In the classroom, there is a bust of Zeus on the wall. Shortly before the director Knauer enters the room, the bust is faded in, at the same time a camera is directed at Knauer's face and for a few seconds both faces can be seen one above the other, so that the similarity between Knauer and the bust is emphasised. With the help of this camera technique, the figure of Knauer is ironically stylised into the father of the gods by means of exaggeration and comparison.

Compared to *So ein Flegel,* the film music of *Feuerzangenbowle* by stage and film composer Werner Bochmann is dramaturgically functionalised. Instead of a dance song, which is the leitmotif of *So ein Flegel*, there is now much more differentiated music, corresponding to the character of the scenes, which is intended to reflect the current mood. For example, in the frame story, in memory of the deceased teacher "Baboon", quiet, sad music with violins is played, while in the music lesson the boys sing the lively spring canon "Der Frühling liebt das Flötenspiel" by Erich Knauf[27] (text) according to their age. Particularly outstanding is the musical background to the scene in which Principal Knauer walks through the empty schoolhouse in a furious stormy stride and tears open all the doors. The rhythm of the music accompanies Knauer's steps with pinpoint accuracy, accentuating the tearing open of the doors. The furious principal's hurrying down the stairs is accompanied with swelling, beady melody that seems to giggle at Knauer. The orchestral music contains increasing dissonance in this scene, swelling to the dissonant finale of the brass instruments (at the moment of the discovery of the prank), to make the audience aware of Knauer's increasing rage.

Despite some concessions to the Nazi regime contained in this film, Ohmann and Lowry consider it "a neutral and inoffensive film". Overall, it would "hardly qualify as a Nazi film" (Lowry 1991, 236). In the next sentence, however, Lowry points out that the film would confirm very conservative morals and gender roles, with the "typical taming of eroticism" and stereotypes common to films of the Nazi era (ibid., 237). On the question of whether the film is harmless, Lowry contradicts himself in that he argues in the first chapter of his research on Nazi films that it was precisely the harmless films that had been the captious ones. Nazi propagandists deliberately exploited the special power of so-called harmless films. Lowry quotes the Reichsfilmdramaturg Hippler, who in 1942 said that "the effect of a film is what counts"; it should be "artistically well designed, plausible, genuine in plot

---

[27] Knauf was beheaded in the Brandenburg penitentiary on May 2, 1944, three months after the film's premiere, for "defeatist remarks" (see Eckert 2018, 226).

construction, motivation", and also credible and probable, this being "much more important than the factuality of a *story*", because a film character must in any case "be an offer of identification", according to which the viewer can orientate his values and behaviour patterns (ibid., 7 f.).

Regardless of this, this film shines through Rühmann's top acting performance, but also through Erich Ponto as Professor Crey (Schnauz), Paul Henckels as Professor Bömmel and Hans Leibelt as Director Knauer (Zeus), who rightly made it a film deeply integrated into German popular culture over the years. Thus, this film turns out to be an artistic product that was born double-sided as a child of its time: The inimitable brilliance of the actors on the one hand and the terrifying context that took its toll on the film on the other.

The remake (1970) by the "successful and prominent director of the post-war period" (Mehlinger/Ruppert 2008, 3), Helmut Käutner[28] (1908–1980), ultimately had to fail because of this brilliant acting performance in the 1944 film version. Perhaps Käutner intended to free *Feuerzangenbowle* from the burden of its entanglement in the contexts of Nazi film production. He produced[29] a colour film version in connection with the successful "Lümmelfilmen" with renowned actors of the late 1960s: with Uschi Glas as Eva, Nadja Tiller as Marion, Theo Lingen as Professor Crey and Walter Giller as Pfeiffer.

The plot of the film was not – as one might assume – moved to the time around 1970, but remains in the time around 1910. It is oriented in large parts to both the 1944 film adaptation and the book. The complete frame narrative was taken from the 1944 film adaptation,. What this remake has in common with the book is the greater emphasis on the love story. Pfeiffer and Crey are again obvious rivals; the teeter-totter scene that finally consigns Crey to ridicule was carried over in the remake. Some school pranks were modified, shortened or expanded. For example, while discussing the fake construction sign, the teachers are locked in by the students in the staff room. There are no ideological aphorisms in this film version. A special feature is the appearance of Hans Richter as Dr. Brett, since the actor had already appeared in the 1944 film version in the role of the pupil Rosen. This clever

---

[28] Notable films by Käutner were: *Unter den Brücken* (1946); *Romanze in Moll* (1943); *Große Freiheit No. 7* (1944). Käutner was "at home in almost all genres of West German film, demonstrating stylistic variance." (Mehlinger/Ruppert 2008, 4) Käutner also already had experience with school stories: in 1964 he filmed Ludwig Thomas's *Lausbubengeschichten* (cf. Plaß 2008, 49).

[29] Seven-part series: 1. *Die Lümmel von der ersten Bank* (D, 1968), 2. *Zum Teufel mit der Penne* (1968), 3. *Pepe, der Paukerschreck* (1969), 4. *Hurra, die Schule brennt* (1969), 5. *Wir hau'n die Pauker in die Pfanne* (1970), 6. *Morgen läuft die Schule aus* (1971), 7. *Betragen ungenügend* (1972). "Alexander Wolf's [i.e. Herbert Rösler's] 1963 novel had already been a hit with audiences. The films initially took up the satirical impulses of the original, but then dissolved more and more into adolescent-like clamour: The students, above all the main character Pepe Nietnagel, rebel against the outdated teaching methods and authoritarian teachers as well as the repressive system of the school through numerous pranks and intrigues. In the context of the time, the films not only address the then current criticism of traditional school pedagogy, but also take up an anti-authoritarian and hedonistic impulse that massively influenced youth culture. [...] Even older originals such as *Die Feuerzangenbowle* (1970, Helmut Käutner, based on the novel by Heinrich Spoerl 1933) were re-adapted within the stylistic horizon of the crammer film." (Amann 2012).

combination of 'premake' and remake is also explicitly referred to in Richter's character speech.

So ein Flegel and *Die Feuerzangenbowle* from 1944 were pure studio films. The exterior shots took place on the studio lot in front of artificial backdrops. In the remake, real locations were chosen in the Alfred Wegener School in Berlin Dahlem and in the city of Wolfenbüttel. Only the interior shots took place in the Ufa film studio. The real filming locations give the film a far greater naturalness than the other two. Basically, it can be stated that Käutner's filming strictly followed the historical model of the time around 1910 in terms of equipment, costume, interior and scenery. The secondary school shown here is presented in picture and sound as a humanistic, educated bourgeois grammar school. Behind Principal Knauer's desk hangs a picture of the famous nineteenth-century scholar of antiquity, Theodor Mommsen, and in the background Brahms or the tradition of student songs (*gaudeamus igitur*) or Verdi's *Aida* (music: Bernhard Eichhorn) are played, which should not even give the appearance of being artificially made.

Nevertheless: The reviews of the remake are rather scathing, as the audience accustomed to seeing it cannot help but compare this version with the Rühmann film version of 1944: "Compared to the 1944 version, this school satire – despite being directed by Helmut Käutner – lacks atmosphere, wit and charm."[30] In Filmportal, Falk Schwarz writes: "When Käutner delivered this remake of *Feuerzangenbowle,* he had to put up with bitter criticism." Theo Lingen was not up to Erich Ponto. Giller was too old for the role of Pfeiffer. This film was "pretty" to look at: "A light form of entertainment that does not reach the original." (Schwarz 2014). "Käutner's superfluous remake of *Feuerzangenbowle* [...] is not necessarily an opus that inspires great anticipation." (Pflaum 2008, 5).

Summary

With Schmidt's media compact concept, it was possible to place the analysis of the media network *Feuerzangenbowle* on a theoretical foundation. This justifies taking into account the context of creation, the producers involved in the process and their interests, in the interpretation of the individual media in this network and evaluating the media on the basis of theory. Dynamics of the exponential dissemination of the *Stoff* could be shown, which show the extent of how deeply *Die Feuerzangenbowle* has engraved itself into the collective memory and how it (unconsciously) transmits values and norms inscribed in the text to this day. Schmidt's thesis that the process results carry the conditions of the respective media system as specific characteristics can be confirmed.

This first became clear in Spoerl's novel. It is an entertainment product of the culture industry, which works with interchangeable elements for rapid marketing:

---

[30] Cf. https://www.filmdienst.de/film/details/24839/die-feuerzangenbowle-1970 (25.08.2019).

with types and clichés from the genre of the folk comedy according to the principle of seriality. In doing so, it serves the expectations of the intended readership, who want to have their ideas and experiences confirmed and their need for an ideal world satisfied. The main character, Dr. Pfeiffer, functions as an identification figure for the "little man". As such, the character conveys the wisdom of the regulars' table, bourgeois-folk sentiments and simple solutions to complicated problems. Complex contexts are not pointed out; they are also not wanted by the readership: "The joke is everything. No great value needs to be placed on the rest" (Kruse 2008, 209), states the editor of the reprint 65 years after the publication of the first edition.

The first film adaptation (1934) by Reimann belongs to the beginnings of the sound film, at a time when the cinema was beginning to establish itself as a mass entertainment institution. It was produced in a very short time in order to lure viewers into the cinemas with humour and a star-studded cast. Nevertheless, beyond its apparent triviality, this film can be said to have a certain literary quality. The tale of a bachelor turns into a love story with the swaggering character of a comedy of mistaken identity. An ironic play within the play arguably serves as a sideswipe at his fellow poet who is in the business of (erotic) literature.

The second film version (1944) by Spoerl, Weiss and Rühmann became a masterpiece in the media network, which advanced to become a film of German popular culture, regardless of the frightening context in which it was made. The Nazi state was able to earn good money from the so-called *H-films*, finance the armaments industry and distract the population from the surrounding death, suffering and deprivation under the hail of bombs. *H-films* were considered very useful during the "holding out" period. The Nazi censors nevertheless demanded certain concessions from the film producers. These could be shown in the character Dr. Brett, however the film as a whole seems to have been purposefully made non-political in order to be considered harmless.

Käutner's third film version (1970) was made in the context of the production of the Lümmel films. Due to the permanent comparison of the audience with the extremely popular 1944 film version, with the unforgettable Erich Ponto as Schnauz, Paul Henckels as Bömmel and with Rühmann, this remake, regardless of its artistic quality and innovations, is condemned by critics and condemned to insignificance in this media network system.

This media network analysis should make us aware of the fact that such a network system is capable of spreading *literarische Stoffe* as well as interests, ideologies, values and norms enormously in a very short time and transmitting them over a long period of time. In this context, this media network already ranks among the historical networks of print and audiovisual storage media. An investigation of the effects of the presence of the film and a digital copy of the first edition on the Internet is still pending.

References

Primary Media

Spoerl, Heinrich: Die Feuerzangenbowle. Eine Lausbüberei in der Kleinstadt. 1.–20. Tsd. Düsseldorf: Mittag-Bücherei, 1933. 21–50 Tsd. Düsseldorf: Droste 1937; 51–80 Tsd. Düsseldorf: Droste, 1938; 141–173 Tsd. Düsseldorf: Droste, 1940; 301–350. Tsd. Düsseldorf: Droste, 1941; Riga 1942 und 1943; 596.–515. Tsd. Düsseldorf: Droste, Feldpostausg. 1943; Düsseldorf: Droste, Wehrmachtsausg. 1944; Düsseldorf: Drei Eulen, 1946; Berlin: Dt. Buch-Gemeinsch. 1957; Die Feuerzangenbowle. Man kann ruhig darüber sprechen. Stuttgarter Hausbücherei, Stuttgart 1959; Gütersloh: Bertelsmann Lesering, 962; Die Feuerzangenbowle. Der Maulkorb. Werke. Klagenfurt: Buch und Welt, 1963; Die Feuerzangenbowle. Der eiserne Besen. Sonderausg. Köln: Lingen, 1963; Ausw. und erl. von Gert Engel, Haase & Søns, København 1967; Bearb. und erl. von A. V. Jurdzin, Den Haag: van Goor Zonen, 2 1968; München: dtv, 1973; Die Feuerzangenbowle. Der Gasmann. Zürich: Neue Schweizer Bibliothek, 1978; Hamburg: Dt. Bücherbund, 1979; Die Feuerzangenbowle. Für d. Theater bearb. von Wilfried Schröder. Berlin: Kiepenheuer, 1980; Die Feuerzangenbowle. Der Gasmann. München: Piper, 1981; dtv Großdruck. München: dtv, 1984; Die Feuerzangenbowle. Roman. München: Heyne, 1990; Ges. Werke. Zürich: Piper, 1990; Die Feuerzangenbowle. Der Gasmann. Augsburg: Weltbild, 1994; Großdruck. Hameln, 1997; Das Beste. Die Feuerzangenbowle. Der Maulkorb. Der Gasmann. Zürich: Piper, 2001; Reprint [1933], mit einem Nachw. von Joseph Anton Kruse. Dusseldorf: Droste, 2008; Digitale free Version der Erstausgabe: https://archive.org/details/DieFeuerzangenbowle/page/n2 (02.03.2019).

Filmography

So ein Flegel (D 1934). Regie: Robert Adolf Stemmle Drehbuch: Hans Reimann, Musik: Harald Böhmelt, Cicero-Film GmbH, Berlin. Video-Kassette, BMG Video, München 1997, https://www.youtube.com/watch?v=ZdbAOxSoFNo (08.03.2019), https://www.dailymotion.com/video/x21bl8h (08.03.2019).

Die Feuerzangenbowle. Ein heiterer Film (D 1944). Regie: Helmut Weiss, Musik: Werner Bochmann, Terra Film, Babelsberg, https://www.youtube.com/watch?v=Bs3WSNwgOnU (09.03.2019), https://www.dailymotion.com/video/x483dpb (09.03.2019) Außerdem: Super-8-mm-Film, Atlas Film, Edition Atlas Super 8, Duisburg ca. 1976; VHS-Video-Kassette, Taurus Video, München 1990; DVD, Kinowelt Home Entertainment, München, Leipzig 1999; DVD, Universum-Film, München 2004; DVD, restaurierte Fassung, Arte 2006; DVD und CD, Kinowelt, Berlin 2007; Blu-Ray-Disc, Kinowelt Home Entertainment, München 2008.

Die Feuerzangenbowle (D 1970). Nach nach dem alten Rezept von Heinrich Spoerl neu angerichtet. Regie: Helmut Käutner, Rialto-Film, Berlin. Video-Kassette, o. O., o. J.

Audiography

Die Feuerzangenbowle von Heinrich Spoerl. Gelesen von Götz Alsmann. Hörbuch, 4 CD, Roof Musik, Bochum 2003.

Heinz Rühmann in Heinrich Spoerls *Die Feuerzangenbowle*. Ein Hörspiel unter Verwendung des berühmten Filmtons. Hörspielregie: Peter Geyer & Florian Fickel, 2 CD, Die Audiothek, Universal Vertrieb, Berlin 2004.
Die Feuerzangenbowle. Hörspielfassung: Bernd Grashoff, Regie: Heinz-Günther Stamm. Mit Hans Clarin, Fritz Rémond, Paul Verhoeven u. a., [Bayrischer Rundfunk 1970], CD, München 2006.

Secondary Literature Before 1945

Gefährliche „Reform"-Pläne. In: Der Kinematograph 28 (1934) 26, 1 f.
So ein Flegel. In: Der Kinematograph 28 (1934) 31, 2.

Secondary Literature After 1945

Amann, Caroline: Paukerfilm, auch Lümmelfilm. 2012. In: Lexikon der Filmbegriffe, http://film-lexikon.uni-kiel.de/index.php?action=lexikon&tag=det&id=7966 (25.08.2019).
Assmann, Aleida: Werden was wir waren. Anmerkungen zur Geschichte der Kindheitsidee. In: Antike und Abendland 24 (1978), 98–124.
Brenner, Sabine: Ich bin kein großer Sprecher, sondern ein stiller Schreiber. Ein Streifzug durch Heinrich Spoerls literarisches Schaffen. In: Kruse, Joseph A. (Hg.): Heinrich Spoerl. Buch-Bühne-Leinwand. Düsseldorf 2004, 11–16.
Curstädt, Lucas: Die Feuerzangenbowle. In: Beyer, Friedemann/Grob, Norbert (Hg.): Der NS-Film. Stuttgart 2018 (Stilepochen des Films; 2), 403–412.
Dorn, Margit: Film. In: Werner Faulstich (Hg.): Grundwissen Medien. Paderborn 2004, 218–239.
Eckert, Wolfgang: Heimat, deine Sterne. Leben und Sterben des Erich Knauf – Biografi e. Berlin 2018.
Görtz, Franz Josef/Sarkowiz, Hans: Heinz Rühmann. 1902–1994. München 2001.
Grimm, Edith/Rieger, Ursula: Das Lehrerbild in H. Spoerls „Die Feuerzangenbowle". In: Grunder, Hans Ulrich (Hg.): „Der Kerl ist verrückt!" Das Bild des Lehrers und der Lehrerin in der Literatur und in der Pädagogik. Zürich 2011, 63–73.
Hickethier, Knut: Film- und Fernsehanalyse. Stuttgart 2007.
Hickethier, Knut: Einführung in die Medienwissenschaft. Stuttgart 2010.
Hoffmann, Kay: Zwischen Tradition und Moderne. Zum NS-Kulturfilm 1933–1945. In: Rother, Rainer/Thomas, Vera (Hg.): Linientreu und populär. Das Ufa-Imperium 1933–1945. Berlin 2017, 82–92.
Horkheimer, Max/Adorno, Theodor W.: Dialektik der Aufklärung. Philosophische Fragmente. Frankfurt a. M. 2002 [EA 1944].
Kiesel, Helmuth: Nachwort: In: George, Stefan: Geheimes Deutschland. Gedichte. München 2018, 121–156.
Kruse, Joseph Anton: Nachwort. In: Spoerl, Heinrich: Die Feuerzangenbowle, Reprint 1933, Düsseldorf 2008, 205–216.
Lowry, Stephen: Pathos und Politik. Ideologie in Spielfilmen des Nationalsozialismus. Tübingen 1991 (Medien in Forschung + Unterricht; 31). Zugl.: Bremen, Univ., Diss., 1990.
Mailänder, Elissa: Ich fl ieg auf dich! Frauen, Krieg und Flieger. In: Rother, Rainer/Thomas, Vera (Hg.): Linientreu und populär. Das Ufa-Imperium 1933–1945. Berlin 2017, 105–119.
Mehlinger, Claudia/Ruppert, René: Vorwort. In: Dies/Dies. (Hg.): Helmut Käutner. München 2008 (Film-Konzepte; 11), 3–4.

Nusser, Peter: Trivialliteratur. Stuttgart 1991 (Sammlung Metzler; 262).
Ohmann, Oliver: Heinz Rühmann und „Die Feuerzangenbowle". Die Geschichte eines Filmklassikers. Leipzig 2010.
Püschel, Almuth: Namen, die in keinem Abspann stehen. Zwangsarbeit bei der Ufa von 1940 bis 1945. In: Rother, Rainer/Thomas, Vera (Hg.): Linientreu und populär. Das Ufa-Imperium 1933–1945. Berlin 2017, 161–173.
Pflaum, Hans Günther: Große und kleine Freiheiten. In: Mehlinger, Claudia (Hg.): Helmut Käutner. München 2008 (Film-Konzepte; 11), 5–23.
Plaß, Robert: Das Verhalten und Verhältnisse. Die kaberettistische Perspektive im filmischen Werk Helmut Käutners. In: Mehlinger, Claudia (Hg.): Helmut Käutner. München 2008 (Film-Konzepte; 11), 47–57.
Richter, Dieter: Hexen, kleine Teufel, Schwererziehbare. Zur Kulturgeschichte des ‚bösen Kindes'. In: Deutsches Jugendinstitut (Hg.): Was für Kinder. Aufwachsen in Deutschland. Ein Handbuch. München 1993, 195–205, auch unter: http://docplayer.org/22907722-Hexen-kleine-teufel-schwererziehbare.html, 1–15 (11.03.2019).
Rother, Rainer: Die Ufa 1933. Dokumente und Kommentare. In: Rother, Rainer/Thomas, Vera (Hg.): Linientreu und populär. Das Ufa-Imperium 1933–1945. Berlin 2017, 11–29.
Sallhoff, Daniel (2017) Carmen Nebel stoppt Abwärtstrend bei den Älteren, Die „Feuerzangenbowle" ist erfolgreicher, http://www.quotenmeter.de/n/97993/carmen-nebel-stoppt-abwaertstrend-bei-den-aelteren-die-feuerzangenbowle-ist-erfolgreicher (24.08.2019).
Schmidt, Siegfried J./Zurstiege, Guido: Orientierung Kommunikationswissenschaft. Was sie kann, was sie will. Hamburg 2000.
Schmidt, Siegfried J.: Der Medienkompaktbegriff. In: Münker, Stefan/Roesler, Alexander (Hg.): Was ist ein Medium? Frankfurt a. M. 2008, 144–157.
Schwarz, Falk: Ein Regisseur verabschiedet sich. 2014. In: filmportal.de, https://www.filmportal.de/film/die-feuerzangenbowle_5821b22324d046ca959695544f0e3ebb (24.08.2019).
Straßner, Erich: Schwank. Stuttgart 1978.
Urwand, Ben: Der Pakt. Hollywoods Geschäfte mit Hitler. Darmstadt 2017.
Vitz, Georg: Heinrich Spoerl und Düsseldorf – biografische und literarische Spuren. In: Kruse, Joseph A. (Hg.): Heinrich Spoerl. Buch-Bühne-Leinwand. Düsseldorf 2004, 17–26.
Winkler, Willi: Der Finsterling. 1992, https://www.zeit.de/1992/46/der-finsterling/komplettansicht (03.03.2019).
Witte, Karsten: Lachende Erben, Toller Tag. Filmkomödie im Dritten Reich. Berlin 1995.

Crime and the Scandalous on the Big Screen

Emotionalisation Between Sexuality, Generational Conflict, and Discourse on Power

The *Steglitzer Schülertragödie* as a Media Network

Marlene Antonia Illies

Introduction

In the early morning of June 28, 1927, Günther Scheller, a high school student, shoots 18-year-old chef apprentice Hans Stephan and then himself in his parents' flat. His classmate Paul Krantz, who is present at the time of the crime, is arrested on suspicion of complicity – he spends the next eight months at a remand facility. There are two reasons for suspicion against Krantz: on the one hand, the murder weapon belongs to him, on the other hand, two suicide notes from the night before the crime survived, which were jointly written by Krantz and Scheller. In them they reveal the plan of a suicide killing four: Günther wants to shoot Hans, Paul then Günther, then his sister Hilde and finally himself.[1] Behind this project are a sleepless night with high alcohol consumption and a complicated relationship structure. The prehistory as well as the exact course of the (suicide) murder are difficult to reconstruct, even if this was intensively attempted through witness interviews by the police as well as in the trial against Paul Krantz. What is certain: Günther declared Hans, with whom he was once friends as his archenemy. Hilde and Hans are lovers. Paul is in love with Hilde and the two of them became closer on the night of June 26–27, 1927. Hilde welcomes Hans on June 27, 1927, at her parents' flat, who are out of town, and is surprised by Günther and Paul. She hides Hans, but Paul learns

---

[1] The farewell letters of Paul Krantz and Günther Scheller, written on the night of 27 June 1927, can be found in Sack 2016, 134.

M. A. Illies (✉)
Faculty of Linguistics and Literary Studies, German Studies, Bielefeld University, Bielefeld, Germany
e-mail: marlene.illies@uni-bielefeld.de

that he is there. Hilde asks Paul not to tell her brother, but at some point, during the night Günther does find out. On the morning of June 28, 1927, Günther discovers Hans in his parents' bedroom and shoots him.

Some certainties as well as different versions of and speculations about the incident spread quickly – the Berlin morning papers already reported on it. For the bourgeois society of the Weimar Republic, this constellation of facts and conjectures offered all the aspects of a scandal: (student) (suicide) murder, homosexuality, a "vicious" girl who not only lets her boyfriend spend the night, but also consorts with several men, and based on this, the question: Is this how our youth is? The first and for a long time most prominent medium for the dissemination of this story was the daily press, but it was to be followed by other institutions and medial parties. This article aims to clarify whether and to what extent a) one can speak of a media network in this respect and b) this was received by children and/or young people. Following the question, the underlying understanding of media networks will first be clarified and theoretically substantiated. Subsequently, the press coverage and its reception will be presented, meetings and political confrontations with the process will be reported on, the literary system of references as well as the cinematic adaptations of the *Stoff* will be traced, and at the end the overlapping points with a further contemporary media network – Peter Martin Lampel's *Revolte im Erziehungshaus* – will be shown.

The *Steglitzer Schülertragödie* as a Media Network?

Initially, it should be explained why the *Stoff* at hand – the core element of a media network[2] – is referred to here as the *Steglitzer Schülertragödie*. A similar turn of phrase can already be found in the *B. Z. am Mittag* on June 28, 1927, in the headline *Schüler-Tragödie in Steglitz. Ein Neunzehnjähriger erschießt seinen Freund und sich* (cf. Sack 2016, 123). In the evening edition of the *Deutsche Zeitung* of the same day, the same phrase appears: *Großstadtjugend und ihr Ende. Schülertragödie in Steglitz* (cf. ibid., 236). It is not possible to say for certain where the *Steglitzer* was first placed before the *Schülertragödie*, but this designation became established in the press and continues to shape the research literature on the subject to this day, which is why the *Stoff* is named in this particular way here as well. Nevertheless, the wrong conclusions to which this designation can lead are immediately revealed: there is no obvious connection between the criminal case and the institution of school. Paul Krantz, Günther and Hilde Scheller were still pupils, and in later paratexts it is explained that Krantz – a proletarian child who received a free place at an upper secondary school – had problems settling into the bourgeois milieu of the higher school; moreover, Paul Krantz and Günther Scheller had already been skipping school for several days at the time of the crime. There are no more

---

[2] Cf. in this volume the introduction, chapter *Spectrum of media networks*.

connections. The rapid designation as a *Schülertragödie* is an early reference to a literary genre system that was known and used to develop and interpret the events, as will be explained below.

Can a criminal case be or become a media network? Kurwinkel (2017) describes a media network as a "system consisting of individual media that has emerged from an *original text*" (ibid., 15). The original text is not necessarily characterized as fictional, as in Maiwald (2010),[3] but rather with a broad concept of text according to Nöth (2000):

> In its broadest definition, the concept of text encompasses a verbal, non-verbal, visual, and auditory communication that is directed from a sender to a receiver by means of a code. Accordingly, not only spoken, and written discourses, but also films, theatre performances, ceremonies, ballet performances, happenings, circus acts, pictures or pieces of music are texts. (Ibid., 392; quoted from Kurwinkel 2017, 15)

This broad concept of text covers all (media) post processing of the *Steglitzer Schülertragödie*: the first reports in the newspapers, the entire coverage of the trial, the films, and books in which the incident was processed, as well as the motions by politicians that were submitted to the Reichstag, for example, with reference to the case. Nevertheless, this textual term does not yet cover the actual incident. Therefore, I propose to understand the *Steglitzer Schülertragödie* as a transmedial phenomenon. Rajewsky (2002) describes transmediality as

> the occurrence of the same Stoff or the implementation of a certain aesthetic or a certain type of discourse in different media, without the assumption of a contact-giving original medium being important or possible here or becoming relevant for the constitution of meaning of the respective media product. (Ibid., 12f.)

As an example, she mentions parody as a genre or discourse type that was developed in the literary medium, but whose rules are not specific to the medium, which is why it can be implemented in both literature and film, for example, using the means inherent to the respective medium (cf. ibid., 13). In the case of the *Steglitzer Schülertragödie*, too, the public discourse shows numerous transmedial references; particularly striking here is the generational conflict with reference to the effects of the caesura of the First World War (see below). That it itself grows into a transmedial phenomenon will be shown in the following remarks.

Kurwinkel points out that the original text and the individual media are "in intra- and/or intermedial relationships among and with each other" (Kurwinkel 2017, 15). According to Rajewsky, intermediality refers to the "totality of all phenomena that cross media boundaries" (Rajewsky 2002, 12), from which intramediality is to be distinguished "as a term to designate those phenomena [...] that [...] exist *within* [emphasis in the original] a medium, i.e. with which a crossing of media boundaries is not accompanied" (ibid.). An example would be the references of literary texts to

---

[3] Maiwald (2010) defines media networks as "systemically planned aggregates of media offers on one and the same fictional *Stoff*, which enable not only reception but also interaction behaviour. Thus, media networks form fictional-aesthetic zones of experience and consumption" (ibid., 140).

a specific single text (ibid.). In relation to the *Steglitzer Schülertragödie, interme*dial references in different spaces of action are particularly noticeable.

In contrast to other definitions of the term *media network,* one aspect should be mentioned here that does not apply, or only to a limited extent, to the *Steglitzer Schülertragödie.* Consequently, Maiwald (2010) demands of a media network, "that it does not simply arise randomly as a juxtaposition of different media offers but is generated in a planned manner at the social-systemic level, that is, by media organizations and institutions" (ibid., 139). In fact, the *Steglitzer Schülertragödie* was definitely adapted in a planned way by media organizations and institutions – the generation of the *Stoff* in a (spontaneous) action preceded these individual acts. They can be described as individual since they actually emerge "as a juxtaposition of different media offers" – only the term "random" is to be denied here. The widespread exploitation of the *Steglitzer Schülertragödie* is related to the social, societal, and cultural issues of its time and its high connectivity for different disciplines. This example suggests that media networks can arise unplanned and by chance. Although the individual actors and institutions still need a planned action to use the *Stoff,* they can nevertheless have been inspired independently of each other. The high popularity of a *Stoff* unmistakably contributes to its intensive further distribution and processing. Following on from this, it is also worth mentioning Möbius (2013), who characterises media networks and also crossmediality as marketing strategies that "[are] production and product-oriented, it is a coupling of different types of media for commercial reasons" (Möbius 2013, 225). It is precisely these marketing strategies that can be observed in the *Steglitzer Schülertragödie,* with the caveat that they were not collaboratively planned by the institutions but used spontaneously. The multiple marketing of the discourse topics around the *Stoff* literally offered itself to various institutions.

With Siegfried J. Schmidt's terminology of media as a compact concept (2008),[4] the social actors and institutions of the observed media network can be focused on.[5] With their specific means of communication and technical variations, the press and film ensured the timely dissemination and processing of the *Stoff*. The newspaper can be described as the primary medium of public discourse; the film industry also reacted directly (as can be seen in advertisements and announcements) but was only able to bring its own adaptations to market with a time lag in 1929. At the level of discourse, state institutions – most presently the judiciary – and private organizations – production companies and newspaper publishers – encountered each other in alternating agency roles of production, distribution, reception, and post processing as a "self-organizing interaction" (Schmidt 2008, 145). Unlike the planned modern media networks on which most definitions of the term are based, the actors and institutions were only in contact with each other in isolated instances; the network emerged spontaneously. This interaction of "many components in the context of their spheres of action and in interaction with other social subsystems, such as

---

[4] Cf. the introduction in this volume, section *Media Networks: Theoretical Frameworks.*
[5] The following explanations and usage of terms follow Schmidt (2008), 144 f.

economy, art, politics or education" (Josting 2013, 235) will be considered here with a focus on different subsystems. Schmidt's extension of media as a compact concept to include the concept of emotions (Schmidt 2014, 134–147) also becomes relevant here, showing the interdependency of emotions and media. The consciousness of the participating roles is "a dynamic process structure" in which four folders or "attractors" are involved – "cognition, emotion, morality (normative orientation) and empraxis (assessment of practical relevance to life)" (Schmidt 2005, 18).

If one breaks down the *Steglitzer Schülertragödie* on this basis, the following statements can be made: There is a cross-media dissemination of a *Stoff* which represents a transmedial phenomenon and which – following Nöth's broad concept of text – is shaped as a text in different spaces of action. The reference character of the individual media to the *Stoff* is explicit – the *Steglitzer Schülertragödie* is at the very centre of public discourse – but the mutual reference to each other is extremely different.

The Press as a Medium of Documentation and Emotionalisation

The media perception and thus the narration of the *Steglitzer Schülertragödie* already began on the morning of the crime. Heidi Sack (2016), who has worked through the reporting in detail, shows that the vast majority of both local and national newspapers reported on the incident on the same day (cf. ibid., 123). The press spread information as well as rumours and assumptions. As late as June 28, 1927, alternative versions of the motive for the murder were circulated: violent quarrel between Günther and Hans or jealousy on the part of the presumably homosexual Günther (ibid., 139). When on 30 June 1927 news broke that the murder weapon belonged to Paul Krantz, the headlines changed and were directed against him as the suspect (cf. ibid., 140). However, the murder case was quickly overshadowed by the intimate details of the witness interrogations, and the focus of press coverage shifted to the (sexual) lives of the youths (ibid., 238).

The trial opened on February 9, 1928, and lasted 12 days.[6] On February 20, 1928, Krantz was sentenced to three weeks in prison for possession of the murder weapon (which had already been served with the pre-trial detention); he was acquitted on all other charges. This trial is to be understood as part of the *Steglitzer Schülertragödie*, the reporting of which first turned the incident into a journalistic and then quickly into a transmedial phenomenon. Public interest – fueled by the coverage – was massive, reflected in the attempts of how many people tried to attend the trial, for which

---

[6] The trial was originally scheduled to last only two days, but it ended up taking 50 hours of trial time, spread over two weeks, caused by an increasing number of witnesses and expert witnesses called, as well as a brief interruption of the proceedings (cf. Sack 2016, 144).

tickets were sold. It turned into a show trial, thus becoming a public event, and becoming more and more similar to the theatre.

The trial is presented to the newspaper readers in written and visual[7] form, turning them into observers of the trial and giving them the feeling of being there. In the various descriptions, dramatic and cinematic means of staging are noticeable: the events of the trial are written down as in a theatre script or screenplay, the sensational character is heightened, and the emotional participation of the reader is incited. Some lines seem like stage directions, such as the commentary on Hilde Scheller's appearance when she is called to the witness stand: "[t]he girl, 16 years old, is fully developed physically, her pretty but inexpressive face shows no movement" (Krantz schildert die Mordnacht 1928) – or the atmosphere in the courtroom: "[u]nder breathless tension of the auditorium, the court announces the following decision after a few minutes of consultation" (Verhandlung wegen Totschlag 1928, 1). Journalists themselves frequently drew theatrical comparisons, allusions to Wedekind's children's tragedy *Frühlings Erwachen* (1891) were particularly popular.[8] The drama tells the story of several adolescents who, in the course of their puberty and the sexual curiosity that comes with it, are confronted with the problems of psychological instability and social intolerance on the part of adults. The play premiered at the Berliner Kammerspiele on November 20, 1906 and had been a regular feature on Berlin playbills ever since. The implicit criticism of sexual morality in the Wilhelminian Empire encouraged comparisons, but even more obviously the characters Moritz, a fifteen-year-old schoolboy who commits suicide, and Wendla, a fourteen-year-old sexually active girl.

The intimate details of the lives of those involved, which were revealed during the hearings and disseminated via the press, aroused the voyeurism of readers and at the same time led to massive criticism. It was suspected that the reports on the behaviour of the defendant, the state witness Hilde Scheller as well as the witness Elinor Ratti[9] would have negative effects on the "morality" of the youth. The daily press was accessible to persons of all ages and – especially in this case – was also consumed by young people. It was again the press that commented critically on the reception by young people, for example the *Germania* of February 26, 1928:

> The press has a responsibility to the essential. It is capitalist abuse when such delicate things are printed in blocking print and in bold type to spur on the course of the lunchtime papers. I was told in Steglitz that half editions were given away to minors. The apprentices

---

[7] Drawings, caricatures, photographs.

[8] Two plays were actually produced: Edgard Walsemann's *Die Schülertragödie* was performed in Hamburg in March 1928, and *Der Kindergarten* by Sylvia von Harden, who was among those attending the trial, was completed during the proceedings, and premiered at a Berlin theatre during the current season (cf. Sack 2016, 175 f.).

[9] Also *Ellinor* Ratti – the spellings differ. Ratti was present on the evening before the crime and on the morning of the crime. According to her own statement, she and Krantz kissed the previous evening, while Günther Scheller had temporarily disappeared and Hilde Scheller was alone in a room with Hans Stephan. Ratti, however, left the apartment afterwards, slept at her parents, and came by in the morning to pick up Hilde Scheller for school. When the shots were fired, she was talking to Hilde in the hallway (cf. Sack 2016, 133 and 138).

devoured the report which had just been pulled out of the press. [...] The flood of erotic sensations that has now been reaching even the last village and the last youth in our own country for over a week is unforgivable. Such publicity is a disaster. No state can permit it. (Sonnenschein 1928, 5)

This reception is what makes the media network around the *Steglitzer Schülertragödie* a de facto (also) youth literary one; it was made possible by a medium that was uncensored in its distribution and accessible to all ages. However, it did not stop at pure reception, young people began to participate, they became, in the sense of Möbius (2013), co-producers, produsers (cf. ibid., 226), within the framework of contemporary media possibilities, i.e. above all through letters to the editor, which were also printed in a wide variety of newspapers.[10]

Transmedial Extensions of the *Stoff*: Sexuality, Generational Conflict

Both the desire of young people to participate in this discourse and the actual publication of such letters cannot be surprising: The so-called Krantz trial had become the trigger for a debate whose subject was *youth*. More than the legal disputes, the soul life of these young people, who were interpreted and portrayed as prototypical of the contemporary young generation, was of interest. The focal points of discussion were the plight of today's youth, the role of adults, and adolescent sexuality, the latter strongly focussing on Hilde Scheller, whose contact with men in the trial was expanded well beyond what was necessary and made known to the public through often verbatim reporting.[11] The view of the older generation led to strong reactions from younger readers, ranging from approval to outright rejection (cf. Siemens 2007, 274). The youth under discussion saw themselves as the subject of adult debates "in which their age group was either over-idealized or pathologized in a generalizing way" (Sack 2016, 432 f.). The phenomenon was not new; rather, it reflected a general discourse theme of the Weimar Republic: the generational conflict. The youth of the Weimar Republic grew up – in many cases without fathers – under the bleak conditions of the postwar years, moreover in a time of rapid social and technological change. Mommsen describes the growing tension between the worlds of experience of the young and the old, which prevented "the skills of the fathers from being passed on directly to the sons; they proved increasingly worthless in the face of changing job descriptions and educational requirements."

---

[10] After the verdict was pronounced, Hilde Scheller and Paul Krantz also contributed their share to these remarks. Scheller, who was largely cast in a bad light by the press, asked Karl Kraus, the editor of the *Fackel*, for a rebuttal, which the latter published in June 1928 with the article *Für Hilde Scheller* (Kraus 1928). Krantz expressed his views in a serial under the title *Mein Prozess von Paul Krantz,* which appeared in the *Welt am Abend* from February 24 to March 2, 1928 (cf. among others Krantz 1928).

[11] On these points, also see Siemens 2007, 273 f.

(Mommsen 1985, 53) Young people separated from the family earlier, there was a pronounced overrepresentation of younger people, especially in urban centres like Berlin, youth lacked role models. It was the hope of the nation, a myth, and at the same time it was eyed critically and without understanding. Youth became – as Mommsen states – the "leitmotif" of Weimar culture, and the relationship to the younger generation dominated the humanities, literature, education, and above all psychology (cf. ibid., 62). It only became clear time and again that the rift "which had opened up between the Republic and its youth and which was basically a legacy of the First World War" (ibid.) could no longer be bridged. The *Steglitzer Schülertragödie* provided another occasion to explore this topic in depth; many letters from young people dealt with it or at least referred to it. The newspapers recognized the participation desired by young people as a means of increasing circulation – in addition to numerous letters from readers, there was also a deliberate attempt to collect statements, for example from the *Welt am Abend,* which, in a politically correct manner, had "a young employee collect voices of the proletarian and also the bourgeois high school youth" (Stimmen der Jugend 1928).

The views expressed, in this as in many other contributions,[12] split into exactly the same categories as those of the elders: "One side stressed that the case was typical of the youth of the time and their sexual life, the other emphasized that it was an inglorious exception that should not be generalized under any circumstances." (Sack 2016, 320)[13] Broken down according to Nöth's concept of text, young people address recipients of all ages as senders by means of the code of a "letter to the editor" and call on them to take note of their opinions, thus as producers becoming actors within and co-creators of the media network.

Discourse on Power in the Media Network

In the daily press as well as in the research literature, there are numerous references to public meetings called in the context of the *Steglitzer Schülertragödie,* often with renowned speakers, and not infrequently expert witnesses of the trial appeared.[14] Young people were also among the organisers; for example, on February 20, 1928, a meeting of the *Sozialistischer Schülerbund Berlin* took place, "for which invitations had previously been distributed to all Berlin schools, also calling for a statement on the Krantz trial" (Sack 2016, 321). This mobilization was not welcomed by the conservative political forces and, after heated debate in the Prussian parliament – with reference to the low age of the participants and their high numbers – was banned for the future (cf. ibid., 321).

---

[12] See, among others, *Schiffbruch der Eltern* (1928); *Wir Jungen und der Primaner Krantz* (1928); Kämpfer (1928); *16 Oberprimanerinnen lehnen ab* (1928); Stumpfe (1928), and many others.

[13] Cf. also Siemens 2007, 275.

[14] Among them were the philosopher and educator Eduard Spranger, the pedagogue Siegfried Bernfeld, the sexologist Magnus Hirschfeld and the grammar school teacher, lecturer and SPD politician Hildegard Wegscheider.

Assemblies of this kind are also to be understood as part of the media network and, in Nöth's sense, as a text: The youth organizers, as transmitters, invited the youth recipients to participate in the discourse by means of the code of the distributed invitations. At the same time, this meeting also exemplifies the produser behaviour of the young people and their factual reception of the *Stoff*. The subsequent discourse in the state parliament is to be evaluated in a similar way: the politicians (senders) decide on a ban (code) of such meetings, which affects the young people (recipients).[15]

This was not the only political measure triggered by the *Steglitzer Schülertragödie*. The public interest, especially from young people, led to various (attempts at) media censorship measures. Thus, the caricatures and especially the photographs from the courtroom were criticized.[16] The latter were a relative[17] novelty in trial reporting: the photo reporter Erich Salomon, unknown at the time, managed to get into the courtroom with a camera hidden in a pocket or his hat and took pictures during the trial[18] (cf. Siemens 2007, 282 f.). The photographs were published in various daily newspapers and additionally illustrated the trial, suggesting to the recipients an even greater proximity to the events and putting the protagonists even more in the public eye. The publication of Salomon's photographs led to a letter from the Anwaltskammer[19] calling on the Minister of Justice to ban court photography, but to no avail, as the transcript of a press conference held on September 26, 1928, attests. The Minister of Justice in office at that time, Erich Koch-Weser, even

> laconically stated that everything was filmed nowadays; it was not necessary to make an exception for the court. Moreover, someone who had committed a sensational crime had become a person of contemporary history who had to accept the dissemination of his image. (Siemens 2007, 286f.)

Salomon's photographs led to a further emotionalization of the trial coverage. Their production was clandestine and, like their publication, a scandal in itself. The pictures provided insights into the courtroom, which was closed to most recipients, allowed them to form a picture – in the truest sense of the word – of those acting in

---

[15] Mention must also be made of the event organized by the *Deutsche Liga für Menschenrechte, Der Krantz-Prozess und seine Lehren,* which took place on 29 February 1928 in the Spichern Halls in Berlin. Here, among other things, trial reporters, trial experts and writers discussed with numerous young people the introduction of coeducation, the expansion of competences of the juvenile court, the publicity of court proceedings and the generational conflict. A controversy between the editor Rudolf Olden and the then 24-year-old Hans Litten ended in Olden's call to the youth to take action themselves. Litten then founded the youth counselling centre "Jugend hilft Jugend" together with his friend Max Fürst, which existed until 1930 (cf. Sack 2016, 322 ff.).

[16] For a detailed discussion of photographic pictorial coverage of crime in the Berlin tabloid press from the Weimar Republic to 1945, see Tribukait 2017, 204–296; esp. on the *Steglitzer Schülertragödie* 232–247.

[17] Weise states in this regard: "The legend that there were no photos from German courtrooms before Salomon must be contradicted. As early as 1922, Robert Sennecke had taken photos in the Rathenau murder trial [...]." (Weise 2004, 28 f.)

[18] In fact, Ernst Salomon's career as a photojournalist began with the Krantz trial, cf. Weise 2004.

[19] Roughly translated: lawyers' association.

it, and thus once again fueled interpretations of the personalities of those depicted and general speculation. Through their photographic images, the young people who had involuntarily become persons of contemporary history became even more familiar media figures; the recipients believed they were even closer to them, knew them even better, and were even more entitled to pass judgment on them.

Not only the photos of Krantz, Scheller and Ratti, but also the reporting as a whole illuminated and discussed them from all sides and also came under criticism for this. The general "sensationalism" and again the "moral endangerment" of the youth was considered alarming, especially because of the many sexual details that were asked in the trial and published by the press. Politicians took this case as a welcome opportunity to discuss the already frequently discussed topic of "press and justice" and to make proposals for reform, also because of the criticism of justice present in the reports (cf. Sack 2016, 207 f.). Only two days after the start of the trial, the German Nationalist MP Reinhard Mumm submitted a motion to amend the Reichspressegesetz to include the following wording: "Trial reports that are likely to overstimulate or mislead the sexual feelings of youth are forbidden." (Quoted in Sack 2016, 208 f.) The press itself largely reacted with criticism and defended itself, but the so-called *Lex Krantz* nevertheless had an impact: the Berlin district association of the *Reichsverband der Deutschen Presse* adopted a resolution at its general meeting on February 20, 1928, in which it opposed the exceptional law, but promised that, out of its own "sense of responsibility, counterproductive court reporting" would be excluded in the future (ibid., 214). The effect of this resolution, however, proved to be short-lived in practice (cf. ibid., 217).

The communist city council faction, in turn, introduced a motion in the city parliament "deal[ing] with the failure of the schools to meet the needs of the youth" (Stadtparlament und Krantz-Prozeß 1928). Demands were made for co-education, sex education from the first year of school onwards, and appropriate courses for all teachers. Although these demands were not followed word-to-word, the trial influenced Berlin school policy in the context of the already broad debate on educational policy. The Prussian Minister of Education felt compelled to make school reform commitments, and in Berlin there was a "resolution on the innovation of the school system through the joint education of the sexes" (Hansen-Schaberg 1999, 289). The coeducational classes introduced as a result were able to last in Berlin until the National Socialist takeover (cf. ibid., 288).

The public discourses thus went far beyond trial reporting, reaching political institutions and leading to resolutions and legislation that in turn affected young people.

The Student Drama as a Literary Reference System

Lange notes that the *Steglitzer Schülertragödie* was understood as symptomatic of a "crisis of youth" that "had until then occurred mainly in novels and drama" (Lange 1985, 412). Reference is made here to the genre system of student dramas, novels, and narratives, which had been increasingly published in Germany since Wedekind's *Frühlings Erwachen* (cf. Noob 1998, 103 f.) and experienced a new rise in popularity in the Weimar Republic.[20] As already explained, there was no clear line of reference between the criminal case and the school, but the naming of it precisely as a *Schülertragödie,* as well as Günther Scheller's suicide, had the effect of a system reference in public perception; intermedial references to individual literary texts can be found in numerous articles on the event. Wedekind's *Frühlings Erwachen* was often mentioned in the same breath as the *Steglitzer Schülertragödie.* Another Wedekind reference was to his character Lulu from *Der Erdgeist* (1895) and its sequel *Die Büchse der Pandora* (1902), who, as the epitome of a permissive girl, invited constant comparison with Hilde Scheller; Rutschky states succinctly, "Hildegard Scheller was Lulu" (Rutschky 1993, 32). The Wedekind comparisons are so present and manifest that they are even consciously contradicted, for example by Manfred Georg: "Nothing is further away and would be more wrong than to see in the young girl Hilde a depraved creature that has sprung from a Wedekindian comedy [sic!]." (Georg 1928) From the variety of further references,[21] two will be presented as a means of example:

A reader's letter in the *Berliner Lokal Anzeiger* refers to Max Halbe's tragedy *Jugend* (1893). The writer concludes from the familiarity of the subject:

> So [...] what are we actually to gain from the broad treatment of the sexual problem at the court, except the sad realization of how unfortunately young people today can be indiscriminate and unrestrained in their libido, and how unfortunately today some parents make it easy for themselves with the upbringing and supervision of their growing children. (Grabein 1928)

The raising of his literary-historical example, which is supposed to testify to knowledge of the problem, is not taken further by him. For the fact that Halbe's drama also raises the problems and questions – which are still unanswered and preferably kept quiet – ultimately shows that little has happened within 35 years since its publication. As a solution to the problem, he only advises the older ones to be a good friend and support the younger ones, the younger ones to seek advice from the older ones and "not to seek enlightenment secretly from their peers in dark nooks and crannies" (ibid.). There would be no other solution to the problem, after all, one could not let "adolescents already marry each other or unite in free love" (ibid.). He concludes with a moral appeal in a militaristic tone: "[More] discipline, more self-discipline, and for the rest enough of this confusing talk." (Ibid.)

The article *Primaner Krantz und seine Generation,* which appeared in the *8-Uhr-Abendblatt* the day before the trial began, on February 8, 1928, chooses a more current example and uses it to try to explain "this youth": *Das Tagebuch des Schülers*

---

[20] On this aspect, see also the contributions by Petra Josting on *Traumulus* and Gabriele von Glasenapp on *Mädchen in Uniform* in this volume.

[21] These include *Die Leiden des jungen Werther* (Goethe, 1774), *Die Ehre* (Sudermann, 1890), *Nicht der Mörder, der Ermordete ist schuldig* (Werfel, 1920), *Tor zur Welt* (Thiess, 1926), *Krankheit der Jugend* (Bruckner, 1924). Lange also suspects that Bruckner's contemporary play *Die Verbrecher* (first performed in 1928) may have been inspired by the trial (cf. Lange 1985, 423 f.).

Kostja Rjabzew by the Russian author Nikolai Ognyev, published in 1928 in a German translation by Maria Einstein. In this "[highly interesting] document of the Russian school" one finds

> carefully and honestly recorded all the problems of a young heart, but where they become quite personal, where, for example, as sexual ones, they often grow over the diarist's head, the solution of the private conflict nevertheless results for him through its orientation to general events. (Georg 1928)

Krantz and the other people involved in the affair – who would come from a "sinking and sociologically barren" middle class – would, on the other hand, not be able to step back from their personal conflicts in this way. They had "just come to life" and were not "prepared for puberty [...] tearing up all the soil of the soul" (ibid.). Also, the article *Jugend von heute. Ihre Geheimnisse und die Hilflosigkeit der Alten*, which appeared in *Welt am Abend* on February 18, 1928, draws on Ognyev's novel, through which one "[at least] learned something of Russian youth [...]" (Ali Baba 1928). In comparison, "[of] German youth [...] unfortunately nothing is known". The Krantz trial, too, "as a result of its purely criminalistic direction, brought none of this to the public" (ibid.). Literary texts are thus used to understand "this youth", to gain insight into it – the success of this endeavor remains to be seen.

The *Steglitzer Schülertragödie* was also itself processed in and into literary texts. Well-known adaptations include Paul Krantz's novel *Die Mietskaserne*, which is a kind of literarized autobiography of the author and appeared in 1931 as the first publication under his pseudonym Ernst Erich Noth. In this novel, a friend of the protagonist also commits suicide, but the circumstances do not recall the familiar narratives of the night of the crime. The writer Clara Viebig, who took part in the trial, adapted the *Stoff* in the opening of her novel *Insel der Hoffnung* (1933). Rutschky also lists various retrospective narratives of the incident by contemporaries (cf. Rutschky 1993, 23–27), although these were not published until after 1945 and thus transcend the period focused on here. The intermedial references to a genre system as well as to individual texts and the literary treatments of the *Stoff* form a further core element in the perception of the *Steglitzer Schülertragödie* as a transmedial phenomenon.

The *Steglitzer Schülertragödie* in the Film Media System

A *Stoff* as popular as the *Steglitzer Schülertragödie* also left its mark on the film industry, and in four different forms: it was discussed, it was banned, it was used for commercial purposes, and it was produced.

The *Lex Krantz* played a prominent role in the discussion. This was gratefully received by the film press, as it allowed the frequent vituperations and alleged dangers of cinema to be taken up, as well as the *Schmutz- and Schunddebatte* that the film industry had been exposed to since its inception and which was to accompany it constantly until the end of the Weimar Republic.[22] The Krantz trial offered a welcome point of contact on the subject of *film and young people,* for – as the subtitle of an article of the same name put it – *[t]he cinema is uninvolved.* In the "Krantz circle [there was] much more interest in the theatre [...] than in the cinema, which was only occasionally attended" (Film und Jugendliche 1928). Incidentally, it was not clear why film, of all things, should corrupt young people:

> They are allowed to go to the theatre and revues. And if they are working-class children who live in the same room with adults, in the same bed in a backyard apartment, then there is no need to worry about their sexual education. So, no sensible person will afterwards declare the press, the revues, the books as the sole culprits. (Ibid.)

The relativisation goes much further. One participant in the debate uses the trial as an opportunity to call for a lowering of the age for the protection of minors:

> The cinema is forbidden to young people up to the age of 18 if they do not want to be with 8–9-year-old tots. They, the youths, are not allowed to go to the cinema, but they can get literature that excites their senses for 20 pf. at any newspaper cart. They are not allowed to go to the cinema, but at the fairgrounds they can romp about with extremely questionable performances. They are not allowed to go to the cinema, but in public places they can send their often still pure souls to the devil. They are not allowed to go to the cinema, but they can go to the revues, where nudity or semi-nudity is the trump card. They are not allowed to go to the cinema because, because yes because? [...] The process is over, a sad chapter has been closed, and in the final analysis, what remains for our industry is the demand: get rid of the youth protection age of 18! (Templiner 1929)

The *Steglitzer Schülertragödie* quickly aroused the interest of production companies, as it offered a quasi-finished *Stoff* that captivated the audience, whose script seemed to have already been written and which could easily be turned into a successful sensational film. No less than three film companies wooed Hilde Scheller and Paul Krantz to either star in their planned films or write the screenplay (cf. Sack 2016, 174). The companies advertised their plans early on. The first to react was SM[23] -Filmproduktion, which announced a film adaptation in the *Film-Kurier* on February 10, 1928 – one day after the start of the trial:

> Furthermore, preparations are in full swing for a film that deals with a Schülertragödie based on an idea by Otto K. Ronde, and whose title is "Entgleiste Jugend", the confession of a high school student. The subject, currently topical, deals with the story of the present generation, which at the most dangerous age, through concealment and suppression in education, derails and wreaks disasters. (Von kommenden Filmen 1928)

That this film directly alludes to the *Steglitzer Schülertragödie* is shown by the advertisement (Fig. 1) with the text:

> Germany's lender! We're making the latest film of our time: Entgleiste Jugend. The confession of a high school student. A Schülertragödie of our time [...]. The great trial has begun and is being read by millions of people in the daily newspapers. (Anzeige *Entgleiste Jugend* 1928)

---

[22] Cf. also the contribution by Tobias Kurwinkel in this volume.

[23] Divergent: Essem film production.

Fig. 1 Ad for *Entgleiste Jugend*, from: *Film-Kurier* 10 (1928) 36 of 10.02., 4

Fig. 2 Ad for *Primanerliebe* (D 1927a), from: *Film-Kurier* 10 (1928) 41 from 16.02., Beibl. 2

Ultimately, this film was never produced, perhaps a consequence of the general criticism of the production companies' immediate interest, which culminated in the industry organizations' self-commitment to "neither screen nor distribute such a film" (Sack 2016, 174 f.), reported in the newspapers on February 17.

The topical theme was used for reprises of two older films, which were re-advertised with reference to the *Schülertragödie*. The Strauß-Film-Gesellschaft again advertised a film from the previous year – *Primanerliebe* (R. Robert Land, D 1927a). An advertisement in the *Film-Kurier* of February 16, 1928 literally states (Fig. 2):

> The Schülertragödie. At the center of a highly topical trial are the aberrations and hardships, torments, and desires of the maturing school youth. The burning interest of the whole world today is directed towards the secrets in which these young people live. Deep insight into

these processes is provided by the great school film by Strauß-Film Ges., starring Grete Mosheim, Wolfgang Zilzer and Fritz Kortner, which has been recognized as artistically valuable by the Central Institute for Education and Instruction, *Primanerliebe*. (Anzeige Primanerliebe, 1928)

The film had its premiere on June 3, 1927 – before the night of the crime – and was the ideal film to accompany the events of the day. It is about a primary school student who is in love with his teacher's daughter. He comes into conflict with the teacher and is expelled from school. He wants to kill himself, but then surprises an opera singer who gets too close to his beloved. With the weapon intended for his suicide, he injures the rival. The circumstances of the crime are clarified before the examining magistrate, and the adolescent is allowed to return to his school (cf. Primanerliebe 1927a, b). A schoolboy, an unhappy love affair, a weapon, a planned suicide, a courtroom – the thematic complex fitted in perfectly with the current discourse and was immediately integrated into the media network of the *Schülertragödie*.[24]

Germania Film-Verleih acted similarly, advertising the film version of Wedekind's *Frühlings Erwachen* from 1923 (directed by Luise and Jakob Fleck) with the new title *Frühreife Jugend* and the advertising text "Eine zeitgemäße Schülertragödie" (Anzeige Frühreife Jugend 1928). As early as May 1928, moreover, Terra announced the remake of the drama *Frühlings Erwachen*, numerously cited in the *Steglitzer Schülertragödie* (cf. Die Pressebüros melden 1928), and on November 14, 1929, it finally screened at the Stella-Palast in Berlin (cf. Frühlingserwachen 1929).[25] The film, directed by Richard Oswald, was awarded the rating of *künstlerisch* by the state review boards and was banned for young people (cf. Crăciun 2018, 142 f.). The youth ban also affected most of the cinematic exploitations of the *Steglitzer Schülertragödie*, which were made despite the above-mentioned resolution.

In the preface to his detailed handbook on German film of 1929, Gandert states that a whole series of films – sometimes serious, sometimes with speculative intent – "took on youth and its hardships" (Gandert 1993, XIV f.). In addition to *Frühlings Erwachen*, he names the titles *Die Halbwüchsigen, Zwischen vierzehn und siebzehn, Verirrte Jugend, Geschminkte Jugend, Revolution der Jugend, Jugendsünden,* and *Jugendtragödie* (cf. ibid.). As an example, let us first consider the film *Geschminkte Jugend* (1929), which was directed by Carl Boese and premiered on April 17, 1929, at the Titania-Palast in Berlin-Steglitz (!). It is about the schoolgirl Olga Hiller, who is often left alone by her pleasure-seeking mother. Following her mother's example,

---

[24] Director Robert Land tackled a similar subject in 1930 with the film *Boykott (Primanerehre)*, based on the novella of the same name (*Boykott*) by Arnold Ulitz from the same year. Here, too, the ad text emphasizes the reference to contemporary issues: "Ulitz's book, which quickly became famous, was the basis for this film, which gives a mirror image of our days, a faithful chronicle of the events that so often scream out at us from the newspapers. Primaner X committed suicide. Why? An "unhappy love affair"? Injured sense of honor? In „Boykott" the soul is illuminated, seriously, ravishingly" (Advertisement Boykott 1930).

[25] With *Die Büchse der Pandora* (R. G. W. Pabst, D 1929), an adaptation of *Erdgeist* and *Die Büchse der Pandora* also reached the big screen with great success in the same year.

she puts on make-up and parties with her friends, sometimes in her parent free flat, sometimes on a car trip to the countryside. On the latter, she refuses the pushy Arthur, who nevertheless won't let go of her. In a fierce conflict between Arthur and a better mannered suitor, a fatal shot is fired. In court, a dedicated defense lawyer seeks to blame society, with success: the defendant, the moral admirer, is acquitted.

Even the surname of the protagonist, Hiller[26] (played by Toni van Eyck), refers as a kind of Kofferwort[27] to Hilde Scheller, whose person (or rather her portrayal in the press) is clearly quoted on here. Olga sometimes kisses one, sometimes the other, and withdraws when Arthur (Kurt von Wolowski) gets too close to her. Olga Hiller's swearing-in can also be seen as a direct quotation of Hilde Scheller's swearing-in. The seventh and final part of the film, set in court, opens with it, and although the scene is entirely silent,[28] almost an entire minute is devoted to it (01.27.37–01.28.25). Scheller's swearing-in was a widely covered topic, both legally and journalistically. The scene is all the more significant because Hiller's role afterwards is only that of a spectator; the questioning of the witness is not shown. The plot leads directly into the closing arguments of the prosecutor and the defense attorney. The swearing in therefore makes no sense in the dynamics of the plot, even contradicts it, and thus gains all the more significance in relation back to the trial. Hardly any reviewer[29] has refrained from referencing the "Krantz-Scheller catastrophe" (Lange 2006, 105). As an example, the opening of Maraun's ironic critique in the *Deutsche Allgemeine Zeitung* is cited here, which takes up the audience reaction:

> The Steglitz girls have won all along the line. They bravely took sides. When, at the end of the film, the prosecutor cries, "Look at this youth, how it comes to school made up – discipline and fear must be reacquainted with it!" the fathers applaud, but the girls hiss him down with a hearty malice. "Fear stands separating young and old, you must do away with it, made-up lips are only an externality and do not touch the attitude of the soul!" says pathetically the defender, and the fathers whistle and hiss. But the girls give an enthusiastic bravo of hands and are disappointed when Tony van Eyck, the heroine, sadly wipes the make-up from her beautiful, already very feminine, suffering face in close-up. Some of them respond with a stunned contradiction. The Steglitz girls are in favor of make-up. (Maraun 1929)

A popular cultural behaviour is portrayed here: The youth ignore the pompous plot and adores the female star, thus enjoying the film in an anarchic way, while the older ones – quite deliberately grouped together as "fathers" – are outraged (probably also by this). The actual target group, whose reactions are described here, was officially excluded by a youth ban, which was critically commented by the trade press:

---

[26] Olga is the first name in the French version that I was able to view in person. On filmportal.de the first name is given as "Margot".

[27] Also, box word or portemanteau word. An artificial word created from at least two morphologically overlapping words that merge to form a new term in terms of content.

[28] It is a silent film, but at this point text panels are also omitted.

[29] Manfred Georg, reporter of the Krantz trial for the *8-Uhr-Abendblatt*, was also among them (cf. Georg 1928).

A film is being made, with young people, for young people. The subject: youth in make-up. Youth of today, where the little bit of make-up is no more than an imitation of adult conventions. That's what's shown. The backgrounds, class issues, sexual confusion can only be hinted at. Because the German film censors are watching. They make sure that no film appears that takes a stand on the present, on life. And so, in short order, they ban the youth film, which at least insipidly hinted at what it meant, for young people. Characteristic of the mentality of the examiners is a title: "Thus the main blame lies with those who have failed the young, with the educators." This may well be printed, spoken, written, but not projected. Film censors don't know guilty educators; or rather, only in the fooled, approved final version of the title: "So the blame for this lies as much with the young as with the educators, who have not set a good example for the young or paid enough attention to their lives and doings." Uff -. (F[eld] 1929)[30]

The plots of the other films mentioned by Gandert reveal sometimes more, sometimes less clear references to the *Steglitzer Schülertragödie*. What they have in common is that they all deal with young people. In many of them we find a Paul Krantz or a Hilde Scheller. These two became *characters* through the trial coverage that (involuntarily) shaped this media network. Hengst (2014) defines *character* as a "nexus, the instance that connects various media, objects, and services to each other and to their (human) addressees." (Hengst 2014, 153) For the public, Krantz and Scheller were familiar protagonists who were used accordingly in media treatments. Krantz formed the more mobile imaginary platform: a spiritualized, melancholic youth from a proletarian milieu who makes friends with socially superior people. Krantz *characters* can be found in *Geschminkte Jugend, Jugendsünden*, and *Jugendtragödie*. "The" Hilde Scheller is an easy-going girl who parties and flirts with various men. Visually, she is committed to the haircut and fashions of the *New Woman*, making her easy to identify in cinematic treatments. Manifestations of this *character* appear in *Geschminkte Jugend, Die Halbwüchsigen*, and *Verirrte Jugend*.

Furthermore, motifs are cited such as murder and suicide *(Geschminkte Jugend, Jugendsünden, Verirrte Jugend, Zwischen vierzehn und siebzehn, Jugendtragödie)*, police and justice *(Geschminkte Jugend, Die Halbwüchsigen, Verirrte Jugend, Jugendtragödie)*, the sibling-friend relationship between the Schellers and Krantz *(Jugendsünden, Die Halbwüchsigen)*. In addition to these references, the perception of the films as quoting the *Steglitzer Schülertragödie* is evident in the film reviews. The verdict on *Die Halbwüchsigen* is: "A filmed courtroom report. Very clearly visible is the youth tragedy that took place in a Berlin suburb last year" (Die Halbwüchsigen 1929b). On *Verirrte Jugend*: "This a quarter of a century after 'Frühlings Erwachen'. No sober courtroom report nowadays gives such problems so superficially, so clueless of the inner ongoings. Reminiscences of the Krantz-Scheller trial, etc." (Jacobi 1929; quoted in Gandert 1993, 689). On *Jugendtragödie*:

> The films about tragedies of youth are multiplying. In this "tragic" film there is love and murder, one welfare child kills another – out of jealousy. A little Krantz trial conjuncture mixed with Manasse Friedländer, the necessary dose of welfare conjuncture, that's how the making of this film came about. (Jugendtragödie 1929; quoted from Gandert 1993, 332)

---

[30] In a correction of October 15, 1929, the defused title criticized here (Act 7, Title 12) was banned altogether (cf. Gandert 1993, 244).

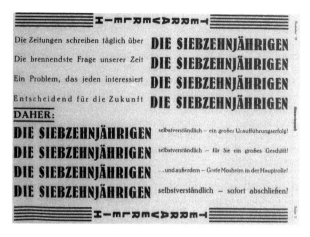

Fig. 3 Advertisement for *Die Siebzehnjährigen* (D 1929a), from: *Der Kinematograph* 23 (1929) 10 from 13.01., 3

The reviews already hint at a dynamic that can be observed in all films: the *Stoffe* are mixed, different themes are taken up and combined with each other. For this purpose, we will conclude by looking at another film adaptation of a play, *Die Siebzehnjährigen* (1929b) after Max Dreyer (1904), from the Terra production.[31] This drama, too, is not filmed in close proximity to the trial by chance, but is linked to the *Steglitzer Schülertragödie* and modernized. As in the original, father and son love the same woman, but in the film the son does not kill himself but shoots his father, who is only slightly injured. The son ends up in juvenile court, where he is acquitted and reconciled (cf. Die Siebzehnjährigen 1929b). The advertisement still notes rather inconspicuously: "The newspapers write daily about the most burning question of our time." (Anzeige Die Siebzehnjährigen, 1929; Fig. 3) The film review reflects on the convergence of different sources of inspiration:

> In the age of Schülertragödien, the subject, taken from a play by Max Dreyer, gains in topicality. One might object that the problem of young people is different today than it was when the play was written. But it is precisely this provincial business that this film will do by not pursuing hypermodern lines of thought, by doing without "Revolten im Erziehungshaus", although of course it cannot do without dramatic-tragic conflict. (Die Siebzehnjährigen, 1929b)

Here three *Stoffe* are united in one critique: the *Steglitzer Schülertragödie*, Dreyer's *Die Siebzehnjährigen* and Lampel's *Revolte im Erziehungshaus*.

---

[31] Terra also filmed *Frühlings Erwachen* (1929), in both movies Grete Mosheim played the leading role, who also appeared as a teenage heroine in *Primanerliebe* (1927a).

Revolte im Erziehungshaus

In his enumeration of youth films, Gandert also mentions the film version of Peter Martin Lampel's *Revolte im Erziehungshaus* by Georg Asagaroff, a film that "made it to sad fame insofar as it was banned four times and in the end was only released in a mutilated form" (Gandert 1993, XV). Already in the films mentioned above, intermingling of the themes of the *Revolte* and the *Steglitzer Schülertragödie* can be seen frequently, both in terms of content and in the critiques. However, the lines of connection between the *Stoffe* extend even further. Lampel's volume of reports *Jungen in Not* (1928), in which he documents his experiences as an intern in youth welfare, discusses the Krantz trial and its effects at the educators' conference. Starting with a discourse about revolts in various homes, the director comes to speak about the "sexual question":

> A delicate thing: the sexual question. But I do not think it is that important. We have again heard with indignation from the Krantz trial that certain circles are trying, with forced meanness, to bring about things, even to artificially expose them, which are not in themselves the focus of interest. From such mudslinging, as Mr. Sanitätsrat Hirschfeld has expressed himself under the guise of an expert, we quite decidedly refrain. (Lampel 1928, 50)

After a thematic excursion on coeducation, which is rejected by the director, he returns to the subject:

> Consider how the moral core German being is stirring. Nineteen female Lyceum students have written a public letter declaring that the German female youth does not wish to be lumped together with Fräulein Hilde. That must convince me. (Ibid., 50 f.)

Lampel, incidentally a proponent of co-education, provides in his report a coincidental testimony to the preoccupation of educators with the *Steglitzer Schülertragödie*. The director also refers to one of the published reactions of young people, which in turn proves that these too were received by the public and became visible (and discussed) treatments of the *Stoff*. The text referred to here is probably the letter *16 Oberprimanerinnen lehnen ab* (1928), printed in the *Berliner Lokal-Anzeiger* on February 21, 1928. The reference to this letter of protest again emphasizes the explosive nature of the *Stoff* in the pedagogical context and Hilde Scheller's strong presence as a *character.* An entire class of girls felt so pressured that they felt compelled to distance themselves from this media figure – a reaction welcomed by pedagogues, as Lampel shows. He finds this single reference so important that he also integrates it into the play. Here he puts the same words into the mouth of the priest, only the "Schmutzereien" become "Schweinereien" (cf. Lampel 1929, 69). In his *Erinnerungen,* Noth reports on the premiere of the play, to which the editor and publicist Walter Hammer took him and at which he was also introduced to Lampel himself (cf. Noth 2009, 178). The play had made him

> naturally [...] extraordinarily [interested], and my sympathy belonged all the more to the prisoners driven to despair, as I had met numerous young inmates in the remand prison who had confided in me the most hair-raising things about events in these institutions; unfortunately, there was not the slightest reason to doubt the truth of their statements. (Noth 2009, 177f.)

Thus, a delicate literary and personal line of connection can indeed be observed between the *Steglitzer Schülertragödie* and the *Revolte*. The fact that both *Stoffe* shaped the youth discourses and youth films of their time in terms of their topicality and relevance could be made clear in the selected film reviews.

Concluding Remarks

The *Steglitzer Schülertragödie* is a media network that is fraying at the edges. It could be thought about for a long time because the incident became a catchword, a symbol. The public debates about *youth* were always thought of in context. The transitions to the comparable media network *Revolte im Erziehungshaus* are fluid; here, too, the incidents were real and only literarised in retrospect; they were about influencing legislatures, about real action, about politics and general (media) attention. It is no coincidence that old *Stoffe* such as Dreyer's *Die Siebzehnjährige* and Wedekind's *Frühlings Erwachen* were re-filmed and re-performed during this period; it is also no coincidence that the *Steglitzer Schülertragödie* itself has repeatedly shone through, even after 1945.[32] It has appeal, both as a story of suffering and in its potential for discussion, and manifests itself as a transmedial phenomenon.

It is crucial to note here that the last and best-known film adaptation, Achim von Borries' *Was nützt die Liebe in Gedanken* (2004),[33] finally also reflects in its production and distribution (approximately) what this *Stoff*, this incident, has always been. *Was nützt die Liebe in Gedanken* is a youth film, was produced and advertised as such. Here, according to the FSK release, at least the youth from 16 years of age are allowed to see what has always been their subject – themselves and their questions. Romanticized and historically transfigured, in soft tones and forms, yet with the same explosiveness and intensity that this *Stoff* has always had. What has changed are the technical dispositives. Lange (2006) reports on the "large media accompanying effort", which included, among other things, a "website of the distributor", on which both the historical events and the "message" of the film were disseminated, which was aimed at the target group "youth" and addressed them directly: "Do you believe in love? In the one big one? Or in the many, smaller ones?" (Ibid., 96 f.) The Internet presence described by Lange no longer exists in this form today, but the content,[34] possibilities and functions he describes show how the approach to the subject has changed.

---

[32] For detailed information on the processing after 1945, see Lange 2006.

[33] Based on Arno Meyer zu Küingdorf's novel *Der Selbstmörder-Klub* (1999), which promises to "historically faithfully re[tell] the *Steglitzer Schülertragödie* and document[s] the novelistic account with long quotations from the interrogation transcripts at the trial" (Lange 2006, 112).

[34] Today's official website for the film at X Distribution, https://www.x-verleih.de/filme/was-nuetzt-die-liebe-in-gedanken (18.02.2020), offers only general information about the film. The address given by Lange in 2006, http://liebe-in-gedanken.de/filminhalt, no longer exists.

In the limited possibilities of a media network at the end of the 1920s due to the availability of only a few forms of media compared to today, the *Steglitzer Schülertragödie* proved to have a great scope – involuntarily, as a fad, as hitting the zeitgeist. Its *Stoff* can be seen as a transmedial phenomenon that is closely intertwined with other transmedial phenomena. It is a media network received by young people. The narration of the actual criminal case was certainly not primarily intended for the youth – however, they consumed these narrations, since the case concerned them and was accessible to them in the uncensored medium of the press, they even participated in it. The media network was not planned, conceived, designed, at least not in the first instance. In the development of public interest, the obvious scandalousness of the topic, producers from various sides took up the *Stoff* and transformed it according to their needs and goals. This was true for film production companies, which advertised their films with motifs and catchwords from the *Steglitzer Schülertragödie*, as well as for the experts in the trial, who appeared as experts at meetings and marketed their individual trial experiences and findings. Behind the *Steglitzer Schülertragödie* was not a company, an author, a brand that wanted to make a profit; there were many individuals who took advantage of its scandalous character and public interest.

References

Primary Literature

Lampel, Peter Martin: Jungen in Not. Berichte von Fürsorgezöglingen. Berlin: J. M. Spaeth, 1928.
Lampel, Peter Martin: Revolte im Erziehungshaus. Schauspiel der Gegenwart in drei Akten. Berlin: Gustav Kiepenheuer, 1929.
Meyer zu Küingdorf, Arno: Der Selbstmörder-Klub. Leipzig: Reclam 1999.
Meyer zu Küingdorf, Arno: Was nützt die Liebe in Gedanken. Roman. Berlin: Aufbau, 2004.
Noth, Ernst Erich: Die Mietskaserne [1931]. Stuttgart: Huber Frauenfeld, 1982.
Noth, Ernst Erich: Erinnerungen eines Deutschen. Die deutschen Jahre [1971]. Frankfurt a. M.: glotzi, 2009.
Viebig, Clara: Insel der Hoffnung. Roman. Stuttgart [u. a.]: Deutsche Verlagsanstalt, 1933.
Wedekind, Frank: Frühlings Erwachen. Eine Kindertragödie. Zürich: Schmidt, 1891.
Wedekind, Frank: Der Erdgeist. Eine Tragödie. Paris: Langen, 1895.
Wedekind, Frank: Die Büchse der Pandora. Tragödie in drei Aufzügen. Berlin: Cassirer, 1902.

Filmography

Die Halbwüchsigen [Stummfilm] (D 1929a). Regie: Edmund Heuberger, Drehbuch: Edmund Heuberger/Eduard Andrés, Musik: Anton Pointner, Aco-Film GmbH.
Die Siebzehnjährigen [Stummfilm] (D 1929a). Regie: Georg Asagaroff, Drehbuch: Fritz Falkenstein, Musik: Guiseppe Becce, Terra-Film AG.

Frühlings Erwachen [Stummfilm] (D 1923). Regie: Jakob Fleck/Luise Fleck, Drehbuch: Jakob Fleck/Adolf Lantz, Wiener Kunstfilm. Nach dem Bühnenstück *Frühlings Erwachen* von Frank Wedekind (EV: 1891, EA: 1906). 1928 vertrieben unter dem Titel *Frühreife Jugend*.
Frühlings Erwachen. Eine Kindertragödie [Stummfilm] (D 1929). Regie: Richard Oswald, Drehbuch: Friedrich Raff/Herbert Rosenfeld, Musik: Walter Ulfig, Hegewald-Film. Nach dem Bühnenstück *Frühlings Erwachen* von Frank Wedekind (EV: 1891, EA: 1906).
Geschminkte Jugend [Stummfilm] (D 1929). Regie: Carl Boese, Drehbuch: Martin Land, Musik: Hansheinrich Dransmann, Carl Boese-Film GmbH/National-Film Verleih und Vertriebs-GmbH.
Jugendsünden [Stummfilm] (D 1929). Regie: Carl Heinz Wolff, Drehbuch: Toni Dathe/Carl Heinz Wolff, Aco-Film GmbH.
Jugendtragödie [Stummfilm] (D 1929). Regie: Adolf Trotz, Drehbuch: Adolf Lantz, Musik: Werner Schmidt-Boelcke, Luna-Film.
Primanerliebe [Stummfilm] (D 1927a). Regie: Robert Land, Drehbuch: Alfred Schirokauer/Curt Wesse, Musik: Walter Ulfig, Domo-Strauß-Film GmbH.
Revolte im Erziehungshaus [Stummfilm] (D 1929). Regie: Georg Asagaroff, Drehbuch: W. Solsky/ Herbert Rosenfeld, Musik: Werner Schmidt-Boelcke, Grohnert-Film-Produktion. Nach dem gleichnamigen Bühnenstück von Peter Martin Lampel (EA: 1928, EV: 1929).
Revolution der Jugend (Jugend am Scheideweg) [Tonfilm] (D/A 1929). Regie: Conrad Wiene, Drehbuch: Conrad Wiene/Ludwig Netz, Musik: Bernhard Homola, Gold-Film GmbH.
Verirrte Jugend [Stummfilm] (D 1929). Regie: Richard Löwenbein, Drehbuch: O. Karpfen/C. C. Fürst, Musik: Beer, Mondial-Film GmbH.
Was nützt die Liebe in Gedanken [Drama] (D 2004). Regie: Achim von Borries, Drehbuch: Achim von Borries/Hendrik Handloegten, Musik: Thomas Feiner/Ingo L. Frenzel/Uwe Kirbach, X Filme Creative Pool. Nach dem Roman *Der Selbstmörder-Klub* von Arno Meyer zu Küingdorf (1999).
Zwischen vierzehn und siebzehn [Stummfilm] (D 1929). Regie: E. W. Emo, Drehbuch: Herbert Nossen/Franz Roswalt, Musik: Pasquale Perris, Strauß-Film-Fabrikation und Verleih GmbH.

Secondary Literature Before 1945

16 Oberprimanerinnen lehnen ab... In: Berliner Lokal-Anzeiger 46 (1928) vom 21.02. (MA), 1. Beibl., 1.
Ali Baba: Jugend von heute. Ihre Geheimnisse und die Hilflosigkeit der Alten. In: Die Welt am Abend 6 (1928) 42 vom 18.02., 2. Beibl., 1.
Anzeige Boykott in: Der Kinematograph 24 (1930) 202 vom 30.08., 6.
Anzeige Die Siebzehnjährigen: Der Kinematograph 23 (1929) 10 vom 13.01., 3.
Anzeige Entgleiste Jugend: Film-Kurier 10 (1928) 36 vom 10.02., 4.
Anzeige Frühreife Jugend: Film-Kurier 10 (1928) 70 vom 21.03., Beibl., 2.
Anzeige Primanerliebe: Film-Kurier 10 (1928) 41 vom 16.02.1928, Beibl., 2.
Die Halbwüchsigen. In: Der Kinematograph 23 (1929b) 224 vom 25.09., 3.
Die Pressebüros melden: Neuverfilmung von „Frühlingserwachen". In: Film-Kurier 10 (1928) 118 vom 18.05., 3.
Die Siebzehnjährigen. In: Der Kinematograph 23 (1929b) 8 vom 10.01., 2.
Film und Jugendliche. In: Film-Kurier 10 (1928) 38 vom 13.02., 2.
„Frühlingserwachen". In: Der Kinematograph vom 09.11.1929, Nr. 263, 8.
Georg, Manfred: Primaner Krantz und seine Generation. Qual der Jugend. In: 8-Uhr-Abendblatt (1928) vom 08.02.
Grabein, Paul: Alte und Junge. In: Berliner Lokal-Anzeiger (1928) (MA) vom 21.02., 1. Beibl., 1.
Kämpfer, H.: Ihr und wir. In: Berliner Lokal-Anzeiger 46 (1928) vom 17.02., (MA).
Krantz, Paul: Mein Prozess von Paul Krantz. In: Die Welt am Abend 6 (1928) 47 vom 24.02., 1–2.
Krantz schildert die Mordnacht. Zusammenstöße zwischen Verteidiger und Staatsanwalt. In: Die Welt am Abend 6 (1928) 35 vom 10.02., 3.

Kraus, Karl: Für Hildegard Scheller. In: Die Fackel 3 (1928) 781–786, 40–46.
Maraun: „Geschminkte Jugend". In: Deutsche Allgemeine Zeitung (1929) 183 vom 20.04., Beibl., 1.
Primanerliebe (Filmkritik). In: Der Kinematograph 21 (1927b) 1059 vom 05.06., 22.
Schiffbruch der Eltern. In: Die Welt am Abend 6 (1928) 36 vom 11.02., 2. Beil., 1.
Sonnenschein, Carl: Der Prozeß der Schüler. In: Germania (1928) vom 26.02., (MA), 5–6.
Stadtparlament und Krantz-Prozeß. In: Die Welt am Abend 6 (1928) 44 vom 21.02., 3.
Stimmen der Jugend. Zwei Klassen kommen zum Wort. In: Die Welt am Abend 6 (1928) 42 vom 18.02., 2. Beil., 1.
Stumpfe, Ortrud: Nach der äußeren die innere Freiheit. In: Berliner Lokal-Anzeiger 46 (1928) vom 21.02., (MA), 1. Beibl., 1–2.
Templiner, A.: Die Steglitzer Schüler-Tragödie, der Krantz-Prozeß, das Kino und das Jugendschutzalter von 18 Jahren. In: Film-Kurier 10 (1929) 49 vom 25.02., 2. Beibl., 1.
Verhandlung wegen Totschlags. In: Die Welt am Abend 6 (1928) 38 vom 14.02., 1–2.
Von kommenden Filmen. Entgleiste Jugend. In: Film-Kurier 10 (1928) 36 vom 10.02., 3.
Wir Jungen und der Primaner Krantz. In: 8-Uhr-Abendblatt (1928) vom 14.02.

Secondary Literature After 1945

Crăciun, Ioana: „Möchte doch wissen, wozu wir eigentlich auf der Welt sind!" Zur Inszenierung von Kindheit und Jugend im Weimarer Kino. In: Herbst-Meßlinger, Karin/Rother, Rainer/Schaefer, Annika (Hg.): Weimarer Kino neu gesehen. Berlin 2018, 120–143.
Gandert, Gero: Der Film der Weimarer Republik 1929. Ein Handbuch der zeitgenössischen Kritik. Berlin [u. a.] 1993.
Hansen-Schaberg, Inge: Jugendgemäßheit und Lebendigkeit in der Schule. Eine „Schülertragödie" und ihre Auswirkungen auf bildungspolitische Entscheidungen in der Weimarer Republik. In: PÄD Form 27/12 (1999) 4, 285–292.
Hengst, Heinz: Am Anfang war die Biene Maja. Medienverbund und Japanisierung der kommerziellen Kultur. In: Weiss, Harald (Hg.): 100 Jahre Biene Maja – Vom Kinderbuch zum Kassenschlager. Heidelberg 2014 (Studien zur europäischen Kinder- und Jugendliteratur; 1), 143–165.
Josting, Petra: Medienkonvergenz im aktuellen Handlungssystem der Kinder- und Jugendliteratur. In: Weinkauff, Gina/Dettmar, Ute/Möbius, Thomas/Tomkowiak, Ingrid (Hg.): Kinder- und Jugendliteratur in Medienkontexten. Adaption – Hybridisierung – Intermedialität – Konvergenz. Frankfurt a. M. [u. a.] 2013 (Kinder- und Jugendkultur, -literatur und -medien. Theorie – Geschichte – Didaktik; 89), 233–252.
Kurwinkel, Tobias: Zur Theorie von Medien- und Produktverbänden und ihren Sammlungen am Beispiel von Bibi und Tina. In: kjl&m 69 (2017) 2, 14–21.
Lange, Thomas: Der „Steglitzer Schülermordprozess" 1928. In: Thomas Koebner/Janz, Rolf-Peter/Trommler, Frank (Hg.): „Mit uns zieht die neue Zeit". Der Mythos Jugend. Frankfurt a. M. 1985, 412–437.
Lange, Thomas: „Moderne Jugend" als Medienereignis (1928–2004). In: Geschichte in Wissenschaft und Unterricht 57 (2006) 2, 96–113.
Maiwald, Klaus: Literatur im Medienverbund unterrichten. In: Rösch, Heidi (Hg.): Literarische Bildung im kompetenzorientierten Deutschunterricht. Freiburg/Br. 2010, 135–156.
Möbius, Thomas: Adaption – Verbund – Produsage. Implikationen des Begriffs Medienkonvergenz. In: Weinkauff, Gina/Dettmar, Ute/Möbius, Thomas/Tomkowiak, Ingrid (Hg.): Kinder- und Jugendliteratur in Medienkontexten. Adaption – Hybridisierung – Intermedialität – Konvergenz. Frankfurt a. M. [u. a.] 2013 (Kinder- und Jugendkultur, -literatur und -medien. Theorie – Geschichte – Didaktik; 89), 219–232.

Mommsen, Hans: Generationskonflikt und Jugendrevolte in der Weimarer Republik. In: Koebner, Thomas/Janz, Rolf-Peter/Trommler, Frank (Hg.): "Mit uns zieht die neue Zeit". Der Mythos Jugend. Frankfurt a.M. 1985, 50–67.

Noob, Joachim: Der Schülerselbstmord in der deutschen Literatur um die Jahrhundertwende. Heidelberg 1998 (Beiträge zur neueren Literaturgeschichte; Folge 3; 158). Zugl.: Oregon/ USA, Univ., Diss., 1997.

Rajewsky, Irina O.: Intermedialität. Tübingen [u. a.] 2002.

Rutschky, Katharina: Jugend als literarische Inszenierung. In: Mitteilungen des Instituts für Jugendbuchforschung (1993) 2, 16–33.

Sack, Heidi: Moderne Jugend vor Gericht. Sensationsprozesse, „Sexualtragödien" und die Krise der Jugend in der Weimarer Republik. Bielefeld 2016. Zugl.: Düsseldorf, Univ., Diss., 2015.

Schmidt, Siegfried J.: Medien und Emotionen: Zum Management von Bezugnahmen. In: Ders. (Hg.): Medien und Emotionen. Münster 2005 (Media, 11), 11–39.

Schmidt, Siegfried J. (2008): Der Medienkompaktbegriff. In: Münker, Stefan/Roesler (Hg.): Was ist ein Medium? Frankfurt a. M. 2008, 144–157.

Schmidt, Siegfried J.: Kulturbeschreibung – Beschreibungskultur. Umrisse einer Prozessorientierten Kulturtheorie. Velbrück 2014.

Siemens, Daniel: Metropole und Verbrechen. Die Gerichtsreportage in Berlin, Paris und Chicago 1919–1933. Stuttgart 2007 (Transatlantische Historische Studien; 32).

Tribukait, Maren: Gefährliche Sensationen. Die Visualisierung von Verbrechen in deutschen und amerikanischen Pressefotografien 1928–1938. Göttingen 2017. Zugl.: Bielefeld, Univ., Diss., 2013.

Weise, Bernd: „Ich muß jetzt fort zum Reichstag". Dr. Erich Salomon – Beruf: Photojournalist. In: Frecot, Janos (Hg.): Erich Salomon. „Mit Frack und Linse durch Politik und Gesellschaft". Photographien 1928–1938. München 2004, 27–46.

The Commercial Genre Supersystem of Early Cinema Screen Detectives

On the Media Networks Surrounding Sherlock Holmes, Nick Carter, Stuart Webbs and Joe Deebs

Tobias Kurwinkel

Preliminary Remarks

Peter Hasubek describes Erich Kästner's novel *Emil und die Detektive* as a "climax and a provisional goal" (Hasubek 1974, 32) of the detective narrative for children and young people. Kästner's first novel, written in the context of *Neue Sachlichkeit*, in which both the big city and crime are typical motifs, is characterised by a cinematic narrative style – implements what Alfred Döblin called for in 1913 with the "courage of kinetic imagination" (Döblin 1963, 19) and Bertolt Brecht sought after in 1926 with the "technification of literary production" (Brecht 1967, 156). Thus, the multiple cinema and film comparisons are worth mentioning, as is the integration of rapid scene and perspective changes that characterise the novel's cinematic narrative style (see, among others, Kümmerling-Meibauer 2012, 106).

Three years after the publication of the novel, the film version celebrated its premiere on December 2, 1931 at the Ufa Theater on the Kurfürstendamm in Berlin. The film, for which Erich Kästner, Emmerich Pressburger and Billy Wilder wrote the screenplay and Gerhart Lamprecht directed, is convincing as an illustration of the novel, especially through its portrayal of the characters: what Siegfried Kracauer calls democratisation in *Von Caligari zu Hitler* means the self-empowerment of children and the accompanying emancipation from adults, which Lamprecht effectively stages with cinematic means (cf. Kracauer 1979, 236 f.). *Emil und die Detektive* as a film is – to take up Hasubek's dictum – "the climax and a provisional goal" of a series of early detective films that are the subjects of this article. These films are not *Primarily*, but *Actual Children's and Youth Films*, since their recipients also – and in particular – included children and young adults.

T. Kurwinkel (✉)
Faculty of Humanities, German Studies, University of Duisburg-Essen, Essen, Germany
e-mail: tobias.kurwinkel@uni-due.de

The content-related and aesthetic conventions of the films can be derived from literature: Thus, the pure form of the detective film, as a subgenre of the crime film, tells primarily about the solving of a crime (cf. Alewyn 1998); the gangster film, on the other hand, which is referred to in literature as crime poetry, focuses on the crime. The gangster film, as put by Knut Hickethier, represents "a world below bourgeois society, the world of shadows, where not only gambling, drugs, prostitution, but also robbery and murder are at home" (Hickethier 2005, 19 f.). The thriller, after all, is about preventing a crime; it is dominated by a future-oriented suspense that is directed towards events yet to come. Other sub-genres of the crime film are the court film and the police film.

In the following, I will trace the history of these early detective films using selected examples such as Sherlock Holmes, Nick Carter, Stuart Webbs and Joe Deebs, which form a genre system in the form of media networks. Thus, this article is concerned on the one hand with the diachronic as well as synchronic perspectivation of the networks with their constituent *Medienangebote* as understood by Siegfried J. Schmidt (cf. Schmidt 2008), and on the other hand with the interaction of the media networks and their media texts as and within the genre supersystem.

I understand such media networks [*Commercial Supersystem*] (cf. Kinder 1991) or *Children's Global Multimedia* (cf. Seiter 2000) as "cross-media dissemination of popular cultural *Stoffe*" (Weinkauff 2014, 131), which can be accompanied by a large array of merchandising opportunities as a product network. Basically, two different types of media networks can be distinguished (cf. Kurwinkel 2020; 2017): the starting point of the first, to which the networks discussed below correspond, is an *Originärtext*, which is based on a narrative realised as a novel, film, etc.. This *Originärtext* stands in intra- and/or intermedia relations with further media texts: On an intramedial level, these relationships take place within a medium; on an intermedial level, they cross media boundaries as *media transpositions* and *intermedia references*. Different types of media do not displace each other in such systems; instead, they converge (cf. Jenkins 2006) and coexist, they refer to each other.

I would like to briefly concretise these theoretical remarks with an example: Transferred to *Emil und die Detektive,* the *Originärtext* of the media network is the novel from 1929; the sequel is in intramedial relation to this, which appears in 1935 under the title *Emil und die drei Zwillinge.* In an intermedial relationship, *media transpositions* are the drama, which Kästner arranged in 1930 (cf. Kümmerling-Meibauer 2012, 110), the film by Lamprecht mentioned at the beginning, and the musical from 2001, whose music is by Marc Schubring and whose libretto is by Wolfgang Adenberg.

In the following, I will begin with the media network of Sherlock Holmes and the detective film of the pre-war years (1900–1914), after which I will deal with the series[1] of the war years (1914–1918) and then with the decline of the genre at the

---

[1] The detective films in series dealt with here are series: "The series is characterised by the specific internal structure of the episodes, each of which exhibits cohesiveness, i.e. each episode tells an independent story. The term series is used [...] as a translation of the term *series*" (Klein/Hißnauer 2012, 11).

end of the 1910s (1918–1920). This will be supplemented by remarks on children and young people as recipients of early film and a brief consideration of contemporary debates about *Kinoschund* and trivialisation. Finally, I will discuss the structure of the genre supersystem at the level of the networks and their *Medienangebote*, including the significance of the media networks for the further development of the genre.

Such an account of film and media history can only be exemplary in the present scope, and can only trace and depict individual developments and their lines prototypically.

The Beginnings of the Detective Film: Sherlock Holmes

The birth of detective films can be dated back to 1900; it begins with the analytical, rational private detective from London's fictional No. 221b Baker Street, who first appears in Arthur Conan Doyle's 1887 novel *A Study in Scarlet,* the *Originärtext* of the media network: 13 years later, on April 26, 1900, Arthur W. Marvin released the 35-second silent film *Sherlock Holmes Baffled* for the US production company Biograph for the mutoscope.[2] The content of the film, thought to have been lost[3] before it was found by Michael Pointer in the Library of Congress in 1968,[4] is quickly summarised: A burglar is interrupted by Sherlock Holmes during a theft and escapes the situation by vanishing into thin air. Holmes, dressed in a dressing gown, settles into a chair and lights a cigar (Fig. 1), whereupon the burglar appears out of nowhere. The detective draws a pistol and shoots the intruder, who in turn disappears and reappears a short time later. Holmes attempts to apprehend the thief, but he again turns invisible. The short film ends with Holmes trying to leave the room with the stolen goods, but they are taken from him by the invisible burglar. What remains in the scene is a confused and baffled master detective.

It is difficult to identify this master detective as Sherlock Holmes at first glance, as he wears neither the Deerstalker cap nor the Inverness cloak, those iconic garments with which Sidney E. Paget outfitted the character. Paget first illustrated the master detective for the story *A Bohemian Scandal,* which appeared in *The Strand*

---

[2] The mutoscope is a kind of mechanical flip-book: a large number of photographs are mounted radially on a shaft; as the shaft rotates, the images are briefly stopped one after the other and are thus shown to the viewer for a fraction of a second. The overall impression of these photographs, which follow one another quickly and stand still for a short time, is cinematic, similar to that of the kinetoscope.

[3] Georg Seeßlen declared the film lost as late as 1981 in his famous work *Mord im Kino. Geschichte und Mythologie des Detektiv-Films* as lost, and he still holds to this in the new editions of the work in 1998 and most recently in 2011.

[4] Before me I have the letter dated May 25, 1968, in which Michael Pointer indicates and comments on the finding of the film in the *Library of Congress* to the *Sherlock Holmes Journal*. I thank the *Sherlock Holmes Society of London,* in personam Roger Johnson, for making the document available.

Fig. 1 *Sherlock Holmes Baffled* (1900), https://www.youtube.com/watch?v=KmffCrlgY-c (24.01.2020)

Magazine in July 1891; the cap and coat can be found in the illustrations for *The Boscombe Valley Mystery* three months later.

The outward appearance of the detective in Arthur Marvin's silent film, however, was not unknown to contemporary connoisseurs of the early media network, as it was based on William Gillette's portrayal of the detective in *Sherlock Holmes: A Drama in Four Acts* (cf. Pointer 1975, 31). The popular play, which Gillette co-wrote with Doyle, premiered on Broadway at the Garrick Theatre on November 6, 1899. Both the calabash pipe and the *signature phrase* "Elementary, my dear Watson" originate from this play; they belong – like the cap and overcoat – to the "emblem[s] [...] which to this day, after more than a hundred years, are immediately decoded as [...] a signet of the detective" (Hügel 2003, 157).

James Stuart Blackton, director and producer of the second Holmes film *Adventures of Sherlock Holmes; or, Held for Ransom* (Vitagraph) from 1905 was already familiar with these emblems: His Sherlock Holmes obviously wears the Deerstalker cap. The film, also US-American, starring Gilbert M. Anderson and H. Kyrle Bellew, is based partly in a few scenes on Doyle's second novel *The Sign of the Four* from 1890 (cf. Klinger 1998). Theodore A. Liebler Jr. was responsible for the scenario of the film with a length of 220 m.

Due to their technical limitations, the first two Holmes films, like all silent films of the genre, focus less on analysis and deduction of the main character than on *action elements* and narrative or dramaturgical aspects such as *mystery* and *suspense* (cf. Moody 2003, 228). This is particularly evident in *Sherlock Holmes Baffled*, whose plot is written around the stop trick that Georges Méliès developed in 1896 (cf. Ezra 2000, 15). Here, a shot is taken, the camera is stopped, and an object is removed or added. Afterwards, the recording is continued. When the shot is played back, the object disappears or appears at once (cf. Kurwinkel/Schmerheim 2013, 57).

The early media network of the master detective is characterised by intra- and intermedial references between the *Medienangebote*; the latter particularly constitute the media texts for which Doyle was not responsible as the author. In the case of the film texts, the references are *Systemreferenzen* such as the narrative and dramaturgical aspects described above, which are already present in the *Originärtext* in the form of mystery and suspense, as well as *Einzeltextreferenzen* such as the signets.

These references resulted from economic considerations: Film producers were simply concerned with reaching paying audiences through references to popular *Stoffe* and works. "Plagiarism", writes Pointer in this context:

> was the order of the day in the earliest years of moving pictures. No sooner was an interesting scene or successful comic or dramatic subject issued by one company than all the others dashed off to copy it, and so from the crude beginnings of the peepshow machine and kinematograph up till about 1912 it was the practice of many, though not all, American filmmakers [...] (Pointer 1975)

Detective Movies in Series: Sherlock Holmes, Nat Pinkerton and Especially Nick Carter

Three years after *Adventures of Sherlock Holmes,* the first series formats of the detective film were established with the *Sherlock Holmes-series of* Nordisk Film Kompagni from Denmark, with *Nat Pinkerton* (Eclipse) from Germany and the *Nick Carter* adaptations of the French film company Éclair.

The films before 1914 strive for an internationally comprehensible film language; accordingly, the foreign as well as domestic productions shape the viewing habits of Wilhelmine cinema and, apart from minor national idiosyncrasies, respond to the collective dispositions of a pan-European, if not international audience (cf. Hesse 2003, 11). With these detective films, filmmakers from 1908 onwards adapted serial storytelling, which developed with trivial literature in the nineteenth and early twentieth centuries in various written media: The French journalist Emile Gaboriau was one of the first writers to publish his novels in newspapers from 1863 onwards; the structure and dramaturgy of his stories about the detective Lecoq correspond to the medium: in Gaboriau's work, there is no character without conflict and no sentence without emphasis, yet the intensity of the reader's attention was not allowed to diminish in any episode (cf. Seeßlen 1998, 24).

The success of Sherlock Holmes can also be explained by the *Medienangebote* through which his tales were disseminated: After Doyle had initially tried his hand at an epic large-scale project, he subsequently confined himself mainly to the short story form à la Edgar Allan Poe. It proved ideal for the magazines that were widely distributed in the 1880s.

The detective as a serial hero was born in these magazines, writes Georg Seeßlen, and comes to blossom in the dime novels, as they emerge in the USA (cf. Seeßlen 1998, 25):

> This form of entertainment literature eventually replaced the previously common form of 'colporte novels' in Europe, those extensive stories with never-ending ramifications and variations of the plot, which were brought to the house in weekly deliveries by colporteurs and continued to be spun by the authors as long as the interest of the subscribers continued. (Ibid.)

The structure of the *Medienangebote* in the networks of this period is characterised accordingly by a specific sequence: the stories about the early detectives were first published in newspapers and magazines, then in story collections and novels; at the turn of the century, the dime novels were added, followed by films. There is thus a "close formal and aesthetic interlocking" (Hesse 2003, 11) between the dime novels and the films, which, from an intermedial perspective, manifests itself in *media transpositions*, but especially in various references.

In terms of content, the dime novel detectives were mostly indebted to their great role model Sherlock Holmes; however, an element that is hardly significant for the upscaled detective novel comes into play in their case, which also characterises the first two film examples: Action. The detective is not so much determined by his function in the game of detection alone; he is not a "thinking machine with some quirks" (Seeßlen 1998, 26), but as a hero he is the bearer of dreams and desires projected into him. The most famous of these detectives is Nick Carter, whose first case appeared in the *New York Weekly* magazine in thirteen parts beginning in September 1886 (Fig. 2); since 1906, he celebrated success in Germany as *Amerikas größter Detektiv* in the dime novels of the Dresden Verlagsbuchhandlung A. Eichler. This detective, as Pierre Boileau and Thomas Narcejac put it, inherited from Kit Karson and Buffalo Bill; he embodied the lonely man as a hero in the metropolis of boards and concrete (cf. Boileau/Narcejac 1967, 92 f.).

Victorin-Hippolyte Jasset, the technical director of Éclair at that time, adapted this counter-design to the classic, bourgeois and conservative detective for the screen with Pierre Bressol in the leading role from September 1908. Under the title *Nick Carter – Le Roi des Detectives,* the first season is produced with a total of six self-contained episodes. Two further three-part seasons followed in 1909 with *Les Nouvelles Aventures de Nick Carter* and *Les Merveilleux Exploits de Nick Carter.* Georges Hatot developed the scenarios of the first season mainly by referring to the stories of the *Nick Carter* magazines and dime novels; the episodes, which ranged in length from 185 to 235 m, are not adaptations of individual stories.

Le Guet-Apens, the first episode from September 8, 1908, has the now classic two-part narrative structure: In the first half, the crime is committed; in the second half, the detective solves the very crime. The film opens with the wedding of an emphatically bourgeois doctor; criminals loiter outside the church, following the newlyweds as they make their way home through the streets of Paris. They eventually ambush the doctor and force him to write a ransom note. In the second half of the film, the wife calls in the detective, who succeeds in finding the criminals. At this point, the film shocks with an eerie interlude à la dime novel: the criminals torture their victim by starting a fire under his bare feet. At the last second, Nick Carter comes to the rescue; at the end, the reunited couple, a stereotypical "representation of restored bourgeois happiness" (Hesse 2003, 60), hold each other in their arms.

Fig. 2 Movie poster of the first *Nick Carter episode Le Guet-Apens* (1908b), https://en.wikipedia.org/wiki/File:Nick-Carter-b.jpg (24.01.2020)

The images of Paris are striking in this film; Jasset clearly places the American Nick Carter in the French capital, in the living world of the audience. Jasset shoots the big city scenes predominantly on location, striving for the greatest authenticity possible; accordingly, the images unfold a poetry by themselves in addition to their documentative qualities (cf. Hesse 2003, 57). "The open-air atmosphere of natural decors in the suburb of Montreuil," writes Hans Gerhold,

> spreads during a robbery or a chase that poetic charm found in many sérials [...]. Scenes on the banks of the Seine or the Saint-Martin canal cleverly incorporate barges, automobiles, piers, and bridges as realistic details and backgrounds useful for pictorial composition. (Gerhold 1994, 185)

These images have their origins in the *flânerie* of the *fin de siècle*, in the flâneur's impressions of surface stimuli and sensations, as first described by Poe in December 1840 in *The Man of The Crowd*. They form an essential feature not only of the early detective film; they are equally found in Lamprecht's *Emil und die Detektive* as big-city images, as shots of the railway stations Zoo and Friedrichstraße as well as boulevards and squares like Kurfürstendamm, Motzstraße and Nollendorfplatz. The shots are more than a cinematic representation of the space where the action takes place; they are aspects of detective film's *narrato-aesthetic*.

With the last season *Les Merveilleux Exploits de Nick Carter*, Jasset explicitly integrates references to other *Stoffe*; the title and plot elements of the episode *Nick Carter: Le club des suicidés* from September 20, 1999, for example, represent intermedial references to *The Suicide Club,* a story by Robert Louis Stevenson from 1887. The film, which has only survived in fragments, is about a mysterious circle of men whose members follow archaic rituals and, as a result, have decided to end their lives. The selection of the person to commit suicide is made by a card game: Whoever draws the ace of spades will die. Jasset takes over only this core of the plot: [5] instead of a Bohemian prince and his colonel, who fall into the circle in search of new sensations, in the film it is a journalist who becomes a member of the mysterious club on behalf of his editor-in-chief. Needless to say, he pulls the wrong card: Nick Carter, alerted as in *Le Guet-Apens* by the worried wife, will save him. Jasset's images are, writes Sebastian Hesse, "codifications of those dark, irrational forces of nature as whose antipode the enlightened detective functions" (Hesse 2003, 62).

In 1911, Jasset placed a criminal figure at the centre of a film serial: *Zigomar, roi des voleur* is an adaptation of the 1910 novel of the same name by the Parisian journalist Léon Sazie. Jasset's *Zigomar film* marks the transition in the production history of the Éclair to the feature-length film (Fig. 3): the film has a duration of 51 min, however no continuous plot: rather, it consists of a sequence of three short, equal individual episodes or acts that are somewhat longer than the *Nick Carter episodes*.

With the *Zigomar films*, Jasset creates a new type of detective film in terms of genre typology: the plot no longer focuses solely on the detective, but also on the criminal: the result is a first *genre hybrid* of detective and gangster film. Zigomar, who is at least the equal of the detective – first a police investigator named Paul Broquet, then Nick Carter in *Zigomar contre Nick Carter* (1912) – in the core disciplines of analysis and deduction, becomes the second main character as a master mind. This character is no longer defeated, is not identified as the perpetrator, arrested and brought to punishment; owing to the serial conception of the films, the master mind escapes both at the level of the act and the episode. Moral categories are still confirmed on the first level by the triumphs of the detective, but are suspended on the second level: "The viewer should remain ambivalent," writes Hesse:

> [j]udicial victory by one of the antagonists would put an end to the sérial. Here lies the subversiveness of the Zigomar series: It valorises a morally reprehensible character into a sympathetic figure. Zigomar embodies an alternative value system of immorality that stands on equal footing with the bourgeois one of Nick Carter (Hesse 2003, 63).

According to Hesse, the three Zigomar films – *Zigomar, peau d'anguille* completes the trilogy on March 21, 1913 – represent the final stage in the development of the early detective film: The first stage of his three-stage model describes the detective

---

[5] Hesse refers to *Nick Carter: Le club des suicidés* as the earliest adaptation of Stevenson's short story (cf. Hesse 2003, 60), but is mistaken here: four months earlier, on 3 May 1909, D. W. Griffith's *The Suicide Club* premiered.

Fig. 3 Film poster of the first *Zigomar film* (1911), https://ru.wikipedia.org/wiki/%D0%97%D0%B8%D0%B3%D0%BE%D0%BC%D0%B0%D1%80#/media/%D0%A4%D0%B0%D0%B9%D0%BB:Zigomar.jpg (24.01.2020)

film as an "illustration of the abstract principle of *ratio*" (Hesse 2003, 23), alongside which, on the second stage, the shaking of the normative, the reliance on reality in general, becomes increasingly dominant. The effort to achieve originality and the differentiation of the genre then produces, on the third level, varieties in which the "*de-tabooing of crime and the immoral* is stylised as the central attraction" (ibid.).

Kinoschund and Trivialisation, Censorship: And How Children Got into the Cinema

The contemporary critical reception becomes precisely clear in relation to this third stage of development in the form of the Nick Carter films: for example, in the social democratic periodical *Die Gleichheit* from 1912, one reads:

> We turn with all our energy against the trash literature [...] of the Nick Carter books; but this cinema trash has a far more haunting and dangerous effect, where one does not only have

to imagine the ugliness, but where one sees everything happening vividly and really before one's eyes. (Roland 1912/1913, 128 f.)

The theatre critic Heinrich Stümcke is also convinced that *Kinoschund* poses a far greater threat than "Schundliteratur":

> It is not enough to fight the battle against Nick Carter and the heroes of Karl May's grace on the book market and to pursue them into the last nooks and crannies of the small bookbinder's shops, newspaper kiosks and journal reading circles; the [...] film, which is watched by hundreds at the same time, with its glorification of daring criminals, its blood-soaked bullfights and brutal execution scenes, has a far more inciting and lasting effect than the printed word read in silence. (Stümcke 1912, 239 f.)

These statements on cinema and film in general, as well as on Nick Carter in particular, refer primarily to the brutalising depictions of crime and sexuality. In addition, the contemporary texts also express concern about trivialisation through the new medium and its content, about the "Strudel Trivialität" (Pfemfert 1911, 560), as Franz Pfemfert put it in the 18th issue of *storm of triviality* in June 1911. In *Kino als Erzieher*, the editor of the journal laments that the advance of progress is accompanied by a cultural decay that is fundamentally apparent in all areas of society. This is visible above all in the supposed omnipresent soullessness, which he defines as the opposite of individuality. This lack of individuality also characterises architecture, which can be seen as the "fairground style in the new West Berlin," where "triviality [...] celebrates veritable orgies" (Pfemfert 1911, 561). The cinema, in particular, was helping the rampant triviality towards triumph and was devastating the "taste of the people" through "brutal picture reporting" (ibid., 562), as Pfemfert explains. Consequently, he declares apodictically: "Nick Carter, cinema and Berlin tenements, this trivial trinity belongs together" (ibid.). Thus the cinema is the "entertainer of the broad masses" and their "most dangerous educator" (ibid.). This also and especially applied to children, after all, the cinema had "now also opened up the schoolrooms" (ibid.). What Pfemfert alludes to are short films in which Kaiser Wilhelm II presents himself at military celebrations, parades and maneuvers, staged theatrically and pompously. Of the 82 films (cf. Petzold 2009, 128) showing the Kaiser at parades and maneuvers, some were shown to schoolchildren in special performances – the "good Prussian military spirit turns cartwheels before children's souls" (ibid.), as Pfemfert comments.

At that time, however, children and young people came into contact with film much less at school than in the cinema itself; after cinema's first years, the time of travelling and fairground cinemas, stationary cinemas were also established in Germany from 1906 onwards, initially with the shop cinemas and later with the film palaces based on the US model. Children and young people in particular are among the visitors – just as they have been the recipients of moving pictures since the birth of film in 1895. Early cinema did not yet know how to address an elaborate target group; the screenings were attended by children as well as adults, but in the afternoons the cinemas were effectively in the hands of the children (cf. Maase 2008, 128). Wild West and detective films were particularly popular (cf. Clemens 1931, 27).

As is clear from the sources, the German public followed what the children saw in the cinema with great attention and concern. First and foremost, authors of brochures and books, of daily newspapers and magazines – as in Pfemfert's case – had their say.

> Pastors and teachers dealt with the problems of children going to the cinema in sermons and lessons, in missives and at parents' evenings – after they themselves had discussed the subject among their professional colleagues and on the basis of institutional instructions. The cinema industry also sought to bring its view to the media, but had a difficult time with the children's issue in particular. Parliaments at all levels treated the cinema question and discussed it, as did the nation as a whole, essentially as a children's question. After all, we know that even in the spheres of encounter in everyday life – in the pub, on the street, in the hallway – the topic of conversation was what was probably happening to the children in the darkness of the cinema halls. (Maase 2008, 138)

A central control of children's and adolescents' cinema attendance only came into being with the passing of the Reichslichtspielgesetz of May 12, 1920; after this date, all films had to be inspected by Prüfstellen in Berlin and Munich before being shown. Films that have a harmful effect on the moral, mental or health development or overstimulate the imagination of young people" (quoted in Räder 2009, 24) could only be seen from the age of 18.

The adolescents who were excluded, however, continued to see films such as *Kaliber fünf Komma zwei* from the *Joe Deebs* series, which the Reichsfilmzensur imposed a ban on for young people (No. 207) on August 11, 1920: they smuggled and cheated their way into the cinemas, which was often not even necessary in the suburbs: these cinemas did good business with the films that were not suitable for young people. When the authorities checked, the usual excuses were given, such as "a copy of the film has just been mixed up" or "the wrong film was delivered" and they didn't know the content. In some cinemas, someone at the entrance even indicated to the projectionist that control officers had entered the cinema (cf. Schäfer 2015).

The Detective Film of the War Years: Stuart Webbs and Joe Deebs

Joe Deebs, from which *Kaliber fünf Komma zwei* originates, was a detective film series by director and producer Joe May at the time of WWII – those years in which the boom in detective films reached unimagined proportions: "Half of all the feature films that dominated the cinema in wartime were detective films" (Kalbus 1935, 39). The German market was flooded with series about investigators with English names; the first of these detectives – the direct ancestor of Joe Deebs – is Stuart Webbs, played by Ernst Reicher. The actor himself is said to have devised the character – in reference to a detective he had met in London (cf. Kalbus 1935, 38). Joe May directed these films for Continental-Kunstfilm Berlin. Oskar Kalbus, one of the earliest German film historians, writes about the first episode with the title *Die geheimnisvolle Villa:*

> What nobody expected happened. This film did the biggest business imaginable up to that time. Everywhere it appeared, at home and abroad, audiences were lining up at the box office. It wasn't long before the second Stuart Webbs film was made, then the third, the fourth, the twentieth. Ernst Reicher must have made 40-50 films in which he was "Stuart Webbs", that amiable, chevalier, highly intellectual, athletically trained detective who saw his noblest task in the tireless service of justice. (Kalbus 1935, 38)

The films of this period are, on the one hand, testimonies to the political developments of the time, and on the other, to the discourse of legitimacy in early film. Accordingly, a *Kinematograph* article on the premiere of the second *Stuart Webbs* episode *Der Mann im Keller* reads:

> English and sensation are two expressions our opponents would cling to if everything about and around this film were not genuinely German and the sensational did not refer to its quality. (O.V, 1914, 71)

"[G]enuinely German" – that is war propaganda; that is the attempt to align the genre nationally, to Germanise it. Parallel to this development is the attempt to free the detective film from the accusation that it comes up with a "hair-raising stringing together of the most implausible sensations" (Hesse 2003, 148); shortly after the premiere of *Die geheimnisvolle Villa Licht-Bild-Bühne* states:

> The suspense and interest is not aroused by the plot (the situations are sufficiently familiar to us through detective literature), the keen interest in Webbs' fate was kept alive by the way the scenes were brought, from the directorial as well as the acting point of view. (o. V. 1914, 37)

May's detective films are less sensational or attraction cinema; they are convincing on the level of *histoire* through realism and plot logic as well as through psychologically differentiated characters. Thomas Elsaesser describes the films of this early narrative cinema as unmistakable quality products with recognition value and describes how the individual responsibilities in the production process presented themselves:

> May's aim is not only to create the brand name "Stuart Webbs" and thus bring audiences to the cinemas on a regular basis, but also to provide cinema owners with an advertising campaign centrally controlled by the production company. Richer's contribution, in turn, is to shape the given pattern of the gentleman detective in such a way that he is also able to break it ironically and build a strategically important bridge between legitimate theatre and disreputable *Kintopp*. (Elsaesser 1991, 15)

After three highly acclaimed films, May and Reicher and the production company Continental broke up in the summer of 1914. Reicher produces further films in the series on his own, deviating more and more from the features and characteristics of the new detective film.

May founded his own production company in 1915, and on June 3, 1915, the first episode of the *Joe Deebs* series, *Das Gesetz der Mine,* premiered. By 1922, 30 films in the series had been made (cf. Wlaschin 2009 59), with May directing more than ten. May differentiated the character and thus the genre by integrating the investigator's private life into the narratives – in contrast to earlier films. Accordingly, the 6th episode of the series from 1916 is entitled *Wie ich Detektiv wurde,* in which Deebs tells his friends in a club his life and love story.

During the war, numerous production companies attempted to copy the success of May and Reicher; to this end, detectives from pre-war cinema returned to the screen in the form of Sherlock Holmes and Nick Carter, which had been prepared to a certain extent by May's and Reicher's films: Stuart Webb explicitly refers to Sherlock Holmes in his characterisations, while Joe Deebs refers to Nick Carter.

Apart from this, new detective characters such as Joe Jenkins and Harry Higgs establish themselves: directed by Rudolf Meinert, the *Higgs* series, which celebrates its premiere with the episode *John Rool* at Berlin's Tauentzienpalast in September 1916, bears clearly parodic features. It is these traits, as well as the integration of the private, the romantic, that deprive the detective film of credibility, as Hesse writes: "It is not its brutalising effect that breaks the genre's neck, but its ridiculous one" (Hesse 2003, 184).

After the end of the war, the 23-year-old Carlo Mierendorff reckons with the detective film in his essay *Hätte ich das Kino!*, which Kalbus attests that "in 1919 [...] it was as good as rushed to death" (Kalbus 1935, 38): "Once upon a time there was the imaginative backstairs novel," Mierendorff writes,

> He died long ago. Even the detectives are gone. Instead of pistols and flashing lights, they're already handling hearts, they've become love heroes. Crooks whose authenticity no one believes any more. How great once the ingenuity of Sherlock Holmes [was]. How thin, by contrast, the invention of Harry Higgs, Joe Deebs, Stuart Webbs. How pale the entanglement. How dull and perfumed. (Mierendorff 1972, 303)

The Genre System of the Early Screen Detectives

The media networks of the early detective films are, as shown, both diachronically and synchronously perspectivised, internationally and intermedially; they are inconceivable without their literary forebears: If Charles Dickens and Willie Collins are considered pioneers for the detective novel, Edgar Allan Poe, Emile Gaboriau and Arthur Conan Doyle are for the detective narrative, which is first published in newspapers and magazines, later in story collections and novels, then in the dime novels.

The serial narration in these *Medienangebote*, above all in the dime novels, forms the preconditions for the film series of the genre both structurally and in terms of content and dramaturgy. Among other things, the emphasis on action-oriented events should be mentioned, which allows the analytical process and deduction that structured the classic detective story to recede into the background. Also worthy of mention are the fight scenes and chases, which in their dramaturgy anticipate those in the early detective film; and last but not least, the detective assistants, who assume different functions than in Poe's or Doyle's stories: they are no longer interlocutors to whom the master detective explains his chains of deduction, but assistants who investigate independently. They follow up individual leads, thus enabling multiple, parallel narrative strands; these strands correspond to the cinematic storytelling of parallel montage, as first seen in Edwin S. Porter's *The Great Train Robbery* in 1903.

The media networks of the early detective films encompass countless *Stoffe* in various *Medienangebote*; the films, especially in the early years, rarely present themselves as adaptations, but rather as film texts whose content is composed of a mosaic of intra- and intermedial references: Accordingly, for example, in the second episode of the first *Nick Carter season*, *L'Affaire des bijoux* from September 22, 1908, plot aspects such as the wife hiring the detective in dire need are taken from the previous film and combined with motifs taken from other media and sources. An example of such a combination are the references to Stevenson's *The Suicide Club* in the first episode of the third season, *Les Merveilleux Exploits de Nick Carter*.

Another similar example is the 1908 film *Sherlock Holmes in the Great Murder Mystery*, which echoes Gillette's play and Blackton's film in terms of emblems, but in which Sherlock Holmes and Dr. Watson solve a case that took place in a Rue Morgue and whose perpetrator is an orangutan – as is famously the case in Poe's 1841 short story *The Murders in the Rue Morgue*. At the time, then, fidelity to the work and/or questions of copyright were less likely to prevent filmmakers from invention and variation (cf. Seeßlen 1998, 56).

The organisational structure of the media networks of the genre supersystem is rhizomatic, is not vertical, not strictly hierarchical in nature; instead, to speak with the words of Gilles Deleuze and Félix Guattari, it exhibits principles of connection and heterogeneity as well as the principle of asignificant rupture: like a rhizome that can be broken at any point and continues to proliferate along its own or other lines (cf. Deleuze/Guattari 1977, 16), many of the media networks continue and carry on. Examples of this are the countless Sherlock Holmes adaptations as well as the media network of Nick Carter: after the third season as well as the *Zigomar* period 1912, Nick Carter found its way back into the cinemas in the 1960s: French film production company Chaumiane's *Nick Carter va tout casser* premiered on June 17, 1964, starring Eddie Constantine. The film picks up where its predecessors left off in terms of content and dramaturgy – and takes a self-referential look at the media network: in one scene, Carter enters an apartment where he finds countless *Nick Carter* dime novels and memorabilia.

Many of the narrative features and conventions that the early films adopted on the one hand from the serial detective narratives, but also (further) developed on the other, are not only to be found in *Emil und die Detektive,* but are also to be found in current productions. These include the division of the narrative structure into two parts as well as action, mystery and suspense, parallel montages and the big city as a plot space.

References

Primary Literature

Kästner, Erich: Emil und die Detektive: Ein Roman für Kinder. Hamburg: Dressler, 2010 [EA 1929].
Kästner, Erich: Emil und die drei Zwillinge. Zürich: Atrium, 2018 [EA 1934].
Doyle, Arthur C.: The Adventures of Sherlock Holmes II. A Scandal in Bohemia. In: The Strand Magazine 1 (1891), 61–75.
Doyle, Arthur C.: The Adventures of Sherlock Holmes IV. The Boscombe Valley Mystery. In: The Strand Magazine 1 (1891), 401–416.
Doyle, Arthur C.: The Sign of the Four. In: Lippincott's Monthly Magazine 41 (1890), 145–223
Doyle, Arthur C.: A Study in Scarlet. London [u. a.]: Penguin, 2004.
Poe, Edgar A.: The Man of the Crowd. In: Burton's Gentleman's Magazine 4 (1840), 267–270.
Poe, Edgar A.: The Murders in the Rue Morgue. In: Ders.: Selected Tales. London: Penguin, 1994, 118–153.
Stevenson, Robert L.: The Suicide Club. New York: Charles Scribner's Sons, 1896.

Filmography

Adventures of Sherlock Holmes; or, Held for a Ransom (USA 1905). Regie: J. Stuart Blackton, Vitagraph Company of America.
Emil und die Detektive (D 1931). Regie: Gerhard Lamprecht, Universum Film (Ufa).
Harry Higgs: John Rool (D 1916). Regie: Rudolf Meinert, Meinert-Film Bürstein & Janak.
Joe Deebs: Das Gesetz der Mine (D 1915). Regie: Joe May, May-Film.
Joe Deebs: Wie ich Detektiv wurde (D 1916). Regie: Joe May, May-Film.
Joe Deebs: Kaliber fünf Komma zwei (D 1920). Regie: Willy Zeyn, Projektions-AG Union (PAGU).
Nick Carter: L'affaire des bijoux (F 1908). Regie: Victorin-Hippolyte Jasset, Société Française des Films Éclair.
Nick Carter: Le Guet-Apens (F 1908). Regie: Victorin-Hippolyte Jasset, Société Française des Films Éclair.
Nick Carter: Le club des suicidés. (F 1909). Regie: Victorin-Hippolyte Jasset, Société Française des Films Éclair.
Nick Carter va tout casser (F/I 1964). Regie: Henri Decoin, Chaumiane, Florida Films.
Sherlock Holmes Baffled (USA 1900). Regie: Arthur W. Marvin, American Mutoscope & Biograph.
Sherlock Holmes in the Great Murder Mystery (USA 1908). Regie: Fred J. Balshofer, Crescent Film Company.
Stuart Webbs: Die geheimnisvolle Villa (D 1914). Regie: Joe May, Continental Kunstfilm GmbH.
Stuart Webbs: Der Mann im Keller (D 1914). Regie: Joe May, Continental Kunstfilm GmbH.
The Great Train Robbery (USA 1903). Regie: Edwin S. Porter, Edison Manufacturing Company
The Suicide Club (USA 1909). Regie: D. W. Griffith, American Mutoscope & Biograph.
Zigomar, roi des voleur (F 1911). Regie: Victorin-Hippolyte Jasset, Société Française des Films Éclair.
Zigomar contre Nick Carter (F 1912). Regie: Victorin-Hippolyte Jasset, Société Française des Films Éclair.
Zigomar, peau d'anguille (F 1913). Regie: Victorin-Hippolyte Jasset, Société Française des Films Éclair.

Theatrography

Emil und die Detektive (UA Berlin 2001). Text: Wolfgang Adenberg; Musik: Marc Schubring. Hamburg: Verlag für Kindertheater, 2008.
Sherlock Holmes. A Drama in four Acts. (UA New York 1899). Text: Arthur C. Doyle und William Gillette. London: Samuel French, 1922.

Secondary Literature Before 1945

Clemens, Walter: Der Kinderfilm. Untersuchungen über seine psychologischen, pädagogischen und methodischen Grundlagen. Braunschweig, TU, Diss., 1931.
Der Mann im Keller. In: Der Kinematograph 8 (1914) 379 vom 01.04., 64.
Die Detektiv-Filme. In: Lichtbild-Bühne 1 (1914) 14, 28–37.
Kalbus, Oskar: Vom Werden deutscher Filmkunst. 1. Teil: Der stumme Film. Altona-Bahrenfeld 1935.
Pfemfert, Franz: Kino als Erzieher. In: Die Aktion 1 (1911) 18, 560–563.
Stümcke, Heinrich: Kinematograph und Theater. In: Bühne und Welt 14 (1912), wiederabgedr. In: Schweinitz, Jörg (Hg.): Prolog vor dem Film. Nachdenken über ein neues Medium 1909–1914. Leipzig 1992, 239–240.
Roland [sic!]: Gegen die Frauenverblödung im Kino. In: Die Gleichheit 23 (1912/1913), wiederabgedruckt in: Schweinitz, Jörg (Hg.): Prolog vor dem Film. Nachdenken über ein neues Medium 1909–1914. Leipzig 1992, 128–129.

Secondary Literature After 1945

Alewyn, Richard: Anatomie des Detektivromans. In: Vogt, Jochen (Hg.): Der Kriminalroman. Poetik, Theorie, Geschichte. München 1998 (UTB für Wissenschaft; 8147), 52–72.
Boileau, Pierre und Thomas Narcejac: Der Detektivroman. Berlin 1967.
Brecht, Bertolt: Über Film. In: Ders.: Gesammelte Werke, Bd. 18: Schriften zur Literatur und Kunst 1. Frankfurt a. M. 1967, 135–216.
Döblin, Alfred: An Romanautoren und ihre Kritiker. Berliner Programm. In: Ders (Hg.): Aufsätze zur Literatur. Olten/Freiburg i. B. 1963, 15–19.
Deleuze, Gilles/Guattari, Félix: Rhizom. Berlin 1977.
Elsaesser, Thomas: Filmgeschichte – Firmengeschichte – Familiengeschichte. Der Übergang vom Wilhelminischen zum Weimarer Film. In: Bock, Hans Michael/Lenssen, Claudia (Hg.): Joe May – Regisseur und Produzent. München 1991, 11–30.
Ezra, Elizabeth: Georges Méliès: the birth of the auteur. Manchester 2000.
Gerhold, Hans: Der Zufallslyrismus der Serie und die Vorläufer des Kriminalfilms: Von Dolly's Abenteuer (The Adventure of Dolly, 1908) bis Die Vampire (Les Vampires, 1915–1916). In: Korte, Helmut/Faulstich, Werner (Hg.): Fischer-Filmgeschichte, Bd. 1: 1895–1924. Frankfurt a. M. 1994, 182–200.
Hasubek, Peter: Die Detektivgeschichte für junge Leser. Bad Heilbrunn 1974.
Hesse, Sebastian: Kamera-Auge und Spürnase. Der Detektiv im frühen deutschen Kino. Basel 2003 (KINTOP Schriften; 5).
Hickethier, Knut: Einleitung. In: Ders. (Hg.): Filmgenres. Kriminalfilm. Stuttgart 2005 (Reclams Universal-Bibliothek; 18408), 11–41.
Hügel, Hans-Otto: Detektiv. In: Ders. (Hg.): Handbuch Populäre Kultur. Begriffe, Theorien und Diskussionen. Stuttgart 2003, 153–159.

Jenkins, Henry: Convergence culture. Where Old and New Media Collide. New York 2006
Kinder, Marsha: Playing with Power in Movies, Television and Video Games. Los Angeles [u. a.] 1991.
Klinger, Leslie S.: Was Maurice Costello The First Screen Sherlock Holmes? In: The Baker Street Journal 48 (1998) 2, 27–30.
Klein, Thomas/Hißnauer, Christian: Einleitung. In: Dies. (Hg.): Klassiker der Fernsehserie. Stuttgart 2012 (Reclams Universal-Bibliothek; 19025), 7–26.
Kracauer, Siegfried: Schriften. Hg. von Karsten Witte, Bd. 2: Von Caligari zu Hitler. Eine psychologische Geschichte des deutschen Films. Übers. von Ruth Baumgarten und Karsten Witte. Frankfurt a. M. 1979.
Kurwinkel, Tobias/Schmerheim, Philipp: Kinder- und Jugendfilmanalyse. Konstanz 2013 (UTB für Wissenschaft; 3885).
Kurwinkel, Tobias: Zur Theorie von Medien- und Produktverbünden und ihren Sammlungen am Beispiel von Bibi und Tina. In: kjl&m 17 (2017) 2, 14–21.
Kurwinkel, Tobias: Medien- und Produktverbund. In: Kurwinkel, Tobias/Schmerheim, Philipp (Hg.). Unter Mitarbeit von Stefanie Jakobi: Handbuch Kinder- und Jugendliteratur. Stuttgart 2020. [in Vorber.].
Kümmerling-Meibauer, Bettina: Erich Kästner: Emil und die Detektive (1929). In: Dies. (Hg:): Kinder- und Jugendliteratur. Eine Einführung. Darmstadt 2012, 101–110.
Maase, Kaspar: Kinderkino. Halbwüchsige, Öffentlichkeiten und kommerzielle Populärkultur im deutschen Kaiserreich. In: Müller, Corinna/Segeberg, Harro (Hg.): Kinoöffentlichkeit (1895–1920). Entstehung, Etablierung, Differenzierung/Cinemas Public Sphere (1895–1920): Emergence Settlement Differentiation. Marburg 2008, 126–148.
Mierendorff, Carlo: Die Romantik des Kapitalismus. In: Witte, Karsten (Hg.): Theorie des Kinos. Ideologiekritik der Traumfabrik. Frankfurt a. M. 1972, 301–304.
Moody, Nickianne: Crime in Film and on TV. In: Priestmann, Martin (Hg.): The Cambridge Companion to Crime Fiction. Cambridge 2003, 227–244.
Petzold, Dominik: Der Kaiser und das Kino. Herrschaftsinszenierung, Populärkultur und Filmkultur im Wilhelminischen Zeitalter. Paderborn 2012. Zugl.: München, Univ., Diss., 2009.
Pointer, Michael: The Public Life of Sherlock Holmes. London/Vancouver, 1975.
Räder, Andy: Der Kinderfilm in der Weimarer Republik. In: Schäfer, Horst/Wegener, Claudia (Hg.): Kindheit und Film. Geschichte, Themen und Perspektiven des Kinderfilms in Deutschland. Konstanz 2009, 21–38.
Schäfer, Horst: Kinder und Jugendliche in den Kinos der Weimarer Republik (2015) http://kinderundjugendmedien.de/index.php/component/content/article/105-mediageschichte/filmgeschichte/1261-2-kinder-und-jugendliche-in-den-kinos-der-weimarer-republik (10.05.2019).
Schmidt, Siegfried J.: Der Medienkompaktbegriff. In: Münke, Stefan/Roessler, Alexander (Hg.): Was ist ein Medium? Frankfurt a. M. 2008, 144–157.
Seeßlen, Georg/Roloff, Bernhard: Mord im Kino. Geschichte und Mythologie des Detektiv-Films. Mit einer Filmografi e von Georg Seeßlen und einer Bibliographie von Jürgen Berger. Reinbek bei Hamburg 1981 (Grundlagen des populären Films; 8).
Seeßlen, Georg: Detektive. Mord im Kino. Überarb. u. akt. Neuaufl . Marburg 1998 (Grundlagen des populären Films).
Seiter, Ellen: „Gotta Catch 'Em All – Pokémon". Problems in the Study of Children's Global Multi-Media. In: Research in Childhood: Sociology, Culture & History. A Collection of Papers. Odense 2000, 189–196.
Weinkauff, Gina: Das Sams. Betrachtung eines prominenten kinderliterarischen Medienverbundes und seiner Rezeption in der Fachöffentlichkeit. In: Weinkauff, Gina/Dettmar, Ute/Möbius, Thomas/Tomkowiak, Ingrid (Hg.): Kinder- und Jugendliteratur in Medienkontexten. Adaption – Hybridisierung – Intermedialität – Konvergenz. Frankfurt a. M. [u. a.] 2014 (Kinder- und Jugendkultur, -literatur und -medien; 89), 127–146.
Wlaschin, Ken: Silent Mystery and Detective Movies. A Comprehensive Filmography. Jefferson, NC 2009.

"Donnerwetter, das ist famos"

Mediale Mobilmachung in the Nazi Girls' Film *Was tun, Sibylle?*

Caroline Roeder

„Vorspann
Ruhevoll und in makel-
loser Reinheit liegt die
Landschaft im Schnee –

Dunkle Wälder –
weite Schneeflächen –
weiche Bergsilhouetten –

da saust plötzlich ein
Mädel auf Skiern ins Bild,
bremst rasch ab,

wendet sich und
ruft fröhlich:

„Hallo – – !"[1]

With this snappy greeting, which resounds from a snowy landscape in the Ore Mountains, the Nazi youth film *Was tun, Sibylle?* opens. (1938). The first long shot is followed by scenes in which other girls gradually join the picture. The entire opening credits are accompanied by shots of a snow-covered mountain landscape. The images of the female skier, who draws graphically artfully arranged tracks in the snow, have an impressive effect. The lighting design and choreography of the

---

[1] Line break as in the original: Quote from the script *Was tun, Sibylle?* (Neumeister/Bierkowsky o.J., 2).

C. Roeder (✉)
PH Ludwigsburg, Ludwigsburg, Germany

descent as well as the atmospheric natural scenery evoke impressions in the visual memory that must have been well present to the cinema audience of those years through the contemporary Nazi propaganda films of Leni Riefenstahl, but also through the films of Luis Trenker.

The ski trip leads right into the life of the *Volksgemeinschaft*, which is presented in the film as a positive völkisch[2] model. It also serves as a loose framing to lead to the central theme, which will take its actual setting into the school. The feature film *Was tun, Sibylle?* was directed in 1938 by Peter Paul Brauer, a successful film director during the Nazi era. Brauer directed around thirty films, most of them comedies.[3]

The literary model for the youth film is the girls' book by the author Sofie Schieker-Ebe, which was published in 1930 and has the same title. Little[4] is known about the author Schieker-Ebe today,[5] although she wrote over twenty books for children and young people that were published between 1925 and 1952. Schieker-Ebe's texts are primarily addressed to a younger reading public; some of the titles are regionally oriented, while some are seasonal publications such as a *Krippenspiel* (1950); *Was tun, Sibylle?* is addressed to a female, youthful audience. It is not insignificant that Schieker-Ebe's husband, Friedrich Schieker, was a well-known author of reform pedagogical publications[6] and made a name for himself in this pedagogical environment as head of the primary school *Schule am Kräherwald* in Stuttgart.[7] There are no relevant writings by Sofie Schieker-Ebe, however, it can be assumed that she can be located in this context.

The novel *Was tun, Sibylle?* (1930) was first published by the small Stuttgart publishing house *Silberburg*. All later editions were published by Thienemann Verlag, also based in Stuttgart.[8] The book proved successful on the market and achieved a total circulation of around 70,000 copies. The publication history ranges from the first publication through the National Socialist era to the post-war period of the 1960s.[9] In 1931 Schieker-Ebe continued the *story* with the follow-up volume *Sibylle blickt ins Leben* (1931), which also had a total print run of 44,000 until 1950. It probably contributed to the novel's success that the book was made into a film. In

---

[2] On the concept of the *völkisch*, cf. Hopster 2005, 353; cf. also Josting 2020.

[3] On the importance of comedies in Nazi film, see Grimm 2000.

[4] The author was born in Ulm in 1892 and died in Stuttgart in 1970.

[5] The Wikipedia entry of only a few lines mentions as first sentence: "Sofie Schieker-Ebe was married to the pedagogue Friedrich Schieker since 1920." https://de.wikipedia.org/wiki/Sofie_Schieker-Ebe (05.09.2017).

[6] Cf. Friedrich Schieker: *Die Grundschule und das Kind* (1924).

[7] The school became known far beyond the region. Among the school's patrons was the philosopher Martin Buber. The clientele of the students was middle-class and offered Jewish children in particular a liberal environment until the time of National Socialism. Schieker's pupils included Friedrich Wolf's sons Markus and Konrad (cf. Jacobsen/Aurich 2005, ch. 1).

[8] It has not yet been clarified whether the Silberburg publishing house was a publishing house that had Jewish publishers and was incorporated into the Thienemann publishing house after 1933, or whether the reason for the change in publishing house was due to better marketability, for example.

[9] There are also school editions for the Netherlands and Sweden and a translation into Finnish.

1938 the film was shown for the first time. After 1945 it was classified as a so-called *"Vorbehaltsfilm"*[10] and is therefore not accessible to the public today, but can be viewed for research purposes in the archives of the Deutsche Kinemathek.[11] A copy of the film can be viewed in the Bundes Filmarchiv in Berlin;[12] the corresponding screenplay or the third version of the same (Neumeister/Bierkowski o.J) can also be found in the archive of the *Deutsche Kinemathek*. There you will also find a number of promotional materials that prove that the film was advertised and distributed at great expense.[13]

The research question: This article focuses on the representation of the construction and shaping of girl characters in the media context, namely in the temporal framework of the 1930s. To this end, the book *Was tun, Sibylle?* by Sofie Schieker-Ebe will be used as an example in order to relate the image of the girl created in this book to contemporary drawings of female protagonists,[14] which have found their way into literary and art research on the New Objectivity under the catchwords *Neue Frau (*cf. Becker 1993; Karrenbrock 2003; Drescher 2003) and *Neue Mädchen* (cf. Tost 2003). In a second step, the film version of the novel will be consulted and changes will be shown that are not solely due to the media adaptation, but that reveal possible shifts in the evaluation of gender images and arrangements. On the one hand, the focus is on gender discourse and the revanchist image of women under National Socialism; on the other hand, it explores the question of the extent to which further ideological inscriptions of National Socialism can be traced in the literary adaptation. In other words, it asks which tendencies can be made visible in children's and youth media published during the Nazi era and whether characteristics of a "reactionary modernity" (Nassen 1987, 10; cf. Herrmann/Nassen 1993) can be detected in the media. The media-theoretical considerations of Harro Segeberg (2004) are drawn upon, who examined *strategies of mediale Mobildmachung* his study of Nazi film. Segeberg's investigation follows the dictum not to "foreground (the) ideologisation of the medial, but the medialisation of the ideological." (Segeberg 2004, 11) Segeberg concretizes this approach when he writes:

> Therefore, mediale Mobilmachung in the context of the project does not mean [...] the instrumentalisation of cinema in favor of a political-ideological mobilisation, but the mobilisation of the medium, which achieved political effects precisely by aiming far more consistently than previously assumed to transform political references into media references. (Ibid., 11 f.)

---

[10] On the conditional film, cf. Krah/Wünsch 2000.

[11] File number Film Deutsche Kinemathek, archive signature 1/86.

[12] On *Film im NS-Staat*, see essay and contemporary historical documents at: https://www.filmportal.de/thema/film-im-ns-staat (01.07.2019).

[13] As promotional material, one finds posters and advertisements; as cinematic material, also an opening credits announcing the film.

[14] "With their writings, the authors attempt to expand the circle of addressees within children's literature and, moreover, to remove limitations to adult literature. Their girls no longer stand on the sidelines as patient minor characters, but act as significant plot devices whose intervention is crucial to the course of the story." (Tost 2003, 242)

In the following, the literary model of the later film adaptation under National Socialism will be presented.

The Girls' Book *Was tun, Sibylle?*[15]

"'Donnerwetter,' sagte plötzlich Sibylle Brant, 'mein Geld ist weg.'" (WtS 15) The laconically announced news bursts into an extraordinarily tranquil classroom situation: the A level pupils of a secondary girls' school just immersed themselves in the contemplation of a statue of Buddha. The figure served as an introduction to the planned class reading of "eine(r) Erzählung über Indien" (WtS 13), meaning Rudyard Kipling's *The Jungle Book* (EA 1894; German version 1898). Sibylle's exclamation signals an *incredible event* that disrupts the contemplative school scene. What is *incredible* is not only that the theft takes place in the middle of the lesson, but also that there can be no doubt that it must be a perpetrator from within the class. The girls' book begins with this suspenseful exposition.

The novel is 130 pages long and is divided into ten short chapters. The content can be summarised quickly: The 15-year-old Sibylle Brant finds herself in an emotional conflict by the theft of a 10 Mark note, with which she wanted to pay the contribution to a class trip. Suspicion falls on her classmate Lene, who claims the note belongs to her when a banknote falls out of her book. But Sibylle identifies it because the note has an unusual number that she had memorised. The question arises for Sibylle: what should she do? Should Sibylle believe the factual evidence at hand or her personal (high) esteem of her classmate?

> Sibylle Brant sah das alles, und sie schüttelte ein wenig verzagt den Kopf. Es war ihr nicht um das Geld zu tun. Aber wenn sie nun schwieg – und sie wußte, dass das Schicksal dieser Stunde an ihr hing – so war ja nicht Recht getan. Man bestahl einander nicht. Man belog einander nicht. Sibylle Brant war nicht in ihrer Person verletzt. Die Welt, das Leben war verletzt worden. Irgend so etwas spürte sie. Sie war erst fünfzehn Jahre alt. Aber sie nahm das Unrecht nicht hin. (WtS, 20)

Although all the facts speak against Lene, the girl stubbornly insists on her innocence. The plot that develops from this conflict is transferred into a detective's search for clues. Not only the motif of the stolen and marked banknote is reminiscent of Erich Kästner's children's novel *Emil und die Dektektive* (*Emil and the Detectives*. 1929), which was published just one year before Schieker-Ebe's girls' book. There are also moments of comparison in the solving of the theft, when Schieker-Ebe's protagonists move around the urban space in a mobile manner as they work on the case. In the girls' novel, however, the focus is not on a gang of children, but rather on the criminalistic model of the investigative duo consisting of Sibylle and her friend and secret admirer Peter, who quickly gains her trust. In the

---

[15] In the rest of the text, quotations from *Was tun, Sibylle?* are taken from the 1941 edition and identified by the sigle (WtS plus page number) for ease of reading.

following chapters, the search for clues leads to different locations and is pursued with different concepts. For example, while Sibylle seeks to talk to Lene (and travels by train to her hometown to do so), suspicions lead Peter to his own school, a boys' high school. Here he observes a situation between pupils which he interprets as a blackmail scene.

In the popular children's gang motif of the 1920s and 1930s, the young protagonists often prove to be more understanding than the adults (as in Erich Kästner or Kurt Held).[16] In Schieker-Ebe's case, the investigative duo is to be judged differently. Although the young characters also act independently, it is clear that the teacher Dr. Fromann (as an experienced pedagogue) has an overview of the situation throughout the entire (plot) time. In this respect, the independence of the protagonists appears to be *guided*. In *Was tun, Sibylle?* moral questions of the community in particular are at the centre of the plot. The young people's investigative work appears in an educational light and can be understood as a learning and moral maturation process that takes place *under guidance*. Eventually, the case is solved and it turns out: the classmate Käthe stole the money because her little brother was being blackmailed by another boy. So Käthe stole to help and thus tried to save her brother, who is also subject to family violence, from being expelled from school (since he takes a so-called exemption position, he is not allowed to commit any misdeeds).

The novel makes it clear that although Lene lied (so as not to betray Käthe) and although Käthe stole in order to help her brother, both girls are actually free of guilt. What is essential are the motives for the behavior, which are not greed or self-interest, but morally motivated. Social causes that condition the deeds become recognisable and further emphasise the high moral integrity of the female protagonists. Both Lene and Käthe come from *poor backgrounds*. The social issue raised here, however, is not explored more deeply, and is mainly turned into the pedagogical. The bad boy, on the other hand, who blackmailed the little brother, is drawn stereotypically as a villain compared to the other characters: 'Peter Kurre sah in ein breites, plattes Gesicht mit merkwürdig dünnen Lippen und kleinen tiefliegenden dunklen Augen' (WtS, 77). Significantly, the thief is the only character in the novel to remain nameless. Interestingly, he is not held accountable, but gets off with a moral warning.

Lines of Tradition and References of the Novel

Schieker-Ebe's novel can be assigned to various children's or youth literature traditions. It shows similarities to the traditional girl's book, or the bakery-fish or boarding school novel (cf. Dahrendorf 1978; Grenz 2008). The genre of the girls' book is supported not only by the almost universally female characters of the schoolgirls

---

[16] On the children's gang, cf. Steinlein 1999.

and the setting of the girls' school, but also by the novel's focus on adolescence and the process of maturation and socialisation that the protagonists undergo. Whereas in the traditional boarding school story the school location presents itself as a "pedagogical island life" (cf. Wilkending 1997) or transit space of a female community (cf. Roeder 2008), in Schieker-Ebe's *story* the school takes on a central role as a setting, but does not signify a heterotopically conceived space of action. Rather, the school serves as a (pedagogical) starting point for the protagonists' independent activities and actions.

It is striking that the opening scene of the novel contains intertextual references to Emmy von Rhoden's classic girls' book *Trotzkopf* (1885 ff.). This can be read both in the constellation of characters in the family and in the drawing of the girl Sibylle. Both the (intimately drawn) father-daughter constellation (Sibylle's mother died giving birth to her; her father's sister lives with her in the family) and the character design of the girl's impetuous nature are reminiscent of the familiar pre-text and the familiar opening scene (cf. Grenz 1997; Roeder 2015). To speak of a *model of Trotzkopf* (Dahrendorf 1978), however, is out of the question in Schieker-Ebe's case. Although Sibylle's maturation process is the focus of the novel, it is clear from the way it is structured that the girls' book is by no means about the *taming of the Shrew*; rather, the process of maturing and forming one's own moral judgements is placed in a more modern context of reformist pedagogy.

The girl character Sibylle exhibits, in addition to the already mentioned spirited (and also somewhat tomboyish nature), a contemporary characterisation of the *Neue Mädchen that is* to be understood in the sense of the *New Objectivity* (cf. Tost 2003). Thus, Sibylle does morning exercises and is described as athletic; she dashes around the apartment or runs to school with her dog; the language given to the protagonist is *brisk* and rather *ungirly* for the time (as exemplified by her exclamation "Donnerwetter" (WtS 15)). The text is characterised by literal speech and thus *authentically* reproduces the conversations between the young people.

Other attributes, such as the urban setting or the urbanity of the literary setting, identify the text as belonging to the *New Objectivity*.[17] Although Schieker-Ebe's novel does not mention a specific place by name, the opening scene already leads the reader's gaze into a metropolitan setting when the novel begins with the sentences:

> Sibylle Brant lehnte sich weit zum Fenster hinaus und suchte den Himmel über dem engen Hof zwischen den Häusern. Es war gar nicht einfach ihn zu finden, denn man schaute von diesem untersten Stockwerk wie auf der Tiefe eines Schachtes hoch an kahlen Mauern empor. (WtS 5).

Sibylle's searching gaze (which can certainly be interpreted symbolically for the following text and its focus on the girl's maturing process) refers to the cramped

---

[17] "The New Objectivity is an urban movement, the emancipation of women and authors is also bound to the metropolitan space [...] The newly won freedoms are tested here, the urban space is the place where the female sex experiences or has experienced the departures to freedom, the city is the place where authors or women realize new life concepts and designs". (Becker 1993, 193 f.)

living conditions often found in tenements (in urban settings). The fact that the apartment is on the lowest floor also gives a first indication of the social situation of the Brant family, which does not seem to be wealthy.[18] (In the rest of the plot, the journeys of the investigating duo refer to the (urban) mobility of the characters and also to the urban environment). Other features of the *New Objectivity* can be identified, including the girls' aspirations for their careers, which reflect developments in young women at the time: Lene wants to study chemistry later on and lives alone in a neighbouring town.

What seems essential in Schieker-Ebe's novel is the model of educational ideas that are represented in her novel and point to the reform pedagogical background. This model becomes particularly impressive in the shaping of the role of the teacher. In the novel, teacher Fromann proves to be a modern pedagogue; instead of education through punishment, he relies on persuasion. Questions of guilt are answered by him in a differentiated way and social causes are included as well as those of the personal maturity of his pupils. A programmatic scene makes this attitude of the teacher clear when Sibylle asks him a *cardinal question* (here it is whether he has already reported the theft):

> „Haben Sie es eigentlich schon nach oben weitergemeldet?"
> „Was ist ‚oben'?"
> „Rektorat."
> Doktor Fromann schüttelte nur den Kopf.
> „Donnerwetter", sagte Sibylle, „das nenne ich nobel. Denn von Rechts wegen hätten Sie es doch tun müssen, nicht?"
> „Von Rechts wegen?"
> „Ich meine die Vorschriften und Verordnungen und so", erklärte Sibylle.
> „Es gibt allerhand Vorschriften und Verordnungen", sagte Doktor Fromann,
> „äußere und innere. Und dann gibt es Fälle, bei denen die äußeren, und solche, bei denen die inneren Vorschriften maßgebend sind."
> „Und hier waren es die inneren, ja?"
> „Hier waren es die inneren." (WtS, 112 f.)[19]

---

[18] The living situation also becomes clearer on the first page, when we read that Sibylle has such a small, narrow room that she can only do her morning gymnastics if she has to.

[19] "Have you actually reported it upstairs yet?"
"What's 'up'?"
"Principal's office."
Doctor Fromann just shook his head.
"By golly," said Sibyl, "I call that noble. For by rights you ought to have done it, oughtn't you?"
"By rights?"
"I mean the rules and regulations and stuff," Sibylle explained.
"There are all sorts of rules and regulations," said Doctor Fromann, "external and internal. And the living situation also becomes clearer on the first page, when we read that Sibylle has such a small, narrow room that she can only do her morning gymnastics if she has to."
"And here it was the inner ones, yes?"
"Here it was the inner ones." (WtS, 112 f.)

Fromann evidently not only resists Wilhelmine obedience (or even subservient spirit), but applies his own standards; interesting here is the reference to the hierarchical above. The teacher's educational maxims are also clearly expressed, for example when Fromann provides a pedagogically framed explanation for what is happening in the school:

> Es war wahrscheinlich nicht das erste mal [sic!], daß aus Angst und Verwirrung, aus Angst vor Strafe und vor Vätern und Lehrern Schuld und wieder Schuld eines Kindes herauswuchs, und daß dieses Kind dann keinen Ausweg mehr sah. Keinen als Lüge und Betrug und Diebstahl.
> Aber vielleicht war es das erstemal in Doktor Fromanns Leben, daß ein junger Mensch – fast ein Kind noch – mit solcher Tapferkeit und Aufrichtigkeit durch das Schicksal ging und – es meisterte. (WtS, 111)[20]

In summary, it can be stated: Schieker-Ebe's novel for girls is indebted to traditional narrative models such as the Bildungsroman or the *Trotzkopf model*; at the same time, the character design shows modern traits, which are oriented towards the reformist pedagogical narrative models of the *Neue Sachlichkeit* (*New Objectivity*) and depict social realities; changed ideas of childhood and girls' roles can be found.

The titular protagonist Sibylle is no *Kunstseidenes Mädchen* (Irmgard Keun), but a self-confident schoolgirl. With Lene and Käthe, the author places other strong female characters at the protagonist's side; Lene in particular embodies a prototype of the *Neues Mädchen* with her desire to study chemistry later on[21] and also with her independent life in the city.

The film version of the girls' novel has some deviations that seem significant, especially with regard to the ideological potential of the film.

The Film as an Educator or *Die kleinen Ladenmädchen gehen ins Kino*[22]

Film took on a significant role in National Socialism. Joseph Goebbels saw the young medium as a powerful means of propaganda, as one of the "most modern and far-reaching means of influencing the masses".[23] In his speech at the opening of the film work of the Hitler Youth in 1941, Goebbels refers to film as a „nationales Erziehungsmittel" (Goebbels 1969; quoted in Albrecht 1969, 480). While for a

---

[20] It was probably not the first time [sic!] that out of fear and confusion, out of fear of punishment and of fathers and teachers, guilt and guilt again grew out of a child, and that this child then saw no way out. None but lies and deceit and theft. But perhaps it was the first time in Doctor Fromann's life that a young person – almost a child – went through fate with such bravery and sincerity and – mastered it. (WtS, 111)

[21] Cf. on the girl's career choice in an academic and, moreover, scientific field also the title *stud. Chem. Helene Willfüer* by Vicki Baum from 1928, which was filmed in 1929.

[22] cf. Kracauer 1963.

[23] Goebbels on 09.02.1934 in front of filmmakers; quoted from Albrecht 1969, 22.

long-time media studies research project focused primarily on Nazi propaganda films, the focus of interest increasingly shifted to entertainment offerings as well (cf. Grimm 2000). In 1941, Goebbels proclaimed before the Reichsfilmkammer in Berlin that entertainment had the task of "ein Volk für seinen Lebenskampf auszustatten, ihm die in dem dramatischen Geschehen des Tages notwendige Erbauung, Unterhaltung und Entspannung zu geben"; after all, the best propaganda was not that "bei der die eigentlichen Elemente der Propaganda immer sichtbar zutage treten", sondern die, die "sozusagen unsichtbar" sind. (Goebbels 1969; quoted in Albrecht 1979, 260 f.).[24]

The importance of film for propaganda under National Socialism is also evident in the significance that was attached to youth film. Stahr points out in his study that film consumption for young people was extraordinarily promoted under National Socialism: "According to the media theorist Hans Traub, the concepts of 'youth', 'film' and 'National Socialism' were closely linked in their essence as forces overcoming all bourgeois conventions and traditions and opening up new forms of expression" (cf. Stahr 2001, 84). In order to effectively install this propaganda tool, legal conditions were created to be able to implement direct control measures in schools and the HJ (Hitler Youth), such as the HJ's regular youth film lessons. The visitor statistics of these years also show that women were among the strongest groups of visitors. No other population group was so extensively represented. This was certainly aided by the fact that "films in which women played a leading role [made up] about 40 to 50 percent of the total productions." (Scheidgen 2009, 264).

In his sociological study *Nationalsozialistische Filmpolitik* (1969), Gerd Albrechts sets the figures for the total production of feature films under National Socialism at 1094 and divides them into four categories. Bianca Dusdar, in her study on *Film als Propagandainstrument in der Jugendpolitik des Dritten Reichs*, filters out the figures for youth film from this and states:

> Of the entire film production of the Third Reich, 297 films received the censorship rating "adult". This means that only 26% of the entire feature film production was accessible to children and young people without age restrictions. They had no access to the vast majority of feature films.
> A further 149 feature films were released for the 14 to 18 age group, so that with a total of 446 feature films, 41 per cent of German feature film production was accessible to them. (Dusdar 1996, 46 f.)

It also seems interesting to examine gender aspects in Nazi film (cf. Bechdolf 1992; Jatho 2007; Frietsch/Herkommer 2009). Irina Scheidgen shows in her study *Frauenbilder im Spielfilm, Kulturfilm und in der Wochenschau des > Dritten Reiches<* (2009) that there are

> there [was] no uniform image of women in the Nazi feature films, nor were all images of women identical to the stereotype of the German woman as wife and mother. However, if in most fictional films a concession was made to the Nazi ideal despite all the depictions of working women, in the cultural film and in the newsreel the scope for the thematisation of

---

[24] Goebbels in a speech on the occasion of the war conference of the Reichsfilmkammer on 15.02.1941; quoted after Albrecht 1979, 260 f.

female emancipation was much broader and was also no longer questioned, especially after 1939. (Ibid., 268)

The occupation of women, however, is one of the major themes of these films. From today's perspective, it is surprising that, despite the predominance of female stereotypes in Nazi films, after 1939 there was an increase in the number of working women, although they were not usually married. In particular, it seems important to note that by no means were only stereotypical drawings of female images prevalent. Rather, there is a palette of different images of women and patterns of behaviour that the protagonists go through:

> It does not seem to make much sense to establish a fixed typology of certain female characters in the entertainment film, since a woman could embody several types within her character development in the course of the film plot. Nevertheless, certain recurring portrayals of women stand out in the film, which are given an evaluation and thus positioning by the end of the film. (Ibid., 264)

The Film Version *Was tun, Sibylle?*

In the following, central elements of the filmic implementation of the literary model will be briefly presented. Here, the chronology of the plot will not be followed, but the film will be examined for ideological inscriptions, *modernisations,* questions of pedagogy and dramaturgy.

On the frame story with the setting of nature: As introduced in the scene presented at the beginning, the film begins with emotionally powerful images of nature that serve as the opening credits. Thus, the film expands the final chapter of the book version and places it at the beginning. The book ends with a pleasurably amorous scene at the bathing lake where Sibylle and Peter are alone. In the filmic frame story, the summer scene is transformed into a winter landscape, and at the same time a line of development can be read. Whereas the opening images in the film depict the group and community of the schoolgirls, the closing sequence focuses only on Sibylle and Peter. The interpretation suggests that the maturation process that the young girl has gone through in the film is now sealed with a (marital) partnership. In this respect, this framing can be understood as leading from the *Volksgemeinschaft* and jointly experienced companionate togetherness to the tete à tete on the alpine pasture, as successful female socialisation that is transferred into marriage. The *natural* destiny of the woman is staged here in an emotionally powerful way.

Fig. 1 Sibylle absorbedly contemplating the female figures. Film still (© Bundesarchiv Berlin, 18821_3)

The Ideal of Women in National Socialism as Measured by the Reading *Stoff* of the Class

The motif of the *book* plays a leading role in the plot – both in the book version and in the film version. One can name different levels that are called up. One example would be the school reading that the A level pupils read. If in the novel the *Jungle Book* is handed out (and the screenplay follows this template) in the film the book-[25] gives way to a non-fiction text. Thus, the girls' class is handed a work about Gothic female characters. Interestingly, a didactic introduction to the *Stoff* occurs here as well. To this end, teacher Fromann (portrayed by Hans Leibelt) throws various images of female figures onto the wall using a modern light-screen projector. The girls are introduced to two female figures from Naumburg Cathedral (Fig. 1); the teacher refers to these figures as "Erbe aus dem Gut unserer Ahnen"[26] (04:07:02). These are the figures of Reglindis and Uta of Naumburg. The leitmotif seen here, according to the teacher, is: "Gläubigkeit und Schönheit";[27] in an exemplary manner, the original artist understood how to capture the "Typische der deutschen Frau schlechthin."[28] Fromann continues: "Sehen Sie das aufgeschlossene Antlitz dieser Frau (die Stifterfigur Riglindis, Anm. CR): klar, wahr, heiter", im Gegensatz dazu Uta "und ihren nach innen gekehrten Blick; welch adliges Antlitz."[29] While the lec-

---

[25] "8th image classroom of UI B" (Neumeister/Bierkowski o.J., 113 f.).
[26] heritage from the estate (genome) of our ancestors.
[27] faith and beauty.
[28] what is typical of the German woman par excellence
[29] "See the open-minded face of this woman (the Stifter figure Reglindis, note CR): clear, true, cheerful"), in contrast to Uta ("and her inwardly turned gaze; what a noble countenance").

ture is heard off-screen, Sibylle is seen dreamily close-up in long shot; the girl seems to be completely absorbed in these women's countenances (cf. 04:02:09). The projection serves to capture: "Das Typische der deutschen Frau schlechthin."[30] (04.07; 2nd reel).

Dramaturgically, the use of image projection serves on the one hand to underline the modernity of media-supported teaching; on the other hand, however, it serves as a dramaturgical aid, because in order to make the theft in the classroom plausible, this process appears conceivable during the darkening of the classroom. But the *book*, as a medium, also has a plot-constituting function in the crime story. For regardless of its content, which is turned propagandistic here, it is the place where the stolen banknote was hidden and then discovered.[31]

Social Situation

Changes in the social role design are made above all in the character Sibylle. In the novel, the girl lives with her father in a rented apartment; in the film, Sibylle and the family environment are socially upgraded.

In the film version, Sibylle turns into a pony-hatted A level pupil, even if she is not as theatrical as Kästner's protagonist. The character is played by Jutta Freybe; she embodies an attractive blonde-haired young woman who rests in her pillows

Fig. 2 Sibyl at home. Film still (© Bundesarchiv Berlin, 18821_2)

---

[30] the typical nature of the German woman par excellence.

[31] The social attitude of Dr. Fromann's teacher can also be read from the book motif. It turns out that the teacher pays for the books for his students out of his own pocket, even though he claims to have received them as a gift. With this commitment, Fromann on the one hand supports booksellers and on the other hand makes it possible for his students to come into possession of reading *Stoff*. The fact that Fromann thus also knows how to direct the reading in terms of content is certainly not without significance.

like a diva (Fig. 2). Even her dog, which gave the protagonist more androgynous features in the novel, appears in the film adaptation as the young lady's expensive and loyal companion. In contrast, Lene and Käthe correspond to the book in terms of social drawing. The casting of the characters clearly indicates that Lene in particular (cast with Christine Grabe) does not have it easy in life.

Design of the Film with Attributes of *Modernity*

Ulrich Nassen has extensively studied texts of the Nazi era and pointed out the paradox that in literature of National Socialism reactionary and modern tendencies are merged. He has coined the term *reactionary modernity* for this phenomenon (Nassen 1987). Nassen defines this characteristic more precisely when he writes: "Atavistic Germanicism and progressivist technocracy are the two extremes of this ambivalent conglomerate." (Nassen 1987, 9).[32]

This observation appears to be a perfect match for the aforementioned scene, in which images of the Gothic female figures are projected onto the wall with the light show projector. Further signs of modernism, or rather quotations of it, can be found in an opening image of the film that is to be judged programmatically. Here one sees a train signal in long shot (cf. screenplay 21. part). In its design, the motif is reminiscent of Ruthmann's *Sinfonie einer Großstadt* (*Symphony of a Big City*), but also in its photographic form of contemporary photographs of the avant-garde. The girls are driving home from their ski trip, the signal mast switches to *Freie Fahrt* ("*free to go*"). This motto can be understood ambiguously.

In addition, the plot is given a *modern* charge with modern technology and props. The teacher's slide projector has already been mentioned; further attributes of modernity would be: Sibylle on the telephone she uses in her investigative work; Peter riding a motor scooter; and various settings on the train used for trips to Lene's. However, one scene in particular is programmatic and was added to the plot. These are dramatically staged images that hint at the climax of the action. Here, the camera follows the girl Lene as she walks distraught through the city; in the montage of images, one repeatedly sees a bridge railing that suggests suicide. Lene eventually stumbles through the roaring traffic without looking right or left. Finally, the girl is hit by a vehicle. The whole scene is reminiscent of Fritz Lang's legendary film *M – eine Stadt sucht einen Mörder* (1931) in its metropolitan dynamics and in the girl's wandering. This parallel is also evident in the scene photo (Fig. 3). In the screenplay, the urban locations of Dresden and Pirna are specifically named as the setting (Neumeister/Bierkowski n.d., 2).

---

[32] "National Socialism presented itself as a *myth of the abolition of divisiveness and alienation*, whereby the individual and the community could appear suspended in a 'higher' unity [...] where, by being embedded in the security of a 'Volksgemeinschaft', people were supposed to be relieved of their *fear of the future*." (Herrmann/Nassen 1993, 9)

Fig. 3 Accident scene with Lene. Film still (© Bundesarchiv Berlin, 18821_7)

Fig. 4 In the card room. Film still (© Bundesarchiv Berlin, 18821_6)

Racial-Propagandistic Iconography

In most comedies and full-length entertainment films, there are hardly any references to National Socialism in the form of swastika flags or uniforms, as was common practice during this period and desired by the Ministry of Propaganda. However, there is one specific reference in a telling scene. It takes place in the school's map room, a location that is to be taken with much hindsight. The room is where the maps and charts are kept that depict the racial and geopolitical policies of Nazism in a particular way. In the scene, the teacher Fromann, who works here during recess, and Sibylle meet for an important discussion (Fig. 4).[33]

In the film still you can see the inscription of the card: It reads: *Bilder deutscher Rassen 1 (Pictures of German Races 1)*. 9 pictures with busts of men and women in

---

[33] In the script "102nd pic: Humboldt School/Map Room" (Neumeister/Bierkowski o.J., 256).

Fig. 5 Theatrical scene *Wallenstein's* Camp. Film still (© Bundesarchiv Berlin, 18821_5)

profile and frontal shots are depicted on it; the card refers to the racist practices of National Socialism.

The scenes at the very beginning of the film can also be interpreted propagandistically. The pupils of the girls' school, named here as the Humboldt School, undertake a visit to the nearby Goethe High School, where boys go to school. Here, *Wallensteins Lager* is performed in a school play. The film shows the pupils in masquerade and costume and the merry goings-on at rehearsals. While the young actors transform themselves into warlike masks, Peter belts out the famous lines from Schiller's *Wallensteins Lager* (Fig. 5):

> Ein Reich von Soldaten wollt' er gründen,
>   Die Welt anstecken und entzünden,
>   Sich alles vermessen und unterwinden. (Neumeister/Bierkowski o. J., 35)[34]

Theft: *Volksgemeinschaft*

In addition to these mass scenes at the theatrical performance, which pay homage to martial life and German cultural assets, the film invokes the *Volksgemeinschaft*. An example of this is a scene that deals with the assessment of theft. Fromann postulates before the teaching staff:

> Sibylle Brant hat recht –
>   ... Sie haben es richtig
>   erkannt: Es geht nicht um
>   verlorene Dinge –
>   es geht um das verlorene

---

[34] An empire of soldiers he would found,
    Infect and ignite the world,
    To measure everything and to suppress it. (Neumeister/Bierkowski o.J, 35)

V e r t r a u e n! (Ebd., 123; Hervorh. i. O.)[35]

When opposition is raised from the college, he argues further:

> Nun hören Sie mal zu!
> Wir sind eine Kameradschaft -
> Kameradschaft ist Vertrauen -
> und dieses Vertrauen wollen wir auch einem
> Kameraden erhalten, der sich einmal verirrt hat -
> dann wird er von selbst wieder zu sich kommen.[36]

Alongside these militant passages, the National Socialist ideological inscriptions are also discernible in the pedagogical.

School and Educational Maxims

Comparable to the book, the film version emphasises the importance of the pedagogical and educational attitude of the teacher. To this end, various scenes are inserted that reflect discussions between the teacher Fromann and the staff, who are identified as *backwards oriented*. At the same time, the school becomes a political arena. Fromann is stylised as a star pedagogue who receives media attention and an award. Sibylle's father discovers during his morning newspaper reading that the teacher is successful with his pedagogical publication. Fromann is also praised by the school's headmaster, who offers him the prospect of a lectureship at the university. But there are also angry opponents who contradict Fromann's teaching methods, which are *based on trust*. Turbulent scenes ensue in the staff room with angry exchanges. Fromann therefore initially keeps quiet about the theft in his class. But the incident comes to light and the teacher has to justify himself. At a teachers'

---

[35] Sibylle Brant is right -
... you got it right:
It's not about
lost things -
it's about the loss in
Trust! (Ibid., 123; emphasis in the original)

[36] Now you listen!
We are a comradeship -
Camaraderie is trust -
and we want to give this trust to a
comrade who once lost his way -
then he will come to his senses on his own. (Ibid.)

conference he is confronted and insists on his approach, which is now turned from the pedagogical into the ideological when he postulates:

> Fromann steht wie ein Kämpfer,
> sagt männlich:
> „Es geht nicht nur um meine Berufung an die Universität,
> Herr Rektor .. hier steht
> meine ganze W e l t a n s c h a u u n g auf dem Spiel ...! (Ibid., 177; emphasis in the original).[37]

Ulrich Nassen and Norbert Hopster have pointed out comparable coincidences in their studies on National Socialism and education. Although, according to Nassen, there was no genuine National Socialist pedagogical theoretical stance, the educational stance was shaped by Nazi ideals. This can also be seen in teaching and German lessons:

> In this definition of the function (school as an educational function, CR) of the school, German lessons were given their own status, i.e., they became the first and most important educational instrument in the school, from which clear effects on other subjects were also expected. The most important tendency was to directly link school and life through German lessons – in contrast to the period before 1933, which was still strongly influenced by reform pedagogy; to de-subjectify school and lessons, so to speak. (Hopster/Nassen 1983, 12)

Conclusion and Outlook

The aim was to show with which complex entanglements to ideological positions and political-racist ideologemes in National Socialism entertainment or youth films were charged, which was illustrated by an exemplary example of a "medial mobilisation" (Segeberg 2004, 11). This means that it was not "the instrumentalisation of cinema in favour of a political-ideological mobilisation [...], but the mobilisation of the medium, which achieved political effects precisely by aiming even far more consistently than previously assumed to transform political references into media references" (ibid., 11 f.), that became effective.

It is interesting to see how the girls' book *Was tun, Sibylle? is* transformed in the media adaptation and how the Nazi ideologemes are implanted in the filmic realisation. The findings of media studies on entertainment films under National Socialism and on the significance of youth films for Nazi propaganda can be read from this

---

[37] Fromann stands like a fighter,
   says manly:
   "It's not just about my appointment to the university",
   Mr. Rector ... it says here
   my whole world view is at stake ...!

exemplary *Stoff*. The results of the contribution show that children's and youth media of this specific period are extremely productive types of literary material and can expand upon the already profound research on National Socialism and film with additional aspects.

References

Primary Literature

Neumeister, Wolf/Bierkowski, Heinz: Was tun, Sibylle? [Drehbuch]. Film Nr. 944 (Dritte Fassung). Ufa, Herstellungsgruppe Peter Paul Brauer. Akte: Deutsche Kinemathek Museum für Film und Fernsehen Berlin, Aktennummer: 4.4 – 80/19.100.
Schieker-Ebe, Sofi e: Was tun, Sibylle? Abenteuer eines Mädchens. Stuttgart: Thienemann, 1941 [EA 1930].
Schieker-Ebe, Sofi e: Sibylles Weg ins Leben. Stuttgart: Thienemann, 1948 [EA 1931].

Filmography

Was tun, Sibylle [Spielfilm] (D 1938). Regie: Peter Paul Brauer, Drehbuch: Wolf Neumeister und Heinz Bierkowski, Ufa, Berlin (Bundesarchiv, Friedrich-Wilhelm-Murnau-Stiftung; Archivsignatur 1/86).

Secondary Literature After 1945

Albrecht, Gerd: Der Film im Dritten Reich. Karlsruhe 1979.
Albrecht, Gerd: Nationalsozialistische Filmpolitik. Eine soziologische Untersuchung über Spielfilme im Dritten Reich. Stuttgart 1969.
Brandt, Kerstin: Sentiment und Sachlichkeit. Der Roman der Neuen Frau in der Weimarer Republik. Köln 2003 (Literatur, Kultur, Geschlecht. Große Reihe). Zugl.: FU Berlin, Univ., Diss., 1999.
Bechdolf, Ute: Wunsch-Bilder? Frauen im Nationalsozialistischen Unterhaltungsfilm. Tübingen 1992 (Studien & Materialien des Ludwig-Uhland-Instituts der Universität Tübingen; 8).
Becker, Sabina: Urbanität und Moderne. Studien zur Großstadtwahrnehmung in der deutschen Literatur 1900–1930. St. Ingbert 1993 (Saarbrücker Beiträge zur Literaturwissenschaft; 39). Zugl.: Saarbrücken, Univ., Diss., 1992.
Dahrendorf, Malte: Das Mädchenbuch und seine Leserin. Jugendlektüre als Instrument der Sozialisation. Völlig neu bearb. Aufl . Weinheim [u. a.] ^{3}1978.
Drescher, Barbara: Die ‚Neue Frau'. In: Fähnders, Walter/Karrenbrock, Helga (Hg.): Autorinnen der Weimarer Republik. Bielefeld 2003 (Aisthesis Studienbuch; 5), 163–186.
Dusdar, Bianca: Film als Propagandainstrument in der Jugendpolitik des Dritten Reiches. Alfeld 1996 (Aufsätze zur Film und Fernsehen; 32).
Fähnders, Walter/Karrenbrock, Helga: Einleitung: In: Ders./Dies. (Hg.): Autorinnen der Weimarer Republik. Bielefeld 2003 (Aisthesis Studienbuch; 5), 7–19.

Film im NS-Staat (o. V.): „Film im NS-Staat", https://www.filmportal.de/thema/film-im-ns-staat (19.08.2019).
Frietsch, Elke/Herkommer Christina: Nationalsozialismus und Geschlecht. Eine Einführung. In: Dies. (Hg.): Nationalsozialismus und Geschlecht. Zur Politisierung und Ästhetisierung von Körper, „Rasse" und Sexualität im „Dritten Reich" und nach 1945. Bielefeld 2009, 9–44.
Goebbels, Joseph: Der Film als Erzieher. Rede zur Eröffnung der Filmarbeit der HJ. Berlin, 12. Oktober 1941. In: Ders. (Hg.): Das eherne Herz. Reden und Aufsätze aus den Jahren 1941/42. München 1943, 37–46. Abgedr. in: Albrecht, Gerd: Nationalsozialistische Filmpolitik. Eine soziologische Untersuchung über Spielfilme des Dritten Reiches. Stuttgart 1969, 480–483.
Grenz, Dagmar: Mädchenliteratur. In: Wild, Reiner (Hg.): Geschichte der deutschen Kinder- und Jugendliteratur. Überarb. und erw. Aufl. Stuttgart ³2008, 379–393.
Grenz, Dagmar: Der Trotzkopf – ein Bestseller damals und heute. In: Dies./Wilkending, Gisela (Hg.): Geschichte der Mädchenlektüre. Mädchenliteratur und die gesellschaftliche Situation der Frauen vom 18. Jahrhundert bis zur Gegenwart. Weinheim [u. a.] 1997 (Lesesozialisation und Medien), 115–122.
Grimm, Petra: Herzensfreund und Herzensleid – Anmerkungen zur deutschen Filmkomödie im diachronen Vergleich. In: Krah, Hans (Hg.): Geschichte(n) NS-Film – NS-Spuren heute. Kiel: 2000 (LIMES – Literatur- und Medienwissenschaftliche Studien; 1), 51–64.
Herrmann, Ulrich/Nassen, Ulrich: Die ästhetische Inszenierung von Herrschaft und Beherrschung im nationalsozialistischen Deutschland. Über die ästhetischen und ästhetischpolitischen Strategien nationalsozialistischer Herrschaftspraxis, deren mentalitäre Voraussetzungen und Konsequenzen. In: Dies. (Hg.): Formative Ästhetik im Nationalsozialismus. Intentionen, Medien und Praxisformen totalitärer ästhetischer Herrschaft und Beherrschung. Weinheim [u. a.] 1993 (Zeitschrift für Pädagogik; 31. Beih.), 9–12.
Hopster, Norbert: Heimat und Volkstum. In: Ders./Josting, Petra/Neuhaus, Joachim: Kinder- und Jugendliteratur 1933–1945. Ein Handbuch, Bd. 2, Stuttgart 2005, 353–410.
Hopster, Norbert/Nassen, Ulrich: Literatur und Erziehung im Nationalsozialismus. Deutschunterricht als Körperkultur. Paderborn [u. a.] 1983 (Informationen zur Sprache und Literaturdidaktik; 39).
Jacobsen, Wolfgang/Aurich, Rolf: Der Sonnensucher. Konrad Wolf. Biographie. Berlin 2005
Jatho, Gabriele: City Girls. Aufbruch in den Zwanzigern. In: Dies./Rother, Rainer (Hg.): City Girls. Frauenbilder im Stummfilm. Berlin 2007, 10–13.
Josting, Petra: „Gehe niemals vom Wege ab …" Fritz Genschows Rotkäppchen -Verfilmungen ideologisch auf Kurs. In: Roeder, Caroline (Hg.): Parole(n) – Politische Dimensionen von Kinder- und Jugendmedien. Stuttgart 2020 (Studien zu Kinder-und Jugendliteratur und -medien; 2), 271–284.
Karrenbrock, Helga: „Das Heraustreten der Frau aus dem Bild des Mannes". Zum Selbstverständnis schreibender Frauen in den Zwanziger Jahren. In: Fähnders, Walter/Karrenbrock, Helga (Hg.): Autorinnen der Weimarer Republik. Bielefeld 2003 (Aisthesis Studienbuch; 5), 21–38.
Kracauer, Siegfried: Die kleinen Ladenmädchen gehen ins Kino. In: Ders. (Hg.): Das Ornament der Masse. Essays. Frankfurt a. M. 1963, 279–294.
Krah, Hans/Wünsch, Marianne: Der Film des Nationalsozialismus als Vorbehaltsfilm oder ‚Ufa-Klassiker'. Vom Umgang mit der Vergangenheit. Eine Einführung. In: Ders. (Hg.): Geschichte(n) NS-Film – NS-Spuren heute. Kiel 2000 (Literatur- und Medienwissenschaftliche Studien; 1), 9–29.
Nassen, Ulrich: Jugend, Buch und Konjunktur 1933–1945. Studien zum Ideologiepotential des genuin nationalsozialistischen und des konjunkturellen ›Jugendschriftentums‹. München 1987.
Roeder, Caroline: Vom Trotzkopf bis Tschick, von Moritz bis Marsmädchen. Nonkonforme adoleszente ProtagonistInnen im Spannungsfeld von (literarischen) Regel-Diskursen. In: Freudenberg, Ricarda/Josting, Petra (Hg.): Norm und Normüberschreitung in der Kinder- und Jugendliteratur und ihren Institutionen. München 2015 (kjl&m 15.extra), 44–57.
Roeder, Caroline: Vom *Trotzkopf* zum *Stargirl* – von der traditionellen Mädchen-Pensionats-Geschichte zum aktuellen College-Außenseiterinnen-Adoleszenzroman. In: Zabka, Thomas (Hg.): Schule in der neueren Kinder- und Jugendliteratur. Baltmannsweiler 2008, 157–176.

Scheidgen, Irina: Frauenbilder im Spielfilm, Kulturfilm und in der Wochenschau des „Dritten Reiches". In: Frietsch, Elke/Herkommer, Christina (Hg.): Nationalsozialismus und Geschlecht. Zur Politisierung und Ästhetisierung von Körper, „Rasse" und Sexualität im „Dritten Reich" und nach 1945. Bielefeld 2009 (GenderCodes; 6), 259–281.

Schieker, Friedrich: Die Grundschule und das Kind. Einblicke in Notwendigkeiten für Schule und Haus. Stuttgart 1924.

Segeberg, Harro: Erlebnisraum Kino. Das Dritte Reich als Kultur- und Mediengesellschaft. In: Ders. (Hg.): Mediale Mobilmachung I. Das Dritte Reich und der Film. Mediengeschichte des Films, Bd. 4, München 2004, 11–42.

Stahr, Gerhard: Volksgemeinschaft vor der Leinwand? Der nationalsozialistische Film und sein Publikum. Berlin 2001. Zugl.: Berlin, Freie Univ., Diss., 1998.

Steinlein, Rüdiger: Gemeinsam sind wir stark. Die Kindergruppe als soziales Modell bei Erich Kästner und anderen Autoren der 20er und 30er Jahre. In: Deutschunterricht 52 (1999) 6, 449–460.

Tost, Birte: Nesthäkchens freche Schwestern. Das ‚Neue Mädchen' in kinderliterarischen Texten von Autorinnen der Weimarer Republik. In: Fähnders, Walter/Karrenbrock, Helga (Hg.): Autorinnen der Weimarer Republik. Bielefeld 2003 (Aisthesis Studienbuch; 5), 239–255.

Wilkending, Gisela: Man sollte den *Trotzkopf* noch einmal lesen. Anmerkungen zu einer anderen Lesart. In: Grenz, Dagmar/Wilkending, Gisela (Hg.): Geschichte der Mädchenlektüre. Mädchenliteratur und die gesellschaftliche Situation der Frauen vom 18. Jahrhundert bis zur Gegenwart. Weinheim [u. a.] 1997 (Lesesozialisation und Medien), 123–138.

Politics Conquer Book and Film

Pacifist Anti-War Films of the Pre-Fascist Era

The Media Network Surrounding *Im Westen nichts Neues*

Ricarda Freudenberg

Introduction

This article aims to reconstruct the media network surrounding the film adaptation of the 1930 novel *Im Westen nichts Neues*. It does so with the help of Schmidt's (2008/2012) notion of media as a compact concept and systemises the descriptive aspects according to Schmidt's modelled spheres of action "production", "distribution", "reception" and "post processing" (cf. Schmidt 2008). At the same time, it becomes clear that the heuristics of the model have their limitations in several places: This is the case, on the one hand, where a "post processing" format becomes the new starting point and is examined from the perspective of "production", which in turn leads to marketing and reception – the model is unable to depict this shift in focus. A more dynamic model is needed here, one that makes the cluster structure of a media network visible. A network-like structure could also bring out a phenomenon such as interpictoriality more strongly, which can be observed in the present case on the basis of book covers, posters, film shots and panels. On the other hand, the question arises as to whether a media network is actually founded solely on the direct reference of these spheres of activity to one another, or whether a virulent problem, a controversial question in socio-political or cultural-political discussion, to which media formats devote themselves in parallel, is not also sufficient as a nucleus. Possibly a media network, conceived in this way, does not constitute itself, but is subsequently contoured and profiled through attribution and assignment at the moment of "post processing" by film criticism and cultural policy.

This article will take these questions into account when it focuses on the first film adaptation of Remarque's novel in order to examine the dimensions of this media

---

R. Freudenberg (✉)
PH Weingarten, Weingarten, Germany
e-mail: freudenberg@ph-weingarten.de

network, first from a synchronic and then from a diachronic perspective. Two German films produced at roughly the same time, *Niemandsland* (*No Man's Land*) and *Westfront 1918,* are included, as is an adaptation of the novel as a graphic novel from the 2014 commemorative year, when the subject experienced a renewed boom.

The article will also examine whether and in which regards the films discussed can be described as *anti-war films*. In doing so, the production as well as reception perspective and the attribution practice will be taken into account: Does the film open up an "ostensibly war-critical perspective" (Röwekamp 2011, 13)? Is it "capable of deconstructing media and cultural constructions of the truth of war" (ibid., 209)?[1] Does it use means to do so that are antithetical to those of war films? Is it advertised accordingly? Or is it rather received and discussed retrospectively by the audience, by critics, by the social debate in the feuilletons, for example, as an anti-war film? Qualifying these films as *l'art engagé* runs the risk of reducing them to their cultural and socio-political function. This would mean ignoring the fact that they are aesthetic entities, literary fiction, modern, innovative film art, sometimes even cinematic experiments. And indeed, as will be shown, these perspectives are not expanded upon sufficiently in contemporary reactions.

Im Westen nichts Neues (*All Quiet on the Western Front*) (USA 1930)

This first of the two literary adaptations based on the novel by Erich Maria Remarque (1928/1929)[2] was certainly predicated on the market-strategic intention to participate in the success of the original.[3] As a reminder: after the typescript had been initially rejected by the publisher S. Fischer – on the grounds that the Great War no longer interested anyone (cf. Schneider 2015, 337) – and then also because of the supposedly strong pacifist tendencies[4] by the Scherl-Verlag, which had been responsible for the magazine *Der Kinematograph*[5] since 1923, the manuscript was finally accepted by the bourgeois-liberal Ullstein-Verlag in the summer of 1928, albeit with manifold requirements for it to be edited (cf. ibid.). Preprints were published from 10.11. to 09.12.28 in the *Berliner Vossische Zeitung. Berlinische Zeitung von*

---

[1] Incidentally, the anti-war films of the period between the two world wars discussed here seem more visionary than backward-looking in this respect.

[2] For a comparison of the two film adaptations, see Boeckh 2018.

[3] On the background to the creation of a film adaptation in which "artistic motivations and economic objectives" intertwine, cf. Schwab 2006, 30.

[4] On the reasons for the rejection, cf. also the interview with Fritz Lucke, chief editor at Scherl-Verlag, in *Geschundenes Zelluloid. Das Schicksal des Kinoklassikers* Im Westen nichts Neues, Documentary, ZDF (1984), 2:33–3:17.

[5] Film magazine (1907–1935); from 1923 published by August Scherl, part of the national-conservative Hugenberg Group. The Jewish editor-in-chief Alfred Rosenthal emigrates in 1933 and is murdered in Riga in 1942.

Staats- und gelehrten Sachen, which also belonged to the Ullstein-Verlag. Remarque's novel was published in book format on 29.01.29 by the Imprint Propyläen-Verlag.[6]

As early as July 1929, the Jewish American of German descent Carl Laemmle, head of Universal Pictures, bought the film rights. Filming began in November. The director was Lewis Milestone, who in World War I as an employee of the Army Signal Corps "had gained experience in cinematic war photography and in making military training films, so he was very familiar with the media conditions of war." (Röwekamp 2011, 80)

Novel and Film Adaptation (*Post Processing*): A Comparison from a Narratological Perspective

"The screenplay of ALL QUIET ON THE WESTERN FRONT shows hardly any changes compared to the novel." (Ibid.) This thesis will be decisively contradicted in the following; rather, the screenplay shows serious changes. The fact that the change of media as a whole leads to the fact that it is not merely an adaptation, but a transformation, should not come as a surprise in view of two different types of media, each with its own "aesthetic conventions" (Schwab 2006, 39). This will be shown by means of three selected aspects (theme, dramaturgy, narrative perspective).

There is an observable shift in subject: the novel *Im Westen nichts Neues* is conceived as the first part of a trilogy. It is mainly concerned with the question of how a continuation of life, a resocialisation of the so-called lost generation, might be possible. This problem is reflected in prominent places in the novel, with shockingly disillusioned views being voiced: "Albert spricht es aus. 'Der Krieg hat uns für alles verdorben.'"[7] (Remarque 2015, 93) Paul Bäumer, protagonist and first-person narrator, confirms, "Er hat recht."[8] (Ibid.) In the novel, the conversation is divided into two scenes: First, young recruits and veteran soldiers sit together; later, the boys alone exchange ideas about their chances for a civilian life in peace.

However, in the film adaptation this theme is pushed back: it is only late in the story[9] that the soldiers start talking about the time after the war. Unlike the novel, the question is motivated by the fact that the homeland gains access to the front by means of a letter from his wife to Detering. Now a type of awareness seeps in that, parallel to the fighting at the front, relatives at home are struggling for their daily survival. The aforementioned two scenes are drawn together in the film so that the contrast is visibly stronger. The young confront the old directly with their envy of their family and civilian life: "Ihr alten Knochen habt gut reden. Ihr habt ja etwas,

---

[6] A spin-off of the Ullstein publishing house in 1919, sold in 1934.
[7] "Albert pronounces. 'The war has spoiled us for everything.'"
[8] "He's right."
[9] From 1:07:35 of the German DVD version (2004), which is also quoted from below.

das auf euch wartet: Frau, Kinder, Arbeit. Aber was ist mit uns? Was haben wir schon groß zu erwarten [...]?"[10] The scene ends on a far more somber and fatalistic note than in the novel. Leer enumerates what has become of the classmates and concludes, "Eines Tages werden wir alle tot sein. Also was reden wir noch darüber?"[11] (1:09:53).

These moments of reflection and discussion are rare in the film. Instead, it focuses on the experiences at the front, which on the one hand are contrasted with scenes at home, and on the other hand are illustrated in all their agonising dimensions through the constant alternation of combat and waiting phases. Another thematic focus is put on the staging of industrialised war, which includes not only machine warfare but also the constant flow of human supplies: very young, mostly naïve, and ideologically blinded, cheerful boys grow up prematurely into hardened and disillusioned men before they fall in battle and are replaced by even younger ones; the article will return to this later. In this respect, one can indeed speak of thematic shifts, which are most certainly also based on the fact that no sequel was intended.[12]

On a dramaturgical level, enrichments, condensations, and restructurings are observable. After the prologue, for example, the film enters the plot via a dialogue scene between two civilians (according to the script, the caretaker couple of a school) that does not exist in the novel. As they sweep, the door to the outside is opened, and endless platoons of soldiers march by: "30.000!" "Alles Russen?" "Nein, Franzosen. Russen nehmen wir jeden Tag so viele gefangen."[13] Consequently, while the novel begins *in medias res*, "neun Kilometer hinter der Front"[14] (Remarque 2015, 9), the film places scenes at home at the beginning, within civilian life, into which the effects of the war break: the march of prisoners; the enlistment of civilians, such as the postman Himmelstoß, "Feldwebel der Reserve"[15] (Schrader 1992, 291), as he explains to the butcher, seen on his last day in his civilian job. Himmelstoß comes across as a friendly man to the viewer who tends to be servile – all the more reason to ask how he could become such a sadist.

A second scene is inserted. On home leave, the disillusioned Paul tells his former class teacher Kantorek in class about the war as he has experienced it. Full of childish arrogance and naivety, the younger ones are outraged by the older man's descriptions and yet are next to die on the battlefield. Certainly because of this flaming anti-war plea, the film is perceived and discussed as a pacifist anti-war film. This scene, however, like several others, is cut out before the first screening in Germany.

---

[10] "You old bones can talk. You've got something waiting for you: Wife, kids, job. But what about us? What great thing have we to look forward to [...]?"

[11] "One day we'll all be dead. So what are we still talking about?"

[12] Remarque's sequel to the novel *Der Weg zurück* was published three quarters of a year after the American premiere of the film adaptation of *Im Westen nichts Neues*.

[13] "30,000!" "All Russians?" "No, French. Russians we capture so many every day."

[14] "nine kilometers behind the front".

[15] "sergeant of the reserve".

Other scenes in the novel, as mentioned, are contracted in the film. As a result, instead of two, there is only one furlough. After being wounded and hospitalised, Paul is allowed to visit his family. Consequently, his answer to his mother's question (which she also asks in the novel) about whether he is wounded is a lie in the film: "Nein, Mutter, ich habe Urlaub."[16] (1:46:17) And the character of Peter from the Catholic military hospital is dispensed with; his role – of protesting, filled with terrible foreboding, against his transfer to the death chamber – is taken by Paul himself. The film here follows its principle of concentrating on the protagonist. In doing so, it imbues the scene with a tremendous dramatic mood and Paul's justified extreme fear of dying with a vehemence that the viewer can hardly escape. But similar to Peter against all odds, Paul will also return from the death chamber.

The most modern cinematic means of the time are used to charge some scenes, some moments with high symbolic power. This is sometimes done in a striking way and conveys quite obvious comments and evaluations. Here, the boot scene is certainly one of the most prominent – it, too, is cut out for the German screening. Franz Kemmerich, one of Paul's classmates, loses not only his leg but also his life. Müller unsentimentally accepts the inheritance in the form of a good pair of boots; a rarity on the front. As the events take place at the beginning of the novel, the first-person narrator Paul feels he still has to justify his comrade's pragmatic actions – later he relies on the reader knowing how to classify the actions, motives for action and corresponding linguistic expressions of the front-line soldiers. This apologia of the narrator to the reader is realised in the film[17] as a dialogue: Müller himself now explains and excuses his unsentimental actions to Paul, who – on behalf of the viewer – plays it down, shows forbearance, and forgives.

In the novel, the boots are only mentioned again towards the end, with the death of Müller, as Paul now inherits them and plans to pass them on to Tjaden after his own demise. The film is different, condensing this succession into an impressive 56-second sequence of images. It uses the camera for this, which always places the boots prominently instead of their wearers. The sequence, which works without editing but with cross-fading, ends with the boots being shown again. They become a concrete material symbol, "outlive" their wearer, experience a "resurrection" to new service in order to carry their next owner marching to his death. By means of the boots, which are medially staged as a symbol, the tireless cycle of human wear and replenishment, a death machinery indifferent to individual fate, is brought into focus.

A scene in the dugout makes similarly clear allusions to the fact that the soldier at the front loses not only his life but also his dignity: the comrades beat rats to death before they go into battle to kill opponents and be killed themselves. The film devotes a full 8 minutes to this fight scene (attack and counterattack).

---

[16] "No, Mother, I'm on leave."

[17] Since the film follows the chronology of events in its structure, the scene is found at a much later point, after about 60 min in the DVD version.

Even the death scene, deliberately kept laconic in the novel, is symbolically charged in the film: Paul reaches out of the dugout for a butterfly and is shot in the process. The final sentence, which also contains the title, is spoken from off-screen. The film ends with a dissolve of the military cemetery by marching youths in uniform, who look back at the viewer.[18]

Unlike the novel, the film is structured chronologically. As previously stated, the beginning of the film shows the eve of Paul's and his comrades' experiences at the front at home. This includes their recruitment, a scene that is taken as a memory sequence from a later passage in the novel. The students in one class are encouraged by their teacher to volunteer. The film brings the events out of the subjective memory of the protagonist and first-person narrator Paul into observable, present, attested, and shared reality. At the same time, it becomes clear that the film rearranges the structure of the novel, it narrates chronologically, while the novel, which in any case begins later in the temporal course of the plot, breaks through the chronology in order to narrate in retrospective, to provide insights into memories. This can be justified in terms of both effect and media aesthetics. In her comparative analysis of the film adaptations from 1930 and 1979, Klara Boeckh argues that the older of the two makes the entire genesis of the students into young soldiers, their development and change, visible and comprehensible through the chronological structure (cf. Boeckh 2018, 97 f.). Overall, the chronological arrangement relies entirely on the "continuously" dramatic culmination, which finds "its climax in the death of Katczinsky, the boys' father figure, as well as the death of the leading figure Paul, which immediately follows." (ibid., 98)

In terms of media aesthetics, the restructuring can be justified by the change of media and the abandonment of a narrator. Paul's memories are inserted into the chronologically arranged plot structure, his reflections on the events as an autodiegetic narrator are reworked into character monologues and dialogues. In this respect, scenes that drive the action forward alternate with scenes of a retarding character in which the individuals reflect on what they have experienced, their homeland and their future.

Internal focalisation and autodiegesis are consequently abandoned: The film tells the story of Paul Bäumer and his comrades by means of non-personal camera work, not from Paul's perspective. Nevertheless, Paul remains at the centre, he is absent as the protagonist in only a few scenes. We are thus dealing with the dissolution of the identity of narrative instance and character, with the detachment of the narrative perspective from the character Paul; the consequence is overview instead of insight. The film does transform Paul's speech of thought in the novel: it is now put into the character's mouth as direct speech, for example when he tells Müller how he saw Kemmerich die and felt all the more intensely what it means to live on his way back (from 1:03:40).[19]

---

[18] Cf. in detail Bronfen 2013.
[19] In the novel: Remarque 2015, 41.

Paul's narration, however, is different. By dispensing with a *voice-over procedure*, his reflections seem to be omitted, for example those on the connection between physiognomy and malice, stemming from his experiential knowledge:

> Es ist übrigens komisch, daß das Unglück der Welt so oft von kleinen Leuten herrührt, sie sind viel energischer und unverträglicher als großgewachsene. Ich habe mich stets gehütet, in Abteilungen mit kleinen Kompagnieführern zu geraten; es sind meistens verfluchte Schinder.[20] (Remarque 2015, 18 f.)

Retrospective observations of the narrator Paul are transposed by means of camera and sound: "Wir wurden hart, mißtrauisch, rachsüchtig, roh, […]"[21] (Ibid., 34). However, unlike the novel, the film can only visualise the result of military education, but not that Paul is aware of this transformation and evaluates it: "[…] – und das war gut; denn diese Eigenschaften fehlten uns gerade. Hätte man uns ohne diese Ausbildungszeit in den Schützengraben geschickt, dann wären wohl die meisten von uns verrückt geworden."[22] (Ibid.)

This does not mean, however, that there is no narrative instance and that the film does not evaluate what it tells – on the contrary, its *point of view* becomes discernible on different levels, as was shown, for example, under "symbolism". For films distribute "the narrative activity among several functionaries" (Schwab 2006, 81). According to Schwab, they thus come even closer to "the original [oral, RF] narration" with its factors of "spontaneity", "affectivity", "vividness" and "continuity" (ibid.). Reflection and evaluation, in the novel bound to the instance of the narrator, are consequently transformed with the help of the technical possibilities offered by the medium of film. Finally, this will be examined using camera and sound technology as examples.

The Production of the Film from a Media-Aesthetic Perspective

A whole series of technical achievements open up previously unknown staging possibilities; for example, the crane to which the camera is attached and the rails on which this construction can travel along, thus providing an overhead view of the trenches and at the same time an insight. This creates proximity, for example in the bomb crater scene (1:15:02 to 1:22:45). The viewer is trapped in the bomb crater with the two figures and is a direct witness to the events. The camera shows Paul

---

[20] "It's funny, by the way, that the misfortunes of the world so often come from little people; they are much more energetic and intolerable than tall ones. I have always been careful not to get into detachments with small company leaders; they are usually cursed drudges."

[21] "We became hard, suspicious, pitiless, vindictive, raw, […]".

[22] "[…] – and that was good; because we lacked these qualities just then. If we had been sent to the trenches without this period of training, I think most of us would have gone mad."

Fig. 1 *Im Westen nichts Neues* (*All Quiet on the Western Front*), bomb crater scene (1:15:46)

Bäumer and Gérard Duval as individuals in close-ups, even before Paul finds the ID card[23] and family photo of his opponent and victim (Fig. 1).

As early as in the martinet scene, which virtually testifies to the merciless drill in the barracks yard in preparation for deployment to the front, the close-up shot, in addition to the shot and counter-shot, documents how Paul's muddy face reflects humiliation, but also defiance, on behalf of all the boys.

Another innovation concerns sound technology, advertised as "Licht- und Nadelton"[24] (Im Westen nichts Neues [Anzeige] 1930). Needle tone as the older process, in which film and sound were synchronised by needle technology and the sound carrier played in parallel with the film carrier (which only worked to a limited extent), is replaced by the light-tone process, "in which sounds were transformed into a pulsating beam of light that was preserved on film and could be reconverted into sound made audible via amplifier and loudspeaker during projection" (Hüningen 2012). This process was developed in the USA and used by Western Electric. The aforementioned crane, on which the microphone was mounted, made it possible to record the spoken word at the same time as the image, for example in the bomb crater scene. The sounds and music were mixed in later.

The innovative sound technology plays a central role in the film. On the one hand, this is evident in view of the media staging of the war, for the shell impacts, the drum fire, the machine-gun salvos are not just background noise. The film tells of how thunderous noise alternates with threatening silence, the fateful low hum before the shell impacts. The danger that announces itself in such a way is acoustically anticipated by the characters, but also by the recipients (of whom, one may assume, quite a few knew how to interpret these signals from their own experience at the time).

---

[23] On the cover page of the card, the first name is Gérald, inside it is Gérard.
[24] "light and needle tone".

On the other hand, one of the quietest and most compassionate scenes in the film relies on sound rather than image. In the coitus scene, Paul and Suzanne are not shown, but their intimacy is respected by the camera. The viewer remains with it in the anteroom of the bedroom, with only shadows suggesting that the two characters are in the next room. Only their whispering – which fails semantically but not pragmatically as a conversation because of the language barrier – is the focus.

Distribution: Posters and Advertisements

Even before production began (shooting started on 11.11.1929 at Universal City studios), Carl Laemmle was warned by Ufa[25] that it would not distribute the film. Instead, it was distributed by Deutsche Universal Film AG, Laemmle's own company (founded in 1921, acquired by Rota-Film-AG in 1934). The film version of the novel is advertised with the obvious intention of participating in its success.[26] In the same month in which Laemmle acquired the film rights, this was announced in a full-page advertisement in the film magazine *Der Kinematograph*, the upper half of which is printed with the author's name and the title of the novel: "We alone have acquired the film rights to this most widely read book of recent years, which has now been translated into 20 languages." At the same time, it warns against "infringing our ownership rights in any way" (Im Westen nichts Neues [Anzeige] 1929). Deutsche Universal Film AG thus also reserved the exclusive right to advertise this media network, consisting of novel and film adaptation. What is more: this advertising, for example through posters and advertisements, is equally part of the media network, as will be shown.

Advertisements include the purchase of the film rights for "the greatest book success of recent decades" (Wir beginnen heute [Anzeige] 1929), for – note the increase – "the most widely read book of all time" (*Unsere Produktion* [ad] 1929) and for a film "based on the work of the same name by Erich Maria Remarque, published in millions" (*Voranzeige!* [ad] 1930), "based on the world-famous novel of the same name by Erich Maria Remarque" (*Im Westen nichts Neues* [ad] 1930). To underline the close relationship to the original visually, this advertisement (Fig. 2) quotes the Fraktur typeface of the cover of the first edition in white on a black background. In contrast to this, the informative, clearly smaller text modules in the right margin (black on a white background) are designed in antiqua.

American posters advertise with the face or the uniformed bust of Lew Ayres, the largely unknown leading actor. The subject and style of these posters are reminiscent of the dust jacket of the American first edition,[27] designed by Paul Wenck. It

---

[25] In 1927 Alfred Hugenberg buys Ufa and transfers it to the NSDAP in 1933.

[26] The rigid media network concept according to Möbius 2014 could be applied to this phenomenon, which is "primarily production and product-oriented"; it is "a coupling of different media for commercial reasons." (Möbius 2014, 225)

[27] Boston: Little, Brown, and Company 1929.

Fig. 2 *Im Westen nichts Neues* [ad] (1930), from: *Kinematograph* 24 (1930) 279 of 29.11., 5

shows a uniformed, helmeted soldier looking past the viewer, in the style of a carefully coloured pencil drawing (grey uniform, reddish-brown face, pale yellow background).[28] The model for this cover, in turn, is a German propaganda poster from 1917, designed by Fritz Erler in the style of an etching, with the appeal: "Helft uns siegen! zeichnet die Kriegsanleihe".[29] An early German poster version takes the American one as its inspiration; here, too, the soldier with Lew Ayres' face is the focus, supplemented by the film title in the familiar Fraktur font and production information.

---

[28] Different the English first edition of 1929 (London: Putnam), whose dust jacket is without illustration. Only a 1930 edition by the same publisher shows the color drawing of an unknown soldier in the familiar pose in front of white flowering trees.

[29] "Help us win! draw the war bond".

This brief overview reveals several things: firstly, the continuity of the advertising strategy around a staged figure, which extends from a political poster from Munich during the First World War to the distribution of the US translation of the novel (by A. W. Wheen) to the promotion of first the American, then the German film version. Secondly, with the translation and publication in the USA, the protagonist Paul Bäumer is given a face for the first time via the dust jacket. The marketing of the film takes advantage of this by basically retaining the arrangement, but exchanging the face of one unknown for that of the other, the young Lew Ayres. Consequently on the one hand, the Unknown Soldier, over whose grave the soldiers will pass by means of cinematic devices such as dissolves at the end of the film, is brought out of his anonymity: he now has not only a name and a biography, but also a countenance. On the other hand, however, he retains "the generality of the 'Everyman'" (Wulff 2006, 48), remains an exemplary representative of his generation. The mention of actors' names thus recedes into the background. Louis Wolheim, who plays Katczinsky, is far better known than the leading actor which is why he is mentioned first on posters and advertisements that mention names at all. Regardless, a July 1929 advertisement flaunts that the film will be made "as a German-speaking talkie in Germany and America with a very large cast." (Der größte Bucherfolg [Anzeige] 1929) What seems exaggerated in view of the acting renown may well be valid in view of the sheer quantity of extras and collaborators.

The publicity for the film does not refer solely to the popularity of the novel. From the beginning, the innovative technology of the film was also pointed out: It was a sound film (not a matter of course at the time, and to that extent necessarily effective in advertising), specified with the reference to the "light and needle tone" discussed, i.e. to the state of the art sound technology at the time. For the German audience, the addition of "German-speaking talkie" is supposed to be attractive; the film is dubbed by Rhythmographie GmbH in Berlin.[30] At the same time, attention is drawn to a silent film version for cinemas that have not yet been converted: A "*silent* (underlined in the original) version has been specially shot" (… und unsere große stumme Produktion 1930/31 [Anzeige] 1930).

The film is not advertised as an *anti-war film*. Carl Laemmle is aware that the film adaptation would be just as polarising as the novel. As a result it was difficult enough to break into the German market with the film – it had to be shortened by crucial passages and the American screenplay had to be rewritten in some dialogues. In March 1930, the producer was still apparently politically reticent:

> Mr. Laemmle said at the time that he was making neither a war film nor a pacifist story. He was portraying life as a poet sees it, objectively and without bias. (Anti-German Films in America 1930)

---

[30] On the rhythmographic process according to Carl Robert Blum, cf. Wedel 2011, 192 ff. Wedel discusses the initial lack of audience acceptance of post-synchronized films despite good technical results.

Three quarters of a year later, however, they say:

> Among other things, Uncle Carl literally told the representative of this (American, RF) correspondence office that he was proud to have brought out Remarque's film, and that it would be wonderful if the film could be shown throughout Germany. For through this film one could counteract the propaganda which was being carried on by the armaments industry, and work against the revival of German militarism. (Zirkus Nollendorfplatz 1930)

The difference in the producer's assessment of his work – non-political work of art, pure literary adaptation or use for enlightened political purposes – can be explained by looking at the addressees: in the one case the German market, in the other the American public, his second home.

In the reviews and the well-documented censorship process, however, the political and ideological readings dominate. The attribution of *anti-war film* is thus *post festum*.

Reception: Political Debates and Censorship

The premiere took place in April 1930 in Los Angeles. Already for this, the film was shortened by 10 minutes compared to the original version. The film was shown for the first time in New York on April 29, 1930. At the beginning of June 1930 the film was premiered in London, at the beginning of November in Strasbourg. In the same month it won Academy Awards for Best Film and Best Director.

As early as March 1930, political debates begin in Germany about supposed "anti-German inflammatory films" (Antideutsche Filme in Amerika 1930) in America with blatant reference to *All Quiet on the Western Front*. *Der Kinematograph* defends Carl Laemmle: he is the only American producer who also produces in Germany and thus creates jobs (cf. Vom Westen was Neues 1930). The film passed censorship by the Filmprüfstelle Berlin on 21.11.30. The premiere of the German-language version took place within the framework of a festive event on Thursday, 04.12.30, at 8.30 pm (and in a late screening at 11.00 pm) in the Berlin Mozartsaal (Theater am Nollendorfplatz). The version shown was, as mentioned, considerably shortened, for example by Paul's haunting account of his experiences at the front on home leave, so that Siegfried Kracauer comes to the conclusion:

> Paul [...] is occasionally called upon by the school professor during his vacation to appear before the class and inflame it with a short speech. He refuses to second the professorial heroic patter, desperately protesting that he cannot speak. This muteness marks the highly contestable neutrality of the film (and, of course, the novel). It is inimical to cognition. It elevates war to the status of mythical fate, which it is not, and leaves it with the inevitability that it does not have. (Kracauer 1930)

The same issue also describes massive disturbances of the performance on 05.12.1930 by National Socialists under the leadership of Joseph Goebbels, which ultimately led to an abrupt stop of the 7 pm performance and the cancellation of the 9 pm performance. A prominent witness at the time reported:

> On December 3, Else Lasker-Schüler writes to Robert Asher that she has "2 beautiful tickets for next door in the Mozart Hall": "Nothing New in the West Film: Première" (KA, vol. 8. p. 252). [...] On February 4, 1931, Else Lasker-Schüler informs Adolf Grimme: "I am not yet healed from the Nollendorf battle. Still a wound in the upper arm and lower foot, so I fought with the Nazis & society still outside in front of the film posters fists flew like grenades." (KA, vol. 8. p. 262). (Skrodzki 2015)

The Jewish director of the cinema, Hanns Brodnitz,[31] from then on showed the film under massive police protection, as there were demonstrations every evening. These were banned on 10.12.1930 by the Minister of the Interior Severing and the Police President Grzesinski.[32] However, at the request of the governments of Saxony, Bavaria, Württemberg, Thuringia, and Brunswick, but not Prussia, the film censorship was carried out on 11.12.1930 by the Film-Oberprüfstelle Berlin, which thus revoked the approval by the Filmprüfstelle Berlin of 21.11.1930. The film was then shown in the cinema.[33] On the same day, the Berlin government approved the screening of the film in a debate of the Prussian parliament.[34] The film was then re-approved by the Berlin Film Board on 08.06.1931, but initially with restrictions (no young people and only closed events),[35] which were successively lifted later in the year. Hanns Brodnitz, however, was expressly refused permission by Deutsche Universal to show the film in the Mozartsaal. As a direct consequence, the Mozartsaal ran out of money and was forced to close. On 13.03.1933 the Landesfilmstelle Süd applied for a definitive ban. The illustrious list also included *Niemandsland* and *Westfront 1918*. In accordance with the application, the films were banned from 22.04.1933 onwards. In November 1937, the *Film-Kurier* reports that the film was going to be the subject of the Munich exhibition *Der ewige Jude* (*The Eternal Jew*) in the library building of the Deutsches Museum (cf. Filmprodukte der Verfallszeit 1937).

---

[31] Brodnitz had to go into hiding from 1938, was arrested in 1943 and murdered in Auschwitz in 1944. His notes on the events can be found in the autobiography *Kino intim*, which is well worth reading, the proofs of which survived the war and were published in 2005.

[32] Cf. http://www.remarque.uni-osnabrueck.de/iwnnfilm.htm (24.08.2017).

[33] Cf. http://www.difarchiv.deutsches-filminstitut.de/zengut/dt2tb154z.pdf (29.06.2019).

[34] Cf. http://www.remarque.uni-osnabrueck.de/iwnnfilm.htm (24.08.2017).

[35] http://www.difarchiv.deutsches-filminstitut.de/zengut/dt2tb154z.pdf (29.06.2019).

Post Processing: Reactions and Debates in the Feature Pages of the Daily Press and in Film Magazines

Heinz Pol[36] documented the reaction of the public in the morning edition of the *Vossische Zeitung* on December 5, 1930:

> Well, the almost sensational tension that filled the theater before the film began very quickly turned into deep shock during the unrolling. The audience, which in the middle of the film had still demonstratively applauded some of the dialogues directed against the war, left the house at the end, silent and agitated to the core, unable to express applause. Never before has a film work had such an immediate effect on the viewers and listeners. The film also stands purely technically and artistically [...] at an outstanding height ... (Pol 1930; quoted from Schrader 1992, 105).

This testimony is interesting because the tension triggered by the politically motivated debate, the effect on the audience and media-aesthetic remarks are related to each other. Accordingly, the facets of film criticism will be systemised in the following.

In a historical-critical dimension, the question is: "Was it really like that" (Redmann 1930). Unlike Pol, many reviewers, as already noted at the outset, lacked an eye for innovative cinematography. Instead, the film was widely received as a quasi-documentary testament to what (supposedly) was. Accordingly, reactions to the film present factual arguments or, as in the following *Germania*, a contrary "truth":

> The people in Remarque's film – and in this film it seems even more blatant – are *no* longer *people* with body and soul, but soulless schemata, only concerned with their body's necessities, with gluttony and drunkenness, who shiver in all their limbs as soon as they lie in the trench or have to endure the shellfire. The German soldier did not look like this even in the autumn of 1918, when attrition was rapidly advancing. No one who has been there will take the scene in the dugout during the barrage seriously. He will know that in the most difficult hours there was usually something like a leaden calm and serious silence over the fighters, and that their thoughts in battle and hardship were directed to deeper things than this film wants to admit. If one wants to draw the truth, then one cannot arbitrarily pick out the cases where people broke down soullessly and shaken to and fro by the external events, where the terrible struggle naturally lost all meaning when seen from the point of view of the individual. Otherwise one would be doing bitter injustice to the majority of German soldiers, whose inner fortitude gave them the strength to perform such superhuman feats as the world war demanded of them. Nor can the aim of infaming the war ever justify such a distortion of true humanity as the film version of Remarque reveals anew (Remarque im Film 1930; quoted by Schrader 1992, 117 f.)

This excerpt works with the word "true" in a conspicuously frequent manner. The review struggles for interpretive sovereignty, to counter the film with its own, indeed *the* historically attested truth of "who has been there". The reviewer of the *Kinematograph* argues similarly, accusing those responsible from America of not having been eyewitnesses at the time and therefore of being ignorant. He scolds: "In

---

[36] Actually Pollack. Left-wing critic who leaves the newspaper in 1931 in protest against the interference of Ufa and thus of the Hugenberg concern (for which Remarque also works for a time as a journalist: *Sport im Bild*).

the process, the Anglo-American version flawlessly produced a work that sensitively offends the feelings of the broadest strata of the German people" (Im Westen nichts Neues [Rezension] 1930) Even though the reviewer praises, "The film is technically extraordinarily well made in parts. The individual battle scenes are of shattering authenticity", he nevertheless arrives at the verdict: "But there are also pictures which seem almost comical to the front-line fighter, because they portray the military situation as it could not possibly have been at the front." (Ibid.)

The fact that the film is measured against the historical authenticity of what it shows is related on the one hand to the legend surrounding the novel, which is received and also advertised as autobiographical testimony, although the typescript submitted to Ullstein contains the genre classification *novel*. On the other hand, the production and marketing of the film promote the nimbus of authenticity: for example, former German military officers were hired as advisors for the training scenes in the barracks and for the battle scenes. The reviews nevertheless ignore the fact that the film, as an adaptation, like its original, the novel, is allowed to claim precisely this freedom of perspective qua aesthetic staging and fiction and does not have to orient itself to the standards that are rightly applied to historical documentation and scholarly processing.

In a political dimension, the question "defamation or plea for peace?" is discussed. Those who judge that the film does not correspond to the historical facts usually also interpret it as hostile to Germany, inciting hatred among the people, devaluing their honour:

> But a fundamental question remains open. Namely, whether we should show films in Germany that degrade and damage the reputation of the German and the German soldier abroad. [...] We would like to think that this film should not be shown, if only to convince the Americans in a tangible way that we do not put up with the denigration of national things outside our borders and that we subsequently do business with us with the same picture strip, dubbed differently." (Im Westen nichts Neues [Rezension] 1930)

The same review warns (justifiably) of political unrest that could indirectly lead to losses for individual cinema operators. Siegfried Kracauer also reports debates even before the film's release:

> A small German nationalist request received by the Prussian Landtag also sought to prevent alleged mischief in advance, stating bluntly that in the film 'our German youth is ridiculed and portrayed as unmanly. The tendency amounts to a disparagement of the sacrificial love of the fatherland'. (Kracauer 1930)[37]

---

[37] A similar tenor can also be found in the applications for a ban to the film review board, for example on the part of the Württemberg government representative: "Im Beschauer werde der Anschein erweckt, so sei der deutsche Unteroffizier gewesen, wie auch in den jämmerlichen und klagenden Kriegsfreiwilligen der deutsche Soldat gesehen werde. Keine Szene zeige den Opfermut und die Opferbereitschaft im Kriege. Eine derartige Darstellung müsse das deutsche nationale Bewusstsein beleidigen [...]." ("The viewer is given the impression that this is what the German non-commissioned officer was like, just as the German soldier is seen in the pitiful and complaining war volunteers. No scene showed the courage and willingness to make sacrifices in war. Such a portrayal must offend the German national consciousness [...].") (http://www.difarchiv.deutsches-filminstitut.de/zengut/dt2tb154z.pdf (29.06.2019)).

If the film is perceived by German nationalists as a film of tendencies, the next reviewer sees the warning against supposed heroism and the plea against the war as arising precisely from the complete abstention from anything tendentious:

> Just like Remarque's book, the American film based on it, which is in no way biased, leaves it up to the viewer to form his own opinion about the terrible genocide, which is portrayed here in horrible clarity, without embellishment and without exaggeration. Young people should recognize from it that heroism, as it exists in the phraseology of nationalistic big mouths, does not exist in reality [...]. It is highly commendable that this film, by depicting the unvarnished truth, places itself in the defensive struggle against warmongering and ignorance, for it cannot be hammered into people's brains often enough that war is the greatest crime against humanity. (E. K. 1930)

While Kracauer on the one hand criticises "the highly contestable neutrality of the film" (Kracauer 1930), this reviewer sees it precisely as a sign of quality and trusts in the power of the cinematic depiction. Kracauer, on the other hand, struggles with this: "Instead of posing the question of its [the war's, RF] origins or getting to the heart of it with political and social arguments, film and book remain stuck in petty-bourgeois outbursts of discomfort, which are unable to lend sufficient support to the images of horror." (Ibid.)

In a media-aesthetic dimension, staging and technique are discussed. What Hans Wollenberg of *Licht Bild Bühne*[38] praises in the acting of the young artists in particular: "bears the stamp of convincing reality" (Wollenberg 1930; quoted after Schrader 1992, 115; there "Ernst" Wollenberg), the reviewer of *Filmwoche* condemns: "The main character of the film is Louis Wolheim in the role of Katczinsky; a front pig, tangibly real and genuine. For the sake of this Wolheim, one can watch the film; he is the experience. The youthful roles are, of course, dull; it is not worth while to single out their performers." (Erstaufführungen in Berlin 1930, 2) Conversely, Wollenberg judges, "Not quite so genuine by a fine little nuance: the Himmelstoß of John Wray [...]" (Wollenberg 1930; quoted in Schrader 1992, 115), while *Filmwoche* is torn: "Excellent again is John Wray as Himmelstoß: genuine as a barracks yard sergeant. Unfortunately, he becomes an actor in the front pictures." (Erstaufführungen in Berlin 1930, 2) Strikingly, the assessment of the quality of the performance depends on whether the actors credibly perform historical reality – whether their characters are "tangibly real and genuine". Even more: *avant la lettre*, film critics in the feuilletons seem to claim to practice *method acting*, that is, not "just" to play the character, but to merge with the character – to be the character.[39]

Some comments refer to the dubbing, which is not a pure transfer of the American screenplay into German, but is aimed at the German market. It is "made with all the chicanery. The illusion that it is Germans, not Englishmen, who are speaking is

---

[38] *Illustrierte Tageszeitung des Films* (1908–1939); barely three years after this very favourable review by Hans Wollenberg, a lead story in the same newspaper polemicises against *Im Westen nichts Neues on* the occasion of Joseph Goebbels' upcoming birthday and praises the uproar instigated by Goebbels at the time as a "commitment to German film" (*Licht Bild Bühne*, 28.10.33, 1).

[39] For a problematisation, see Freudenberg 2018.

ninety percent perfect." (Im Westen nichts Neues [Rezension] 1930) Also, "the overall effect [...] is hardly diminished by the dubbing into German" (E. K. 1930) Kracauer disagrees:

> Unfortunately, the German words, which were added after the fact, often do a poor job of matching the mouth movements of the Americans. (If the sound film is to retain the internationality of the silent one, one must either shift the emphasis from the dialogues back to the images and also to the sounds, or shoot every film in all the main languages from the outset. The attempt to pass off American speakers for German ones is an absurdity).
> (Kracauer 1930)

Regarding the much advertised cinematic technique, critics are quite unanimous. Like Pol, quoted at the beginning, and the reviewer of the *Kinematograph* ("Technically undoubtedly a remarkable work." (Im Westen nichts Neues [Rezension] 1930)), Kracauer also praises sound engineering and camera work:

> Directed by Lewis Milestone, the film was made with great apparatus, admirable technical skill and an extraordinary fidelity to reality. The old-fashioned thunder of battle differentiates itself into the interplay of the most diverse sounds of hell, and all war images of earlier times pale before the close combat scenes, which fight their way close to the viewer here.
> (Kracauer 1930)

Last but not least, the film as novel adaptation is examined in a literary and media-critical dimension. The function of the cinema will also be discussed: Does it see itself as an institution of enlightenment or of diversion? The reviewers of both *Kinematograph* and *Filmwoche* assume "that the cinema is a place of entertainment for everyone." And on that premise "such a book is quite unsuitable for film editing." (Im Westen nichts Neues [Rezension] 1930) Nevertheless:

> In view of the fact that most sound films cater predominantly to the audience's need for entertainment and are less attuned to artistic moments, we henceforth apply a more serious critical standard only when the artistic intentions of the producers are openly discernible. [...] Those who are in the fortunate position of not knowing the novel (I don't) don't need to make any comparisons; they see the film as it is, – and add nothing to it. (Erstaufführungen in Berlin 1930, 1)

The Media Network Around *Im Westen nichts Neues* from a Synchronous Perspective: *Niemandsland* and the *Westfront 1918*

At the beginning, we already asked how media networks can be constituted and adequately conceptualised and modelled. The question now arises again and concretely: in view of the anti-war films discussed here, can one actually speak of a media network? Superficially, this does not seem to be the case: The films are too little explicitly related to each other to stand in a production and processing context to each other. Rather, the novels *Im Westen nichts Neues* and *Vier von der Infanterie* and their cinematic adaptations each form a network in their own right. But the films are implicitly connected, if one considers the zeitgeist, the virulence of certain themes and the use of media techniques to stage them. It seems worthwhile to show this comparatively by means of *Niemandsland*. The films in question are also subsequently, from the perspective of reception and post processing, to remain in the terminology of Schmidt's (2008/2012) notion of media as a compact conecept, placed in a closer context and ultimately sanctioned in terms of cultural policy. This will be demonstrated comparatively with *Westfront 1918*.

All three films, two German and one American production, including two literary adaptations, premiered in Germany between May 1930 and December 1931. They struck a chord with National Conservatives and National Socialists as well as with those with socio-political to communist tendencies. It would be wrong to treat them indifferently. They are received as films with a tendency, whose presumed intention is to have a moral or political effect. In contrast, perceiving them as artistic-aesthetic works is relegated to the background, as demonstrated by *Im Westen nichts Neues* (*All Quiet on the Western Front*).

Niemandsland from a Production Perspective

The St. Petersburg-born Victor Trivas, who had previously worked as a set designer on the film *Die Liebe der Jeanne Ney* (1927) under Georg Wilhelm Pabst who directed *Westfront 1918*, was responsible for the directing, manuscript and screenplay of *Niemandsland* (Germany, 1931). Assistant director is George Shdanoff. The film implements elements of an idea of the writer and pacifist Leonhard Frank. The film music is by the Austrian composer Hanns Eisler. The cast list includes renowned actors (in addition to the American dancer Louis Douglas, who toured Europe with Josephine Baker in the 1920s, Ernst Busch and Vladimir Sokoloff, who also played a small role in *Westfront 1918*), some of whom had to emigrate or flee in 1933.

As with Milestone, the newspaper reports on the production process document the effort to stay close to reality:

> Viktor Trivas, who is making 'Niemandsland' for Resco Film, has gone to France and England for field shoots. Trivas, in addition to French milieu shots, will shoot an original 'Bal Musette' in Paris and large street scenes in London. (Aus der Produktion 1931)

The civilian past life of the five protagonists, who will meet as soldiers in the vastness of the European metropolises of Berlin, London and Paris, the diversity of their different religious-cultural and linguistic contexts, their professional and private-family constellations – the film gives a lot of space to this macrocosm: 32 minutes and thus a third of the film. As a microcosm in spatial-scenic concentration, the cellar of a shot-up building between the fronts, i.e. in *Niemandsland,* is held up against it, where a chamber play, an experiment in a confined space with an uncertain outcome now takes place (Fig. 3). Consequently, the movement of the film appears star-shaped: The protagonists are drawn together to this place from all points of the compass. This place, which belongs to no one, is symbolically charged: as the eye of the storm, as a melting pot, as the site of an eutopia from which global

Fig. 3 *Niemandsland* (00:54:04)

hope germinates for a peaceful future, overcoming linguistic and cultural barriers, abandoning hatred and violence.

This film is thus far more of a trendy film than *Im Westen nichts Neues* (*All Quiet on the Western Front*), its pacifist plea is unmistakable, and the events told take a back seat to the message. It is received accordingly, with reviewers sometimes crediting it for this tendency, sometimes holding it against it; more on this later. At the same time, however, the film is highly interesting from a media-aesthetic perspective, since it works with forms, rhythms, and sounds, and in addition to the camera, editing and montage techniques are used for staging purposes.

Consequently the film, supported by Eisler's music, celebrates the dawn of modernity, in particular the mechanics and dynamics of traffic and the world of work. A street scene in Paris focuses in close-up on the wheels of the tram cutting against those of a horse-drawn carriage. In London, the Englishman watches Towerbridge opening from the window of his apartment. The machines on which the Frenchman and his colleagues are happily working are shown in close-up in their vertically and horizontally pounding rhythm. The workers adapt their mechanical movements to this rhythm; indeed, via editing and montage, the entire working world seems to submit to it, until finally the vertical brushstrokes of a painter high up on a scaffold (filmed from below) lead into the horizontal planing movements of the German at the bench of his small workshop and into the Jew's treading motion at his sewing machine.

The fact that scenes from different spheres of life and geographical locations are mounted directly next to one another, thereby recombined, and related to one another in surprising ways, follows a structural principle of the film: the Frenchman shoots at a fairground stall, and with the detaching bang – cut – a boy bowling hits "all nines", so that the acoustic signal functions as a link. Another cut: some gentlemen in a summerhouse applaud as if they were applauding the boy. Another example: For mobilisation, various barracks yard scenes are juxtaposed with the insertion of national coats of arms. For minutes the same scenery can be seen: Flags waving in the wind, and in front of them hats being thrown into the air, musically accompanied by the hymns in edited versions.

Compared to Milestone's film, *Niemandsland* is the more committed, the more resolutely political. It in no way conceals its trendiness as a pacifist anti-war film; the whole film is a parable and a didactic piece. The fact that the film is still tremendously appealing today is due to its consistent use of the technical possibilities of its time. At the same time, it also celebrates modernity *in* the image by elevating this very technology to the subject matter.

On the Reception of *Niemandsland* in the Mirror of Post Processing

The film is approved by the censors on 25.11.1931 and premiered on 10.12.1931, like *Im Westen nichts Neues* (*All Quiet on the Western Front*) before it, in the Mozartsaal of the Berlin Theater am Nollendorfplatz. The reviewer of the *Kinematograph* clearly classifies it as a pacifist film. He considers it "technically excellently made" and "artistically serious", but reproaches it for the fact that the ideological message does not carry a whole feature film and that the film "therefore packs itself with various accessories, so that the events finally drag on." (Niemandsland [Rezension] 1931) This sounds different in Manfred Georg(e) Cohn's[40] review in *Tempo*:[41] "The film is extraordinary and significant." (Cohn 1931) Cohn celebrates the "exciting effect," the "good deed" (ibid.), consequently the film's commitment and radiance. Aesthetically, above all he emphasises the film's music:

> Eisler is one of the most courageous creators of modern music. He achieves what most of them get stuck in the theoretical: the unleashing of the musical effect not to obscure but to expose the feelings. At least he works brilliantly with the film director Trivas in the acoustic montage incidence here. The effect of the following image, for example, is almost phenomenal: the drafted muskots march sadly to the barracks yard, laden with the grief of their wives and children on top of everything else. And sad music hangs in ragged tones around their shoulders, until suddenly everything changes into marching rhythms, and under the cheering din the marchers' gait tightens, their breasts heave, their eyes begin to flash – music as the promoter of idiocy, here it is unmasked in a wonderful example, a prime example that beautifully demonstrates the 'political moment' in music." (Ibid.)

---

[40] Jewish journalist and translator as well as politically active pacifist. His exile leads him via Prague to the USA.

[41] Berliner Zeitung (evening paper) of the Ullstein publishing house, 1928–1933. Among the authors are Kurt Tucholsky and Erika Mann.

Hans Siemsen[42] also attests the film "a pronounced, clear, political tendency [...] and indeed a thoroughly 'leftist', thoroughly democratic, pacifist and internationally oriented tendency" (Siemsen 1931). And he finds it "technically and artistically [...] much much better 'made' than all German amusement and entertainment films." (Ibid.) – with a significantly smaller budget, as he points out. He highlights the performance of Louis Douglas in particular, "the director's mastery of all the means of sound film, often using them in a completely new way" and Hanns Eisler's music – which speaks "more clearly than words" (ibid.).

In all three reviews, the audience is targeted: *Der Kinematograph,* for example, predicts that the film will find its audience only among those who share the same worldview (cf. Niemandsland [Rezension] 1931). Cohn underscores the political significance of the film, "which, with its defensible spirit and courage, boldly stands out in a time in which almost everything seems to revolve around two polar phenomena, around big mouths and full pants. This film lies in the middle of them, so it is an act." (Cohn 1931) Siemsen however, reflects:

> But more important than all that is the question: *What will become of this film?* The other two excellent films ('Kameradschaft' and 'Mädchen in Uniform') barely managed to stay in the big cinemas for a week. The decent and demanding cinema audience has to do something for good films! Does it want to leave the cinema to the philistines and idiots? *Every* pacifist, *every* democrat and republican, *every* socialist, *every* 'prolet' in Germany has the *duty* to see to it that these really good, courageous films do their work and also have the financial success they deserve! If the better part of the German cinema audience is not capable of seeing such films through to success, *then it deserves nothing other* than the filth that the amusement industry puts before it and its shameful assertion: 'The audience *wants* nothing but trash and filth!' (Siemsen 1931; emphasis in original, RF)

However, already a quarter of a year later, the ban on showing the film in France is reported (cf. Pariser Notizen 1932),[43] and Bavaria's application to ban the film of 13.03.1933 is granted on 22.04.1933.[44] Remarkable for the present question of the constitution of media nerworks via common themes, social, political, ideological orientations and representation strategies is the connection opened up by Siemsen with two "other excellent films", which he concedes to have "a pronounced, clear, political tendency" (Siemsen 1931). Subsequently, from the perspective of reception and post processing, a visible classification takes place.

---

[42] Writer and journalist, left-wing oppositionist, and homosexual. He is a friend of Joachim Ringelnatz. In exile he lives in Paris and in the USA.
[43] However, it is reported on 24.11.1932 that the film is running in Toulouse (cf. *Kinematograph of* 24.11.32, 2).
[44] http://www.difarchiv.deutsches-filminstitut.de/zengut/df2tb000z.pdf (30.06.2019).

Reception and Post Processing of *Im Westen nichts Neues* (*All Quiet on the Western Front*) in Comparison with *Westfront 1918*

Finally, we will briefly discuss *Westfront 1918* (Germany, 1930), as Milestone's work is compared to the older German production by film critics and how it is banned from movie theaters by cultural policy. The film adaptation of the novel *Vier von der Infanterie. Westfront 1918* by Ernst Johannsen (published by Fackelreiter-Verlag in 1929)[45] premiered at Berlin's Capitol am Zoo on 23.05.1930. The director is Georg Wilhelm Pabst, the screenplay is written by Ladislaus Vajda, the music is by Alexander Laszlo.[46] At this point, we will explain by way of example the context in which criticism places Milestone's and Pabst's film – which Angelika Müller claims was made "in a hurry" as a "German answer" to *Im Westen nichts Neues* (*All Quiet on the Western Front*) (Müller 1985, 231).[47] Siegfried Kracauer, who at the time had quite critically classified *Westfront 1918* as clearly pacifist, but had accused it of not inquiring into the causes of the war, but of losing itself in general appeals (cf. ibid., 233; Kagelmann/Keiner 2014, 90), now points out precisely this, however, in a direct comparison: "Both works agree with each other in their basic attitude; only the German one emphasizes more than the American one the monotony of the trench years and also perhaps takes a somewhat more explicit stand against the madness of war." (Kracauer 1930) The review ends with a general doubt about the relevance of both films: "Visual instruction is undoubtedly useful. But it seems to me that even more useful now would be films that showed us not only the horrors of wars, but exposed their causes of origin and their real consequences." (Ibid.) The *Filmwoche* reviewer judged Milestone's film to be "not an actual soldier film, like 'Westfront 1918'; this American film is the tragedy of some youths." (Erstaufführungen in Berlin 1930, 1) In this respect, the German production served the genre more appropriately: "[…] what the film 'Westfront 1918' did better: this American film knows no German officers. Neither at the front nor in the stage. Somewhere, however, the officers, without whom one cannot make a war film, must have been." (Ibid., 2)

---

[45] Pacifist-socialist publishing house (1922–1933). The publisher Walter Hammer (actually Walter Hösterey) is a pacifist, not least because of his experiences in the First World War on the Western Front. He is interned in the Sachsenhausen concentration camp and later sentenced to five years in prison in Brandenburg.

[46] For information on the film, its status, and its relationship to the novel, see Kagelmann/Keiner 2014.

[47] In her contribution, she provides an overview of reactions to the film, including those by Kracauer, and compares the two films with each other. Despite all the structural similarities, she sees differences in the "assessment and representation of the same values" (Müller 1985, 236) and attests to *Westfront 1918* having "built up and upheld the value of 'comradeship' in a sentimental, unrealistic way" (ibid.).

Both films, together with *Niemandsland*, are listed under the heading "films with a pacifist tendency" on the aforementioned application list for censorship of 13.03.1933. Three days after *Niemandsland*, *Westfront 1918* was also banned on 27.04.1933.[48]

The Media Network around *Im Westen nichts Neues* from a Diachronic Perspective

The media adaptations and transformations that follow Remarque's novel can be found in large quantity: so far, two film adaptations,[49] stage versions, a comic book in the *Classics Illustrated* series from 1952, an opera (published on CD in 2002, premiered in 2003), a song by Elton John (recorded in 1981, on the album *Jump up* and released as a single in 1982, the year of the Falklands War), another by the Toten Hosen (published in 1999, a swan song to the modern working world). Especially around the 2014 commemorations, publications increased, including: an audio book (2013, voiced by August Diehl), two radio plays (2014),[50] a Plain Language version of the novel (2014), and a graphic novel (2014).

Im Westen nichts Neues: *Eine Graphic Novel* (2014)

Interesting in the present context are those adaptations that also refer to Milestone's film. The graphic novel by Peter Eickmeyer and Gaby von Borstel is one such case. In its narrative structure, it basically follows the novel with its retrospectives, and in the text, which is printed in typewriter font in full justification on a light background, it takes over the original word for word with a few exceptions, but cuts back decidedly (for example, Peter, who is seriously injured in the Catholic military hospital, is not mentioned) and sometimes summarises scenes (for example, the visit of the comrades to Kemmerich and his final death, at which only Paul is still present). This occasionally results in rearrangements compared to the novel, but the declared adherence to its structure remains visible. Text and image are mostly conceived as meta-panels and arranged in such a way that the typed text on the word panel appears as if laid on transparent sheets of paper over the mostly double-page background image ("the majority of *Im Westen* consists of mostly double splash pages",

---

[48] Cf. http://www.difarchiv.deutsches-filminstitut.de/zengut/df2tb733z.pdf (30.06.2019).

[49] In the meanwhile another film adaptation was released in 2022 which won four Academy Awards, amongst others for Best International Film.

[50] The radio play by Jan Decker, which emerged from a seminar at the University of Osnabrück, addresses Remarque's life and work more comprehensively. *Im Westen nichts Neues* is included insofar as the original report by the British soldier Alexander Donald from his time in Afghanistan shows clear parallels to the descriptions in the novel (cf. Decker 2014).

Kutch/Grammatikopoulos 2015, 272), whose colourations and contours delicately shimmer through. These large-format paintings, rendered in oil or gouache, sometimes with pen-and-ink strokes, have a function that goes far beyond illustration: it is primarily through the use of colour that they create the atmospheric framework for the narrative, enrich the text (when, for example, the abbreviated text is written in a shaded manner), and provide the reader with a sense of the narrative. When, for example, the abridged text simply mentions "the flowering meadow" and the "tender panicles of grasses", the picture makes it clear that, according to the novel, these are poppies and focuses on details in order to heighten them to symbolic[51] or metaphysical[52] proportions. In turn, white-framed *image panels* are often superimposed on the text; at the beginning, they introduce the characters as *character panels,* but as the text progresses, they primarily illustrate individual moments described in the text, occasionally to the point of pain and beyond in their explicitness (e.g. in battles on the battlefield).

To what extent in this case can we speak of a reference to the film of 1930? "The principle of repetition is formative for the comic not only on the level of content as well as on the structural-compositional level, but also under the aspect of intermediality," Monika Schmitz-Emans emphasizes, because:

> Comics quote from the literary tradition […] and one could at least ponder whether the literary comic, the adaptation of the literary by the comic, is not a particularly 'typical' comic from this point of view. The history of images and pictorial media is also connected to in a variety of ways; chains of citations link the history of comics to the history of painting, photography, and other pictorial forms of representation. (Schmitz-Emans 2012, 10 f.)

In his epilogue to Eickmeyers/von Borstel's adaptation, Thomas F. Schneider accordingly points out the manifold interpictorial references.[53] He establishes thematic and artistic-technical references to Otto Dix and Pablo Picasso, but also points out that the image design is linked to the two film adaptations:

> He (Peter Eickmeyer, RF) is aware that with a visual adaptation of Remarque's international icon of anti-war literature he is moving in a field of tension of the most diverse medial traditions and predecessors: From the text *Im Westen nichts Neues* itself, to the two film adaptations by Milestone and Delbert Mann, the adaptations in comics, but also in the field of illustration, to the image of the First World War as the first 'modern', industrialized war, anchored in cultural memory, generated by countless photographs and a few historical documentary shots in film. (Schneider 2018, no pages available.)

---

[51] For example, Paul's eye, in which two fighting soldiers are reflected; the pupil seems to have become a bomb crater.

[52] Thus the emperor's head with pimple cap and moustache, who, as the text and an image panel tell us, is visiting troops: he appears on the left half of the double page like a larger-than-life vision in light blue and opaque white in the firmament.

[53] On the intertextual and interpictural references of the graphic novel, see Kutch/Grammatikopoulos 2015, who also discuss Milestone's film adaptation and interpret its opening scene, the opening of the door, metaphorically, which allows them to draw comparisons with the opening of a book and the presentation of the characters (in Eickmeyer/von Borstel through *character panels*).

Consequently, Paul Bäumer resembles Lew Ayres in individual panels, and the *double splash page* that concludes the bomb crater scene (to which several panels are devoted altogether) is reminiscent in its structure, arrangement and drawing of the figures of shots from the first film adaptation, which has become iconic. Beyond these references, both works achieve their power through their pictorial technique, which does not rely on illustration but on the creation of atmosphere, staging sometimes masses, sometimes the individual (in the close-up with the focus on the face, the facial expression).

Conclusion

On the one hand, the investigation of this exemplary media network has shown that the early film adaptation of Remarque's novel, itself initially a form of "post processing", as a "product" becomes the core and starting point of its own media network and in this respect emancipates itself at least in part from the novel. Its images are iconic, its technical and media-aesthetic innovation is ground-breaking. On the other hand, it has been confirmed that Schmidt's notion of media as a compact concept is not sufficient to adequately describe the dynamics of the media network, the change in the perspective taken on a medium, the interlocking and intertwining of levels, the explicitness or implicitness of the reference to one another – in other words, the flexible network and cluster structure in spatial and temporal dimensions. In addition, this modelling only allows for a descriptive-reconstructive view of a media network, but not for a differentiated examination of whether and under which conditions or presuppositions it is such a network at all.

References

Primary Literature

Eickmeyer, Peter/von Borstel, Gaby: Im Westen nichts Neues. Eine Graphic Novel nach dem Roman von Erich Maria Remarque. Bielefeld ⁵2018.
Johannsen, Ernst: Vier von der Infanterie. Westfront 1918. Hamburg-Bergedorf 1929.
Remarque, Erich Maria: Im Westen nichts Neues [1929]. Köln ³2015.

Filmography

Geschundenes Zelluloid. Das Schicksal des Kinoklassikers *Im Westen nichts Neues*. Dokumentation, ZDF (1984), https://www.youtube.com/watch?v=Ytkcu2Q65XE (06.07.2019).

Im Westen nichts Neues (USA 1930). Regie: Lewis Milestone. Nach dem Roman von Erich Maria Remarque [EA 1929], Universal (DVD).
Niemandsland (D 1931). Regie: Victor Trivas, http://www.europeanfilmgateway.eu/de/detail/Niemandsland/dk::579a5f660bc8bfd5308dc4a921f9360a (28.08.2019).
Westfront 1918 (D 1930). Regie: Georg Wilhelm Pabst. Nach dem Roman von Ernst Johannsen [EA 1929], Universum (Ufa Klassiker Edition) (DVD).

Secondary Literature Before 1945

Antideutsche Filme in Amerika. In: Kinematograph 24 (1930) 73 vom 27.03., 3.
Aus der Produktion. In: Kinematograph 25 (1931) 212/213 vom 15.09., 2.
Cohn, Manfred Georg(e): „Niemandsland". Ein erregender Film, ein durchschlagender Erfolg (Mozartsaal). In: Tempo 4 (1931) 288 vom 10.12., 2. Beibl.
Der größte Bucherfolg der letzten Jahrzehnte [Anzeige]. In: Kinematograph 23 (1929) 174 vom 29.7., 15.
Do. Remarque im Film. Die deutsche Fassung von „Im Westen nichts Neues". Germania. Zeitung für das Deutsche Volk (Berlin) vom 05.12.30. In: Schrader, Bärbel (Hg.): Der Fall Remarque. „Im Westen nichts Neues" – Eine Dokumentation. Leipzig 1992, 116–118.
Erstaufführungen in Berlin. In: Filmwoche (1930) 51 vom 17.12., 1–2.
Filmprodukte der Verfallszeit. In: Film-Kurier 19 (1937) 264 vom 12.11., 2.
Im Westen nichts Neues [Anzeige]. In: Kinematograph 23 (1929) 159 vom 11.7., 2.
Im Westen nichts Neues [Anzeige]. In: Kinematograph 24 (1930) 279 vom 29.11., 5.
Im Westen nichts Neues [Rezension]. In: Kinematograph 24 (1930) 284 vom 05.12., 4.
E. K.: Vom Film. „Im Westen nichts Neues" (Mozartsaal). In: Die Welt am Montag 36 (1930) vom 08.12.
Kracauer, Siegfried: „Im Westen nichts Neues." Zum Remarque-Tonfilm. In: Frankfurter Zeitung und Handelsblatt vom 06.12.1930.
„Niemandsland" [Rez.]. In: Kinematograph 25 (1931) 285 vom 10.12., 4.
Pariser Notizen. In: Kinematograph 26 (1932) 44 vom 03.03., 4.
Pol, Heinz: „Im Westen nichts Neues". Der Film im Mozart-Saal. Vossische Zeitung (Berlin) vom 05.12.30. In: Bärbel Schrader (Hg.): Der Fall Remarque. „Im Westen nichts Neues" – Eine Dokumentation. Leipzig 1992, 105.
Redmann, Walter: „Im Westen nichts Neues." Der Remarque-Film im Mozartsaal. In: Berliner Morgenpost (1930) 291 vom 06.12., 2. Beibl.
Siemsen, Hans: Der Film der Woche. Niemandsland. In: Die Welt am Montag 37 (1931) vom 14.12.
…und unsere große stumme Produktion 1920/31 [Anzeige]. In: Kinematograph 24 (1930) 279 vom 29.11., 9.
Unsere Produktion 1929–30 [Anzeige]. In: Kinematograph 23 (1929) 221 vom 22.09., 28.
Vom Westen was Neues. In: Kinematograph 24 (1930) 89 vom 15.04., 4.
Voranzeige! [Anzeige]. In: Kinematograph 24 (1930) 193 vom 20.08., 2.
Wir beginnen heute mit der Vermietung [Anzeige]. In: Kinematograph 23 (1929) 174 vom 29.07., 5.
Wollenberg, Hans: „Im Westen nichts Neues" nach Erich Maria Remarque. Universum Film – Deutsche Universal – Mozartsaal. Licht Bild Bühne. Illustrierte Tageszeitung des Films (Berlin) vom 05.12.30. In: Bärbel Schrader (Hg.): Der Fall Remarque. „Im Westen nichts Neues" – Eine Dokumentation. Leipzig 1992, 112–115.
Zirkus Nollendorfplatz. In: Kinematograph 24 (1930) 289 vom 11.12., 1.

Secondary Literature After 1945

Boeckh, Klara: Zwischen Eindeutigkeit und Irritation, Nähe und Distanz. Ein Vergleich der Verfilmungen von Erich Maria Remarques *Im Westen nichts Neues*. In: Schneider, Thomas F. (Hg.): Remarque und die Medien. Literatur, Musik, Film, Graphic Novel. Göttingen 2018 (Erich Maria Remarque Jahrbuch/Yearbook; 28), 93–116.

Brodnitz, Hanns: Kino intim. Eine vergessene Biographie [1933]. Mit Beiträgen von Gero Gandert, Wolfgang Jacobsen. Teetz 2005 (Jüdische Memoiren; 14).

Bronfen, Elisabeth: Hollywoods Kriege. Geschichte einer Heimsuchung. Aus d. Amerik. von Regina Brückner. Frankfurt a. M. 2013.

Decker, Jan: [remark]. Ein Werkstattbericht. [remark]. Hörspiel. In: Schneider, Thomas F. (Hg.): Erich Maria Remarque, *Im Westen nichts Neues* und die Folgen. Göttingen 2014 (Erich Maria Remarque Jahrbuch/Yearbook; 24), 85–102.

Freudenberg, Ricarda: „Wer seid das ihr?" Zur Rolle des Autors im Literaturunterricht. In: Führer, Carolin/Heins, Jochen (Hg.): Autorschaft im Unterricht. Literaturdidaktische Facetten am Beispiel von Interviews. Baltmannsweiler 2018, 121–134.

Hüningen, James zu: Art. Phonofilm. In: Lexikon der Filmbegriffe (2012), http://filmlexikon.uni-kiel.de/index.php?action=lexikon&tag=det&id=4360 (06.07.2019)

Kagelmann, Andre/Keiner, Reinhold: „Lässig beginnt der Tod, Mensch und Tier zu ernten." Überlegungen zu Ernst Johannsens Roman *Vier von der Infanterie* und G. W. Pabsts Film *WESTFRONT 1918*. In: Dies. (Hg.): Ernst Johannsen: *Vier von der Infanterie. Ihre letzten Tage an der Westfront 1918*. Kassel 2014 (Filme zum Lesen; 2), 80–113.

Kutch, Lynn Marie/Grammatikopoulos, Damianos: Intertextual References in Eickmeyer's *Im Westen nichts Neues*: Eine Graphic Novel. In: Colloquia Germanica 48 (2015) 4, Themenheft German Comics, 267–292, https://www.jstor.org/stable/26431159 (06.07.2019).

Möbius, Thomas: Adaption – Verbund – Produsage: Implikationen des Begriffs Medienkonvergenz. In: Weinkauff, Gina/Dettmar, Ute/Möbius, Thomas/Tomkowiak, Ingrid (Hg.): Kinder- und Jugendliteratur in Medienkontexten: Adaption – Hybridisierung – Intermedialität – Konvergenz. Frankfurt a. M. 2014 (Kinder- und Jugendkultur, -literatur und -medien. Theorie – Geschichte – Didaktik; 89), 219–232.

Müller, Angelika: Aus der Chronik des Antikriegsfilms. In: Harth, Dietrich/Schubert, Dietrich/Schmidt, Ronald Michael (Hg.): Pazifismus zwischen den Weltkriegen. Deutsche Schriftsteller und Künstler gegen Krieg und Militarismus 1918–1933. Heidelberg 1985 (Heidelberger Bibliotheksschriften; 16), 229–239.

Röwekamp, Burkhard: Antikriegsfilm. Zur Ästhetik, Geschichte und Theorie einer filmhistorischen Praxis. München 2011 (edition text + kritik).

Schmidt, Siegfried J.: Der Medienkompaktbegriff. In: Münker, Stefan/Roesler, Alexander (Hg.): Was ist ein Medium? Frankfurt a. M. ^{2}2012.

Schmitz-Emans, Monika: Comic und Literatur – Literatur und Comic. Zur Einführung. In: Dies. (Hg.): Comic und Literatur. Konstellationen. (linguae & litterae; 16). Berlin [u. a.] 2012, 1–13.

Schneider, Thomas F.: „Wir passen nicht in die Welt hinein." Zur Entstehung und Publikation von Erich Maria Remarque *Im Westen nichts Neues*. Köln ^{3}2015, 330–353.

Schneider, Thomas F.: Erich Maria Remarque *Im Westen nichts Neues* als Graphic Novel. Einige Anmerkungen zu Peter Eickmeyers Adaption. Bielefeld ^{5}2018, o. S.

Schrader, Bärbel (Hg.): Der Fall Remarque. „Im Westen nichts Neues" – Eine Dokumentation. Leipzig 1992.

Schwab, Ulrike: Erzähltext und Spielfilm. Zur Ästhetik und Analyse der Filmadaption. Berlin 2006 (Geschichte, Zukunft, Kommunikation. Untersuchungen zur europäischen Medienforschung; 4).

Skrodzki, Karl Jürgen: Else Lasker-Schüler und der Film (2015), http://www.kj-skrodzki.de/Dokumente/Text_076.htm (29.06.2019).

Wedel, Michael: Filmgeschichte als Krisengeschichte. Schnitte und Spuren durch den deutschen Film. Bielefeld 2011.

Wulff, Hans J.: *Im Westen nichts Neues*. In: Klein, Thomas/Stiglegger, Marcus/Traber, Bodo (Hg.): Filmgenres: Kriegsfilm. Stuttgart 2006, 46–56.

Boyish Romance in a Timeless Idyll?

Depoliticising Entertainment Using the Example of Alfred Weidenmann's *Jakko*

Winfred Kaminski

Preliminary Note

The focus of the following remarks is *Jakko. Roman eines Jungen* (1939) by the author and director Alfred Weidenmann (1916–2000) and its 1941 film adaptation of the same name. In order to approach the book and the film, some detours are necessary. There are, in fact, only a few detailed contributions to the discussion of Weidenmann's literary and cinematic work for young people. It therefore makes sense to trace his career in more detail. In doing so, we will take a look at the contents of this book and its film adaptation, and also examine other books and films by Weidenmann, such as his adventurous entertainment readings or numerous non-fiction titles, as well as his films that present themselves as documentaries. The contemporary and present-day reception of Weidenmann's work also requires investigation, also and because only fragments can ever be found.

Finally, the director Fritz Peter Buch and the composer Hans Otto Borgmann are introduced, both of whom were jointly responsible for the cinematic adaptation of the literary model. We owe Weidenmann, Buch and Borgmann the youth feature film *Jakko*, which with its triad of instruction, probation and conversion corresponded in a special way to the expectations of the National Socialists for the film industry and films for the youth.

W. Kaminski (✉)
Frankfurt a. M, Germany
e-mail: winfred.kaminski@th-koeln.de

Career Steps

When the name Alfred Weidenmann is mentioned, many people think of his long-selling young adult book *Gepäckschein 666* (1953)[1] and his successful films from the 1950s and 1960s, i.e. literary adaptations such as *Die Buddenbrooks* or *Der Schimmelreiter*, as well as the films of a different kind *Canaris* and *Stern von Afrika*. He is even more tangible in his lifelong collaboration with screenwriter Herbert Reinecker as the TV series director of *Derrick, Der Alte* and quite a few *Tatort thrillers*. However, the parts of his literary and cinematic oeuvre that belong to the Federal Republic of Germany are readily recorded on their own, and his beginnings as a writer of books for young people and filmmaker since the mid-1930s in National Socialist Germany are passed over.

The year 1939, when the Second World War began, played a prominent role. It was also the year of the first publication of *Jakko. Roman eines Jungen* (Fig. 1). This temporal proximity was no mere coincidence. For, I would like to put forward the thesis, Alfred Weidenmann contributed to the mobilisation of German youth on a literary, cinematic, and political-organisational level since the so-called seizure of power by the National Socialists through depoliticising entertainment.

First and foremost, I would like to mention his trilogy *50 Jungen im Dienst* (*Jungzug 2, Kanonier Brakke Nr. 2,* and *Trupp Plassen,* published in 1936/1937), which won a prize from the National Socialist Teachers' Association (NSLB). It tells of the development of young people, or more precisely young men, into soldiers and marks the institutional stages from Hitler Youth (HJ) to Reich Labor Service (RAD) to the Wehrmacht, and each new step towards the fighter and warrior, the soldierly type.

The second level on which Alfred Weidenmann contributed medially to mobilisation was film and photography, as in his early cine film *Jungbann 2* (1935/36), and also with his photographs for *Junges Europa* (1940) as well as for travel books he wrote about the fascist youths from Portugal to Romania, which were also illustrated with his own photographs.

And on a third level, Alfred Weidenmann was someone who specifically mobilised politically and had become active in the Württemberg Hitler Youth at an early age, making it to the position of Leiter der Filmabteilung of the Reichsjugendführung in Berlin (cf. Galle 2016, 48). During his "steep career in Reichsjugendführung of the Third Reich" (ibid.), he cleverly linked his party-political and organisational rise with his literary, pictorial, and cinematic projects.

---

[1] Brunken 1995 has presented a detailed account of this post-war novel by Weidenmann.

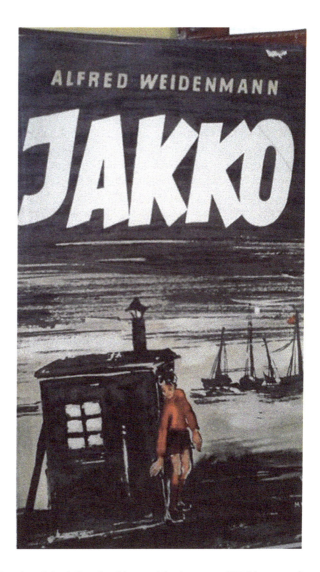

Fig. 1 Dust jacket of the young adult novel *Jakko* (Weidenmann © Stuttgart: Loewe, 1939)

The journalist Ernst Klee listed the following biographical stages of Weidenmann[2] in his *Personenlexikon zum Dritten Reich* (2016): 1934 entry into the NSDAP, press

---

[2] These would have to be supplemented by the hint of Hans Peter Mahnke, who points out that Weidenmann had attended the Stuttgart Dillmann-Realgymnasium up to the Mittlere Reife (i.e. about 1932) and had been active in the Catholic Youth *Neu-Deutschland* (cf. Mahnke 2009, 194 f.). In an essay on Stuttgart in the *Third Reich,* Burkhardt writes that the group to which Weidenmann belonged had been "transferred to the HJ by a chaplain" (Burkhardt 1984, 267). Another historian who has studied youth organisations around 1933 notes that a "preference for uniforms," "playing soldier," and "pre-militaristic avocations" were also evident in the Catholic youth movement (Beyerle 1985, 181). Rolf Eilers goes even further when he points out that many in the Bund Neudeutschland were not fundamentally opposed to the "idea of a fascist-style Führer state" (Eilers 1985, 23), in contrast to the negative experience of the Weimar Republic.

And in *Cinegraph. Lexikon zum deutschsprachigen Film* (1984 ff., Lfg. 34 D1-D8) the name of Weidenmann's parents can be found: Ludwig Weidenmann and his wife Clara, née Göttle. Here also the statement that Weidenmann had wanted to become a commercial artist and had therefore taken three semesters of art history at the Stuttgart Art Academy.

and propaganda department of the HJ, head of the film department in the propaganda department of the HJ area leadership Württemberg, 1936 Wehrmacht, 1939 soldier, later released, 1941 directorial debut with *Hände hoch* (1942) and finally – barely thirty years old – the breakthrough as a director with *Junge Adler* (1943/44).

Alfred Weidenmann was firmly integrated into the organisations and institutions of the Nazi state. In his study *Totale Erziehung für den totalen Krieg* (2003), the historian Michael Buddrus notes that the HJ propaganda apparatus established a "far-reaching system for directing consciousness and guiding people that was previously unknown in German youth history" (ibid., 91). With regard to youth literature, Buddrus further emphasises that a "not inconsiderable number of Nazi literati" came from the "highest echelons of the HJ" (ibid., 106 f.).[3] In the biographical appendix of his study, it is stated that Alfred Weidenmann held the rank of Bannführer of the HJ, and Heinz J. Galle (2016) was even given the rank of SS-Untersturmführer for the year 1944.[4]

Alfred Weidenmann was considered a "bearer of hope for National Socialist cultural policy"; his "ideological-propagandistic project" had made him an "ideal representative of Nazi youth culture" (Steinlein 2007, 224 f.). This assessment by Rüdiger Steinlein gains further facets if we consider some of the few statements Alfred Weidenmann made about his personal and professional development.

A book about his lifelong colleague and screenwriter Herbert Reinecker contains retrospective statements by Weidenmann. He states there that he came from the Boy Scouts movement and was "alliance-oriented": "I can claim to have preserved in my books and films the boyish romanticism that was the essential characteristic of the alliance idea" (Weidenmann, quoted in Aurich et al. 2010, 101). He further emphasises that he was "no propagandist" and that his film *Junge Adler*, for example, was "downright civil" and "purely human" in its orientation (ibid., 101). Nevertheless, it is not difficult to interpret these statements as mere "rhetorical red herrings" (ibid.).[5]

Upright and Down to Earth

In the preface to *Jakko. Roman eines Jungen*, the author states that he had spent time in Lisbon at the beginning of 1939 in order to dream all the more emphatically of *home and the Reich* in these foreign surroundings. Alfred Weidenmann therefore

---

[3] In the study by Adam 2010, 316 we not coincidentally come across the note that since 1933 there has been an enormous professionalisation of the "cross-connections between film and book" (ibid.).

[4] In view of these career moves, it is difficult to follow Kanzog when he writes: "Alfred Weidemann [sic!] certainly kept his distance from the National Socialist rulers at the time, but behaved loyally" (Kanzog 2016, 42).

[5] Knowing Alfred Weidenmann's self-assessment, it does not seem entirely conclusive when Rüdiger Steinlein claims to have recognized "features of modernity" (Steinlein 2007, 220) and the "pathos of intentional sobriety" (ibid., 221) in the author's cinematic and youth literature.

Fig. 2 Cover of the youth non-fiction book *Junges Europa* (© Stuttgart: Loewe, 1940)

dedicated the novel *Jakko* to "the Hitler Youth of Lisbon". At the very end of the book there is a publisher's advertisement for *50 Jungen im Dienst*. There is also a reference to the *Hans Schemm Prize* 1937/1938 of the NSLB for Weidenmann's trilogy. Furthermore, the chief of the Press and Propaganda Office of the Reich Youth Leadership is quoted in a promotional manner with the sentences: "What makes the three books particularly valuable is the attitude resting in them and the type of modern German boys' book expressed both in content and outward form."[6] Additionally, a reference to the series of travel books *Junges Europa* was forgotten (Fig. 2) by the twenty-two-year-old author.

---

[6] In 2005, Hopster offered a different assessment in the large-scale and altogether impressive survey of *Children's and Youth Literature 1933–1945* in the second volume, where he writes of the first two books of Weidenmann's trilogy: "Erlebnisliteratur makes it clear that an aesthetically innovative children's and youth literature could also emerge under the conditions of the Nazi regime, in cases where literary competence and a belief in the new, revolutionary nature of National Socialism coincided, in those cases, that is, where National Socialist ideology of revolution turned into a subjectively progressive consciousness, an attitude of departure" (Hopster 2005, 156). It is considered outstanding that the author Weidenmann wrote from the perspective of the protagonist or the collective we (cf. ibid., 157).

The boys' novel *Jakko* was published by Loewe Verlag and reached seven editions by the end of the war.[7] Nevertheless, the story about Jakko does not necessarily have to be regarded as an HJ book. The HJ as an organisation remains conspicuously in the background in comparison with Alfred Weidenmann's other books for young people. The dust jacket of the first edition nevertheless offers a subtle reference to the colors of the Nazi flags through the colors black, white and red. Darkness, mystery and seafaring are also played with.

At the beginning of the depicted experiences and events around Jakko, he is 15 years old, lives and works in a circus. He is an orphan because his father died at the end of the First World War and his mother had an accident while working in the circus. However, on his birthday, Anton the clown, his foster father, informs Jakko that his mother did not die in an accident, but that the circus director killed her deliberately. This leads to a conflict with the ringmaster, and Anton and Jakko are forced to leave the circus. They then arrive in a small town.

Earlier, Jakko had received a pocket watch as a birthday present from Anton, an heirloom from his father, with the inscription *Never bend.* Throughout all the adventures and tensions of the story, this motto is constantly on Jakko's mind: how can, will and must he prove himself and behave if he wants to remain faithful to this motto and, that is, to his father? Is he worthy of friendship with the smallest and weakest of his school class? Can he hold his own in a wrestling match with the shipowner's son Jochen? Whether it's school pranks and their consequences, the HJ's battle with the dock boys, the detection or exposing robbers and smugglers, the core moral challenge remains "Never bend" and find your own way while persevering. Does Jakko live up to the expectations placed on him from all sides?

Jakko matures in his inner confrontation with the accidental death of little Kurt Buske. For he knows that he shares responsibility for the accident and that he cannot evade it (cf. Weidenmann 1939, 296). In the end, he stands before himself and all others as "fundamentally decent" (ibid., 301); as Jochen puts it, HJ leader, son of an upper middle-class family and his friend. The epilogue (cf. ibid., 302/303) of the volume finally describes how the two protagonists, the former circus boy Jakko and the bourgeois child Jochen, meet again on the same level when they join the Reich Labor Service as part of the Volksgemeinschaft. In the future, both offer themselves for "sacrifice and service" (ibid., 296).

Fight and Play

After the *Jakko*-book, Alfred Weidenmann limited his youth writing, which may have had something to do with his wartime deployment. He nevertheless remained associated with his Stuttgart publishing house in the years from around 1938 as the

---

[7] The page numbers in the various editions vary between 343 pages and 303 pages. This is due to the fact that the first editions were printed in Fraktur typeface; when these were defamed as *Jewish* by the National Socialists from about 1941 onwards, further editions appeared in Antiqua.

editor of a series of books for boys, or he wrote and worked under the pseudonym W. Derfla for the *Kriegsbücherei der deutschen Jugend* (from 1939).[8]

Instead, his work as a film director came to the forefront after, as mentioned above, his Hitlerjungen film *Jungbann 2* – a silent film shot with a narrow film machine – had already been shown in public in the presence of Reich Governor Murr in the mid-1930s,[9] as the daily newspaper *Film-Kurier* (Premiere of a Hitlerjungen-Film 1936) enthusiastically reported at the time.

Five years later, the *Film-Kurier* then reported that the Reichsjugendführung had shown further short films by Alfred Weidenmann: *Soldaten von morgen* (1941) as well as *Hände hoch* (1942).[10] Alfred Weidenmann was responsible for both as screenwriter and director. The first film was explicitly directed against Great Britain and celebrated the military training of German youth and their superior paramilitary training; the second was characterised by a slight detective-like touch; it reports on a stay of the Hitler Youth in Slovakia. Weidenmann's film *Außer Gefahr* (1941), which dealt with the challenges of the Kinderlandverschickung, is also primarily about playfully proving oneself in combat and everyday life. Reports on these films rarely failed to mention that they were made in cooperation with the Reich Youth Leadership. In these films, too, Alfred Weidenmann skillfully combined advertising and propaganda for National Socialist ideology and its organisations with entertainment.

In a similar, albeit varied way, he combined the one with the other in his documentary film series (seven episodes were made) *Junges Europa,* which were coupled with the cinema newsreels during their public screenings. The first episode

---

[8] Weigand explains that the *Kriegsbücherei der deutschen Jugend* was launched shortly after the invasion of Poland and that this launch was accompanied by numerous articles in daily newspapers, mostly official government texts, announcing the new series: it was published "on behalf of the youth leader of the German Reich" (Weigand 2010, 7) as well as the High Command of the Army, Navy and Air Force. At the end of the Second World War, the booklets of the *Kriegsbücherei* consequently contained "appeals to young readers to volunteer" (ibid., 9).

[9] Further evidence that Alfred Weidenmann was already involved in the Nazi organisations and their ideology as a young man is his collaboration on the youth book by Ernst G. Erich Lorenz *Pimpfe drehen einen Film: Die Rache des Inkas,* Stuttgart: Loewe (1935), which is based on a Jungvolk play film of the same name. The illustrating photographs are also taken from this film. The book also contains a large number of drawings by Alfred Weidenmann. The author of the book *Pimpfe drehen einen Film (Pimpfe Shoot a Film)* had previously appeared with adventure books as well as with ns-typical youth writings. So here we find not only the ideological-political closeness that Alfred Weidenmann shares with him, but also the linking of Jungvolkspielfilm and Jugendbuch with its genre-typical characteristics, which were adopted by Alfred Weidenmann in his books and especially in his boys' novel *Jakko.*

[10] Alfred Weidenmann was awarded the prize for the best European youth film for *Hände hoch!* in Florence on the occasion of a film competition (cf. Henseleit 1942a). The prize consisted of a "bust of the Führer" designed by the then very famous sculptor Fritz Klimsch (1870–1960), who had been placed on the *list of* the twelve most important visual artists of the Nazi regime by Adolf Hitler in 1944. The premiere of *Hände hoch!* marked the beginning of the Jugendfilmstunden 1942/43 and took place in the presence of Reich Propaganda Minister Josef Goebbels and Reich Youth Leader Artur Axmann (cf. Henseleit 1942b). The film was said to usher in a "new era of youth film" (ibid.).

showed pictures and scenes of the HJ's constant readiness and willingness for action in connection with the fire brigade or by highlighting the war-important work of young girls as tram conductors. It also advertised the so-called „Wall aus Fleisch und Blut" in the Eastern mission and sentimentally recorded a performance by the *Mozart Choir of the HJ* while taking care of the troops in the military hospital. The submarine war was present and the fight against Bolshevism. The Regiment *Groß-Deutschland* was also celebrated, which was said to have been constituted only by HJ leaders. The film also pointed at the Nazi women's organisation *Faith and Beauty*. Justification for the war campaign against the Soviet Union was provided by such images, which were said to prove poverty and mental illness as a direct result of the Soviet political system. In the 7th episode of *Junges Europa*, the coalition with the fascist states of Slovakia and Spain and once again the common anti-Bolshevik struggle were invoked; the thought that the youth was now needed in the armaments production in order to work was taken for granted.[11]

Nevertheless, the film images were dominated by the fun of sports and games and "idealising, romantic images," as Peter Zimmermann and Hoffmann (2005, 633) puts it. In his account of the history of documentary film in the *Third Reich,* Zimmermann's formula of "steely romanticism" also captures the character of these projects by Weidenmann, which he subsumes under the motto: "modernisation, mobilisation and medialisation" (ibid., 231).

I would like to describe these film projects – in the words of Daniel Uziel – as contributions to the "consolidation of the German home front" (Uziel 2008). For this purpose, Alfred Weidenmann offered his young readers and viewers a literary and cinematic strategy that reinterpreted *service to the people,* i.e. mostly war deployment or preparation for it, as an adventure (cf. Kaminski 1987, 207 ff.) and made it consumable.

Defensible Bodies

After Alfred Weidenmann had become a director and screenwriter by 1942 at the latest, one might have expected him to use his own novels for boys as a template for a film. But that did not happen. His next film *Junge Adler* from 1944 was based on a script by Herbert Reinecker, at the time a well-known and sought-after journalist, active for the National Socialist advertising magazine *Signal,* published in many languages, war correspondent and high-ranking member of SS propaganda companies.[12]

The film *Junge Adler* was set in the milieu of the Flieger-HJ. It relied on young people's fascination with technology and served to inculcate a sense of militancy

---

[11] Roschlau's book (2008) is accompanied by a CD that offers the opportunity to view some of Weidenmann's documentary films.

[12] For details see Aurich 2008.

(cf. Seubert 2003). In this work by Weidenmann, the technically modern was amalgamated with the socially and politically reactionary. Rolf Seubert characterises this with the formula "reactionary modernity" (ibid., 376). The intended target was the "soldierly young man" and the "motivational vehicle" (ibid., 382), with which this Nazi youth film aimed at the "permanent mobilisation for National Socialism and the war" (ibid., 399); in relation to the year in which it was made, we are also dealing with a "perseverance film" (ibid., 395).[13]

In addition, what had already been formulated in contemporary criticism of Weidenmann's other films applies to *Junge Adler,* namely that the film shows "steely, elastic bodies" (Henseleit; quoted in Roschlau 2008, 44), as well as forcing the "enthusiasm of the youth", their "cheerful detachment" and the military education of the Hitler Youth (Henseleit; quoted in ibid., 45). It was probably these elements that at the time disguised the unreality of the situation and the atmosphere (according to Erhard Schütz), which is recognisable from today's perspective. Whichever way one turns it, these productions always vary the "incorporation or reintegration into a group or community", individuals are socialised[14] and resocialised (cf. Roschlau 2008, 40 f.).[15]

Bold Realism or a Trendy Film?

At the beginning of 1941, the *Film-Kurier* informed about the beginning of the production of *Jakko* in the unsigned article *Der Film und die Erlebniswelt der Jugend.* This article asked about problems of the German youth film and informed about the fact that the Reichsjugendführer Artur Axmann (successor of Baldur von Schirach) had attended the set. A few weeks later there was even a supplement in the *Film-Kurier* (Deutsche Jugend in neuen Spielfilmen 1941) in which the then current youth film projects (besides *Jakko* there were *Jungens* and *Kopf hoch, Johannes*)

---

[13] On the occasion of an obituary in *Film-Dienst* (2000), Weidenmann's *Junge Adler is* called a "blatant exercise piece". In this obituary in 2000, Rainer Heinz draws parallels to Weidenmann's post-war films such as *Canaris* (1954), which he sees as "pseudo-authentic", and calls *Stern von Afrika* (1958) a "propagandistic hero's song".

[14] The Munich film scholar Kanzog also accentuates in his reflections that the "subject of the film is the socialisation" of Theo Brakke and states that the "normative sentences of the film may claim general validity" (Kanzog 2016, 41); at the same time, however, he knows that "they can hardly be separated from the historical context of National Socialist educational principles" (ibid.).

[15] As time warped as all this may seem, for some young actors who were either at a Napola or one of the Adolf Hitler schools at the time, this appearance became the start of their film careers, such as for Dietmar Schönherr and Hardy Krüger. For more details, see Barbara Stambolis 2016, 210–232. In his 2017 autobiography, the pop singer Roberto Blanco describes how he met Weidenmann and how he helped him get his first film role. And the Berlin musician Rüdiger Trantow also recalled his cinematic collaboration with Weidenmann and the film *Jakko in* his *Mosaik meines Lebens* (2007). Before that, Walter Kempowski had already recounted in his 1971 novel *Tadellöser & Wolff* how he and a friend almost *took part in* the film *Junge Adler.*

had been photographically processed. In *Film-Kurier*, Gerd Eckert praised the film work of the *Third Reich* and in particular the film *Jakko* for its "courageous realism" (Eckert 1941, 1).[16] Since the completion of the film, additional reference was made to the text by Alfred Weidenmann and to the fact that with this film a successful step had been taken in the creation of the youth film.

Fritz Peter Buch (1894–1964), who had very successfully worked for the cinema since the mid-1930s after beginning in the theatre, was enlisted for the film adaptation of Weidenmann's book *Jakko* (1941). The premiere took place on 12 October 1941 on the occasion of the opening of the Jugendfilmstunden 1941/1942 at the *Ufa-Palast am Zoo in* Berlin in the presence of the Reich Minister of Propaganda Joseph Goebbels (Dr. Goebbels opened the Jugendfilmstunden 1941).[17] In his speech, Goebbels defined cinema films as "a national educational tool of the first order" and listed such films as *Jud Süß, Ohm Krüger* and *Ich klage an* in a row with *Jakko*. In the same speech, Joseph Goebbels also took up the cudgels for the form of indirect propaganda he favoured (cf. ibid.).[18]

The then head of the Press and Propaganda Office of the Reich Youth Leadership, Oberbannführer Memminger (1941), repeated and reinforced Goebbels' positioning of youth film work in his editorial for the *Film-Kurier* a few days after the premiere, saying that *Jakko* (Fig. 3) was just as successful an example of National Socialist film work as Steinhoff's filming of Schenzinger's *Der Hitlerjunge Quex* (1932) almost a decade earlier. Memminger pointed out as a quality feature of the *Jakko* adaptation that in it the "main value was placed on the purely human and boyish" (ibid., 4). In 1941, the censors awarded the film the ratings of *state-political value, popular value*, and *youth value*. The political leadership of the Propaganda Ministry as well as the Reich Youth Leadership felt that the institutional promotion that this film had additionally received through the Navy-HJ, National Political Training Institutes (Napola) and Adolf Hitler Schools had been rewarded.

In addition to looking at the quasi-partisan reception, it further helps to hear other voices from the 1940s on *Jakko:* Swiss film scholar Ernest Prodolliet uncovered a review from the *Neue Zürcher Zeitung* (1942) that praised the film for its "hearty idealism of benign comrades" (quoted in Prodolliet 1999, 152). The Swiss *Tages-Anzeiger* of 29.08.1942, however, recognised in *Jakko* an "only weakly disguised 'trendy film'" (quoted after ibid.).

In Germany, the film publicist Libertas Schulze-Boysen,[19] who had worked professionally for one and a half years at the Kulturfilmzentrale of the Reich Propaganda

---

[16] Discussions of other NS youth films can be found in Brücher 1995, 17 ff., Hobsch 1995, 39 ff. and Strobel 1995, 57 ff.

[17] Hoffmann 1988, 100 ff. has taken a closer look at youth film lessons.

[18] Korn 2017, in a recent newspaper article on Veit Harlan's *Jud Süß film* about the propaganda techniques favored by Joseph Goebbels, emphasized that it was true of many of the cinematic projects of the Nazi era that they communicated their propagandistic intentions "indirectly."

[19] To discover Libertas Schulze-Boysen as a Nazi cultural journalist is surprising, because she was at the same time a member of the anti-fascist resistance group *Rote Kapelle* around Arvid Harnack and her husband Harald Schulze-Boysen.

Fig. 3 Cover page of the *Illustrierter Film-Kurier* (1941) on the occasion of the film release of *Jakko* with the two main actors Norbert Rohringer as Jakko and Eugen Klöpfer as his fatherly friend Anton Weber

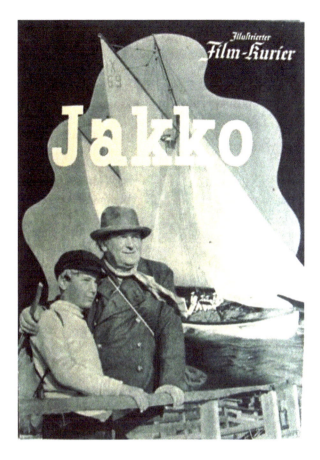

Ministry and wrote for the Essen-based NS-oriented *National-Zeitung* (10.16.1941), had reported on *Jakko* under the title *Echte Jungens*. She singled him out because with him the youth film lessons had been heralded. In her opinion, it was a film to which "cleanliness and ethical value" (Schulze-Boysen 2008, 159) were to be attested. The adjective *"genuine"* occurs strikingly often in her text.

A comprehensive study of Nazi youth film and also of *Jakko* can be found in the article *Jugend und Film* by Anneliese U. Sander (1944/1984).[20] Sander was also familiar with Weidenmann's 1935 film *Jungbann 2*, which she called *Jungenzug 2*. She defined it as a "report film" from the life of the Jungvolk, which could be described as the "first successful experiment in this direction" (Sander 1944/1984, 23). It is not surprising that Weidenmann's other films were also positively evaluated by her (cf. ibid., 24) and that she also emphatically praised the literary

---

[20] After the end of the Nazi regime, a conspicuously large number of film scholars refer to Sander's remarks and make use of her data, figures, and evaluations. This must be surprising, since the article was a text published by Eher Verlag, the central publishing house of the NSDAP, and in no way represents an independent professional discussion.

adaptation *Jakko*. According to Sander, we are dealing with the "style of young Germany" (ibid., 34) in these projects, *Hitlerjunge Quex* at the forefront.

In Sander's assessment of the film, it is noticeable that although she is aware of the party and youth political ties and does not leave them out, the way she writes about the products is reminiscent of themes and phrases of the traditional bourgeois art education and youth writing movement. Theodor Storm's dictum, for example, emerges that whoever writes for youth must not write for youth (cf. ibid., 45). This formula had been raised to the fanfare of youth writing criticism at the turn of the century by the elementary school teacher Heinrich Wolgast. Sander consequently prefers the novel *Jakko to* the film adaptation by Fritz Peter Buch: "The slender, black-haired, spirited circus boy of the novel is Aryanized blond as a mother's boy to increase his effect in the film – they meant too well with him" (ibid.).[21] This could well be understood as a form of criticism directed at the director Fritz Peter Buch and his otherwise highly praised youth film *Jakko*. Alfred Weidenmann's own works, books, and films, however, are understood by Sander as "harmoniously balanced works of youth art" (ibid., 51).

Director and Composer

There is some information about Fritz Peter Buch in various biographical and/or lexical reference works, for example in the *Deutsches Theater Lexikon* (1953), *Metzler Kabarett Lexikon* (1996) or in the *Grosses Personenlexikon des Films* (2001). However, the information contained therein is not very informative or is limited to the most necessary.

It is therefore surprising when in the catalogue of the *German National Library* searching for Fritz Peter Buch's publications one quickly discovers that he had been active as a writer on a large scale since the beginning of the 1920s and had increasingly been active in theatre. This ranged from working on and with Gerd von Bassewitz's *Peterchens Mondfahrt*[22] and Buch's own Christmas fairy tale *Princess Huschewind* (1922), illustrated by Hans Baluschek, which had also been brought to the stage as a *prankster's tale in* the same year, to adapting a comedy of Bill Bjelozerkowsky's *Mond von links* (1930). Here Buch cooperated with the Austrian communist fairy-tale writer Hermynia zur Mühlen. Even after 1933, Buch produced

---

[21] Sander's reference to Jakko's *Aryanisation* from black-haired to blond unspokenly draws attention to the fact that racism does occur in Weidenmann's books for young people, but not anti-Semitism! In *Jakko,* however, on page 79 ff. we come across an episode about a member of the ship's boys, the *nigger, to* whom Weidenmann has given the pejorative nickname "Kakke"; this is given a number of problematic stereotypes to demonstrate his inferiority. Weidenmann had portrayed the Bolsheviks in particular in a similarly disparaging manner in his films.

[22] Cf. the contribution by Julia Benner in this volume.

several stage plays, which were distributed and performed by theatre publishers. As late as 1980, the Südwest Verlag reissued Buch's first work, *Prinzessin Huschewind,* with the old illustrations by Hans Baluschek. For the Frankfurt Städtische Bühnen, he staged Franz Werfel's *Paulus drama* and Ernst Barlach's play *Sündflut* before 1933, for example, and after 1945 he worked at the Schauspielhaus in Düsseldorf, where Gustav Gründgens had become director.

The second facet of his artistic work was film,[23] for which he directed regularly since 1934 and this as about 1937 with up to three films per year. He achieved special success with the crime movie *Der Fall Deruga* in 1938. In 1952 he shot *Cuba Cubana* with Zarah Leander, with whom he had already worked during the *Third Reich,* and in 1956 his last movie *Verlobung am Wolfgangsee.*

It is thanks to the theatre researcher Bettina Schültke (1997) that today more than a few scrawny sources of data are known about Fritz Peter Buch. In her large-scale study of the Frankfurt Städtische Bühnen, she devotes several pages to him. It is clear from her information that Buch had come into contact with left-wing political positions and people during the Weimar Republic. In Schültke's study it is therefore not surprising to find that he was summarily dismissed from his position as dramaturge and head of the Frankfurt Schauspiel on May 23, 1933. The accusation against him was that he had a "tendency towards a communist world view" (ibid., 64). This was substantiated by a list of his productions of so-called left-wing authors: Friedrich Wolf, Ferdinand Bruckner, Sergei Tretyakov, Bill Bjelozerkovsky and Hermann Kesser's *Rotation.*

Fritz Peter Buch, however, took decisive action against his dismissal (cf. ibid., 65) because he had never – as pointed out by himself – belonged to a political party and had never been politically active. He did not want to be excluded from the current "cultural renewal" (ibid.) and equally did not want to be "labelled as a communist for all eternity" (ibid.). Before the Prussian theater committee Hans Hinkel (at that time one of the managing directors of the Reichskulturkammer and later head of the film department in the Ministry of Propaganda)[24] stood up for Fritz Peter Buch with the result that he could start anew at the *Prussian Theater of Youth* in Berlin as early as September 1, 1933 (cf. ibid.).

This by no means completely secured his position, for from voices located in Frankfurt attempts continued to defame him as "dangerous to the state" or "morally destructive of the state" (ibid., 99). Elsewhere, his work was also characterised as "conjunctural nationalism" (ibid., 100). In parallel, however, Buch enjoyed numerous theatrical successes. His play *Katarakt*, for example, was performed over 70 times between 1934 and 1944 (cf. ibid.); his comedy *Ein ganzer Kerl* (1938) was

---

[23] The complete list can be found at www.filmportal.de
[24] On Hans Hinkel, cf. Werner 1987.

one of the most successful plays in the *Third Reich,* with around 140 performances, and was successfully filmed in 1939 with Heidemarie Hatheyer in the leading role.[25]

Fritz Peter Buch was professional as a writer, as a dramaturge, as a screenwriter and as a director. That made him interesting and he knew how to use that, the breadth of his undertakings indicates. Ultimately then, it was no surprise when the screenplay and direction of the film adaptation of the novel *Jakko* were handed to him in 1941. He used the elements laid out in Weidenmann's youth novel: Circus and vaudeville parts, the speakeasy milieu of the *Klein St. Pauli* pub, the world of ports and shipping with smuggling and exposure of crime, courtship for friendship, etc. His film *Jakko* became an entertainment film and at the same time a kind of cinematic glossy brochure for the Marine-HJ.[26]

Fritz Peter Buch did not touch the moral appeal structure of "Never bend" from the original text. In the film too, it boils down to decency and to "being a man". In Buch's film, the circus world and the bourgeois world stand opposite each other, as do the world of the naval H.J. and that of the non-organised, or even the H.J. and the school. The tension arises from the fact that Jakko doesn't know exactly where he belongs for a long time, and only towards the end, purified by experience, does he realise that there must be something else for him than just himself. He succeeds in dissolving a bad suspicion against himself, restoring his honour and being ready for friendship and trust. At last the time has come for Jakko to be allowed to join the naval HJ, after he brilliantly passes his test in front of everyone.

The film closes – typical of National Socialist youth films – with a joyful, rousing marching song, *Where one stands for the other,* by the then well-known film composer Hans Otto Borgmann (1901–1977).[27] Borgmann had already composed the melody to the HJ hymn *Unsere Fahne flattert uns voran* for the film *Der Hitlerjunge Quex*[28] in 1933, to lyrics by Baldur von Schirach. And Borgmann also composed the film music for Alfred Weidenmann's *Junge Adler.* From 1931 (then for Ufa) to 1961, Borgmann was responsible for numerous film scores for a wide variety of genres;[29] also for *Der große König* (1940–1942) by Veit Harlan.

---

[25] One of the biggest fans of director Fritz Peter Buch and his films was Joseph Goebbels (cf. Schültke 1997, 100).

[26] Even today *Jakko* belongs to the reserved films and may not be performed in public.

[27] Wanderscheck 1942 celebrated the artist Borgmann as one of the outstanding film composers of his time. Biographical information about Borgmann can be found in Noack 1995 as well as on the website http://www.nurembergfilm.org (31.03.2020). It is also important to note, for example, that as early as 1948 Borgmann created the background music for a documentary film about the Nuremberg Trials, for which the former Ufa producer Eric Pommer (an employee of *OMGUS* after his return from forced emigration in 1948*)* was jointly responsible and who probably knew Borgmann from his early days at Ufa.

[28] Cf. most recently on Schenzinger's book Schumann 2013, 131 ff.

[29] Cf. http://www.nurembergfilm.org (31.03.2020).

Instruction, Probation, Conversion

The interplay between Weidenmann, Buch and Borgmann[30] contributed significantly to the fact that this film could be assigned the role of a propaganda instrument in the youth policy of the *Third Reich*. This assessment by Bianca Dustdar (1996) and by Barbara Stelzner-Large (1996), which is based on the fact that the Jugendfilmstunde of the HJ are said to have had an audience of more than 30 million,[31] can hardly be disputed, but is well evidenced.

The film *Jakko* was and still is considered by today's film critics to be close to the Hitler Youth film *Quex* in terms of motif (cf. ibid., 223), especially because of the similar intention of integrating an outsider into the Hitler Youth. However, *Jakko* shows additional characteristics that distinguish it from other Nazi youth films (cf. ibid., 237). One of these is that in *Jakko* the *negative influence* of the parental home is not as clearly expressed and – despite all the hallmarks of an HJ film – it nevertheless remains a friendship film first and foremost (cf. ibid., 238). Although the HJ is typically shown as a "dynamic mass" of "extraordinary activity" (ibid.), a "timeless idyll" (ibid., 239) dominates in the film and this was determinant for the entertainment film of the *Third Reich* in general (cf. ibid.). Thus, this youth feature film and the few others for a young cinema audience (only 1.2% of the total production) fit into the framework of the other 1100 full-length feature films released in Germany since 1933 (cf. ibid., 13).

The film version *Jakko* also has something special going for it: *Jakko* is a representative of the circus film. This attribution can be found in Matthias Christen's study *Der Zirkusfilm. Exotisches, Konformität, Transgression* (2010). However, both Weidenmann's novel and Fritz Peter Buch's film adaptation have the effect that the exotic of circus life remains décor, conformity prevails, and any transgression is prevented. The circus, according to the tenor of both book and film, is a – as Christen traces – "morally questionable social form" (ibid., 154), from which the main character must free himself as quickly as possible. Jakko's circus life was considered acceptable, at best as an intermediate stage on the way to a superior, openly political form of community like the Hitler Youth (cf. ibid., 155).

Matthias Christen has traced that the promotional materials for the film *Jakko* explicitly emphasised the "devaluation of the circus milieu" (ibid., 156). The *Tobis-Film-Gesellschaft* also controlled the reception not least by enforcing, together with the Reich Youth Leadership, that cinema operators were instructed to coordinate with the local leadership of the Hitler Youth when showing the film. The intention was to render ineffective the dimension of transgression traditionally peculiar to the circus milieu and the irritation and/or attraction that might emanate from it.

---

[30] Thiel 1996 describes how Borgmann was also active as a film composer in the then SBZ and in the early GDR.

[31] In Stelzner-Large's 1996 study, 227 ff. there is also a detailed film analysis of *Jakko*, which provides revealing information about scenes and camera angles.

After 1945, the fact that he was responsible for a National Socialist propaganda film par excellence with *Menschen im Sturm* (1941) hardly hindered Fritz Peter Buch in continuing to produce films. The HJ song composer Hans Otto Borgmann wrote for popular productions in the post-war period and taught at a Berlin music college. In the same way, the youth author and film director Weidenmann continued to have a public presence.

Otto Borgmann, Fritz Peter Buch and Alfred Weidenmann were wheels and not just cogs within the National Socialist propaganda apparatus. The media network of film production company, party-political organisations, the special performance mode of *Jugendfilmstunde* and not least the reception guidance by the Hitler Youth led to the fact that for the artistic-media functional elite – here consisting of author, director and composer – the years between 1933 and 1945 acted as a career accelerator, which did not slow down the aforementioned even in the early post-war period and then in the Federal Republic of Germany as well as partly also in the early German Democratic Republic. Each of them was able to continue his career and celebrate further successes in his profession after the war and the end of the *Third Reich*.

References

Primary Literature

Blanco, Roberto: Roberto Blanco. Von der Seele. Die Autobiographie Kulmbach: Plassen, 2017.
Kempowski, Walter: Tadellöser & Wolff. Ein bürgerlicher Roman München Hanser, 1971.
Trantow, Rüdiger: Mosaik meines Lebens. Berlin: Transit, 2007.
Weidenmann, Alfred: Jungzug 2. Text, Photos und Zeichn. von Alfred Weidenmann. Stuttgart: Loewe, 1936 (Jungen im Dienst; 1).
Weidenmann, Alfred: Trupp Plassen. Eine Kameradschaft der Gräben und der Spaten Fotos vom Verf.. Stuttgart: Loewe, 1937a (Jungen im Dienst; 2).
Weidenmann, Alfred: Kanonier Brakke Nr. 2. Sämtliche Fotos von Alfred Weidenmann. Zeichn.: Heiner Rothfuchs. Geleitw.: Dollmann. Stuttgart: Loewe, 1937b (Jungen im Dienst; 3).
Weidenmann, Alfred: Jakko. Der Roman eines Jungen. Stuttgart: Loewe, 1939.
Weidenmann, Alfred: Junges Europa. Mit 100 eigenen Aufnahmen des Verfassers. Stuttgart: Loewe, 1940 (Verlag der Jungen; 1332).

Filmography

Außer Gefahr [Kurz-Dokumentarfilm] (D 1941). Regie und Drehbuch: Alfred Weidenmann; Deutsche Filmherstellungs- und Verwertungs-GmbH, Berlin-Tempelhof.
Hände hoch! [Spielfilm] (D 1942). Regie und Drehbuch: Alfred Weidenmann, Musik: Horst Hanns Sieber; Deutsche Filmherstellungs- und Verwertungs-GmbH, Berlin-Tempelhof.
Jakko [Spielfilm] (D 1941). Regie: Fritz P. Buch, Musik: Hans O. Borgmann; Tobis-Filmkunst GmbH, Berlin.

Jungbann 2 [Dokumentarfilm] (D 1935/36). Regie und Drehbuch: Alfred Weidenmann; Produktionsfirma: HJ, Gebietsführung 20, Referat Film, Stuttgart.
Junge Adler [Spielfilm] (D 1943/44). Regie: Alfred Weidenmann, Drehbuch: Alfred Weidenmann und Herbert Reinecker, Musik: Hans O. Borgmann; Ufa-Filmkunst GmbH
Soldaten von morgen [Kurz-Dokumentarfilm] (D 1941). Regie und Drehbuch: Alfred Weidenmann, Musik: Horst Hanns Sieber; Deutsche Filmherstellungs- und Verwertungs-GmbH Berlin-Tempelhof.

Secondary Literature Before 1945

Deutsche Jugend in neuen Spielfilmen. In: Film-Kurier 23 (1941) 45 vom 22.02, Bilderbogen 1–2.
Der Film und die Erlebniswelt der Jugend. In: Film-Kurier 23 (1941) 10 vom 13.01., 1–2.
Eckert, Gerd: Unsere Filmtendenz ist ein mutiger Realismus. Es geht um die große Wahrhaftigkeit, die unseren gegenwärtigen Kampf auszeichnet. In: Film-Kurier 23 (1941) 49 vom 27.02., 1–2.
Uraufführung eines Hitlerjungen Films. „Jungbann 2". In: Film-Kurier 18 (1936) 232 vom 03.10, 2.
Henseleit, Felix: Der europäische Jugendfilm in Florenz. In: Film-Kurier 24 (1942a) 151 vom 01.07., 1–2.
Henseleit, Felix: Die Eröffnung der Jugendfilmstunden 1942/43. In: Film-Kurier 24 (1942b) 251 vom 26.10., 1–2
Memminger: Jugend im Film. In: Film-Kurier 23 (1941) 244 vom 17.10., 1–2 und 4.
Dr. Goebbels eröffnete die Jugendfilmstunden 41/42. In: Film-Kurier 23 (1941) 240 vom 13.10., 1–3.
Wanderscheck, Hermann: Musikalische Temperamente. In: Film-Kurier 24 (1942) 252 vom 27.10., 2.

Secondary Literature After 1945

Adam, Christian: Lesen unter Hitler. Autoren, Bestseller, Leser im Dritten Reich. Berlin 2010
Albrecht, Gerd: Der Film im 3. Reich. Karlsruhe 1979.
Aurich, Rolf [Red.]: Libertas Schulze-Boysen. Filmpublizistin. Mit Aufsätzen und Kritiken von Libertas Schulze-Boysen und einem Essay von Wenke Wegner. München 2008.
Aurich, Rolf/Beckenbach, Niels/Jacobsen, Wolfgang (Hg.): Reineckerland. Der Schriftsteller Herbert Reinecker. München 2010.
Beyerle, Hermann: Neudeutsche Jungengemeinschaft – Stuttgart im Umbruch der Nazizeit. In: Eilers, Rolf (Hg.): Löscht den Geist nicht aus. Der Bund Neu-Deutschland im Dritten Reich. Mainz 1985, 181–189.
Brücher, Bodo: Der Film als Mittel der Massenkommunikation in der NS-Jugenderziehung. In: Lauffer, Jürgen/Volkmer, Ingrid (Hg.): Kommunikative Kompetenz in einer sich verändernden Medienwelt. Opladen 1995, 17–27.
Brunken, Otto: Ein schwieriger Fall. Alfred Weidenmanns „Gepäckschein 666". In: Hurrelmann, Bettina (Hg.): Klassiker der Kinder- und Jugendliteratur. Frankfurt a. M. 1995, 479–501.
Buddrus, Michael: Totale Erziehung für den totalen Krieg: Hitlerjugend und nationalsozialistische Jugendpolitik. Berlin [u. a.] 2003.
Burkhardt, Bernd: Aus Spiel wird Ernst – Die Hitlerjungen: „Unser Leben heißt Kampf!" In: Fuchs, Karlheinz (Hg.): Stuttgart im Dritten Reich. Anpassung, Widerstand, Verfolgung. Die Jahre von 1933 bis 1939. Stuttgart 1984, 238–269.
Christen, Matthias: Der Zirkusfilm. Exotismus – Konformität – Transgression. Marburg 2010 (Zürcher Filmstudien; 23). Zugl.: Bochum, Univ., Habil., 2009.

Dustdar, Bianca: Film als Propagandainstrument in der Jugendpolitik des Dritten Reichs. Alfeld 1996 (Aufsätze zu Film und Fernsehen; 32).
Eilers, Rolf (Hg.): Löscht den Geist nicht aus. Der Bund Neu-Deutschland im Dritten Reich. Mainz 1985.
Epping-Jäger, Cornelia (Hg.): Freund, Feind & Verrat. Das politische Feld der Medien. Köln 2004 (Mediologie; 12).
Galle, Heinz J.: Die Mobilisierung der Medien. Propagandakompanien und ihre Akteure im Zweiten Weltkrieg und in der Nachkriegszeit. Lüneburg 2016.
Heinz, Rainer: Nachruf Alfred Weidenmann. In: Filmdienst 53 (2000) 15, 18.
Hobsch, Manfred: Ideologie für Kopf und Herz der Jugend. In: Schäfer, Horst/Wegener, Claudia (Hg.): Kindheit und Film. Geschichte, Themen und Perspektiven des Kinderfilms in Deutschland. Konstanz 1995, 39–55.
Hoffmann, Hilmar: „Und die Fahne führt uns in die Ewigkeit." Propaganda im NS-Film. Frankfurt a. M. 1988.
Hopster, Norbert: Literatur der Organisationen und der Dienste. In: Ders./Josting, Petra/Neuhaus, Joachim (Hg.): Kinder- und Jugendliteratur 1933–1945. Ein Handbuch, Bd. 2.: Darstellender Teil. Stuttgart 2005, 121–186.
Kaminski, Winfred: Weidenmann, Alfred. In: Doderer, Klaus (Hg.): Lexikon der Kinder- und Jugendliteratur, Bd. 3, Weinheim [u. a.] 1979, 773–774.
Kaminski, Winfred: Dienst am Volk als Abenteuer. In: Thunecke, Jörg (Hg.): Leid der Worte. Panorama des literarischen Nationalsozialismus. Bonn 1987 (Abhandlungen zur Kunst-, Musik- und Literaturwissenschaft; 367), 207–226.
Kanzog, Klaus: Militärische Leitbilder in Spielfilmen der Bundesrepublik der 50er Jahre. Faktizität, Kunstfreiheit, Rhetorik. Nordhausen 2016 (Libri nigri; 56).
Kersting, Franz-Werner: Militär und Jugend im NS-Staat. Rüstungs- und Schulpolitik der Wehrmacht. Wiesbaden 1989.
Klee, Ernst: Das Personenlexikon zum Dritten Reich. Wer war was vor und nach 1945. Hamburg 2016.
Kleinhans, Bernd: Ein Volk, ein Reich, ein Kino: Lichtspiel in der braunen Provinz. Köln. 2003 (Neue kleine Bibliothek; 88).
Korn, Salomon: Jud Süß. In: Frankfurter Allgemeine Zeitung (2017) 157 vom 10.07., 6.
Mediale Mobilmachung; Teil: 1: Das Dritte Reich und der Film. Paderborn [u. a.] 2004 (Mediengeschichte des Films; 4).
Noack, Hans: Borgmann, Hans Otto. In: Bock, Hans Michael/Bergfelder, Tim (Hg.): The Concise Cinegraph. Encyclopaedia of German Cinema. München 2009, 52.
Pöttker, Horst: Abgewehrte Vergangenheit. Beiträge zur deutschen Erinnerung an den Nationalsozialismus. Köln 2005.
Prodolliet, Ernest: Der NS-Film in der Schweiz im Urteil der Presse 1933–1945. Eine Dokumentation. Zürich 1999.
Roschlau, Johannes (Hg.): Alles in Scherben! …? Film – Produktion und Propaganda in Europa 1940–1950. Cinefest, V. Internationales Festival des Deutschen Film-Erbes, Hamburg, Kommunales Kino Metropolis. München 2008.
Rother, Rainer/Prokasky, Judith (Hg.): Die Kamera als Waffe. Propagandabilder des Zweiten Weltkrieges. München 2010.
Schruttke, Tatjana: Die Jugendpresse des Nationalsozialismus. Köln [u. a.] 1997.
Sander, Anneliese U.: Jugend und Film. Berlin 1944 (Sonderveröffentlichung 6 für „Das Junge Deutschland" Amtliches Organ des Jugendführers des Deutschen Reiches); ND als: Jugendfilm im Nationalsozialismus. Dokumentation und Kommentar. Münster 1984.
Schültke, Bettina: Theater oder Propaganda? Die Städtischen Bühnen Frankfurt a. M. 1933–1945. Frankfurt a. M. 1997 (Studien zur Frankfurter Geschichte; 40).
Schumann, Dirk: Karl Aloys Schenzinger, Der Hitlerjunge Quex. In: Bräuer, Christoph/ Wangerin, Wolfgang (Hg.): Unter dem roten Wunderschirm. Lesarten klassischer Kinder- und Jugendliteratur. Göttingen 2013, 131–140.

Schulze-Boysen, Libertas: Filmpublizistin. Mit Aufsätzen und Kritiken von Libertas Schulze-Boysen und einem Essay von Wenke Wegner [Red.: Rolf Auruch]. München 2008 (Film & Schrift; 7).

Seubert, Rolf: Junge Adler. Technikfaszination und Wehrhaftmachung im nationalsozialistischen Jugendfilm. In: Chiari, Bernhard (Hg.): Krieg und Militär im Film des 20. Jahrhunderts. Im Auftr. des Militärgeschichtlichen Forschungsamts. München 2003 (Beiträge zur Militärgeschichte; 59), 371–400.

Stahr, Gerhard: Volksgemeinschaft vor der Leinwand? Der nationalsozialistische Film und sein Publikum. Berlin 2001.

Stambolis, Barbara: Der Film „Junge Adler" (1944) in generationellen Kontexten. In: Dies./Köster, Markus (Hg.): Jugend im Fokus von Film und Fotografie. Zur visuellen Geschichte von Jugendkulturen im 20. Jahrhundert. Göttingen 2016 (Jugendbewegung und Jugendkulturen; 12), 210–232.

Steinlein, Rüdiger: Der nationalsozialistische Jugendspielfilm. Der Autor und Regisseur Alfred Weidenmann als Hoffnungsträger der nationalsozialistischen Kulturpolitik. In: Köppen, Manuel/Schütz, Erhard (Hg.): Kunst der Propaganda – der Film im Dritten Reich. Bern [u. a.] 2007 (Publikationen zur Zeitschrift für Germanistik; 15), 217–246.

Stelzner-Large, Barbara: „Der Jugend zur Freude"? Untersuchungen zum propagandistischen Jugendspielfilm im Dritten Reich. Weimar 1996.

Strobel, Heidi: Formung der Gefühle – Kinderfilm in NS-Diktatur und früher Nachkriegszeit. In: Schäfer, Horst/Wegener, Claudia (Hg.): Kindheit und Film. Geschichte, Themen und Perspektiven des Kinderfilms in Deutschland. Konstanz 1995, 57–71.

Thiel, Wolfgang: Klänge aus dem Osten. Wer komponierte die Musik der DEFA-Filme? abgedruckt in: film-dienst 17,19/1996) zit. nach https://www.defa-stiftung.de/defa/publikationen/artikel/17191996-klaenge-aus-dem-osten/ (25.07.2020).

Uziel, Daniel: The propaganda warriors: the Wehrmacht and the consolidation of the German home front. Oxford [u. a.] 2008.

Weigand, Jörg: Frontlektüre. Lesestoff für und von Soldaten der deutschen Wehrmacht im Zweiten Weltkrieg. Hameln 2010 (Lesesaal; 33).

Werner, Wolfram [Bearb.]: Reichskulturkammer und ihre Einzelkammern, Bestand R 56. [Bundesarchiv Koblenz] Koblenz 1987 (Findbücher zu Beständen des Bundesarchivs; 31).

Zimmermann, Peter/Hoffmann, Kay (Hg.): Geschichte des dokumentarischen Films 1933–1945 Bd. 3. Stuttgart 2005.

Printed in the USA
CPSIA information can be obtained
at www.ICGtesting.com
LVHW010737200324
774517LV00073B/610